THE LEGAL PROCESS AND THE PROMISE OF JUSTICE

Malcolm Feeley, one of the founding giants of the law and society field, is also one of its most exciting, diverse, and contemporary scholars. His works have examined criminal courts, prison reform, the legal profession, legal professionalism, and a variety of other important topics of enduring theoretical interest with a keen eye for the practical implications. In this volume, *The Legal Process and the Promise of Justice*, an eminent group of contemporary law and society scholars offer fresh and original analyses of his work. They assess the legacy of Feeley's theoretical innovations, put his findings to the test of time, and provide provocative historical and international perspectives for his insights. This collection of original essays not only draws attention to Professor Feeley's seminal writings but also to the theories and ideas of others who, inspired by Feeley, have explored how courts and the legal process really work.

ROSANN GREENSPAN is executive director of the Center for the Study of Law and Society at the University of California, Berkeley. She is the author of *The Transformation of Criminal Due Process in the Administrative State* (2014) and co-editor of the Law Section of the *International Encyclopedia of the Social and Behavioral Sciences* (Second edition, 2015). She received the Western Society of Criminology's Fellows Award for important contributions to the field of criminology.

HADAR AVIRAM is the Miller Professor of Law at the University of California, Hastings College of Law. Professor Aviram's research focuses on the criminal justice system and examines policing, courtroom practices, and corrections through social science perspectives. She is the author of *Cheap on Crime: Recession-Era Politics and the Transformation of American Punishment* (2015) and the former President of the Western Society of Criminology.

JONATHAN SIMON is the Lance Robbins Professor of Criminal Justice Law at the University of California, Berkeley. He is the author of several books on emerging trends in crime control and the role of crime in contemporary governance. Among these books are *Governing Through Crime: How the War on Crime Transformed American Democracy and Created a Culture of Fear* (2006) and *Mass Incarceration on Trial: A Remarkable Court Decision and the Future of Prisons in America* (2014).

CAMBRIDGE STUDIES IN LAW AND SOCIETY

Founded in 1997, Cambridge Studies in Law and Society is a hub for leading scholarship in socio-legal studies. Located at the intersection of law, the humanities, and the social sciences, it publishes empirically innovative and theoretically sophisticated work on law's manifestations in everyday life: from discourses to practices, and from institutions to cultures. The series editors have longstanding expertise in the interdisciplinary study of law, and welcome contributions that place legal phenomena in national, comparative, or international perspective. Series authors come from a range of disciplines, including anthropology, history, law, literature, political science, and sociology.

Series Editors
Mark Fathi Massoud, *University of California, Santa Cruz*
Jens Meierhenrich, *London School of Economics and Political Science*
Rachel E. Stern, *University of California, Berkeley*

A list of books in the series can be found at the back of this book.

The Legal Process and the Promise of Justice

STUDIES INSPIRED BY THE WORK OF
MALCOLM FEELEY

Edited by

ROSANN GREENSPAN
University of California, Berkeley

HADAR AVIRAM
University of California, Hastings College of the Law

JONATHAN SIMON
University of California, Berkeley

CAMBRIDGE
UNIVERSITY PRESS

University Printing House, Cambridge CB2 8BS, United Kingdom

One Liberty Plaza, 20th Floor, New York, NY 10006, USA

477 Williamstown Road, Port Melbourne, VIC 3207, Australia

314-321, 3rd Floor, Plot 3, Splendor Forum, Jasola District Centre, New Delhi - 110025, India

103 Penang Road, #05-06/07, Visioncrest Commercial, Singapore 238467

Cambridge University Press is part of the University of Cambridge.

It furthers the University's mission by disseminating knowledge in the pursuit of education, learning and research at the highest international levels of excellence.

www.cambridge.org
Information on this title: www.cambridge.org/9781108401975
DOI : 10.1017/9781108234979

© Rosann Greenspan, Hadar Aviram and Jonathan Simon 2019

This publication is in copyright. Subject to statutory exception and to the provisions of relevant collective licensing agreements, no reproduction of any part may take place without the written permission of Cambridge University Press.

First published 2019
First paperback edition 2022

A catalogue record for this publication is available from the British Library

ISBN 978-1-108-41568-2 Hardback
ISBN 978-1-108-40197-5 Paperback

Cambridge University Press has no responsibility for the persistence or accuracy of URLs for external or third-party internet websites referred to in this publication, and does not guarantee that any content on such websites is, or will remain, accurate or appropriate.

Contents

About the Contributors   page vii

Introduction: Past as Prologue   1
Hadar Aviram, Rosann Greenspan, and Jonathan Simon

PART I   THE PROCESS IS THE PUNISHMENT   17

1. **Adversarial Bias and the Criminal Process: Infusing the Organizational Perspective on Criminal Courts with Insights from Behavioral Science**   19
Hadar Aviram

2. **Malcolm Feeley's Concept of Law**   36
Issa Kohler-Hausmann

3. **Process as Intergenerational Punishment**   55
Kay L. Levine and Volkan Topalli

4. **The Process Is the Problem**   72
Shauhin Talesh

PART II   COURT REFORM ON TRIAL   95

5. **Regulating E-Cigarettes: Why Policies Diverge**   97
Eric A. Feldman

6. **Japanese Court Reform on Trial**   122
David T. Johnson and Setsuo Miyazawa

7. **Court Reform and Comparative Criminal Justice**   139
David Nelken

| 8 | The Birth of the Penal Organization: Why Prisons Were Born to Fail
Ashley T. Rubin | 152 |
| 9 | The Misbegotten: Infanticide in Victorian England
Lawrence M. Friedman | 172 |

PART III   JUDICIAL POLICYMAKING AND THE MODERN STATE 191

| 10 | Judicial Deference in the Modern State
Lauren B. Edelman | 193 |
| 11 | The Law of the Workplace
Paul Frymer | 215 |
| 12 | Administrative "States" of Judicial Policy on Gender-Motivated Violence
Christine B. Harrington | 230 |
| 13 | Can Courts Abolish Mass Incarceration?
Jonathan Simon | 259 |
| 14 | Policy Making by Out-of-Court Settlements: Palestinian Informers at the Israeli High Court of Justice
Menachem Hofnung | 273 |

PART IV   POLITICAL LIBERALISM AND THE LEGAL COMPLEX 287

| 15 | The International Legal Complex: Wang Yu and the Global Response to Repression of China's Rights Lawyers
Terence C. Halliday | 289 |
| 16 | The Legal Profession's Promise of Justice: Choices and Challenges in Legal and Sociolegal Work
Mark Fathi Massoud | 314 |
| 17 | The Varieties of Judicial Independence and the Judiciary's Role in Political Reform
Edward L. Rubin | 335 |
| 18 | The Legal Complex and Lawyers-in-Chief
Kim Lane Scheppele | 361 |

Index   385

About the Contributors

Hadar Aviram is the Thomas Miller '73 Professor of Law at the University of California, Hastings College of the Law.

Lauren B. Edelman is the Agnes Roddy Robb Professor of Law and professor of sociology at the University of California, Berkeley.

Eric A. Feldman is professor of law at the University of Pennsylvania Law School.

Lawrence M. Friedman is the Marion Rice Kirkwood Professor of Law and (by courtesy) professor of history and political science at Stanford University.

Paul Frymer is professor of politics and director of the Program in Law and Public Affairs at Princeton University.

Rosann Greenspan is executive director of the Center for the Study of Law and Society at the University of California, Berkeley School of Law.

Terence C. Halliday is research professor at the American Bar Foundation and codirector of the Center on Law and Globalization, American Bar Foundation and University of Illinois College of Law.

Christine B. Harrington is professor of politics at New York University

Menachem Hofnung is professor of political science at the Hebrew University of Jerusalem.

David T. Johnson is professor of sociology and adjunct professor of law at the University of Hawaii at Manoa.

Issa Kohler-Hausmann is associate professor of law at Yale Law School and associate professor of sociology at Yale.

Kay L. Levine is professor of law and associate dean of faculty at Emory University School of Law.

Mark Fathi Massoud is associate professor of politics and legal studies at the University of California, Santa Cruz.

Setsuo Miyazawa is senior professor of law and senior director of the East Asian Legal Studies Program at the University of California, Hastings College of the Law and professor of law at Aoyama Gakuin University.

David Nelken is professor of law at King's College, London and distinguished professor of legal institutions and social change at the University of Macerata.

Ashley T. Rubin is assistant professor of sociology at the University of Toronto.

Edward L. Rubin is university professor of law and political science at Vanderbilt University.

Kim Lane Scheppele is the Laurance S. Rockefeller Professor of Sociology and International Affairs in the Woodrow Wilson School and in the University Center for Human Values at Princeton University.

Jonathan Simon is the Lance Robbins Professor of Criminal Justice Law and faculty director of the Center for the Study of Law and Society at the University of California, Berkeley School of Law.

Shauhin Talesh is professor of law and (by courtesy) professor of sociology and criminology, law and society at the University of California, Irvine.

Volkan Topalli is professor of criminal justice at Georgia State University.

Introduction: Past as Prologue

Hadar Aviram, Rosann Greenspan, and Jonathan Simon

We live in what some sociolegal scholars might be tempted to call a Feeleyian moment in the course of law and liberal societies. "What?" you might say, "Feeleyian?" That would be a reference, of course, to the influential and wide-ranging scholarship of political scientist and legal scholar Malcolm Feeley. While history may not repeat itself, its well-known propensity for echoing or rhyming (the latter being attributed with no apparent evidence to the writer Mark Twain) seemed evident when a group of noted scholars in sociolegal scholarship gathered in Berkeley to present new work in the fields that Feeley sowed in some cases decades earlier. What links these diverse fields, besides the farsightedness of one of our most productive scholars (as marked by the 2015 Kalven Prize of the Law & Society Association)? We think it lies in the fact that his work was planted directly in the agonistic struggles (Goodman, Page, and Phelps 2017) and occasional seismic moves of that lingering sense of justice in the procedures of law that we sometimes call due process, without quite knowing what authorities and responsibilities it conjures. Consider, to take one example, the cascading interest in urban criminal trial courts, including those dealing with less serious crimes (Gonzalez Van Cleve 2016; Kohler-Hausmann 2018). Feeley explored the emerging war on crime from the vantage of lower criminal courts in one of his most famous studies (and indisputably best titles), *The Process is the Punishment: Handling Cases in a Lower Criminal Court*, which was first published in 1979. Feeley's argument was quite well summarized in his title – for most people whose cases were being handled by lower criminal courts, it was not the prospect of conviction and prison time, the dominant concerns of appellate courts and television dramas both, but the petty indignities and discomforts of being processed through arrest, jail detention, and the chaos of court itself.

These lessons have never really been forgotten (as is marked by the fact that the book never went out of print and continues to be read by students), but in the age of mass incarceration (Alexander 2010; Simon 2014) sociolegal scholars and criminologists, among others, could be forgiven for shifting focus to the importance of incarceration (Zimring and Hawkins 1991; Feeley and Simon 1992; Garland 2001). In the last few years, however, a four-decade-long escalation of imprisonment rates in the United States (paralleled in some other countries including the United Kingdom) has come under sustained attack from within the political and legal establishment (even if by no means a consensus), and has modestly declined since 2012. As state criminal justice systems in the United States begin to look for ways to reduce their reliance on imprisonment (and jails) while not reducing the overall scale of their commitment to governing through crime (Simon 2007), the lower portions of the court systems have returned as important sites of both policy entrepreneurship (Feeley 2018) and critical social science inquiry. With the long-dominant value of increasing incapacitation through maximizing the potential of the pre-trial phases of the criminal process to yield prison sentences (or at least jail time) more contested than ever, it is possible to see, as Feeley did in his study, that criminal courts manage myriad social problems and address many community goals (some of them now objectionable, like maintaining white supremacy).

Feeley's next topic, the subject of a second Russell Sage Foundation study, *Court Reform on Trial: Why Simple Solutions Fail* (1983), addressed a range of reforms undertaken by states eager to improve criminal courts along a number of dimensions (and not just maximizing prison time), including fairness and equality. They story of these reforms and the landscape of public problems they capture is another reminder of the diversity of values that were replaced by the turn to the monoculture of mass imprisonment and the logic of incapacitation that unexpectedly followed. The criminal court has many roles to play in a democratic society, and *Court Reform on Trial* provides a reminder of how many of those other vital values have suffered under the hegemony of mass incarceration. Today, a tremendous amount of interest is again focused on reforming courts as a way now of shrinking the carceral state, including bail reform and more aggressive pretrial case management to reduce time to resolution, while plea bargaining is once again coming under fire (Lynch 2016).

A third example of renewed activity in an area historically captured by Feeley's work is courts as engines of social and institutional reform. The major framework is laid out in his study, done with Ed Rubin (1999), of the judicial revolution in prison reform that began in the 1960s using the traditionally spare authority of the Eighth Amendment's ban on "cruel and unusual punishments." Today, much research suggests that at the state level these court battles failed to achieve their goals to reduce reliance on incarceration. The legal challenges to prison conditions, which prisoner advocates hoped would force states to adopt alternatives to imprisonment, instead seemed to push fiscally conservative legislatures past their reluctance to fund a prison boom (Lynch 2010; Schoenfeld 2018). Building new prisons, rather than closing them, turned out to be a common outcome.

But if the politics of court reform are always unpredictable in a Feeleyian universe, *Court Reform on Trial* captured a more enduring institutional feature of federal courts in our constitutional system. The long debate about whether courts should be policy makers had ignored the conditions under which they could be policy makers. Here history matters. Today, with a new set of brutal and underinvested prison systems, many times the scale they were in the 1970s, we see federal courts cautiously weighing back in using just the kind of methodology Feeley and Rubin would expect (Simon 2014). How far any new period of judicial policy making in the penal field can be expected to go depends on developments beyond the courts that can provide sources of objectification and restraint (see Simon this volume).

Ironically, one of these developments may be what Feeley and Simon (1992) called "the new penology," i.e., the shift toward penal justice being framed in terms of risk management. Then, the authors saw the focus on offender risk as an analog to the rapidly spreading logic of mass imprisonment. As they later acknowledged, punitive populism, not actuarial categorization, seemed a more proximate cause of more and longer prison sentences. Yet today, as greatly expanded prison systems face escalating financial costs associated with aging and health care, as well the threat of renewed court challenges, many are turning to actuarial risk assessment as a possible framework for ordering or managing prison downsizing.

Prisons are not the only parts of the control state facing legitimacy challenge in the United States and other advanced democracies, and courts are not the only sources of policy making that need structures of objectivity, including expanding roles for both national and transnational executive power. Police, immigration detention and deportation, and the treatment of homeless people as well as people living with disabilities and with mental illnesses are frontiers of emerging legalities.

A final example does not rhyme with history because it is history in the making. The rise of liberal democracies seemed to have momentum as recently as the Arab Spring of 2012. Today, with illiberal political parties growing in both new and established democracies, the direction of history is less clear. Feeley's work with Terrence Halliday and Lucien Karpik (2007; 2012) on the role of the "legal complex" of lawyers, judges, and other legal professionals in establishing the anchors of political liberalism (which itself is quite close to the rule of law and constitutional democracy) confronts these issues as they occur.

Across these examples, we observe the agonistic struggles over bureaucratic control and human dignity playing out in those institutions that place the liberal state most pointedly in danger of legitimacy deficit (if not crisis). Moreover, we observe the role of law, not as an autonomous source of legitimacy, but as an incomplete project of legitimation and of the possibility of justice as dynamic that is simultaneously emerging and necessarily "unfinished." There is also a sense of conjunctural change coming through this research, at least as to the role of the criminal side of the state in the United States, although with broader repercussions for the legitimacy of political liberalism there and elsewhere. Feeley began his career as the war on crime and its parallel campaigns to reform and expand the criminal justice side of state and local government was unfolding, and his work has in many respects chronicled its integration with and influence on American government more broadly. Today the size and power of the criminal apparatus is under stress, and the whole range of insights Feeley's work generated, based on the quite different set of baselines he documented, should be reassessed and reinterpreted.

We organized the conference and this book largely around these central axes, inviting authors to present their own work in light of one or another of these classics. The reader will recognize Feeley's distinctive book titles in the headings of each section: Part I: The Process Is the Punishment; Part II: Court Reform on Trial; Part III: Judicial Policymaking and the Modern State; Part IV: Political Liberalism and the Legal Complex. Before discussing the authors' contributions, we proceed to discuss Feeley's intellectual path along each of these axes in turn.

PART I. FEELEY AS AN ORGANIZATIONAL SOCIOLOGIST: THE PROCESS IS THE PUNISHMENT

Feeley came to the study of criminal courts at a pivotal moment in scholarship. As a graduate student in political science at the University of Minnesota in the mid-1960s, he was fortunate to be exposed to a richer framework than the average legal scholar of that time. In addition to Sam Krislov and Harold Chase, his mentors in political science, he studied positive political theory with Ed Fogelman, anthropology of law with E. Adamson Hoebel, sociology of law with Arnold Rose, legal history with Robert Gerstein, and the philosophy of law with Jeffrey Murphy, and wrote a dissertation on state supreme courts. This eclectic training led him to move beyond the law in the books and law in action dichotomy that framed so much of the empirical work on law the time. The Vietnam War, the civil rights struggles and the findings of the presidential crime commission further prompted him to look skeptically at the much-hailed Warren Court's due process revolution (Packer 1968). These guideposts came in handy in his observations, interviews, and data collection on the New Haven lower court during his postdoctoral study at Yale. Taking a page from organizational sociologist Amitai Etzioni (1961), Feeley looked at the court through fresh eyes: not as a Weberian, rational beacon of justice with clear goals and coordinated effort to achieve those goals, but as a system comprised of different personal and institutional actors, each of which might pursue different goals. Feeley recognized that the courts that affect citizens most and bustle with the most courthouse activity are those at the bottom of the courthouse hierarchy, the misdemeanor courts.

The result was the landmark study of lower criminal courts, *The Process Is the Punishment*, Feeley's answer to the question of "why, even after winning these due process rights and guarantees in the Supreme Court, do so many people plead guilty in lower courts?" His insights were fresh and original. The problem did not lie in heavy caseloads; it lay in the complex organization of law in the dance of cooperation and competition among the courtroom actors trying to do justice, and the costs of the process and the toll it took on defendants. Nevertheless, as Mark Massoud notes in his contribution to this volume, "In his empirical studies of lower courts, Feeley watched prosecutors, defense lawyers, and judges toil for justice, despite the obstacles they faced and regardless of whether they succeeded. Even prosecutors, he found, had a sense of role morality." Feeley was aware of broader societal issues underlying these mechanisms – he explicitly discusses race and class in the introduction with acute awareness of their importance. His contribution lies in the multilevel complexity of his explanation.

The authors in Part I grapple with and extend Feeley's legacy in the study of the legal process as theory, method, and substance. Hadar Aviram's "Adversarial Bias and the Criminal Process: Infusing the Organizational Perspective on Criminal Courts with Insights from Behavioral Science" is an effort to reconcile the "big-time evils" we see on the news – colossal miscarriages of justice, prosecutorial misconduct, and wrongful convictions (supposedly stemming from unhealthy hyper-adversarialism) – with the daily evils Feeley observed: assembly line justice that is frustrating and impenetrable to everyday defendants and other visitors to the court (supposedly stemming from inappropriate cooperation). Aviram relies on the work of Kahneman, Tversky, and others to explain that both types of evils, which appear to be contradictory, can be explained by the same set of heuristics and biases on the systemic level.

Issa Kohler-Hausmann's "Malcolm Feeley's Concept of Law" considers how and why *The Process is the Punishment* "has achieved canonical status in the field of law and society." After a careful review of Feeley's empirical findings and his explanation of those findings, Kohler-Hausmann offers a surprising linkage between Feeley's deeply pragmatic approach to the study of law as revealed in lower courts and John Dewey's concept of normative ordering. As she observes, *The Process Is the Punishment* became a canonical text precisely because its approach differed from the more common "law in action" writings about the court; the book offers an examination of law as a "normative ordering" that is, always and necessarily, itself ordered in concrete organizational settings.

In *The Process is the Punishment*, Feeley showed that the experience of criminal court processing can feel like punishment to a defendant, separate and apart from the outcome of the criminal case. In their contribution, Kay Levine and Volkan Topalli explore how that effect extends beyond defendants to their families, particularly children, and whether this effect exists even before incarceration is imposed. In "Process as Intergenerational Punishment: Are Children Casualties of Parental Court Experiences?" the authors interviewed prosecutors and active offenders in a major southeastern city to identify their perceptions of the short- and long-term effects of witnessing court processing on children of offenders. Their interviews suggest that such experiences could have deleterious effects similar to those observed in research on the effects of parental incarceration. They conclude by offering some policy suggestions for how the court system might mitigate these effects in the future.

Finally, Shauhin Talesh's "The Process Is the Problem" extends Feeley's analysis into civil litigation and alternative dispute resolution processes. Talesh argues that in these contexts the process is not the punishment, but rather the problem. Focusing largely on the procedural rules in court and alternative dispute processes, this chapter highlights how the United States Supreme Court has trimmed procedural protections in civil courts and alternative dispute forums. With the advocacy and support of private organizations and the defense bar, due process rights and procedural protections have been redefined, and consequently citizens' access to justice is significantly undermined. When individuals do invoke their procedural and due process rights and seek substantive relief in court or arbitration, they are subject to a process filtered with organizational values and influence in subtle and sometimes not-so-subtle ways.

PART II. FEELEY AS AN EVALUATOR OF THE LEGAL PROCESS: COURT REFORM ON TRIAL

In a recent article, Feeley wrote, "The American criminal court system rests upon the quest for perfection ... I want to explore the reasons why this quest for a Rolls Royce has led to the acquisition of a wreck ... I want to focus on the machinery of criminal justice ... My argument is that the institutional design of the adversary process fails in fundamental ways to provide a workable system of misdemeanor justice, and that its problems are compounded by the American governmental structure" (Feeley, 2018: 70). That article was the culmination of many years of observing and analyzing and hoping for better from the legal process. In *Court Reform on Trial*, Feeley centered on the issue of disappointment: why do so many seemingly good ideas, such as bail reform, pretrial diversion, speedy trials, and determinate sentencing, fail to bring positive change to the system? The typical answer to this question among both legal scholars and some social scientists has been to blame the plea bargaining system, which has granted prosecutors immense power over charging decisions and, as a consequence, over the system in general. But Feeley's unique organizational lens saw plea bargaining not as an evil undermining the adversarial system, but as its logical outcome (Feeley 1983). The problem with reforms, he argues in the book, has to do with the nature of reform itself. Reformers – typically outsiders to the system – come to the task of reform with unrealistic expectations, where they encounter a splintered system with fragmented decision making, politicians who are counterincentivized to resist change, voiceless constituencies, and the demons of their own grandiosity. The book is not only a tour de force in mapping the clashing forces for and against court reform, but it is also an example of Feeley's real investment in change: his tone and style address the reformers themselves, offering some guidelines toward change.

The chapters in Part II continue in Feeley's footsteps in exposing the cultural and political underpinnings of policy and reform, as well as their unintended consequences. Also in the spirit of Feeley's exploration as a comparativist across space and time, these authors take us on geographic and historical journeys.

As Eric Feldman says in "Regulating E-Cigarettes: Why Policies Diverge," Feeley's work often engages complex policy choices, and analyzes the range of policy approaches available to state actors. This study follows his example by exploring a thorny policy question – the regulation of e-cigarettes – and examining a spectrum of policy approaches. Moreover, Feeley's "work is almost always concerned with the law in action, and demonstrates a deep engagement with how legal rules and practices affect the populace, particularly marginalized populations." Feldman follows in Feeley's comparative footsteps in his examination of systemic problems and challenges in the legal control of electronic cigarettes in the United States, Japan, and China. Conflict over the regulation of this novel product has emerged throughout the industrialized world, with policymakers in small towns, large nations, and international organizations debating the pros and cons of nicotine vaporizing devices. As major multinational tobacco companies have increasingly taken control of the e-cigarette industry, what was at first a battle between small business and government regulators has become a fight involving billions of dollars and fundamental issues of public health. Feldman examines the legal and policy principles at stake in the conflict over the regulation of e-cigarettes and compares the regulatory markets in three nations. He finds considerable differences in the set of legal controls that each jurisdiction deems appropriate, and also finds that the different policy choices generate different consequences, both intended and unintended.

In "Japanese Court Reform on Trial" David Johnson and Setsuo Miyazawa consider some major changes in the Japanese court system that have been introduced in recent years: the creation of lay judge panels to adjudicate serious criminal cases, and changes in legal education aimed at reshaping the legal profession by introducing postgraduate professional law schools and increasing the number of new lawyers admitted to the bar. Citing *Court Reform on Trial*, they point to one of Feeley's important insights in that study: "One of the central problems of the courts is that there is no agreement on what constitutes acceptable practice and hence no agreement on what improvements should be made. Practices that are regarded by some as signs of decline may, when seen through someone else's eyes, be seen as strengths." As it is early days in the reforms Johnson and Miyazawa examine, they recognize that "it will take more time to make a sound assessment of the changes." Moreover, if Feeley is correct, as they believe he is, "when the conclusion comes it will be a hung jury because different people expect different things from the Japanese reforms, and they are not all compatible."

In "Court Reform and Comparative Criminal Justice," comparative criminologist David Nelken considers *Court Reform on Trial* and its lessons for comparative methodology. Nelken takes us on a journey through not only what the book can teach, but importantly what it can learn from comparative criminal justice. Applying Feeley's ideas to a foreign jurisdiction – the Italian criminal justice system – raises new questions about the role and limits of generalizing through explanatory social science. Nelken considers whether all social science is inherently comparative as Feeley suggests, or whether, as in Nelken's more interpretative approach, many of the instructive lessons of looking abroad come from seeing the difficulty of generalizing and the challenges of cross-cultural translation.

The last two chapters in this section apply the spirit and insights of *Court Reform on Trial* to historical settings. In "The Birth of the Penal Organization: Why Prisons Were Born to Fail," Ashley Rubin argues that, like courts, prisons are the subject of exaggerated claims and unrealistic expectations grounded in a fundamental misunderstanding of prisons' nature and operation. The prison itself was a significant reform – one that repeatedly failed, only to be replaced through reform by a new iteration of itself. Her chapter examines the transition away from capital punishment, an informal, ad hoc, temporary ritual, and the location of punishment within a formal, rational, semipermanent organization. She argues that moving punishment inside an organization – housed in a semipermanent building, employing administrators and staff charged with following ambiguous rules – introduces a wide range of nonpenal logics, goals and problems that compete with and ultimately displace penal goals. This process, which Rubin calls "organizationalization," is attended by many of the problems Feeley has identified with court reforms' conception, implementation, and routinization. It also creates a context of inevitable failure that leads to the prison's history of ongoing cycles of reform. With this understanding in mind, the question becomes not why prisons fail, but why we repeatedly expect prisons to succeed.

Finally, legal historian Lawrence Friedman's "The Misbegotten: Infanticide in Victorian England" is a nod not only to the issue of unintended consequences in *Court Reform on Trial*, but also to another area of Feeley's scholarship – the history of female offenders. While working on historical plea bargaining in the Old Bailey, Feeley came across a curious phenomenon: a large percentage of female offenders, even in areas of crime that are not "typically female." He expanded this study to other European courts, finding a similar pattern that transcended local changes and incidents. In works with Deborah Little (1996) and Hadar Aviram (2011), and relying on work by social historians of gender, Feeley explained the "vanishing" of female offenders from the criminal court map as part of a shift in patriarchy styles from public to private. Friedman's chapter in this volume examines cases from the Old Bailey in the Victorian period, in which young unmarried women in domestic service were accused of murdering their newborn children. Although it was considered a significant social problem in the period, the defendants were almost never convicted of this crime; almost half were acquitted, and most of the rest were found guilty only of a lesser crime (concealing the birth of an illegitimate child). The cases reveal a kind of Victorian paradox. On the one hand, a strict and harsh moral code bore most heavily on women, and made their situation truly desperate if they gave birth out of wedlock – particularly if they were poor women in domestic service. And yet the (all-male) juries were extremely lenient. Scattered evidence from other parts of England confirms the findings from London. Gender stereotypes may explain the paradox: the idea that women were in general naive, innocent, and easily seduced, and that they, despite their sins, were actually victims in these cases, may have acted to save them from the gallows.

PART III. FEELEY AS AN ANALYST OF THE COURTS' POWER IN BRINGING ABOUT SOCIAL CHANGE: JUDICIAL POLICY MAKING AND THE MODERN STATE

A more optimistic perspective on the power of reform is in evidence in Feeley's 1998 collaboration with Edward Rubin. In *Judicial Policy Making and the Modern State*, they argue that, between 1965 and 1990, federal judges in almost all of the states handed down sweeping rulings that affected virtually every prison and jail in the United States. Without a doubt, judges were the most important prison reformers during this period, though they collaborated with reform-minded litigators and corrections professionals to challenge state prison systems with the worst conditions. Activist judges relied upon standards that had been devised within the corrections field to combat recalcitrance and pressure prisons into ending inhumane practices. Feeley and Rubin use their account of this process to explore the more general issue of the role of courts in the modern bureaucratic state. They provide detailed analyses of how the courts formulated and sought to implement their orders, and how these actions affected the traditional conception of federalism, separation of powers, and the rule of law.

But can courts bring about social change in other contexts as well? And if not, why not? The chapters in Part III compare Feeley and Rubin's analysis of prison reform with other legal areas in which activists sought to increase dignity and equality through litigation and found varying degrees of success.

In "Judicial Deference in the Modern State," Lauren Edelman argues that judicial reliance on organizational standards does not always have the positive consequences Feeley and Rubin found in the deference to professional correctional standards in prison litigation. Focusing on civil rights in the employment arena, Edelman shows that judicial deference to organizational structures is becoming increasingly common in the modern state. Yet because organizations create compliance structures that symbolize legality, judges tend to assume that the mere presence of these structures constitutes compliance with antidiscrimination law irrespective of whether those structures are effective in combating discrimination. Judicial deference to symbolic structures helps to explain why race and gender inequality persist in the American workplace more than a half-century after the landmark 1964 Civil Rights Act. Citing recent work by scholars studying prison litigation, Edelman suggests that, at least in recent years, judicial deference to symbolic compliance also occurs in this arena.

Paul Frymer finds a similar judicial reluctance to intervene in the context of labor. In "The Law of the Workplace," he begins with a thematic extending from the first to the second Gilded Age: judges, as argued by legal academics and illustrated in repeated judicial decisions that interpret labor statutes, have consistently been resistant to extending the rights of workers who wish to organize and join unions. Furthermore, courts have been unwilling to extend legal protections to individuals on the basis of economic class, even during a revolutionary era when such rights were expanded to other demographic categories. The reasons for this judicial bias are multifaceted. In part, it stems from straightforward economic elitism. It is also the result of regulatory features of labor law that resist judicial cultures and sensibilities that are geared toward individual justice and resistant to group empowerment. And in part it reflects judicial criticism of the strategies of labor litigation. Frymer surveys this conversation and focus on federal court decisions in the modern era with the hope of further understanding this critical institutional dynamic that too frequently serves to recreate economic inequality.

Christine Harrington recognizes in Feeley and Rubin's classic analysis of the institutional dynamics of judicial policy making a more general framework for understanding how policy making is both legally and politically contested. In "Administrative 'States' of Judicial Policy on Gender-Motivated Violence" Harrington applies this framework to the example of the Violence Against Women Act of 1994 (VAWA), a statute that created a comprehensive new federal civil right for individuals to be protected against a wide array of sexually charged violent acts. In the 2000 decision of *Morrison* v. *Olson*, the Supreme Court invalidated the central component of VAWA, holding that Congress exceeded its authority under the Commerce Clause and the Fourteenth Amendment, and was impinging on the proper authority of the states under the broad conservative doctrine of federalism. Harrington focuses in on this judicially led countermobilization against a newly established right and shows how Feeley and Rubin's dynamics can be used by a conservative judiciary to push back against new rights in favor of traditional values and legal doctrines. Feeley and Rubin showed how individual federal judges could use a combination of traditional doctrinal tools like metaphor, analogy and classification along with a new recognition of the "bureaucratic element" in doctrinal implementation to become policy-making powers in the modern administrative state. Harrington shows how the federal judiciary as a whole, and through its leadership, has built since the 1920s a formidable bureaucratic power of its own to help shape the modern administrative state through complex negotiations and lobbying with Congress and, ultimately, as in *Morrison*, to draw on both bureaucratic imperatives (like efficiency and scientific management) along with revitalized conservative ideals of federalism to stymie those pieces of rights legislation that are enacted over its objections.

Jonathan Simon extends the analysis of *Judicial Policy Making and the Modern State* well into the 2010s in "Can Courts End Mass Incarceration?" In his chapter, Simon observes that federal courts in the 1970s and 1980s were able to use the Eighth Amendment to find numerous substantive requirements for the humane and decent treatment of prisoners that effectively dismantled a system of southern plantation-style prisons that had survived Reconstruction, the New Deal, and the Great Society. Ironically, the very success of the prisoners' rights revolution, however, helped lay the foundation for mass incarceration by forcing states to build new prisons not vulnerable to the interventions of courts. The resulting transformation of American corrections largely undermined the jurisprudential basis of judicial reform of prisons. Courts began to defer more comprehensively to prison managers and their expertise, a trend codified by the Prison Litigation Reform Act. Simon asks whether the landmark 2011 *Brown* v. *Plata* decision of the US Supreme Court, affirming the most comprehensive prison system reform order in history on California's overcrowded and medically incompetent prisons, may mean that a new era of judicially-led prison reform is upon us. Comparing the jurisprudential and social foundation of court-led reform in the past and today, Simon asks whether court-led efforts can help dismantle mass incarceration, a system of penal harm vastly larger and perhaps even more degrading than the plantation-style prisons addressed by the courts in Feeley's study.

Finally, Menachem Hofnung extends Feeley's framework to argue that, sometimes, courts effect social change not by open rulings, but by procedural encouragement of out-of-court settlements. In "Policy Making by Out-of-Court Settlements: Palestinian Informers at the Israeli High Court of Justice," Hofnung argues that courts can serve as effective policy makers by avoiding detailed rulings and installing legal standards by forcing state agencies to accept out-of-court settlements. The database for this research is comprised of close to 600 petitions by thousands of Arabs (mostly Palestinians) who are turning to the Israeli High Court of Justice and asking to be formally recognized as "informers" (a term commonly used in Israel to denote Palestinian collaborators with the Israeli secret services). In the absence of direct legislation, the court is handling dozens of these petitions every year. Out of the nearly 600 cases, there has been only one clear victory for the petitioner. Interestingly enough, notwithstanding the negligible chance of winning, the number of petitions has risen steadily since the early 1990s. Hofnung argues that by quietly settling petitions through out-of-court settlements instead of setting precedents that would be binding in the future, the Court can become an effective policy maker, while at the same time refraining from a direct clash with both the elected authorities and the security establishment.

PART IV. FEELEY AS A THEORIST OF LEGAL EVOLUTION: THE LEGAL COMPLEX AND POLITICAL LIBERALISM

The project that Terence Halliday and Lucien Karpik embarked upon, to examine the role of lawyers in the construction of liberal political regimes, what they called "political lawyering," began in the 1990s. But it gained momentum and indeed complexity when Malcolm Feeley joined the political liberalism project, paying more attention to the role of courts as political actors and the relationship between the bench and the bar, and developing the term "the legal complex." As Edward Rubin says in his contribution to this volume, "The quality of the relationship between judges and lawyers can powerfully contribute to the process of securing basic human rights and imposing constraints on governmental power – the hallmarks of political liberalism, in Professor Feeley's view. Thus, this relationship, which lies at the center of the legal complex, is a major factor that determines whether liberal regimes flourish or founder." As Feeley explains in a Postscript to their 2012 volume,

> Studies of political liberalism consistently emphasize that the fortunes of liberal politics are inextricably intertwined with not only the politics of the bar but the politics of the bench ... In our extension of the political liberalism project to other continents, times and places, it became clear that turns toward and away from political liberalism also often turned on alliances between judges and lawyers: when the bar acted alone, and sometimes in opposition to the judiciary, its capacity to facility or defend political liberalism was greatly impeded ... When the bench, and especially constitutional judges, and the bar fought together, the political conflict with the state became more radical as a result the prospect of political liberalism brightened perceptibly unless the state was prepared to brutally escalate its repression ... Because we observed, historically and comparatively, that the politics of courts are intertwined with those of the bar, we introduced a new concept, the legal complex, a notion that acknowledges the expanded importance of legally trained, law-practicing actors in the political process in the modern state. (493)

The chapters in Part IV consider the role of the legal complex in a range of contexts, both theoretical and material, beginning with one of Feeley's coauthors, Terrance Halliday. Halliday further expands the notion of the legal complex to the promising concept of an "international legal complex." As Halliday recognizes in "The International Legal Complex: Wang Yu and the Global Response to Repression of China's Political Lawyers," "A central element of Feeley's work on lawyers and political liberalism has revolved around the politics of the legal complex ... Feeley has argued that the concept of legal complex is particularly valuable insofar as it embraces what previously had been a study of judicial politics without lawyers." In the spirit of Feeley's inquiries, this chapter advances the concept of the international legal complex. It argues that since the nineteenth century, the political struggles by lawyers for basic legal freedoms in many parts of the world were not simply a national but an international phenomenon. It explores the dimensions of an international legal complex through an unprecedented repressive turn by China's Party-State, the case of Wang Yu, a leading human rights lawyer, who was "disappeared" on July 11, 2015. This was the opening move by the state security apparatus against almost 200 human rights lawyers and activists, quite possibly the most extraordinary state action against lawyers by any major country in the last several decades. The response by lawyers outside China, by international rights organizations, NGOs, foreign governments, and international media provide a rich body of data through which to explore the mobilization of an international legal complex, both in the structure of ties among legal professions and in their relationships with international civil society and global publics. It also opens up the question of how far an international legal complex can mobilize as a collective actor beyond legal practitioners and legal academics.

In "The Legal Profession's Promise of Justice," Mark Massoud builds on Feeley's scholarship on how lawyers and judges work to secure the promise of justice, and how scholars consider both empirical context and humanistic values when studying the legal profession. As he notes, "Feeley's solo and collaborative scholarship, sometimes based on empirical research in and on courts, has been central to literature on the practices of judges and lawyers in diverse political contexts, from lower courts in the United States to apex courts in East Asia and former British colonies." Massoud illuminates a social theory of justice derived in part from Feeley's scholarship, in which Feeley's conception of justice links the legal profession's idealism with its materialism. To show how Feeley's theory of justice is part of a broader call for normative sociolegal scholarship, the paper also engages with, among others, Philip Selznick's work on morality and personhood and Martin Krygier's work on the rule of law. Ultimately, Massoud argues, Feeley's scholarship on the legal profession's promise of justice invites law and society scholars to "think comparatively, to consider the margins, and to be contrarian."

In "The Varieties of Judicial Independence and the Judiciary's Role in Political Reform," Edward Rubin examines the notion of judicial independence, which he argues is a necessary condition for the legal complex – as defined by Malcolm Feeley and his colleagues – to serve as a force for advancing political liberalism. Rubin argues that judicial independence is not an inevitable element in democratic regimes, nor is it limited to these regimes. Second, it exists at different levels, what he calls "ordinary judicial independence" and "judicial hyperindependence," in which the judiciary is independent not only of the executive but of the legislature. He considers these issues generally and in the specific context of the two forms of judicial hyperindependence that exist in the American legal system: common law and constitutional law. He argues that the hyperindependence of the common law was replaced by ordinary independence as the administrative state took hold, while the hyperindependence of constitutional law continued, but in modified form.

Kim Scheppele considers the role lawyers in power can play in undermining political liberalism, as in the examples of Russia and Hungary. In "The Legal Complex and the Legal Loophole," she argues that while legal complex scholarship has shown that lawyers think about politics differently than other politicians and often pull even illiberal governments toward liberalism, lawyers in power can also undermine liberalism by taking advantage of legal loopholes to evade the full force of the law. In Russia, President Vladimir Putin trained as a lawyer, and his legalistic style shows in his governance. The use of "little green men" in Crimea – men said to be "volunteers" associated with no state army – evaded a clear legal prohibition against foreign invasion and annexation of territory. In Hungary, Prime Minister Viktor Orbán, also trained as a lawyer, took the bits and pieces of laws of other European Union Member States and stitched together these provisions to produce an illiberal constitution, a "Frankenstate." But Orbán evaded EU sanctions by invoking other states' comparable laws in self-defense – even though those laws were used in very different contexts. These two cases show that lawyers in power can use their legal training to find legal loopholes as much as they can use their legal talent for bringing governments closer to liberal legality.

CONCLUSION

In conclusion, on offer here is not the work of one scholar, even a great one at that, but a suite of recent scholarship by established and emerging leaders in fields of law, sociolegal studies, political science, and criminology, addressing the institutions that continue to determine the meaning of law and human dignity in liberal and not so liberal societies. With one eye toward the transformative history of the twentieth century that shaped the modern administrative state and one toward the unfinished possibilities of justice, these chapters now invite you in to take the next steps.

REFERENCES

Alexander, Michelle. 2010. *The New Jim Crow: Mass Incarceration in the Age of Colorblindness*. New York: The New Press.

Etzioni, Amitai. 1961. *A Comparative Analysis of Complex Organizations: On Power, Involvement, and their Correlates*. New York: Free Press.

Feeley, Malcolm M. 1979. *The Process is the Punishment: Handling Cases in a Lower Criminal Court*. New York: Russel-Sage.

Feeley, Malcolm M. 1983. *Court Reform on Trial: Why Simple Solutions Fail*. New York: Basic Books.

Feeley, Malcolm M. 2018. "How to Think About Criminal Court Reform." *Boston University Law Review* 98: 669–726.

Feeley, Malcolm M. and Hadar Aviram. 2010. "Social Historical Studies of Women, Crime, and Courts." *Annual Review of Law and Social Science* 6: 151–71.

Feeley, Malcolm M. and Deborah Little. 1991. "The Vanishing Female: The Decline of Women in the Criminal Process, 1687–1912." *Law & Society Review* 25: 719–57.

Feeley, Malcolm M. and Edward L. Rubin. 1999. *Judicial Policy Making and the Modern State: How the Courts Reformed America's Prisons*. New York: Cambridge University Press.

Feeley, Malcolm M., and Jonathan Simon. 1992. "The New Penology: Notes on the Emerging Strategy of Corrections and Its Implications." *Criminology* 30.4: 449–74.

Garland, David. 2001. *The Culture of Control: Crime and Social Order in Contemporary Society*. Chicago: University of Chicago Press.

Gonzalez Van Cleve, Nicole. 2016. *Crook County Racism and Injustice in America's Largest Criminal Court*. Stanford: Stanford University Press.

Goodman, Philip, Joshua Page, and Michelle Phelps. 2017. *Breaking the Pendulum: The Long Struggle Over Criminal Justice*. New York, NY: Oxford University Press.

Halliday Terence C., Lucien Karpik, and Malcolm M. Feeley. 2007. *Fighting for Political Freedom: Comparative Studies of the Legal Complex and Political Liberalism*. Oñati: Hart Publishing.

Halliday Terence C., Lucien Karpik, and Malcolm M. Feeley. 2012. *Fates of Political Liberalism in the British Post-Colony*. New York: Cambridge University Press.

Kohler-Hausmann, Issa. 2018. *Misdemeanorland: Criminal Courts and Social Control in an Age of Broken Windows Policing*. Princeton: Princeton University Press.

Lynch, Mona. 2010. *Sunbelt Justice: Arizona and the Transformation of American Punishment*. Stanford: Stanford University Press.

Lynch, Mona. 2016. *Hard Bargains: The Coercive Power of Drug Laws in Federal Court*. New York: Russell Sage Foundation.

Packer, Herbert L. 1968. *The Limits of the Criminal Sanction*. Stanford: Stanford University Press.

Pound, Roscoe. 1910. "Law in Books and Law in Action." *American Law Review* 44.1: 12–36.

Schoenfeld, Heather. 2018. *Building the Prison State: Race and the Politics of Mass Incarceration*. Chicago: University of Chicago Press.

Simon, Jonathan. 2007. *Governing Through Crime: How the Warn on Crime Transformed American Democracy and Created a Culture of Fear*. New York: Oxford University Press.

Simon, Jonathan. 2014. *Mass Incarceration on Trial: A Remarkable Court Decision and the Future of Prisons in America*. New York: The New Press.

Zimring, Franklin E. and Gordon J. Hawkins. 1991. *The Scale of Imprisonment*. Chicago: University of Chicago Press.

PART I

The Process Is the Punishment

1

Adversarial Bias and the Criminal Process: Infusing the Organizational Perspective on Criminal Courts with Insights from Behavioral Science

Hadar Aviram

INTRODUCTION

Generations of criminal courtroom scholars were raised on Malcolm Feeley's book *The Process Is the Punishment* (1979b) as the gold standard of criminal courtroom ethnography. In the book, and in some of his other work from the 1970s and early 1980s (Feeley 1973; Feeley 1977; Feeley, 1982), Feeley examined lower criminal courts from an organizational perspective, a view that shaped several of the classic criminal court studies, such as Eisenstein and Jacob's *Felony Justice* (1978) and Nardulli's *The Courtroom Elite* (1978). In the first of Feeley's works in this vein, "Two Models of the Criminal Process: An Organizational Perspective" (1973), he offered a sociological counterpart to Herbert Packer's *The Limits of the Criminal Sanction* (1968) and a primer on courts as organizations. In "Pleading Guilty in Lower Courts" (1978), and in *The Process Is the Punishment*, he examined the pressures and incentives generated by the court's organizational culture and their impact on defendants' decisions to plead guilty and avoid trials. And in "Plea Bargains and the Structure of the Criminal Process" (1982), Feeley used the organizational framework to argue that plea bargains were not an aberration of adversarialism, but its natural corollary.

Feeley's organizational framework led him to develop a fresh and unique perspective on the adversarial system. Where common portrayals of the adversarial process showed warfare, games, and rivalry, Feeley saw convergence, cooperation, and workplace convenience. While much has changed in the criminal justice system since Feeley sat and observed case processing in New Haven courts in the 1970s, his insights about the nature of adversarialism are as true and useful today as they were then. The rates of guilty pleas and the assembly-line style of case processing confirm his findings about institutional collaboration in efficient disposal of cases, and even though the decades since his early publications have seen a rise in punitive legislation and in power concentration in the hands of prosecutors, much of the current crisis of mass incarceration can be attributed to aggressive felony charging, overcharging, and charge bargaining (Pfaff 2011, 2017).

As Feeley was developing an understanding of adversarialism as collaborative, however, scholars in other disciplines were exposing factors that suggested otherwise. The Nobel-winning work of Amos Tversky and Daniel Kahneman (1974; 1981), as well as that of their students, has yielded rich findings about motivation, heuristics, and biases, which affect human ability to think rationally, accurately perceive reality, obtain and assess information. Some of these mechanisms, particularly attitudinal and confirmation biases, would suggest that actors in the criminal justice system, like everyone else, are susceptible to the rigidity and "tunnel vision" that can hinder collaboration and compromise and, what is worse, generate serious miscarriages of justice.

How are these two views of adversarialism to be reconciled? In this chapter, I argue that Feeley's groundbreaking understanding of adversarialism is not undermined by subsequent insights from behavioral sciences. To the contrary: the tendency of "repeat players" in the criminal justice system, such as prosecutors and defense attorneys, to reach agreements that allow them to quickly and efficiently process the vast majority of cases, stems from the same biases that lead them to fight bitterly in court about a small minority of cases. The high-profile, dramatic miscarriages of justice predicted by heuristics and biases stem from the same "banality of evil" that produces the low-key, everyday miscarriages of justice that Feeley witnessed in lower courts, and that we still witness today. I refer to the phenomenon that generates both of these problems as adversarial bias.

The chapter begins, in Section 1.1, with an exposition of Feeley's ideas about the organizational features underlying courtroom culture, and particularly the idea of a "functional system" where rivaling goals and interests meet institutional concerns. Section 1.2 elaborates on the classic courtroom ethnographies and the extent to which their findings lended support to the "functional systems model" and to the idea of cooperation between the parties. Then, Section 1.3 presents the problems of adversarialism as highlighted by behavioral research, which at first glance seems to contradict the ethnographic insight about courtroom cooperation. The two understandings of the adversarial courtroom setting – unhealthy cooperation and unhealthy competition – are taken to their extreme in Section 1.4, which presents them as two "parades of horribles." Section 1.5 reconciles these visions by explaining that tunnel vision and unhealthy cooperation are two sides of the same coin, and that courtroom adversarialism can breed both problems, though they typically manifest in different settings. I end by offering an agenda for future research.

1.1 RATIONAL GOALS AND FUNCTIONAL SYSTEMS

In 1968, Herbert Packer published *The Limits of the Criminal Sanction*. Part II of the book, based on a prior article, formulated the now-famous two models of the criminal process. Crime control, argued Packer, was a framework that focused on promoting efficiency in case processing. In such a system, the police and the prosecution enjoyed vast amounts of power and trust; any defendant whose case proceeded to trial past a rigorous police investigation and the scrutiny of prosecutorial discretion was likely guilty, which meant that lengthy trials and punctilious technical protections were unnecessary, as were post-conviction remedies. By contrast, due process focused on quality control in an effort to avoid wrongful conviction. Under the due process model, the biases of the law enforcement apparatus had to be countered by powerful constitutional protections and zealous representation, and an array of post-conviction remedies was necessary to prevent mistakes. Rather than describing actual legal systems, Packer argued that the models represented "ideal types" that could be useful for analyzing longitudinal trends or comparing systems to one another.

It is no coincidence that Packer wrote his book as he witnessed the Warren Court revolution, which equipped state defendants nationwide with powerful constitutional protections. For his intended audience – law professors, like Packer himself, in elite law schools, who were making sense of the new Supreme Court jurisprudence – the book was innovative and visionary. At the time, elite legal scholars focused their energy on doctrinal commentary on Supreme Court cases, and Packer's book offered a comprehensive framework for understanding these changes (Aviram 2011). But for social scientists, who were discovering the rich world of lower courts and the immense potential of courtroom ethnography, Packer's models seemed naïve. Among the first critics of Packer's book was Abraham Blumberg (1969), who argued that the models hid a reality that was closer to the crime control model: a system guided mostly by efficiency and plea bargaining. Blumberg critiqued the detachment of legal scholars from the everyday realities of courtroom dynamics, particularly in lower courts.

In a similar, but more sophisticated, critique, Malcolm Feeley (1978; 1979a; 1979b) argued that the two models were not made of the same cloth. Due process, Feeley argued, was a normative, idealized concept generated by the court, masking the empirical reality, which was actually much closer to crime control.[1] As someone who had come to the study of law via a strong background in social science, Feeley's interest was in models that facilitated useful and informative empirical work; the gap between what the law strove to achieve and what it actually achieved interested him less than studying the motivations and pressures that shaped actual behavior by criminal justice agents. And, indeed, the eponymous models in his essay "Two Models of the Criminal Process: An Organizational Perspective" (1973) are very different from those proposed by Packer.

Feeley's analysis was strongly influenced by a typology created by organizational sociologist Amitai Etzioni. Adapting Etzioni's typology to the lower criminal court

[1] This conceptual problem was later echoed in Stuart Macdonald's critique of the models: "Packer's dialogue between the two models . . . reveals two voices speaking at cross-purposes: a crime control model that fails to articulate its model clearly, and a due process voice that has failed to understand the model of its opponent" (Macdonald 2008, 276).

setting, Feeley identified two new models: the rational goal model and the functional systems model.

The rational goal model, Feeley argued, was a manifestation of Weber's rationality, and in this context reflected the activities of the criminal justice system as guided by rigid rules, professionalism, division of labor, and a supervision apparatus. Indeed, this model:

> seem[ed] to be the dominant view or ideal of the criminal justice process held by appellate judges and lawyers, and many of the academic students of the courts. Much of their discussion and research, therefore, has centered on the problems with the formal rules of operation, i.e., increasing the "rationality" by minimizing discretion and arbitrary administration, through specifying with increasing precision the roles of the actors. Lawyers under the auspices of the American Bar Association go to great lengths to articulate and refine the precise role of the advocate in criminal justice; many appellate court decisions are attempts at further defining and refining the rules and roles for the various actors in the organization; law journals and appellate court opinions are filled with discussions of the proposals for rules to minimize discretion and more completely define the rules of procedure; and social scientists continue to point out that no one is following the formal rules. (Feeley 1973, 410–411)

Studies relying on a rational goal model, argued Feeley, sought to measure the extent to which the criminal justice system lived up to its goals and aspirations – such as, for example, an examination of whether police interrogatory behavior conformed to the requirements of *Miranda v. Arizona* (1966).

What these studies failed to do, claimed Feeley, was take into account the possibility that some behaviors and practices in the criminal justice system occurred not in relation to the set of formal rules, but rather to other factors. These factors are more adequately addressed via the more realistic functional systems model. Rather than strictly obeying the formal rules of the system, the actors in the criminal justice system are more likely to follow:

> the "folkways" or informal "rules of the game" within the organization; the goals they pursue are likely to be personal or subgroup goals; and the roles they assume are likely to be defined by the functional adaptation of these two factors. These three features of the organization then are the objects to be accounted for, and the functional-systems approach is likely to begin to identify and examine the adaptation of the actors to the environment, the workload and the interests of the persons placed within the system, i.e., other goals of the actors within the organization. (Feeley 1973, 414)

Some of these informal folkways and personal/partisan interests include, explained Feeley, a push toward convenience and away from formalities and time-consuming tasks. Jerome Skolnick's *Justice Without Trial* (1968) exemplified research based on this perspective; Skolnick's ethnography of police officers, prosecutors, and defense attorneys showed how the actors gravitated toward cooperation and "cutting corners" in case processing, and how attorneys who insisted on formalities, thus jamming the efficiency machine, were eventually transferred out. Similarly, Feeley found the functional model to be supported by Blumberg's analysis of defense counsel (1967a; 1967b), who presumably under the formal rules were supposed to zealously work on behalf of their clients, but due to organizational pressures and repeat-player connections in the system ended up cooperating with the law enforcement apparatus and "conning" their clients into accepting plea bargains.[2]

1.2 COURTROOM ETHNOGRAPHIES AND ADVERSARIALISM

Feeley's analysis, and particularly his functional systems model, perfectly captured the scholarly zeitgeist. The 1960s and 1970s saw a lively flow of scholarship that examined lower criminal courts through an organizational lens – including Feeley's own empirical work. These works, which exposed the often opaque inner workings of police investigations, prosecutorial decision making, and plea bargaining, highlighted the interpersonal and bureaucratic pressure to process cases efficiently, through collaborations and agreements. By doing so, they showed how the official rules of criminal procedure failed to fully capture the realities that shaped decision-making and negotiations in the criminal justice system.

David Sudnow's "Normal Crimes" (1965), for example, exposed the irrelevance of the offense definitions in the criminal code for case disposition. The sentence a defendant received for a given offense, he demonstrated via observations, was a far cry from the Beccaria-esque structure of criminal codes, which strove to ascribe punishment to each offense based on its severity. Actual plea negotiations did not rely on such definitions or on formal scales of severity, but rather on reaching an understanding to classify the given case in the appropriate category according to the circumstances. This classification did not rely on the penal code, but rather on the cumulative expertise of defense attorneys and prosecutors, who would have already seen numerous cases that resembled the one in question. The plea agreement would reflect this shared understanding, thus allowing to process these common, "normal crimes" quickly and saving time for the few unusual outliers that did not lend themselves to such classification.

Similar cooperation was uncovered in James Eisenstein and Herbert Jacob's *Felony Justice* (1977), which revealed that even when cases came to trial they were no more than "slow pleas." This work, as well as Milton Heumann's *Plea Bargaining* (1968) and Peter Nardulli's *The Courtroom Elite* (1979), marshaled observations,

---

[2] Notably, Feeley's later work, *Court Reform on Trial* (2013[1983]) and "The New Penology" (Feeley and Simon 1992), reflects a functional perspective – the evolution of sentencing and corrections into a full-fledged risk assessment model, which classifies people according to an actuarial assessment of risk and controls them accordingly, and which does not subscribe to an express penological goal, but rather to "warehousing" out of organizational convenience.

interviews, and quantitative findings to show that criminal justice actors – prosecutors, defense attorneys, and judges – were motivated by factors other than their official roles in the system. The need for efficiency, docket management, and preserving interpersonal relationships among repeat players provided strong motivation toward plea bargaining and other concessions.

Feeley's own book, *The Process Is the Punishment* (1979b), is the quintessential example of such extraneous motivation – this time, that of the defendants themselves. As opposed to the "rational" analysis of plea bargaining, Feeley concluded that defendants pleaded guilty because showing up for trial, in itself – as well as experiencing the trial process – was, from their perspective, "punishment." By contrast, plea bargains were a predictable time saver, more akin to a price list at a supermarket than to the Middle Eastern bazaar (1978; 1979a) envisioned by doctrinal students of pleas.

Lest it be concluded that this scholarship rejected the idea of the adversarial process, Feeley's later work showed how plea bargains were the natural corollary of adversarialism, rather than its unintended nemesis. In "Plea Bargaining and the Structure of the Criminal Process" (1982), he writes:

> Plea bargaining is not a cooperative practice that undermines or compromises the adversary process; rather, the opportunity for adversariness has expanded in direct proportion to, and perhaps as a result of, the growth of plea bargaining. As the requirements of due process have expanded, as resources have become more accessible to both the prosecution and the criminally accused, as the substantive criminal law has developed, and as the availability and role of defense counsel have expanded, the opportunity for both adversariness and negotiations has increased. (340)

It is easy to see how Feeley's conclusion can only flow from a functional systems model. A rational goal perspective would support a limited understanding of adversarialism as a performative "contest" or "game" during a criminal trial, which allows for the best exposition of the truth; indeed, some rational goal scholars reject settlements because of their strong belief in adversarialism (Fiss 1984). A functional systems perspective, however, is sensitive to the opportunities for cooperation that are born out of the historical changes in substantive and procedural criminal law, such as offense definition, prosecutorial discretion, and increased defense representation. This perspective is supported by later works on plea bargaining (Bibas 2004).

Whether one adopts the rational goal critique of plea bargaining as antithetical to the goals adversarialism is supposed to achieve, or Feeley's more sophisticated perspective that sees plea bargaining as a natural consequence of adversarialism, the classic courtroom ethnographies have focused on the pathologies of cooperation. The most obvious one is defense attorneys' failure to keep their clients' interests in mind when tempted by the powerful incentive to cooperate and maintain efficient operation and smooth working relations with other members of the courtroom workgroup. But other pathologies, highlighted by later commentators (Emmelman 1996; Frohmann 1997) have to do with the realistic assessment by prosecutors and defense attorneys of the "value of the case" – the potential that it will end in conviction – and recursive charging and pleading strategies. For rational goal scholars, these calculations thwart the goal of the adversarial process. For functional system scholars, they confirm and reflect the pressures in the system, but are nonetheless undesirable.

But do all organizational pressures in the workplace lead to more cooperation? And is cooperation a necessary outcome of adversarialism? Insights from behavioral science scholarship suggest powerful disincentives for cooperation, which we now turn to examine.

1.3 ADVERSARIAL BIAS

Both the rational goal model and the functional systems model see criminal justice professionals as rational actors; in the former model, the actors rationally respond to the official goals of the process, and in the latter, they rationally respond to the organizational and interpersonal conditions and pressures in which they are placed. But neither model takes into account the possibility that the actors' rationality may be impaired by their worldviews and ideologies in ways that are impermeable to the actors themselves.

The groundbreaking work of Amos Tversky and Daniel Kahneman (1974; 1981) and their many followers (Nickerson 1998; Klayman 1995; Friedrich 1993; Ganzach and Schul 1995) showed that human decision making, far from conforming to assumptions of absolute rationality, is plagued by biases and heuristics, two of which include confirmation bias (a preference for information that confirms, rather than contradicts, existing information) and attitudinal bias (a preference for information that supports, rather than undermines, the decision-maker's worldview). These biases and heuristics have been studied extensively in the context of legal decision making, demonstrating the vulnerability of so-called objective judgment to partisanship and existing worldviews. In a study by Simon, Stenstrom, and Read (2009), respondents confronted with an academic disciplinary procedure formed opinions about the facts that significantly differed in correlation with the different levels of partisanship that they were assigned. In his book *In Doubt* (2012), Simon compiles extensive experiential evidence confirming the effect of partisanship. Similarly, studies conducted by scholars working in the context of the Cultural Cognition Project have demonstrated that people form opinions not only about just outcomes, but about the facts, in congruence with their existing worldviews, such as in the context of self-defense (Kahan and Braman 2008), consent in acquaintance rape cases (Kahan 2010), and police use of force (Kahan, Hoffman, and Braman 2009).

There has also been an effort to gauge biases in the context of professional identity: Kassin and Kiechel (2005) presented police officers and students with true and false confessions, finding that police officers did worse than the students in identifying which confessions were true and which were false, but exhibited more certainty than the students in their own judgment. There have also been abundant studies of cognitive biases in judicial decision making (Teichman and Zamir 2013).

These studies generate strong hypotheses about professional biases, suggesting that partisanship, worldview, and professional identity may produce such biases in perceiving and interpreting facts. While no study so far has attempted to gauge and measure fact assessment among practicing prosecutors and defense attorneys, abundant literature expresses grave concerns about prosecutorial "tunnel vision" and its disastrous effects on case disposition (see generally Davis 2007; Medwed 2012), particularly that of innocent defendants (Findley and Scott 2006).

The arc of influence of this adversarial bias extends beyond the prosecutors themselves: Shelton (2015) found that expert witnesses present their opinions as stronger when employed by the prosecution. And Levine (2007) has found that prosecutors do not function well when forced to perform tasks beyond their traditional job identification. Critical literature raises concerns that evidentiary law, as well as criminal procedure, support and give preference to the prosecutorial perspective (McBarnet 1981; Davis 2007; Alexander 2010). These studies raise interesting and unanswered questions about the locus and source of prosecutorial biases.

The existing literature on the perspectives of defense attorneys has seen a generational shift from studies that maligned defense attorneys, and particularly public defenders, to studies that viewed their performance with more sympathy. Early literature portrayed defense attorneys as "con artists" who swindle their clients into plea bargaining (Blumberg 1967a) or as strategists whose presentation of the facts of the case is an opportunistic effort to procure a bargain (Sudnow 1965; Maynard 1984). Defense attorneys, particularly public defenders, were presented as differing from their clients in being "repeat players" (Galanter 1974), whose goals were mostly aligned with the organizational interest in case processing (Feeley 1979). Even trials were seen as no more than "slow pleas" (Eisenstein and Jacob 1977), and the adversarial system prescribed by doctrinal law was more of a collaborative "courtroom workgroup" for producing guilty pleas (Nardulli 1979). But literature from the 1980s and beyond presented a more benign view of defense attorneys, who were motivated by trial work (McIntyre 1988) but bound by the systemic discrimination against their clients (Emmelman 2003). Miscarriages of justice stemming from the quality of defense services have been viewed in a forgiving light by courts, who required a very low professional standard for a determination of ineffective assistance of counsel – for the most part in cases in which defense attorneys demonstrate a defeatist approach toward their clients' case (Aviram, Dyer, and Thomas 2015).

Arguing for a difference in values, goals, and perception of justice between prosecutors and defense attorneys (Packer 1968; Griffiths 1969; Whitebread and Slobogin 2007; Medwed 2012) may be less controversial than arguing for a difference in the perception of evidence and facts. However, as highlighted above, social psychology literature has identified biases and heuristics in fact perception. Sociolegal scholarship on testimonial and forensic evidence indicates that disagreements on its strength and value are possible and common. Abundant scientific evidence has probed into the contribution of false confessions to wrongful convictions (Leo 1996; Leo 2009; Leo and Ofshe 1998). Eyewitness identification, which may provoke sympathy especially in cases in which the witness was a victim of violent crime, has also been found to be malleable to problems in perception (Kramer et al. 1990), retention of memory (Loftus and Hoffman 1989; Loftus, 2005), and retrieval, as influenced by procedure at the police station (Wells and Bradfield 1998.) Forensic evidence is also far from being neutral and uncontested. As Simon Cole found, fingerprints, once considered a definitive form of identification, are actually malleable to subjective interpretation (Cole 2002). Even DNA evidence is, apparently, open to interpretation (Butler 2013) to the point of yielding serious miscarriages of justice (Thompson 2015). Moreover, the presentation of forensic evidence by experts can, in itself, yield different interpretations of its value (Cole 2008). This literature strongly supports the view that there is a range of possible ways to interpret both testimonial and forensic evidence. When taken in conjunction with insights from social psychology, it suggests that adversarial bias can color perceptions of evidence.

1.4 TWO PARADES OF HORRIBLES

It is valuable to contrast courtroom ethnographies and behavioral science studies in terms not only of their empirical findings, but also of the pathological implications. As explained above, the organizational analysis in courtroom ethnography raises the concern that concepts of truth and culpability lose their importance given the criminal justice system's emphasis on efficiency and case disposition. Indeed, cooperation among criminal justice professionals, which is presumably a rational response to organizational pressures, yields a mass-produced criminal process, in which truth and innocence may be buried under hasty agreements, and the population of defendants is regarded as a faceless herd rather than as individual people with individual cases and circumstances.

However, the insights from the behavioral sciences give rise to a different "parade of horribles" – one that has already yielded disconcerting evidence about miscarriages of justice resulting in wrongful convictions. Medwed (2012) refers to this phenomenon as representing "prosecution complex" – a form of tunnel vision, or attitudinal bias, supported by the vast discretion awarded to prosecutors in American criminal procedure, and made worse through the propagation of the idea that prosecutors are "officers of the court." The University of Michigan's National Registry of Exonerations lists "official misconduct" as the cause of wrongful conviction in 738 of its 1,617 entries; Bedau and Radelet (1987) cite data suggesting that 10 percent of wrongful convictions resulted from violations of the prosecutorial duty to disclose exculpatory evidence to the defense, as required by *Brady* v. *Maryland* (1963) (for a different perspective, see Markman and Cassell, 1988).

The legal framework through which such miscarriages of justice are assessed, both in the context of exonerations and of compensation for the wrongly accused, typically approaches them through a limited doctrinal perspective that employs the "language of guilt" and malice (Burke 2010). In some cases, such as when the evidence has been destroyed, there is no relief for the defendant absent a finding that the state exhibited "bad faith." Most recently, in *Connick* v. *Thompson* (2012), the Supreme Court denied compensation to an exonerated man who had spent eighteen years on Louisiana's death row because he had not been able to prove that the failure of the prosecutor to disclose a blood test taken from the scene of the crime stemmed from "deliberate indifference." Remarkably, the Court stated that legal education – from law school, through bar preparation, to continuing legal education courses – provides the necessary training to prosecutorial offices by teaching them the standards of *Brady*.

The legal focus on malice and intent draws attention away from a more mundane, and probably more common, explanation for prosecutorial failures to disclosed exculpatory material: confirmation and attitudinal biases, colloquially known as "tunnel vision" (Burke 2006; Burke 2007; Aviram 2013). Commentators on prosecutorial misconduct (Medwed 2012; Davis 2007; Dershowitz 1996) have pointed out that such biases, and the organizational culture that surrounds them, may more fully explain these occurrences, as well as the often dogged adherence to the original case outcome and strong resistance to reopening cases that may reveal mistakes in evidence assessment at the post-conviction phases (Swisher 2012). I refer to the combination of attitudinal bias (prosecutorial tendency to view evidence as inculpatory, and defense tendency to view evidence as exculpatory) and confirmation bias (the tendency to interpret subsequent pieces of evidence as confirming one's original view of the case) among legal professionals in the context of a criminal case as "adversarial bias."

Adversarial bias raises graver concerns with regard to the prosecution than to the defense, due to the privileged and powerful position held by prosecutors as "ministers of justice" (Medwed 2009), responsible for charging decisions and, to a great extent, via the plea bargaining process, for case disposition (Bibas 2004; Pfaff 2011). But defense attorneys who are persuaded of their client's innocence may also suffer from adversarial biases, which could lead them to discount the evidence against the client, which could result in a faulty defense or in ethical violations of their own discovery duties. The extent to which the professional value systems of prosecutors and defense attorneys might impact not only their adherence to due process or their overall worldview, but their assessment of testimonial and forensic evidence strength, has not yet been systematically measured. As a result, there is no "best practices" manual providing prosecutorial offices with practical advice on managing adversarial bias in the context of hiring practices, intra-office culture and training, and work assignments.

Moreover, there has been no systematic effort yet to uncover the extent and sources of adversarial bias. Case studies provided by Medwed (2012), as well as work by Levine (2005; 2007) and Wright and Levine (2015), suggest several important factors: the organizational culture within the prosecutorial office and the seniority of the prosecutor (Levine and Wright identify a "young prosecutor complex"). Emmelman (2003) identifies an ethos among contract defense attorneys. Some research suggests that judges with a prosecutorial background leave behind the socialization on the job, and their decisions correlate better with their ideology than with their professional history (Robinson 2011; Robinson's data is limited to the Supreme Court and the US Courts of Appeals).

If lawyers self-select into prosecutorial and defense positions in accordance with inclinations they develop before or during law school (forming their professional identity early on: Thomson 2014), questions arise as to whether legal education should address the potential of adversarial bias and tailor its pedagogy to generate more open-minded lawyers. This is particularly true for contemporary legal education, which sees many law schools shift to a more skill-based education that includes placing law students in prosecutorial and defense offices for academic credit (Amsterdam 1984; Kotkin and Rivkin 2010).

1.5 RECONCILING ADVERSARIAL BIAS WITH THE FUNCTIONAL SYSTEMS MODEL

The insights from behavioral science suggest that adversarialism is a complicated and multifaceted phenomenon, which creates both incentives and disincentives for cooperation. How are these insights to be reconciled with the classic ethnographies' findings of adversarialism as encouraging cooperation and bargaining?

Part of the answer lies in the particular locus and time of the classic ethnographic inquiries. The lower court studies of the late 1970s preceded much of the public hysteria regarding drug offenses, which meant that, while the process was the punishment, the punishment itself was less onerous than it would be ten or even thirty years later. Pamela Utz's distinction between instrumental and expressive prosecution (1978) is also relevant here: in "normal crimes" – small-time, nonviolent offenses – prosecutors would not experience the same pressures to manifest their allegiance to their mission as in high-profile cases, and would be primarily driven by instrumental goals – maximizing numbers of convictions at a small expense via guilty pleas – rather than by expressive goals of "seeing justice done" or conforming to the will of their perceived community of constituents. In other words, the cooperative adversarialism of Feeley's New Haven lower court is not the combative, theatrical adversarialism of Vincent Bugliosi in his prosecution of the Manson Family (1974) because the context is different.

But another part of the answer is that, inherent in the seemingly cooperative system of plea-bargaining are biases that affirm, rather than blur, prosecutorial tunnel vision. The procedural and evidentiary rules, as well as courtroom conventions and negotiation mores, conform to the idea that Packer encapsulated in his "presumption of guilt," that is, that defendants who remain in the system following a police investigation and a prosecutorial charging decision are likely to be guilty (otherwise they would have been screened out). The nonconsequential, low-key, presumably amicable negotiation on sentencing among the courtroom workgroup hides an assumption that defendants are largely guilty and that the individual differences between cases are far less consequential than the similarities. In short, as Doreen McBarnet observed, "due process is for crime control" (1981).

Punitive perspectives that fuel either self-selection into prosecutorial roles, socialization into the prosecutorial culture, or both, manifest themselves both at the normal and abnormal crime version. A classic example is the application of so-called three strikes laws. Since its enactment in California in 1994 (Tyler and Boeckman 1997), and leading to its modification in 2012 (Aviram 2015), this draconian habitual offender law had drawn negative media because of its perceived unjust applications in cases in which the "third strike," leading to a life sentence, was a minor nonviolent felony. But the vast majority of cases affected by the three strikes system did not consist of lifers, who even at the heyday of the law were no more than 9,000 people out of California's 170,000-strong inmate population. They consisted of people who agreed to plead guilty to lesser offenses under the threat of receiving life imprisonment following a trial. The adversarial bias fueling the administration of "three strikes" did not manifest solely in the grandiose examples of severe punishment, but also in the daily plea bargains that occurred in the shadow of the law. These negotiations, which undoubtedly ended up in relatively lenient punishment for the would-be third strikes, are not antithetical to adversarialism, nor do they reflect benign cooperation. Rather, they affirm and support the extreme cases in making the outcome of the case acceptable and mundane.

As to defense attorneys, it seems that allegiance to the ideals of defense would contradict the cooperation involved in guilty pleas, but later ethnographies reveal that mass pleadings stem more from necessity and realism than from a faltering loyalty to one's role as a defense attorney. As Debra Emmelman shows in her interviews with defense attorneys in *Justice for the Poor* (2003), representatives of indigent defendants are no less committed to their adversarial role – they simply define victory, and the best interest of their clients, in accordance with what they realistically think they can obtain from the process.

Feeley's organizational analysis, I believe, is not contradicted by the behavioral findings. The existence of systemic pressures to cooperate and process cases quickly via bargaining does not undermine the doctrinal requirement of an adversarial system. Punitive declarations and mass pleadings are two sides of the same coin, both reflecting the same kind of bias and allegiance to one's "side" in the criminal process.

1.6 EPILOGUE

Like many of Feeley's students, I ended up teaching at a law school, where our scholarship is expected to offer normative prescriptions. Given the empirical findings about functional systems and the pressures they exert on actors in the criminal justice system, and given the behavioral science insights about adversarial bias and its discontents, it is fairly unlikely that a rational-goal solution, in the form of a legislative fix, will prevent miscarriages of justice, whether dramatic or mundane. Solutions must lie, instead, in modifications to the organizational culture that produces these miscarriages of justice, in a way that encourages thoughtful collaboration and discourages both tunnel vision and mindless organizational shortcuts.

First, to the extent that adversarial bias is generated through workplace socialization, a modification in hiring practices may alleviate some of its insidious effects. Prosecutorial offices should offer not only a chance, but also a preference, to applicants who have a background of working for the other side. Greater transition between positions may dilute blind loyalties and produce more scrutiny and self-examination within the office.

Second, to the extent that the bias consists of self-selection during law school, curricula, exams, and other activities should be crafted with special care to expose students to work for both sides of the system. The hypothetical fact pattern, that quintessential law school and bar exam tool, should require students to think both as prosecutors and as defense attorneys, and to do their best for each side. Criminal justice clinics might be better structured if they allow students practical exposure to prosecutorial and public defense offices in the course of their studies.

Finally, empirical research should turn its attention toward measuring adversarial bias and its manifestations not among laboratory subjects simulating partisan work, but among actual, practicing prosecutors and defense attorneys. Producing an experimental design in which the subjects bring in existing, real adversarial biases, will bridge the gap between the classic courtroom ethnographies, which offer a window into real courtroom dynamics, and behavioral science studies, which offer the ability to measure and control the biases in these dynamics. The increased attention to the effects of adversarialism both in extremely punitive and combative trials and in day-to-day bargaining practices, it is hoped, will create an impetus to rethink our adherence to the rational goal presumably shared by the entire system: to see justice done in a fair and reasonable manner.

REFERENCES

Alexander, M. 2010. *The New Jim Crow: Mass Incarceration in the Age of Colorblindness.* New York: The New Press.
Amsterdam, A. G. 1984. "Clinical Legal Education–A 21st Century Perspective." *Journal of Legal Education* 34 (4): 612–18.
Aviram, H. 2011. "Packer in Context: Formalism and Fairness in the Due Process Model." *Law & Social Inquiry* 36 (1): 237–61.
Aviram, H. 2012. "What Would You Do? Conducting Web-Based Factorial Vignette Surveys." In *Handbook of Survey Methodology for the Social Sciences*, edited by Lior Gideon, 463–73. New York: Springer.
Aviram, H. 2013. "Legally Blind: Hyperadversarialsm, Brady Violations, and the Prosecutorial Organizational Culture." *St. John's Law Review* 87 (1): 1–46.
Aviram, H., Dyer, D., and Thomas, S. C. 2015. "Check, Pleas: Toward a Jurisprudence of Defense Ethics in Plea Bargaining." *Hastings Constitutional Law Quarterly* 41 (4): 775–843.
Bedau, H. A. and Radelet, M. L. 1987. "Miscarriages of Justice in Potentially Capital Cases." *Stanford Law Review* 40 (1): 21–179.
Bibas, S. 2004. "Plea Bargaining Outside the Shadow of Trial." *Harvard Law Review* 117 (8): 2463–547.
Bibas, S. 2012. *The Machinery of Criminal Justice.* Oxford: Oxford University Press.
Blumberg, A. S. 1967a. "The Practice of Law as Confidence Game: Organizational Cooptation of a Profession." *Law & Society Review* 1 (2): 15–40.
Blumberg, A. S. 1967b. *Criminal Justice.* Chicago: Quadrangle Books.
Blumberg, A. S. 1969. "Book Review: The Limits of the Criminal Sanction." *University of Pennsylvania Law Review* 117 (5): 790–94.
Bowen, G. A. 2005. "Preparing a Qualitative Research-Based Dissertation: Lessons Learned." *The Qualitative Report* 10 (2): 208–22.
Bugliosi, V. and Gentry, C. 2001 [1974]. *Helter Skelter: The True Story of the Manson Murders.* New York: W. W. Norton and Company.
Burke, A. S. 2006. "Improving Prosecutorial Decision Making: Some Lessons of Cognitive Science." *William & Mary Law Review* 40: 1587–633.
Burke, A. S. 2007. "Neutralizing Cognitive Bias: An Invitation to Prosecutors." *N.Y.U. Law and Liberty Journal* 2: 512–30 (symposium).
Burke, A. S. 2010. "Prosecutorial Agnosticism." *Ohio State Journal of Criminal Law* 8: 79–100 (symposium).
Butler, J. 2013. "DNA Mixture Interpretation: History, Background, Thresholds, Statistical Methods, and SWGDAM." New York: National Institute of Standards and Technology, available at: www.cstl.nist.gov/strbase/pub_pres/FordhamLaw-June2013.pdf (accessed on July 23, 2015).
Cole, S. A. 2002. *Suspect Identities: A History of Fingerprinting and Criminal Identification.* Cambridge: Harvard University Press.
Cole, S. A. 2008. "The 'Opinionization' of Fingerprint Evidence." *BioSocieties* 3: 105–13.
Davis, A. J. 2007. *Arbitrary Justice: The Power of the American Prosecutor.* Oxford: Oxford University Press.
Dershowitz, A. 1996. *Reasonable doubts: The OJ Simpson Case and the Criminal Justice System.* New York: Simon and Schuster.
Eisenstein, J. and Jacob, H. 1977. *Felony Justice: An Organizational Analysis of Criminal Courts.* Boston: Little, Brown.

Emmelman, D. S. 1996. "Trial by Plea Bargain: Case Settlement as a Product of Recursive Decisionmaking." *Law & Society Review* 30 (2): 335–60.
Emmelman, D. S. 2003. *Justice for the Poor: A Study of Criminal Defense Work.* Aldershot: Ashgate.
Feeley, M. M. 1973. "Two Models of the Criminal Justice System: An Organizational Perspective." *Law & Society Review* 7: 407–26.
Feeley, M. M. 1978. "Pleading Guilty in Lower Courts." *Law & Society Review* 7: 461–66.
Feeley, M. M. 1979a. "Perspectives on Plea Bargaining." *Law & Society Review* 13 (2): 199–209.
Feeley, M. M. 1979b. *The Process is the Punishment: Handling Cases in a Lower Criminal Court.* New York: Russel-Sage.
Feeley, M. M. 1982. "Plea Bargaining and the Structure of the Criminal Process." *The Justice System Journal* 7: 338–54.
Feeley, M. M. 2013 [1983]. *Court Reform on Trial: Why Simple Solutions Fail.* New York: Quid Pro Quo.
Feeley, M. M. and Simon, J. 1992. "The New Penology: Notes on the Emerging Strategy of Corrections and Its Limitations." *Criminology* 30 (4): 449–74.
Findley, K. A. and Scott, M. S. 2006. "The Multiple Dimensions of Tunnel Vision in Criminal Cases." *Wisconsin Law Review* 2006: 291–397.
Fiss, O. 1984. "Against Settlement." *Yale Law Journal* 93 (6): 1073–90.
Friedrich, J. 1993. "Primary Error Detection and Minimization (PEDMIN) Strategies in Social Cognition: A Reinterpretation of Confirmation Bias Phenomena." *Psychological Review* 100 (2): 298–319.
Frohmann, L. 1997. "Convictability and Discordant Locales: Reproducing Race, Class, and Gender Ideologies in Prosecutorial Decisionmaking." *Law & Society Review*, 31 (3): 531–56.
Galanter, M. 1974. "Why the Haves Come Out Ahead: Speculations on the Limits of Legal Change." *Law & Society Review* 9 (1): 95–160.
Ganzach, Y. and Schul, Y. 1995. "The Influence of Quantity of Information and Goal Framing on Decision." *Acta Psychologica* 89: 23–36.
Griffiths, J. 1969. "Ideology in Criminal Procedure or a Third 'Model' of the Criminal Process." *Yale Law Journal* 79 (3): 359–417.
Heumann, M. 1968. *Plea Bargaining: The Experiences of Prosecutors, Judges, and Defense Attorneys.* Chicago: The University of Chicago Press.
Kahan, D. and Braman, D. 2008. "The Self-Defensive Cognition of Self-Defense." *American Criminal Law Review* 45 (1): 1–65.
Kahan, D. 2010. "Culture, Cognition, and Consent: Who Perceives What, and Why, in 'Acquaintance Rape' Cases." *University of Pennsylvania Law Review* 158: 729–98.
Kahan, D., Hoffman, D., and Braman, D. 2009. "Whose Eyes Are You Going to Believe? Scott v. Harris and the Perils of Cognitive Illiberalism." *Harvard Law Review* 122 (3): 838–904.
Kassin, S. M. and Kiechel, K. M. 2005. "The Social Psychology of False Confessions: Compliance, Internalization, and Confabulation." *Psychological Science* 7 (3): 125–28.
Kotkin, M. J. and Rivkin, D. H. 2010. "Clinical Legal Education at a Generational Crossroads: Reflections from Two Boomers." *Clinical Law Review* 17: 197.
Klayman, J. 1995. "Variaties of Confirmation Bias." In *Decision Making from a Cognitive Perspective: Advances in Research and Theory*, edited by Jerome Busemeyer and Reid Hastie, 385–418. New York: Academic Press.
Kramer, T. H., Buckhout, R., and Eugenio, P. 1990. "Weapon Focus, Arousal, and Eyewitness Memory: Attention Must Be Paid." *Law and Human Behavior* 14 (2): 167–84.

Leo, R. 1996. "Miranda's Revenge: Police Interrogation as a Confidence Game." *Law & Society Review* 30 (2): 259–88.

Leo, R. 2009. *Police Interrogation and American Justice*. Cambridge: Harvard University Press.

Leo, R. and Ofshe, R. 1998. "Consequences of False Confessions: Deprivations of Liberty and Miscarriages of Justice." *Journal of Criminal Law and Criminology* 88 (2): 422–96.

Levine, K. L. 2005. "The New Prosecution." *Wake Forest Law Review* 40 (4): 1125–214.

Levine, K. L. 2007. "Can Prosecutors Be Social Workers?" *Studies in Law, Politics and Society* 40: 127–54.

Loftus, E. F. and Hoffman, H. G. 1989. "Misinformation and Memory: The Creation of New Memories." *Journal of Experimental Psychology* 118 (1): 100–04.

Loftus, E. F. 2005. "Planting Misinformation in the Human Mind: A 30-year Investigation of the Malleability of Memory." *Learning and Memory* 12: 361–66.

Macdonald, S. 2008 "Constructing a Framework for Criminal Justice Research: Learning from Packer's Mistakes." *New Criminal Law Review* 11 (2): 257–311.

Markman, S. J. and Cassell, P. G. 1988. "Protecting the Innocent: A Response to the Bedau-Radelet Study." *Stanford Law Review* 41 (1): 121–60.

Maynard, D. 1984. *Inside Plea Bargaining: The Language of Negotiation*. New York: Plenum Press.

McBarnet, D. 1981. *Conviction: Law, the State, and the Construction of Justice*. London: Macmillan Press.

McIntyre, L. J. 1988. *The Public Defender: The Practice of Law in the Shadows of Repute*. Chicago: University of Chicago Press.

Medwed, D. S. 2009. "The Prosecutor as a Minister of Justice: Preaching to the Unconverted from the Post-Conviction Pulpit." *Washington Law Review* 84: 35–66.

Medwed, D. S. 2012. *Prosecution Complex: America's Race to Convict and Its Impact on the Innocent*. New York: New York University Press.

Nickerson, R. S. 1998. "Confirmation Bias: A Ubiquitous Phenomenon in Many Guises." *Review of General Psychology* 2 (2): 175–220.

Nardulli, P. 1978. *The Courtroom Elite: An Organizational Perspective on Criminal Justice*. New York: Harper Collins.

Packer, H. 1968. *The Limits of the Criminal Sanction*. Stanford: Stanford University Press.

Pfaff, J. F. 2011. "The Micro and Macro Causes of Prison Growth." *Georgia State University Law Review* 28 (4): 1237–71.

Pfaff, J. F. 2017. Locked In: The True Causes of Mass Incarceration – And How to Achieve Real Reform. New York: Basic Books.

Robinson, R. 2011. "Does Prosecutorial Experience 'Balance Out' a Judge's Liberal Tendencies?" *Justice System Journal* 32 (2): 146–68.

Shelton, D. 2015. "Closing the Gate on Biased Expert Testimony: The Judicial Perspective." Paper presented at the annual meeting for the American Academy of Forensic Sciences, Orlando, Florida, February 16–21.

Skolnick, J. 2011 [1968]. *Justice Without Trial: Law Enforcement in Democratic Society*. New York: Quid Pro.

Simon, D., Stenstrom, D., and Read, S. J. 2009. "Partisanship and Prosecutorial Decisionmaking: An Experiment." Paper presented at the annual conference for Empirical Legal Studies, Ithaca, NY.

Simon, D. 2012. *In Doubt: The Psychology of the Criminal Justice Process*. Cambridge: Harvard University Press.

Sudnow, D. 1965. "Normal Crimes: Sociological Features of the Penal Code in a Public Defender's Office." *Social Problems* 12 (3): 255–76.

Swisher, K. 2012. "Prosecutorial Conflicts of Interest in Post Conviction Practice." *Hofstra Law Review* 41 (1): 181–215.
Tarrow, S. 1995. "Bridging the Quantitative-Qualitative Divide in Political Science." *American Political Science Review* 89 (2): 471–74.
Teichman, D., and Zamir, E. 2013. "Judicial Decisionmaking: A Behavioral Perspective." In *Oxford Handbook of Behavioral Economics and the Law*, edited by Eyal Zamir and Doron Teichman, 664–702. New York: Oxford University Press.
Thomson, D. I. C. 2014. "Defining Experiential Legal Education." University of Denver Legal Studies Research Paper no. 14–50, available at: http://papers.ssrn.com/sol3/papers.cfm?abstract_id=2497505 (last accessed July 23, 2015).
Thompson, W. C. 2015. "A Setback for Forensic Science." *The Washington Post*, May 8, 2015, available at: www.washingtonpost.com/opinions/a-setback-for-forensic-science/2015/05/08/540273f2-f350-11e4-84a6-6d7c67c50db0_story.html (last accessed July 23, 2015).
Tversky, A. and Kahneman, D. 1974. "Judgment Under Uncertainty: Heuristics and Biases." *Science* 185 (4157): 1124–31.
Tversky, A. and Kahneman, D. 1981. "The Framing of Decisions and the Psychology of Choice." *Science* 211 (4481): 453–58.
Wells, G. L. and Bradfield, A. L. 1998. "'Good, You Identified the Suspect': Feedback to Eyewitnesses Distorts Their Reports of the Witnessing Experience." *Journal of Applied Psychology* 83 (3): 360–76.
Whitebread, C. H. and Slobogin, C. 2007. *Criminal Procedure: An Analysis of Cases and Concepts*. New York: Foundation Press.
Wright, R. F. and Levine, K. L. 2015. "The Cure for Young Prosecutor's Syndrome." *Arizona Law Review* 56: 1066–128.

CASES

Brady v. Maryland, 373 U.S. 83 (1963)
Connick v. Thompson, 563 U.S. 51 (2011)
Miranda v. Arizona, 384 U.S. 436 (1966)

ADDITIONAL SOURCES

The University of Michigan's National Registry of Exonerations (www.law.umich.edu/special/exoneration/Pages/about.aspx)

2

Malcolm Feeley's Concept of Law

Issa Kohler-Hausmann

INTRODUCTION

Malcolm Feeley's *The Process Is the Punishment* has undoubtedly reached canonical status. Perhaps because Feeley bestowed it with a dangerously catchy title, the book is often cited for a fairly straightforward empirical conclusion: the burdens and hassles that defendants experience in lower criminal courts as their cases are processed more often than not outweigh formal sanctions imposed when the cases are concluded. Behind that conclusion – in fact premising it – are a set of complex and nuanced propositions about how we ought to conceptualize the law and what that conceptualization means for our study of it.

This essay details what I discern to be the *concept of law* that animates Feeley's approach to the study of lower courts. The first section of the essay revisits the empirical puzzle behind the book and how Feeley explained the findings that made *The Process Is the Punishment* so famous. But the study has achieved canonical status in the field of law and society not merely because it provides a surprising answer to the empirical puzzle stated at the start of the book. Rather, it is the way he approaches the study of law that makes the book so rich and rewarding. Feeley conceptualized law as a "normative ordering" that is always and necessarily ordered in concrete organizational settings. That is, he insists that to enact law is to make a series of ethical and moral judgments situated in a particular place and time. In his site, he shows that the concrete organizational setting of the lower criminal court is configured in a specific way and that configuration has implications for how law is used in the site. Furthermore, he explores how the various methods legal actors might use as they go about solving the recurrent practical – yet deeply value-laden – tasks that constitute their daily work entail different costs and resources. These mundane facts about the context of conducting legal work end up having profound consequences for the concept of law Feeley develops throughout the book.

In the second part of the essay I take some creative license to expand on the concept of law that I discern to be operative in *The Process*. I hope that license allows me to enhance and not distort the concept of law at work in the book. Drawing on

John Dewey and others, I argue that Feeley's concept of law is one that is deeply pragmatist in that it presents law as taking form only in relation to actual instances of use in concrete situations. Understanding *how* the process comes to be the punishment reveals the means by which law as "scraps of paper or voices in the air" are translated into an active social and normative ordering (Dewey 1988, 118). It also reveals a rewarding way to conceptualize what we are studying when we study the life of the law in other concrete contexts.

2.1 WHAT IS *THE PROCESS IS THE PUNISHMENT* ABOUT?

In this section I review the themes and arguments presented in *The Process Is the Punishment*. I organize my review to highlight how the evidence and arguments of the book are interwoven in a way that makes out a particular concept of law. Eventually, I draw on a few of Feeley's other works and interpret them in the light of pragmatist writing on action and law in order to sketch out what I understand to be his operative concept of law.

Malcolm Feeley has written a lot. Despite all of this productivity, I am not aware of any particular piece where he lays out a detailed, overarching theory of analytic jurisprudential philosophy or the ontology of law. As I will argue, that is only appropriate because I understand Feeley's concept of law to be deeply grounded in the American pragmatist tradition. This tradition is less concerned with abstract conceptual refinement than active use of conceptual tools. It is one that approaches abstract questions such as "How do we know what law is?" or "What is the nature of law?" by putting forward studies that successfully illuminate the law in operation, or that show us a way of studying it that is, well, intellectually satisfying. *The Process* is an exemplar of working out a concept of law in this way. Feeley reveals his conceptual apparatus by way of explicating social phenomena of interest, showing us what it means to talk about law as both an explanatory variable and an object of explanation.

The book does not begin with an extensive history of lower courts in the United States, but it does briefly locate the relevance of the study in the historical moment in which it took place. And that historical moment provided an opportunity to study law in action in an exciting way because changes in formal rules, doctrines, and rights opened up a new set of possibilities and expectations for those charged with interpreting the law and those subject to its powers.

At the start of the book Feeley notes that lower criminal courts have long been considered "a world apart" (Feeley 1979, 3). He recounts Roscoe Pound's 1930 indictment of lower courts – "the bad physical surroundings, the confusion, the want of decorum, the undignified offhand disposition of cases at high speed" (Feeley 1979, 6, citing Pound, *Criminal Justice in America*, 1930). From these and other such observations Pound concluded that, "[u]nder such circumstances rules were being applied arbitrarily" (Feeley 1979, 6).

Feeley does not belabor the point, but I will. Pound's indictment was but the first in a short but influential string of impeachments of the operations of lower criminal courts during the first two-thirds of the twentieth century. Scholarly and professional reports that looked at lower courts exposed both the breadth of criminal law's prohibitions and the dearth of procedural protections afforded those accused of violating its myriad prohibitions. From Caleb Foote's famous 1955 study of the processing of vagrancy-type criminal cases in Philadelphia's magistrates' courts to the President's Commission on Law Enforcement and Administration of Justice Task Force of 1967, the picture of lower courts that was consistently returned was one of a lawless holding site for society's despised and dislocated (Task Force on the Administration of Justice 1967; Foote 1956). These courts trafficked in "essentially violations of moral norms or instances of annoying behavior," (Task Force on the Administration of Justice 1967, 126) and "process[ed] massive numbers of pathetic and impoverished people through clumsy and inappropriate procedures" (Kadish 1968, 28).

These studies thus produced a set of critiques around which mid-century criminal law reform efforts crystallized.[1] The first was an attack on overbroad and vague criminal statutes that essentially criminalized a status, such as vagrancy or addiction, instead of an overt wrongful act.[2] The second was an attack on procedures by which courts adjudicated guilt and punishment. Indeed, it was these twin critiques of criminal law – largely forged in the dismaying inspection of lower criminal courts – that ended up being the defining issues in the criminal law reforms that led to Feeley's research puzzle. Legal victories addressing the first line of critique included a series of court rulings striking down some "status" crimes as unconstitutionally vague, limiting the overbroad terms of others, or legislative enactments reforming penal law provisions to adhere to those evolving notions of specificity and legality.[3] Legal victories addressing the second line of critique included the now familiar Due Process Revolution and the extension of certain procedural rights to defendants (Stuntz 2011; *Argersinger v. Hamlin*, 407 U.S. 25 (1972)).

Enter Malcolm Feeley. Against this backdrop the import of Feeley's project comes into relief. If lower courts had been the poster child of unruly and unjust adjudication that incited these legal reforms, how did they fare after the reforms?

---

[1] As Deborah Livingston has argued, the "assembly-line justice meted out in lower criminal courts for offenses like drunkenness, disorderly conduct, vagrancy, gambling, and prostitution ... was itself one of the surest signs that the criminal sanction was being misapplied" (Livingston 1997, 586).

[2] See Goluboff 2016) for an excellent discussion of reform efforts around vagrancy statutes.

[3] E.g., *Robinson v. California*, 370 U.S. 660 (1962) (striking down California's misdemeanor offense to be addicted to narcotics); *Powell v. Texas*, 392 U.S. 514, 532-34 (1968) (upholding a conviction for public drunkenness and distinguishing that crime from the status of being an alcoholic because the former entailed a positive "act"); *Papachristou v. City of Jacksonville*, 405 U.S. 156, 162 (1972) (finding that the vagrancy "ordinance is void for vagueness, both in the sense that it 'fails to give a person of ordinary intelligence fair notice that his contemplated conduct is forbidden by the statute,' and because it encourages arbitrary and erratic arrests and convictions.") (internal citations omitted).

Without so much as a "spolier alert," Feeley lists the major findings of the study on page nine of the book. He paints a picture of an institution little changed by the legal revolution that went on around it. At least in terms of the formal outcomes legal scholars tend to look at for indicia of meaningful change, he informs us that none of the defendants in his study availed themselves of the right to a jury trial, many proceeded without counsel, adjudication and sentence still often proceeded *en masse*, twice as many people were in jail before disposition than were jailed after disposition, and the duration of a process rarely correlated with legal or factual complexity.

These findings set up the puzzle of the book: why, after all of those monumental legal changes, do certain features of lower courts long noted by observers persist?

Feeley did not approach his topic by asking how the Due Process Revolution was thwarted. Nor did he try to explain the recalcitrance of judges and prosecutors, or why defendants were such dupes. He did not, as many scholars were doing at the time (and many are still), conduct a classic "gap study" of why law-on-the-books fell short in when put in action (Feeley 1976; Nelken 1981). Rather, he tried to figure out how law intervened in a complex interactive system. He asked how the actors that comprised that system were using the law, and investigated the costs that legal processes imposed on those subject to them. He surveyed what shaped the strategic choices of the constitutive actors in lower criminal courts. The "findings" of the study for which the book is so often cited turn out to be the way into an examination of *what it means* to study the law as it is given effect and felt by its subjects.

Early in the book, Feeley lays out three major claims that he develops richly throughout the work. He argues that these three claims make sense of why the Due Process Revolution failed to revolutionize due process in New Haven's lower courts. First, "courts are complex institutions, and what they do is in part a function of how they are organized" (Feeley 1979, 14). Second, "law is above all, a normative ordering" (Feeley 1979, 15). And third, "legal processes are costly" (Feeley 1979, 15). There are of course many other arguments and insights in the book. I focus on these three in order to show that *how* he develops these claims to explain his findings illuminates a concept of law. But before turning to what I believe that concept of law to be, I want to review how these claims are deployed in the service of explanation, because the concept of law emerges through how he analyzes his explanatory puzzle.

First, "courts are complex institutions, and what they do is in part a function of how they are organized" (Feeley 1979, 14). Indeed, chapters two, three, and four of the book meticulously document just how complex courts are by unpacking the jurisdictional and organizational structure of New Haven's criminal courts. These chapters detail the relationship of the court to the police, the nature and makeup of the court's cases, the physical and organizational structure of the court, and the way the daily work is ordered and carried out. He addresses the important yet neglected roles of "supportive figures," such "bail commissioners, bondsmen, counselors, screeners, clerks, stenographers, sheriffs, investigators, and secretaries" (Feeley 1979, 94). A key revelation from these chapters is the importance of political and patronage systems in staffing the offices of the Court of Common Pleas. From the judges, prosecutors, and public defenders through the support staff, most offices were filled by "sponsorship" from the local party power structures. All of this careful detail establishes that courts are indeed complex institutions.

But this material also establishes that one of the reigning models in the study of criminal courts is thoroughly unsuitable for his field site. These chapters essentially undermine any notion that it would be appropriate to approach this site with the classic Weberian ideal-type bureaucracy, where legitimate legal authority is exercised by a rational ordering of tasks undertaken by personnel selected on "their proficiency in mastering the technology and rules in which they must work" (Feeley 1979, 57). One of the defining elements of rational legal authority exercised through bureaucracies is that power is impersonal, it inures in the law and office, not in the person (Weber 1978, 217–19). Other defining elements include a hierarchy of offices with powers strictly delimited by laws and rules, and appointment as opposed to election to those offices. "Election," of course, includes selection by any political means. As Weber put it, "election" of lower-ranked officials in a bureaucracy "modifies the rigidity of hierarchical subordination" because the official then "derives position not from above but below" (Weber 1978, 960).

As Feeley documents, New Haven's Court of Common Pleas challenges every one of these defining elements of bureaucracy. The court actors' work was not governed by abstract generalizable rules but by wide discretion, "the ability to base decisions on individual judgments rather than rules" (Feeley 1979, 16). Most important (and even unimportant!) positions were filled via party patronage, such that the head of both the prosecutors and public defender organizations rarely had substantial control over staffing (Feeley 1979, 70–75; 86). Although some of the personnel sponsored by the local party might have ended up being competent workers, they were not actually selected for competence in technical skills, nor were they advanced up the organizational hierarchy on the basis of mastery of legal rules and procedures.

But Feeley resists the temptation to talk about lower criminal courts as failed or faulty bureaucracies, and then commits the rest of his book to searching for the "cause" of this distortion. In fact, he rejects some of the other reigning models of criminal courts, such as "assembly-lines" or nominally adversarial systems that have degenerated into cooperative shams. He was skeptical of claims that assumed the "goal model" of courts, which presumed that, absent certain distorting influences, such as high caseloads, criminal court actors would somehow invariably and naturally fall into adversarial roles and practices as provided for by the formal rules of the criminal procedure law.[4] Instead, he insists that what these complex organizations called lower criminal courts *do* "is in part a function of how they are *organized*" and proceeds to propose a better way for thinking about how they are organized (better than, say, bureaucracy, failed bureaucracy, or assembly-line).

This work was one of the first to propose that we think about courts as an "open system," which he defines as "any set of elements in which there are regular and recurring patterns of interaction" (Feeley 1979, 19). On this approach, the "task of the social scientists is to identify and understand the multiplicity of incentives and interests" that are at work in the component actors and sub-organizations that make up the system. It is "open" in that the system is extremely interpenetrated by its environment. Exogenous forces such as police and state laws largely determine the court's workload and composition. The people populating the court's offices come from specific political, social, and cultural communities from which they bring decisional norms and substantives values that shape how they use their discretion on the job.

This brings us to the second point: law is, after all, "a normative ordering" (Feeley 1979, 15). Courts, Feeley reminds us, are "staffed by representatives of this society, and what *they* do is in part a function of their own sense of justice" (Feeley 1979, 15). What defines courts as courts of law is that they are supposed to be applying universalistic principles to particular disputes. And the animating force of the Due Process Revolution was to insist that justice obtained not merely in a correct outcome, but by correct procedures. Feeley argued that "[t]he meaning of due process has reached its height in the criminal law, and a concern with justice is inextricably linked to the notion of due process" (Feeley 1979, 22).

The point of procedurally proper adjudication is to "narrow the focus of relevant concern," to direct the decision makers to what are authorized lines of inquiry to resolve a factual and legal controversy. But Feeley reminds us that the actors that work the actual machinery of criminal law bring to it their own notions of what it means to do justice when they arrive at work. Feeley found in New Haven's lower criminal courts in the mid-1970s that instead of being concerned with procedural justice, those on the front lines of misdemeanor adjudication were concerned with what he termed *substantive justice*. That is, "they tend to respond directly to the incident and the defendant; they feel their primary task is not to prove or disprove specific assertions, but to come to an understanding about the defendant's

---

[4] For example, he was critical of a contemporary study that seemed to take the constituting rules of an adversarial system as an empirical expectation for how actual courts would work, saying "the implication of Blumberg's argument seems to be that, in the absence of heavy caseloads, the actors would 'naturally' tend to perform their 'proper' adversarial roles as defined by the full-fledged fight theory of the adversary system, and as outlined in some of the rational-goal models of the process" (Feeley 1973, 418).

involvement in a troublesome situation in order to arrive at an appropriate disposition" (Feeley 1979, 283).

Substantive justice cannot be formulated with universal rules or rote formalism. Feeley argued that we could only understand what substantive justice meant in this site at this time by examining the actual content of the infractions the legal actors were called on to process, and their understandings about the defendants who stood accused of those infractions. So why might these legal actors eschew procedural justice in favor of a substantive justice in approaching their tasks?

This brings us to the third claim: "legal processes are costly" (Feeley 1979, 15). This point is simple, and yet it simply eluded many observers and commentators on courts. Any process of administration entails costs and consequences because it engages time, resources, bodies, and cogitative capacities to carry out the actual tasks of administration. The question is, how do legal actors respond to and strategically act as a consequence of this unavoidable fact?

In engaging this claim, Feeley forges his own model of the criminal process that diverged from the two dominant accounts of the time. What he called the "Due Process Model" seemed to assume that the overarching orientation towards formal adjudication (in the Lon Fuller sense of providing reasoned proofs and arguments in favor of a finding of guilt or innocence) should somehow naturally instill itself in court actors independently of the logistical entailments of the forms of adjudication. What he called the "Plea Bargaining Model" essentially also assumed the natural default of the due process model, but explained that it degenerated into cooperation or assembly-line pleas out of "pressures of heavy caseloads, organizational security, and bureaucratic self-interest" (Feeley 1979, 25).[5] Whereas the former seems to imagine a frictionless translation of legal ideas into action, the latter presents a friction-determinative world where cost avoidance is the only driving mechanism shaping the criminal process.

But Feeley wants us to see that just because legal actors are avoiding formal adversarial process, this does not mean that they have abandoned all notions of doing justice. These actors might not believe formal adversarial process is necessary to do the type of justice they see as fitting in this context. Here he reminds us *what* it is these courts are processing: these cases were "universally labeled as 'garbage,' 'junk,' 'trash,' 'crap,' penny ante,' and the like" (Feeley 1979, 4). Although factual and legal adjudication is what the rules of courts are officially about, Feeley finds that in the grand majority of cases there is no felt need to engage those rules to adjudicate the facts or law of such cases in order to come to a decision about how to dispose of the case.

---

[5] Early versions of these models were formulated in his 1973 article "Two Models of the Criminal Justice System: An Organizational Perspective" (Feeley 1973).

2.2 FEELEY AND DEWEY

Prior to writing this paper, I never had the occasion to ask Feeley if his concept of the law or method of approaching the study of it was informed or inspired by Dewey and the pragmatist tradition. And if Google is worth its estimated market capitalization on the NASDAQ, it seems Feeley has never himself written anything citing to Dewey.[6] So I am admittedly taking some artistic license in this section by claiming that the concept of law operationalized in *The Process* is a deeply pragmatist one. But I hope that the artistic license yields valuable insights into the original work.

Consistent with pragmatist philosophy, I propose in this section that the best concept of law for the purposes of social science is one that is grounded in a particular theory of action, a concept that guides interesting research and that produces exciting findings. By "concept of law" I mean an operational notion of what sort of thing law is and how it operates and produces outcomes. An operational notion of what law *is* might not match the rigor or specificity of a philosophical account because it is produced for different uses, but it must have boundaries and content in order to do what it needed for the purposes at hand.[7] And for us in this volume honoring Malcolm Feeley – consisting of social scientists interested in understanding the operations of actually existing legal institutions – our purposes at hand are investigating and explaining. A concept of law proposes a range of hypotheses about how we would go about investigating its relevance and operation, because a concept of law entails an understanding about how law engages our practical reasoning. A good concept of law by pragmatists leads to rewarding lines of inquiry and new (not novel necessarily, but at least not obvious and predictable) and gratifying insights.

What does it mean to say a concept of law must be grounded in a theory of action? Well, what social scientists are interested in knowing is how the law orders (or fails to order) human affairs. To get at those sorts of questions we need to have a framework of human action more broadly; "the law" as a social enterprise is not a world apart but part of the world, the social world that is. As Dewey said: "law is through and

---

[6] Google Scholar, to be specific, revealed three published articles authored by Malcolm Feeley containing the proper noun "Dewey" anywhere in the text or title. All three referenced someone else's work in relation to Dewey. After reading this paper, Malcolm reported to me that he believed the pragmatist influence on his thinking to be largely vicariously transmitted by his reading of Philip Selznick and legal anthropologists.

[7] Approaching these questions from the standpoint of analytic jurisprudence is about trying to wrestle out an answer to "What is the nature of the law?" from a set of truisms; this might yield a slightly different set of answers than approaching the question from the point of empirical inquiry. The questions of analytic jurisprudence might, for example, ask the "identity question: what properties make the thing the thing and not something else?" or the "implication question: what necessarily follows if the thing is what it is?" The pragmatist approach to the question of the nature of law might be thought of a particularly grounded version of the "implication question," asking what are the practical and methodological upshots of a particular conceptualization of the thing. For an extended discussion of the "identity question" of law from a rigorous philosophically analytic approach, see Shapiro (2011).

through a social phenomenon; social in origin, in purpose or end, and in application" (Dewey 1988, 117).

Dewey concedes that this statement "tries to explain what is obscure, namely the nature of law, by reference to something still more obscure, namely, society," but he insists that if we understand social to mean "human *activities*" that are necessarily "*inter*-activities," there is something more than circular abstraction to his assertion. He goes on to explain that his definitional claim "signifies that law must be viewed both as intervening in the complex of other activities, and as itself as a social process, not something that can be said to be done or to happen at a certain date" (Dewey 1988, 117). I understand this pragmatist notion of law to motivate the following questions: In what ways does the law intervene in human activities? How do social actors that are charged with something under the law understand what they are doing? When in the course of their daily activities do they consult legal texts or sources, under what conditions, and to what ends? I take the pragmatist claim to be as follows: if we can understand *how* the law intervenes in human affairs, then we can articulate what the proper conceptualization of the law is.

> A given legal arrangement *is* what it *does*, and what it does lies in the field of modifying and/or maintaining human activities as going concerns. Without application these are scraps of paper or voice in the air but nothing that can be called law. (Dewey 1988, 118)

A defining aspect of the pragmatist approach is to insist that experience is primary, and in fact prior to conceptualization: "practice – experience – supplies the impetus for all inquiry; it also reveals the meaning of ideas and provides the ultimate test of their truth" (Emirbayer and Maynard 2010a, 225). The practical bearing on how we understand and do things is what determines how we ought to conceptualize the objects of study.

Feeley's critique of how others conceptualized law in their studies around the same time *The Process* was published offers a helpful illustration of this approach. For example, in *The Process* and in other writing from that time Feeley explicitly rejected an Austinian sanction-backed command concept of the law. He rejected any concept that posited the law as a set of external, clear, specific directives or unambiguous normative principles straightforwardly accessible from text. Feeley questioned the value of studies that asked about the "effectiveness" of law or that examined "the 'gap' between the ideal of the law and the actual practices flowing from it" (Feeley 1976, 497). Classic "gap studies" were premised on the notion that abstract rules have obvious and specific meanings in the world of action, meanings that are plainly available to guide actors in specific choice situations, and therefore are susceptible of being held up as a standard against which the uses and choices that actors actually select are compared.[8] But, he noted that it is theoretically thorny to "identify, operationalize, and measure the goals of the law" in order to define the

---

[8] There is a long history of law and society scholars studying what has been termed the "gap question." For example, David Nelken discussed an academic schism between sociology of law and sociolegal

standard against which the gap is measured (Feeley 1976, 500). That standard is not self-evident, but rather must be selected and specified by the researcher. As Feeley stated: "What is posited in the name of detached objectivity as 'the' goals or purposes of the law can in fact be a substitution of the researcher's own – or someone else's – goals and values for those held either by the promulgators or the 'recipients' of the law" (Feeley 1976, 509).

Furthermore, some of the most interesting topics that sociolegal scholars study are legal organizations, sites that are not structured by legal commands, prohibitions, or even decision rules elaborated by the common law tradition, but rather "power-conferring" rules, rules that establish a menu of authorized actions or set forth a "manner and form" by which a delegated power must be exercised (Hart 2012, 28).[9] Power-conferring rules, for example, establish the legal capacities of criminal court judges, the range of sentences authorized for given offenses, or the proper methods by which a criminal complaint or indictment can be filed. They cannot be said to establish an obvious expectation about *how* the frontline legal actors will in fact use these powers or capacities because they are just not duty-imposing rules (Kohler-Hausmann 2018, chapter 3). (It is interesting to note that organizational sociologists writing around the same time *The Process* was published had essentially come to the conclusion that it was no longer a fruitful research program to compare formal organizational plans to the practices of living organizations, as it would consistently – and predictably – reveal unanticipated or unplanned practices and structures [see, e.g., Etzioni 1960; Kohler-Hausmann 2017 and sources cited therein]).

For those reasons, Feeley worried that conceptualizing law in terms of a "goal" would be theoretically uninteresting because it would regularly produce findings about the researcher's personal disappointment: why things turned out differently from how the researcher had wanted/expected things to have turned out. The findings would also be predictable: consistently showing a gap between formal law and actual practice. Yet, the precise ways in which they would differ would be

---

studies as characterized by the former criticizing the latter for making "implausible assumptions concerning the way in which norms might be expected to affect conduct," or Carroll Seron and Susan Silbey, documenting law and society scholarship on various subject matters – from courts to policing to administrative agencies – noted that most of the seminal scholarship is focused on documenting the gap between law on the books and law in action (Seron and Silbey 2008; Nelken 1981).

[9] Feeley argued that even with duty-imposing rules, "the language of the law is frequently so vague that the specific behavior it 'commands' is not unambiguous or clearly derivable from it." However, he was particularly concerned with the inadequacy of concepts of law that did not cover the most common forms that were essentially constitutive of the functioning of legal organizations: "My point is merely to emphasize that social scientists have not drawn on a concept of law that adequately addresses forms of law other than commands, a conceptual failure that has led to improperly drawn boundaries of investigation. More importantly, empirical investigations premised upon this initial failure have led to generalizations about law and society that are of questionable usefulness" (Feeley 1976, 509).

thoroughly dependent upon the model's assumptions – the effects we assume the law ought to have produced will determine what explanations we proffer for its failure (or success). Furthermore, once we broaden our gaze beyond sanction-backed commands to look at status and power-conferring or definitional laws, it is less clear how to even approach specifying the "goal" or "aim" of the law (Feeley 1976, 505–08).

If law does not express a clear goal, purpose, or value, dictate a specific command, or state a prohibition, then how does it intervene in human affairs? Feeley proposed that "[t]hus it [the law] must be understood as only one of a number of interrelated factors in complicated systems of interaction" (Feeley 1976, 518). The best way to formulate a concept of law is to take the "complicated system of interaction" as a starting point, and then to study the ways in which it intervenes in the patterned interactions in that system.

This is much in line with the pragmatist notion of law and, in turn, with pragmatist theory of action. According to Dewey, we do not undertake any action because goals or ends draw us towards some external fixed state. We encounter an "indeterminate situation," one that challenges habitual or routine lines of action and thought. An indeterminate situation is reformulated into a "problematic situation" through inquiry, meaning the constituents of the troubling indeterminacy are systematized into familiar structures. As Emirbayer and Maynard explain, "all practical reasoning begins with a problematic experience, a 'fork in the road,' which it attempts experimentally to resolve ... [t]hinking is what occurs most especially in situations where regular channels of action no longer suffice, where conflicts or ruptures in practice cause perplexity" (Emirbayer and Maynard 2010b, 227–28).

Utilities and values do not sit inside us as prefabricated directions to act, just as the law does not sit outside actors as an instruction to right action. Dewey expressed confusion about what sort of exercise we would even be engaged in if we asked normative questions unmoored to a concrete problem situation:

> Without a problem there is blind groping in the dark. The way in which a problem is conceived decides what specific suggestions are entertained and which are dismissed; what data are selected and which rejected; it is the criterion for relevancy and irrelevancy of hypotheses and conceptual structures. On the other hand, to set up a problem that does not grow out of an actual situation is to start on a course of dead work . . . [p]roblems that are self-set are mere excuses for seeming to do something intellectual, something that has the semblance but not the substance of scientific activity. (Dewey 2013)

This problematic situation then requires some resolution. In the course of deliberation and creative problem solving we come to formulate what Dewey called "ends-in-view," or aims that would point the way out of the current problem situation. These ends-in-view are not "outside- and-beyond" activity, "something necessary to induce action and in which it terminates" (Dewey 1922, 335). Rather, "[e]nds are foreseen consequences which arise in the course of activity and which are employed to give activity added meaning and to direct its further course. They are in no sense ends *of* action. In being ends of *deliberation* they are redirecting pivots *in* action" (Dewey 1922, 338–39).

What Feeley criticized in others' concepts of law was the notion that it produces outcomes in the social world by supplying actors with ultimate ends or determinate values, which in turn clearly and predictably guide behavior. Why should we assume to know what a natural or obvious instantiation of "the law" would be before knowing anything about the context in which legal actors deployed the law?

To use the pragmatist language, the law does not shape human affairs because at every salient and important juncture people ask, "How does the law direct me now?" It does not sit outside our material life beckoning us towards right action. Rather, people find themselves at salient and important junctures, and for some reason they must or can consult the law in order to proceed. The situation beckoned us to the law, not the other way around. And the precise contours of the situation that beckoned us to engage the law will necessarily shape what we understand the law to be, to demand of us, or to mean. It did not have a determinate meaning prior to that action situation simply because we did not have an occasion to think about it.

Said another way, we do not start the day asking what the law is and how we ought to be guided by it. We start the day with a set of concrete tasks, and then might encounter what pragmatist thinkers have called problem situations that force us to ask what the law is or how the law affects some element of a potential course of action, and then we proceed from there. The law is brought to bear to make situated judgments undertaken because some situation demands action. As Dewey said, we often formulate general principles of law inductively from successfully solved problem situations:

> Men do not begin to thinking with premises. They begin with some complicated and confused case, apparently admitting of alternative modes of treatment and solution ... The problem is not to draw a conclusion from given premises ... [t]he problem is to find statements, of general principle and of particular fact, which are worthy to serve as premises. (Dewey 1924, 23)

This is not to say that law does not bind, command, restrict, or perhaps even engage practical reasoning in a special way by simultaneously supplying evaluative and prescriptive grounds of action (although we can still debate if there is a distinctly legal way our practical reasoning is engaged, but that is a much longer argument). The Feeley-Dewey fusion I hope to develop here is that it does so *only in grounded action situations*, inside organizations with real cultural contours and actual resource constraints, where actors are facing concrete questions with material and moral dimensions particular to the situation, where they must choose to act with tools available at that time and place.

The relevance of this concept of law for an explanation is best discussed in reference to a specific set of questions and not in the abstract. So let's revisit the explanation of Feeley's primary findings from *The Process* summarized in the prior section using these tools.

2.3 WHAT IS THE CONCEPT OF LAW IN *THE PROCESS IS THE PUNISHMENT*?

Malcolm Feeley wants us to understand law by looking at the way in which the daily work of legal actors is organized, how they interact, and what pressures bear on their immediate decisions. In *The Process*, he urges the reader to think of lower courts as "open systems" as opposed to bureaucratic or even goal-oriented organizations. Lower courts do not fit the classic Weberian model of bureaucracy in which actors are cabined by hierarchical jurisdictional spheres, their decisions regulated by definite articulable rules directed at coordinating behavior towards some clear fixed end. He explains that a defining element of how legal work is organized in lower courts is that prosecutors, judges, and defense attorneys have substantial discretion to make decisions in each individual case. The open system concept is one that analyzes the "regular and recurring patterns of interaction" among these actors with wide discretion (Feeley 1979, 19).

In this way, Feeley, while never explicitly claiming to do so, goes about developing a concept of law in a classic pragmatist fashion: not by stipulating some notion of what the law ought to look like or the researcher's own assumptions regarding what the law could look like as the standard by which to measure a "gap," but by studying the concretely situated ways in which legal questions arise and in which legal powers and rights are exercised. *The Process* carefully details how actors interact in the setting of New Haven's Court of Common Pleas. Cases come to disposition through the interaction and negotiation of actors with conflicting interests. It is their wide discretion – not adherence to prefabricated detailed rules – that made the outcomes he observed possible. Indeed, it is "the discretionary capabilities of the prosecutor and judge and the many options of the defense which facilitate rapid processing of vast numbers of cases" (Feeley 1979, 16).

However, the disposition outcomes are not random, nor are they merely a function of personal proclivities and preferences. There are patterns, and Feeley traces those patterns. Remember the "findings" for which the book is so often cited are revealed just as the book pagination breaks into the double digits: not a single defendant insisted upon a jury trial; about half were processed without legal counsel; defense attorneys engaged in short interviews and rarely conducted factual investigations or legal research; many defendants were processed *en masse*; more defendants were detained pretrial than sentenced to prospective jail time after conviction; many seemingly simple cases dragged out, and other seemingly complex cases were disposed with lightning speed; nonconviction dispositions were common and jail sentences were rare. I hope to show in this final section that it is the way Feeley *explains* those findings that reveals his concept of law that, in turn, makes the book such a classic.

These patterned outcomes that are the "findings" cannot be understood as merely the result of an explicit directive from the law to proceed in a particular manner, the sacrificing of clear legal goals or values to organizational imperatives of efficiency or expediency, or the signal of blatant disregard of due process values on account of self-interest (although some of each may be true). The findings of the book can only be understood by studying the ways in which law is operationalized in a grounded setting. As I understand it, Feeley organizes his grounded approach to explaining the findings of the book by developing the three claims discussed in Section 2.1 of this essay: (1) "courts are complex institutions, and what they do is in part a function of how they are organized"; (2) "law is above all, a normative ordering"; and (3) "legal processes are costly" (Feeley 1979, 15).

With this framework, we can see that the rules and rights of the Due Process Revolution would not enter the scene of lower criminal courts as a new set of dictates that could automatically and radically rupture prior practice. Nor is it clear that we need evidence of actors intentionally or even consciously circumventing or undermining the spirit of those laws and holdings in order to make sense of his findings. These new rules and rights entered the scene as a set of possibilities. They represented possible adjustments to the costs and consequences for taking certain actions in legal proceedings.

Take the right to counsel in misdemeanor cases where a prospective jail sentence is imposed that was articulated in *Argersinger v. Hamlin*.[10] That "right" could be conceptualized as a directive to judges and prosecutors to make sure defense attorneys are present in all cases where the prosecution intends to seek a prospective jail sentence as part of the disposition. Or it could be conceptualized as a point of consideration in a strategic action situation that shapes the very ends-in-view that actors adopt. That is, the fact that prosecutors and judges know they must provide counsel if a jail term is imposed is itself a fact about the strategic situation of plea bargaining and seeking dispositions to cases that forms the very values, goals, and ends legal actors will consider in a given case. Remember, courts are complex interactive sites, the constitutive actors bring in their own value orientations to their assigned tasks, and legal processes impose costs. Those three claims are interdependent: actors consider the costs they can impose on others by taking various lines of action, they consider the costs others in the system can impose on them as they both seek their own interests, and they consider those costs in an evaluative framework specific to the types of substantive issues they are addressing in their daily work. A newly articulated "right" can be thought of as presenting a new problem situation

---

[10] 407 U.S. 25 (1972). The year *The Process* was published the Supreme Court made clear the constitutional right to appointment of counsel was triggered only by "actual imprisonment." *Scott v. Illinois*, 440 U.S. 367, 373 (1979).

to the legal actors populating New Haven's Court of Common Pleas by disrupting established disposition practices that were able to be achieved without the costs and interference of defense attorneys. The rule does thereby alter their conduct, but not by directing one thing or prohibiting another. Rather, it does so by shaping what they think they might want to do and altering the costs and payoffs for doing it in a certain way.

We can think of the newly articulated "right" as presenting the prosecution and judge with a new problem situation. They must ask: "What do I want out of this case? Does what I want out of this case require a prospective jail sentence, or is there another way to bring about an acceptable disposition in this case? Is my want of a jail sentence worth triggering the rule requiring defense attorneys?" In pragmatist talk, the existence of this new right in an old and familiar action situation – rapidly disposing of "petty" cases – provides an occasion to evaluate habitual practices and to engage in situated evaluation of values and desired (or acceptable) end states – the value of jail sentences versus the punishment value of legal processes. The prosecutor and judge must now ask if there are other ways to satisfactorily dispose of the case (to use the courtroom vernacular that is quite appropriate to a pragmatist theory of action) that would satisfy their sense of fairness within available means, means that are not too costly relative to what was at issue in the case. It seems that in a substantial number of cases it was not worth it to prosecutors and judges to trigger the right to counsel rule in order to get something satisfactory out of the case. Feeley reports that "[f]ully 40 percent of all defendants had no representation and were charged with a wide variety of offenses" (Feeley 1979, 182).[11]

The overarching interest of legal actors in finding suitable dispositions given the "worth" of the case and the relative costs of adjudication is what Feeley called a concern with "substantive justice." His account was that judges and prosecutors negotiate with defense attorneys over what they think the case is worth, and it is this assessment that guides how they dispose of the case. Formal due process adjudication is not so much being avoided in these cases as it is determined to be *unnecessary* to what the actors think of as a proper way of disposing of the case. Feeley insisted that the normative ordering of law can be achieved either by adherence to a predetermined vision of fair procedure or by a substantive vision of the quantum of deprivation or discomfort merited by different types of wrongdoing. He argued that legal actors in lower courts are predominantly concerned with the latter (substantive justice), because the former (procedural justice) does not seem "worth" the costs of process given that the cases were given such labels as "garbage," "penny ante," and others epithets as previously mentioned (Feeley 1979, 4).

Therefore, unsurprisingly, many of the dispositions did not involve a conviction, much less a custodial sentence. *The Process* reports that prosecutors decided to *nolle*

---

[11] It is worth noting that Feeley observed a handful of cases where defendants were given prospective jail sentences without being represented by counsel, so in some instances it seems they were just ignoring or violating the rule.

prosequi over one-third of the cases and offered noncustodial sentences in the grand majority of the guilty pleas.[12]

This brings us back to the proposition for which most people cite the book's title – that lower courts impose mainly process burdens, these burdens are what "cause" defendants to abjure their due process rights, which thereby allows legal actors to undermine a processually fair adjudication process. Certainly, the first two claims are in the book, and in some sense the third only without the evaluative presumption that procedural justice is the only and best form of justice. But focusing only on these findings misses Feeley's concept of the law – the concept of law that is elucidated in the way the book *explains* these findings. He carefully shows that these dispositions are the result of an interactive process. It is true that certain parties, namely the defense and defendant, come to the interaction from a position of relative disempowerment. Their choices are sharply circumscribed once an arrest is made because there is no way out but through the system.

But the ability of the defendant and defense attorneys to invoke newly extended rights is itself a power to impose process punishment on the other actors, namely the court and the prosecutors, if they don't offer a reasonable disposition. And the other actors are aware of that potential cost imposition, which is why these rights should be thought of as a feature of a strategic action situation as opposed to a directive to any party. Feeley made the prescient observation – one that I think anyone who has worked or observed in any lower court would agree is still universally true – that "there will always be too many cases for many of the participants in the system, since most of them have a strong interest in being some place other than in court" (Feeley 1979, 47).

Consider, for example, the prosecutor on page 183 who pressures the unrepresented defendant to take a $10 fine today instead of fighting his case, saying: "Don't fuck around. Take a small fine. Why come back again or perhaps two or three times? Why miss a few days' work and end up with a stiffer sentence than you would get from me?" When he warns him that "[i]f you go to trial, you may go to jail," he is clearly leveraging a threat of a more serious sentence to keep the defendant from invoking his due process rights out of a concern for his own increased workload from contested cases, not just the defendant's welfare (Feeley 1979, 183).

But prosecutors and judges do not merely offer so-called "discounted" dispositions to defendants so that they can go home early, although that is certainly the case sometimes.[13] They do so also because it satisfies their sense of substantive justice. As one judge quoted in the book put it:

---

[12] He reports that about 5 percent of the convicted cases resulted in a jail sentence during his study period (Feeley 1979, 127, 138, 249, 255).

[13] I put "discounted" in quotes because I do not believe one can really use that term in either a descriptive or normative sense without a sense of what the retail disposition would be in the case; but most people understand the term to mean at least something discounted relative to penalties authorized by law.

> What do you do in these petty cases? They're not serious enough to put a person in jail; yet you want to do something to show society's disapproval. Normally a fine would be appropriate, but so many of these people don't have any money. So we end up giving meaningless conditional discharges or probation, and it becomes something of a joke. It's frustrating; there's little we can do. (Feeley 1979, 69)

Sometimes the thing "to do in these petty cases" is to recognize the value of a byproduct that was not necessarily intentionally inflicted. Whether or not anyone *intends* them to be, processes impose costs. These costs can be refigured as punishments after they occur when actors encounter a situation that demands a decision: pursue the case, or settle for a disposition that involves recognizing the process costs that the defendant has already experienced *as a punishment*. Actors need to decide if the process was sufficient punishment as exemplified in this defense attorney's appeal recounted in the book and reproduced here:

> Your Honor, my client has already been punished enough. He has made six separate appearances in court and each time his case has been continued. If he had pled guilty the first time, his sentence would have caused fewer problems than those encountered by having to come down here so often. (Feeley 1979, 177)

And in a substantial number of cases it seems prosecutors and judges were moved by that logic, even when no one explicitly argued the point to them. Prosecutors, without any protest from judges, agreed to *nolle* a significant proportion of misdemeanor cases according to the data in the book. This is not because, as Feeley explains, they actually thought there were some legal or factual problems with the cases. As he explains:

> [I]t is impossible to know if [the rate of *nolles*] would rise if a more adversarial stance were taken, certainly defense attorneys and prosecutors believe that many defendants who now have their charges *nolled* are guilty and could have been convicted. These *nolles*, they believe, are "equitable" resolutions of cases in which a finding of guilt or a sentence would have no meaning or positive benefit for anyone. (Feeley 1979, 274)

Therefore, the fact that process is often more costly relative to dispositions offered early in the case does dissuade defendants from invoking due process rights. But the fact that process imposes burdens was also a *justification* for legal actors to offer and accept formally lenient dispositions, dispositions that made them feel satisfied in not having to fully adjudicate and trigger due process rights in order to achieve a formal punishment.

In sum, Feeley's findings in *The Process* show that law does in fact reorder human affairs. But the way he explains how the law reorders human affairs proceeds in what I would call a classically pragmatist way. He does not look for direct channels of coercion or internalization of obvious norms, but rather analyzes complex interactive sites where changes in the law become an occasion for actors to evaluate their values, ends-in-view, and the appropriateness of means to realize those values and ends-in-view. Thus, the law does not stand outside of the organizational setting as an ideal or value towards which the actors direct their activity. Rather, it is a feature of the organizational setting. What these actors are doing is trying to figure out in real time what these rules mean for practical concerns, namely finding suitable dispositions for so-called "petty" cases. The relevance of law is visible only in reference to the situated practical features of the actual work that legal actors must accomplish with the law.

This way of conceptualizing the law, I believe, is truly a model for us all to embrace.

REFERENCES

Dewey, John. 2013 [1938]. *Logic: The Theory of Inquiry*. Redditch: Read Books Ltd.
Dewey, John. 1988. *The Later Works of John Dewey, 1925–1953: Essays, Reviews, and Miscellany, 1939–1941*. Carbondale: Southern Illinois University Press.
Dewey, John. 1924. "Logical Method and Law." *Cornell Law Review* 10: 17–27.
Dewey, John. 1922. *The Human Nature and Conduct: An Introduction to Social Psychology*. New York: Henry Holt and Company.
Emirbayer, Mustafa and Douglas W. Maynard. 2010. "Pragmatism and Ethnomethodology." *Qualitative Sociology* 34: 221–61.
Etzioni, Amitai. 1960. "Two Approaches to Organizational Analysis: A Critique and a Suggestion." *Administrative Science Quarterly* 5 (2) (September): 258.
Feeley, Malcolm. 1979. *The Process Is the Punishment: Handling Cases in a Lower Criminal Court*. New York: Russell Sage Foundation.
Feeley, Malcolm. 1976. "The Concept of Laws in Social Science: A Critique and Notes on an Expanded View." *Law & Society Review* 10: 497–523.
Feeley, Malcolm. 1973. "Two Models of the Criminal Justice System: An Organizational Perspective." *Law and Society Review* 7: 407–26.
Foote, Caleb. 1955. "Vagrancy-Type Law and Its Administration." *University of Pennsylvania Law Review* 104: 603.
Goluboff, Risa. 2016. *Vagrant Nation: Police Power, Constitutional Change, and the Making of the 1960s*. Oxford: Oxford University Press.
Hart, H. L. A. 2012. *The Concept of Law*. Oxford University Press.
Kadish, Sanford H. 1968. "The Crisis of Overcriminalization." *American Criminal Law Quarterly* 7: 17.
Kohler-Hausmann, Issa. 2017. "Jumping Bunnies and Legal Rules: The Organizational Sociologist and the Legal Scholar Should Be Friends." In *The New Criminal Justice Thinking*, edited by Sharon Dolovich and Alexandra Natapoff, 246–70. New York: New York University Press.
Livingston, Debra. 1997. "Police Discretion and the Quality of Life in Public Places: Courts, Communities, and the New Policing." *Columbia Law Review* 97: 551–86.
NCJRS. 1967. "Task Force on the Administration of Justice, The Report by the President's Commission on Law Enforcement and the Administration of Justice, The Challenge of Crime in a Free Society," available at www.ncjrs.gov/App/publications/Abstract.aspx?id=147397 (last accessed November 8, 2012).
Nelken, David. 1981. "Gap Problem in the Sociology of Law: A Theoretical Review." *The Windsor Yearbook of Access to Justice* 1: 35.

Pound, Rosco. 1930. *Criminal Justice in America*. London: Routledge.
Seron, Carroll and Susan Silbey. 2008. "Profession, Science and Culture: An Emergent Canon of Law and Society Research." In *The Blackwell Companion to Law and Society*, edited by Austin Sarat, 30–59. John Wiley & Sons.
Shapiro, Scott. 2011. *Legality*. Cambridge: Harvard University Press.
Stuntz, William. 2011. *The Collapse of American Criminal Justice*. Cambridge: Harvard University Press.
Weber, Max. 1978 [1922]. *Economy and Society: An Outline of Interpretive Sociology*. Oakland: University of California Press.

3

Process as Intergenerational Punishment

Kay L. Levine and Volkan Topalli

INTRODUCTION

In *The Process is the Punishment*, Malcolm Feeley exposed the lower criminal court as a powerful institution in American life, an important counterpart to both the more glamorous federal courts and the more highly charged superior courts that preside over serious crimes within a jurisdiction. Although it typically handles only low-level criminal charges, the lower criminal court's reach is both broad and deep; in its functioning and process it has the capacity to change the lives of many who come before it – sometimes for the better, sometimes for the worse – irrespective of guilt or innocence, conviction or dismissal.

Toward that end, one of the book's primary themes is the cost of pretrial process in an organization characterized by high-volume, low-intensity cases. Feeley powerfully demonstrates that for many – if not most – defendants, the costs of being accused are often greater than the costs of being punished. Finding and meeting with a lawyer, obtaining bond or experiencing pretrial detention, and the delays due to continuances all can lead to lost wages and pull resources from the defendant's wallet that can easily exceed whatever fine he might ultimately be sentenced to pay. In addition to these clear financial burdens, defendants experience uncertainty associated with not knowing the case outcome for months or sometimes years. While due process has generated many of these pretrial process mechanisms, Feeley argues that most defendants would prefer a cheaper alternative that allows them to return to their lives more quickly and with more actual money in their pockets.

The aim of this chapter is to expand upon Feeley's insight into the American trial court's reach by considering the court's impact on the children of the defendants who are brought before it. Might they suffer from the criminal court process too? What might be the emotional impact on a young child who witnesses a parent being processed by the court, dressed in a jail uniform, manhandled by the deputies, harangued by attorneys, and led away in handcuffs? In essence, we explore the extent to which the children of the accused ought to be considered co-victims, not of the original offense but of the process they witness their parents endure in court. The long-term and short-term effects on children of these more distal experiences may be less easily subject to analysis and investigation than those suffered by their parents, but they may be far-reaching and long-standing nonetheless.

The emotionally harmful influence of the carceral state on nonoffending children has received significant scholarly attention in recent decades. Scholars have linked parental incarceration to risk of criminal activity by children, as well as to public health impacts like depression, behavioral problems, anxiety, peer relationship difficulty, and school performance issues (Eckenrode, Laird, and Doris 1993; Farrington 1997; Shonk and Cicchetti 2001; Thornberry 2009; Wakefield and Wildeman 2011; Turney 2014). There is also a significant relevant literature on the criminological impact of early childhood trauma (including maltreatment and neglect) that demonstrates such experiences increase a child's risk of engaging in criminal behavior at a later age (see, e.g., Curry and Tekin 2012). In light of these findings, we believe the emotional impacts of children's courtroom exposure *before* parental incarceration ought to be studied too. That is, scholars and policymakers working in these areas ought to determine whether children who witness their parents processed by the court for alleged criminal behavior experience this event as traumatic, and consequently suffer in terms of health, education, relationships, and criminal behavior.

This essay is meant to begin a conversation about the potentially corrosive effects of early courtroom exposure. We use original interview data with two populations of courthouse regulars – prosecutors and repeat offenders – to preliminarily explore the ways in which children might become casualties of the criminal court processing of their parents. Prosecutors offer several different narratives to explain what they, as professionals working in the courtroom, see as the negative impacts on children who attend their parents' court hearings. The offenders share more personal accounts, as they sometimes describe how they as children felt watching their own parents in court, and secondly report how they as defendants feel when their children attend court. Offenders' narratives sometimes compete with and sometimes reinforce the prosecutors' perceptions, but they are uniformly negative as well.

What we learned from these interviews suggests that scholars interested in the collateral consequences of parental offending and the linkage between childhood experiences of trauma and later criminality ought to begin their inquiries in the courthouse, rather than in the jail or prison setting. Moreover, if the process is a form of punishment for the children of offenders, and not just for the offenders themselves, courthouse communities should limit the exposure of children to courtroom proceedings by providing child-care facilities or other alternatives for partners of offenders who have preschool aged children.

This essay is organized as follows. In Section 3.1 we take the reader on a quick tour of the two criminology literatures that principally frame our inquiry: the collateral consequences of parental incarceration and the criminological effect of exposure to trauma early in life. In Section 3.2 we say a few words about methodology before introducing our interview data from prosecutors and offenders. We conclude with an outline for better planning by courthouse communities to reduce children's access to the inside of criminal courtrooms.

3.1 FRAMING THE PROBLEM

3.1.1 Collateral Consequences of Parental Incarceration

Criminologists have long observed that crime tends to run in families (Glueck and Glueck 1950; West and Farrington 1973; Rowe and Farrington 1997; Besemer 2012). The association between parent and child criminality builds on Sutherland's differential association theory of criminal behavior (1947), but also draws on social learning perspectives (see, e.g., Akers 1990; Akers 2008). Recently, the interest in intergenerational offending has generated a parallel interest in the intergenerational influence of parental incarceration, as scholars have tried to parse whether childhood offending correlates more with the parent's criminality or instead with the losses caused by prolonged absence during the incarceration term. Because parental incarceration often imposes "the strains of economic deprivation, the loss of parental socialization through role modeling, support and supervision, and the stigma and shame of societal labeling," (Hagan and Dinovitzer 1999, 123), strain, socialization, and stigmatization theories provide theoretical underpinnings for much of this recent work.

Focusing on the parent's carceral status rather than on the underlying behavior, studies have documented the relation between a parent's incarceration for criminal activity and the risk of criminal activity by the child (Farrington 1997; Thornberry 2009; Murray, Loeber, and Pardini 2012). The risk may not be consistent across all kinds of criminal activity or children, though. As to criminal activity, Wakefield and Wildeman (2011, 799) document "global" effects of father incarceration on children of both sexes in terms of aggression and delinquency, while Murray and his colleagues (2012) found the effect with theft but not with marijuana use. As to age, children aged 7–18 at the time of their parent's incarceration are more likely to show later criminal activity than are children who were much younger at the time the parent was sent away (Besemer et al. 2011; cf. Murray, Janon, and Farrington 2007). Moreover, young boys appear to be more prone than girls to aggression and delinquency following their father's incarceration (Wildeman 2010).

The documented effects on children extend far beyond criminal behavior, however, suggesting that the public health impact of parental incarceration might be far more troublesome than the straight criminological impact. Children of incarcerated parents have higher rates of depression, behavioral problems, anxiety, and learning disabilities (Turney 2014; Wakefield and Wildeman 2011), as well as significant problems with school attendance, academics, and peer relationships (Parke 2001).

They are also at risk for performing poorly in school (Shonk and Cicchetti 2001; Eckenrode, Laird, and Doris 1993). These "internalizing" stress effects are particularly striking in girls (Wakefield 2007). Moreover, "[s]tigma from incarceration produces isolation and shame, which impedes social ties, reduces support systems, and challenges the social integration of already detached families and children" (Turney and Haskins 2014, citing Braman 2004; Goffman 1963; Murray and Farrington 2008a; Murray and Farrington 2008b).

To be sure, the effects of incarceration can be difficult to isolate (Johnson and Easterling 2012), given the comingling of race and class with the populations most likely to be incarcerated and the fact that many of these families live in disadvantaged neighborhoods before the parent's incarceration begins. Yet even with that concern, there is little doubt that for many children, the incarceration of a parent is a "unique" traumatic experience (Wildeman, Wakefield, and Turney 2013) that often leads children to "duplicate destructive family patterns in their own adult interpersonal lives" (Laird 1981, 110; Johnston and Gabel 1995). In short, "[parental] incarceration has the effect of additionally burdening already vulnerable children" (Wakefield and Wildeman 2011, 800).

3.1.2 Early Childhood Exposure to Trauma

Early childhood exposure to trauma, either through witnessing traumatic events or being subjected to them, has been implicated in a wide variety of later negative outcomes. For example, studies have shown a particular link between early childhood traumatic experiences and later in life developing a drug habit (Chauchan and Widom 2012), engaging in dating violence (Tomsich et al. 2015), participating in street crime (Frederick, McCarthy, and Hagan 2013), and joining a gang (Hennigan, Kolnick, Vindel, and Maxson 2015).

Some childhood traumas are experienced directly, as in the case of childhood abuse, maltreatment, or neglect. But others are experienced vicariously, as the child learns of events through direct observation or through transmission of experiences from others. For example, growing up in a disadvantaged neighborhood has been shown to produce significant and predictable adverse effects on mental and physical health and psychological adjustment (see, e.g., Evans 2004; Hackman and Farah 2009; Leventhal and Brooks-Gunn 2011; McLoyd 1998). Community context and socioeconomic disadvantage are strongly linked to later participation in violent crime (Sampson, Morenoff, and Gannon-Rowley 2002; Elliott et al. 1996). One possible explanation for this association is that neighborhood disadvantage may indoctrinate a set of cultural beliefs favorable to the use of violence in social situations (Anderson 1990; Anderson 1999; Shover 1996).

Notably, trauma researchers tend to exclude the court experience as part of their definition of neighborhood disadvantage. This exclusion appears to imply that courts, because they are part of the formal criminal justice system, are somehow separate from the daily lives of most people. We would argue the opposite, particularly in the case of disadvantaged populations in urban contexts. For many of these individuals, the criminal justice system is a fact of daily life, and the exposure of children to its maneuverings is far more commonplace than one might expect or wish. Children in disadvantaged neighborhoods regularly view police action and treatment of residents, whether through stops, arrests, or searches, and many of them have incarcerated parents (and have had to deal with the bureaucracy of the correctional system to see or communicate with their parents). Many have witnessed the process that placed their parents in that incarcerated state to begin with – not only the arrest, but also the criminal court hearing.

For this reason, exposure to court proceedings in criminal cases should be viewed as part of the overall life experience for children coming from disadvantaged neighborhoods. If such proceedings serve to dehumanize parents, to frighten or disturb children, or to portray officials of the court as punitive or threatening, these experiences might contribute to the negative outcomes accruing from early childhood exposure to disadvantage in general.

3.2 METHODOLOGY AND DATA

Lower criminal courts are noisy, bustling, chaotic, confusing assemblages of people from socioeconomically lower-status groups, accused of crimes that are regularly characterized by the people who work there as "garbage, junk, trash, crap, penny ante, and the like." (Feeley 1992, 4). Repeat players know what to expect when they enter the courtroom; they are familiar with the relationships between professionals, with the delays that inevitably occur, with the obvious indicia of state coercion and control of the defendant population. But what must this environment look like to a child whose parent has been accused of a crime? When faced with this barrage of humanity and the inescapable signs of raw state power, how might children react?

To begin to frame a set of answers to these questions, we draw on our original interview data with prosecutors and offenders, collected as part of a larger project about drug enforcement patterns in a large southeastern city. The data we report below is not comprehensive or representative; it is instead meant to convey recurrent themes we heard when talking with court professionals and active dealers about this issue.

We interviewed eighteen prosecutors and ten active street offenders during the summer and fall of 2015. The interviews lasted approximately sixty to ninety minutes, and proceeded according to a semi-structured format. Each interview was audio recorded and transcribed. Respondents in the prosecutor group were variously white, African American, and Asian, ranging in age from late twenties to late fifties. Approximately 70 percent were female. Respondents in the offender group were uniformly African American, ranging in age from eighteen to thirty-seven. All but one were male. These offenders were "active" and noninstitutionalized.

We interviewed offenders in the community instead of incarcerated offenders for two reasons. First, although one's incarcerated status is often seen as the ultimate indicator of deviance, prison subjects are frequently reluctant to be honest about their participation in offending. Second, their status as "caught" and "unsuccessful" as an offender may cloud or alter their recollections of their offending, as well as their memories of childhood experiences that affected their decision to offend (see Topalli 2005; Belli and Loftus 1996).

We first report the narratives offered by prosecutors, detailing their perceptions of how children might be affected by witnessing their parents or close relatives being processed in court. Next, we introduce readers to the offenders themselves, speaking both as former children of offenders and as current parents, describing their views of how children experience the criminal court. Notably but unsurprisingly, offenders' views align imperfectly with the stories told by prosecutors – they emphasize the immediate emotional impact felt by a child who sees their parent suffering, rather than the linkage between this trauma and their own later behavior.

3.2.1 *Prosecutorial Perspectives*

Prosecutors identify five ways in which children are likely to be negatively affected by witnessing their parents' courtroom experience, even before conviction and sentencing. We call these narratives: *normalization, loss of authority, brutality, manipulation*, and *home-court comparison*. These characterizations are often interrelated, and they mostly signal that court processing of one's parent is likely to leave a lasting harmful impression on a young child.

3.2.1.1 Normalization

When children come to court, they learn to see criminal justice violation and processing as a normal part of life that everyone experiences. They no longer regard the criminal law as an institution that maintains an important moral boundary or defines proper behavior, because the people they love regularly break those laws. Though they see the justice system meting out consequences for violation, these children don't learn that violations should be avoided. Rather, they come to see violation followed by consequences as just another pattern that people from their family and community experience, devoid of stigma or shame (see Anderson 2000; Anderson 1997; see also Akers and Lee 1999). Having learned that this is the expected relationship people have with the law, children of offenders are more likely to become offenders themselves, and to develop an unhealthy disrespect for the police and the rule of law more generally.

Consider this comment from a prosecutor who has been in the profession for decades. She emphasizes that children who attend court learn that crime is a way of life, that the police should be regarded as the enemy, and that drug dealers are normal members of the community. Part of her evidence for this viewpoint comes from listening to jail calls, where she hears offenders casually talking about all of the people they know in neighboring cells, and she notes that this recitation is not met with shock or disapproval by the listener.

> I think it's astonishing that anyone would bring kids to see daddy coming out of the holding cell or you know, whatever. I guess they're there for support for the defendant, and I understand that, but it's just inconceivable to me why you would expose your child to that, except that it's a way of life and the police are the enemy and not the drug dealers, and I think it's so relevant to today and all the stuff that's going on with the anti-police sentiment . . . I think it's an accepted way of life, almost, that this is just part of, you know, growing up, there's no stigma, there's no shame to it . . . [F]rom listening to jail recordings I hear "guess who's locked up with me?" And they go over all the people that they know that either got out since they've been in there or just came in or – and it's kind of like who they know who's in jail with them and it's just kind of like, "Oh, yeah?" and it's not shocking or horrifying or anything else. It's just kind of accepted as a way of life and it's always, "the police are the bad guys" (Prosecutor 114).

A more junior prosecutor agrees that normalization of crime is likely to result from childhood courtroom exposure. She regrets that small children of defendants seem to get "acclimated" to the criminal justice system at a very young age, both from attending court and from visiting relatives in jail. They thus come to see contact with the criminal justice system as a normal process, "not that big of a deal," rather than as something that provokes shock, sadness or anger.

> A lot of my defendants' families will come and they'll have very small children. And they get very acclimated to the criminal justice system at a very young age. To the extent that it is a normal process for them to talk to an uncle or brother in jail. And so, I think as you get used to it, it's not that big of a deal. You know, you have communities where that's not the norm and you know, jail is like, "Oh my God, you know, what happened?!" And in these communities, it's like . . . "oh, you went to jail, ok, how long do you think you gonna be there?" . . . They see the handcuffs, like I say they talk to them in jail, they go to the visitations, and things like that, it's a very real part of their world (Prosecutor 103).

Several other prosecutors built on this theme in equally colorful language, commenting that bringing children to court is "horrible" because "the criminal justice process is oftentimes brutal, faceless," and when children develop an "unfortunate familiarity" with the criminal justice system, they will consequently have "no basic respect for law and order" (Prosecutor 112). Others felt that young people may be "indoctrinated" into adopting antisocial values (Prosecutor 116). Lacking a foundation of respect for rule of law values, "[t]here's nothing to scare them when they get older . . . it doesn't scare them not to do bad things" (Prosecutor 109). Moreover, these children learn to place blame for their criminal behavior on others and to regard the justice system as unfairly stacked against them. They learn to think: "The Man's constantly just trying to get up on your stuff" (Prosecutor 112). One prosecutor acknowledged that the normalization effect might vary by child, with some being shocked into compliance while others turn into lawbreakers: It might "spur [one] child to say 'never me!' [but] a different kid to emulate what they see" (Prosecutor 110).

3.2.1.2 Loss of Authority

Aside from developing a sense of disrespect for law and law enforcement, children who see their parents in court may come to disrespect those parents. "It sets a bad example to see your dad coming out in shackles," we were told by Prosecutor 117. With its myriad formalities and authority rules, the court can be an infantilizing place for a defendant; a child who sees a parent in handcuffs, subject to visible forms of authority, perhaps even treated in a humiliating fashion, is likely to lose the impression of that parent as an authority figure. Hence, regardless of whether these parents are ever convicted of the crime of which they were accused, their perceived role and place in the family could be permanently and negatively altered. This concern is consistent with Lynne Haney's observations of children who accompany their mothers to prison; she found that inmates lost the ability to exert parental authority over their children because the children saw them belittled by prison authorities (Haney 2013, 114–15).

Commenting on the court's institutional processes that undermine an adult's ability to parent, one prosecutor exclaimed, "I wouldn't want [my] daughter seeing me in handcuffs!" (Prosecutor 110). Another remarked that for a child to see a parent "being put in a child's place" by the criminal court, "to see [a] parent disciplined this way must be very negative," and would likely cause the parent to lose "authority status" (Prosecutor 105). Still another emphasized that it can't be good to see your "father figure, this is someone you follow in his steps," treated in this fashion (Prosecutor 115).

The loss of authority does not simply result from the way in which court officials speak to the accused. Prosecutors acknowledge that visible signs of control in criminal court (handcuffs, jail uniform, holding cell) are likely to produce a particularly lasting influence on children's view of their parents:

> I mean, I don't understand how you explain to your child – and it depends on the age of your child, too, obviously, if they're old enough to understand what's going on, and where are we and what's happening here – but to see your father in handcuffs and a jail uniform coming out of a holding cell when you're in court that he's being prosecuted for a criminal offense, I don't understand why people do that (Prosecutor 114).

Yet another prosecutor offered an anecdote regarding a defendant who brought her children to court expecting to receive probation, but was instead sentenced to jail and taken into custody immediately; her children, bewildered, went home with her attorney (Prosecutor 107). Having one's parent's authority directly transferred to an actor in the criminal justice system is an experience no child is likely to forget.

3.2.1.3 Brutality

A child's experience in the courtroom is not limited to seeing one's own parent; the child who comes to court will see and hear other defendants and other cases at the preliminary hearing or bond hearing stage. Prosecutors describe the environment as follows:

> The courtroom is not a good place to be. There are lots of defendants sitting in the audience near the kids. There can be serious cases set for prelim (murder, rape, child molestation) – we shouldn't want kids hearing that (Prosecutor 110).

> In court, kids are learning things they don't want to know – not necessarily about the legal process, but simply just because . . . it's a revolving door that's constantly exposing them to a heavily skewed population of people accused of crimes sitting in the gallery watching (Prosecutor 112).

> It's a negative impact to sit in that courtroom, hear what's going on, they hear things they shouldn't hear. They hear bond hearings for rape cases, bond hearings for murder cases (Prosecutor 109).

State courtrooms are a rough-and-tumble assemblage of people and cases. Sitting in the audience for hours at a stretch, children may be exposed to a range of crimes that have ugly and/or frightening facts. Instead of attending school to learn math and science, they are likely to learn about the destructive features of, and dysfunctional people in, their community. The criminal court thus unveils the brutality of the human condition, at a time when children are entitled to a bit more innocence (see, e.g., Finkelhor, Turner, Ormrod, and Hamby 2009).

Beyond this dynamic, there are likely long-term traumatic consequences from being exposed to the unexpurgated brutality of life in poor, violence-prone communities that can set children up for failure in a variety of ways. Trauma researchers, criminologists, and sociologists have described in detail a host of negative outcomes associated with early exposure to negative social and physical stimuli – everything from poor school attainment to drug use and participation in violent crime (see, e.g., McCoy, Roy, and Raver 2015; Gulley, Oppenheimer, and Hankin 2104; Evans and Kim 2013). Surely there is good reason to fear that the circumstances to which the children of offenders in court are exposed – "conduct that isn't pretty," according to Prosecutor 117 – would produce similar effects.

3.2.1.4 Manipulation

Prosecutors believe that sometimes children are brought to court as a prop or a ploy to make the defendant appear more sympathetic to the judge or jury. In this scenario, defendants try to manipulate the decision-makers by inflating their parenting role in a very public way (referred to as "impression management" in the psychological literature; see, e.g., Tedeschi 2013; Aronsson, Jönsson, and Linell 1987).

According to this narrative, the presence of children in court is predominantly strategic: the goal is to inspire the decision-maker to go easy on the defendant, thereby lessening the family's suffering. Irrespective of whether the strategy works, prosecutors believe there is something unethical or immoral with using one's children this way, that it is a fraud on the court, and that children will eventually pick up on the fact that they are being exploited. This is ultimately harmful to the parent-child relationship, even if it does result in a lesser sentence being imposed on the offender.

Prosecutor 109 told us a particularly colorful story about how this tactic is used, based on her time as a defense attorney intern:

> When I was in law school I had to do an internship . . . with the PD's Office. The guy I sat with – was supposed to be like the best PD in Mississippi – he was getting ready to try a case . . . and we actually picked a jury. And he told his defendant to pick one baby mama, an attractive baby mama, and get all your other kids together and put them in their Easter suits and have them sit in the back of the courtroom while we pick a jury. Put them in pigtails, the ruffled socks – he says, "My intent is to try to get grandmothers and mothers and people who work with kids on my jury, and when they see those kids they'll feel sorry for you and then they won't find you guilty."
>
> And I knew that tactic, so when I came here, it's just a tactic. They bring them in the courtroom, pinch 'em, make 'em cry, and the whole thing is to make you feel sorry for – or make the judge feel sorry for them – all of sudden you see men holding them, giving them bottles and you know they don't do that at home – it's just a show.
>
> It basically says to me when I see them, "Please don't put me in prison 'cause I got this baby." And when it comes to men, I doubt they have any interaction with those babies. They just call their baby mamas, "May I borrow your . . . " It's just a prop. It pisses me off . . . I think it's horrible for any parent who takes their young kids into the courtroom as a ploy to try to get them off charges or reduced charges. Shame on them (Prosecutor 109).

Some prosecutors believe that judges have gotten wise to this tactic; one related to us an incident in which a judge halted the proceedings to separate the defendant from his manufactured family image:

> We had this one case where the judge was like, "I am not getting ready to take this plea with you holding that baby – you have to figure something out" (Prosecutor 106).

This same prosecutor once required a defendant to come back with photos of his children, notes from their teachers, and the like to prove his family involvement as a reason to stay out of jail. She was pleasantly surprised when he complied.

3.2.1.5 Home-Court Comparison

Finally, some prosecutors minimize the potentially negative effects of courtroom experience by comparing the child's courtroom exposure to his or her home environment – what one prosecutor (116) referred to as "tragically disintegrated home lives" (see Bandura 2002 for work on moral disengagement and the use of advantageous comparison techniques). Prosecutors invoking this narrative tended to refer to the child's home life only in abstract terms, steering clear of more concrete criticisms of the negative influences the child experiences every day. But however this home environment is understood, what the child sees in court pales by comparison, and thus is not a particular cause for concern.

> I think, I mean, it's not a place that I would want kids to be. I don't think it's a good thing for them to learn, but there's also like what's going on at their home, and I'm sure that's worse than whatever's happening in court, so – I'm not sure. I don't know ... I'm sure that if they are actually using drugs then whatever is going on at home is probably more upsetting than what's happening in court, but I don't think it is a great place for children to be (Prosecutor 113).

> I can't imagine [the impact] would be good. I imagine, and I don't want to paint with too broad a brush, if their parents, their mother, father, whatever, is in that situation, in many of those cases, unfortunately, they've probably seen a lot worse than that [at home] ... I can't imagine it would be good (Prosecutor 107).

> I think they have seen so much, I just really think they have seen so much, to where what they see in the courthouse probably is a whole lot less than what they see at home. I really, really, really think that they just see so much. (Prosecutor 106).

When asked to comment more specifically about the effects of a negative home environment, Prosecutor 106 offered the following observation:

> I volunteer in schools and I know what they tell me, and I know their behavior, I know what teachers feel about their behavior, and I know oftentimes they're products of their environment. Because they're too young to be out there – learning – it's what they're exposed to, why they do what they do. Because they're not born that way. They're not born saying certain things, doing certain things, having certain behaviors – they're learning it from somewhere.

To sum up: from the point of view of the prosecutors who work in lower criminal courts every day, the presence of children in the courtroom is a purely negative development. It inspires future criminal behavior, contributes to the deterioration of family, introduces children to the ugliness of the world before they are ready, and perpetrates a fraud on the court. While for some prosecutors these negatives are outweighed by the harmful influences in the child's home environment, there is no doubt that children do not belong in the courtroom.

3.2.2 Offender Perspectives

Having recounted prosecutorial perspectives on how children experience court, we now turn the lens in a different direction, to hear from offenders themselves about their own courtroom experiences. These offenders had all witnessed the court process as children when their parents were accused of a crime, or had to see their own children sitting in the audience during their own hearings. In most cases, these criminal proceedings were for relatively serious offenses such as drug possession and distribution, violent offenses such as robbery or carjacking, or property crimes such as burglary. In all cases, drug distribution and use were central features of the offender's day-to-day world.

Young children who see their parents as defendants in criminal court experience a sense of upheaval; the experience delegitimizes the authority of the court and creates an antagonistic or adversarial relationship with the criminal justice system in general. This is particularly important because many children also witness their parents being arrested or questioned by the police before going to court, and/or being subject to the harsh and seemingly capricious rules of engagement after the parent has been sentenced and is serving time in prison. Thus, the child's experience with and assessment of the criminal justice system in general, and court in particular, is negative, often from beginning to end (see Murray 2012, 257, recounting studies that establish post-traumatic stress for children who witness the arrest of a household member). These negative assessments remain with such children as they move forward in life, influencing their interactions with the police and placing them at risk for criminal justice involvement later in life. None of our offenders suggested that their early experiences normalized the criminal justice system for them, nor altered the role of law as a meaningful boundary between right and wrong. If there's diminishment in law as an authority, it's because the legal system seems to them brutal and unfair.

Thus, while offenders and prosecutors agree about the harmful effect of humiliation/degradation experienced by the offender and witnessed by the child (pursuant to the loss-of-authority prosecutor narrative we described above), offenders see this humiliation and degradation as more than just a loss of authority. For them it appears to be a critical component of the criminal justice process itself, a purposeful strategy implemented by those who operate the court system to gain compliance and affirm the court's authority over certain citizens, particularly those who are poor or of color. Prosecutors acknowledge this harshness but deny its centrality; they see it as at most an unfortunate side effect of an otherwise fair system meant to impose consequences on lawbreakers.

But offenders and their children assume that this harshness is built into the court process, viewing it as an exercise in domination and disrespect meant to break down not only the offender's rebelliousness to the system, but that of others who may be contemplating such rebelliousness. For that reason, they are likely to respond in kind – with rebellion and disrespect.

> My moms took me to court this one time because [my pops was] busted in the summer and we was out of school and my cousins and sister weren't around to look after me so I went. And you know it was fucked up. You see your pops up there with his head down and the judge was mean and there's like cops around. He in chains man. Chains! It just hit you, you know, that this is messed up, even a little kid know that. My moms was crying, I guess, when the judge gave him the sentence like five years. And the worst was when she cried the judge yelled at her and we got kicked out the court. You see that, how you gonna be ok with this bullshit justice system we got? (Butter, age 30, robber)

> I hated it. When you in court seeing them take away your mom it make you feel like you the one did something. That's what they do to you. It's heartless for a kid to see that shit (Nukie, 25, carjacker).

> It was messed up. I got busted for an ounce, just an ounce, man. And this judge, she was there saying I was [poisoning] the neighborhood and I was messing up the kids in the neighborhood and my daughter and my daughter's mama sitting right there while this woman is shitting on me. Look man, I never sold to no kids, OK? But here's this crazy ass judge saying all this shit and then she was asking me if I was feeling bad or guilty about it, and I said yeah, cuz you know I wanted to get out of there, and when I didn't say it loud enough, she yelled at me and was like, "What? I did not hear you mister! You will please speak up in my court and sit up straight!" I'm like, serious? You talkin' to me like that? I know she heard me, she just trying to make me look bad. My girl lookin' at me like, damn daddy, I thought you was the boss, you ain't shit. That's how I felt like (Rez-boy, 24, drug dealer).

As these passages show, offenders acutely feel the degradation that seems embedded in the criminal court process. As children they sensed what was happening to their parents; as offenders they sense how their children perceive what is happening to them. Faced with that display of raw state power and disrespect, they unsurprisingly turn away from both law and their parents as legitimate sources of authority in their lives. Having become untethered to formal and informal means of behavioral control, they are predisposed to high-risk futures. In other words, individuals exposed to the circumstances we describe above become more, not less, at risk for participating in exactly the kinds of behaviors the justice system wishes to deter. In public health circles this is referred to as an iatrogenic effect, where the cure becomes the cause of the disease one is trying to prevent. In such circumstances the cure itself should be reevaluated or recalibrated.

3.3 CONCLUSION

Our preliminary data suggest that, in addition to the financial costs borne by the accused that Malcolm Feeley (1979) documented decades ago, exposure to the criminal court packs an emotional punch for the accused's children. Prosecutors offer five different narratives to explain the ways in which children may become casualties of the criminal court; offenders' narratives both enrich and complicate the stories prosecutors tell about the deleterious effects of courtroom exposure. But whichever lens we choose to adopt, these comments leave little room for doubt that the practice of bringing children into the courtroom ought to be seriously investigated by scholars working in the collateral consequences arena, as well as by those working on childhood trauma.

Aside from the scholarship prompt, we hope to sow the seeds of policy change with our observations about this phenomenon. The first-best response to the problem identified here would be to make courts more humane institutions. But until that lofty goal can be reached, we believe that courthouse communities ought to focus on a second-best alternative. They should offer child-care facilities on site, to make child care available when a family member is involved (whether as a defendant, a victim, or a witness) on the criminal court calendar. We recognize that for many families, the choice to bring children to court is not deliberately made; the noninvolved parent may simply have no other option for children who are not in school full-time. But if as a community we care about the harmful intergenerational effects of criminal court exposure, noninvolved parents need to have somewhere safe to leave their children for the entire day, since criminal court calendars oftentimes last for hours. A comprehensive, on-site day-care facility, staffed by professionals and free or low-cost to the families of offenders, victims, and witnesses would help limit children's exposure to the brutality, degradation, and callousness that criminal courts often (appear to) embrace. Several states have already adopted this model on a limited basis,[1] but we believe it should implemented on a much larger scale.

The policy message is more complicated for nonoffending parents who bring children to court so that they can see the accused (and so the accused can see them), aiming to nurture the emotional bond between parent and child on the eve of the parent being sent away for an extended period of incarceration. Children who do not have the chance to say goodbye to the soon-to-be-incarcerated parent might suffer emotionally and blame themselves for the parent's absence. To offer alternatives, courthouses ought to set aside interview rooms for contact visits between parents and children, so that a child's ability to see the parent does not hinge on the criminal court setting itself. In the absence of private rooms, parents ought to at least be

---

[1] See https://www.ncsc.org/Topics/Courthouse-Facilities/Courthouse-Design-and-Finance/State-Links.aspx?cat=Childrens%20Waiting%20Rooms%20and%20Day%20Care%20Centers (accessed on October 2, 2018). The website contains the National Center for State Courts' list of state initiatives to create children's waiting rooms and day care centers in courthouses.

reminded – by the defense attorney, perhaps – that while furthering the parent-child bond is an honorable goal, bringing the child to court poses real risks for the child's future. In fact, the bonding goal might be thwarted by the child's attendance, as the loss of authority narrative and Haney's research in the prison context suggest.

In sum, to prevent the sorts of intergenerational harms our interviewees describe, both courthouse communities and families need to be attentive to providing alternative pathways for family bonding and court work to take place. Comingling them in the courtroom for the sake of time and space efficiency does not appear to be in the best interests of the children, nor in the best interests of a society interested in preventing future crime and public health problems.

REFERENCES

Akers, R. L. 1990. "Rational Choice, Deterrence, and Social Learning Theory in Criminology: The Path Not Taken." *Journal of Criminal Law & Criminology* 81: 653–76.

Akers, R. L. 2008. "Self-Control and Social Learning Theory." In *Out of control: Assessing the General Theory of Crime*, edited by Erich Goode, 77–89. Palo Alto: Stanford University Press.

Akers, R. L. and G. Lee. 1999. "Age, Social Learning, and Social Bonding in Adolescent Substance Use." *Deviant Behavior* 20 (1): 1–25.

Anderson, E. 1997. "Violence and the Inner-City Street Code." In *Violence and Childhood in the Inner City*, edited by Joan McCord, 1–30.

Anderson, E. 2000. *Code of the Street: Decency, Violence, and the Moral Life of the Inner City*. New York: W.W. Norton & Company.

Aronsson, K., L. Jönsson, and P. Linell. 1987. "The Courtroom Hearing as a Middle Ground: Speech Accommodation by Lawyers and Defendants." *Journal of Language and Social Psychology* 6 (2): 99–115.

Besemer, S. and D. P. Farrington. 2012. "Intergenerational Transmission of Criminal Behaviour: Conviction Trajectories of Fathers and Their Children." *European Journal of Criminology* 9 (2): 120–141.

Besemer, S., V. Van der Geest, J. Murray, C. C. Bijleveld, and D. P. Farrington. 2011. "The Relationship Between Parental Imprisonment and Offspring Offending in England and the Netherlands." *British Journal of Criminology* 51 (2): 413–37.

Belli, R. F. and E. F. Loftus. 1996. "Misinformation and the False Memory Problem." In *Remembering Our Past: Studies in Autobiographical Memory*, edited by David C. Rubin, 157–79.

Chauhan, P. and C. S. Widom. 2012. "Childhood Maltreatment and Illicit Drug Use in Middle Adulthood: The Role of Neighborhood Characteristics." *Development and Psychopathology* 24 (3): 723–38.

Currie, J. and E. Tekin. 2012. "Understanding the Cycle Childhood Maltreatment and Future Crime." *Journal of Human Resources* 47 (2): 509–49.

Eckenrode, J., M. Laird, and J. Doris. 1993. "School Performance and Disciplinary Problems Among Abused and Neglected Children." *Developmental Psychology* 29 (1): 53–62.

Elliott, D. S., W. J. Wilson, D. Huizinga, R. J. Sampson, A. Elliott, and B. Rankin. 1996. "The Effects of Neighborhood Disadvantage On Adolescent Development." *Journal of Research in Crime and Delinquency* 33 (4): 389–426.

Evans, G. W. 2004. "The Environment of Childhood Poverty." *American Psychologist* 59 (2): 77–92.
Evans, G. W. and P. Kim. 2013. "Childhood Poverty, Chronic Stress, Self-Regulation, and Coping." *Child Development Perspectives* 7 (1): 43–48.
Farrington, D. P. 1997. "Early Prediction of Violent and Non-Violent Youthful Offending." *European Journal on Criminal Policy and Research* 5 (2): 51–66.
Feeley, M. M. 1979. *The Process is the Punishment: Handling Cases in a Lower Criminal Court*. New York: Russell Sage Foundation.
Finkelhor, D., H. Turner, R. Ormrod, and S. L. Hamby. 2009. "Violence, Abuse, and Crime Exposure in a National Sample of Children and Youth." *Pediatrics* 124 (5): 1411–423.
Frederick, T. J., B. McCarthy, and J. Hagan. 2013. "Perceived Danger and Offending: Exploring the Links Between Violent Victimization and Street Crime." *Violence and Victims* 28 (1): 16–35.
Glueck S, Glueck E. 1950. *Unraveling Juvenile Delinquency*. Cambridge, MA: Harvard University Press.
Goffman, E. 1963. *Behavior in Public Places*. New York: The Free Press.
Gulley, L. D., C. W. Oppenheimer, and B. L. Hankin. 2014. "Associations Among Negative Parenting, Attention Bias to Anger, and Social Anxiety Among Youth." *Developmental Psychology* 50 (2): 577–585.
Hackman, D. A. and M. J. Farah. 2009. "Socioeconomic Status and the Developing Brain." *Trends in Cognitive Sciences* 13 (2): 65–73.
Hagan, J. and R. Dinovitzer. 1999. "Collateral Consequences of Imprisonment for Children, Communities, and Prisoners." *Crime and Justice* 26: 121–62.
Haney, L. 2013. "Motherhood as Punishment: The Case of Parenting in Prison." *Signs* 39 (1): 105–30.
Hennigan, K. M., K. A. Kolnick, F. Vindel, and C. L. Maxson. 2015. "Targeting Youth at Risk for Gang Involvement: Validation of a Gang Risk Assessment to Support Individualized Secondary Prevention." *Children and Youth Services Review* 56: 86–96.
Johnson, E. I. and B. Easterling. 2012. "Understanding Unique Effects of Parental Incarceration on Children: Challenges, Progress, and Recommendations." *Journal of Marriage and Family* 74 (2): 342–56.
Johnston, D. and K. Gabel. 1995. "Incarcerated Parents." In *Children of Incarcerated Parents*, edited by K. Gabel and D. Johnson, 3–20. New York: Lexington Books.
Laird J. 1981. "An Ecological Approach to Child Welfare." In *Parents of Children in Placement*, edited by P. A. Sinanoglu and A. N. Maluccio, 97–132. New York: Child Welfare League of America.
Leventhal, T. and J. Brooks-Gunn. 2011. "Changes in Neighborhood Poverty from 1990 to 2000 and Youth's Problem Behaviors." *Developmental Psychology* 47 (6): 1680–98.
McCoy, D. C., A. L. Roy, and C. C. Raver. 2015. "Neighborhood Crime as a Predictor of Individual Differences in Emotional Processing and Regulation." *Developmental Science* 19(1): 164–74.
McLoyd, V. C. 1998. "Socioeconomic Disadvantage and Child Development." *American Psychologist* 53 (2): 185-204.
Murray, J. and D. P. Farrington. 2008a. "Parental Imprisonment: Long-Lasting Effects on Boys' Internalizing Problems Through the Life Course." *Development and Psychopathology* 20 (1): 273–90.
Murray, J. and D. P. Farrington. 2008b. "The Effects of Parental Imprisonment on Children." *Crime and Justice* 37 (1): 133–206.

Murray, J., C. G. Janson, and D. P. Farrington. 2007. "Crime in Adult Offspring of Prisoners: A Cross-National Comparison of Two Longitudinal Samples." *Criminal Justice and Behavior* 34 (1): 133–49.

Murray, J., R. Loeber, and D. Pardini. 2012. "Parental Involvement in the Criminal Justice System and the Development of Youth Theft, Marijuana Use, Depression, and Poor Academic Performance." *Criminology* 50 (1): 255–302.

Rowe, D. C. and D. P. Farrington. 1997. "The Familial Transmission of Criminal Convictions." *Criminology* 35 (1): 177–202.

Sampson, R. J., J. D. Morenoff, and T. Gannon-Rowley. 2002. "Assessing 'Neighborhood Effects': Social Processes and New Directions in Research." Annual Review of Sociology : 443–78.

Shonk, S. M. and D. Cicchetti. 2001. "Maltreatment, Competency Deficits, and Risk for Academic and Behavioral Maladjustment." *Developmental Psychology* 37 (1): 3–14.

Tedeschi, J. T., ed. 2013. *Impression Management Theory and Social Psychological Research*. Cambridge: Academic Press.

Thornberry, T. P. 2009. "The Apple Doesn't Fall Far from the Tree (or Does It?): Intergenerational Patterns of Antisocial Behavior – The American Society of Criminology 2008 Sutherland Address." *Criminology* 47 (2): 297–325.

Tomsich, E., W. G. Jennings, T. N. Richards, A. R. Gover, and R. A. Powers. 2015. "Childhood Physical Maltreatment and Young Adult Dating Violence: A Propensity Matching Approach." *Journal of Interpersonal Violence* 3(22): 3475–96

Topalli, V. 2005. "When Being Good Is Bad: An Expansion of Neutralization Theory." *Criminology* 43 (3): 797–836.

Turney, K. 2014. "Incarceration and Social Inequality Challenges and Directions for Future Research." *The ANNALS of the American Academy of Political and Social Science* 651 (1): 97–101.

Turney, K. and A. R. Haskins. 2014. "Falling Behind? Children's Early Grade Retention After Paternal Incarceration." *Sociology of Education* 87 (4): 241–58.

Wakefield, S. and C. Wildeman. 2011. "Mass Imprisonment and Racial Disparities in Childhood Behavioral Problems." *Criminology & Public Policy* 10(3): 793–817.

West, D. J. and D. P. Farrington. 1973. *Who Becomes Delinquent? Second Report of the Cambridge Study in Delinquent Development*. Abingdon: Taylor & Francis.

Wildeman, C. 2010. "Paternal Incarceration and Children's Physically Aggressive Behaviors: Evidence from the Fragile Families and Child Wellbeing Study." *Social Forces* 89 (1): 285–309.

Wildeman, C., S. Wakefield, and K. Turney. 2013. "Misidentifying the Effects of Parental Incarceration? A Comment on Johnson and Easterling (2012)." *Journal of Marriage and Family* 75 (1): 252–58.

4

The Process Is the Problem

Shauhin Talesh

INTRODUCTION

Malcolm Feeley's pathbreaking book *The Process Is the Punishment* is a classic study of the gap between the law on the books and the law in action. In particular, Feeley exposes the tension between the ideal of "due process," which seeks to allow individuals an opportunity to be heard at a meaningful time and in a meaningful manner, with the reality of how criminal processes and procedures impact a litigant navigating through the criminal justice process in powerful ways. Although due process protections in theory protect defendants and preserve the ideal of serving justice, they developed largely without regard to cost. Feeley's book highlights the challenges and costs of invoking due process rights in various criminal settings.

Acknowledging the paucity of trials in the routine flow of criminal cases, Feeley's ethnographic exploration of lower criminal courts in New Haven reveals that most of the court's work gets done in the process of arraignment and other pretrial processes. In these settings, cases are often dismissed, guilt is pleaded, and fines are imposed. Feeley's exploration of the decision making at pretrial detention and release, the appointment of public defenders, adjudication, sentencing, and pretrial processes reveals that defendants often incur the costs of loss of pay, inconvenience, auto impoundment charges, and attorneys' fees. Efforts to slow the process and make it truly deliberative might lead to harsher treatment of defendants and more lost time for complainants and victims. Expanded procedures designed to improve the criminal process are not invoked because they might be counterproductive. Mechanisms to inhibit discretion by institutional actors and litigants do not perform their expected functions. Defendants suffer the indignities of dispute and defense, and often navigate a distinctly unfamiliar courtroom setting.

Feeley's in-depth exploration of lower criminal courts leads him to conclude that the process is the punishment. That is, the cost to criminal defendants of invoking their due process rights in lower criminal courts ultimately ends up being greater than the benefits of the rights themselves (Feeley 1979). In doing so, Feeley reveals how the costs of the pretrial process are not only important sanctions in their own right, but also how they in turn shape and are shaped by the nature of the court organization and the conceptions of substantive justice.

Feeley's book highlights a paradox that our criminal justice system continues to wrestle with: in the name of "due process," American law tries to establish rules that guard against the possibility that innocent individuals will suffer sanctions and endure unfair consequences. Our criminal justice system seeks to curb this fear by fostering an ideal of perfectibility and a preoccupation with procedure. The reality, however, is that the process is so complex and cumbersome that these due process protections serve limited functions in the vast majority of criminal cases. The costs of invoking many due process rights render many of these rights shallow symbols of fairness that are often not invoked.

As perceptive as Feeley's account is, he focused only on criminal courts. What about civil courts in the United States? Are procedural protections and due process rights in the civil justice system so costly that they make achieving substantive relief difficult? Similar to the criminal context, United States Supreme Court cases seek to preserve due process protections in civil courts. Moreover, the drafters of the Federal Rules of Civil Procedure in 1938 tried to create a system that leads to efficient, speedy, and just results. The following examines how process impacts the civil justice system, both among courts and in alternative dispute forums. I argue that in the civil context, the process is not the punishment, but rather the problem. Focusing largely on the procedural rules in court and alternative dispute processes, this article highlights how the United States Supreme Court has trimmed procedural protections in civil courts and alternative disputing forums. With the advocacy and support of private organizations and the defense bar, due process rights and procedural protections have been redefined, and consequently citizens' access to justice is significantly undermined. When individuals do invoke their procedural and due process rights and seek substantive relief in court or arbitration, they are subject to a process filtered with organizational values and influence in subtle and sometimes not-so-subtle ways.

4.1 THE DEFORMATION OF CIVIL PROCEDURE IN THE UNITED STATES

The establishment of the Federal Rules of Civil Procedure in 1938 reflected a policy of citizen access for civil disputes. The Federal Rules promote the resolution of disputes on the merits rather than on the basis of the technicalities that characterized earlier procedural systems. Concerned that the outcomes of trials turned not on the merits of the case but on the skills of lawyers or the financial resources of the parties, the drafters were determined to implement a system that would allow the parties to obtain the "fullest possible knowledge of the issues and facts before trial" (Bell et al. 1992, 6). The drafters believed that wide-ranging discovery would ensure a fair and just determination in cases and remedy the imbalance of power between the wealthy and the poor. As noted in FRCP Rule 1, the federal rules contemplate a system that ensures a "just, speedy, and inexpensive determination of every action and proceeding." Fed. R. Civ. Pro. 1. Similar to criminal courts, the procedures established in non-criminal courts in the United States – at least when such rules were promulgated in 1938 – was to ensure that a procedurally fair system leads to substantively just results.

However, over the past twenty-five years, there has been a dramatic shift in the way the Federal Rules are conceptualized and interpreted by the United States Supreme Court. This shift has led to an increasingly early procedural disposition of cases prior to trial. Moreover, litigants have far less access to courts. Even though litigants enjoy more consumer and civil rights protections than ever before, litigants using the civil justice system encounter a procedural system that narrows a person's ability to effectuate these rights. The Supreme Court's shift has been in line with large corporations' desire for less discovery and fewer trials. Trials are now few and far between. The focus on case disposition has led to a series of procedural hurdles and transformed the relatively uncluttered pretrial process that the drafters of the rules established into one where the process is now the problem. The following highlights how the various phases of civil procedure have changed in ways that limit due process rights and access to justice.

4.1.1 The Pleading Process is the Problem

Recent Supreme Court decisions in *Bell Atlantic Corp.* v. *Twombly* (2007) and *Ashcroft* v. *Iqbal* (2009) made plaintiffs' ability to survive a motion to dismiss at the pleading stage for failing to state a claim upon which relief could be granted much harder. Since 1938, Rule 8, the core federal pleading provision, required only "a short and plain statement . . . showing that the pleader is entitled to relief" (Federal R. Civ. Proc. Rule 8(a)(2)). The rulemakers drafted this rule in this manner in order to make it easy for plaintiffs to enter federal courts without technicality or formality. Thus, pleadings were to simply give "notice" to the other side of the claims.

Subsequent discovery and motion practice would eliminate non-meritorious claims. The Supreme Court in *Conley* v. *Gibson* (1957, 47) indicated that complaints should simply "give a defendant fair notice of what the . . . claim is and the grounds upon which it rests." As long as there were "no set of facts" such that plaintiffs could not establish its claim, the motion to dismiss should be dismissed.

Twombly and *Iqbal* radically changed the pleading standard from a "notice" pleading standard to a heightened "plausibility pleading" standard. As opposed to simply providing notice of a claim, the plaintiff's complaint requires facts, not conclusions, "showing" a "plausible" claim. In particular, these cases read in tandem suggest that the long-standing principle that a court must accept as true all of the allegations contained in a complaint is inapplicable to legal conclusions. Moreover, only a complaint that states a plausible claim for relief will survive a motion to dismiss. Determining whether a complaint states a plausible claim for relief will "be a context-specific task that requires the reviewing court to draw on its judicial experience and common sense" (Iqbal 2009, 679). In an attempt to textually ground its holding in Rule 8(a)(2), these cases suggest this rule requires that a complaint contain a statement "showing that the pleader is entitled to relief." The Supreme Court offered a two-pronged approach that requires courts to eliminate conclusory allegations from a complaint and evaluate whether the remaining claims give rise to an entitlement to relief.

One of the great contributions of Feeley's *The Process Is the Punishment* is the subtle focus on the costs of due process rights. The costs of the Supreme Court's decisions in *Twombly* and *Iqbal* on civil procedure are potentially significant. Prevailing empirical research as to the impact of these recent Supreme Court decisions on litigant behavior is inconclusive. In particular, there are serious methodological challenges to studying the impact of these cases on pleadings, such as case selection effects, sample size problems, and nonrepresentative samples.

More basically, we do not know in how many cases the plaintiffs' lawyers choose not to file a lawsuit because they fear they cannot plead facts in a complaint that satisfy the heightened pleading standard. There is some research that suggests that defendants are filing motions to dismiss at higher rates, but these motions are not necessarily being granted at higher rates than prior to when *Twombly* and *Iqbal* were decided (Gelbach 2012; Hubbard 2017). There is also research that shows that plaintiffs' complaints now enumerate fewer causes of action (Boyd et al. 2013) and that tort causes of action are now pled in more lengthy and complex ways (Hazelton 2015). Much more empirical research is needed to tease out the full impact of *Twombly* and *Iqbal*.

What is clear, however, is that these changes are more likely to negatively impact plaintiffs than defendants. If we accept that at least some cases never end up being filed because of a concern over failing to satisfy *Twombly* and *Iqbal*, then this heightened pleading standard ultimately denies court access to those who, although have meritorious claims, cannot satisfy its requirements either because they lack the resources to engage in extensive pre-filing investigation or because of informational asymmetries.

Higher pleadings standards make it especially difficult for *pro se* plaintiffs or plaintiffs challenging or bringing discrimination lawsuits (Moore 2010, 2012; Gelbach 2012; Hubbard 2017). Without the benefit of discovery, it is often difficult to plead the facts plausibly suggesting illegal conduct. Defendants often possess information suggesting disparate treatment or impact in their institutional policies and practices. Thus, these cases are particularly vulnerable to motions to dismiss under the standard set forth in *Twombly* and *Iqbal*.

Moreover, courts are supposed to use "judicial experience and common sense" to evaluate plausibility. This standard is very subjective and fails to give judges enough guidance on how to determine whether a complaint should be dismissed. To the extent there are significant differences in perception among racial groups over the existence and pervasiveness of racial discrimination, plaintiffs may be at a disadvantage in court, especially when the majority of judges are white.

The fact that civil rights cases are at risk of being dismissed in federal courts is an important problem because it potentially undermines civil rights enforcement and compromises deterrence. Under the legislative scheme of most civil rights statutes, individuals are empowered to act as private attorney general and seek relief. Thus, similar to the criminal defendants Feeley studied in New Haven, while plaintiffs are afforded many due process rights, statutory or otherwise, litigants in the civil justice system face an uphill battle trying to survive a motion to dismiss and have their case heard in court. The heightened pleading standard, therefore, undermines the fundamental right to be heard, which is a core part of conceptions of due process in the United States. Moreover, denying plaintiffs access to the courts undermines the preference to have cases decided on the merits as opposed to procedural technicalities. The current pleading procedure as set forth by *Twombly* and *Iqbal* appears to be the problem, not the punishment.

4.1.2 *The Civil Discovery Procedures are the Problem*

The rules of discovery have taken a similar path to pleading. Discovery rules were initially broad in order to allow broad access to information to help people prove their cases. However, discovery rules have become increasingly limited because of concerns over excessive and costly discovery. Due in part to the careful lobbying of the defense bar and large corporations who have actively influenced the rule-making process, the Supreme Court and those involved in revising the Federal Rules continue to retract the scope of discovery.

While pretrial discovery did not occur at common law the majority of the time, the introduction of the Federal Rules of Civil Procedure in 1938 was, ironically, supposed to lower the cost of litigation (Beisner 2010). As one scholar notes, "[b]y mandating a full exchange of information, the drafters thought they could help less powerful litigants prove their legal claims and thus redress the imbalance" (Blaner 1998, 8). At least since the 1970s, the scope of permissible discovery extended to "any matter, not privileged which is relevant to the subject matter involved in the pending action," subject to many other specific rules and trial court discretion to restrain excessive or abusive discovery. Fed. R. Civ. P 26(b)(1), 398 U.S. 977, 982 (1970) (amended 2000).

However, plaintiffs' ability to conduct discovery has shrunk in the past thirty years. Under the 2000 amendment to Rule 26(b)(1), the default definition of the scope of discovery was narrowed to "any matter, not privileged, that is relevant to the claim or defense of any party." Fed. R. Civ. P. 26(b)(1). This was part of a series of amendments that sought to curb costs and excessive discovery. The Federal Rules did note, however, "[f]or good cause, the court may order discovery of any matter relevant to the subject matter involved in the action. Relevant information need not be admissible at the trial if the discovery appears reasonably calculated to lead to the discovery of admissible evidence." Fed. R. Civ. P. 26(b)(1). These amendments in 2000, coupled with changes in 1983 and 1993 to the Federal Rules,[1] reflect a general trend toward managing the discovery process in a way that reduces costs and prevents abusive tactics by lawyers.

The narrowing of the scope of permissible discovery is continuing with recent amendments. On December 1, 2015, new amendments to discovery rules in the Federal Rules of Civil Procedure went into effect that alter discovery and increase the burden on plaintiffs. The new rules alter the presumptions and burdens of proof in discovery proceedings as well as impose specific limitations on how discovery is conducted.

The biggest change alters the scope of discoverable information, which of course impacts virtually every discovery activity. The prior standard permitted the production of any matter relevant to the subject matter as long as the discovery appears reasonably calculated to lead to the discovery of admissible evidence. The new rule eliminates the language referring to the likelihood of leading to the discovery of admissible evidence, and instead requires that discovery be "proportional" to the needs of the case. When evaluating "proportionality," courts are now permitted to consider the amount in controversy, the importance of the issues at stake in the action, the parties' resources, the importance of the discovery in resolving the issues, and most notably, whether the burden or expense of the proposed discovery outweighs its likely benefit.

The costs of these changes will be largely absorbed by plaintiffs. The revised rule places a larger burden on the requesting party to demonstrate proportionality. In the past, the concept of "proportionality" was used in Rule 26(c). Previously, Rule 26(c) authorized a party to seek a protective order by arguing that the burden or expense of discovery outweighs its likely benefit. By moving the concept of proportionality into the definition of the scope of discovery under FRCP Rule 26(b), defendants have an additional weapon that they can use to limit every discovery request. Moreover, the enumerated factors that parties may use when evaluating whether discovery is proportional provides defendants specific grounds to avoid producing relevant information that plaintiffs may need to prove their cases.

At a minimum, the revised rule undoubtedly shifts the procedural burden to the requesting party to raise the issue with the court in the face of a proportionality objection by a responding party. This challenge is especially glaring in cases where the information is largely in the defendant's possession, such as civil rights, discrimination, employment, and product liability cases. In those situations, plaintiffs

---

[1] Though not the focus of this article, I want to note that the 1980, 1983, and 1993 amendments were in large part a response to private organizations and the defense bar calling for less discovery abuse. These amendments in part centered around disclosure rules and the level of involvement and oversight judges should maintain in the process.

have to argue that the likely benefit of the unknown information outweighs the quantifiable cost to the defendant. Defendants can simply object and argue that the information is too expensive or burdensome to produce even if the information is relevant and critical to plaintiffs' case. The changes will also likely increase the costs for plaintiffs who will have to file additional motions to compel and engage in discovery battles with opposing counsel over the right to gain access to documents. Given that many states adopt or incorporate the Federal Rules as their own, state and federal courts will maintain discovery procedures that are problematic and against the ideal of allowing individuals access to courts. In sum, although the Federal Rules affords litigants the opportunity to conduct discovery, the process here becomes harder and more problematic, especially for plaintiffs involved in complex litigation or where the defendant holds a disproportionate amount of information compared to the plaintiff.

4.1.3 The Motion for Summary Judgment Process is the Problem

Summary judgment was initially instituted into the Federal Rules as a method for promptly disposing of lawsuits in which there was no genuine issue of material fact and a party was entitled to a judgment as a matter of law. Passed in 1938, Federal Rule of Civil Procedure Rule 56 opened the door to prompt adjudication by allowing a party to defeat unfounded claims or defenses with little expense. Evaluating the state of summary proceedings around the country, Charles E. Clarke, one of the individuals involved in drafting the Federal Rules in 1938, framed the value of summary adjudicatory proceedings in the following way: "Except where trial is necessary to settle an issue of fact, the judicial process is, by this procedure, made to function more quickly and with less complexity than in the ordinary long drawn out suit" (Clarke and Samenow 1929, 423).

At the outset, when the rule was created, there were concerns over its wide scope, the vague standard for determining whether an issue of fact existed, and the significant level of discretion judges maintained to dismiss a lawsuit (Wood 2011). The potential problems posed by judicial discretion did not occur during the first forty years after Rule 56 was adopted. Federal judges approached summary judgment very cautiously and set a high bar for granting relief. Federal judges perceived summary judgments as threatening a denial of such fundamental guarantees as the right to confront witnesses and the right of a jury to make inferences and determinate credibility. In 1962, the Supreme Court discouraged summary judgments in antitrust cases by noting "[t]rial by affidavit is no substitute for trial by jury which so long has been the hallmark of 'even handed justice'" (*Poller* v. *CBS, Inc.* 368 U.S. 464, 473 (1962)).

The problem is that this procedural rule, through judicial decisions, has evolved in a way that makes it hard to accomplish the original goal of Rule 56. Significant resources go into preparing summary judgment motions, courts spend considerable time evaluating such motions before ruling, and appellate courts often deal with appeals from parties who insist that the trial court overlooked a critical disputed issue of material fact or misapplied the law. In particular, the summary judgment standard changed in 1986, when the Supreme Court added another procedural weapon to the arsenal of defendants. In a trilogy of cases addressing the standards for summary judgment, *Celotex Corp. v. Catrett*, *Anderson v. Liberty Lobby*, and *Matsushita Electrical Industrial Corp. v. Zenith Radio*, the Court expanded the applicability of summary judgment under Rule 56. Collectively, these cases eased the initial burden placed on the party moving for summary judgment and allowed the district court discretion in determining the existence of issues that required a trial. Prior to these three cases, the Supreme Court's decision in *Adickes v. S. H. Kress & Co.* (1969) put the responsibility on the moving party to "carry its burden of showing the absence of any genuine issue of fact." 398 U.S. 144, 153 (1969).

Celotex relieved the defendant moving for summary judgment of any significant burden of production to establish the absence of a material issue of fact, and placed the burden of production on the nonmoving party to come forward with evidence of facts in dispute. Thus, a defendant's initial burden of production could be satisfied even without submitted sworn testimony revealing the absence of a genuine issue of material fact. In *Anderson*, the Supreme Court held that to avoid summary judgment in a case presenting a "clear and convincing" standard of proof at trial, the nonmovant must show that the record would sustain a verdict in her favor over the heightened clear and convincing burden. In *Matsushita*, the Supreme Court upheld summary judgment despite unrebutted expert reports supporting the plaintiffs' claims because "the [expert's] claim was one that simply makes no economic sense" 475 U.S. at 574, 587 (1986). The Court noted that a party opposing summary judgment "must do more than simply show that there is some metaphysical doubt as to the material facts" 475 U.S. at 586. Thus, courts can at the summary judgment stage evaluate the merits of expert testimony as opposed to simply determining whether triable issues of material fact remain.

As a result of these three cases, summary judgment, which prior to the Federal Rules was largely a plaintiff's motion, has become largely a defendant's motion (Denlow 1998). The category of issues being decided by judges as a matter of law is now enlarged. Due process rights, such as having an opportunity to have your case heard in court and the constitutional right to a jury, are compromised as parties increasingly engage in summary judgment motions. Indeed, discovery is now guided by preparing for winning or defending against summary judgment, not trial. An American Bar Association survey in 2009 revealed that 50 percent of plaintiffs' lawyers, 47 percent of defense lawyers, and 44 percent of all other lawyers believe that discovery's primary utility is to develop evidence for summary judgment, not to prepare for trial (Hornby 2010).

These cases impact litigation strategy in significant ways. A plaintiff maximizes her position through the possibility of trial. A defendant maximizes her position by discouraging and avoiding trial. Summary judgment provides defendants with a major tactical advantage because it creates leverage over plaintiffs. Summary judgment creates an additional hurdle for a plaintiff because it forces her to engage in a paper mini-trial just to ensure that her case will continue. This allows the defendant a preview of the key elements of plaintiff's case. Even when summary judgment motions are unsuccessful, summary judgments are expensive to prepare, time-consuming, and can drain plaintiffs' will to continue to trial. Moreover, they often lead to delays in the case. Often a defendant will not engage in meaningful settlement discussions until a plaintiff survives summary judgment.

Summary judgment was established to try to expedite cases and reduce costs. However, the Supreme Court's decisions made litigating cases lengthier and costlier. Similar to Feeley's inquiry into lower criminal courts, the trilogy of summary judgment cases impacts the information balance between, and incentives operating on, both parties. In turn, these cases impact the range of decisions facing litigants, from the filing of lawsuits to the choice between settling and litigating a claim through to trial. Although a party has the right to pursue a case with the idea that jurors will evaluate her case, the summary judgment standard makes it more likely the case will be resolved by a judge. Once again, the process is not the punishment, but the problem.

4.1.4 The Class Action Process is the Problem

The class action rule as set forth in Rule 23 of the Federal Rule of Civil Procedure has often been thought of as a device to protect the liberties of ordinary citizens. Class actions represent the law's best effort at procedural democracy and access to justice for marginalized groups, whether they are consumers, employees, or small business owners that would otherwise be unable to have their claims and grievances adjudicated in court. Big businesses are often immunized from complying with the law because those with small claims and limited resources are unlikely to challenge them. Moreover, individually, litigation costs and attorneys' fees may exceed the value of the recovery. Even if individuals are able to seek redress for individual harms, they cannot successfully challenge widespread misconduct in the absence of collective action. Although individual cases may motivate employers to change their relevant policies and practices to avoid similar lawsuits, this comes nowhere near the remedies and scope of injunctive relief plaintiffs can craft in class or group-based actions. During the golden era of class actions in the 1960s and early 1970s, public interest lawyers used the class action rule to integrate school systems, deinstitutionalize mental health facilities, reform conditions of confinement for inmates in prison systems, challenge discriminatory public accommodation and housing laws, and deal with various kinds of employment discrimination. Thus, FRCP 23 was a procedural mechanism to enhance substantive justice.

This procedural weapon for plaintiffs has been largely curtailed by a series of legislative and judicial decisions. Wary of having to defend aggregate litigation claims, private organizations used the legislative process and court cases to narrow the likelihood that a class action will be certified. Courts increased standards relating to the certification of damages and injunctive classes, and created new standing requirements for consumer class actions. Congress also enacted a series of laws such as the Private Securities Litigation Reform Act and the Class Action Fairness Act that have essentially pushed litigants towards non-collective, non-adjudicatory remedies.

In particular, when George W. Bush signed into law the Class Action Fairness Act (CAFA) in 2005, he indicated that this law was a "critical step toward ending the lawsuit culture in our country" (White House signing ceremony, Feb. 18, 2005). CAFA is the product of significant institutional lobbying by businesses. Concerned with the perceived rate with which state courts grant class certification, CAFA seeks to curb perceived abuses of the class action device. In particular, CAFA expands federal diversity jurisdiction over interstate class actions and also expands removal powers.

CAFA is especially illustrative of how procedural changes impact one's ability to achieve substantive justice. Prior to the passage of CAFA, there were specific restrictions that applied if a defendant wanted to remove a case from state to federal court. First, a defendant could not remove a case if the defendant was a resident of the state in which the lawsuit was originally filed. Also, if there were multiple defendants, all the defendants had to consent to removal for the removal to be proper. Lastly, Congress issued an express, one-year time restriction on the removal of cases when the original jurisdiction was based on diversity as opposed to a federal question.

CAFA essentially removes all three of these requirements. In doing so, CAFA removes the traditional barriers to federal jurisdiction for many class action cases. The class action may be removed without regard to whether any defendant is a citizen of the state in which the action is brought. This essentially curtails the past practice of plaintiffs' attorneys who frequently would name a plaintiff or defendant in the action in order to avoid diversity jurisdiction. Also, the defendant may remove a case without the consent of other defendants. Finally, CAFA eliminates the one-year limitation on removal of claims based upon diversity jurisdiction. Once again, we see the procedure is the problem for litigants seeking access to courts and substantive relief. By expanding federal diversity jurisdiction and removal capabilities, CAFA makes it easier for defendants to remove cases from state court to federal court, where federal judges are less liberal in granting certification to multistate, state-law-based class action lawsuits.

Legislative curtailment of class action as a procedural weapon is coupled by Supreme Court decisions that disapprove massive class actions. The most significant recent decision is *Wal-Mart Stores, Inc. v. Dukes* (2011). In this case, former and current female employees brought a class action against Wal-Mart Stores, Inc. on behalf of approximately 1.5 million women, alleging nationwide gender discrimination in violation of Title VII of the Civil Rights Act of 1964. The plaintiffs argued that Wal-Mart gives its local managers undue discretion when making pay and promotion decisions, and that this results in women being underpaid and disproportionately denied promotions.

The Supreme Court concluded that the case failed to meet the requirement of a class action. In doing so, the Supreme Court in *Wal-Mart* made class certification much more difficult by raising the standard for satisfying the "commonality" requirement that the class has a common question that it seeks resolution toward. The Court indicated Wal-Mart plaintiffs were required to prove, with significant evidence, that there exists a general policy of discrimination in order to receive certification. Moreover, the class members must each suffer the "same injury" rather than the same Title VII violation.

Thus, class members must make common contentions whose resolution will decide critical issues affecting each one of the claims. The court elevated the evidentiary burden that plaintiffs face when trying to certify that there are common questions of fact. By requiring a higher level of commonality and raising the evidentiary burden at the outset than was previously thought necessary by class members, the Supreme Court made it very hard for litigants to reach the commonality requirement in the future.[2] It is important to note that nothing in the history of the rule, the language of FRCP Rule 23, or prior case law suggests that these limitations should exist. Shifting the burden of pretrial persuasion reflects a very subtle way that class certification may be denied before a decision on the merits.

The Supreme Court's decision in *Wal-Mart* impacts the procedures relating to class action lawsuits. Class certification is now another procedural hurdle for plaintiffs to gain entry into federal courts. The Court's decision in *Wal-Mart* reduces the prospect of class certification and the likelihood that a class action will be brought. Plaintiffs' attorneys will have to invest significant resources in discovery before moving for certification. Because fewer cases will be certified, plaintiffs will have less settlement leverage in these large cases. The broader impact of *Wal-Mart* as well as legislation such as CAFA is that they reduce defendants' potential exposure to class-wide liability. They also reduce the deterrent effect of class actions generally. Similar to pleading, discovery, and summary judgment, what was supposed to be a procedural tool to broaden a litigant's ability to seek access to justice is now an impediment.

4.1.5 Alternative Dispute Resolution Processes are the Problem

Given the problems with the civil justice system, many suggest using alternative dispute resolution processes such as mediation or arbitration to resolve disputes

---

[2] The commonality requirement could have been discriminatory bias as a result of a policy of excessive subjectivity as opposed to requiring a common contention of discriminatory bias on the part of the same supervisor.

that would otherwise go to court. Alternative dispute resolution advocates argue that such venues provide a more informal, faster, and flexible forum that gives the parties greater voice and involvement in the resolution of their case. Despite these worthy goals, arbitration has become a procedural tool for private organizations (Talesh 2013). Moreover, courts and legislators have allowed arbitration to gain legitimacy in society. Beginning as early as the 1940s, private organizations began inserting in their contracts arbitration provisions forcing or mandating disputes be arbitrated before the American Arbitration Association or the National Arbitration Forum rather than litigated in courts (Gilles 2012). Initially, courts were hesitant to enforce arbitration provisions. However, by the 1980s, the Supreme Court, relying largely on the Federal Arbitration Act, reinterpreted this law and other statutes to permit rather than forbid enforcement of arbitration contracts. In the 1980s and 1990s, the United States Supreme Court deferred and upheld arbitration clauses, often finding that the Federal Arbitration Act applies in state as well as federal court proceedings and preempts state legislation affecting arbitration. The Supreme Court consistently maintains the position that procedural protections in arbitration systems preserve all parties' ability to achieve substantive justice.

Most recently, businesses have begun inserting class action waivers into contractual arbitration provisions provided consumers. The Supreme Court in *AT&T Mobility* v. *Concepcion* (2011) upheld such provisions and essentially followed a long line of cases permitting arbitration of a variety of claims such as admiralty, age discrimination, and securities fraud. Thus, while plaintiffs in theory have the ability to use the procedural weapon of class actions to unite, form a class, and sue a defendant in court, the arbitration clause dismantles their ability to do so. More recently, in *American Express Co.* v. *Italian Colors Restaurant* (2013) the Supreme Court held that the Federal Arbitration Act does not permit courts to invalidate a contractual waiver of class arbitration on the ground that the plaintiff's cost of individually arbitrating a federal statutory claim exceeds the potential recovery. In 2018, the Supreme Court held in *Epic Systems Corp.* v. *Lewis* that employers can require employees to arbitrate disputes with the employer individually and waive their right to pursue or participate in class or collective actions against their employer. Coupled with the *Wal-Mart* decision, *AT&T, American Express,* and *Epic Systems Corp.* limit plaintiffs' ability to use class actions to seek relief. As a result, powerful businesses can impose no-class-action arbitration clauses on individuals who are trying to invoke their consumer rights but who have little to no bargaining power. Thus, despite the initial goals of improving a litigant's ability to achieve justice, arbitration forums are now being used as a tool to funnel cases from the public courthouse to the private courthouse where the economic "haves" are able to more directly control the process.

Scholars, policymakers, legislators, and advocates and opponents of arbitration argue over the pros and cons of arbitration and whether arbitration leads to increased victories by businesses. However, less empirical attention is paid to how arbitration systems are set up with the support of legislators and how these arbitration systems are implemented in action. That is, there is less interrogation of the Supreme Court's claim that "the streamlined procedures of arbitration do not entail any consequential restrictions on substantive rights" *Shearson/American Express, Inc. v. McMahon*, 482 U.S. 220, 232 (1987). Do arbitration processes impact substantive justice? If so, how?

My own empirical work explores how the institutional design of arbitration systems help facilitate and inhibit consumer inequality in alternative disputing forums (Talesh 2009, 2012, 2014, 2015). Institutional design and the procedures put in place for arbitration systems matter. Process is equally problematic in alternative disputing forums, especially arbitration settings. I have examined how arbitration processes were codified into law for consumers to use when resolving warranty disputes, especially warranties issued by automobile manufacturers. My work pays particular attention to how private organizations often shape the content and meaning of legislation and regulatory rules that are designed to regulate them.

Drawing on neo-institutional ideas of organizational fields and legal endogeneity, I show how institutionalized logics operating among organizations play an important role in determining the form and structure of legislation and administrative processes. Focusing on the evolution of California's consumer protection laws, I review how institutional and political forces come together to shape the dispute resolution process in the consumer protection context. Although political mobilization and contestation remain prevalent in the legislative process, the political frames used by organizations lobbying the legislature reflect logics that are derived from institutionalized norms and structures developed by and through the organizational field.

In 1970, California passed the first consumer warranty protection law in the United States, the Song-Beverly Act, in order to limit manufacturers' ability to perpetuate social and economic advantage through the manufacturer-consumer relationship. The Song-Beverly Act specified that if manufacturers were unable to make repairs under warranties after being given a "reasonable number of attempts," consumers could seek relief in court and obtain full restitution or replacement, attorneys' fees, and a civil penalty. Despite granting consumers powerful legal weapons, the Song-Beverly Act did not specify the meaning of a "reasonable number of attempts."

In the early 1980s, the California legislature attempted to curb any ambiguity in the warranty law by creating a "lemon law" that established a "legal presumption" as to what constitutes a "reasonable number of attempts" to fix a problem that consumers could specifically invoke against automobile manufacturers. During the legislative lawmaking process automobile manufacturers alerted the legislature that they (the manufacturers) had during the 1970s created dispute resolution structures to resolve automobile warranty disputes outside court. This institutional form of dispute resolution quickly spread, and by 1981 over 2,000 automotive dealers across the United States had jointly funded and controlled a third-party dispute resolution process to resolve warranty complaints. Manufacturers eventually used such third-party organizations to administer these programs in order to legitimize them.

As manufacturer advocacy coalitions lobbied the legislature concerning the terms of the lemon law, Ford, General Motors, and Chrysler framed the purpose and benefits of their dispute resolution processes in terms of legitimacy, efficiency, informality, and customer satisfaction, as opposed to consumer protection (Talesh 2009, 2014). Manufacturers collectively claimed that their institutional venues were primarily created to benefit consumers and to provide less costly, more effective ways of resolving disputes.

Without formally evaluating the merits of these procedures, the legislature subsequently incorporated these institutionalized organizational practices into legal doctrine by making consumer rights and remedies contingent on first using certified third-party manufacturer dispute resolution structures in compliance with cursory federal regulation. Specifically, the legal presumption as to what constitutes a "reasonable number of attempts" – the main purpose of the lemon law – could not be asserted in court unless the consumer first resorted to the existing "qualified third-party dispute resolution process" to the extent a manufacturer maintained one (Civil Code § 1793.22(c)). The lemon law provided that no civil penalties or attorneys' fees could be recovered in dispute resolution processes unless the manufacturer-run program permits such recovery. Further, unlike the all (restitution, replacement) or nothing (no award) remedies at trial, arbitrators are permitted to award consumers the opportunity to allow manufacturers another repair attempt. Decisions under dispute resolution processes were binding on manufacturers but not consumers. Moreover, in a display of deference to manufacturer venues, the lemon law indicated if the consumer chose to reject the arbitrator's ruling and sue, the arbitrator's findings could be admitted at trial without any need for evidentiary foundation.

Once organizational logic as to what constitutes a fair process became formally codified into law, legislative amendments had less to do with protecting consumer rights and more to do with giving legal legitimacy to institutional venues through cursory regulatory monitoring and oversight, and bolstering the degree to which consumers, manufacturers, legislators, and regulators defer to institutional venues designed and funded by manufacturers (Talesh 2009, 2014). In particular, changes to the regulatory structure and certification process aimed at strengthening the legitimacy of these forums ultimately allowed arbitrators from manufacturer-sponsored programs to retain flexibility and final authority regarding the legal standards, statutory or otherwise, they chose to ultimately apply in particular cases. Thus, as businesses "legalized" their domains with law-like structures, business logics – anchored in informality, efficiency, discretion, and problem solving – flowed back into core public legal institutions through the efforts of advocacy coalitions, who reframed the meaning of consumer protection for legislators and regulators.

Thus, my research offers an important intervention to those debating the benefits of using courts versus arbitration. Similar to courts, the rules – the procedures and processes parties use to seek relief in alternative forums – matter. Although consumers are afforded considerable rights in the lemon law context, the process – as set forth by automobile manufacturers and codified into law by legislators – is the problem. In response to powerful consumer protection laws aimed at manufacturers standing behind their warranties issued to consumers, my research shows how automobile manufacturers first created internal dispute resolution structures to adjudicate public legal rights outside the judicial process, and then ceded control of these structures to third-party dispute resolution organizations for legitimacy purposes (Talesh 2009, 2013). The legislature ultimately codified these privatized adjudicatory systems into law and afforded considerable deference to these quasi-private and quasi-public regimes. Thus, in the civil context, private organizations are impacting the meaning of process simultaneously among public and private institutions.

Through participant observation and interviews, I continued my analysis by comparing how two different alternative dispute resolution forums (one created and administered by private organizations in California, and the other administered and run by the state of Vermont) operating outside the court system resolve consumer disputes. In this respect, my work is similar to Feeley's exploration of lower criminal courts because I unpacked how law is constructed in these forums. Unlike the single-arbitrator system in private dispute resolution programs, Vermont uses an arbitration board consisting of a five-person panel of arbitrators (three citizens, an automotive dealer representative, and a technical expert).

I find that the institutional design of dispute resolution, and how business and consumer values and perspectives are translated by field actors in different dispute resolution systems, leads to two different meanings of law operating in California and Vermont. The former is influenced by business values while the latter balances business and consumer values. The implementation of different dispute resolution processes has a very real impact. As business values flow through California dispute resolution structures, organizational repeat players gain subtle opportunities for advantages.

Moreover, in terms of consumer outcomes in these hearings, consumers do far worse in private than in state-run disputing structures (Talesh 2012).

In California, managerial and business values of efficiency, managerial discretion and control, productivity, and customer retention flow into the rules, procedures, and meaning of law operating in dispute resolution structures mainly through the training and socialization process for California arbitrators. Third-party administrators hired by automobile manufacturers to run their dispute resolution programs teach a set of rationales and scripts that emphasize eliminating consumer emotion and individual voice from the process and narrowing the fact-finding role of arbitrators. Arbitrator training programs reshape the meaning of law by building discretion and flexibility into legal procedure and remedies, while recontextualizing legal rules and arbitrator decision making around a set of business values. As a result, arbitrators are taught to deploy an altered version of the lemon law that mirrors formal law, but is filtered through business values and influence. Moreover, organizational repeat players gain subtle advantages through the operation of the dispute resolution structure (Talesh 2012).

In contrast to California's managerial justice adjudicatory model, Vermont uses a collaborative justice model that balances various interested stakeholders, reflecting both business *and* consumer values in a state-funded and designed dispute resolution structure. As a result, Vermont's structure is far less likely to emphasize business values at the expense of consumer interests and prevents many repeat player advantages enjoyed by manufacturers in California.

To the extent business values are introduced into the process by the presence of an automotive dealer and technical expert board members, they are balanced with competing consumer logics by the presence of three citizen arbitrators on Vermont arbitration board (the Lemon Law Board) and a program administrator who oversees the program. In particular, citizen arbitrators balance the fact-finding and deliberation process with a consumer perspective that often allows emotion and individual voice to enter the process. Furthermore, the technical expert on the Lemon Law Board counterbalances manufacturers' repeat player advantages, e.g., greater knowledge, experience, and ability to offer expert testimony or reports.

Professional training is a key mechanism for the diffusion of organizational constructions of law in manufacturer-sponsored training programs. The dispute resolution programs in California and Vermont train and socialize their arbitrators in different ways. In California, arbitrators are taught to disregard any prior knowledge of legal processes and strictly follow what they are taught in the training processes. Trainers emphasize discretion and flexibility with respect to applying formal law in these processes. This philosophical orientation is a key mechanism for explaining how organizations shape the meaning of law.

Conversely, Vermont's panel of arbitrators receives minimal formal training and socialization. The little training they do receive largely focuses on assuring that they apply formal law. Vermont arbitrators believe the effectiveness of the Lemon Law Board is contingent on the right mixture of people offering different consumer and business perspectives while still operating within the strictures of formal law. The legitimacy of California's dispute resolution training programs administered by the third-party administrators is based on the idea that professional training and socialization produces impartial and neutral decision makers. In Vermont, these same core legal principles rest on interest representation and balancing consumer and business logics in the structure. Thus, the different adjudicative orientations in

California and Vermont facilitate and inhibit the conditions under which and the degree to which business values are more or less likely to flow into law.

Similar to Feeley's account of lower criminal courts in New Haven, manufacturer-sponsored and state-run dispute resolution programs in California and Vermont both devote attention to preserving due process during their training. However, in the manufacturer-sponsored hearings, other non-legal values like efficiency, rationality, and discretion alter how policies and procedures should be implemented.

For example, the amount of independent expert information offered into evidence concerning automobile defects is guided by a series of business values. California training programs teach arbitrators that they may appoint a technical expert to examine a vehicle and issue an expert report if necessary. However, by focusing on efficiency, time delay, and resource conservation, trainers dissuade arbitrators from using technical experts (Talesh 2012).

By framing technical experts as potentially unnecessary or an inefficient use of time, California training programs exclude neutral technical experts who may have the requisite experience and mechanical equipment to identify vehicle problems, while leaving evaluation to the lay knowledge of arbitrators who usually have only manufacturer testimony to rely on. In fact, manufacturers that I interviewed indicate that they often bring mechanical experts to hearings.

Under these circumstances, arbitrators are especially captive to manufacturers' technical evaluations and testimony because they are trained to avoid appointing independent experts. In this way, the dispute resolution structure subtly gives repeat players control over the degree and scope of technical information admitted into the hearing. Moreover, California state regulators repeatedly lamented in interviews how efficiency concerns guide the way facts are offered into evidence and hinder the overall fairness of the third-party administrators' dispute resolution programs. In Vermont, arbitrators indicate having a technical expert on the Lemon Law Board prevents parties from misleading the Board regarding technical defects or problems with vehicles, combats information asymmetry between manufacturers and consumers, and leads to better evaluation of the technical issues involved in the case.

The dispute resolution design also impacts how cases are resolved in these two disputing processes. For example, while both Vermont and California dispute resolution programs emphasize impartiality and neutrality, they construe the meaning of these terms differently. The divergent fact-finding approaches arbitrators deploy in both states illustrate the way impartiality and neutrality mean different things. In California, impartiality and neutrality are considered compromised when arbitrators actively investigate facts. California arbitrators are instructed to rely solely on parties' production of relevant factual evidence. In Vermont, actively investigating facts is considered a necessary component for establishing impartiality and neutrality. Vermont arbitrators indicate it is their responsibility to actively gather information and facts regardless of whether the parties offer information on their own. According to Vermont arbitrators, active investigation assures a procedurally fair and neutral process (Talesh 2012).

This distinction is important because passive arbitrators in California provide structural advantages for repeat players whereas the inquisitorial role of arbitrators in Vermont offsets repeat player advantages. Active investigation by Vermont arbitrators also counterbalances any experiential and informational advantage manufacturers maintain, such as manufacturers' unilateral access to repair history records and ability to bring experts or expert reports into evidence. Actively investigating facts in Vermont also includes preventing intimidation from repeat players against one-shotters during questioning. Thus, according to the arbitrators and training programs in California and Vermont, active fact-finding preserves arbitrator impartiality and neutrality in Vermont whereas active investigation compromises the process in California.

My empirical research highlights other differences and how dispute resolution system design matters (Talesh 2012, 2013, 2014, 2015). However, overall, my data suggests that the design of Vermont's arbitration process has less tendency to emphasize business interests at the expense of consumer interests, and prevents some of the repeat player advantages enjoyed by manufacturers in California. In terms of consumer outcomes, consumers win twice as often in state-run dispute resolution structures as in private-run structures (Talesh 2012).

Similar to lower criminal courts (Feeley 1979), the design of the dispute resolution process may facilitate or inhibit whether a consumer ultimately prevails. Arbitration does not always work well and does not always work poorly. Consumers do not always win or lose.

Rather, the process really matters, and in the lemon law context, the arbitration process in California is problematic, while the Vermont process seems to curb some of the repeat player advantages enjoyed by manufacturers in California. Through the legislative process and subsequent control of the arbitration system through organizational surrogates such as third-party administrators, private organizations have been able to redefine and control consumer rights in California.

In a world where private actors are increasingly involved in handling functions traditionally run by the government, organizational repeat players no longer simply play for favorable rules in the public arena, but rather play for removing the entire disputing game from the public arena into the private arena, actively create the terms of legal compliance, and reshape the meaning of consumer rights and remedies. This is a critical way in which the "haves" come out ahead. However, contrary to most studies that demonstrate how repeat players gain advantages in disputing structures, my comparative research design also allows me to explore how dispute resolution structures can also inhibit repeat player advantages. Simply stated, I reach a similar conclusion to Feeley's conclusion in *The Process is the Punishment*: process matters.

In this instance, the institutional design can facilitate and inhibit repeat player advantages.

4.2 CONCLUSION

In the tradition of Feeley's approach in *The Process Is the Punishment*, this article exposes the tension between the ideal of "due process," which seeks to allow individuals an opportunity to be heard at a meaningful time and in a meaningful manner, with the reality of how civil processes and procedures impact a litigant navigating through the civil justice system.

When the Federal Rules were established in 1938, they embodied a desire for creating a system that would allow parties to seek justice in a public forum. The drafters of the Federal Rules believed in citizen access to the courts and in the resolution of disputes on their merits. The rules for the most part were comprehensible, plainly worded, and nontechnical. As Federal Rule 1 notes, the goal was "just, speedy, and inexpensive determination of every action and proceeding." Court cases initially protected an individual's due process rights, especially the opportunity to be heard at a meaningful time and in a meaningful manner. The broad "notice" pleading was followed by liberal discovery rules that enabled parties to seek information relevant to the subject matter of the lawsuit and have equal access. Litigation was resolved based on the facts. A summary judgment procedure was available only for situations where there was truly no genuine dispute as to material fact. The ideal model of federal civil dispute resolution was a trial, often by a jury. Procedures were established to preserve this ideal. Coupled with these procedural protections was the establishment of powerful civil and consumer rights that provide substantive protections and private causes of action.

Even though the process was supposed to preserve due process and procedural protections so that individuals can seek access to justice, this article demonstrates that the process is now an impediment or problem. Advocating an agenda that seeks to curtail individuals' access to courts or simply move the case to private arbitration, private organizations succeed in the legislative process and use the court system to recreate a system in their favor.

The Supreme Court plays a critical role. *Twombly* and *Iqbal* heightened pleading requirements for plaintiffs and emboldened defendants to bring more motions to dismiss. Discovery rules continue to narrow the permissible scope of inquiry and encourage defendants to raise objections and entrench litigation in discovery battles. Summary judgment is now a weapon for defendants to end cases prior to trial under a standard that increasingly puts pressure on plaintiffs. Supreme Court decisions concerning class actions and legislation such as CAFA make it harder for plaintiffs to constitute class action lawsuits. Moreover, the Federal Arbitration Act, mandatory arbitration clauses, and a series of Supreme Court decisions concerning arbitration often redirect litigants to private dispute resolution venues where large bureaucratic organizations are more likely to come out ahead. Thus, when people invoke their civil or consumer rights, they bear the costs of dealing with a procedural system tilted in the direction of businesses.

Thus, I am left reaching a similar conclusion to the one that Malcolm Feeley found in *The Process Is the Punishment*: procedure affects substance. The procedural costs of invoking your rights in civil courts end up being greater than the rights themselves. The cost of invoking your rights in the civil context is that a litigant will likely adjudicate her case in a private forum via arbitration. If a litigant is permitted to sue in court, she faces a system flooded with procedural hurdles. As the federal rules recognized during its creation, American law has always been motivated by the ideals of rule of law, access to justice, a level litigation playing field, and equal justice under law. It sought to preserve these goals through procedural rights and due process protections under the Constitution. However, similar to Feeley's conclusion in the criminal context, these rules have been altered in civil litigation in ways that make achieving substantive justice very difficult. Moreover, similar to Feeley's conclusion in the criminal context, the civil litigation system is so complex, cumbersome, and expensive that these procedural protections serve limited functions at best. As long as the process is the problem, the adjudicative ideal will continue to conflict with the substantive goals civil and consumer rights enforcement.

REFERENCES

Beisner, John H. 2010. US Chamber Inst. for Legal Reform. "The Centre Cannot Hold: The Need for Effective Reform of the U.S. Civil Discovery Process," at 7, available at www.instituteforlegalreform.com/sites/default/files/ilr_discovery_2010_0.pdf.

Bell, Griffen D., Chilton Davis Varner, and Hugh Q. Gottschalk. 1992. "Automatic Disclosure in Discovery – The Rush to Reform." *Georgia Law Review* 27: 1–58.

Blaner, Kathleen L., Alfred W. Cortese, and Donald H. Green. 1998. "Federal Discovery: Crown Jewel or Curse?" *Litigation* 24(4): 8–65.

Boyd, L. Christina, David A. Hoffman, Zoran Obradovic, and Kosta Ristovski. 2013. "Building a Taxonomy of Litigation: Clusters of Causes of Action in Federal Complaints." *Journal of Empirical Legal Studies* 10: 253–87.

Clark, Charles E. and Charles U. Samenow. 1929. "The Summary Judgment." *Yale Law Journal* 38: 423–71.

Denlow, Morton. 1998. "Summary Judgment: Boon or Burden?" *The Judges' Journal* 37: 26–31.

Feeley, Malcolm. 1979. *The Process is the Punishment: Handling Cases in a Lower Criminal Court*. New York: Russell Sage Foundation.

Gelbach, Jonah. 2012. "Note: Locking the Doors to Discovery?: Assessing the Effects of Twombly and Iqbal on Access to Discovery." *Yale Law Journal* 121: 2270–345.

Gilles, Myriam. 2012. "Procedure in Eclipse: Group-Based Adjudication in a Post-Concepcion Era." *St. Louis Law Journal* 56: 1203–29.

Hazelton, L. W. Morgon. 2015. "Quit Your Complaining? Considering the Impact of Supreme Court Decisions on Strategic Litigants." Unpublished working paper.

Hornby, D. Brock. 2010. "Summary Judgment Without Illusions." *Green Bag 2d* 13: 273–88.

Hubbard, H. J. William. 2017. "The Effects of Twombly and Iqbal." *Journal of Empirical Legal Studies* 14: 474–526.

Moore, Patricia Hatamyar. 2012. "An Updated Quantitative Study of Iqbal's Impact on 12(b)(6) Motions." *University of Richmond Law Review* 46: 603–58.

Moore, Patricia Hatamyar. 2010. "The Tao of Pleading: Do Twombly and Iqbal Matter Empirically." *American University Law Review* 59: 553–634.

Talesh, Shauhin. 2009. "The Privatization of Public Legal Rights: How Manufacturers Construct the Meaning of Consumer Law." *Law & Society Review* 43: 527–62.

Talesh, Shauhin. 2012. "How Dispute Resolution System Design Matters: An Organizational Analysis of Dispute Resolution Structures and Consumer Lemon Laws." *Law & Society Review* 46: 463–96.

Talesh, Shauhin. 2013. "How the 'Haves' Come Out Ahead in the Twenty-First Century." *DePaul Law Review* 62: 519–54.

Talesh, Shauhin. 2014. "Institutional and Political Sources of Legislative Change: Explaining How Private Organizations Influence the Form and Content of Consumer Protection Legislation." *Law & Social Inquiry* 39: 973–1005.

Talesh, Shauhin. 2015. "Rule-Intermediaries in Action: How State and Business Stakeholders Influence the Meaning of Consumer Rights in Regulatory Governance Arrangements." *Law & Policy* 37: 1–31.

Wood, Diane P. 2011. "Summary Judgment and the Law of Unintended Consequences." *Oklahoma City University Law Review* 36: 231–52.

White House signing ceremony, Feb. 18, 2005; transcript and official press release available at www.whitehouse.gov/briefings-statements/.

CASES

Adickes *v.* S.H. Kress & Co., 398 U.S. 144 (1969).
Anderson *v.* Liberty Lobby, 477 U.S. 242 (1986).
Ashcroft *v.* Iqbal, 556 U.S. 662 (2009).
AT&T Mobility *v.* Concepcion, 563 U.S. 333 (2011)
Bell Atlantic Corp. *v.* Twombly, 550 U.S. 544 (2007).
Celotex Corp. *v.* Catrett, 477 U.S. 317 (1986).
Conley *v.* Gibson, 355 U.S. 41 (1957).
Epic Systems Corp. *v.* Lewis, 138 S. Ct. 1612 (2018).
Matsushita Electrical Industrial Corp. *v.* Zenith Radio, 475 U.S. 574 (1986).
Poller *v.* CBS, Inc., 368 U.S. 464 (1962).
Shearson/American Express, Inc. *v.* McMahon, 482 U.S. 220, 232 (1987).
Wal-Mart Stores, Inc. *v.* Dukes, 564 U.S. 338 (2011).
American Express Co. *v.* Italian Colors Restaurant, 570 U.S. 228 (2013).

RULES

Fed. R. Civ. Pro. Rule 1
Fed. R. Civ. Pro. Rule 8
Fed. R. Civ. Pro. Rule 23
Fed. R. Civ. Pro. Rule 26
Fed R. Civ. Pro. Rule 26(b)(1) 398 U.S. 977, 982 (1970) (amended 2000)

STATUTES

Civil Code § 1793.22(c)

PART II

Court Reform on Trial

5

Regulating E-Cigarettes: Why Policies Diverge[1]

Eric A. Feldman

INTRODUCTION

From their origins in the laboratory of a Chinese pharmacist in 2003 to their place in the portfolios of the world's largest tobacco companies, electronic cigarettes have emerged as one of the most popular and controversial products of the twenty-first century. Some current smokers see e-cigarettes as offering an opportunity to reduce their dependence on conventional combustible tobacco products and instead make use of a potentially less dangerous substitute. Others, particularly young nonsmokers, embrace e-cigarettes because they offer a taste of the unknown, a chance to assert independence by using a new product that they see as edgy and experimental. Public health professionals are divided about the health consequences of e-cigarettes, with some arguing that they will perpetuate or even exacerbate the public health harms caused by conventional cigarettes and others claiming that they will reduce tobacco-related morbidity and mortality. For many, e-cigarettes represent an attractive business opportunity; from single-proprietor vaping shops in suburban malls to multinational companies with global tobacco holdings, e-cigarettes have taken root as an important new consumer product.

Faced with such diverse perspectives, what are regulators doing to control the manufacture, sale, and use of e-cigarettes? The answer, perhaps surprising in this age of supposed globalization, depends in large part upon where those regulators are located. Public Health England (PHE), for example, has embraced the e-cigarette, recently stating that "vaping is at least 95% less harmful than smoking" and highlighting "the large difference in relative risk" between smoking and vaping "so that more smokers are encouraged to make the switch" (McNeill et al. 2018). PHE's enthusiasm for e-cigarettes is reflected in the widespread use of e-cigarettes in England, where 6 percent of the adult population are vapers, almost all of whom are smokers or ex-smokers (McNeill et al. 2018, 14). In contrast, regulators in twenty-

---

[1] I am grateful for the exemplary research assistance of Brian Ruocco and abundant bibliographical help from Timothy Von Dulm. Support for this paper was generously provided by a University of Pennsylvania Law School Summer Research Grant.

five countries as diverse as the UAE, Brazil, Panama, and Singapore have banned the sale and/or use of e-cigarettes. Where e-cigarettes are not banned, they are regulated in widely different ways, ranging from the stringent imposition of pharmaceutical regulations to lax consumer product controls (Kennedy et al. 2017).

Although the texture of e-cigarette regulations is highly variable, it would be an exaggeration to suggest that the forces of globalization are entirely absent. The most significant example of transnational e-cigarette regulation is found in the European Community, where the European Parliament approved a revision of the Tobacco Products Directive (TPD) in 2014 (Directive 2014/40/EU). The revised TPD, which came into force in May 2016, applies many preexisting tobacco control policies to e-cigarettes, such as banning advertising, requiring childproof packaging, and including packet health warnings. In addition, it includes regulations specific to e-cigarettes, such as setting the maximum size of e-cigarette refill containers (10 ml), the maximum concentration of nicotine in e-liquid (20 mg/ml), the maximum size of liquid tanks (2 ml), and requirements that e-cigarettes use liquids "that do not pose a risk to human health in heated or unheated form," that "electronic cigarettes deliver the nicotine doses at consistent levels," and that the packaging include a detailed list of ingredients.

Even within the European Union, however, policy differences remain, and beyond the EU the regulation of e-cigarettes varies dramatically across borders. What explains the divergence of e-cigarette policies globally? Why haven't we seen the opposite – general convergence of laws and regulations governing the sale and use of e-cigarettes?

This paper explores the landscape of e-cigarette policy globally by looking at three jurisdictions that have taken starkly different approaches to regulating e-cigarettes – the United States, Japan, and China. Each of those countries has a robust tobacco industry, government agencies entrusted with protecting public health, an active and sophisticated scientific and medical community, and a regulatory structure for managing new pharmaceutical, tobacco, and consumer products. All three are signatories of the World Health Organization's (WHO) Framework Convention on Tobacco Control (United Nations 2003),[2] all are signatories of the Agreement on Trade-Related Aspects of Intellectual Property Rights,[3] and all are members of the World Trade Organization. Which legal, economic, social and political differences between the three countries explain their diverse approaches to regulating e-cigarettes? Why have they embraced such dramatically different postures toward e-cigarettes?

Although Malcolm Feeley has not (yet!) studied e-cigarettes, this paper builds on his legacy in several ways. First, a great deal of Feeley's work is explicitly or implicitly comparative. He is always thinking about the full spectrum of possible answers to the

---

[2] In addition, both China and Japan have ratified the FCTC, but not the US.
[3] TRIPS Agreement, World Intellectual Property Organization (1995).

questions he poses; considering cross-border similarities and differences between legal institutions; questioning assumptions about how politics, economics, law, and society interact; and probing to see how different institutional configurations might lead to different legal outcomes. E-cigarette regulation invites exactly that type of analysis. What differentiates policy approaches to e-cigarettes has little to do with science or with the nature of e-cigarette devices. Instead, the differences are institutional, political, economic, sociological, and legal. In that way, e-cigarette regulation provides a window through which to examine the foundation, and the operation, of different legal systems – Feeley's stock in trade.

This paper also owes a debt to Feeley's work on complex policy choices, in which he undertakes an almost surgical dismantling of policy options. He would surely relish the opportunity to put the full set of e-cigarette regulatory options on the operating table and use his analytical scalpel to demonstrate their costs and benefits. Third, Malcolm Feeley is a brilliant theorist, but I have always been even more impressed by his commitment to the law in action, and particularly by his focus on the impact of legal rules and practices on those who are less fortunate. E-cigarettes invite exactly that set of concerns; at root, the issues raised by e-cigarettes implicate basic questions of values and social justice, and the degree to which e-cigarettes might exacerbate or alleviate the disproportionate harm combustible tobacco imposes on those with less education and income.

5.1 E-CIGARETTE POLICY: CONVERGENCE AND DIVERGENCE

Over the past several decades the idea of policy convergence has garnered increasing attention among legal scholars, political scientists, scholars of international relations, and others who have identified specific regulated activities in which policies converge and theorized the how(s) and why(s) of convergence (Linos 2013; Simmons, Dobbin, and Garrett 2006).[4] This paper takes a different approach. It highlights a concrete policy question – whether and how to regulate electronic cigarettes – and asks why the regulatory paths followed in three countries have led one to treat e-cigarettes as tobacco products (the United States), another as pharmaceutical products (Japan), and a third as ordinary consumer products (China). Scientific and epidemiological data about e-cigarettes travels easily across borders; public health officials in those countries have multiple points of connection; political leaders have a shared interest in limiting unnecessary health risks and avoiding unnecessary expenditures; for those and other reasons, convergence rather

[4] See generally Linos, Katerina. 2013. *The Democratic Foundations of Policy Diffusion: How Health, Family and Employment Laws Spread Across Countries* (arguing that policy convergence occurs because of the backing of a technocratic elite and because of the support of ordinary voters); Simmons, Beth A. et al. 2006. "Introduction: The International Diffusion of Liberalism." *International Organization* 60: 781 (positing that the worldwide spread of political and economic liberalism is produced interdependently – i.e., that governments adopt new policies not in isolation, but in response to coercion, cross-border learning, and emulation).

than divergence would appear to be the most likely policy outcome. Why, then, have the United States, Japan, and China – each of which is home to one of the world's most successful tobacco companies, has a large segment of the population that suffers from tobacco-related diseases, and spends billions of dollars caring for people whose deaths are preventable – followed such different paths?

There is, of course, a short and simple answer. Policies in the United States, Japan, and China frequently diverge, be it trade policy, tax policy, health care policy, and more (KPMG 2015).[5] The three nations are differently situated economically, diplomatically, politically, and culturally, and those differences generate different policy preferences. Indeed, one might argue that policy convergence in the area of e-cigarettes, not policy divergence, would be the greater surprise. But to do so would ignore the burgeoning literature on globalization and policy convergence, which makes a compelling argument for why there should be at least some degree of e-cigarette policy convergence in the Unite States, Japan, and China (Linos 2013; Simmons, Dobbin, and Garrett 2006; Fullerton and Alvarez 2012; Scherer 1997).[6]

Recent scholarship on cross-border cooperation and global networks in the area of finance, for example, like Terry Halliday and Greg Shaffer's *Transnational Legal Orders*, highlights the growth of powerful transnational financial institutions. Halliday and Shaffer argue that the influence of cross-border financial institutions has muted the differences between national regulatory approaches and increased the degree to which they overlap. Countries across the globe, in their view, when confronted by similar policy questions, deploy common regulatory strategies and construct similar regulatory institutions (Halliday and Shaffer 2016).

Anne-Marie Slaughter's *A New World Order* offers a related set of arguments about the increasing amount of policy commonality among the world's nations. She

---

[5] Japan, China, and the United States have very different tax structures. See, e.g., KPMG. 2015. "Global Tax Trade Survey." www.kpmg.com/CN/en/IssuesAndInsights/ArticlesPublications/Documents/global-tax-rate-surevy-2015-O-201510.pdf (recording, for instance that social security taxes on employers is 35% in China, 14.7% in Japan, and 7.65% in the United States, and the corporate tax rates are 25% in China, 33.06% in Japan, and 40% in the United States). These countries have had divergent experiences with healthcare policy. See The Economist. 2015. "The Shifting Landscape of Healthcare in Asia-Pacific: A Look at Australia, China, India, Japan, and South Korea." www.eiuperspectives.economist.com/sites/default/files/The%20shifting%20landscape%20of%20healthcare%20in%20Asia-Pacific_Oct%205_0.pdf; Ikegami, Naoki and Gerard F. Anderson. "In Japan, All-Payer Rate Setting Under Tight Government Control Has Proved to Be An Effective Approach to Containing Costs." *Health Affairs*. 31: 1049 (comparing the healthcare paying systems for Japan and the United States). The trading policies and outcomes for these countries differ as well. See "Trade Profiles," World Trade Organization, http://stat.wto.org/CountryProfile/WSDBCountryPFReporter.aspx?Language=E (select China, Japan, and United States, then select "continue").

[6] See generally Linos, Katerina. 2013. *The Democratic Foundations of Policy Diffusion: How Health, Family and Employment Laws Spread Across Countries*; Simmons, Beth A. et al. 2006. "Introduction: The International Diffusion of Liberalism" *International Organization* 60: 781; see, e.g., Fullerton, Larry and Megan Alvarez. 2012. "Convergence in International Merger Control," *Antitrust* 26: 20 (discussing policy convergence regarding merger control regulations); Scherer, F. M. 1996. "Competition Policy Convergence: Where Next?" *International Business Law* 24: 485 (describing the convergence in national competition policies as a result of the intensification of globalized trade).

highlights the importance of global networks – judges, legislators, the police, bankers, ministers, trade officials, and others – and argues that they have become critically important actors in the shaping of both national and global policy.[7] Hers is a vision of governance that has its locus not in unitary state action, but in the simultaneous interaction of multiple networks, which negotiate and influence each other as they address common problems (Slaughter 2005, 5). Viewed through this lens, one should expect e-cigarette policy to be shaped not by isolated nation-states, but through the cross-border interaction of public health experts, tobacco and pharmaceutical company executives, government officials specializing in finance, health, and drugs, legislators, and more. Such interaction would presumably lead to a set of policy outcomes that share at least some key features, not outcomes that are fundamentally at odds.

One network of actors with a strong interest in e-cigarette regulation is made up of scientists, epidemiologists, and other public health experts and policymakers whose work involves the collection and interpretation of data about the health impact of e-cigarettes. The network is relatively small and tightly knit; many members train at the same schools, attend the same conferences, read and publish in the same journals, and are invited to the same international meetings at the WHO and elsewhere. Network members also share a common goal, reflective of the public health field more generally – to limit preventable illness and death. Given those circumstances, one might expect similar, if not identical, epidemiological findings and policy prescriptions for managing e-cigarettes to emerge from such a group.

Despite the various reasons for expecting some degree of e-cigarette policy convergence, it is difficult, at least so far, to find any evidence of such convergence. Instead, e-cigarette regulations in the United States, Japan, and China have taken dramatically different forms. Three factors help to explain why.

First, some degree of scientific consensus, which is often a necessary (though rarely a sufficient) condition for policy convergence, is missing. Although scientists around the world are studying the health consequences of e-cigarettes on users and bystanders, even basic scientific and epidemiological agreement is lacking. To what extent do e-cigarettes imperil the health of those who use them? How risky is the secondhand vapor of e-cigarettes to children and other bystanders? Does the use of e-cigarettes among youth make it more likely that they will become smokers of combustible tobacco? As will be discussed in more detail below, the honest response to all of these questions is "we don't know." Consequently, policy makers are relatively unconstrained by the data; they can advocate a wide variety of policy approaches, all of which are defensible in light of current scientific uncertainty.

Second, economic and political interests are rarely divorced from policy outcomes, and in the area of e-cigarettes those interests are particularly pronounced. In

---

[7] One might see Slaughter's approach as a similar but somewhat thicker web of actors as that described by Feeley et al. in Halliday, Terence C., Lucien Karpik, and Malcolm M. Feeley eds. 2007. *Fighting for Political Freedom: Comparative Studies of the Legal Complex and Political Liberalism.*

the United States, for example, the growth, manufacture, and sale of tobacco products has been left to the corporate sector, which evaded substantial regulation by the federal government until 2009. In contrast, the Japanese government created a monopoly in the early twentieth century that controlled all aspects of the tobacco business. The monopoly was turned into a publicly traded company, Japan Tobacco, Inc., in 1985, but even today the Ministry of Finance continues to hold one-third of its stock. The Chinese central government also has a tobacco monopoly (the China National Tobacco Corporation, or CNTC), but unlike Japan there has not been a move toward privatization. It is the world's largest manufacturer of cigarettes in a country that consumes approximately 30 percent of the world's tobacco products, and is a critical source of revenue for the central government. In each of the three countries, the distinctive institutional configuration and financial interests of the tobacco sector have powerfully influenced e-cigarette policy, and help to explain their divergent approaches.

Third, although the role and prominence of courts as policymaking bodies clearly differs across borders, courts are not often highlighted as an explanation for policy divergence. When it comes to e-cigarettes, however, litigation and judicial decisions have been active components of policymaking in the United States, whereas in both Japan and China the courts have been silent. Indeed, were it not for litigation over e-cigarette regulation in the United States, the government's approach to e-cigarettes would look much more like Japan's. This is not to suggest that courts in the United States are engaged in inappropriate judicial activism, but simply to point out that interested parties there quickly turned to the courts to adjudicate different perspectives on how e-cigarettes should be regulated, and the courts obliged by issuing judgments that have fundamentally shaped government regulation. Each of these three factors will be discussed in greater detail below.

5.2 E-CIGARETTES: TECHNOLOGY, USE, AND IMPACT ON HEALTH

5.2.1 *What is an Electronic Cigarette?*

Before regulating any product, regulators must describe and define what it is they are regulating. For e-cigarettes, that turns out to be extremely difficult (Lempert, Grana, and Glantz 2014).[8] The first e-cigarettes to reach the market, and the ones that are most visually similar to combustible cigarettes, are known as cig-a-likes because they have the shape, look, and feel of a conventional cigarette. Manufacturers quickly realized that cig-a-likes had an important downside – by mimicking the aesthetic of

---

[8] Although there is a generic term for e-cigarettes – electronic nicotine delivery systems (ENDS) – it covers a wide variety of products. For simplicity, this paper uses the term e-cigarette to refer to the complete range of available devices. See Lempert, Lauren K. 2014. "The Importance of Product Definitions in US E-Cigarette Laws and Regulations." *BMJ: Tobacco Control* http://tobaccocontrol.bmj.com/content/early/2014/12/14/tobaccocontrol-2014-051913.full.pdf.

cigarettes, consumers sensibly associated them with cigarettes. For many consumers that was a negative association, given the well-known health risks of smoking and the pejorative moral undertones of doing so. Indeed, many e-cigarette users are keen to distinguish themselves from smokers and disassociate their devices from conventional cigarettes.[9]

As a result, a plethora of other products now use a similar technology to cig-a-likes but take a different form. Those products, collectively known as vaporizers and sometimes called vaping pens, e-hookahs, and more, can take a variety of forms (Mistic E Cigs 2015).[10] Some are rectangular, others look like skulls, a particularly popular device (Juul) is shaped like a USB drive, and a few appear to have come out of Apple's creative department, with slick and appealing contours and colors. The market for vaporizers has expanded rapidly and the devices have changed apace, with some of the newest products featuring options like adjustable wattage, which allows consumers to change the amount of vapor inhaled from each puff.

Despite their aesthetic differences, all e-cigarettes are based on a common technology. They include a rechargeable battery, a liquid (or in a few cases a chamber that can be filled with leaf) that generally contains nicotine, an atomizer that converts liquid into vapor, an LED light to simulate a burning cigarette, and a computer chip that senses inhalation and triggers the atomizer. Some e-cigarettes come prepackaged with a liquid-filled container and are discarded when all of the liquid is vaporized. Others operate on the same principle as Nescafe coffee machines, i.e., a reusable device that is recharged with disposable pods. Still others contain liquid chambers that can be refilled by consumers with whatever e-liquid they prefer, or vaporize leaf tobacco rather than liquid.

One factor that makes it difficult to regulate e-cigarettes, therefore, is the rapidity with which the technology has, and continues to, evolve. The question "What is an e-cigarette?" does not have a simple or clear answer, and without a crisp definition of an e-cigarette regulators have struggled to develop a regulatory strategy. Japanese officials in the Ministry of Health, Labor, and Welfare, for example, have stated that they are not able to specify the meaning of "e-cigarette," and as a result they worry about the coherence of e-cigarette regulation (MHLW officials, personal communication with author, December 2014).

5.2.2 How Popular Are E-Cigarettes?

While the US e-cigarette market is still modest in comparison to the $94 billion in annual sales of combustible cigarettes, some analysts, like Bonnie Herzog at Wells Fargo, have predicted that over the next two decades the market for e-cigarettes may surpass that for combustible cigarettes (Euromonitor International 2017; NACS

---

[9] Those who use vaporizers, and e-cigarettes more generally, call themselves vapers, not smokers.
[10] These devices are sometimes lumped into a category called vapor-tanks-mods, or VTMs. See www.vaporworldexpo.com/PDFs/Vapor_World_Expo_Key_Takeaways.pdf.

2013). Overall, electronic cigarette sales in the United States have been increasing rapidly, from just $20 million in 2008 to an estimated $5.5 billion in 2018. The global market for e-cigarettes has also exploded, and is projected to grow at least 20 percent annually, reaching an estimated $48 billion by 2023 (Business Wire, 2018). Retail outlets for e-cigarettes have also proliferated. Just a few years ago there were no specialty vaping stores. Today, every major city in the United States has dozens, often hundreds, of such shops, which in total numbered over 15,000 in 2015 (Mincer 2015). Those shops are frequented by the ever-increasing number of vapers. Although estimates vary, the Centers for Disease Control and Prevention (CDC) in 2016 reported that 15.4 percent of adults aged eighteen years of age or older had tried e-cigarettes, and 11.3 percent of high school students had used e-cigarettes in the past thirty days (CDC 2017; CDC 2018). In Japan, because of strict regulation (see below), vaping is almost nonexistent. Data on e-cigarette use in China is spotty, but since 2013 China's domestic e-cigarette market has grown quickly, with knowledgeable insiders claiming that over the next five to ten years the market will increase by more than 30 percent annually, and in the coming decades will overtake conventional combustible cigarettes (Feldman and Yue 2016; People 2014).

5.2.3 Are E-Cigarettes Harmful?

Not only is it difficult to identify the key qualities and market size of e-cigarettes, it is also challenging to determine whether e-cigarettes will ultimately harm or enhance public health. A growing number of researchers globally are studying the health consequences of vaping, particularly: What is the impact of vaping on the health of vapers? Does vaping harm the heath of bystanders? Will e-cigarettes substitute for, or be used in addition to, combustible cigarettes? How popular will e-cigarettes be among people below the age of eighteen? Are the chemicals used to flavor e-liquid harmful? Will e-cigarettes be an effective harm reduction device for those who want to quit smoking? Might e-cigarettes create an atmosphere of public tolerance toward vaping that risks "re-normalizing" the use of combustible cigarettes?

Because data collection and analysis will take many years, at this point it is impossible to accurately answer any of the key questions involving e-cigarettes and health. Surely there are reasons for both optimism and concern. If e-cigarettes are capturing the interest of youth, for example, who first vape and then turn to combustible cigarettes, long-running declines in tobacco consumption could level off or be reversed. If current smokers turn to e-cigarettes to supplement but not substitute for cigarette consumption, then e-cigarettes might be reducing the number of people who quit smoking. If certain components of e-cigarettes, perhaps contained in e-liquid base ingredients or flavorings, turn out to be harmful, then e-cigarettes could be ushering in a new era of cancers and other diseases. On the other hand, e-cigarettes might be helping current smokers quit, keeping youth from initiating smoking, and playing a key role in reducing tobacco-related morbidity and mortality.

Scientific uncertainty appears to have heightened the tenor of the debate between those who see little but danger in e-cigarettes and those who embrace them as the centerpiece of a harm reduction strategy.[11] Stanton Glantz, for example, who runs the Center for Tobacco Control Research and Education at the University of California, San Francisco, argues that his research demonstrates that "among youth who had experimented with cigarettes but had not progressed to established smoking, additional use of e-cigarettes was positively associated with future onset of current established smoking" (Chaffee, Watkins, and Glantz 2018). Thomas Glynn of the American Cancer Society offers a different interpretation, arguing that "[t]he data in [Glantz's] study do not allow many of the broad conclusions that it draws." Glynn, in a review of e-cigarettes, expanded upon his view.

> If, at some point in the very near future, the preponderance of objective data show e-cigarettes to be demonstrably unsafe and/or ineffective, we will want to move on to other approaches that can lower the appalling toll from cigarette smoking. Or, in a similarly abbreviated time span, if objective data demonstrate their safety compared with combusted cigarettes and their effectiveness compared with current treatment approaches for tobacco dependence, then smokers can add e-cigarettes to the menu of options they can use to end their combusted cigarette habit and extend their lives (Glynn 2014).

If Glantz represents the critical end of the spectrum of views about the health impact of e-cigarettes, and Glynn is positioned in the middle, other respected scientists have a decidedly positive view of e-cigarettes. David Abrams, the Executive Director of the Schroeder Institute for Tobacco Research and Policy Studies at the Legacy Foundation, is perhaps the most prominent example. Abrams is enthusiastic about the potential of e-cigarettes to greatly reduce tobacco-related morbidity and mortality, arguing that "if most current American smokers switched to vaping e-cigarettes over the next 10 years, there could be as many as 6.6 million fewer premature deaths and 86.7 million fewer life years would be lost" (New York University 2018).

For now, the weight of objective, professional opinion favors the middle ground. As the US Food and Drug Administration (FDA) has stated,

> [e]-cigarettes have not been fully studied, so consumers currently don't know the potential risks of e-cigarettes when used as intended, how much nicotine or other potentially harmful chemicals are being inhaled during use, or whether there are

---

[11] Combustible tobacco has approximately eighty carcinogens and the scientific evidence of their negative impact on health is overwhelming. Most (but not all) e-cigarettes vaporize a nicotine-containing liquid, which makes them potentially addictive. But nicotine is not what kills smokers and is not likely to be the key vector of whatever harm may be caused by e-cigarettes. Although it is possible that e-cigarettes contain certain carcinogens in concentrations that will affect vapers, such harms are, at least at this point, hypothetical.

any benefits associated with using these products. Additionally, it is not known whether e-cigarettes may lead young people to try other tobacco products, including conventional cigarettes, which are known to cause disease and lead to premature death (US Food and Drug Administration 2017).

Similarly, an August 2015 report of the US National Institute on Drug Abuse notes that e-cigarettes "have not been thoroughly evaluated in scientific studies. This may change in the near future, but for now, very little data exists on the safety of e-cigarettes, and consumers have no way of knowing whether there are any therapeutic benefits or how the health effects compare to conventional cigarettes" (National Institute on Drug Abuse 2017). That finding was echoed in an authoritative review conducted by the National Academies (2018), which concluded that "e-cigarettes cannot be simply categorized as either beneficial or harmful to health. The net public health outcome depends on the balance between adverse outcomes (increased youth initiation of combustible tobacco cigarettes, low or even decreased cessation rates in adults, and a high-risk profile) and positive outcomes (very low youth initiation, high cessation rates in adults, and a low-risk profile)."

In contrast to the uncertainty about e-cigarettes expressed by government officials in the United States, policymakers in England have been far more enthusiastic. Public Health England, for example, has vigorously embraced e-cigarettes, declaring that "vaping poses only a small fraction of the risks of smoking and switching completely from smoking to vaping conveys substantial health benefits over continued smoking" (McNeill et al. 2018). In contrast, although China manufacturers over 90 percent of the world's electronic cigarettes, there have been no Chinese studies on the health consequences of vaping, and the government has devoted scant energy to studying the impact of e-cigarettes on youth, on current smokers (of which China has more than any other country in the world), or on bystanders (Feldman and Yue 2016). In Japan, one finds a similar cleavage between public health researchers as in the United States. Some experts, like those working at the National Cancer Center in Tokyo, express strong reservations about the safety of e-cigarettes, whereas others, particularly those based in Osaka, have endorsed e-cigarettes as an effective harm reduction technology (Personal communication with author).

Public health policy rarely rests on a bed of scientific certainty. But the wide range of views among experts about the safety of e-cigarettes goes well beyond the usual lack of consensus. Some researchers consider e-cigarettes themselves to be harmful, or believe that e-cigarettes will encourage the use of combustible tobacco, and insist that they be banned or aggressively regulated. Others conclude that e-cigarettes are an effective harm reduction tool and should be made available to the many people for whom they could provide a benefit. These opposing policy options, both lacking strong empirical support, help to explain the lack of policy convergence in the regulation of e-cigarettes. Faced with an array of policy options and little scientific support for any particular policy outcome, policymakers have instead based their policy choices on other factors – political pressure, financial opportunities and constraints, their perception of the public good, and more. One can see the result of the lack of scientific consensus in the current e-cigarette policies of the United States, Japan, and China. In the United States, the FDA has moved haltingly toward e-cigarette regulation; after an initial effort to regulate e-cigarettes as pharmaceutical products was challenged in court, the agency decided to treat them as tobacco products, but has so far failed to issue specific regulations. Various municipalities, cities, and states have developed their own e-cigarette policies, most of which fold e-cigarettes into existing tobacco control law.

Compared to the absence of national policy in the United States, Japan has followed a much more aggressive path. Policy makers in the Ministry of Health, Labor, and Welfare have concluded that the nicotine in e-cigarettes is a drug, meaning that e-cigarettes fall under the umbrella of pharmaceutical regulation.[12] To market their products, manufacturers of e-cigarettes are therefore required to submit data to the Ministry demonstrating that their products are both safe and effective. Since they currently have no such data, nicotine-containing e-cigarettes cannot be marketed. Japan's de facto e-cigarette ban stands in stark contrast to the Chinese government's approach. There, health officials, finance officials, pharmaceutical regulators, and others have seemingly ignored the debate over e-cigarettes in the United States, Europe, Japan, and elsewhere, and have allowed e-cigarettes to be manufactured, sold, and consumed in a regulatory vacuum.

In an era when scholars so often see policy convergence as the norm, the inconsistency one finds in e-cigarette policy is notable.[13] The absence of robust scientific data about the health impact of e-cigarettes is critical to explaining that inconsistency. Freed from the constraints of robust epidemiological and scientific findings, policymakers in the United States, Japan, and China have adopted three dramatically different approaches to e-cigarette regulation, ranging from the de facto prohibition of e-cigarettes to a highly permissive, unregulated posture. But science is not the only factor that explains regulatory divergence. The political and economic forces that have shaped tobacco policy in different nations are also a crucial part of the explanation.

5.3 LAW, POLITICS, AND MARKETS: THE IMPACT OF TOBACCO POLICY ON E-CIGARETTE REGULATION

When e-cigarettes entered the global marketplace in 2003, they did so against a background that was etched by over a century of conflict over tobacco regulation. In the United States, industrialists in the early twentieth century worked hard to ensure

---

[12] E-cigarettes that do not contain nicotine are not affected by the regulations.
[13] See note 3 above for a small sample of the literature on policy convergence.

that tobacco products escaped government control (Kluger 1997; Brandt 2009). They used their growing wealth – soon, they would be among the largest companies in the United States, and the world – to influence local politicians, hire prominent law firms, and recruit top advertising agencies, and for over a century succeeded in minimizing the regulation of combustible tobacco products. The FDA, created in 1927 as the Food, Drug, and Insecticide Administration and renamed in 1930, had no jurisdiction over tobacco, so federal regulation came primarily from the Federal Trade Commission (FTC), which in 1966 imposed limits on tobacco advertising and required warnings on cigarette packets (US Food and Drug Administration 2018; Federal Cigarette Labeling and Advertising Act of 1966). Over time, states and municipalities picked up some of the regulatory slack, and by the late twentieth century had developed a web of clean air and workplace restrictions.

Calls for more government regulation of tobacco started early in the twentieth century, but it was not until the publication of the Surgeon General's 1964 Report "Smoking and Health," which clearly identified smoking as a cause of lung cancer, that tobacco control advocates had a firm scientific footing (US Department of Health, Education, and Welfare 1964). The report catalyzed the emergence of a powerful tobacco control movement, triggered a long, steady decline in tobacco consumption, and ushered in a half century of tort litigation brought by smokers who accused the industry of acting negligently and marketing defective products. Most of their claims failed, but they spawned additional lawsuits against the industry by state and federal government (Rabin 1991–1992; Rabin 2001). In 2009, Congress granted the FDA authority to regulate tobacco products, and some optimistic tobacco control advocates declared that "the end of tobacco" was at hand (Tobacco Control 2013; Family Smoking Prevention and Tobacco Control Act 2009).[14]

At least initially, e-cigarette companies have little in common with their twentieth century predecessors. The industry, if one can call it that, was made up of individual entrepreneurs who imported small quantities of merchandise from e-cigarette manufacturers in China and sold it either online or in small shops. As the popularity of e-cigarettes increased, however, the nature of the e-cigarette business quickly changed, and what was originally a niche product is now a multibillion-dollar global industry controlled by some of the world's richest companies. Lorillard, for example, purchased the US market-leading e-cigarette, Blu, for $135 million in 2012 and sold it in 2014 (along with several of its tobacco brands) to Imperial Tobacco in a $7.1 billion deal (Solomon 2014).[15] Altria Group, the parent company of Philip Morris, joined with its international spinoff, Philip Morris International, to develop and market MarkTen,

---

[14] Tobacco control, special issue on tobacco endgame; "Family Smoking Prevention and Tobacco Control Act." H.R. 1256, Public Law 111–31, June 22, 2009. It is the 2009 law that the FDA is using to assert regulatory authority over e-cigarettes.

[15] The sale to Imperial was part of a deal in which Reynolds American bought Lorillard for $27.4 billion. www.forbes.com/sites/briansolomon/2014/07/15/reynolds-lorillard-dump-blu-e-cigarettes-in-27-billion-merger/#4849ab5bd1c6.

Green Smoke, and iQOS, and in 2014 purchased UK e-cigarette company Nicocigs. R. J. Reynold's popular e-cigarette, Vuse, was released in 2014, and for a while controlled almost 1/3 of the US market (Craver 2015). British American Tobacco developed and markets Vype. Japan Tobacco Inc. first acquired UK-based E-Lites and later purchased Logic, a major US e-cigarette brand (JTI 2014; JTI 2015).[16] A notable exception to the dominance of global tobacco brands is Pax Labs, originally founded in 2007 as Ploom, which developed a novel e-cigarette product called Juul in 2015 and founded a new company, Juul Labs, in 2017. Sales of Juul increased more than 600 percent in 2017, and by mid-2018 Juul accounted for over 60 percent of all e-cigarette sales in the US (Campaign for Tobacco Free Kids 2018).

Collectively, these companies bring to e-cigarettes an extraordinary amount of wealth, market savvy, and regulatory experience. They have pumped significant resources into marketing and advertising, carefully avoiding claims about the intended use of their products (claiming that e-cigarettes are intended to help smokers quit, for example, invites regulation as a smoking cessation device, which brings them under the ambit of pharmaceutical regulators). They hire top law firms that provide expert corporate advice and litigation defense. And they have teams of lobbyists who know how to work the corridors of power and influence regulators. Globally, e-cigarette regulators must contend with companies that successfully evaded government regulation for most of the twentieth century.

The key forces at play in US tobacco regulation have greatly influenced the regulation of e-cigarettes. First, the tobacco industry consists of a number of private companies, some of which have grown into the world's most robust multinational corporations. Those corporations now control the US e-cigarette industry. Second, tobacco companies have worked hard and spent aggressively to protect themselves from regulation, and are doing the same to fend off and/or shape e-cigarette regulation. Third, for over a century the government has taken a relatively hands-off approach to tobacco regulation, which has changed only since the enactment of the Family Smoking Prevention and Tobacco Control Act in 2009. But that Act only allows the FDA to regulate certain enumerated tobacco products, not including e-cigarettes. So the FDA is engaged in a lengthy effort to "deem" e-cigarettes as tobacco products under the Act (Deeming Tobacco Products To Be Subject to the Federal Food, Drug, and Cosmetic Act, as Amended by the Family Smoking Prevention and Tobacco Control Act [Proposed Rule] 2015; FDA 2011).[17] Fourth, a

---

[16] Japan Tobacco also owns a minority interest in Ploom, a California-based leaf vaporizer.
[17] "Deeming Tobacco Products To Be Subject to the Federal Food, Drug, and Cosmetic Act, as Amended by the Family Smoking Prevention and Tobacco Control Act (Proposed Rule)." FDA. August 8, 2015. www.fda.gov/AboutFDA/ReportsManualsForms/Reports/EconomicAnalyses/ucm394922.htm (detailing efforts by the FDA to promulgate regulations that would give the FDA authority to regulate e-cigarettes); "Stakeholder Letter: Regulation of E-Cigarettes and Other Tobacco Products." April 25, 2011. www.fda.gov/NewsEvents/PublicHealthFocus/ucm252360.htm (describing the FDA's intent to extend its authority to regulate e-cigarettes under the Family Smoking Prevention and Tobacco Control Act of 2009).

combination of municipal, state, and federal regulations now restrict the sale and use of tobacco in a variety of ways: only adults can purchase tobacco products, such products can only be used in certain places, advertising tobacco products is restricted, tobacco is subject to various types of taxation, and more. As a matter of convenience if not coherence, e-cigarettes have in some places been folded into those laws. Fifth, the tobacco control community consistently presses for further regulation of tobacco that will improve public health. But it is divided as to how best to manage e-cigarettes, because there is broad disagreement as to whether e-cigarettes are more or a threat or an asset to public health. In short, the spectrum of economic and political interests that shaped US tobacco policy are now defining US e-cigarette policy.

The key institutions and interests at play in the United States are dramatically different from those that characterize the economic and political framework of tobacco regulation in Japan. In the late nineteenth century the Japanese government took control of tobacco leaf cultivation through the Leaf Tobacco Monopoly Law, and the 1904 Tobacco Monopoly Law completed the state's monopolization of the cultivation, manufacture, and sale of tobacco products (Executory Order and Reasons for a Tobacco Manufacturing Monopoly 1991).[18] Creating a tobacco monopoly brought a number of benefits to the government. One was that it facilitated the collection of tobacco-related taxes, which initially helped to fund the Russo-Japanese War and ultimately constituted a significant portion of the country's total tax revenue (Rothacher 1989; Honjo and Kawachi 2000).[19] In addition, and in what foreshadowed tobacco-related trade conflict between the United States and Japan in the 1980s, the government worried about the increasing prominence of the US tobacco industry and its impact on the health of its domestic tobacco market (Levin 1997; Executory Order and Reasons for a Tobacco Manufacturing Monopoly 1991, 7).[20] A tobacco monopoly, in the government's view, was the best way to protect its domestic interests.

There was a third benefit of the tobacco monopoly; it created a set of institutional relationships that continue to serve the needs of key tobacco policy players – the state, tobacco growers, and Japan's dominant political party (the Liberal Democratic Party, or LDP). In the context of tobacco policy, the most significant government actor is the Ministry of Finance (MoF), which oversaw the monopoly

[18] For a detailed official history of the tobacco monopoly, see *Tabako senbaishi: History of the tobacco monopoly*. 6th edn., 1991, volumes 1–6.

[19] At one point, tobacco constituted 18 percent of total government tax-related revenue, a figure that has declined to 1–2 percent today. Rothacher, Albrecht. 1989 *Japan's Agro-Food Sector: The Politics and Economics of Excess Protection*. See also, Honjo, Kaori and Ichiro Kawachi. 2000. "Effects of Market Liberalization on Smoking in Japan." *Tobacco Control* 9: 193, 193–200.

[20] See, for example, Executory Order and Reasons for a Tobacco Manufacturing Monopoly (Tabako seizō sembai seido riyū oyobi shikō junjo), quoted in *Tabako senbaishi: History of the tobacco monopoly*, 6th ed., 1991, vol. 1, 7, translated and discussed in Mark Levin's detailed article about Japanese tobacco regulation. Mark Levin. 1997. "Smoke Around the Rising Sun: An American Look at Tobacco Regulation in Japan." *Stanford Journal of Law and Policy* 8 (1): 99–123.

until 1985 and continues to be the locus of the government's tobacco strategy. MoF told tobacco farmers how much land they could cultivate and how many plants they could grow. It owned and operated cigarette factories throughout the country, licensed tobacco retailers, and set the price of tobacco products. After 1985, when the tobacco monopoly was eliminated, MoF continued to be the controlling shareholder in Japan's only tobacco company, Japan Tobacco (JT), and it (not the Ministry of Health, Labor, and Welfare) makes all important tobacco policy decisions.

Tobacco growers appear to have flourished under this scheme. They were guaranteed a buyer for all of their tobacco leaf, and received a generous price for their crops. In exchange, they were loyal to their patrons by showing up at the voting booth and supporting the LDP. The disproportionate weight accorded to rural votes in Japan made the support of tobacco farmers (and agriculture more generally) particularly valuable. Japan Tobacco, Japan's sole tobacco company, was also a beneficiary of the system. For many years JT was the sole purveyor of tobacco products in Japan, and it continues to be protected from undue foreign competition. The high post-war rate of tobacco consumption in Japan brought significant revenue to MoF and JT, and JT's international division, Japan Tobacco International (JTI), is now a major global tobacco player.

When e-cigarettes appeared in Japan in the early 2000s, everyone could easily evaluate their preferred policy outcomes. JT had not yet invested in the e-cigarette business, so keeping the domestic market free of competition was a priority. From MoF's perspective, the decline in tobacco consumption in Japan since the 1970s had resulted in decreasing tobacco-related government revenue, and a further decline caused by Japanese cigarette smokers switching to foreign e-cigarettes was undesirable (Funatogawa, Funatogawa, and Tano 2013). For health regulators at the MHLW, long excluded from tobacco regulation by MoF, e-cigarettes were an opportunity to extend their regulatory turf. Tobacco growers, retailers, and others in the industry could not have welcomed competition from e-cigarettes, and members of the LDP had little to gain from a policy that opened the Japanese market to e-cigarettes. In short, the political and economic interests of the key players leaned clearly against a liberal regulatory posture for e-cigarettes. By deciding that e-cigarettes were not tobacco products and would instead be regulated under the Pharmaceutical Affairs Law, MHLW and MoF effectively kept nicotine-containing e-cigarettes out of Japan.[21]

Like Japan, China also has a long history of tobacco cultivation and consumption. The commercialized growth of tobacco started in the sixteenth century, and by the 1750s tobacco had become an important source of revenue for both central

---

[21] In contrast, the Japanese government permits the sale of so-called heat-not-burn products, which use a vaporizing technology similar to e-cigarettes but contain processed leaf tobacco rather than liquid. Such products fit the government's definition of "tobacco products," and therefore have been folded into the preexisting regulatory framework for combustible cigarettes.

and local government (Benedict 2011, 2). In 1981, China created a state tobacco monopoly controlled by an agency with two parts: the State Tobacco Monopoly Administration (STMA), charged with regulating and monitoring the tobacco industry, and China National Tobacco Company (CNTC), tasked with the production, procurement, processing, and pricing of tobacco leaf and the marketing of cigarettes (Li 2012, 82).

With 300 million smokers (25 percent of all smokers globally) who consume 40 percent of the world's cigarettes, the political, economic, and health impacts of tobacco in China are enormous (Li 2012, ix).[22] The most significant issue is revenue; the tobacco industry is a cash cow, even in China's rapidly expanding economy, and tobacco-related taxes are critical to the state's coffers (Baojiang 2010; Li 2012, x; USDA and FAS 2000).[23] The tobacco sector is also a major employer, providing jobs for more than 500,000 people, with an additional 20 million deriving some income from tobacco, including 1.3 million farming households and 5 million retail workers (Martin 2014).

The economic importance of tobacco is underscored by the regulatory power of the State Tobacco Monopoly Administration (STMA), which through the China National Tobacco Corporation (CNTC) controls the Chinese cigarette industry. The CNTC oversees tobacco growth, production, sales, human resources, finance, marketing, and trade, and includes thirty-three provincial subsidiaries (Tobacco Monopoly Administrations) and a multitude of industrial and commercial enterprises. At the regional level, a tobacco leaf tax (20 percent) flows directly to local government, together with 25 percent of the national value-added tax. In provinces like Yunnan and Guizhou, the epicenters of China's tobacco production, tobacco is the "pillar of the economy" (Li 2012).

Superficially, the Chinese government has made tobacco control a policy priority. It signed and ratified the WHO's Framework Convention on Tobacco Control, and in 2007 the State Council established the "FCTC Implementation Inter-Ministerial Coordination Leading Group," with members from a spectrum of relevant ministries (World Health Organization n.d.). That group has discussed the possibility of prohibiting tobacco advertising in the mass media, banning tobacco use in indoor

---

[22] China's total cigarette production is approximately four times greater than the United States, the world's second-largest tobacco-producing country.

[23] Li, Baojiang. 2010. "Effects of increasing tobacco taxes on government revenue and consumption in China." Acta Tabacaria Sinica, 16 (5). The central government collects a tobacco excise tax, a value-added tax, and a certain amount of net profit from the China National Tobacco Corporation. Tobacco taxes combined with profit constituted over 6 percent of total government income in 2014, and considerably more in previous years. ("Over the past decade, the tobacco industry has consistently contributed 7–10 percent of total annual central government revenues, similar to a number of lucrative and fast-growing sectors such as real estate and petroleum." Li, Cheng. 2012. *The Political Mapping of China's Tobacco Industry and Anti-Smoking Campaign*.) See also Global Agriculture Information Network, United States Department of Agriculture, "Peoples Republic of China, Tobacco and Products, Tobacco Update 2000," GAIN Report #CH0044, 1, which states that China derives 10 percent of its total tax revenue from tobacco.

public places, and forbidding sales to minors.[24] More recently, the China Tobacco Control Plan proposed measures like prohibiting smoking in public places, strengthening warnings on cigarette packets, and banning tobacco promotion and sponsorship (Feldman and Yue 2016).

Nonetheless, the political and economic importance of tobacco in China ensures that tobacco control policy will remain weak and ineffective (Hong 2014; Lv, Su, Hong 2011; Li 2012, x). Per capita smoking rates are high, secondhand smoke exposure is ubiquitous, youth access is widespread, and public education is poor. Rather than limit per capita tobacco consumption, CNTC's goal is to improve tobacco sales and profits. As a distinguished scholar of Chinese politics puts it,

> [d]espite growing public concern over the smoking epidemic's severe health consequences, as well as the massive long-term economic burden it presents, Chinese authorities have been slow to acknowledge this increasingly devastating public health crisis. Their hesitance to effectively curtail tobacco production and consumption is driven primarily by the fact that the tobacco industry is one of the largest sources of tax revenue for the Chinese government (Li 2012, x)

Likewise, a historian of the Chinese tobacco industry argues that "a major barrier to effective tobacco control in China remains the significant economic clout wielded by China's highly profitable tobacco industry (Benedict 2011, 253).

With these political and economic factors in mind, how should one expect the government to regulate e-cigarettes? One option might be to reign in the proliferation of private e-cigarette manufacturers by including them in the state e-cigarette monopoly, enabling the government to capture revenue generated by the e-cigarette business. Another approach might be to protect the combustible tobacco industry by prohibiting e-cigarettes. A third option could involve regulating e-cigarettes as tobacco products, but allowing private e-cigarette enterprises to operate. Faced with these and perhaps other regulatory options, the government has so far taken no action; it does not regulate e-cigarettes as medical devices, dangerous chemicals, pharmaceutical products, or tobacco products. No government agency has been tasked with the regulation of e-cigarettes, and those agencies that could plausibility take the reins – the Ministry of Health, the CNTC, the State Administration of Work Safety, the State Administration for Industry and Commerce, the State Food and Drug Administration – have each disclaimed responsibility (Feldman and Yue 2016). What one finds in China, therefore, is an e-cigarette market unburdened by

---

[24] The Smoking Control Ordinance of the Shenzhen Special Economic Zone focused on strengthening the enforcement of smoking bans in public places. It created six municipal agencies: Public Security Bureau, Urban Management Bureau, Transportation Commission, Health Supervision Bureau, Sports and Tourism Bureau, and Market Supervision Bureau, responsible for enforcing the Ordinance in their own domains. From March 1 to December 31, 2014, 100,253 public places were inspected and 8,675 people were administratively fined a total of ¥420,100. Shenzhen, where the most aggressive smoking regulations were implemented in 2014, is seen as a model tobacco control city in China.

regulation, at least until the government determines that some form of regulation is politically and economically advantageous.[25]

It is no surprise that political pressures, financial interests, and institutional arrangements play an important role in determining how policies are shaped, which policies are adopted, and how vigorously policies are enforced. When the stakes are high, the influence of such factors can be particularly acute. Tobacco policy is one such area: the financial interests of parties as diverse as multinational corporations and individual farmers are strong; the political stakes are considerable; and a wide array of institutional actors have skin in the game. What is true for tobacco turns out to be true for e-cigarettes, with many of the same players involved in tobacco regulation staking out positions regarding e-cigarette regulation. The different goals and interests of those players help to explain the divergent approaches to e-cigarette regulation in the United States, Japan, and China.

5.4 E-CIGARETTES AND THE COURTS

In addition to the absence of scientific consensus and the influence of political and economic interests, the role of courts in the policymaking process also helps to explain divergent e-cigarette policies in the United States, Japan, and China. Perhaps not surprisingly, there is only one jurisdiction in which the courts have powerfully influenced e-cigarette policy – the United States. In neither Japan nor China have the courts played even a minor role in determining if, or how, the government should regulate e-cigarettes. In the United States, however, courts have been a central actor, arguably *the* central actor, in the evolving debate over e-cigarette regulation.

Between late 2008 and early 2009, as the e-cigarette business was taking off in the United States, the FDA detained a series of e-cigarette shipments at Los Angeles International Airport and ordered the importers to destroy or export their wares (Feldman 2014). The FDA claimed that the importers were violating the Food, Drug, and Cosmetic Act; in the agency's view, e-cigarettes were combination drugs/ drug delivery devices that required FDA evaluation for safety and efficacy (21 U.S.C. § 360d (1938)). Not surprisingly, the merchants held a different view. Their products should not be regulated as drugs, they argued, because they had not made any representations about their impact on health, a fundamental aspect of the legal definition of a drug. Seeking legal relief, the importers filed a claim in the United States District Court for the District of Columbia in *Smoking Everywhere, Inc. v. U. S. Food and Drug Administration*, better known as the *Sottera* case. (Smoking Everywhere, Inc. v. U.S. Food and Drug Administration, 2010).

---

[25] At this point, the most likely scenario was presented in an article by Li Baojiang, deputy director of the STMA, who told China Daily: "Regulating e-cigarettes, like traditional tobacco products under the State monopoly, is highly feasible. And that helps with consumer safety and rights, product quality control and the government coffers."

The FDA's position was complicated by two factors. One was that after a century without the legal authority to regulate combustible tobacco products, in 2009 Representative Henry Waxman introduced the Family Smoking Prevention and Tobacco Control Act, which provided the FDA with the legal authority to regulate certain combustible tobacco products (FDA 2018).[26] Although regulating tobacco had long been a goal of the FDA, the timing was inauspicious. Without regulatory authority over tobacco, the FDA could potentially justify treating e-cigarettes as pharmaceuticals. Once Congress gave it jurisdiction, regulating e-cigarettes as drugs/drug delivery devices became more difficult. Filing their complaint to coincide with the passage of the Tobacco Control Act, plaintiff e-cigarette corporations insisted that their products be regulated as tobacco, not pharmaceuticals, since under the latter e-cigarettes would be subject to a lengthy, costly, and potentially unsuccessful approval process.[27]

The second factor that complicated the FDA's position was presiding judge Richard Leon, who earlier in his career served as Republican chief counsel investigating Whitewater (*Smoking Everywhere, Inc. v. Food & Drug Admin.* 2010). Described as "a conservative ... who does not shrink from criticizing the federal government on matters as varied as pornography, death penalty, drugs, and terrorism suspects at Guantánamo Bay, Cuba," Judge Leon's general antipathy toward government has also surfaced in a series of decisions involving the FDA (Stolberg 2013). In three cases brought against the agency – e-cigarettes, graphic warning labels on cigarette packets, and mentholated cigarettes – the judge handed the FDA stinging defeats.

Judge Leon's ruling in *Smoking Everywhere*, affirmed on appeal, made a relatively straightforward argument. If the FDA wants to regulate e-cigarettes, the judge argued, it can do so. In the absence of claims that the products are being sold as smoking cessation devices, however, it can only regulate them under the Tobacco Control Act, not as pharmaceuticals. Judge Leon did not simply reject the FDA's regulatory approach; he also called into question the FDA's motives.

> This case appears to be yet another example of FDA's aggressive efforts to regulate recreational tobacco products as drugs or devices under the Food, Drug, and Cosmetic Act (FDCA). Ironically, notwithstanding that Congress has now taken the unprecedented step of granting FDA jurisdiction over those products, FDA remains undeterred. Unfortunately, its tenacious drive to maximize its regulatory power has resulted in its advocacy of an interpretation of the relevant law that I find,

---

[26] See Tobacco Control Act, Food and Drug Administration, www.fda.gov/TobaccoProducts/ GuidanceComplianceRegulatoryInformation/ucm298595.htm (accessed on Feb. 23, 2015) (describing how the Tobacco Control Act of 2009 gives the FDA broad authority to regulate the manufacture, distribution, and marketing of tobacco products).

[27] The FDA requires data on safety and efficacy before drugs can be sold, and e-cigarette manufactures have no such data.

at first blush, to be unreasonable and unacceptable (*Smoking Everywhere, Inc.* v. *Food & Drug Admin.* 2010, 72, 78).

Reflecting on *Sottera* and other tobacco-related cases, Matthew L. Myers, President of the Campaign for Tobacco Free Kids, argues that Judge Leon "has fundamentally altered FDA's authority and ability to carry out its congressional mandate" (Levin 2014).[28] Indeed, in the absence of *Sottera*, the United States would have been on the same regulatory path as Japan, with e-cigarettes effectively banned until manufacturers could present evidence that they were safe and effective nicotine replacement therapies. Instead, because of Judge Leon's decision in *Smoking Everywhere*, the FDA can only regulate e-cigarettes as tobacco products, a long and arduous task that is still underway (FDA 2014).[29]

The *Sottera* case has exerted tremendous influence on US e-cigarette policy. It denied the FDA's efforts to apply drug regulation to e-cigarettes, and instead made the new Tobacco Control Act the only plausible regulatory option. Yet the fact that a complex policy choice was fundamentally shaped by the courts is of little surprise in the United States, where scholars have long acknowledged the role of courts in the policymaking process (Kagan 2003). The difference between the influence of the courts on e-cigarette policy in the United States and in Japan/China could not be more vivid. In neither Japan nor China has there been any litigation over e–cigarette policy; it is difficult even to imagine a legal challenge to the regulatory authority of, for example, Japan's Ministry of Finance over e-cigarettes, or of China's CNTC. Judicial policymaking is not the only explanation for the divergence of e-cigarette regulations in the United States, Japan, and China, but it is one important part of the puzzle.

CONCLUSION

A paper on comparative e-cigarette regulation may not seem the obvious way to pay homage to Malcolm Feeley. The topic does not speak to fundamental tensions in criminal law and procedure for which Feeley is so justly celebrated, nor does it directly engage his interest in federalism. Nonetheless, several aspects of Feeley's work are critically important to how the paper is structured. First, like so much of Feeley's work, the paper is explicitly comparative. Rather than focus on e-cigarette regulation in a single jurisdiction, it looks across three different nations so as to better analyze the range of factors that influence policy in each of them. Second, Feeley's

---

[28] Cases are randomly assigned, which meant that Judge Leon's chance of being assigned all three was one in 1,859 www.fairwarning.org/2014/09/fda-batting-0-3-federal-judge/.

[29] To do so requires a number of time-consuming and difficult administrative maneuvers, which the FDA has been pursing since April 2014. Food and Drug Administration. "Deeming Tobacco Products To Be Subject to the Federal Food, Drug, and Cosmetic Act, as Amended by the Family Smoking Prevention and Tobacco Control Act; Regulations on the Sale and Distribution of Tobacco Products and Required Warning Statements for Tobacco Products," 79 FR 23141, April 25, 2014.

work often engages complex policy choices, and analyzes the range of policy approaches available to state actors. This study follows his example by exploring a thorny policy question – the regulation of e-cigarettes – and examining a spectrum of policy approaches. Third, Feeley's work is almost always concerned with the law in action, and demonstrates a deep engagement with how legal rules and practices affect the populace, particularly marginalized populations. This paper indirectly reflects that concern; the use of combustible tobacco has been increasingly relegated to those with lower incomes and less education, and e-cigarette policy will undoubtedly have an impact on the social gradient of smoking, though the details of that impact are not yet clear.

Those central aspects of Malcolm Feeley's work motivate this paper. A comparative analysis of e-cigarette policy reveals that three important jurisdictions – the United States, Japan, and China – have taken starkly different approaches to the regulation of e-cigarettes. Divergence, not convergence, describes the landscape of e-cigarette regulation, for three reasons; the unclear scientific and epidemiological impact of e-cigarettes, the economic and political interests of key actors, and the role of the courts. Although this paper underscores the particular importance of those reasons, one can easily identify other possible explanations that the paper leaves unexplored. Malcolm Feeley gets the final word: "I would hope that the evidence and observations I present here will be tested against additional information . . . Only if such collective work takes place can social science proceed successfully." (Feeley 1992, xxxiv)

REFERENCES

21 U.S.C. § 360d (1938).
New York University. 2018. News Release. "Do Less Harm: E-Cigarettes a Safer Option than Smoking." January 11, 2018. www.nyu.edu/about/news-publications/news/2018/january/do-less-harm–e-cigarettes-a-safer-option-than-smoking.html.
Baojiang, Li. 2010. "Effects of Increasing Tobacco Taxes on Government Revenue and Consumption in China." *Acta Tabacaria Sinica* 16 (5): 82–88.
Benedict, Carol. 2011. *Golden-Silk Smoke: A History of Tobacco in China, 1550–2010*. Berkeley: University of California Press.
Brandt, Alan. 2009. *The Cigarette Century: The Rise, Fall, and Deadly Persistence of the Product That Defined America*. New York: Basic Books.
Business Wire. 2018. "Global E-Cigarette Market Analysis and Forecast 2018–2023 – Market is Forecasted to Attain a Value of $48 Billion – ResearchAndMarkets.com." www.businesswire.com/news/home/20180306005861/en/Global-E-Cigarette-Market-Analysis-Forecast-2018–2023.
Campaign for Tobacco Free Kids. 2018. "JUUL and Youth: Rising E-Cigarette Popularity." www.tobaccofreekids.org/assets/factsheets/0394.pdf.
Centers for Disease Control and Prevention (CDC) 2018. "Youth and Tobacco Use." www.cdc.gov/tobacco/data_statistics/fact_sheets/youth_data/tobacco_use/index.htm.

Centers for Disease Control and Prevention (CDC). 2017. "Morbidity and Mortality Weekly Report." August 25, 2017, 66 (33): 892.

Chaffee B. W., S. L. Watkins, and S. A. Glantz. 2018. "Electronic Cigarette Use and Progression from Experimentation to Established Smoking." *Pediatrics* 141(4): e20173594.

Craver, Richard. 2015. "Blu Chips Away at Vuse's Share." *Winston-Salem Journal*, July 27, 2015. www.journalnow.com/business/business_news/local/blu-chips-away-at-vuse-s-share/article_64e74e38-34b2-11e5-9115-f74b51fccb68.html.

"Deeming Tobacco Products to Be Subject to the Federal Food, Drug, and Cosmetic Act, as Amended by the Family Smoking Prevention and Tobacco Control Act; Regulations on the Sale and Distribution of Tobacco Products and Required Warning Statements for Tobacco Products," 79 Fed. Reg. 23141 (April 25, 2014).

Directive 2014/40/EU of the European Parliament and of the Council of 3 April 2014 on the approximation of the laws, regulations and administrative provisions of the Member States concerning the manufacture, presentation and sale of tobacco and related products and repealing Directive 2001/37/EC Text with EEA relevance. Title III, Electronic Cigarettes And Herbal Products For Smoking, Article 20, Electronic Cigarettes.

Euromonitor International. 2017. "Cigarettes in the US." www.euromonitor.com/cigarettes?PageCode=96650&CountryCode=380&IndustryCode=null&ContentType=null&ReportType=null&SortBy=1&PageNumber=0&PageSize=20&PageType=2.

"Executory Order and Reasons for a Tobacco Manufacturing Monopoly (Tabako seizō sembai seido riyū oyobi shikō junjo)." Quoted in 1991 *Tabako Sembai-shi* [A History of the Tobacco Monopoly] 6th edn., vol. 1 (Tokyo: Nihon Tabako Sangyō K.K. Shashi Hensan-shitsu). Translated and discussed in Levin, Mark. 1997. "Smoke Around the Rising Sun: An American Look at Tobacco Regulation in Japan." *Stanford Journal of Law and Policy* 8 (1): 99–124.

Family Smoking Prevention and Tobacco Control Act, Public Law 111–31 (H.R. 1256) (June 22, 2009).

Federal Cigarette Labeling and Advertising Act of 1966, 15 U.S.C. §§ 1331–1340 (2012).

Feeley, Malcolm. 1992 [1979]. *The Process Is the Punishment*. New York: Russell Sage Foundation.

Feldman, Eric. 2014. "Layers of Law: The Case of E-Cigarettes." *Florida International University Law Review* 10 (1): 111–23.

Feldman, Eric A. and Chai Yue. 2016. "E-Cigarette Regulation in China: The Road Ahead." *University of Pennsylvania Asian Law Review* 11 (3): 409–38.

Fullerton, Larry and Megan Alvarez. 2012. "Convergence in International Merger Control." *Antitrust* 26 (2): 20–25.

Funatogawa, Ikuko, Takashi Funatogawa, and Eiji Yano. 2013. "Trends in Smoking and Lung Cancer Mortality in Japan, by Birth Cohort, 1949–2010." *Bulletin of the World Health Organization* 91 (5): 332–40.

Glynn, Thomas J. 2014. "E-cigarettes and the Future of Tobacco Control." *CA: A Cancer Journal for Clinicians* 64 (3): 164–68.

Halliday, Terence C. and Gregory Shaffer. 2016. *Transnational Legal Orders*. New York: Cambridge University Press.

Hong, Yu. 2014. "The Change of China Tobacco Control Policy: An Advocacy Coalition Framework-based Analysis." *Chinese Journal of Health Policy* 7 (3): 20–26.

Honjo, Kaori and Ichiro Kawachi. 2000. "Effects of Market Liberalization on Smoking in Japan." *BMJ Tobacco Control* 9 (2): 193–200.

Ikegami, Naoki and Gerard F. Anderson. 2012. "In Japan, All-Payer Rate Setting Under Tight Government Control Has Proved to Be an Eoffective Approach to Containing Costs." *Health Affairs* 31 (5): 1049–56.

JTI. 2014. "JTI Acquires Leading E-cigarette Brand E-lites." *JTI*, June 11, 2014. www.jti.com/our-views/newsroom/jti-acquires-leading-e-cigarette-brand-e-lites.

JTI. 2015. "JT Acquires Logic, the Leading Independent US e-Cigarette." *PR Newswire*, April 30, 2015. www.prnewswire.com/news-releases/jt-acquires-logic-the-leading-independent-us-e-cigarette-company-501787281.html.

Juan, Shan. "E-cigarette Controls Considered for Safety." *China Daily*, January 7, 2015. www.chinadaily.com.cn/china/2015-01/07/content_19255939.htm.

Kagan, Robert. 2003. *Adversarial Legalism: The American Way of Law*. Cambridge: Harvard University Press.

Kennedy R. D., A. Awopegba, and E. De León. 2017. "Global Approaches to Regulating Electronic Cigarettes." *BMJ Tobacco Control* 26, 440–45.

Kluger, Richard. 1997. *Ashes to Ashes: America's Hundred-Year Cigarette War, the Public Health, and the Unabashed Triumph of Philip Morris*. New York: Vintage.

KPMG. 2015. "2015 KPMG Global Tax Rate Survey." Last modified October 25, 2015. https://home.kpmg.com/cn/en/home/insights/2015/10/global-tax-rate-survey.html.

Lempert, Lauren K., Rachel Grana, and Stanton A. Glantz. 2014. "The Importance of Product Definitions in US E-Cigarette Laws and Regulations." *BMJ Tobacco Control*, 1–8. https://doi:10.1136/tobaccocontrol-2014–051913.

Levin, Mark. 1997. "Smoke Around the Rising Sun: An American Look at Tobacco Regulation in Japan." *Stanford Journal of Law and Policy* 8 (1): 99–124.

Levin, Myron. 2014. "Tobacco Industry Batting a Thousand with Federal Judge, While FDA Strikes Out." *Fair Warning*, September 3, 2014. www.fairwarning.org/2014/09/fda-batting-0-3-federal-judge/.

Li, Cheng. 2012. *The Political Mapping of China's Tobacco Industry and Anti-Smoking Campaign*. Washington DC: Brookings.

Linos, Katerina. 2013. *The Democratic Foundations of Policy Diffusion: How Health, Family and Employment Laws Spread Across Countries*. Oxford: Oxford University Press.

Lv, Jun, Su Meng, Zhiheng Hong, Ting Zhang, Xuemei Huang, Bo Wang, and Liming Li. 2011. "Implementation of the WHO Framework Convention on Tobacco Control in mainland China." *BMJ Tobacco Control*, 1–6. http://doi:10.1136/tc.2010.040352.

Martin, Andrew. 2014. "The Chinese Government is Getting Rich Selling Cigarettes." *Bloomberg Businessweek*, December 12, 2014. www.bloomberg.com/news/articles/2014-12-12/the-chinese-government-is-getting-rich-selling-cigarettes#p1.

McNeill, A. et al. 2018. *Evidence Review of E-cigarettes and Heated Tobacco Products 2018: A Report Commissioned by Public Health England*. London: Public Health England.

Mincer, Jilian. 2015. "E-cigarette Usage Surges in Past Year: Reuters/Ipsos Poll." *Reuters*, June 10, 2015. www.reuters.com/article/us-usa-ecigarette-poll-analysis/e-cigarette-usage-surges-in-past-year-reuters-ipsos-poll-idUSKBN0OQ0CA20150610.

Mistic E Cigs. 2015. "What Does VTM Mean?" December 4, 2015. http://blog.mistice cigs.com/what-does-vtm-mean.

NACS. 2013. "E-Cigarette Sales to Exceed Traditional Cigarettes by 2021." September 17, 2013. www.convenience.org/Media/Daily/Pages/ND0917134.aspx#.WnIVkainF3g.

National Academies of Sciences, Engineering, and Medicine. 2018. *Public Health Consequences of E-Cigarettes*. Washington, DC: The National Academies Press. https://doi.org/10.17226/24952.

National Institute on Drug Abuse. 2017. "Electronic Cigarettes (E-cigarettes)." *Drug Facts.* Last modified June 2017. www.drugabuse.gov/publications/drugfacts/electronic-cigarettes-e-cigarettes.

People. 2014. "E-cigarette Experience Two Days of Ice." September 2, 2014. http://scitech.people.com.cn/n/2014/0902/c1007-25585378.html.

Rabin, Robert L. 1991–1992. "A Sociolegal History of the Tobacco Tort Litigation." *Stanford Law Review* 44: 853–78.

Rabin, Robert L. 2001. "The Tobacco Litigation: A Tentative Assessment." *DePaul Law Review* 55 (2): 331–58.

Rothacher, Albrecht. 1989. *Japan's Agro-Food Sector: The Politics and Economics of Excess Protection*. London: MacMillan.

Scherer, F. M. 1997. "Competition Policy Convergence: Where Next?" *Empirica* 24 (1): 5–19.

Simmons, Beth A., Frank Dobbin, and Geoffrey Garrett. 2006. "Introduction: The International Diffusion of Liberalism." *International Organization* 60 (4): 781–810.

Slaughter, Anne-Marie. 2005. *A New World Order*. Princeton: Princeton University Press.

Smoking Everywhere, Inc. v. Food & Drug Admin., 680 F. Supp. 2d 62 (D.D.C. 2010).

Solomon, Brian. 2014. "Reynolds, Lorillard Dump Blu E-Cigarettes in $27 Billion Merger." *Forbes*, July 15, 2014. www.forbes.com/sites/briansolomon/2014/07/15/reynolds-lorillard-dump-blu-e-cigarettes-in-27-billion-merger/#2975be341699.

Stolberg, Sheryl Gay. 2013. "Judge Has Record of Wrestling with Thorny Issues, and the U.S. Government." *New York Times*, December 16, 2013. www.nytimes.com/2013/12/17/us/politics/judge-has-never-let-presidents-off-easy-on-pornography-terrorism-or-surveillance.html?_r=1

The Economist Intelligence Unit. 2015. "The Shifting Landscape of Healthcare in Asia-Pacific: A Look at Australia, China, India, Japan, and South Korea," *The Economist*. www.eiuperspectives.economist.com/sites/default/files/The%20shifting%20landscape%20of%20healthcare%20in%20Asia-Pacific_Oct%205_0.pdf.

Tobacco Control. 2013. "The Tobacco Endgame." *BMJ Tobacco Control* 22 (May): i1-i60.

United States Department of Health, Education, and Welfare. 1964. *Smoking and Health: Report of the Advisory Committee of the Surgeon General of the Public Health Service*. Washington DC: U.S. Government Printing Office.

United States Food and Drug Administration. 2011. "Letter to Stakeholders: Regulation of E-Cigarettes and Other Tobacco Products." April 25, 2011.

United States Food and Drug Administration. 2014. "Deeming Tobacco Products to be Subject to the Federal Food, Drug, and Cosmetic Act, as Amended by the Family Smoking Prevention and Tobacco Control Act (Proposed Rule)." 79 Fed. Reg. 23141 (April 25, 2014).

United States Food and Drug Administration. 2017. "Vaporizers, E-Cigarettes, and Other Electronic Nicotine Delivery Systems (ENDS)." Last modified December 20, 2017. www.fda.gov/TobaccoProducts/Labeling/ProductsIngredientsComponents/ucm456610.htm.

United States Food and Drug Administration. 2018. "Family Smoking Prevention and Tobacco Control Act: An Overview." Last modified January 17, 2018. www.fda.gov/TobaccoProducts/Labeling/RulesRegulationsGuidance/ucm246129.htm.

United States Food and Drug Administration. 2018. "Milestones in U.S. Food and Drug Law History." Last modified January 3, 2018. www.fda.gov/aboutfda/whatwedo/history/forgshistory/evolvingpowers/ucm2007256.htm.

United Nations. 2003. WHO Framework Convention on Tobacco Control. May 21, 2003. https://treaties.un.org/pages/ViewDetails.aspx?src=TREATY&mtdsg_no=IX-4&chapter=9&lang=en.

USDA and FAS. 2000. "China Tobacco and Tobacco Products Update 2000." *GAIN Report* #CH0044, Dec. 11, 2000.

World Health Organization. n.d. "Details on Focal Point for Tobacco Control, Tobacco Control Unit and National Coordinating Mechanism for Tobacco Control. World Health Organization." Accessed February 2, 2018. http://apps.who.int/fctc/implementation/database/sites/implementation/scripts/src/tabulardata.php?indicator=5214&region=6.

World Intellectual Property Organization. n.d. "Other IP Treaties." Accessed January 24, 2018. www.wipo.int/wipolex/en/other_treaties/parties.jsp?treaty_id=231&group_id=22.

World Trade Organization. n.d. "Trade Profiles." http://stat.wto.org/CountryProfile/WSDBCountryPFHome.aspx?Language=E.

World Trade Organization. n.d. "Understanding the WTO: The Organization Members and Observers." Accessed January 24, 2018. www.wto.org/english/thewto_e/whatis_e/tif_e/org6_e.htm.

6

Japanese Court Reform on Trial

David T. Johnson and Setsuo Miyazawa

Court reform is on trial in Japan and two things can be said about the verdict: it will take at least several more years to make a sound assessment of the recent changes, and when the conclusion comes, it will be a hung jury, because different people expect different things from the reforms – and they are not compatible. As Malcolm Feeley observed in the Preface to his seminal analysis of court reform in the United States:

> One of the central problems of the courts is that there is no agreement on what constitutes acceptable practice and hence no agreement on what improvements should be made. Practices that are regarded by some as signs of decline may, when seen through someone else's eyes, be seen as strengths (Feeley 1983, xii).

The scope of court reform in Japan has been broad. Over the past two decades it has included the creation of lay judge panels to adjudicate serious criminal cases, and many other changes in the criminal process that have been stimulated by this reform: civil court reforms to reduce the duration of civil trials, the establishment of a specialized High Court for handling intellectual property cases, the expansion of alternative dispute resolution programs, heightened transparency in making judicial appointments and evaluating judges, and changes in legal education aimed at reshaping the legal profession by introducing postgraduate professional law schools along with increasing the number of new lawyers admitted to the bar.

This chapter focuses on the first and last of these reforms, because they are the most consequential for law and society in Japan. Section 6.1 describes the introduction of lay judges in Japan's criminal justice system, the reasons for this reform, and the changes it has and has not stimulated. Section 6.2 summarizes reforms in Japanese legal education, the reasons for the reforms, and the resultant changes and continuities in Japan's legal system. Overall, there have been some significant changes in Japanese criminal justice and legal education, but much of Japan's old legal system remains intact. Our conclusion suggests that there is a clash of opinions in Japan about whether these reforms are succeeding. If Feeley is right – if strengths and weaknesses depend on the eye of the beholder – then we should expect the clash to continue for many years to come.

6.1 CRIMINAL COURT REFORM

Both the lay judge reform and the reform of legal education were introduced on the basis of recommendations presented by the Justice System Reform Council (JSRC) to Japan's central government in 2001. After World War II, there were various efforts to reform Japan's justice system, but there was little opportunity for such efforts to succeed because the Ministry of Justice, the Supreme Court, and the Japan Federation of Bar Associations (JFBA) frequently disagreed on fundamental issues, and because there had been little demand for reform from interest groups with influence on the Liberal Democratic Party (LDP), which had controlled Japan's government since its founding in 1955. This gridlock came undone in 1998, when the influential *Keidanren* (Japan Business Federation) presented the LDP with a proposal for comprehensive justice system reform. *Keidanren* pushed for this package of reforms because it thought business needed a more responsive court system and a legal profession that could handle business-related cases in lieu of the protection by administrative agencies that had declined due to deregulation. *Keidanren*'s pressure prompted the LDP to put justice system reform on the national agenda, and previously unsuccessful reformers joined forces to take advantage of this extraordinary political opportunity. In 1999, Japan's central government established the JSRC directly under the Cabinet (law-related councils in the past had typically been formed under the Ministry of Justice). The JSRC was mandated to discuss public participation in the administration of the justice system and an expansion of public access to legal services. Various interest groups lobbied to preserve the status quo, and many items in the JSRC's final recommendations in 2001 reflected compromise,[1] including public participation in the administration of justice and legal education reform. After the JSRC shut down in 2001, implementation of its recommendations was turned over to a traditional policy-making process that was led by the Ministry of Justice (Miyazawa 2007), and there was a lag of several years between the enabling legislation for these reforms and their actual advent.

In 2009, Japan began a new trial system in which six lay persons sit with three professional judges to adjudicate guilt and determine sentence in serious criminal cases. This lay judge system (*saiban-in seido*) places citizen participation at the center of Japanese criminal trials – and criminal justice – for the first time since 1943, when Japan's original Jury Act was suspended after fifteen years of fitful use (only 484 jury trials were held in the fifteen years before suspension). At a time when adversarial trials in America are declining and perhaps even dying (Burns 2009), Japan has

---

[1] The JSRC's 2001 recommendations can be found at http://japan.kantei.go.jp/policy/sihou/singikai/990612_e.html.

implemented a trial reform that is so fundamental it could remake the country's criminal justice system in the years to come.

But improvement in Japanese criminal justice is far from guaranteed. For one thing, this new form of civilian participation might be marginalized by Japanese legal professionals – prosecutors and judges especially – who aim to maintain their standard operating procedures. This – "marginalization into obscurity and capture by legal experts" – has happened several times in the Japanese past when citizen participation was made a more central part of the country's criminal process (Anderson and Nolan 2004, 970).

6.1.1 *The Lay Judge Reform*

Japan's Lay Judge Law was passed in 2004, five years before it took effect. The Law states that lay judge panels shall hear two types of cases: those involving crimes that are punishable by death, by imprisonment for an indefinite period, or by imprisonment with hard labor; and those in which the victim has died due to an intentional criminal act. The lay judge reform is important even though it has a limited scope. Since it took effect in 2009, approximately 97 percent of all criminal trials continue to be heard by a single professional judge or by a panel of three professional judges, but because lay judge panels try the most serious criminal cases (including homicide), and because other reforms the lay judge reform has stimulated (see below) shape the legal process in all criminal cases, the 2009 change is widely considered the most fundamental shift in Japan's criminal process in more than half a century.

The Lay Judge Law provides for two types of trial: by a panel of three judges and six lay judges, or by a panel of one judge and four lay judges. The large panels are the default option, and the small ones may be deployed when factual issues are undisputed and when prosecutors, defense lawyers, and defendants do not object to its use. In the first five years of the lay judge system (May 2009 – May 2014), the small panels were never used, despite rates of confession for defendants that exceeded 90 percent for all criminal cases and 60 percent for lay judge cases. Concerns about efficiency have long been important in Japan's judiciary (Ramseyer and Rasmusen 2003). Since the advent of this new trial system, there has been much public and media pressure to protect citizens who serve as lay judges from undue physical, psychological, and social "burdens" (*futan*). In this light, the nonuse of the smaller lay judge panels presents something of a puzzle. In our view, the avoidance of small panels seems to reflect the desire of professional judges to maintain control over trial proceedings and outcomes by sitting in judgment with two of their peers.

The Lay Judge Law stipulates that judges and lay judges must reach a verdict based on their recognition of the facts and application of the relevant laws. If they decide to convict they then sentence accordingly. Only professional judges are authorized to interpret the law and make decisions on litigation procedure, though lay judges are allowed to comment on legal issues. Lay judges may also question witnesses, victims, and defendants during trial, but during and after trial they must not reveal information from their deliberations (Article 70). Citizens who leak a deliberation secret or "other secrets learned" while serving as a lay judge are subject to a fine of up to ¥500,000 ($4,200) or imprisonment for up to six months. Former lay judges are also barred from disclosing what they believed the sentence should have been or what facts should have been found, and they may not even state whether they agreed or disagreed with the sentence imposed or the facts found by the court. This "duty of secrecy" (*shuhi gimu*) has been the subject of serious debate in Japan, with some people – including citizens who have served as lay judges – arguing that it is onerous and should be abolished or relaxed. Whatever its propriety, one function of this duty of secrecy is to prevent society from learning how decisions at criminal trials get made, thereby protecting professional judges from scrutiny and criticism (Levin and Tice 2009).

Consensus is not required in lay judge trials. Instead, decisions are based on the majority opinion of the members of the panel, so verdicts and sentencing decisions – including decisions to impose a sentence of death – can be made by a vote of 5–4, provided that at least one professional judge and one lay judge share the majority view. Thus, this "mixed majority rule" gives professional judges a veto over the lay judges by precluding the possibility of a five- or six-person majority that is not joined by at least one professional judge.

6.1.2 Why Reform?

The most important conclusion in John Langbein's trenchant comparison of the parallels between torture and plea bargaining is that "a legal system will do almost anything, tolerate almost anything, before it will admit the need for reform in its system of proof and trial" (1978, 19). There are two reasons for this resistance. The first is practical: "nothing is quite so imbedded in a legal system as the procedures for proof and trial" (Langbein 1978, 19). Since "every institution of the legal system is geared to the system of truth," reform disturbs "virtually every vested interest" (Langbein 1978, 19). The second reason for resistance to trial reform is ideological. Criminal adjudication intrudes deeply into the lives of affected citizens. The power to adjudicate must therefore rest on a theoretical basis that is "palatable to the populace," and the theory of proof that purports to explain the power to make criminal judgments must play "a central role in legitimating the entire legal system" (Langbein 1978, 20).

Viewed through Langbein's lens, the first puzzle about Japan's lay judge reform is how it occurred at all. Japan has not only admitted "the need for reform in its system of proof and trial," it has implemented fundamental changes in who presides at criminal trial and how proof is taken. This puzzle deepens further when one recognizes Feeley's insight that the central obstacle to change in courts is often not resistance to reform per se, but rather something even deeper: "the lack of interest in even thinking about change" (Feeley 1983, 192). Before Japan's lay judge reform, the most powerful actors in Japanese criminal justice – police and prosecutors – had little interest in thinking about changing a system of proof that conferred on them extraordinary powers to "make crime" (Miyazawa 1992, 11) and that enabled them to produce high clearance and conviction rates (Johnson 2002, 35, 215). How, then, did this reform happen?

Japan's lay judge reform was part of a much larger movement for "justice system reform" (*shiho kaikaku undo*) that aimed to generate "huge" and "extensive" changes in "all aspects of Japan's justice system" (Anderson and Johnson 2010, 372). Two principle reasons were given to justify the creation of greater lay participation in Japan's criminal justice system. The first was the claim that lay participation would produce better criminal justice by ensuring that verdicts and sentences reflect citizens' experiences and common sense. Problems in Japanese criminal justice, such as the length, intensity, and intrusiveness of interrogations, procedural rules that favor state interests while providing few formal protections for suspects and defendants, and a paucity of transparency and accountability throughout the criminal process also motivated the push for some form of lay participation. The second justification for the lay judge reform was the perception that civilian participation in criminal trials would promote the development of Japanese democracy by making the legal system more responsive to society's needs and by increasing the legitimacy of criminal court decisions.

In short, Japan's lay judge reform was not driven by "dramatic events" of the kind that stimulated many of the court reforms in America studied by Feeley (1983, 192). Rather, criminal adjudication in Japan changed because of a broad push to "expand the rule of law" in Japanese society (Saegusa 2009). In this sense, Japan's lay judge reform rode a much larger wave of "path-breaking change" that departed from the more "gradualist" approach to reform that had characterized the country in previous decades (Foote 2008, 1). The salience of "justice system reform" in Japanese political circles resulted in the creation of reform commissions and advisory committees that were not dominated by the branches of the legal profession – procuracy, judiciary, and bar – that had curtailed efforts at reform on many previous occasions. The key reform committees and commissions included members from outside the institutions that have traditionally resisted reform. Once it became clear that reform would be debated by a wide range of constituencies, "the door was opened for wide-reaching reforms" that included lay participation (Foote 2008, 10). Eventually, prosecutors and judges came to see some form of lay participation as inevitable, and they tried to avoid the outcome that they believed would be worst for them: a pure jury system. After considerable conflict about what shape Japan's new criminal courts should take, the lay judge system that emerged was a compromise between the more liberal position taken by the bar (in favor of a pure jury system) and the more conservative stances of the procuracy and the judiciary (which favored mixed tribunals).

"Rationality" is often the major means for "making democracy work" in modern societies (Putnam 1993), but when it comes to reform, what counts as "rational" depends on context – and the most critical context of rationality is *power* (Flyvbjerg 1998). In Japan's justice system reform movement, the power of conservative forces frequently blurred the dividing line between rationality and rationalization by ensuring that some subjects that should have been reform imperatives were left off the agenda for change. Most notably, the police are missing in Japan's justice system reform movement – and for no principled reason. Japanese police are powerful (Miyazawa 1992), they misuse their power (Johnson 2015), and they are neither transparent nor accountable to external organs of authority (Miyazawa 1992). In these respects, police constitute the primary impediment to the "rule of law" that was aspired to in Japan's justice system reform movement. It would have been rational to place police at the center of Japan's criminal justice reforms, but that did not happen because police did not want it to. Police and their allies were able to limit the scope of the political process to consideration of those issues that seemed (mostly) innocuous to them (Bachrach and Baratz 1962). They thereby succeeded in keeping critical questions about their power, performance, and accountability excluded from reform discussions. The Japanese police's success at agenda-setting illustrates the truth that power has the capacity to define "reality" by producing knowledge that is conducive to the policies it wants to pursue, and by suppressing knowledge for which it has no use (Johnson 2004).

6.1.3 Change

How has Japan's lay judge system performed so far, and how is it influencing the country's criminal processes and outcomes? There have been changes in law and in practice.

We begin by describing four legal changes that were stimulated by the trial reform and that have shaped how defendants are processed in lay judge and non-lay judge cases. First, in anticipation of the new trial system, a new system of public defense for criminal suspects started operating in 2006, which increased access to defense counsel considerably. Second, a formal pretrial process was created and defendants' discovery rights were expanded. The main purpose of these reforms, like the main purpose of the new system of public defense, is to invigorate criminal defense and thereby shift the chief locus of decision making away from police and prosecutors, who have long dominated Japan's criminal process, and toward the criminal trial. Third, lay judge trials proceed continuously so as not to inconvenience the citizen participants, whereas trials before professional judges proceed at a pace of about one session every month or so, leading to verdicts that come months or even years after the trial started. Fourth, several laws have been passed to encourage greater victim participation in Japan's criminal process (Saeki 2010). In particular, victims and survivors are now permitted to sit next to prosecutors in the courtroom and to state their sentencing requests to the court at the trial's conclusion. These changes give victims more voice and respect in some criminal proceedings, but they also seem to make the trial mood more emotional and trial outcomes more retributive.

Several other changes in practice have occurred as side effects of these formal changes in law. In the long run, the changes to "law in action" may be more influential than the changes to "law on the books."

The first change in practice concerns criminal interrogation. The extreme reliance on confessions in Japan sometimes motivates extreme methods to obtain them, from plea bargaining (which is illegal in Japan) to "third degree" tactics and the composition of police and prosecutor "essays" which fail to accurately represent the statements made by suspects during interrogation. Police and prosecutor resistance to recording has been strong, but because lay judges need information about how confessions are obtained, the door to the most closed and secretive space in Japanese criminal justice is slowly being pried open. Police and prosecutors have started to record some interrogations in some cases, and the future seems likely to bring more transparency still.

Defendants are also being released on bail more often since the lay judge reform took effect. The main mechanism of this change appears to be changing judicial sensibilities about the importance of adversarial contestation in open court and the need to respect the premise that defendants should be allowed to participate in preparing their own defense. Lay judge trials have also become less reliant on dossiers and more aligned with the principles of "trial-centeredness" and "directness" that were largely dormant in Japan's postwar legal culture. For researchers and other trial watchers, one result is that some criminal trials are no longer the tedious, paper-pushing affairs they used to be.

To some observers, the most fundamental change in Japanese criminal justice is in the "mindset" of professional judges (Shinomiya 2013). Invigorating Japan's judiciary requires more than merely adding lay judges to the criminal process. The passivity of judges towards prosecutors must also be addressed – and this is primarily a cultural challenge (Foote 2010). One step towards that end is fostering public discussions about the role that judges *should* play in Japanese criminal justice (Mori 2013; Segi 2014). This seems to be happening, albeit on a scale that is difficult to discern. The main reason for this change in judicial sensibilities appears to be the presence of lay judges. In law as in life, the fresh eyes of the amateur are important because frequently the more one looks at a thing, the less one sees it. Some professional judges report that the fresh perspectives of lay judges have enabled them to stop seeing the courtroom as their own "familiar workshop," and to start seeing more of the humanity of the defendants in the dock and the persons they have victimized (Chesterton 1909).

These changes in judicial mindset are significant, but they are being at least partially offset by changes in prosecutors' practices. Most notably, prosecutors have become more cautious about what crimes to charge and sentences to seek. In the years leading up to the lay judge reform, more than 500 mock lay judge trials were held, as were several surveys of citizens conducted by the Ministry of Justice. Through these means, prosecutors tried to discern how citizens' evaluations of evidence would differ from the evaluations made by professional judges. They concluded that lay judges would be more skeptical of the state's case for conviction, and so adjusted their charging policies in two main ways: by deciding not to charge many suspects who would have been charged in the prereform period, and by reducing the severity of charges for many of the suspects whom they did decide to charge. These changes in charging policy began before lay judge trials started in 2009 and have continued thereafter (Takeda 2014). Critics contend that by becoming more cautious in their charging policies prosecutors are undermining the lay judge reform which aims to give ordinary citizens more influence in the criminal process (Takano 2009). But more cautious charging policies also mean less use of the criminal sanction. For progressives who believe in "the limits of the criminal sanction" (Packer 1968) and fear its capacity to do harm, this could be considered a welcome development.

6.1.4 Continuity

Japan's lay judge reform has stimulated change in formal rules and standard operating procedures in many parts of the criminal process. The net effect might be a shift in the balance of power in Japanese criminal justice – a balance that long has favored law enforcement's interest in obtaining confessions and convictions (Feeley and Miyazawa 2002). But there are also striking continuities before and after Japan's lay judge reform, especially in case outcomes. If the proof is *only* in the pudding, then it could be said that the advent of the lay judge system has not changed much in Japanese criminal justice. Three continuities are especially significant, in conviction rates, sentencing patterns, and capital punishment.

The first continuity concerns Japan's high conviction rate (Johnson 2002, 214–42). In the three years before the lay judge reform took effect (2006–2008), 7,287 defendants who would have been tried by lay judges in the new system were tried solely by professional judges, and 7,243 of them were convicted, for a baseline conviction rate of 99.4 percent. By comparison, in the first five years after the lay judge reform took effect (May 2009 to May 2014), 6,538 defendants were tried by lay judge panels, and 6,504 of them were convicted, for a conviction rate of 99.5 percent (Takeda 2014, 139). Before the lay judge reform, one defendant in every 166 was acquitted, while after the proportion was one in 192. In the main crime category where the conviction rate has declined since 2009 – trafficking methamphetamines – there were sixteen acquittals in the first five years of the lay judge system (almost half the total of thirty-four acquittals), but in several of them prosecutors obtained convictions on appeal. The main reason for the maintenance of Japan's high conviction rate (despite the presence of lay participants who have been known to issue more acquittals than professional judges do in both modern America and in prewar Japan) is prosecutors' shift toward a more cautious charging policy (Takeda, 2014). As suggested above, this conservatism produces parsimony in the use of criminal punishment, which may be welcomed by those who believe the criminal sanction is a "prime threatener of human freedom" (Packer 1968, 366). But this conservative charging policy also sacrifices victims on the altar of the high conviction rate, suppresses the supply of skilled defense lawyering (who wants to do criminal defense when the chance of success is so slim?), and denies the public the extra deterrence that more aggressive charging policies could generate (Johnson 2002, 237–42).

The second continuity is in criminal sentencing. Sentence severity under the lay judge system has increased for rape, sexual molestation, and assault with injury, but the heightened harshness is modest. For other crimes such as homicide, robbery, arson, and trafficking methamphetamines, Japan's prereform and postreform sentencing patterns are so similar that when sentencing averages over time are plotted on the same page, they look almost indistinguishable (Supreme Court of Japan 2012, 83–90). On the whole, there is much more continuity than change in criminal sentencing in the lay judge system, and the main cause of this continuity is again the conservatism of Japan's legal professionals – judges especially. Japan's judiciary lobbied to establish a lay judge trial policy of relying on sentencing norms based on prereform practices. And when deviations from preexisting sentencing norms have occurred in the new system, Japan's appellate courts revise them, usually in a downward direction. This commitment to continuity in sentencing serves the value of consistency in Japanese criminal justice (Johnson 2002, 147), but conservatism in sentencing can also be criticized, for what is the point of empowering citizens to judge if their preferences must conform to those of professional judges?

The third continuity in outcome concerns capital punishment. Before the lay judge reform, panels of three professional judges imposed a sentence of death about two-thirds of the time that prosecutors sought one. Many advocates of this reform expected that citizen participation in sentencing would make criminal courts less likely to impose the ultimate punishment. But that has not happened. In the first three and a half years after the lay judge reform, lay judge panels imposed a sentence of death fifteen of the twenty-one times that prosecutors asked for one. This death sentencing rate of 71 percent is about the same as the rate (66 percent) that prevailed before the reform took effect (Yomiuri Shimbun Shakaibu 2013, 274). But here, too, however, there is complexity, for the propensity to employ capital punishment cannot be measured merely by what happens in criminal court. In Japan as in the United States, the most important determinant of whether a murderer gets condemned to death is the prosecutor's decision about whether to seek a capital sentence in the first place. In Japan, the lay judge system has prompted prosecutors to become more cautious about seeking sentences of death. The probability of obtaining a capital sentence has not changed much in the new trial system, but the probability of prosecutors asking for one has declined by at least one-third (Shikei Haishi Nempo 2013). Here, too, the adaptions of legal professionals to the new trial system have not pushed Japanese criminal justice toward more severe punishment.

In the United States, jury trials have been called the institution "best designed to achieve truth-for-practical judgment" (Burns 1999, 235). Although this view is contested (Langbein 1978), many analysts praise the American jury both for what it does and for what it says about American society (Kalven and Zeisel 1966; Abramson 1994; Vidmar and Hans 2007; Burns 2009). In Japan, too, there is room to celebrate some of the changes in law and practice that the lay judge reform has generated, but the verdict about whether criminal court reform is succeeding is hardly clear-cut. The more things have changed in Japanese criminal justice (interrogation, bail, discovery, defense lawyering), the more they are staying the same (conviction rates, criminal sentencing, and capital punishment). We see similar signs of complexity in the reform of Japanese legal education.

6.2 LEGAL EDUCATION REFORM

In 2004, seventy-two Japanese universities opened the doors of their professional law schools to their first cohort of students. It was the first time that Japan introduced postgraduate institutions designed to train future legal professionals: judges, prosecutors, and attorneys. The following year, two more universities opened law schools, bringing the total number of law students to 5,825. Until these reforms, legal education in Japan was almost exclusively confined to undergraduate programs, with the exception of a handful of graduate programs designed to train academics. Japan's legal education system had survived without professional law schools because the bar examination did not require completion of any university education. Hence, no undergraduate legal education was required to sit for the exam. Moreover, law courses were never considered to be for professional legal education, and so could be taken during undergraduate study. Under the new system, legal education is considered the core of the legal profession and aspiring legal professionals are required to study and train in law schools. Law schools were intended to be the center of a process that combines university legal education, the bar exam administered by the Ministry of Justice, and an apprenticeship in the Legal Training and Research Institute (LTRI) managed by the Supreme Court. In principle, every person who wishes to participate in a legal capacity in a Japanese court must complete law school and sit for the bar exam.

6.2.1 Why Reform?

The reformers who proposed postgraduate professional law schools intended to increase the number of legal professionals while simultaneously improving their quality (Miyazawa 2007, 45–74; Miyazawa et al. 2008; Miyazawa 2013, 336–37; Foote 2013). Under the old system, those who passed the bar examination were required to have an apprenticeship under the LTRI, initially for two years, and more recently for one and a half years. Apprentices received a stipend from the government and the number of seats in the apprenticeship was regulated. In practice, the old bar examination operated as an entrance examination to the LTRI, and since the old bar exam did not require completion of any university legal education, the old system depended totally on the competitiveness of the bar examination to ensure the quality of legal professionals. Such a system produced an extremely competitive bar examination. Only about 2 percent of test takers passed the exam, resulting in roughly 500 new attorneys a year until around 1990. In that year, the total number of practicing attorneys in Japan was approximately 13,000 – the smallest number of attorneys per capita among all developed countries.

Those who proposed the introduction of postgraduate professional law schools criticized the old system for its failure to produce a sufficiently large number of legal professionals to improve public access to legal services. They also criticized the old system for its failure to produce legal professionals with the broad intellectual background required for contemporary legal services. Critics of the old system argued that applicants to the old bar exam only studied the subjects included in the exam at cram schools. As a result, it was difficult to attract people to the legal profession who had a broad intellectual background or meaningful real-life experiences. Critics argued that the nature of the old bar exam produced legal professionals who have intellectually narrow and shallow backgrounds. To address these concerns, a movement appeared among legal scholars and practitioners to change the legal education system. The movement introduced postgraduate professional law schools where students who have already studied other academic fields or who have had meaningful life experiences can be accepted to the newly created law schools, so that a higher quality of legal professionals can be attained. Such a shift was also intended to broaden the scope of backgrounds and to diversify the legal profession.

When the Justice System Reform Council (JSRC) was established by the government in 1999, it defined the reform of legal education as its first priority. A consensus was quickly formed to introduce some system of postgraduate professional law schools, but details were hotly debated among its members and various interest groups. The cram school industry and people who wanted to maintain undergraduate law faculties, the competitive bar examination, and the LTRI lobbied most intensely. The result was a combination of broad vision and compromise in the final recommendations of 2001.

The broad vision was not problematic for people who took a progressive position on legal education reform. Regarding the size of the legal profession, the JSRC recommended that "the aim should be 3000 successful candidates for the new national bar examination in about 2010," and "the number of legal professionals actively practicing is expected to reach 50,000" (JSRC 2001, chapter 3.1.1).[2] Regarding legal education reform, the JSRC recommended that "[a] new legal training system should be established . . . by organically connecting legal education, the national bar examination and legal training as a 'process.' As its core, law schools, defined as professional schools providing education especially for training for the legal profession, should be established," and "[l]aw schools should be established, with the aim of starting to accept students as of April 2004" (JSRC 2001, chapter 3.2.1).

But from the perspective of progressive reformers there were problems in the details. For instance, while progressive reformers wanted to clearly separate new law schools from old undergraduate law faculties in order to increase the number of legal professionals with nonlaw backgrounds, the JSRC recommended that "[t]he standard training term should be three years, and completion in two years as a shortened term should be recognized" (JSRC 2001, chapter 3.2.2(2)), with two-year programs being mainly expected to attract graduates of undergraduate law faculties. And while progressive reformers proposed replacing the LTRI with clinical programs at law schools, the JSRC recommended retaining the LTRI and created a possibility that "[l]aw schools should provide education so that a sufficient ratio of the students who have completed the course (e.g. 70 to 80 percent of such students) can pass the new national bar examination" (JSRC 2001, chapter 3.2.2(2)). But the JSRC failed to require the Ministry of Justice (which would keep its jurisdiction over the bar examination) to administer the exam in a way that would match the expectations of the new law schools. Most problematically, the JSRC proposed that "[p]roper routes for obtaining the qualification of legal professional should be secured for those who have *not* gone through law schools for reasons such as financial difficulty or because they have sufficient practical experience in the real world" (JSRC 2001, chapter 3.2.3). This proposal was widely understood as a measure to appease those opponents of legal education reform who wanted to maintain the old bar exam.

Once the JSRC was closed in 2001, the traditional policy-making process returned whereby prosecutors, judges, and other bureaucrats drafted laws to implement the JSRC's recommendations, thereby exacerbating their problematic elements. The most serious problem was the introduction of a preliminary examination, which would allow its passers to take the bar examination without graduating from a law school. The Ministry of Justice argued that it would be impossible to introduce limitations on eligibility to sit for the bar, and pushed to create an end run around the legal education reform through the creation of a preliminary examination without any limitations.

---

[2] Parenthetical citations reference the Justice System Reform Council's 2001 Recommendations Report by chapter, part, section, and (if applicable) subsection.

6.2.2 Change and Continuity

Japan's new law schools have produced a variety of positive results. Since no professional legal education existed in Japanese universities, the introduction of legal education clearly defined as *professional* was itself a major achievement. At present, legal practitioners play a crucial role in shaping university legal education for the first time in Japanese history. As a result, new fields (such as professional responsibility) and new methods of instruction (such as Socratic dialogue and clinical education) have been introduced. Graduates of nonlaw faculties and students with work experience have also been admitted to the new law schools. Law schools have also been established outside the major metropolitan areas, and some law schools have introduced evening programs, so that more students have opportunity to become legal professionals.

With the advent of law schools, there has been a rapid increase in the number of legal professionals too, particularly practicing attorneys. In 1990, there was one attorney for every 8,957 people in Japan. In 2014, there was one attorney for every 3,632 people, and the increase was greatest outside large metropolitan areas. In Tokyo, for example, there was one attorney for every 820 people in 2014, compared with one attorney for every 1,878 people in 1990, whereas in rural Iwate prefecture, there was one attorney for every 13,081 people in 2014 compared with one for every 42,939 people in 1990. Some scholars even argue that making it easier to pass the bar exam by increasing the number of passers has attracted more qualified people to the legal profession (Ramseyer and Rasmusen 2015).[3]

Although all of these results were produced in a fairly short period after the introduction of new law schools in 2004, the law school system has also been facing a rapidly worsening crisis since its inception. In fact, as early as the fall of 2004, it was reported that the Ministry of Justice had no intention to realize a bar passage rate of 70 to 80 percent or to produce 3,000 new legal professions by 2010. The total number of applicants to law schools was 72,800 in 2004, but it fell to 41,756 in 2005 and continued to decline thereafter. In 2015, only 10,370 people applied to law schools – just one-seventh the number for 2004. This sharp decline is largely the result of low bar exam pass rates. The first bar exam was administered to the first cohort of graduates of the new two-year program in 2006, and 1,009 applicants passed, for a pass rate of only 48.2 percent. At its peak in 2012, the number of passers reached only 2,102 – far short of the goal of 3,000. By 2014, the bar passage rate had dropped to 23.1 percent.

In the meantime, the preliminary examination was introduced in 2011 and was passed by 116 applicants, for a pass rate of 1.8 percent. These applicants went on to take the final bar exam for the first time in 2012, and 68.2 percent of them passed. That pass rate is

---

[3] The number of applicants to the bar exam peaked at 8,763 in 2011 and then started to decline, raising the possibility that the pool of talent for the legal profession could start to shrink if the bar passage rate remains around the present rate of less than one in four.

higher than the pass rates of even the top law schools. The preliminary examination rapidly grew in popularity, attracting 12,543 applicants in 2015, which was larger than the total number of applicants to all law schools in the same year. The characteristics of the individuals who passed the preliminary exam are also problematic. In 2014, 46 percent were law school students, 32 percent were undergraduate law students, 10 percent were unemployed, and only 8 percent were civil servants or company employees. In other words, most of the preliminary exam passers did not fit the expected profile used by the JSRC to justify its recommendation for creating the preliminary exam in the first place. Many observers fear that a further increase in the number preliminary exam passers will so discourage students of top universities from applying to a law school that the new education system will eventually collapse.

At the same time, the Bar has intensified its lobbying efforts to reduce the number of passers of the bar examination. To support this position, the Bar uses statistics showing a decline in the average number of civil litigations per lawyer per year and an increase in the proportion of attorneys who earn small incomes. The Japan Federation of Bar Associations has been proposing to reduce the number of passers to 1,500 a year, and some local bar associations even demand a reduction to 1,000. As a result, the central government decided in 2015 to withdraw the target of producing 3,000 passers a year and instead proposed to produce "at least" 1,500 passers a year.

From the perspective of the new law schools, the best solution to this crisis is to increase the number of passers and the pass rate. But because this is politically impossible, the Ministry of Education, Culture, Sports, Science and Technology has been reducing or withdrawing its financial aid to low-performing law schools in order to increase the bar passage rate by reducing the number of applicants. This means that small law schools outside major metropolitan areas are more likely to be closed. It also means that law schools with more conservative curriculum (emphasizing bar exam courses) are more likely to survive than are those law schools with progressive curriculums that include clinical and international programs. As of January 2016, thirty out of the original seventy-four law schools have either closed their doors or decided to stop admitting students, and more are expected to follow.

In sum, Japan's new law school system has produced significant changes both inside the classroom and outside it, but the schools are facing major obstacles created by the continuation of elements of the old system. In the end, the bar's opposition to an increase in the number of practicing attorneys and the Ministry of Justice's policy of maintaining the competitive bar exam while introducing a preliminary exam without limitations on eligibility may well be a lethal one-two punch that results in the demise of the most ambitious reform of legal education in Japanese history.

CONCLUSION

In *Court Reform on Trial*, Malcolm Feeley concluded that the process of change in criminal courts "often leads to mixed and confusing results" (1983, 35), and he observed that "the more rigorous an evaluation [of court reform] is, the more likely it is to sound inconclusive" (1983, 203). The complexity we have described in the consequences of court reform in Japan is a testament to Feeley's capacity to depict "the nature of criminal courts" (1983, xiv). In some respects that nature transcends national boundaries. Foremost among Feeley's insights is the observation that "courts should not be seen merely as bureaucratic organizations committed to clear and well-defined purposes – they should be understood as arenas in which a range of competing and conflicting interests collide and vie for attention" (Feeley 1983, 9–10). Competing interests and contrasting views are colliding in Japan, too. The lay judge reform has stimulated progressive change in many spheres of Japanese criminal justice, but it also has provoked renewed commitments to conservatism among prosecutors when it comes to charging cases and among judges when it comes to sentencing. Similarly, Japan's new system of professional law schools is producing graduates who are benefitting the public, but the Ministry of Justice's continued control of the bar examination and the bar's vested interests have produced such a serious crisis that the new system may well collapse.

It is too early to conclude what court reform in Japan ultimately means, and it is unrealistic to suppose that anything close to consensus will emerge about institutions and practices that are as deeply contested as the ones examined in this essay. The "hung jury" verdict that we anticipate in the ongoing trial of Japanese court reform comes from recognizing that many competing interests and expectations are colliding in Japanese society. Court reform in Japan has caused a complex mix of continuities and changes, and there is no one who celebrates them all. In Japanese law and society, as in social life generally, "values collide and often cannot be made to run in parallel," and efforts to pursue improvement are complicated by the fact that "some among the Great Goods cannot live together" (Berlin 1988). As Feeley observed in the conclusion to his fine book, "[t]here are no easy answers" (Feeley 1983, 224). But if the Japanese are fortunate, they, too, might be able to make "some halting and partial advances" (Feeley 1983, 224).

REFERENCES

Abramson, Jeffrey. 1994. *We, the Jury: The Jury System and the Ideal of Democracy*. New York: Basic Books.
Adler, Stephan J. 1994. *The Jury: Trial and Error in the American Courtroom*. New York: Times Books.
Anderson, Kent and David T. Johnson. 2010. "Japan's New Criminal Trials: Origins, Operations, and Implications." In *New Courts in Asia*, edited by Andrew Harding and Penelope (Pip) Nicholson, 371–90. London and New York: Routledge.
Anderson, Kent and Mark Nolan. 2004. "Lay Participation in the Japanese Justice System: A Few Preliminary Thoughts Regarding the Lay Assessor System (*saiban-in seido*) from Domestic Historical and International Psychological Perspectives." *Vanderbilt Journal of Transnational Law* 37 (4): 935–92.

Bachrach, Peter and Morton S. Baratz. 1962. "Two Faces of Power." *The American Political Science Review* 56: 947–52.
Berlin, Isaiah. 1988. "On the Pursuit of the Ideal." *New York Review of Books*. Vol. 35, No. 4 (March 17, 1988), www.nybooks.com/articles/archives/1988/mar/17/on-the-pursuit-of-the-ideal/.
Burns, Robert P. 1999. *A Theory of the Trial*. Princeton: Princeton University Press.
Burns, Robert P. 2009. *The Death of the American Trial*. Chicago and London: University of Chicago Press.
Chesterton, G. K. 1909 [2013]. "The Twelve Men," in *Tremendous Trifles*. CreateSpace Independent Publishing Platform.
Feeley, Malcolm. 1983. *Court Reform on Trial: Why Simple Solutions Fail*. New York: Basic Books.
Feeley, Malcolm and Setsuo Miyazawa, eds. 2002. *The Japanese Adversary System in Context: Controversies and Comparisons*. New York: Palgrave Macmillan.
Flyvbjerg, Bent. 1998. *Rationality and Power: Democracy in Practice*. Chicago: University of Chicago Press.
Foote, Daniel H. 2008. "Justice System Reform in Japan." Unpublished paper, available at www.reds.msh-paris.fr/communication/docs/foote.pdf.
Foote, Daniel H. 2010. "Policymaking by the Japanese Judiciary in the Criminal Justice Field." *Hoshakaigaku* 72: 6–45.
Foote, Daniel H. 2013. "The Trials and Tribulations of Japan's Law Schools and Bar Exam System." *Hastings International and Comparative Law Review* 36: 369–458.
Johnson, David T. 2002. *The Japanese Way of Justice: Prosecuting Crime in Japan*. New York: Oxford University Press.
Johnson, David T. 2004. "Nihon ni okeru Shiho Seido Kaikaku: Keisatsu no Shozai to Sono Juyosei" [Justice System Reform in Japan: Where Are the Police and Why It Matters]. *Horitsu Jiho* 76: 8–15.
Johnson, David T. 2015. "Policing in Japan." In *The Sage Handbook of Modern Japanese Studies*, edited by James Babb, 222–43. Los Angeles: Sage.
Justice System Reform Council. 2001. "Recommendations of the Justice System Reform Council: For A Justice System to Support Japan in the 21st Century." Accessed April 2, 2017. http://japan.kantei.go.jp/policy/sihou/singikai/990612_e.html.
Kalven Jr., Harry and Hans Zeisel. 1966. *The American Jury*. Chicago: University of Chicago Press.
Langbein, John H. 1978. "Torture and Plea Bargaining." *University of Chicago Law Review* 46: 3–22.
Levin, Mark and Virginia Tice. 2009. "Japan's New Citizen Judges: How Secrecy Imperils Judicial Reform." *The Asia-Pacific Journal* 7 (19): 1–17. Accessed at www.japanfocus.org/-Virginia-Tice/3141.
Miyazawa, Setsuo. 1991. "Administrative Controls of Japanese Judges." In *Law and the Technology in the Pacific Community*, edited by Philip S. C. Lewis, 263–81. Boulder: Westview Press.
Miyazawa, Setsuo. 1992. *Policing in Japan: A Study on Making Crime*. Albany: State University of New York Press.
Miyazawa, Setsuo. 2007. "Law Reform, Lawyers, and Access to Justice." In *Japanese Business Law*, edited by Gerald Paul McAlinn, 39–89. The Netherlands: Kluwer Law International.
Miyazawa, Setsuo, Kay-Wah Chan, and Ilhyung Lee. 2008. "The Reform of Legal Education in East Asia." *Annual Review of Law and Social Science* 4: 333–61.

Miyazawa, Setsuo. 2013. "Successes, Failures, and Remaining Issues of the Justice System Reform in Japan: An Introduction to the Symposium Issue." *Hastings International and Comparative Law Review* 36: 313–48.

Mori, Hono. 2013. *Shiho Kenryoku no Uchimaku*. Tokyo: Chikuma Shinsho.

Packer, Herbert L. 1968. *The Limits of the Criminal Sanction*. Stanford: Stanford University Press.

Putnam, Robert. 1993. *Making Democracy Work: Civic Traditions in Modern Italy*. Princeton: Princeton University Press.

Ramseyer, Mark J. and Eric B. Rasmusen. 2003. *Measuring Judicial Independence: The Political Economy of Judging in Japan*. Chicago and London: University of Chicago Press.

Ramseyer, Mark J. and Eric B. Rasmusen. 2015. "Lowering the Bar to Raise the Bar: Licensing Difficulty and Attorney Quality in Japan." *Journal of Japanese Studies* 41: 113–42.

Saegusa, Mayumi. 2009. "Why the Japanese Law School System Was Established: Co-optation as a Defensive Tactic in the Face of Global Pressures." *Law & Social Inquiry* 34: 365–98.

Saeki, Masahiko. 2010. "Victim Participation in Criminal Trials in Japan." *International Journal of Law, Crime and Justice* 38: 149–65.

Segi, Hiroshi. 2014. *Zetsubo no Saibansho*. Tokyo: Kodansha Shinsho.

Fukuda, Taku. 2013. *Shikei Haishi Nempo* [The Death Penalty Annual]. Tokyo: Impakuto.

Shinomiya, Satoru. 2013. "Saibanin Saiban: Saibanin Seido wa Keiji Jitsumu o Dono yo ni Kaete Iru ka." Unpublished paper, Kokugakuin University School of Law, Tokyo, March, 1–13.

Supreme Court of Japan. 2012. *Saibanin Saiban Jisshi Jokyo no Kensho Hokokusho*. Tokyo: Saikosaibansho Jimusokyoku. 1–122.

Takano, Takashi. 2009. "Nihon no Kensatsu wa Hetare na no ka", in *Keiji Saiban o Kangaeru*: Takano Takashi@burogu. June 14 and June 23.

Takeda, Masahiro. 2014. "Saibanin Seido Kaishi kara 5nen: Kensatsu wa Taisho Jiken o Shincho ni Kiso: Saibanin Kohosha no Jitairitsu, 60% Koeru." *Journalism* (Fall): 136–43.

Vidmar, Neil and Valerie P. Hans. 2007. *American Juries: The Verdict*. Amherst, NY: Prometheus Books.

Yomiuri Shimbun Shakaibu. 2013. *Shikei: Kyukoku no Batsu no Shinjitsu*. Tokyo: Chuokoron-Shinsha.

7

Court Reform and Comparative Criminal Justice

David Nelken

INTRODUCTION

Malcolm Feeley's *Court Reform on Trial: Why Simple Solutions Fail* (Feeley 1983) is a monograph based on his report commissioned by the Twentieth Century Fund. The book may be less well known than both many of his earlier and later cutting-edge monographs (see e.g. Feeley 1979, or Feeley and Rubin 1998). But returning to it for the purpose of contributing to this collection made me realize just how good a read it is. Feeley offers us a meta-evaluation of selected court reforms from the 1950s to the 1970s, analyzing the problems that the reformers sought to resolve and the flaws in the solutions that they invented. Following a thoughtful introduction, the central chapters take us through the history of efforts to introduce bail reform, extend pretrial diversion, curb sentence disparities and expedite speedy trials. Feeley draws his examples of the creation, implementation and, in particular, efforts to evaluate such initiatives from a variety of states in the USA, seeking to choose the best evaluated examples of each reform effort. His goal is to explain why, in the majority of cases, these reforms failed to achieve the changes they promised. In his conclusion, Feeley generalizes about the role of criminal courts, and draws out the implications of the case studies he has discussed.

In appraising arguments written well over thirty years ago it is important not to make criticisms based only on hindsight. Feeley has developed his ideas and widened his focus since he wrote this book, and there have also been many other relevant contributions to the literature. The larger environment in which the criminal courts operate has also gone through many changes, the most obvious being the rise of what Garland called the 'culture of control' (Garland 2000) and the consequent growth of mass incarceration in the USA. In a famous work, Feeley argued that that 'the process is the punishment' (Feeley 1979). But under conditions of increasing levels of incarceration many offenders do now also face high penalties at the end of the process. On the other hand, if only for reasons of tightened budgets, we are currently entering a phase where efforts to find alternatives to prison and construct court reforms that will deliver this are again in vogue. Given that Feeley set out to understand, as he now puts it (Feeley 2013), why 'so many good ideas put forward by well-intentioned people went astray', as compared to how much has been written about 'the nasty, vindictive and draconian policies that emerged in the 1970s and into the 2000s', this makes the book all the more potentially relevant.

Criminal justice is a graveyard full of unsuccessful so-called 'reforms' and this work gives us a very good idea of why this is so. Feeley tells us that different historical periods each have their favourite solutions for reshaping the work of the courts or creating alternatives to their role. He describes, for instance, the sometimes unthinking enthusiasm for diversion schemes, and the way this was then followed by exaggerated hopes for neighbourhood justice. But his criticisms could be applied *mutatis mutandis* to the later turn to 'just deserts' or the more recent enthusiasm for victim-oriented justice. Even the current call for decarceration could (again) have unanticipated effects (see e.g. Garland, Hogan, Wodahl, Hass, Stohr and Lambert 2014).

As my title suggests, I am especially interested in examining this book in the light of what it can teach us about comparative criminal justice (drawing especially on my experience of studying criminal justice in Italy in particular over the past thirty years). Many of Feeley's more detailed points may indeed be universalizable – at least to modern criminal justice systems. Take, for example, the claim in discussing the problem of sentencing disparity that we cannot easily standardize sentences because crime cases 'spill over from ordinary life' and do not easily fit the categories of criminal law. There may also be an iron 'logic', from the point of view of those engaged in social control, of formal control being reserved for those for whom informal controls are assumed to be least effective, which leads to criminal sanctions being directed at the poor and weak (cf. Black 1976). But not all the points Feeley makes about successful and unsuccessful court reforms may be equally applicable to other societies. Certainly, Feeley's report makes much of the differences between US states. But, although *Court Reform on Trial* has been widely cited, there have been relatively few efforts to apply its lessons to foreign jurisdictions.[1]

Feeley once claimed that there is no such thing as a comparative approach as such. He argued that all social scientific writing is essentially comparative, insofar as the goal is always the identification and explanation of social variation. In practice, comparative work, in his opinion, tends to be merely classificatory and descriptive (Feeley 1997). On the other hand, I am sure that he would agree that we should not underestimate what is involved even in adequate description. Much of the challenge of comparative work has to do with the special difficulties that face us once we go outside familiar cultural contexts and try to translate the larger meanings embodied in foreign languages and practices (Nelken 2010). By engaging in 'thick description' (Geertz 1973, 1983) we can better grasp the significance of the state in continental

---

[1] The book is cited by writers on Latin America (see, for example, Hammergren 2007), as well as Scandinavia and Canada.

Europe, unravel the different meanings of discretion, or pin down contrasts in 'ideals of due process'. In the case of Italy, for example, it was challenging for me to discover early on that Italy's leading critical criminal law theorist characterized the supposed contrast between 'due process' and 'crime control' as 'bizarre' (Ferrajoli 1990, 1993; Nelken 1993). Even the academic term 'criminal justice' itself (and associated questions such as whether it should be considered more of a 'system' or a 'process') are ones most at home in Anglo-American settings. These are concepts and debates that may not 'travel well' (Twining 2005).

Feeley's report was not intended to contribute to comparative criminal justice in the conventional sense of contrasting law in different jurisdictions – except perhaps to the extent to which it compares the effects of reforms in different states in the USA. But, in recent years Feeley has increasingly engaged in comparative work in countries such as Japan, Europe and Latin America, and has written about the need to develop overarching concepts such as 'the legal complex' (see e.g. Halliday, Karpik and Feeley 2007). He is also interested in the way given yardsticks for evaluation spread globally (Melossi, Sozzo and Sparks 2011). Furthermore, comparison is itself a social process which has consequences. It can be a warrant for change – or resistance (Nelken 2015, 2016), as shown by Feeley's own research into the privatization of prisons (Feeley 2014).

When dealing with an unfamiliar system of criminal justice, care must be taken to appreciate what is salient and meaningful to those working in it in order to appreciate the local cultural specificities in what is taken to be a 'problem' or a 'solution' (Nelken 2009). But the same sensibility may be helpful when looking at our own system. Feeley's book seeks to show the connection between problems and solutions in court reform – and how each helps define the other. The suggestion made here is that a comparative perspective can be helpful in showing that solutions to problems often fail precisely because they reproduce the cultural assumptions that they should be challenging. But, by the same token, this approach also raises the question of what cultural influences lay behind the criteria that Feeley himself used when evaluating the evaluators.

7.1 DEFINING THE PROBLEM(S)

Feeley announces in the title of his book that he will tell us why 'simple solutions fail'. But what he means by simple is in fact far from straightforward. Most obviously, it can refer to *over*-simplification. He tells us, for example, that court delay turns out to cover a variety of different problems. At other times, he points out that what seems the simplest in the sense of the most 'obvious' solution is not necessarily the right one. Appointing more judges leads to more court delay, not less. But, above all, he warns us against the temptation to embrace elegant but overly theoretical remedies that rely on 'neat' formalist logic. Deterrence may indeed be an important goal. Rehabilitation may likewise be a valuable ideal. But failure is almost guaranteed when policy-makers try to make such ideas effective as if they had *tabula rasa*, instead of first seeking to map the existing practices that are currently followed by legal actors as they implement their own conceptions of such goals and ideals. Conversely, efforts to bring about change face the challenge of how not to be ostracized or co-opted by the existing set of criminal justice actors and agencies.

As this suggests, however, many of the reasons for failure that Feeley identified had little to do with simplicity or single-mindedness. There is nothing simple about the recurrent problem of finding and maintaining funding for innovative reforms. We also cannot assume that 'complicated' solutions will work any better than simple ones. Too often we end up asking criminal justice actors to pursue multiple but incompatible goals. And perhaps even trying to pursue any overall goal is quixotic. Given that the criminal justice system is set up as an adversarial arena, any provisions designed to influence outcomes will be 'gamed' by parties who are quite legitimately pursuing conflicting agendas. Indeed, it is more worrying when they do not do this. Criticisms have long been made of the way defence lawyers use plea bargaining so as to privilege their continuing collaboration with the prosecution above the interests of their clients (Blumberg 1967). If the trial is indeed a game (or, better, a series of simultaneous games), agencies using bureaucratic logic will obviously have a hard time in imposing linear outcomes. At most what can be done is to try and find the incentives that might move some actors in desired directions.

In keeping with his focus in the book, Feeley actually lays much of the blame for failure of criminal justice reforms at the door of the evaluators. He shows us that what they billed as successful reforms often involved exaggerating favourable results and ignoring others. Poor research often provided a scientific veneer for changes that did not actually come about because of the policy interventions themselves. Thus, for him, the successful results achieved by bail reform or court diversion would have arrived even under existing informal practices. On the other hand, Feeley also notes that even if it fails as a reform, a given social intervention may help solve other problems, or have other unexpected positive outcomes.

It would have been useful to have had more discussion of the question of how far courts are like or unlike other organizations. It is likely that discovering that reforms are not well conceived, not implemented properly, not evaluated thoroughly or not built successfully into the routine operations of the organization concerned, is something that could be true of any or all policy interventions. There will be difficulties in organizing planned change in any environment. And all institutional settings can become prey to the instrumental interests of the individuals and groups who staff them. One of Feeley's key assumptions (widely shared at the time) was that court reforms are difficult to introduce because of the tendency of the system to neutralize change so as to stay in equilibrium. Yet, not so long after this book was published, the criminal justice system changed rapidly, in the direction of much greater punitiveness (Garland 2000).

How far do Feeley's arguments about the operations of the courts apply to jurisdictions outside of the USA? Conversely, what can comparative criminal justice teach us about the problems faced by courts in the USA? Much of what Feeley says about such courts is certainly relevant more widely. In Italy, for example, the lack of a strong empirical sociological tradition of research into courts makes policy-making especially likely to be captured by legally elegant but overly theoretical remedies. There is also a strong temptation to oversimplify the causes of widely criticized dysfunctions. Leading law professor and judge Sabino Cassese is certain that Italy's exceptionally long court delays are due to the way the rise in the numbers of lawyers has outpaced the increase in the number of judges (Cassese 2001). Leading left-wing magistrates, on the other hand, prefer to blame the interests of powerful businessmen, politicians and others ('i poteri forti'). Both of these explanations seem obvious to those who espouse them, but the true picture is likely to be a rather more complex mix that takes in a range of political, economic and religious variables (Nelken 2004).

Feeley has written well about the dangers of trying to learn from other places without taking into account the 'law in action' as well as the 'law in books' (Feeley and Levine 2001). This is all the more necessary where there is no tradition of rigorous evaluation of criminal justice reforms in societies that are taken as models. If we are convinced by his sobering meta-evaluation of the claims of evaluators in the USA, where evaluation and experimentation is most advanced, the need for caution is likely to be still more true elsewhere where approaches to evaluation are less common or rigorous. Again, this is not difficult to show for Italy. Whatever the many merits of their system, the claims about favourable outcomes in dealing with offenders through the juvenile justice system made by the Italian Ministry of Justice, or by social work agencies, are too easily believed by foreign observers. For example, the high rates of success in the use of pretrial probation for juveniles (so-called 'messa alla prova') has much to do with the careful selection of cases where it is employed. In any case, the statistics usually refer to the judge's decision whether or not to go ahead and hold a trial rather than to evidence about any further offending (Nelken 2015). At the same time, comparative criminal justice can warn us to think more carefully about what is being evaluated, why and how. Why should the success of juvenile justice be judged mainly in terms of its ability to reduce recidivism by youngsters? It is likely that the deliberate attempt to achieve this result is itself likely to increase recidivism (Field and Nelken 2007).

Feeley argues that criminal justice should be seen as a site of competition between different actors. But he also tells us that, over time, participants reach a sort of *modus vivendi*. He notes in particular the importance of local court culture – the set of working relationships that characterize different courts (Church 1982). This helps to explain why changes or reforms in one part of the system can be stymied by practices elsewhere. In Italy, likewise, efforts made to cut down court delay in one part of the criminal justice system often only increase bottlenecks in other, often later part of the same system (see Sarzotti 2007 on prosecution practices and the later stages of trial). Insights from comparative criminal justice could help our understanding of such interdependence beyond criminal justice agencies themselves by showing how different legal systems are embedded in wider patterns shaped by politics, economics and general culture (see Nelken 2004; 2011; 2016). The difficulty in changing these patterns often provides the key to explaining the success and failure of reforms that rely on borrowing from other jurisdictions.

7.2 FINDING THE SOLUTION(S)

To provide evidence of the failures of particular reforms, it is necessary to establish what counts as the criteria of success. But who does – and who should – define what success means? Sometimes Feeley considers a given court reform to be a failure in terms of what its proponents wanted it to achieve, without asking whether what they sought to do should itself be considered a worthwhile aim or not. At other times he substitutes his own judgement. The story is often mixed. Not all of the reforms Feeley reports on were complete failures – at least in terms of what they were meant to achieve. For example, in discussing sentencing reforms he tells us that gun law reforms have had some successes in some places. They may not have lengthened sentences for those carrying guns (assuming this is a 'good', or at least the intended outcome), but they did make sure that these offenders all got prison sentences. How much success is enough to count as success?

Feeley thinks genuine solutions to the failings of the criminal justice system are elusive for a plethora of reasons. Some of the problems that he identifies, such as the lack of sufficient or guaranteed funding for reforms, could in theory be solvable. But some of the others that he describes are by definition beyond solution. Law cannot be both universal and particular, or at once certain and yet also responsive. The goals of criminal justice are not only contradictory, they are often nonachievable even in their own right. General deterrence as a policy comes up against the problem that too few criminals are ever apprehended. Rehabilitation as an ideal often confuses crime with disease. It is an exaggeration to say that meta-evaluation of rehabilitation proves 'that nothing works' (Martinson 1974). Many scholars, from very different schools of thought, have since pointed to the scope for constructive social and situational prevention efforts and engagement with those at risk or convicted of crime (Sherman et al. 1998; Ward and Marun 2007). It remains true, however, that it is hard to help many offenders, given the narrow constraints under which criminal justice operates, and the challenges of the difficult social conditions to which most offenders afterwards return.

Feeley makes it very clear that reforms are doomed to failure if exaggerated claims are made for them when first launched, or if they are evaluated too early, before they have been 'routinized' after the initial enthusiasm has died away and charismatic leaders are no longer in charge. On the other hand, could it be otherwise? How could reforms attract funds and attention without their proponents talking big? And, if we want to decide whether to invest in a given initiative, can we afford to wait to evaluate it until it has been fully rolled out? Feeley also warns us that brilliant innovators are not always good administrators. But, again, it is not easy to see how an appropriate time of handover between the one and the other can easily be institutionalized. As we have noted, inasmuch as the trial is a game or conflict, it will not be easy to make bureaucratically organized planned change. But this also means that amongst the wide variety of agencies involved, what is a solution for some can easily constitute a problem for others. The battle for who gets to 'own' a reform often turns out to be crucial to its success. Feeley shows us, for example, how matters changed when the prosecution service ended up running diversion schemes (rather than the agencies that first pioneered them in the interests of defendants). He also tells us that when responsibility for bail reform shifted to the probation department, they then neglected notifying offenders of the dates of meetings.

Feeley's main conclusion, nonetheless, is mildly optimistic. If we eschew overly ambitious programs and learn to accept what he calls proximate (i.e. imperfect) solutions, much can be achieved by working incrementally. Even if bureaucratic logic can never fully grasp or reign in the adversarial system, some organizations make valuable contributions to making things work better. He is especially impressed by the Vera Institute of Justice because of their impartiality and dedication to serious evaluation. He also thinks that we should trust courts and court personnel more rather than less. Often those in the criminal justice system, he argues, find ways of doing what is sensible, despite being part of an adversarial process.

According to Feeley, a rights strategy, focused on prisoners' rights litigation, did bring about many procedural improvements. Thus, appeals to the courts can help achieve change (Feeley 1992; in later writing he showed at some length the ability of the courts to improve prison conditions, see Feeley and Rubin 1998). But he also points out that we often cannot dispense with the need for legislative action. In the case of speedy trial reforms, he mentions that the Supreme Court offered no guidelines about the appropriate length of time to trial, never overturned decisions based on the time taken to reach them and even let pass a trial that ratcheted up a five-year delay.

Would Feeley's solutions be appropriate for all jurisdictions? Some authors encourage the worldwide embrace of the adversarial system because of the procedural protections it offers (Vogler 2005). And the model is certainly attractive to reformers around the world. But comparative studies of prison rates reveal that it is common law countries that often have the highest levels of incarceration (Cavadino and Dignan 2006). This suggests that a type of criminal procedure that provides more protection at the individual level could have the effect of increasing levels of punishment at the systemic level. By contrast, it has recently been argued that when 'strong states' are involved in punishment, they may be more likely to exercise mercy and soften harshness (Whitman 2005).

A challenge for comparative criminal justice research would be to try to analyze how continental European systems of criminal justice handle the problems discussed by Feeley. Some American scholars critical of their own system strongly believe that they do a better job of dealing with them (Kagan 2001). On the other hand, it can be easy to exaggerate the extent to which these jurisdictions are really more 'policy oriented' than the USA (Nelken 2003a). Even in European systems participants in the legal system have – and are intended to have – conflicting interests. In Italy, defence lawyers take full advantage of the strict speedy trial protections that mean that offenders are acquitted automatically if cases run over a certain period (the rules on 'prescription'). They spend much of their energy on what is castigated there as defending the offender 'from the process' rather than 'in the process'. The debate within Italy turns on whether the defendants' due process rights (the so-called 'garanzie') are an inherent safeguard of the system, or whether, on the other hand, they are too open to being exploited as a means for powerful, and especially political, figures to escape justice by relying on so-called 'garanzie pelosi' (hairy guarantees) that make it impossible to apply the criminal law effectively (Nelken 2012).

Another fruitful area for comparative research is the extent to which in different jurisdictions it is even considered right to evaluate criminal justice systems. What criteria of success are considered appropriate? In particular, in what ways do outcomes matter? Even Feeley acknowledges that evaluation can sometimes be counter-productive. He says of some reforms that failure was due to 'too much' information being asked for. He argues that we should disconnect sentencing from crime control goals, and leave it to appellate courts to deal with disparities. More generally, criminal justice reforms that are created in the image of social sciences policy-making may fail to respect the limits and obligations of the legal roles that they seek to reshape (Nelken 2001; Hilderbrandt 2015). Most obviously, in modern criminal trials we often try to keep information from later decision-makers for fear that it will bias them, irrespective of the implications for the effectiveness of penal outcomes.

The rise of neo-liberal models of governance has led to increasing pressure to feed back knowledge of outcomes to actors in the system. Feeley and Simon's influential notion of 'actuarial justice' (Feeley and Simon 1994) sought to capture the way this was emerging at the level of policing and elsewhere. More recent evidence is found in work on 'pre-crime' (Ashworth, Zedner and Tomlin 2013). As these authors show, such developments are deeply controversial amongst those who worry about legal protections. As this also suggests, some of the reasons leading us to have too high expectations of what criminal justice reforms can achieve derive from a false analogy to health or other social policy interventions.

7.3 THE POLITICS OF CRIMINAL JUSTICE

As a political scientist (amongst the other hats he could wear), the last thing one could accuse Feeley of is underestimating the need to appreciate that courts operate in a political context and produce political effects. *Court Reform on Trial* provides ample evidence of the significance of politics, and not only for those willing to read between the lines. Feeley offers, for example, a fierce critique of a drug law sentencing reform that, according to him, was geared to securing Rockefeller's election to higher office. And he ends his book by deploring the institutionalized racial discrimination built into the system. More generally, he tells us that the 'simplicity' of the reform programs that he criticizes is frequently a result of politicians' desire to attack problems such as trial delay or disparities in sentencing as if they can be dealt with as mere problems of social engineering. In this way they fail to pay proper attention to the human choices and dilemmas that produce them. On the other hand, he also acknowledges that reforms can be valuable politically (irrespective of their effects) if they help social mobilization around good causes. Certainly, it is not only in the USA that words can succeed even if policies fail. Politics is certainly crucial in Italy. As compared to the USA, even arcane features of criminal justice, such as whether public prosecutors in Italy have too much – or too little – independence, are argued about (or, as Italians would say, 'politicized') by the political parties and debated in media-related accounts of clashes between the judges and the politicians (Nelken 2003b; Nelken 2014).

Yet Feeley's book stops short of drawing out the full implications of recognizing criminal justice as a field of political struggle. It simply assumes that there is some space for introducing 'scientific' evaluations that could and should be heeded, without articulating any theory of what shapes that space and what conditions the possibility of experts being heard. With the benefit of hindsight, we can now see how much was taken for granted by most of those writing about criminal justice at the time this book was published. Even though crime was understood to be rising – or just because of that – the solutions proposed by academics focused on how to find ways of relieving the perceived pressure on court case loads. Most critics too readily assumed a liberal consensus concerning the negative consequences of pushing offenders too quickly to trial and sentencing.

The significance of this relatively soft political background to the reforms that are discussed in this book is shown by what happened in the thirty years that followed. The new criminal justice 'reforms' helped produce or accompany a seemingly unstoppable growth in the prison population – and this despite all the evidence that showed crime was declining (only very partially as a result of the massive rise in incarceration itself). How could this happen? Those looking to explain such criminal justice outcomes increasingly connect matters such as prison rates to variables outside the system – such as the neo-liberal turn in social policy, the various political benefits for being 'tough on crime' and the local economic investments in building and staffing prisons rather than to intrinsic weaknesses in reforms as such (Cavadino and Dignan 1996; Waquant 2009a, 2009b; Lacey 2008). But such larger variables receive little mention in this book.

If it does one thing, comparative research should help us understand better the ways criminal justice reform is explicitly and implicitly conditioned by such political priorities and social structures. Which variables matter and why? Why have so many politicians in Italy been unwilling to call for stiffer punishments? Why, as compared to the United States, is there less emphasis on 'crime control' in national elections except where it is the state itself being threatened (by political corruption, organized crime and terrorism)? True, public support for more severity is now increasingly stirred up by the media, but this is mainly directed at offences by foreigners. And crucially, many (if not all) of those working in the criminal justice system feel it their professional duty not to give undue attention to public concern about crime (what they call 'allarme sociale'). Correspondingly, (and more problematically) public confidence in the system is not the lodestar that they follow.

To explain why, instead of 'governing through crime' (Simon 2006), we often find ourselves 'ruling through leniency' (Melossi 1994), we would need to make sense of the continual diet of 'crimes of the powerful' that have filled the Italian newspapers, especially since the so-called *Tangentopoly* investigations of corruption of the early 1990s (Nelken 1996). We would also need to explain why this has apparently not done much to change underlying social patterns of collusion between politicians, administrators and businessmen – often helped by more or less organized crime groups. At certain moments it can even seem as if the courts can best be seen as participants in a carnival in which – for brief periods – the powerful and the powerless change places. A comparative perspective would also want to give attention to differences in the way crime is described in different places. In particular, the use of the term 'micro criminality' in Italy to describe crime other than that committed by organized criminals, terrorism and corruption, reflects and shapes its different salience. Significantly, however, with the growth of immigration to the country, as well as the spread of transnational Anglo-American ways of thinking, these kinds of crimes have now come to be re-labelled as 'street crimes' or 'diffuse crime' (Nelken 2000).

REFERENCES

Ashworth, Andrew, Lucia Zedner, and Patrick Tomlin eds. 2013. *Prevention and the Limits of the Criminal Law*. Oxford: Oxford University Press.
Beck, Ulrich. 2007. 'The Cosmopolitan Condition: Why Methodological Nationalism Fails'. *Theory, Culture and Society* 24 (7–8): 286–90.
Black, Donald. 1976. *The Behaviour of Law*. New York: Academic Press.
Blumberg, Abraham S. 1967. 'The Practice of Law as Confidence Game: Organizational Cooptation of a Profession'. *Law & Society Review* 1 (1): 15–40.

Cassese, Sabino. 2001. 'L'esplosione del diritto. Il sistema giuridico italiano dal 1975 al 2000'. *Sociologia del Diritto* XXVIII/I: 55–66.
Cavadino, Michael and John Dignan. 2006. *Penal Systems: A Comparative Approach.* London: Sage.
Church, Thomas. 1982. *Examining Local Legal Culture – Practitioner Attitudes in Four Criminal Courts.* NIJ.
Feeley, Malcolm. 1979. *The Process is the Punishment: Handling Cases in a Lower Criminal Court.* New York: Russell Sage.
Feeley, Malcolm. 1983. *Court Reform on Trial: Why Simple Solutions Fail.* New York: Basic Books.
Feeley, Malcolm. 1992. 'Hollow Hopes, Flypaper, and Metaphors'. *Law and Social Inquiry* 17 (4): 745–60.
Feeley, Malcolm. 1997. 'Comparative Criminal Law for Criminologists: Comparing for What Purpose?' In *Comparing Legal Cultures*, edited by David Nelken, 93–104. Aldershot: Ashgate.
Feeley, Malcolm. 2013. 'Preface'. In Malcolm Feeley, *Court Reform on Trial: Why Simple Solutions Fail.* New Orleans: Quid Pro Books.
Feeley, Malcolm. 2014. 'The Unconvincing Case against Private Prisons'. *Indiana Law Journal* 89 (4): 1401–36.
Feeley, Malcolm M. and Kay Levine. 2001. 'Assaults on the Adversarial Process: Rethinking American Criminal Justice'. *Punishment & Society* 3 (4): 537–45.
Feeley, Malcolm and Ed Rubin. 1998. *Judicial Policy Making and the Modern State: How the Courts Reformed America's Prisons.* Cambridge: Cambridge University Press.
Feeley, Malcolm and Jonathan Simon. 1994. 'Actuarial Justice: The Emerging New Criminal Law'. In *The Futures of Criminology*, edited by David Nelken, 173–201. London: Sage.
Field, Stewart and David Nelken. 2007. 'Early Intervention and the Cultures of Youth Justice: A Comparison of Italy and Wales'. In *European Ways of Law*, edited by Volkmar Gessner and David Nelken, 349–74. Oxford: Hart.
Ferrajoli, Luigi. 1990 [2011]. *Diritto e Ragione: Teoria del garantismo penale.* Bari: Laterza.
Ferrajoli, Liugi. 1993. 'Note critiche ed autocritiche intorno alla discussione su Diritto e Ragione'. In *Le Ragioni del Garantismo. Discutendo con Luigi Ferrajoli*, edited by Letizia Gianformaggio, 459–520. Torino: Giappichelli.
Garland, Brett, Nancy Hogan, Eric Wodahl, Aida Hass, Mary K. Stohr and Eric Lambert. 2014. 'Decarceration and its Possible Effects on Inmates, Staff, and Communities'. *Punishment & Society* 16: 448–73.
Garland, David. 2000. *The Culture of Control.* Oxford: Oxford University Press.
Geertz, Clifford. 1973. 'Thick Description: Towards an Interpretive Theory of Culture'. In *The Interpretation of Culture*, edited by Clifford Geertz. London: Fontana.
Geertz, Clifford. 1983. *Local Knowledge: Further Essays in Interpretive Anthropology.* New York: Basic Books.
Halliday, Terry, Lucien Karpik and Malcom Feeley. 2007. *Fighting for Political Freedom: Comparative Studies of the Legal Complex and Political Liberalism.* Oxford: Hart.
Hammergren, Linn. 2007. *Envisioning Reform: Improving Judicial Performance in Latin America.* University Park: Penn State University Press.
Hildebrandt, Mireille. 2015. *Smart Technologies and the End(s) of Law: Novel Entanglements of Law and Technology.* Cheltenham: Elgar.
Kagan, Robert. 2001. *Adversarial Legalism.* Cambridge: Harvard University Press.
Lacey, Nicola. 2008. *The Prisoners' Dilemma: Political Economy and Punishment in Contemporary Democracies.* Cambridge: Cambridge University Press.

Martinson, Robert. 1974. 'What Works? Questions and Answers about Prison Reform'. *The Public Interest* 22–54.
Melossi, Dario. 1994. 'The Economy of Illegalities'. In *The Futures of Criminology*, edited by David Nelken, 202–19. London: Sage.
Melossi, Dario, Massimo Sozzo and Richard Sparks, eds. 2011. *Travels of the Criminal Question: Cultural Embeddedness and Diffusion*. Oxford: Hart.
Nelken, David. 1993. 'Le giustificazioni della pena ed i diritti dell'imputato'. In *Le ragioni del garantismo: Discutendo con Luigi Ferrajoli*, edited by Letizia Gianformaggio, 275–307. Giappicheli: Torino.
Nelken, David. 1996. 'Judicial Politics and Corruption in Italy'. In *The Corruption of Politics and the Politics of Corruption*: special issue of the *Journal of Law and Society*, edited by David Nelken and Michael Levi, 95–113.
Nelken, David. 2000. 'Telling Difference: Of Crime and Criminal Justice in Italy'. In *Contrasting Criminal Justice*, edited by David Nelken, 233–64. Aldershot: Dartmouth.
Nelken, David. 2001. 'Can Law Learn from Social Science?' *Israel Law Review* 2–3: 1–20.
Nelken, David. 2003a. 'Beyond Compare? Criticising the American Way of Law'. *Law and Social Inquiry* 28 (3): 181–213.
Nelken, David. 2003b. 'Legitimate Suspicion? Berlusconi and the Judges'. In *The Second Berlusconi Government: Politics in Italy*, edited by Paulo Segatti and Jan Blondel, 112–28. Oxford: Berghahn Books.
Nelken, David. 2004. 'Using the Concept of Legal Culture'. *Australian Journal of Legal Philosophy* 29: 1–28.
Nelken, David. 2009. 'Comparative Criminal Justice: Beyond Ethnocentrism and Relativism'. *European Journal of Criminology* 6 (4): 291–311.
Nelken, David. 2010. *Comparative Criminal Justice: Making Sense of Difference*. London: Sage.
Nelken, David. 2011. 'Using Legal Culture: Prospects and Problems'. In *Journal of Comparative Law*, special issue, edited by David Nelken, 14 (2): 1–39.
Nelken, David. 2012. 'Comparative Criminal Justice'. In *Oxford Handbook of Criminology* (5th edn.), edited by Mike Maguire, Rod Morgan and Robert Reiner, 138–57. Oxford: Oxford University Press.
Nelken, David. 2014. 'Can Prosecutors Be Too Independent? An Italian Case-Study'. In *European Penology?*, edited by Tom Daems, Sonja Snacken, Dirk van der vyl Smit, 241–61. Oxford: Hart.
Nelken, David. 2015. 'Foil Comparisons or Foiled Comparisons? Learning from Italian Juvenile Justice'. *European Journal of Criminology* 12: 519–34.
Nelken, David. 2016. 'From Pains-Taking to Pains-Giving Comparisons'. *International Journal of Law in Context* 12 (4): 390–403.
Nelken, David. 2016. 'Comparative Legal Research and Legal Culture: Facts, Approaches and Values'. *Annual Review of Law and Social Science* 12: 45–62.
Sarzotti, Claudio. 2007. *Processi de selezione del crimine. Procure della republica e organizzazione giudiziaria*. Milan: Giuffrè.
Sherman, Lawrence W., Denise Gottfredson, Doris MacKenzie, John Eck, Peter Reuter and Shawn Bushway. 1998. *Preventing Crime: What Works, What Doesn't, What's Promising, a Report to the United States Congress*. NIJ.
Simon, Jonathan. 2006. *Governing through Crime*. Oxford: Oxford University Press.
Twining, William. 2005. 'Have Concepts, Will Travel'. *International Journal of Law in Context* 1 (4): 427–34.
Vogler, Richard. 2005. *A World View of Criminal Justice*. Aldershot: Ashgate.

Waquant, Loic. 2009a. *Prisons of Poverty*. Minneapolis: University of Minnesota Press.
Waquant, Loic. 2009b. *Punishing the Poor: The Neoliberal Government of Social Insecurity*. Durham, NC: Duke University Press.
Ward, Tony and Shadd Maruna. 2007. *Rehabilitation*. London: Routledge.
Whitman, Jim Q. 2005. *Harsh Justice: Criminal Punishment and the Widening Divide between America and Europe*. Oxford: Oxford University Press.

8

The Birth of the Penal Organization: Why Prisons Were Born to Fail

Ashley T. Rubin[1]

INTRODUCTION: FROM COURTS TO PRISONS

A recurring question for students of punishment has been: why, despite more than "one and a half centuries of failure" (Cohen 1979: 341), has the prison persisted? Throughout history, reformers, politicians, voters, and others have assigned prisons myriad tasks associated with crime reduction – various incarnations of rehabilitation, deterrence, and incapacitation. After every significant reform effort, prisons have disappointed. In the 1970s, prisons were accused of failing to rehabilitate (Martinson 1974; Allen 1981), or potentially making prisoners worse through the process of labeling (Becker 1963). The prisoners' rights movement, and the resulting court cases and prison riots, illuminated the inhumane conditions and racialization of prisons (Cummins 1994; Feeley and Rubin 1998). Today, in the midst of hunger strikes (Reiter 2014), penal policies threatening to bankrupt states (Donziger 1996; Aviram 2015), a greater awareness of the racialized nature of prisons (Wacquant 2001; Alexander 2010), and increasing court actions against prison conditions (Simon 2014), American prisons face yet another legitimacy crisis. This is only the latest round of "failure"; yet with each crisis, the prison not only persists, but continues to expand, replaced by a new and seemingly improved version of itself.

In 1983, Malcolm Feeley took up this theme of repeated, seemingly inevitable failure while examining nationwide court reform targeting bail, pretrial detention, disparate sentencing, and lengthy trials. In his already characteristically direct approach, Feeley identified the heart of the problem: "The courts are an institution whose powers are extremely limited; yet they are frequently called upon to perform Herculean tasks" (Feeley 1983, xiii). Too often, we think of courts as organizations in the idealized sense of an efficient vehicle for goal attainment. Indeed, our expectations are so high that we assign to courts the work of other social institutions – "the family, the church, the workplace, and the school" (Feeley 1983, 19). Instead, Feeley

---

[1] I am grateful to Hadar Aviram, Rosann Greenspan, and Jonathan Simon for the invitation to contribute to this volume and the lovely conference that produced it. I would also like to thank Jay Borchert, Brett Burkhardt, Ted Chiricos, Miltonette Craig, David Johnson, Nicole Kaufman and Monica Williams for comments on previous drafts of this paper.

noted that courts are more fragmented than scholars, critics, and reformers expected: courts are full of value conflicts, are fairly decentralized, and are influenced by their environments (Feeley 1983, 9–18). Rather than thinking of courts "as bureaucratic organizations committed to clear and well-defined purposes – they should be understood as arenas in which a range of competing and conflicting interests collide and vie for attention" (Feeley 1983, 9–10). Throughout the twentieth century, reformers and policymakers have failed to understand that courts are organizations, and, as such, they are constrained by factors many of these commentators did not understand. Ultimately, this mismatch between capacity and expectations – caused by our fundamental misunderstanding of how courts work – virtually ensures that courts will disappoint. As Feeley (1983, xiv) explained, "because our understanding of the courts is flawed and our expectations about what the courts can do are unrealistic, many innovations fail."

This chapter applies the wisdom and feisty spirit of Feeley's *Court Reform on Trial* to prisons. The central thesis is: because our understanding of ~~the courts~~ prisons is flawed and our expectations about what ~~the courts~~ prisons can do are unrealistic, our repeated efforts to create a new, more effective version of incarceration constantly fail. Feeley's characterization of courts – and his diagnosis of scholars and policymakers' misunderstanding – can be applied to prisons and their failures. Prisons are often called upon to mete out justice or retribution, rehabilitate prisoners through therapy or education, incapacitate them, and deter them from future offending, sometimes at the same time. We – scholars, policymakers, voters, critics, reformers – place a great burden on prisons to achieve many difficult and often contradictory tasks.[2] Placing on prisons this "Herculean" burden is all the more challenging given their "extremely limited" capacities, which we constantly fail to recognize.

Specifically, I argue that prisons are fundamentally limited by their organizational framework. Throughout history, reformers and policymakers have expected that, as organizations closed off from the outside world, prisons will efficiently pursue the goals assigned to it. Assigning punishment to an organization, however, introduces a wide range of nonpenal logics, goals, and problems. These logics, goals, and problems include the introduction of managerial concerns; the presence of discretion, particularly in the face of conflicting goals (both stated and unstated) and vague laws; and the emergence of informal structures. These new concerns or challenges introduced by the organizational context compete with and sometimes displace formal penal goals – e.g., rehabilitation, deterrence, incapacitation.[3] I argue that prisons' organizational framework virtually guarantees that they will fail to function

---

[2] For the purposes of this paper, I refer primarily to instrumental goals associated with crime reduction. I do not consider the role of expressive goals such as social solidarity, or structural goals such as class/race domination; these goals, though frequently accomplished, are rarely made explicit or adopted as "formal" goals (e.g., Irwin 1980; Beckett 1997; Wacquant 2001).

[3] While these organizational concerns may not *always* be antithetical to the prison's penal goals, the point is that they frequently do compete with, and displace, these penal goals.

as desired. Ultimately, we have been unable to explain the prison's perennial failure because we have failed to realize the limitations imposed by its very structure – the organization itself.

8.1 PRISONS AS ORGANIZATIONS

One of the central insights of classic organizational theorists has been the way in which, as sociologist Philip Selznick (1949, 10) put it, organizations, once formed, "take on a life of their own." He explained, "it is essential to think of an organization as a dynamic conditioning field which effectively shapes the behavior of those who are attempting to remain at the helm. We can best understand the behavior of officials when we are able to trace that behavior to the needs and structure of the organization as a living social institution." Legal organizations are no exception to this trend. For decades, law and society scholars have identified ways in which gaps emerge between "laws on the books" and "law in action" (Skolnick 1965, 8). Indeed, several prison studies that have been more attuned to the prison's organizational context have illustrated some important consequences.

Examining Progressive Era prisons, Rothman (1980) identified some of the organizational context's consequences for punishment. He argued that prison administrators and penal reformers pursued very different goals: penal reformers were interested in rehabilitating prisoners or diverting prisoners from prisons, while prison administrators were primarily interested in controlling their prisoners and in smoothly run prisons (see also Jacobs 1977). Ultimately, "conscience" (penal goals and ideals) gave way to "convenience" (managerial concerns) because reformers were insufficiently distrustful about their prison administrator allies, and failed to question why administrators so enthusiastically accepted some of the new practices. While Rothman also challenged the extent to which prisons can also operate as schools, communities, and hospitals, the largest cause for failure in his account was the way in which reformative strategies can become co-opted for administrative uses.

Classic prison sociologists writing in the 1950s and 1960s also saw the implications for penal goals of recognizing prisons as an organization (e.g., Sykes 1958; Cressey 1961; Cloward et al. 1960; Zald 1965). These studies acknowledged the competing motivations of prisoners, guards, and administrators, including the organizational imperatives toward external legitimacy and internal control and efficiency. Sykes (1958, 13–14) explained:

> We must not view the prison as a machine which simply and automatically translates the dictates of society into action. The tasks assigned to the prison must be given priorities; general social objectives must be transformed into specific organizational aims; assumptions must be made about the nature of the criminal and his reactions to confinement; and the limitations placed by society on what the prison can do in pursuit of its mission must be taken into account. In short, the

regime which the custodians struggle to impose on the inmate population may indeed be a means of fulfilling the objectives allotted by the larger social order and only become explicable in light of these objectives. But the rules and routines of prison officials represent a choice among alternative means and we must examine the basis of this choice as well as the objectives themselves.

Today, the biggest crises inside prisons have less to do with the prison's failure to achieve minimalist penological goals (e.g., incapacitation), and more to do with problems in its peripheral, nonpenological, managerial features: overcrowding, mistreatment, the failure to provide adequate health care, and bloated budgets (Simon 2014; Calavita and Jenness 2015; Aviram 2015). Moreover, we see the power of prison guard unions, motivated to maintain their jobs and certain working conditions, shaping penal policy (Page 2011). The point that I shall emphasize, however, is that these challenges – the way in which the prison's organizational elements have compromised the pursuit of formal penal goals – are not unique to the present period of crisis, but have persisted throughout American history, beginning with the birth of the prison.

8.2 FROM RITUAL TO ORGANIZATION

8.2.1 *Colonial Executions*

In the centuries before incarceration dominated American criminal justice, most serious (and some minor) offenders were punished through capital or corporal punishments. The American colonial execution was a sporadic affair, sometimes occurring (locally) only a few times in one's lifetime. Though highly ritualized, it was in many ways ad hoc. Typically, executions occurred one month after sentencing, with variation from a few weeks to several months. In the interim, the condemned was housed in the local jail. On execution day, at least one minister, the local sheriff (and his deputies), and perhaps a militia escort would convey the condemned to a newly erected scaffold surrounded by a large crowd. In smaller towns, the entire population could attend; in larger cities, more than half of the local population might attend. In either case, those from the surrounding environs may also travel to view the spectacle. On stage, ministers would offer sermons relating the condemned person's life to moral lessons about obedience and vice. The condemned would also speak before he was hooded and "turned off" at the end of a noose. While some members of the crowd remained to inspect the body, most observers dispersed in somber reflection (Banner 2002, 24–52).

The required infrastructure was thus exceedingly minimal and existed either temporarily or independently of the execution. Except in the largest towns, the scaffold was erected for a particular execution and then taken down.

The primary local officials who organized the event were ministers, who attended to the spiritual elements, and sheriffs, who attended to the physical elements. In a sense, they were *ex officio* members of the execution day team; processing executions, or meting out punishment generally, was not their primary role in society nor an integral part of their work. Other contributors to the execution process – carpenters to erect the scaffold and an executioner – were short-term hired help recruited by the sheriff. Except in early Massachusetts and Maryland, executioners were not professionals (as in England and Europe); instead, the sheriff often had to advertise to hire a temporary executioner, offer a condemned person a reprieve in exchange for performing the deed, or perform the execution himself, which some sheriffs refused to do (Banner 2002, 36–38). Finally, the jail that held the condemned for the month prior to execution was a permanent edifice in the town, but one that already served multiple functions: housing witnesses, vagrants, debtors, petty criminals, and even the families of these groups (Rothman 1971, 48).

8.2.2 Modern Prisons

In the mid- and late eighteenth century, however, both execution rituals and extensive capital statutes came under fire. Between the 1780s and 1810s, almost every state substantially reduced its range of capital offenses and authorized imprisonment instead (Masur 1989; Banner 2002; Rubin 2016). The most significant of the early state prisons (or proto-prisons) was Walnut Street Jail in Philadelphia. Built in the 1770s, but restructured between 1786 and 1794, Walnut Street was one of the first state prisons to receive convicted felons from across the state of Pennsylvania and hold them in confinement, often performing hard labor within the prison's walls, for a year or more (Dumm 1987; Meranze 1996). Copied by almost twenty states, this model quickly became the norm in both the American North and South (Rubin 2016).

These early proto-prisons soon experienced the first of many significant declarations of failure in the 1810s and 1820s. In response to riots, escapes, fires, fights, and general disorder, accompanied by a perceived crime wave attributed to the prison itself, reformers rejected their current vision of confinement and created the next generation of prisons. Also intended for the long-term confinement of convicted felons, these modern prisons, hosting larger populations, offered extensive architecture and detailed daily routines, both designed to discipline, control, and ultimately reform their prisoners while achieving some degree of self-sufficiency from prisoner labor. Again, between 1820 and 1860, almost every state built or reconstructed a modern prison. These prisons almost exclusively copied New York's Auburn System of factory-style labor during the day and solitary confinement at night (McLennan 2008; Rubin 2015).

8.2.3 The Birth of Penal Organization

The birth of the prison in the late eighteenth and early nineteenth centuries was a watershed moment in penal history.[4] For early sociologist Emile Durkheim (1893, 1900), the birth of the prison, accompanied by a rejection of sanguinary punishments in favor of the deprivation of liberty, reflected new values of individualism generated by the transition from primitive, homogenous, highly religious societies toward increasingly diverse, democratic, industrialized societies. For Marxist scholars Georg Rusche and Otto Kirchheimer (1939), the prison represented a new method of extracting the labor power of criminals, more appropriate to the needs of industrialization and nascent capitalism, under which the indiscriminate killing and maiming of criminals was no longer efficient. For Michel Foucault (1977), the prison symbolized the transition away from unrestrained displays of monarchical power to more efficient uses of power, a transition from punishment operating on the body (via painful corporal and capital punishments) to punishment targeting the soul (through reformative discipline).

Whatever changes in society the birth of the prison signified, it also entailed the birth of the penal organization. It represents the transition away from punishment as an informal, ad hoc, temporary ritual or event and the location of punishment within a formal, rational, semi-permanent organization.[5] Placing punishment within an organizational context brought about an entirely new set of elements from those associated with executions. By definition, prisons included a permanent edifice whose sole function was confining a unique population (convicted criminals – as opposed to holding those awaiting a trial or execution, debtors, and vagrants as in colonial jails). These prisons also employed a staff whose sole function was managing prisoners, including a full-time warden and overseers (guards) as well as a part-time physician, minister, and board of directors (or "inspectors"). The need to contain and maintain a substantial population of prisoners introduced myriad new activities that were simultaneously peripheral and integral to punishment: prisoners had to be processed, clothed, fed, sheltered, (medically) treated, supervised, disciplined, trained, and counseled. Finally, as a permanent and expensive

---

[4] Some scholars have questioned the innovativeness of this period, pointing to earlier English and European workhouses (Spierenburg 1991; Hirsch 1992). While precursors certainly existed, the arrival of incarceration as the primary form of punishment for serious offenders revolutionized criminal justice and society.

[5] This terminology is specific to organizational theory. As Scott (2003, 20) explains,

> A *formal* social structure is one in which the social positions and the relationships among them have been explicitly specified and are defined independently of the personal characteristics and relations of the participants occupying these positions. By contrast, in an *informal* social structure, it is impossible to distinguish between the characteristics of the positions and the prescribed relations and the characteristics and personal relations of the participants.

> Likewise, rational is not intended as a normative judgment, but refers to "technical or functional rationality" or "the extent to which a series of actions is organized in such a way as to lead to predetermined goals with maximum efficiency" (Scott 2003, 33).

organization, the prison needed to continuously justify its existence. Most prisons were justified by their combined (purported) ability to reduce crime, reform criminals into useful, law-abiding citizens, and generate some revenue from prisoner labor. Each of these features – a building and staff, epiphenomenal activities, and the need to justify itself and its expense – was absent when punishment was an ad hoc ritual with little infrastructure.[6]

This shift from temporary ritual to permanent organization has significant consequences for punishment. Creating organizations to achieve penal goals introduces a host of new goals and challenges common to organizations of all kinds but that are particularly challenging for prisons. As I show below, prison administrators expended great effort on these nonpenal ends, often eclipsing their other work. Ultimately, I argue that placing punishment within an organization virtually ensured the impossibility of discipline, reformation, or any other formal penal goal that might emerge.[7]

8.3 CONSEQUENCES OF PUNISHMENT'S ORGANIZATIONAL CONTEXT

Drawing on lessons from organizational theory and the law and society literature, as well as insights gleaned from my own primary research on Eastern State Penitentiary (1829–79), I illustrate below three sets of challenges endemic to prisons as organizations that prevent them from functioning as intended. First, the introduction of an organizational setting created myriad managerial concerns with which the administrators of punishment would be forever concerned. These concerns include ensuring the prison's continued existence, keeping costs low or working to achieve some measure of profitability, and of course maintaining – feeding, clothing, and medically treating – human beings in cellular confinement. Second, penal officials, as proxies for the state and charged with daily penal administration, look to terse, vague, and sometimes conflicting laws to guide their behavior and to understand

---

[6] The emphasis on the transition from ritual to organization does not imply that prisons are devoid of ritual. Instead, punishment now constituted not a single, occasional ritual, but a series of ongoing, repeated rituals carried out by guards and wardens – personnel hired specifically for their sole employment in the prison – according to specified rules within a place exclusively dedicated to punishment.

[7] I purposely use the term "formal goal" to distinguish from informal or what we might call "social control" goals. These goals include race or class control – goals whose presence have been convincingly suggested by Irwin (1985), Wacquant (2001), and Alexander (2010), among others. These goals also include using prisons as political tools to help politicians get elected and stay in office or political parties to shore up their power (Beckett 1997; Simon 2007). These goals certainly exist, but they are rarely acknowledged. Moreover, when prisons exist for race or class control, or as political footballs, in many ways their internal functioning matters very little: their very existence, their symbolic potential, and their ability to remove unwanted or "excess" populations from view are each more important. Instead, I focus on prisons' formal penal goals related to crime reduction. That is, I seek to analyze prisons on their own terms, or at least the terms that they publicly claim to justify their existence.

their duties. Finally, prison administrators and staff, like other organizational actors, introduce their own culture or approach to their organization's mission, while some actors identify greatly with their status or position within the prison, and would fight to maintain it. These challenges have plagued prisons from the beginning – even throughout the idealistic, reformer-dominated Jacksonian Era – and continue to compete with formal penal goals.

8.3.1 Introduction of Managerial Concerns

The rise of managerialism in late twentieth-century corrections has received much attention since Feeley and Simon's (1992) identification of the "new penology." Managerialism in this sense is characterized by a generic concern with the functioning of a (prison, parole) system – its ability to process people – divorced from attention to substantive penal goals like deterrence or rehabilitation (or crime reduction). However, some critics of this framework have argued that managerialism has long been a feature of modern criminal justice; instead, it just became more explicit in the 1980s (e.g., Lucken 1998). But whereas these scholars have viewed managerialism as a tool for achieving various penal goals, I describe managerialism as a tendency that competes with formal penal goals and sometimes can even displace those goals. Below, I describe three nonpenal, managerial concerns endemic to prisons.

First, the need to hold human beings for long periods in captivity, definitional to imprisonment, introduces a variety of concerns or necessary activities that have very little to do with formal penal concerns. As Goffman (1961) has noted, in prisons, among other total institutions, "all aspects of life are conducted" by the administrators and staff. The prison must take responsibility for all of the activities a person needs to survive. Prisons must feed, clothe, and give provisions to prisoners. Prisons must try to prevent the spread of disease across prisoners, avoid prisoner deaths, or at least maintain some minimum level of health. Prisons must prevent prisoners from escaping, but also track or supervise prisoners' movements. Prisons must orchestrate prisoners' activities, whether these activities are intended to offer skills and good habits to reduce future criminality, to assign prisoners labor that will mitigate the prison's expenses, or to prevent extreme boredom that may lead to behavior problems. Even if the prison's sole job is to contain its prisoners, and pursue no other penological goals (like rehabilitation, deterrence, or retribution), it still must perform all of these other functions. Consequently, prisons will necessarily divert some of their resources and decision making to these functions' performance.

Second, the introduction of a permanent physical structure and staff, as well as the functions necessary to maintain a group of living beings, generates an unprecedented amount of costs, which soon compete with formal penal goals. (Colonial jails extracted a range of fees from their inmates, but inmates were also supported by their families, by extorting money from other inmates, and occasionally by charity. Some fees were still collected in modern prisons, usually under the heading of court costs, but even these fees did not nearly cover the costs of confinement.) Unlike the execution rituals prisons were understood as replacing, prisons carried large budgets, which many state legislators and penal reformers looked to the prison itself to alleviate.[8] Almost all of the early prisons – including both proto-prisons and modern prisons – relied on prisoner labor to some extent to reduce the significant expenses posed by these facilities. Many prisons were leased to private entrepreneurs who leased the prisoners' labor; in many cases, the dictates of business superseded any concern for penological goals, including prisoner reformation (McLennan 2008). Even prisons that ostensibly cared more about reformation than profit – such as Pennsylvania's Eastern State Penitentiary, which eschewed the New York or Auburn System of factory-style labor and its cost-conscious justifications – manipulated practices, even subverting prisoner reformation, to reduce costs and achieve the appearance of good economy. For example, Eastern's administrators soon realized that training unskilled prisoners, particularly those serving short sentences (i.e., under two years), in certain skilled occupations created a deficit: prisoners were released before their work repaid the costs of training. Instead, administrators (who publicly touted the reformative value of labor and the need to provide skills to prisoners) gave unskilled prisoners tasks that required little or no training, or simply left them idle, to avoid exacerbating costs. Similar calculations supported administrators' decisions about when and how to punish refractory prisoners (Rubin 2013, 142–50). Reducing costs was thus a nonpenal goal that not only competed with, but also displaced, penal goals, and prevented prisons from expending more energy on such goals.[9]

Third, locating punishment within an organization introduced new concerns about the longevity of the organization itself. All organizations seek to survive. In part, this drive includes the continuous quest for sovereignty. As Selznick (1949, 10) explains, "The important point about organizations is that, though they are tools, each nevertheless has a life of its own. Though formally subordinated to some outside authority, they universally resist complete control." As later neo-institutional theorists have taught us, one of the major forms of survival is to retain legitimacy, which is frequently achieved by conforming to the expectations of one's

---

[8] Even after removing prisoner labor from prisons, and thus the traditional goal of having prisoners negate some of their living costs, prison and state officials still pay attention to budgets – a staple in Department of Corrections annual reports. Recently, a variety of states have revived the fees and fines of colonial jails, implementing pay-to-stay programs and otherwise charge prisoners for basic necessities (see Aviram 2015).

[9] Importantly, the conflict between formal or technical goals (e.g., penal goals) and informal or survival goals (e.g., balancing costs) is not unique to prisons. As (Scott 2003, 11) has noted, summarizing decades of organizational studies, all organizations are beset by a common curse. All resources cannot be devoted directly to goal attainment; some – in some cases a high proportion – of the resources utilized by any organization must be expended to maintain the organization itself. Although organizations are viewed as means to accomplish ends, the means themselves absorb much energy and, in the extreme (but perhaps not rare) case, become ends in themselves.

environment (Meyer and Rowan 1977; DiMaggio and Powell 1983). In practice, this means symbolically adopting practices or structures popular at the time, even if they do not achieve the technical goals the organization is designed to achieve, while privately continuing the activities that help achieve various organizational goals. In prisons, adopting the language of prisoner rehabilitation while doing little to achieve it is a well-known strategy for maintaining legitimacy and organizational autonomy (e.g., Jacobs 1977; Rothman 1980). In such cases, the need to demonstrate the organization's fitness with the normative environment (the expectations of politicians and voters), rather than the rational need to pursue technically coherent plans to achieve penal goals, shapes important administrative decisions.

8.3.2 *The Problems of Discretion, Conflicting Goals, and Vague Rules*

Once punishment takes place behind closed doors, meted out by proxies for the state, an inevitable gap between theory and practice will emerge for at least three reasons. First, locating punishment within an organization, beyond the gaze of citizens, introduces tremendous discretion on the part of prison staff and administrators (see also Maynard-Moody and Musheno 2003, for discretion among police and other frontline workers). In the nineteenth century, prison administrators, not legislators, in most states wrote the internal rules governing their prisons. Prison administrators also meted out punishments to refractory prisoners without external witnesses present and within frameworks of minimal supervision. Prison officials were largely free to run their prisons as they saw fit (for the early twentieth century, see Jacobs 1977). In Pennsylvania's heavily toured Eastern State Penitentiary, oversight came primarily in the form of reformers who made monthly visits to the prison, local grand juries who visited occasionally, and even more rare visits from state and city officials (see Rubin 2017a). (The word "visit" is intentional and borrowed from the historical record – these "visits" were often more of a social call than a form of formal supervision.) Moreover, prison administrators controlled visitors' access to prisoners to prevent the spread of unflattering information (Foulke October 26, 1848; November 6, 1849).

Indeed, Eastern's prison administration was initially highly discretionary – administrators did not formally write their prison rules until, after several years of operations, the state legislature insisted; the legislature's mandate followed a scandal surrounding tortuous punishments that resulted in the death and insanity of two prisoners. The investigation cleared the administration of wrongdoing, but made suggestions for changes to the prison's operations (Pennsylvania 1835). Such scandals occurred in other states, but rarely resulted in serious changes or greater oversight (e.g., Rafter 1985; Pisciotta 1994).

Today, discretion is still widespread. While prisons are significantly more closed off than the nineteenth century's tourist-magnet prisons, they do have significantly more formal oversight from their departments of corrections, courts willing to intervene (sometimes), and a more robust media. However, few prisoner complaints reach the courts (Calavita and Jenness 2015), and courts seem to intervene in prison business only to address exceptional circumstances (Feeley and Rubin 1998; Reiter 2012a; Simon 2014). Indeed, formal structures for prisoner complaints apparently create new avenues of discretion that subvert those complaints (Bordt and Musheno 1988). Moreover, where departments of correction seek to remedy apparently problematic prisons, particularly where political differences exist between the department and state legislature or department and prison, change is painfully slow (Feeley and Rubin 1998; Lynch 2010; Schoenfeld 2010; Guetzkow and Schoon 2015).

The prison line staff – the guards themselves – also have tremendous control over the daily lives of prisoners. In the nineteenth century, guards frequently secretly disobeyed orders; smuggled letters, drink, and other illicit objects; molested the prisoners; or simply neglected the prisoners (e.g., Rafter 1985; Pisciotta 1994; Rubin 2017b). Dedicated prison administrators at the upper levels did not always catch guards' misconduct, and if they did catch such behavior, they may have ignored it or punished it. Some of these problems persist today, albeit less commonly. More insidiously, however, guards' decisions about when to enforce rules remain discretionary by necessity – they simply cannot enforce every rule, and must use other judgments to determine when to punish and when to turn a blind eye (Sykes 1958; Conover 2001; Ibsen 2013).

Even when prison administrators and line staff diligently apply their discretionary authority, they face sparse, ambiguous, or conflicting rules (see also Edelman 1992; Grattet and Jenness 2005). Statutes authorizing prisons in the nineteenth century were fairly concise and left much to the prison administrators to flesh out. Pennsylvania's penal statutes were some of the country's most descriptive; but even these statutes provided ample discretion. For example, the legislation authorizing Walnut Street Jail (the state's first prison and the prototype other states copied) demanded prisoners' separation "as much as the convenience of the building will admit." Moreover, it ordered prison administrators to assign prisoners to work tasks based on each prisoner's knowledge and the ease with which they might "embezzle" the tools and materials (Dumm 1987, 102–03). The law itself thus enshrined subjective assessments and built discretion into prison administrators' role. Later laws were not only highly discretionary, but vague, authorizing "separate or solitary confinement," which the statutes left undefined. Throughout the nineteenth century, Pennsylvania even passed somewhat contradictory laws, variously requiring "separate and solitary confinement," "separate confinement," or "solitary confinement" in different statutes, and sometimes within the same statute (Rubin 2013, 54). Lest we believe contemporary statutes are more detailed, criminologist and legal scholar Keramet Reiter (2012b, 539–40) notes that the famous "supermax" prison at Pelican Bay was authorized by a California state senate bill calling for a "2000 bed 'maximum security complex in Del Norte County'. However, the bill did not describe exactly what form this 'maximum security complex' would take; these details were left up to executive officials and corrections department administrators."

While we might expect prison administrators to look to the overarching goals of incarceration to guide their discretionary decisions and interpretations of vague laws, here too they face obstacles in the form of conflicting goals (see also Heimer 1999). In addition to the managerial goals described above, the penal goals we assign prisons are themselves conflicting. Prisons are intended to punish, reform, deter, and incapacitate prisoners, all while maintaining low costs and some minimal level of prisoner health. Prison administrators themselves disagree about which purpose of punishment is the most important (e.g., Pennsylvania 1850: 5, 28; Goodman et al. 2015). In this context, we should expect prison administrators to pursue those goals that are most important to them – managerial concerns that are easier to measure (e.g., reduced costs instead of reformed prisoners, avoiding prisoner deaths instead of ensuring good health). As such, we should expect organizational goals to supersede penological goals.

8.3.3 *The Emergence of Informal Structures*

While organizations include a variety of formal structures like official, written rules and staff hierarchies, they also develop extensive informal structures, which are more difficult to observe and control. First, each prison will develop its own organizational culture or approach to and interpretation of its duties (see also, e.g., Fine 2006). Even prisons following the same formal approach (e.g., the Auburn System or the correctional institution approach) or two prisons within the same state subject to the same laws will develop disparate cultures (e.g., Piacentini 2004; Kruttschnitt and Gartner 2005). People who staff prisons identify with their prison's formal goals or methods in greater or lesser degrees; as new staff enter the prison and are trained, they too will become imbued with the local culture's disposition toward these goals (Lerman and Page 2012). This culture can determine the extent to which a given prison closely follows a state's official penal goals or adheres to official dictates (see also Lynch 1998). Ultimately, variation in organizational culture across prisons can result in different experiences of punishment for prisoners confined in different prisons and in different extents to which prison staff and administrators aspire to or actually achieve their formal penal goals (Kruttschnitt and Gartner 2005).

Second, individual members of the prison organization can develop a "commitment" to their job or affiliation with the prison. This can happen in many ways. As Selznick (1949, 51) explained, "the personnel becomes identified with the agency, deriving prestige and disesteem from the fortunes of the organization itself." This affiliation encourages prison actors to protect the prison from criticism in order to insulate themselves from criticism. But members of organizations can also become personally invested in their position within the organization, whether their organizational membership itself or the office they hold. An organization, an office, or a technology can become "infuse[d] with value," causing organizational actors to resist change to these entities, even when their technical value declines (Selznick 1957, 17). Ultimately, organizational actors can become more invested in their position, the organization, or even a technology than in the organization's formal goals.

My own research on Eastern State Penitentiary revealed how influential prison administrators' commitment to their prison could become, and the extent to which it could interfere with penal goals. Since its founding in 1829, Eastern followed a unique and highly criticized system of long-term "separate" (solitary) confinement. However, its administrators firmly defended the system against the criticism, claiming instead that it was the most effective, humane, and benevolent prison system of its day. In the process, Eastern's administrators clothed themselves in positive labels – benevolent, humane, progressive, expert – that they could only legitimately claim in defense of the prison. They also fiercely resisted any attempts by legislators and penal reformers to alter their unique, but highly criticized system. Drawing on a range of primary sources,[10] I found that, in practice, these same prison administrators who expounded on their prison system's superiority persistently violated the prison system's rules and central principles. Prison administrators double-celled prisoners thought to be susceptible to mental illness in violation of the mandate to keep prisoners always separate from one another. Administrators also assigned prisoners to work around the prison (outside of their cells), often resulting in prisoners having illicit contact with unapproved personnel and other prisoners. Despite myriad outcomes seen as problematic for penal goals, prison administrators continued these practices because, they believed, these tactics could reduce incidences of mental illness and the cost of prison management – two problems for which the prison was well known and highly criticized, and which the prison had to formally report annually. Ultimately, prison administrators routinely violated their system's rules and principles in order to protect its reputation, prevent further criticism, and ultimately continue to derive esteem from their affiliation with their "superior" prison (Rubin 2013).

8.4 DISCUSSION

I have described three sets of ways in which the prison's organizational setting creates a life of its own to the detriment of traditional penological goals. The privileging of managerial concerns, the influence of discretion in light of legal ambiguity, and the power of informal structures each create pathways by which formal penal goals must compete with and sometimes lose out to facts of organizational life. Ultimately, I have argued that placing punishment in an organizational setting, beginning with the birth of the prison, virtually ensures the prison's repeated failure to achieve its ostensible penal goals.

---

[10] These sources included annual reports, the testimony and reports from a legislative investigation, the diary of a penal reformer, the meeting minutes of a local penal reform society and from the prison's own board of inspectors, the warden's personal daily log, internal records of labor performed by prisoners, and other primary sources.

How should we respond to the prison's assured failure? Should we return to informal, ad hoc execution rituals of the colonial era as our central form of punishment? Should we abolish prisons altogether? I expect both would be misguided for a wide variety of reasons. Indeed, within a society dominated by organizations (Perrow 1991), it is difficult to conceive of a punishment that would take place outside of an organizational setting, and it would be unrealistic to advocate for one (although restorative justice approximates one alternative). Instead, much as Feeley suggests, this chapter calls for a more realistic understanding of what prisons are and why they cannot do what we want or expect them to do: we must recognize the full impact of punishment's location in an organizational context. Prisons are tools designed for achieving particular ends, but tools that introduce their own complications for those ends. Before we seek to revise the prison yet again, we must recognize why it has failed thus far and try to ameliorate the components of an organizational setting that have interfered with penal goals thus far. Simultaneously, we should recognize that the prison will never be able to fully pursue its official ends and that assigning it "Herculean" tasks reveals unrealistic expectations on our part.

8.4.1 A Comparative Perspective

I have primarily focused on American examples. One may wonder why European prisons are functioning significantly better than American prisons, at least according to how much academic literature describes them (e.g., Whitman 2003; Pratt 2008; Simon 2014). In this case, we may think it is not organizing punishment into prison as such that is the problem, but something more distinctively American. However, prisons outside the USA are not immune to the challenges of prisons as organizations, and many such problems have been caused by organizational factors discussed in this chapter. Despite Scandinavian countries' reputation for humane treatment, for example, they have in fact been subject to numerous charges for human rights violations (Barker 2013). In recent years, Canadian prisons have been increasing their reliance on extreme punishments like solitary confinement to control problematic prisoners, particularly those with mental health issues (Hannah-Moffat and Klassen 2015).[11] Cliquennois (2013) has described the high level of discretion and contradictory goals shaping decisions in French detention prisons, while

---

[11] Recent litigation may have stalled this trend by placing limits on the use of solitary confinement. However, one of the tragedies that precipitated this effort, the Ashley Smith case, illustrates the problem with imposing limitations in a discretionary context. Smith committed suicide after spending a majority of her time in prison – initially a several-month sentence that became a multiple-year sentence following in-prison infractions – in solitary confinement. At the time of her death, Smith had been kept in solitary far beyond the legal limit: prison officials had strategically released Smith from solitary to avoid violating legal restrictions on how much time one can spend on solitary confinement while effectively maximizing her time there. Indeed, a report investigating her death found rule violations at "the individual, institutional, regional and national levels" (Sapers 2008, 4). Thus, new restrictions on the use of solitary confinement may not be enough to curb the trend toward a greater reliance on solitary confinement.

Chantraine (2010) has illustrated the consequences of conflicting pressures on prisons to balance security and prisoners' rights. Prisons elsewhere are thus experiencing some of the same problems described here. However, Canadian and European formal rhetoric and policies tend to be more humane and welfarist, which has helped to divert attention from the inhumane practices behind the scenes. Moreover, many European countries maintain smaller prison populations and rely on shorter sentences, which can help to attenuate some of the consequences discussed here, making them less visible overall.

One may also wonder why organizational settings are problematic for prisons but not, apparently, for most business or governmental organizations. Indeed, organizations, particularly bureaucratic organizations, became increasingly dominant in the modern era because they help to efficiently achieve their assigned goals (Weber 1968). But even the most efficient structures produce unintended consequences, such as informal structures that mitigate against achieving formal goals (Scott 2003, chapter 3). In many organizations, however, the organizational setting does not significantly detract from their formal goals. Most importantly, some traditional organizational goals, such as ensuring organizational persistence and reducing the bottom line, are already aligned with some formal goals, particularly in business organizations. In organizations where formal goals and organizational needs are not aligned, divergence favors organizational needs. For examples, universities and law schools are increasingly subverting their traditional goals of education in favor of improving their rankings and, by extension, donations (Espeland and Sauder 2007; Sauder and Espeland 2009). Prisons are more like universities than business in this respect. For prisons, the organizational context is more of a liability than an asset.

8.4.2 Faith and Failure

Why have we failed to recognize the intrinsic design flaws of prison and continued to place our faith in prisons? Several scholars have offered initial explanations for our continued faith in the prison, despite its repeated failures. David Garland has suggested the prison's versatility enables its endurance. Unlike capital and corporal punishment, Garland argues, the prison can "absorb different elements and adapt to one strategy after another" (Garland 1985, 155). Because the prison is able to constantly reshape itself, it can survive while other punishments are abandoned. The prison is highly versatile indeed: the early penitentiaries' castle-like edifices were revised into larger, factory-like Big House prisons of the 1920s, the correctional institutions of the 1960s, and finally the warehouse prisons of today (e.g., Irwin 2005). As Simon (2007, 144–54) has demonstrated, the prison has also evolved to support different political orders; thus we observe different styles of incarceration in the Early Republic, the era of patronage politics, the New Deal Era, and most recently the Post–New Deal Era.

By contrast, Rothman has suggested that there is something about incarceration that inspires faith, which sustains the prison. The prison's initial reputation as a benevolent and effective tool of rehabilitation, he suggests, may have outlasted actual attempts to reform prisoners. He explains, "it was too easy to succumb to the belief that incarceration in and of itself would accomplish reform, that all wardens had to do was to confine the inmate and the result would be beneficial." For Rothman, "the rhetoric of the reform" offered prisons a "mantle of legitimacy long after the reality of reform had disappeared" (Rothman 1998, 125). Even today, despite the emphasis on deterrence and incapacitation (e.g., Zimring et al. 2001), prison guards retain the name "correctional officers" and the bureaucracies that run state prisons (many still called "correctional institutions") retain the name "Department of Corrections." That the prison experience almost magically reforms criminals apparently remains a persuasive myth administrators encourage.

While both of these explanations seem plausible, this chapter suggests that our continued faith in prisons to perform better in the future despite past failure is even more basic. Just as court reforms fail because of a central misunderstanding about the nature and work of courts, so is our continued faith in prisons the direct result of our own failure to understand what it means that prisons are organizations. The organizational context, I argue, will always introduce extra-penal goals, poorly guided discretion, and informal structures, all of which compete with and can (and frequently will) ultimately displace the penal goals we assign prisons. Our job now is to take these extra-penal factors seriously and try to mitigate their effects, to the extent possible, or at least adjust our expectations about prison's capacity. These moves are essential going forward: it is often the mismatch between our great expectations and discouraging results that precipitate the more punitive turns in penal policy (e.g., Allen 1981). Until we recognize the persistence of this mismatch, we will continue to expect more from prisons than they can reasonably accomplish, just as generations of critics and reformers have misunderstood courts.

REFERENCES

Alexander, M. 2010. *The New Jim Crow*. New York: The New Press.
Allen, F. 1981. *The Decline of the Rehabilitative Ideal: Penal Policy and Social Purpose*. New Haven: Yale University Press.
Aviram, H. 2015. *Cheap on Crime: Recession-Era Politics and the Transformation of American Punishment*. Oakland: University of California Press.
Banner, S. 2002. *The Death Penalty: An American History*. Cambridge: Harvard University Press.
Barker, V. 2013. "Nordic Exceptionalism Revisited: Explaining the Paradox of a Janus-Faced Penal Regime." *Theoretical Criminology*, 17 (1): 5–25.
Becker, H. 1963. *Outsiders*. New York: Free Press.
Beckett, K. 1997. *Making Crime Pay: Law and Order in Contemporary American Politics*. New York: Oxford University Press.

Bordt, R. L. and M. C. Musheno. 1988. "Bureaucratic Co-Optation of Informal Dispute Processing: Social Control as an Effect of Inmate Grievance Policy." *Journal of Research in Crime and Delinquency* 25 (1): 7–26.
Calavita, K. and V. Jenness. 2015. *Appealing to Justice: Prisoner Grievances, Rights, and Carceral Logic.* Oakland: University of California Press.
Chantraine, G. 2010. "French Prisons of Yesteryear and Today." *Punishment & Society* 12 (1): 27–46.
Cliquennois, G. 2013. "Which Penology for Decision Making in French Prisons?" *Punishment & Society* 15 (5): 468–87.
Cloward, R. A., D. R. Cressey, G. H. Grosser, R. McCleery, L. E. Ohlin, G. M. Sykes, and S. L. Messinger. 1960. *Theoretical Studies in Social Organization of the Prison.* New York: Social Science Research Council.
Cohen, S. 1979. "The Punitive City: Notes on the Dispersal of Social Control." *Crime, Law and Social Change* 4 (3): 339–63.
Conover, T. 2001. *Newjack: Guarding Sing Sing.* New York: Vintage Books.
Cressey, D. R. 1961. Introduction to *The Prison: Studies in Institutional Organization and Change*, edited by D. R. Cressey, 1–12. New York: Holt, Rinehart and Winston, Inc.
Cummins, E. 1994. *The Rise and Fall of California's Radical Prison Movement.* Stanford: Stanford University Press.
DiMaggio, P. J. and W. W. Powell. 1983. "The Iron Cage Revisited: Institutional Isomorphism and Collective Rationality in Organizational Fields." *American Sociological Review.* 48 (2): 147–60.
Donziger, S. R. 1996. *The Real War on Crime: The Report of the National Criminal Justice Commission.* New York: Harper Collins.
Dumm, T. 1987. *Democracy and Punishment: Disciplinary Origins of the United States.* Madison: University of Wisconsin Press.
Durkheim, E. 1969 [1900]. "Two Laws of Penal Evolution." *University of Cincinnati Law Review* 38 (1): 32–61.
Durkheim, E. 1984 [1893]. *The Division of Labor in Society.* New York: The Free Press.
Edelman, L. B. 1992. "Legal Ambiguity and Symbolic Structures: Organizational Mediation of Civil Rights Law." *American Journal of Sociology* 97 (6): 1531–576.
Espeland, W. N. and M. Sauder. 2007. "Rankings and Reactivity: How Public Measures Recreate Social Worlds." *American Journal of Sociology* 113 (1): 1–40.
Feeley, M. and E. Rubin. 1998. *Judicial Policy Making and the Modern State: How the Courts Reformed America's Prisons.* Cambridge: Cambridge University Press.
Feeley, M. M. 1983. *Court Reform on Trial: Why Simple Solutions Fail.* New York: Basic Books.
Feeley, M. M. and J. Simon. 1992. "The New Penology: Notes on the Emerging Strategy of Corrections and Its Implications." *Criminology* 30 (4): 449–74.
Fine, G. A. 2006. "Shopfloor Cultures: The Idioculture of Production in Operational Meteorology." *The Sociological Quarterly* 47 (1): 1–19.
Foucault, M. 1977. *Discipline and Punish: The Birth of the Prison.* New York: Vintage Books.
Foulke, W. (1846–1852). Notebooks concerning prisons and prisoners. Box 7, William Parker Foulke Papers. American Philosophical Society, Philadelphia.
Garland, D. 1985. *Punishment and Welfare.* Brookfield: Gower.
Goffman, I. 1961. *Asylums.* Garden City: Anchor Press.
Goodman, P., J. Page, and M. Phelps. 2015. "The Long Struggle: An Agonistic Perspective on Penal Development." *Theoretical Criminology* 19 (3): 315–35.

Grattet, R. and V. Jenness. 2005. "The Reconstitution of Law in Local Settings: Agency Discretion, Ambiguity, and a Surplus of Law in the Policing of Hate Crime." *Law & Society Review* 39 (4): 893–942.

Guetzkow, J. and E. Schoon. 2015. "If You Build It, They Will Fill It: The Consequences of Prison Overcrowding Litigation." *Law & Society Review* 49 (2): 401–32.

Hannah-Moffat, K. and A. Klassen. 2015. "Normalizing Exceptions: Solitary Confinement and the Micro-Politics of Risk/Need in Canada." In Extreme Punishment: Comparative Studies in Detention, Incarceration and Solitary Confinement, edited by K. Reiter and A. Koenig, 135–55. London: Palgrave Macmillan.

Heimer, C. A. 1999. "Competing Institutions: Law, Medicine, and Family in Neonatal Intensive Care." *Law & Society Review* 33 (1): 17–66.

Hirsch, A. J. 1992. *The Rise of the Penitentiary: Prisons and Punishment in Early America*. New Haven: Yale University Press.

Ibsen, A. Z. 2013. "Ruling by Favors: Prison Guards' Informal Exercise of Institutional Control."*Law & Social Inquiry* 38 (2): 342–63.

Irwin, J. 1980. *Prisons in Turmoil*. Boston: Little, Brown.

Irwin, J. 1985. *The Jail: Managing the Underclass in American Society*. Oakland: University of California Press.

Irwin, J. 2005. *The Warehouse Prison: Disposal of the New Dangerous Class*. Los Angeles: Roxbury.

Jacobs, J. B. 1977. *Stateville: The Penitentiary in Mass Society*. Chicago: University of Chicago Press.

Kruttschnitt, C. and R. Gartner. 2005. *Marking Time in the Golden State: Women's Imprisonment in California*. Cambridge: Cambridge University Press.

Lerman, A. E. and J. Page. 2012. "The State of the Job: An Embedded Work Role Perspective on Prison Officer Attitudes." *Punishment & Society* 14 (5): 503–29.

Lucken, K. 1998. "Contemporary Penal Trends: Modern or Postmodern?" *British Journal of Criminology* 38 (1): 106–23.

Lynch, M. 1998. "Waste Managers? The New Penology, Crime Fighting, and Parole Agent Identity." *Law & Society Review* 32 (4): 839–70.

Lynch, M. 2010. *Sunbelt Justice: Arizona and the Transformation of American Punishment*. Stanford: Stanford University Press.

Martinson, R. 1974. "What Works? Questions and Answers About Prison Reform." *The Public Interest* 35: 22–54.

Masur, L. P. 1989. *Rites of Execution: Capital Punishment and the Transformation of American Culture, 1776–1865*. New York: Oxford University Press.

Maynard-Moody, S. and M. Musheno. 2003. *Cops, Teachers, Counselors: Stories from the Front Lines of Public Service*. Ann Arbor: University of Michigan Press.

McLennan, R. M. 2008. *The Crisis of Imprisonment: Protest, Politics, and the Making of the American Penal State, 1776–1941*. New York: Cambridge University Press.

Meranze, M. 1996. *Laboratories of Virtue: Punishment, Revolution, and Authority in Philadelphia, 1760–1835*. Chapel Hill: University of North Carolina Press.

Meyer, J. W. and B. Rowan. 1977. "Institutionalized Organizations: Formal Structure as Myth and Ceremony." *American Journal of Sociology* 83 (2): 340–63.

Page, J. 2011. *The Toughest Beat: Politics, Punishment, and the Prison Officers Union in California*. New York: Oxford University Press.

Pennsylvania 1835. *Report of the Joint Committee of the Legislature of Pennsylvania Relative to the Eastern State Penitentiary at Philadelphia (Mar. 26, 1835)*. Harrisburg: Welsh and Patterson.

Pennsylvania 1850. The Twenty-First Annual Report of the Inspectors of the Eastern State Penitentiary of Pennsylvania. Philadelphia: Edmond Barrington and George D. Haswell.
Perrow, C. 1991. "A Society of Organizations." *Theory and Society* 20 (6): 725–62.
Piacentini, L. 2004. "Penal Identities in Russian Prison Colonies." *Punishment & Society* 6 (2): 131–47.
Pisciotta, A. 1994. *Benevolent Repression: Social Control and the American Reformatory-Prison Movement*. New York: New York University Press.
Pratt, J. 2008. "Scandinavian Exceptionalism in an Era of Penal Excess: Part I: The Nature and Roots of Scandinavian Exceptionalism." *British Journal of Criminology* 48 (2): 119–37.
Rafter, N. 1985. *Partial Justice: Women in State Prisons, 1800–1935*. Boston: Northeastern University Press.
Reiter, K. A. 2012a. "The Most Restrictive Alternative: A Litigation History of Solitary Confinement in U.S. Prisons, 1960–2006." *Studies in Law, Politics, and Society* 57: 71–124.
Reiter, K. A. 2012b. "Parole, Snitch, or Die: California's Supermax Prisons and Prisoners, 1997– 2007." *Punishment & Society* 14 (5): 530–63.
Reiter, K. A. 2014. "The Pelican Bay Hunger Strike: Resistance Within the Structural Constraints of a U.S. Supermax Prison." *South Atlantic Quarterly* 113 (3): 579–611.
Rothman, D. J. 1971. *The Discovery of the Asylum: Social Order and Disorder in the New Republic*. Boston: Little, Brown.
Rothman, D. J. 1980. *Conscience and Convenience: The Asylum and Its Alternatives in Progressive America*. Hawthorne: Aldine de Gruyter.
Rothman, D. J. 1998. "Perfecting the Prison: United States, 1789–1865." In *Oxford History of the Prison: The Practice of Punishment in Western Society*, edited by N. Morris and D. J. Rothman, 111–30. New York: Oxford University Press.
Rubin, A. T. 2013. "Institutionalizing the Pennsylvania System: Organizational Exceptionalism, Administrative Support, and Eastern State Penitentiary, 1829–1875." PhD dissertation, University of California, Berkeley.
Rubin, A. T. 2015. "A Neo-Institutional Account of Prison Diffusion." *Law & Society Review* 49 (2): 365–99.
Rubin, A. T. 2017a. "The Consequences of Prisoners' Micro-Resistance." *Law & Social Inquiry* 42 (1): 138–62.
Rubin, A. T. 2017b. "Resistance As Agency? Incorporating the Structural Determinants of Prisoner Behaviour." *British Journal of Criminology* 57 (3): 644–63.
Rubin, A. T. 2016. "Penal Change as Penal Layering: A Case Study of Proto-Prison Adoption and Capital Punishment Reduction, 1785–1822." *Punishment & Society* 18 (4): 420–41.
Rusche, G. and Kirchheimer, O. 1939. *Punishment and Social Structure*. New York: Columbia University Press.
Sapers, H. 2008. *A Preventable Death*. Office of the Correctional Investigator. www.oci-bec.gc.ca/cnt/rpt/pdf/oth-aut/oth-aut20080620-eng.pdf (last accessed: January 5, 2018).
Sauder, M. and W. N. Espeland. 2009. "The Discipline of Rankings: Tight Coupling and Organizational Change." *American Sociological Review* 74 (1): 63–82.
Schoenfeld, H. 2010. "Mass Incarceration and the Paradox of Prison Conditions Litigation." *Law & Society Review* 44 (3–4): 731–68.
Scott, R. W. 2003. *Organizations: Rational, Natural, and Open Systems*. 5th edn. New York: Sage.
Selznick, P. 1949. *TVA and the Grass Roots*. Berkeley: University of California Press.

Selznick, P. 1957. *Leadership in Administration: A Sociological Interpretation.* New York: Harper & Row.
Simon, J. 2007. *Governing Through Crime: How the War on Crime Transformed American Democracy and Created a Culture of Fear.* New York: Oxford University Press.
Simon, J. 2014. *Mass Incarceration on Trial.* New York: The New Press.
Skolnick, J. H. 1965. "The Sociology of Law in America: Overview and Trends." *Social Problems* 13 (1): 4–39.
Spierenburg, P. 1991. *The Prison Experience: Disciplinary Institutions and Their Inmates in Early Modern Europe.* New Brunswick: Rutgers.
Sykes, G. M. 1958. *The Society of Captives: A Study of a Maximum Security Prison.* Princeton: Princeton University Press.
Wacquant, L. 2001. "Deadly Symbiosis: When Ghetto and Prison Meet and Mesh." *Punishment & Society* 3 (1): 95–133.
Weber, M. 1968 [1922]. *Economy and Society: An Outline of Interpretive Sociology.* New York: Bedminster.
Whitman, J. Q. 2003. *Harsh Justice: Criminal Punishment and the Widening Divide between America and Europe.* New York: Oxford University Press.
Zald, M. N. 1965. "Organizational Control Structures in Five Correctional Institutions." In *Social Welfare Institutions: A Sociological Reader*, edited by M. N. Zald, 451–65. New York: John Wiley & Sons.
Zimring, F., S. Kamin, and G. Hawkins. 2001. *Punishment and Democracy: Three Strikes and You're Out in California.* New York: Oxford University Press.

9

The Misbegotten: Infanticide in Victorian England

Lawrence M. Friedman[1]

INTRODUCTION

In February 1829, Harriet Farrell, aged seventeen, found herself on trial in the Old Bailey (the central criminal court of London), charged with "the willful murder of her bastard child." Harriet was a servant, in the household of Jonathan Cook, a "trunk-maker." Cook's wife had asked her repeatedly if she was in the "family way"; but Harriet had always denied it. She denied giving birth, too; but the Cooks were suspicious, and they found the body of a baby in the privy. At this point, Harriet ended up in the hands of the law, charged with murder. But when she was tried in the Old Bailey, the jury returned a verdict of not guilty. They did find Harriet guilty of a lesser crime, concealing the birth of a child, and she was sentenced to a year in prison.[2]

Harriet Farrell's case was in many ways typical of cases of infanticide in the nineteenth century. A more precise name for her crime is neonaticide, that is, the killing of a newborn child, usually within its first day of life. Killing an older child is a horrific crime; but it is also fairly rare, and usually considered the product of severe depression or some other mental aberration. Neonaticide seems different; at any rate, it was thought different, and handled differently, in the Victorian period. This article will discuss the crime in the context of Victorian England, with a brief look at post-Victorian developments.

The Victorians, of course, were not the first in the English-speaking world to confront neonaticide. Neonaticide in fact has been a feature of many societies, and continues to be practiced in some parts of the world. It was a feature of England in the early modern period, and also in the American colonies: in the colonies, there was both the killing of newborns, and at times the killing of older children as well (Hoffer and Hull 1981). A considerable body of scholarship has dealt with the subject

---

[1] I am indebted to John Butler and to Dante O'Connell for their help in the research for this article; also to the work of Malcolm Feeley and Ashley Rubin, which they were kind enough to share with me; the piece is dedicated to Malcolm Feeley, who has done such pioneering work in this area and others.
[2] *Old Bailey Proceedings Online* (www.oldbaileyonline.org, version 7.1, January 13, 2014) February 1829, trial of Harriet Farrell (t18290219-62).

of infanticide and neonaticide (Langer 1974; Linzer-Schwartz and Isser 2000; Meyer and Oberman 2001; Jackson 2002; Oberman 2003; Rose 1986; Ward 1999; Arnot 2000, 55; Higginbotham 1989; Behlmer 1979; McDonagh 2003, 123; Ward 2014, 101–08; Backhouse 1984; Brennan 2013; Hoffer and Hull 1981; Gartner and McCarthy 2006, 91; Friedman 2018). Strictly speaking, killing a newborn baby is a form of murder, or at least culpable homicide (Ryzner 2013). The penal codes of England and the colonies never had any special clauses dealing with neonaticide or treating it separately from other forms of homicide. Killing was killing. But, of course, societies have always condemned some killings more than others. The penal codes make few distinctions; but the actual behavior of the legal system tells a more complex and nuanced story. This is dramatically the case with regard to neonaticide.

One hundred and ninety-seven cases tried in the Old Bailey between 1828 and 1913 constitute the basic data presented here. The vast majority of the cases were neonaticides; in a few instances, the child was somewhat older. Some of the cases, as reported, present testimony in considerable detail; in others, only a few bare facts are mentioned; and in some, the evidence is (unfortunately) omitted as "being of a nature unfit for publication" – unfit, that is, for the tender sensibilities of the Victorians.[3] Killing a newborn is overwhelmingly a woman's crime; occasionally (in the United States) we find mention of some man who either helped the mother kill the child, or had a role in hiding the body. This is much rarer in the Old Bailey files. In every single case in our data set, the defendant was a woman. Obviously, there is (or was) a man lurking in the background – after all, somebody fathered these children. But men hardly figure at all in the cases. In 1847, Matilda Hewson gave birth to a child, secretly, and put the baby in the privy, where it died. Her father, George John Hewson, was also arrested and charged with concealing the birth.[4] But this is quite exceptional. In a few cases, actual fathers (or supposed fathers) are mentioned. In 1868, Minnie Edwards was charged with murdering her newborn son. She was a servant for a bookbinder. She accused William Byatt, a machinist, of fathering the child. He denied it. According to the defendant, he advised her to walk around all night; the baby would eventually die. She followed his advice, and then left the child on the steps to die. She was found not guilty.[5]

We can distinguish three main reasons why a woman might kill her newborn child. The first is sheer economic desperation. This was a dominant motive in the London cases, as far as we can tell from the reports, which as we said are often rather fragmentary. A second motive was a sense of shame. Virtually all of these women

---

[3] See, for example, Mary Ann Leaver, LCCC, May 14, 1838. She had been "delivered of an illegitimate child, which was discovered in the privy of her mother's house." The verdict was not guilty.

[4] *Old Bailey Proceedings*, October 1847, George John & Matilda Hewson (t18471025-2345). Sarah Ann Fry was tried in 1849, and a man, James Durant, was named as an accessory after the fact. Neither was convicted.

[5] *Old Bailey Proceedings*, December 1868, Minnie Edwards (t18681214-147).

were unmarried, at a time when giving birth out of wedlock was a scandalous and highly stigmatized act, at least in respectable society. A third motive might be mental illness; but the state of the records makes it impossible to speculate about the extent of this motive, and, in any event, the women almost never entered a plea of not guilty by reason of insanity. In a few cases, we do hear about the woman's state of mental health, offered as a kind of excuse or mitigation; Mary Medlin, in 1886, who had killed her infant child, was declared insane, and thus not responsible for what she did.[6] Another woman, Annie Cherry, in 1887, was charged with murder; but evidence was offered to show she was not in her right mind. A doctor said she suffered from "melancholia." She was found guilty, but was "detained for Her Majesty's pleasure"; a pardon or commutation was almost certain.[7] A woman in 1888, charged with murder, was (according to a doctor) suffering from "puerperal mania" and was hence not blameworthy. The verdict: not guilty.[8]

There was considerable discussion and debate about neonaticide in Victorian England, particularly in the 1860s; and there is a sizeable literature on the subject; it also figures in Victorian fiction. To actually measure the problem, however, is almost impossible. The Old Bailey reports, which we rely on here, are a rare and extremely valuable source for studying the issue in social context.[9] But the total number of cases in the Old Bailey was never huge: a bit over two a year, in the eighty-five years covered in this study. The number did, however, increase in the second half of the nineteenth century, though not enormously. The problem is, the Old Bailey papers tell us only about the women who were caught and put on trial. Articles in the London press talk about tiny bodies found floating in the Thames. Who put them there was almost never discovered. In general, it is pretty much agreed that most mothers who killed a newborn baby simply got away with it.

9.1 SEDUCED AND ABANDONED

Harriet Farrell was in most ways quite typical of the young women accused of the crime in London. She was unmarried. She was poor. And she was in domestic service. In nineteenth century England, the crime was committed almost exclusively by women in this situation. Perhaps we should put it more cautiously. Many of the Old Bailey files are quite skimpy, and say nothing about occupation. Where an occupation is listed, the woman is almost always in some form of domestic service. And unmarried. Fragmentary evidence from other parts of England, along with

---

[6] *Old Bailey Proceedings*, October 1886, Mary Spago Medlin (t18861025-1082). A fourth motive is one we find in a few cases in recent times: a very young woman feels completely unready and unprepared for motherhood. She disposes of the child to get rid of this burden.
[7] *Old Bailey Proceedings*, May 1887, Annie Cherry (t18870523-659).
[8] *Old Bailey Proceedings*, January 1888, Maxwell Rae (t18880130-282).
[9] These records are now available online. They will be cited here by the name of the defendant and the date.

secondary sources, confirm the impression the Old Bailey records give us: the defendants in these cases are for the most part unmarried women in domestic service.

Domestic service was a very common occupation for women in Victorian England, perhaps the most common of all. According to one estimate, there were about a million servants in Great Britain in 1851, and the vast majority of them were women (May 1998, 4). Great families had multitudes of servants, as the television fans of Downton Abbey are aware; the Sixth Duke of Bedford, who died in 1839, had 300 servants (May 1998, 4). Smaller households had fewer servants, but even small tradesmen – grocers, plumbers, corn dealers – were likely to have at least a "maid-of-all-work" (Horn 1975, 18). Getting a decent count of the actual numbers, however, is a tricky business (Higgs 1986; Higgs 1983). In general, the literature on these thousands and thousands of women is quite sparse (Horn 1975, 18; Huggett 1977; Lethbridge 2013). We know that girls as young as twelve or thirteen entered households as maids of all work. But servants were supposed to be as invisible as possible. In Victorian literature, on the whole, they hover around the edges of the great novels, presupposed, essential, but hardly ever emerging from obscurity as real people.

But, of course, they were real people with lives, dreams, hopes – and also pain, suffering, and calamity. Life could be hard for a young girl in domestic service – it was a life of hard work for little money, often work from dawn till dusk. And for the domestic servant, unwanted pregnancy was perhaps the calamity of calamities. In many, perhaps most, of the households, this pregnancy could cost the poor woman her job. Her employer would dismiss her, disown her, and send her packing "without a character," that is, without a reference she could use to get another position (Huggett 1977, 126). Her family, if she had one, might also reject her as a fallen woman who disgraced them. The result, in the days long before the welfare state, might well be grinding poverty, or absolute destitution; for some women, prostitution seemed like the only viable alternative.

Middle- and upper-class women simply do not show up in the court files. Were they never guilty of neonaticide? Clearly, such women were not in the same desperate situation as a poor housemaid who found herself pregnant. Money could help a woman find a way out. Women could collude with gravediggers and church sextons; dead babies could simply be buried in graveyards, on payment of a fee (Behlmer 1979, 414). There are certainly hints in contemporary sources, which suggest that neonaticide was not confined to the poverty-stricken. An article from 1863 in *The Observer* fulminated against the practice of carelessly labeling dead babies as "stillborn." He spoke of "connivance or negligence between low and disreputable undertakers, grasping and unscrupulous officials, ignorant nurses calling themselves 'midwives,' aye, and even members of the medical profession," all of whom were said to conspire to cover up suspicious deaths of children. The doctors would sign a death certificate, and the baby would be labeled stillborn, shipped to the undertaker, and hastily buried.[10] And, we are told, there were "establishments" in London "where females, who have fallen and wish to hide their shame, go for the purpose of being confined." The baby is "either allowed to die," or handed over to "some person to be brought up by hand, which, in the majority of cases, means that it shall be allowed gradually to pine away and die."[11]

This last sentence is a reference to the infamous "baby farms." These were in some notorious instances simply a slower and less dramatic way of killing a newborn child. The mother would promise the "baby farmer" a monthly fee, or a lump sum. Mostly, the payments would stop – either because of poverty; or intentionally. The mother would never reclaim the child. These babies soon died. Indeed, that was the point. There were periodic scandals about some of these baby farms, and about the women who, for a price, took in and disposed of newborn babies. Charlotte Winsor, of Torquay, a 45-year-old woman, was defendant in a sensational trial in 1865. Charlotte "put away" unwanted babies for a fee; she did this service for one Mary Harris, who watched while Winsor smothered the child. A jury found Winsor guilty of murder (Behlmer 1982, 20–22). Indeed, Charlotte Winsor had the dubious honor of entering Madame Tussaud's "Chamber of Horrors," in the form of a full-length wax model "taken from life" in Madame Tussaud's establishment on Baker Street; admittance was one shilling; children under ten were half price.[12] A woman named Margaret Waters, who ran a baby farm, was put on trial in 1870; she had drugged and starved more than a dozen infants, wrapped their bodies up, and tossed them into the streets in Brixton.[13] Waters was accused of murder and other crimes; she went on trial, was convicted, and hanged on October 11, 1870 (Behlmer 1982, 29).

Not all baby farms were deliberate, cold-blooded murder factories. Some baby farmers were simply poor women who took up baby farming to make some money; the babies mostly failed to thrive and eventually died, but this was not necessarily part of the plan (Rose 1986, 80). Still, the situation at such baby farms was scandalous enough. Baby farming aroused public outrage; a number of organizations were formed with the goal of protecting the life of infants. Laws enacted in 1872 and 1897 were designed to curb abusive baby farming; people who were paid to care for babies were supposed to register with local authorities. But local authorities probably never had the will or the resources to monitor baby farms (Cretney 2003, 632–33, 650–51).

An unmarried servant who found herself in the "family way" was, as we said, in a terrible bind. She had very few real options. Best if she could get the child's father to marry her, or at least to take responsibility for the child. No doubt this happened; but not for the women who ended up as defendants in the Old Bailey. In almost all of

---

[10] "Facilities Afforded By Law for Infanticide." *The Observer*, September 21, 1863.
[11] "The Society for the Suppression of Infanticide," *The Observer*, September 30, 1863.
[12] Advertisement in *John Bull*, January 6, 1866.
[13] Haller, Dorothy L. "Bastardy and Baby Farming in Victorian England." www.loyno.edu/-history/journal/1989-0/haller.htm. (accessed on September 6, 2013).

these cases, there is no mention of a father or anyone else who could take responsibility for the baby. Abortion was hardly a viable alternative. It was difficult, expensive, illegal, and exceedingly dangerous (Sauer 1978). The defendants, moreover, were on the whole exceedingly poor. A "baby farm" (which was, as we said, often a form of slow infanticide) was one solution; but it cost at least some money. Many of the women probably had no money at all, or, perhaps, no easy way to get access to a baby farmer.

In George Eliot's novel, *Adam Bede* (1839), Hetty, one of the central characters, is seduced, and gives birth to a child, which she abandons; the child dies, and Hetty is tried for murder (Bede 2005, 477–78).[14] Later in the century, infanticide figured in George Moore's powerful novel, *Esther Waters* (1894). Esther, a poor, illiterate (and deeply religious) servant girl, becomes pregnant. The father is another servant, who abandons her and elopes with a different woman. Esther's mistress is kind and understanding, but nonetheless turns her out of the house. She is left almost destitute. She gives birth to a boy, Jack; desperate, she gets employment as a wet nurse, giving the boy to a baby farmer; but when she realizes that the boy will likely die, she leaves the household where she works, takes the boy, and continues the terrible struggle to survive.

Esther Waters has a more or less happy ending; but for most women in her situation, no happy ending seemed possible. A foundling hospital might take the baby in; Thomas Coram established this institution in the eighteenth century (Zunshine 2005; McClure 1981; Jocelyn 2005). Another possibility was the "lying-in house." As one account described it in 1871, the woman goes into these lodgings under a false name; she calls herself Mrs. Smith, and she gives birth under that name. The baby, once born, goes to a baby farm, or is given to adoptive parents.[15] But the women in some of these places were women "in a better condition of life," and they paid from twenty-five to one hundred pounds, which obviously ruled out the poor women in the dock at the Old Bailey.[16] Many girls no doubt returned to their families, or went to a workhouse, some of which had "lying-in wards"; in April, 1971, Kensington Workhouse had about thirteen girls – unmarried girls who had been in domestic service – living within its walls with their babies (Horn 1975, 137). The workhouse experience is described in *Esther Waters*. But for women, this was only a temporary solution to their problem; in the novel, Esther is forced to leave the rudimentary shelter of the workhouse, because a new crop of mothers has appeared and the workhouse needed the space. Babies born in the workhouse would probably

---

[14] Adam Bede, even after hearing the evidence, feels that "Hetty could not be guilty of the crime . . . The little creature had died naturally, and then she had hidden it: babies were so liable to death." *Adam Bede* (Broadview Edition, 2005, 477–78).

[15] The newspaper account uses the term "adoption," but the common law made no provision for formal adoption of children. This did not become possible in England until 1926.

[16] "Horrors of Baby-Farming." *Liverpool Mercury*, August 18, 1871.

be farmed out (and most likely soon die). One wonders, too, about the ultimate fate of the workhouse women, after their babies were born, and after they had to leave.

Some Victorians tried to find humane solutions to the problem of women like Esther Waters; but they could help at best only a few of an army of destitute and abandoned women. James Nugent, a former chaplain in Liverpool prison, writing in 1900,[17] claimed "personal insight" into the "desperate" condition the women found themselves in: "Ruined and often cruelly deserted, and even disowned by their own relatives and friends," they hide their "shame" by committing crimes "from which they would otherwise shrink." He commended the "House of Providence of West Dingle, Liverpool," which admitted "unwedded mothers and their babies." The mothers had to remain for a year to nurse their babies and work with them. But this too could help only a few women, and only temporarily.

In short, the women who ended up on trial in the Old Bailey were women who had seen no easy way out; with nowhere to turn, they used a quick, secret, and violent way to deal with an impossible situation. They had now landed in even deeper trouble. And yet the prosecution had difficulties of its own. The women had given birth in secret. Many of them had been able to hide the very fact that they were pregnant – at least from their master and mistress. An earlier writer had claimed that "Servants and the Poorer sort of Women have seldom an Opportunity of concealing a Big Belly" (Jackson 1996, 62), but in fact this seems incorrect; many of these women *did* hide their big belly. One member of a coroner's jury, in London, 1863, pointed a finger of blame at crinoline: "the rotundity of the dress" made it impossible to tell if a woman was pregnant or not; the coroner agreed, citing the case of a servant wearing crinoline who had "actually waited at the dinner table until within half an hour of her confinement."[18] The "present fashionable mode of extending dresses," another writer pointed out, "so greatly assisted the concealment of pregnancy that persons living not only in the same house, but in the same room, with a young woman were often ignorant that she was in that condition."[19]

When their time came, pregnant servant-girls found ways to get rid of the infant. Some used a privy or water closet. Or the mother might bury the body, or hide it somewhere, or leave it in the street, or (in London) throw it into the Thames or into one of the London canals. In May 1863, the coroner held an inquest "at the Queen's Head Tavern, High-street, Poplar"; the issue was a child found "murdered in the Thames." This was a male child, born full-term and "very healthy"; it had been "put to death by blows on the head." The deputy coroner "remarked upon the extraordinary prevalence of child murder" and the coroner's jury "returned a verdict of Wilful Murder against some person or persons unknown."[20] In 1875, Walter

---

[17] Letter to *Cheshire Observer*, August 11, 1900.
[18] *The Observer*, January 18, 1863.
[19] Quoted in *Huddersfield Chronicle and West Yorkshire Advertiser*, August 15, 1863.
[20] *The Observer*, May 3, 1863.

Hibberd, a riveter, recounted how he was "on the bank of the Regent's Canal, near Cat and Mutton Bridge – there was a black and white dog on the bank and I threw a piece of stick for him to fetch"; but instead of the stick the dog brought "what I thought was a piece of rag," but which turned out to be "a dead child fully dressed."[21] Newspaper accounts give many other examples, from various places in the country.[22] The mothers of the little bodies in the Thames or the canals or elsewhere for the most part remained unknown and unidentified (Oberman 2003, 706–07).[23] Most of the women who gave birth in secret and disposed of the body of a baby were never called to account.

Even when the mother was found, caught, and brought to court, the prosecution had a difficult case to prove. In many instances, the defendant would claim the child had been born dead, or died soon afterwards. This certainly happened often enough; this was an age of high infant mortality, and it was hard to prove that the baby was born alive. Medical knowledge was, by our standards, quite primitive. In some cases, we hear about various "tests" that might or might not shed light on the question. So, in the case of Hannah Maria Pipkins, a twenty-year-old servant accused of "willful murder of a certain male child" in 1855, there is a discussion of the child's lungs, which were "fully inflated, and of a pale pink colour, which would not have been the case had not the child breathed for some little time."[24] It was at one time believed that if a baby's lungs floated in water, the child had been born alive; if the lungs sank, it was a stillborn child (Jackson 1996, 93; Behlmer 1979, 410).

But the main stumbling block for the prosecution was the jury, and, in some instances, the judge himself. There were cases where judges simply dismissed the charges (Higginbotham 1989, 331). And juries seemed to be, on the whole, extremely sympathetic toward the defendant, who was, after all, a poor, suffering, pathetic creature. Many of the women were acquitted. And juries that could not bring themselves to acquit had an alternative: they could find the defendant guilty of concealing the birth of a bastard child, which was an independent crime. As far back as the seventeeth century, Parliament had enacted a law "to prevent the destroying and murthering of bastard children"; the law made it a crime to conceal the birth of a "bastard" child by secretly drowning or burying the child, so that nobody would know whether it was born alive or not. The punishment in the original statute was

---

[21] LCCC, Mary Elizabeth Coward, May 3, 1875. In this case, the mother of the child was tried, and she was found guilty. The jury recommended mercy, but she was sentenced to death. This was, as we shall see, a most unusual outcome.

[22] See, for example, *Western Mall* (Cardiff, Wales), March 2, 1899; a boy found a dead baby in some underbrush, "lying naked on some rags"; a child of six had earlier found the body but "believed it to be a doll." A coroner's inquest returned a verdict of willful murder against persons unknown.

[23] Michelle Oberman (2003) studied homicides in Chicago during the period of 1870 to 1930. She found 136 cases of neonaticide. The majority (115) were never solved; the reports "note only that a newborn child's body was found but no defendant was identified." Evidence suggests that the police reports underestimated the number of dead newborns in the city. As in London, all of the cases that were "solved" involved unmarried women, who delivered their babies alone.

[24] LCCC, Hannah Maria Pipkins, January 29, 1855. The child's throat, however, had been cut.

death (Hoffer and Hull 1981, 20). This aspect of the law ended in 1803; after this, the prosecution could get the death penalty only if the defendant was guilty of murder – which meant proving that the child was born alive, and that the mother had killed the child. It was still a crime to conceal the birth, but a conviction for this crime only brought with it a prison sentence of up to two years. This act was then amended in 1828; now it was a crime to dispose of the body of a dead child, hiding the fact that it was born, even if the baby had died naturally at birth (Jackson 1996, 6–7).[25]

A sympathetic jury, then, could take advantage of this lesser or alternative crime, either because they were not sure the child was born alive, or because they balked at the idea of sentencing these women to death. The Old Bailey records provide many examples. For example, in October 1848, Sarah Freeman was charged with the "willful murder of her infant male child." Sarah was a cook in the household of a man who lived in Eaton Place. The housekeeper, Harriet Nuttall, had suspected Sarah was "in the family-way," but Sarah "always denied it." Then Sarah gave birth. A police inspector found her at home, with a dead baby in a basket; Sarah told the police inspector the baby had died a few minutes after Sarah gave birth. Sarah was, quite understandably, frightened: she asked, "Oh, sir . . . Do you think I shall be hanged?" She claimed she was going to take the body to a "woman in Chelsea, who promised to bury it for me." The medical evidence was inconclusive. Sarah was not, in fact, hanged; instead, she was found guilty of concealing the birth of the child; and given a sentence of twelve months.[26]

The outcome of the cases is shown in Figure 9.1.[27] Almost half of the defendants were acquitted. Seventy-five women, or 38 percent, were found guilty of concealing the birth. Their sentences were, on the whole, quite short. Only one or two of the women actually received a death sentence during the period studied. Early in the nineteenth century, there were a few instances of great harshness. We hear of one Hannah Halley, tried for the "Wilful Murder of her infant Child, by putting it into a Jar and pouring hot water over it." She was married, but "her child was to another man." She was hanged, and her body was "given to the surgeons for dissection" (Jones 2003, 112, 120). Margaret Harvey was executed in 1819; according to a broadside, her crime was "the Murder of her male bastard Child, by cutting its throat . . . and afterwards throwing its mangled body upon a fire." For a mother to

---

[25] Offences Against the Person Act, 1828, 9 Geo. C. 31, § 14, (Eng.).
[26] LCCC, Sarah Freeman, October 23, 1848.
[27] The only other attempt at measuring neonaticide that I know of is Higginbotham, Ann R. "'Sin of the Age': Infanticide and Illegitimacy in Victorian London." at 325. This essay was also printed in Garrigan, Kristine Ottesen. 1992. *Victorian Scandals: Representations of Gender and Class*, 257. Higginbotham looked at sample years between 1839 and 1906, and she did not confine herself to neonaticide, as Table 1, for example, makes clear. In general, however, her results are not in conflict with the ones reported here. Behlmer, George in *Deadly Motherhood* cites a Poor Law report, covering sixty women indicted for murdering illegitimate children between 1730 and 1837 in Middlesex; thirty-seven were acquitted, twelve were found guilty of concealment, and seven were convicted of capital murder (one pleaded guilty, and one case was "quashed on technical grounds"). Probably most of these were neonaticides, but this is not specified.

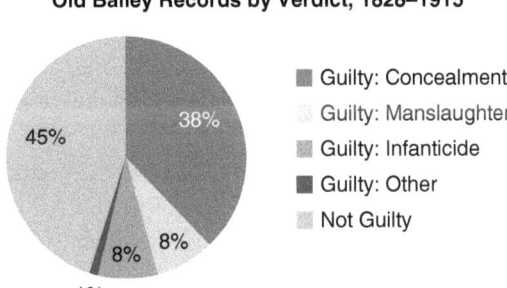

FIGURE 9.1: Old Bailey Records by Verdict, 1828–1915

shed "the blood of her own child," the broadside said, is the "most shocking" of all murders; it is "a matter of horror to reflect, how human nature can be debased" (Jones 2003, 115).

Yet this was clearly not everybody's view of human nature or whether the crime was the "most shocking" of all, at least later in the nineteenth century. The overall impression from the cases, as Figure 9.1 shows, is one of leniency and sympathy. Margaret Arnot has suggested that, in the nineteenth century, the "sense that newborns were not wholly persons appears to have been more pervasive than it is today" (Arnot 2000, 63). For whatever reason, juries clearly did not want these defendants to hang. This was the case in London, and the evidence suggests it was true elsewhere as well. In the late 1850s, in Oxford, seven young servant girls were charged either with murder or concealment; and in the period between 1867 and 1869, another four. All were found guilty, but none were sentenced to death, and some had very short sentences (Horn 1975, 137). In 1898, in Birmingham, a domestic servant, Augusta Villa Robson, was accused of neonaticide. The judge told the jury that "the chance of life of the unborn would be precarious if . . . sympathy with an erring woman might turn the jury into cowards." The jury "returned a verdict of guilty, with the strongest recommendation to mercy." The judge imposed the death sentence, but promised to "forward the recommendation to the proper quarter."[28] In Kent, between 1859 and 1880, no woman was found guilty of killing a newborn child. Women whose newborn children were found dead under "suspicious circumstances" were convicted of the lesser crime of concealment, and the sentences were skimpy; the vast majority were for less than six months (Conley 1991, 110–11).

On the whole, other studies, along with accounts in the newspapers, confirm the strong impression of leniency, which the Old Bailey records so obviously suggest. Apparently, as early as the eighteenth century, this was the norm; we are told, for example, that in the north of England, "there were no convictions for new-born child murder in the eighteenth century after 1757" (Jackson 1996, 134). And this practice was, apparently, not confined to the United Kingdom. Thus, in Canada,

[28] *The Illustrated Police News*, August 13, 1898.

courts would time after time "discharge women accused of infanticide, despite compelling evidence of their guilt." In the Ontario records, between 1840 and 1900, two-thirds (eighteen) of the women accused of killing their infants went free; in six cases, the jury convicted of concealment; in only two cases was the verdict guilty (Backhouse 1984, 458–59, 461–62). Oberman's study of cases in Chicago comes to the same conclusion (Oberman 2003). In short, English juries were not alone in their leniency.

Why did judges and juries treat these women so mildly? Surely, the behavior of juries reflected more general opinion. It must be that judges and juries thought of these women as more to be pitied than censured. In the 1860s, Spencer Walpole, a former Home Secretary, voiced the opinion that people "do not consider that a child just born can be regarded in the same light" as a grown-up; moreover, killing a newborn child lacks "the presupposed malice and malignancy" which is the "foundation" of the law against murder (Behlmer 1982, 20). One writer, in 1869, in London, decried the fact that juries were so soft-hearted; he argued that infanticide was a savage and "cold-blooded" crime that deserved severe punishment (and did not get it).[29] A writer in 1871 stated that it was "a fiction of law" to consider infanticide murder: "We say a fiction, because in no case is capital punishment inflicted," not at least since 1849; in every case of conviction, the sentence was commuted.[30] In 1877, in Aberdeen, Scotland, Sheriff Dove Wilson read an "excellent paper" on infanticide; a "lively discussion" followed in which "several ladies took part." Sheriff Wilson argued – and the audience agreed – that the "eye of the law" should distinguish between infanticide and murder; the present law was "so inoperative that no mother has suffered the penalty of child murder for thirty years past."[31] And the Lord Chief Baron, addressing the grand jury in Belfast, referring to infanticide, expressed the view that the practice of treating these cases leniently "detracts ... from the dignity of the administration of justice"; he felt it was pointless to indict a person "with all the form and ceremony that is necessary in the case of a person on trial for her life, when everybody knows from the commencement of the trial that it can result but one way"; courts, he said, are "assembled for the purpose of serious business, and not for cases that can result in nothing."[32]

Still, whether people thought punishment too light or too severe, they tended to agree that infanticide was a serious problem, with serious dimensions. The court records, along with scattered reports from coroners and other contemporary

[29] "Infanticide." *Pall Mall Gazette*, October 1, 1869. The woman, said the writer, "in some cases for a comparatively small object, such as the wish not to lose a good place," decides to "murder her own helpless infant. Surely, this does not make her a subject for sentimental compassion."
[30] *The Examiner* (London), June 17, 1871. A writer in a woman's magazine, in 1863, called the crime "nationally degrading," and "revolting to every natural and social feeling." Thus it was "lamentable to contemplate the impunity given to the crime ... by our assize courts." *The British Mothers' Journal and Domestic Magazine*, October 1, 1863.
[31] *Aberdeen Weekly Journal*, October 3, 1877, issue 7058.
[32] *Freeman's Journal and Daily Commercial Advertiser* (Dublin), March 16, 1899.

documents, attest, however, that actual trials were uncommon; only a few unlucky women each year. And yet, particularly in the 1860s, some members of the elite looked at neonaticide as some kind of crisis. A writer in *The Observer* talked in 1862 about a "shocking increase of infanticide," which, in London, had reached "fearful dimensions." Every week there were "five or six inquests" on the bodies of newborns, and the verdict was usually "willful murder"; and yet not one in a hundred of the "culprits" were actually punished. Most were not even put on trial. This was because, first, it was very difficult to find the mother of the child; but even when this happened, the woman, in "ninety-nine cases out of a hundred," would be treated as a victim, "betrayed by some heartless seducer," and consequently an object of pity. The poor woman tries to "hide her shame . . . as long as she can"; she is "in service, and she knows that if her folly becomes known her character is gone, and nothing but ruin and the streets await her."[33] This was an insightful observation; and the records basically bear the writer out. Yet the writer, though he decried the situation, had no real solution to offer, other than to call for better foundling homes.

A contributor to the *Morning Post*, in 1865, voiced similar sentiments. The article reported a meeting at "Gray's-in Hotel," to discuss some "practical means" for dealing with this crime, which had "attained hideous proportions." Here too it was observed (almost surely correctly) that the cases concerned women in domestic service. The writer thought that "pressure of circumstances rather than depravity" was the root cause of the problem. In 1866, the coroner of one district in London claimed that in one year he held eighty inquests on children "found dead in the streets"; he estimated that an equal number of dead children simply were never discovered. There were two other districts in London; his estimate, then, was that 480 child murders took place in London each year. This coroner, Edwin Lankester, voiced a rather shocking guess: no less than 16,000 women in London had, at one time or another, murdered a child.[34] He felt that the "chances of discovery were so few" that the practice "continued almost heedlessly of the law."[35] For the central district of Middlesex, there were forty-seven "inquests on infanticide" in the years 1867–68; reportedly, the average number in the preceding ten years was fifty-seven. These cases stemmed from districts "where women are employed in families . . . New-born children found dead in the streets were generally the offspring of domestic servants."[36] And the coroner of Liverpool estimated in 1856 that no less than 300 cases of infanticide occurred in that city each year.[37]

Perhaps these rather hysterical accounts exaggerate the problem. One modern author has found, through careful study of mortality records, that violence

---

[33] "The Increase of Infanticide." *The Observer*, May 24, 1962.
[34] *Times* (London), August 15, 1866.
[35] *The Observer*, January 18, 1863. Lankester, a "strong-willed and articulate medical expert," was a person who believed that "child-murder was rampant and should be exposed in all its horror." Boehlmer, *Deadly Motherhood*, at 424. But his figures may well have been accurate.
[36] *The Times* (London), August 7, 1869.
[37] *The Observer*, September 14, 1856.

"accounted for just 1.5 percent of infant deaths," and that "diarrhea was nearly eight times as lethal as the combined threat of suffocation, burns, and murder." On the other hand, of over 5,314 cases of homicide listed by the Registrar General for a period in the 1860s, an astonishing percentage (63 percent, or 3,355) were cases of dead infants. In 1977, on the other hand, only 6.1 percent of English murder victims were children less than one year old. Mid-Victorian infants, if not "'slaughtered' en masse," were "clearly more apt to be killed than people of all other age groups combined" (Behlmer 1982, 18). In general, it is impossible to tell exactly how many newborn babies were killed; the yearly toll in the London area during the 1860s varied according to different estimates from about 300 to about 1,000 a year, but there is no agreement on any figures, for obvious reasons (Sauer 1978, 86).

The Royal Commission on Capital Punishment, which published its report in 1866, noted the "failure of justice" in cases of infanticide. Infanticide was, legally speaking, simply murder; as soon as a child was born alive, it was "under the protection of the law," the same as an adult. But the Commission pointed out, as it had to, that the sticking point was proof that a child was born alive. The Commission suggested creating a special offense, "unlawfully and maliciously to inflict grievous bodily harm or serious injury upon a child during its birth, or within seven days thereafter," if the child died. The prosecution would not have to show that the "child was completely born alive."[38] This hardly seems like a practical suggestion, and in any event it was not adopted. Perhaps it was unnecessary. The concealment statute did the trick. It provided at least a mild punishment for women who gave birth secretly and whose babies died.

9.2 MODERN TIMES

Victorian sources talked about two motives for infanticide: "pressure of circumstances," that is, economic desperation; and "depravity" (immoral conduct – sex outside of marriage). In England, quite clearly, desperation was the leading motive. The crime was positioned at the juncture of two aspects of Victorian society: its stern sexual code, and the grinding poverty and insecurity of the poor, including women in domestic service. In our times, pressure of circumstance and "depravity" no longer have the same bite that they had in the past. Illegitimacy no longer carries a heavy load of stigma and shame; indeed, sometimes no stigma at all. A poor, unmarried woman who gives birth to a child is no doubt often badly off. But she is not going to starve; she is less likely to scandalize people; and it is much easier to give the child up for adoption. A psychiatrist, writing in 1970, felt that the killing of newborn children had declined. He suggested quite plausible reasons: more

---

[38] "Report of the Capital Punishment Commission, Together with the Minutes of Evidence and Appendix," Royal Commission on Capital Punishment (1866) 50.

effective birth control, more access to abortion, welfare payments which prevent destitution, and easier placement of unwanted children (Resnick 1970, 149).

Indeed, the 1860s and the years just after seem to have constituted some kind of high point (or low point, rather). Apparently, fewer newborn babies were killed in the late nineteenth century, although it is hard to be certain of this fact. In any event, there were fewer stories about the infanticide issue in the newspapers, and less noise about the problem in general. This, of course, does not prove anything about the actual incidence of neonaticide. Perhaps the practice had in fact declined. Whether this was because of better birth control, more access to abortion, or changes in attitudes toward illegitimacy is hard to say (Sauer 1978, 90).

Juries continued to be lenient. Figures for Great Britain for the years 1923 to 1945 showed that the percentage of women who went to prison for the crime declined from 49% to 33%; probation went from 5% to 22.7%. Later figures are even more striking; by the 1960s, 68% of the women were put on probation; only one woman (out of seventy-two charged between 1961 and 1965) went to prison, and her sentence was prison for six months or less (Demme 1978, 16).

Instances of mothers who killed newborn babies are surely rarer today, but they still occur from time to time. Motherhood is not easy. Some women, if they lack a support system, if they are poor, alone, or in an abusive situation, may feel utterly overwhelmed by the misery of their lives; to become pregnant and give birth makes a bad situation worse (Oberman and Meyer 2008). Some of these mothers are no doubt deranged; suffering, perhaps, a severe case of post-partum depression. Such cases were already to be found in the nineteenth century. Medical sources mentioned "puerperal insanity," and as early as 1829 a medical writer remarked on the psychological dangers of childbirth: when "the sexual organs of the human female are employed in forming, lodging, expelling, and lastly feeding the offspring," the mind easily becomes "disordered"; this is especially true of the period right after delivery, and for several months following (Marland 2002, 168, 172; Behlmer 1979, 413).

In England, the Infanticide Act of 1922[39] reduced the punishment for infanticide to manslaughter, if the mother's mind was disturbed at the time she did away with her child. The logic behind this statute, according to one writer, was distinctly odd: the statute "created an apparently psychiatric defence for precisely the category of mothers who were *least* likely to be considered insane" (Ward 1999, 170). But this defense was not really "psychiatric"; the "mental disturbance" was probably nothing more than a recognition that the mother was an unfortunate, suffering woman.

In October 1922, a young woman, Emma Temple, pleaded guilty at Lincoln Assizes to "murdering her newly-born child, adding that at the time she did not know what she was doing." The plea was accepted; she was sentenced to four months in jail. The judge remarked that the law was "most wise and humane"; and stated

---

[39] The Infanticide Act, 1922, 12 & 13 Geo., c. 18, § 1 (Eng.).

that he felt "great pity for the prisoner," who had "suffered punishment enough."[40] In another case, in 1926, Elizabeth Jones drowned her baby (it was fourteen days old); she was unmarried, but lived with a motor bus driver. She testified that she was ill, unable to sleep, and that the baby "was crying and seemed to be in great pain." She "did not realize what she did" and was sorry – she wished she could have the baby back. The jury acquitted her of murder but found her "guilty of infanticide" under the 1922 law. She said that her "mind was unbalanced," and this, along with "her good character," had an impact on the judge, who essentially let her go.[41] The Infanticide Act of 1938[42] gave the mother a defense in cases where the mother's mind was "disturbed by reason of her not having fully recovered from the effect of giving birth to the child or by reason of the effect of lactation consequent upon the birth of the child." This law is still on the books.

9.3 SOME CONCLUDING REMARKS

The Old Bailey papers and the other sources are, in a way, a devastating indictment of Victorian society. They emphasize, once more, if emphasis was needed, how miserable life could be for women in domestic service, how precarious, how full of drudgery and suffering. They emphasize, too, the utter cruelty of the double standard – especially as it bore down on the poor. But the records also are evidence that Victorian norms were more complicated than things appear on the surface. The double standard was indeed a cruel burden on the poor; very likely the cruelty was most pronounced for women in service. These women were under the thumb of the better classes; they were subjected to the rules and regulations which the better classes laid down. Rural and village women who gave birth out of wedlock no doubt faced stigma, degradation, and shame; but apparently, in some parts of the country, they found more tolerance and sympathy than the housemaids who worked in the cities (Horn 1975, 136). Women in domestic service in London and other towns, who had to answer to the command and control of the well-off, were the most at risk, and were likely to suffer the most for their sins.

Yet the Old Bailey papers also show deep social ambivalence. The defendants were unlucky; they got caught. But the system treated them with surprising delicacy; they evoked, apparently, a good deal of sympathy. The all-male juries who heard these cases were hardly harsh upholders of Victorian standards. An 1869 editorial in the *Pall Mall Gazette*, which we have already quoted, fulminated against soft-hearted juries, and also against the people who agreed with these juries. It inveighed in particular against Dr. Elizabeth Blackwell, a vocal advocate of treating the women with kindness (Boyd 2006). There are "few things in morals more curious," said the writer, "than the leniency with which virtuous women

---

[40] "First Case Under 'Wise and Humane' Act," *Manchester Guardian*, October 11, 1922.
[41] *Manchester Guardian*, July 28, 1926.
[42] The Infanticide Act, 1938, 1 & 2 Geo. 6, c. 36, § 1 (Eng.).

regard the crime of child murder in unmarried girls." The writer was appalled at this leniency; that many women felt this way was, in his opinion, an argument against the idea that men and women were morally and intellectually identical.[43] The fact that the lenient juries at the Old Bailey were made up entirely of men is something the writer apparently forgot, or chose to ignore.

These desperate women were almost never convicted of murder. Yet, as we have noted, in a few prominent cases, women who ran baby farms went to the gallows. Society showed little or no pity for the business of infanticide. Women who handed babies over to baby farmers surely knew what fate had in store for these babies; but they almost never suffered the penalties which some baby farmers did. Abortionists too were stigmatized and persecuted; their customers were not. It is easy to call the distinction hypocritical. A young man seduces a housemaid, then runs away; she gives the baby to a baby farmer, who starves it to death. The seducer pays no price at all. The mother pays a price – in money, grief, and shame. The baby farmer, if caught, might pay the highest price of all. She swings from the gallows. The moral calculus of Victorian England, explicit and implicit, is exceedingly complex. Summing it up in a few lapidary phrases would be profoundly misleading.

I have written elsewhere about the so-called unwritten law. A man who killed his wife's lover or seducer was technically guilty of murder, but juries simply would not convict. This happened over and over again in the nineteenth century. The pattern was so consistent that the term "unwritten law" seems completely justified. It was "unwritten," but deserved the name of at least customary "law." Another possible example of an unwritten law might be the exoneration, at least in some periods of history, of those who commit "mercy killings" (Friedman and Havemann 2013). The original unwritten law was, supposedly, an American doctrine; but there is evidence that it found its way to England as well.

Unwritten laws are examples of the way juries, in practice, bent strict norms of criminal law. There are examples on the other side. If you kill a police officer, in the United States, you can expect harsh treatment; and the treatment, in the old South, of African Americans who harmed whites, or violated the code of white supremacy, amounted to an unwritten law of incredible cruelty and harshness.

The Old Bailey records, which newspaper accounts corroborate, suggest a degree of leniency so striking as almost to amount to another unwritten law. The classic unwritten law – the right to kill a wife's lover – was never official doctrine, but it came close; newspapers and lawyers talked about it openly, and often approvingly. There was much less open support for neonaticide (though of course there was some). Some mid-Victorians were scandalized by the death of newborn babies; lenient treatment of the mothers who killed them only compounded the scandal. How many felt this way is, of course, unknown. Yet the cases themselves

---

[43] "Infanticide," *Pall Mall Gazette*, October 1, 1989.

dramatically suggest that great numbers of people disagreed with this stern judgment; the cases suggest, too, that we are in the presence of a kind of unwritten law.

After all, when a man killed his wife's lover, there was little sympathy for the victim. He was condemned as a wretch, a cad, a seducer, a home wrecker. He had also, among other things, violated the sexual code of the Victorians. But the victims of the Old Bailey defendants were newborn, innocent children. Moreover, the defendant herself, an unmarried girl who gave birth, was, in Victorian terms, a sinner and a fallen woman. That was the official story. Victorian literature – and the behavior of the Old Bailey juries – suggest something different.

Perhaps the two types of unwritten law can be reconciled. In the nineteenth century, when a man killed his wife's lover, surprisingly little blame attached to the woman – something that seems odd to our modern sensibilities. She was almost by definition a victim. Of course, she was an adulteress; but the cases rarely treated her as such. She was a woman: assumed to be a weak, innocent creature, sexually naïve (and passionless). And the man who "ruined" her was a devil, a villain, a vile seducer. The men who impregnated the Old Bailey defendants virtually never get mentioned in the records. But they lurk invisibly in the background. They are the real villains, the real criminals, the real murderers.

Again, one confronts a kind of paradox. The double standard was in full flower. It bore down heavily on women. They were held to a higher standard of morality – in theory. A woman who was sexually promiscuous, or who had any sex before marriage, was shut out of polite society. As for the men – well, men were men. There was much more tolerance for their sins. The women in the Old Bailey records, of course, were servants – members of the lower class. But they were dependent on polite society; they worked for polite society; and they were judged by the standards of polite society. The records show no trace of any sort of punishment for the men who made them pregnant.

Only she was on trial. But she did have one (paradoxical) asset: the very gender stereotype which kept her imprisoned in a cage of patriarchy saved her from the gallows. Was it the idea that women were naïve, helpless, easily seduced, that came to their rescue? If so, then the shadowy women in cases of the unwritten law, and the pathetic creatures in the dock of the Old Bailey, were sisters under the skin.

REFERENCES

Arnot, Margaret L. 2000. "Understanding Women Committing Newborn Child Murder in Victorian England." In *Everyday Violence in Britain, 1850–1950: Gender and Class*, edited by Shani D'Cruze, 55–69. London: Longman.

Backhouse, Constance B. 1984. "Desperate Women and Compassionate Courts." *University of Toronto Law Journal* 34: 447–78.

Behlmer, George K. 1979. "Deadly Motherhood: Infanticide and Medical Opinion in Mid-Victorian England." *Journal of History of Medicine* 34: 403–27.

Behlmer, George K. 1982. *Child Abuse and Moral Reform in England, 1870–1908*. Palo Alto: Stanford University Press.

Boyd, Julia. 2006. *The Excellent Doctor Blackwell: The Life of the First Female Physician*. Stroud: The History Press.

Brennan, Karen M. 2013. "'A Fine Mixture of Pity and Justice: The Criminal Justice Response to Infanticide in Ireland, 1922–1949." *Law and History Review* 31: 793–841.

Conley, Carolyn A. 1991. *The Unwritten Law: Criminal Justice in Victorian Kent*. Oxford: Oxford University Press.

Cretney, Stephen. 2003. *Family Law in the Twentieth Century: A History*. Oxford: Oxford University Press.

Demme, Catherine. 1978. "Infanticide: The Worth of an Infant Under Law." *Medical History* 22: 1–24.

Friedman, Lawrence. 2018. *Crime without Punishment: Aspects of the History of Homicide*. Cambridge: Cambridge University Press.

Friedman, Lawrence M. and William F. Havemann. 2013. "The Rise and Fall of the Unwritten Law: Sex, Patriarchy, and Vigilante Justice in the American Courts." *Buffalo Law Review* 61: 997–1056.

Gartner, Rosemary and Bill McCarthy. 2006. "Killing One's Children: Maternal Infanticide and the Dark Figure of Homicide." In *Gender and Crime: Patterns of Victimization and Offending*, edited by Karen Heimer and Candace Kruttschnitt, 91–114. New York: New York University Press.

Higginbotham, Ann R. 1989. "'Sin of the Age': Infanticide and Illegitimacy in Victorian London." *Victorian Studies* 32: 319–37.

Higgs, Edward. 1983. "Domestic Servants and Households in Victorian England." *Social History* 8: 201–10.

Higgs, Edward. 1986. *Domestic Servants and Households in Rochdale, 1851–1871*. Abingdon: Routledge.

Hoffer, Peter C. and N. E. H. Hull. 1981. *Murdering Mothers: Infanticide in England and New England, 1558–1803*. New York: New York University Press.

Horn, Pamela. 1975. *The Rise and Fall of the Victorian Servant*. Dublin: Gill & Company.

Huggett, Frank E. 1977. *Life Below Stairs: Domestic Servants in England from Victorian Times*. London: J. Murray.

Jackson, Mark. 1996. *New-Born Child Murder: Women, Illegitimacy and the Courts in Eighteenth-Century England*. Manchester: Manchester University Press.

Jackson, Mark, ed. 2002. *Infanticide: Historical Perspectives on Child Murder and Concealment, 1550–2000*. Aldershot: Ashgate.

Jocelyn, Marthe. 2005. *A Home for Foundlings*. Toronto: Tundra Books.

Jones, Miriam. 2003. "Fracture Narratives of Infanticide in the Crime and Execution Broadside in Britain, 1780–1850." In *Writing British Infanticide: Child-Murder, Gender, and Print, 1722–1859*, edited by Jennifer Thorn, 112–42. Newark: University of Delaware Press.

Langer, William L. 1974. "Infanticide: A Historical Survey." *History of Childhood Quarterly* 1: 353–66.

Lethbridge, Lucy. 2013. *Servants: A Downstairs History of Britain from the Nineteenth Century to Modern Times*. New York: W.W. Norton.

Schwartz, Lita Linzer and Natalie K. Isser. 2000. *Endangered Children: Neonaticide, Infanticide, and Filicide*. Boca Raton: CRC Press.

Marland, Hilary. 2002. "Getting Away with Murder? Puerperal Insanity, Infanticide and the Defense Plea." In *Infanticide: Historical Perspectives on Child Murder and Concealment, 1550–2000*, edited by Mark Jackson, 168–92. Abingdon: Routledge.

May, Trevor. 1998. *The Victorian Domestic Servant*. London: Shire Publications.

McClure, Ruth K. 1981. *Coram's Children: The London Foundling Hospital in the Eighteenth Century*. New Haven: Yale University Press.

McDonagh, Josephine. 2003. *Child Murder and British Culture, 1720–1900*. Cambridge: Cambridge University Press.

Meyer, Cheryl L. and Michelle Oberman. 2001. *Mothers Who Kill Their Children*. New York: New York University Press.

Oberman, Michelle. 2003. "Understanding Infanticide in Context: Mothers Who Kill, 1870–1930 and Today." *Journal of Criminal Law & Criminology* 92: 707–38.

Oberman, Michelle, and Cheryl L. Meyer. 2008. *When Mothers Kill: Interviews from Prison*. New York: New York University Press.

Resnick, Philip J. 1970. "Murder of the Newborn: A Psychiatric Review of Neoanticide." *American Journal of Psychiatry* 126: 1414–20.

Rose, Lionel. 1986. *The Massacre of the Innocents: Infanticide in Britain, 1800–1939*. Abingdon: Routledge.

Ryznar, Margaret. 2013. "A Crime of Its Own? A Proposal for Achieving Greater Sentencing Consistency in Neonaticide and Infanticide Cases." *University of San Francisco Law Review* 47: 459–83.

Sauer, R. 1978. "Infanticide and Abortion in Nineteenth-Century Britain." *Population Studies* 32: 81–93.

Ward, Ian. 2014. *Sex, Crime and Literature in Victorian England*. Oxford: Hart Publishing.

Ward, Tony. 1999. "The Sad Subject of Infanticide: Law, Medicine, and Child Murder, 1860–1938." *Social & Legal Studies* 8: 163–81.

Zunshine, Lisa. 2005. *Bastards and Foundlings: Illegitimacy in Eighteenth-Century England*. Columbus: The Ohio State University Press.

PART III

Judicial Policymaking and the Modern State

10

Judicial Deference in the Modern State[1]

Lauren B. Edelman

In stark contrast to the ideal of an impartial judge who reaches a decision by impassively applying the law to the facts of a case, decades of research on judicial decision-making show that judicial reasoning is in reality affected by judges' political views and attitudes, by strategic considerations, and by historical and cultural factors. Attitudinal theorists emphasize the impact of judges' ideological values on judicial decision-making and point out that, especially where law is ambiguous, partisan voting tends to influence judicial thinking (Epstein, Landes, and Posner 2013; Pritchett 1948; Segal and Cover 1989). Strategic choice scholars qualify the attitudinal model by arguing that judges take into account the preferences of their colleagues, elected officials, and the public, in part to minimize the likelihood that their decisions will be overturned (Epstein and Knight 1998; Wahlbeck, Spriggs, and Maltzman 1998; Epstein and Knight 2000). Historical institutionalists employ a more interpretive approach that focuses on the contexts, traditions, norms, and cognitive structures that help to constitute judicial preferences and behaviors (Clayton and Gillman 1999; McGuire 2004). In their extensive history of the prison reform movement, Malcolm Feeley and Edward Rubin (1998) take an even stronger position on the politics of the judiciary, arguing that judges – at least in some circumstances – are essentially policy makers in disguise.

Through an in-depth analysis of prison conditions litigation that began in the 1960s, Feeley and Rubin show that some judges adopted an activist policy-making stance. Prior to the 1960s, many state prisons were characterized by inadequate medical services, unsanitary conditions, harsh inmate working conditions, inadequate protection of inmates against violence from other inmates, severe corporal punishment, and rampant racial discrimination and segregation. Prisoner complaints were common but the courts maintained a laissez-faire approach prior to the 1960s. Beginning in the 1960s, however, some southern judges began working

---

[1] The figures in this chapter were originally published in my book, *Working Law: Courts, Corporations, and Symbolic Civil Rights* (University of Chicago Press, 2016). They are reproduced here with permission of the University of Chicago Press. I thank Rosann Greenspan, Melissa McCall, and Aaron Smyth for their very helpful comments on an earlier draft of this chapter.

with reform-minded litigators and corrections professionals to challenge some of the state prison systems with the worst conditions, notably southern prisons, beginning with those in Arkansas and Texas. Many lawsuits began as challenges by individual prisoners, but litigators often combined and expanded them into class actions that lasted decades. Judges in the early prison conditions cases embraced the Eighth Amendment prohibition against cruel and unusual punishment, as well as Section 1983 of the Civil Rights Act of 1871 and legal precedents in nonprison cases to engage in progressive policy-making. By 1975, courts had declared prison systems unconstitutional in more than thirty jurisdictions.

Feeley and Rubin's overarching contribution is in showing how judges in these cases were active policymakers who went far beyond the common understanding of the judicial role as finders rather than as makers of the law. Their contribution is substantial and should be taken seriously by any scholar of judicial decision making. In this essay, however, I focus on an undercurrent in their account, which has broader implications for the relationship between law and organizations: judicial deference to models of compliance that originate in organizations and that become institutionalized within organizational fields. Organizational fields, a construct introduced by organizational sociologists in the 1980s, refer to "those organizations that, in the aggregate, constitute a recognized area of social life: key suppliers, resource and product consumers, regulatory agencies, and other organizations that produce similar services or products" (DiMaggio and Powell 1983, 148). I have shown in previous work that ideas about law and compliance tend to diffuse throughout organizational fields and to influence how organizations comply with relevant laws (Edelman 1992, 2016). Here I argue that in the modern state, judges tend to defer to ideas about law and compliance that arise within organizational fields. Drawing on Feeley and Rubin's impressive social history of prison litigation and reform in *Judicial Policy Making and the Modern State: How the Courts Reformed America's Prisons* (Feeley and Rubin 1998) and on my own analysis of the judicial role in equal employment opportunity (EEO) litigation (Edelman 2016), I suggest that there is a tendency toward judicial deference to organizational practices in the modern state.

10.1 JUDICIAL DEFERENCE IN PRISON LITIGATION

In Feeley and Rubin's (1998) account, the relevant organizational field is the carceral field (Rubin 2015), which includes prisons, corrections professionals, and the many organizations that serve and supply prisons, including food services, medical services, building maintenance, and the like. The activist judges that Feeley and Rubin studied turned to models within the carceral field in devising the standards to which the prisons accused of rights violations ought to be held. First, judges looked to the already published standards of the American Correctional Association (ACA), a voluntary association of prison administrators founded in

1870. The ACA had published a Manual of Correctional Standards in 1946, and revised it in 1959 to include a chapter on the legal rights of prisoners. That manual, as well as standards articulated by the Federal Bureau of Prisons (BOP), became the key resources of the litigators and judges who sought to reform the corrupt state prisons. Second, the judges in these prison conditions cases pointed to other organizations in the carceral field as exemplars that ought to serve as the standard for reform. In particular, the judges treated the federal prison system as a model of good prison governance, and they used that model to seek reforms in state prison systems with egregious conditions. Third, and perhaps most importantly, judges in these cases appointed special masters, often with backgrounds in prison administration, to monitor prison conditions and compliance on the ground. The special masters served as factfinders, mediators, and advisors to the court (Sturm 1979), allowing judges to reach far into prison administration to combat recalcitrance and to challenge continuing violations (Feeley and Rubin 1998, 307–11).

Once the courts began to defer to BOP standards, other professions within the carceral field, including the American Medical Association, the American Bar Association, and the Society of Refrigerating and Heating Engineers also developed new standards for prisons (Feeley and Rubin 1998; Feeley and Swearingen 2004). Regulators within the carceral field participated in the process as well. Federal agencies, such as the Law Enforcement Assistance Administration, the US Department of Justice, the National Institute of Corrections, and the US Public Health Service helped to promulgate these standards in part through funding exemplary programs (Feeley and Rubin 1998; Feeley and Swearingen 2004).

In the prison conditions litigation, then, judges were able to bring about reform – albeit after many years of litigation – by drawing upon sets of standards that originated within the carceral field itself. Feeley and Rubin's (1998) account illustrates a context in which judicial deference to organizational standards has something of a happy ending in that it brings about substantial reform among the subset of prisons that had previously been characterized by the most egregious conditions. Judicial deference to standards that arise within organizational fields, however, does not always have such a happy ending. In the following section, I discuss judicial deference to organizational practices in a different context that occurred during roughly the same time period: EEO litigation. I then turn to a comparison of the prison and EEO contexts, considering why judicial deference resulted in more substantive change in prison litigation than it did in EEO litigation.

10.2 JUDICIAL DEFERENCE IN EEO LITIGATION

Title VII of the 1964 Civil Rights Act prohibits employers from discriminating on the basis of race, color, religion, sex, or national origin. But as I have argued previously (Edelman 1992, 2016), the legislation was highly ambiguous; it neither offered a definition of discrimination nor specified the concrete steps that employers must take to be in compliance. Early regulation by the Equal Employment Opportunity Commission (EEOC), charged with administering Title VII, and the Office of Federal Contract Compliance Programs (OFCCP), charged with monitoring government contracts, was also ambiguous and sometimes contradictory (Edelman 2016).

10.2.1 The Role of Compliance Professionals in Shaping the Meaning of Compliance

This ambiguity left compliance professionals, including management consultants, lawyers, and the personnel profession (which would later come to be called the Human Resource [HR] profession) substantial latitude to define the nature of compliance with Title VII and other antidiscrimination mandates. In part to enhance their own status and power, these professions framed the legal environment as replete with risk and claimed unique expertise at guiding employers through legal landmines (Edelman, Abraham, and Erlanger 1992; Edelman, Uggen, and Erlanger 1999; Dobbin 2009; Talesh 2015; Edelman 2016). Faced with social and government pressure to demonstrate compliance with civil rights mandates but managerial prerogatives resistant to change or interference, compliance professionals saw the creation of new organizational structures as the solution.

Compliance professionals began to create *symbolic structures* such as statements and posters indicating a commitment to civil rights, policies banning discrimination (and later sexual harassment), new compliance officer positions, complaint procedures, and various training and recruitment programs. Although nothing in Title VII or in any other civil rights law explicitly mandated these policies, HR treated the policies as legally required (Edelman 1992; Edelman, Uggen, and Erlanger 1999).

Symbolic structures, which mimic federal policies and principles in form and demonstrate attention to law, are imbued with legal meaning and invoke a sense of compliance and attention to legal ideals. Yet symbolic structures may or may not be effective at protecting employees' legal rights. Some organizations enthusiastically embrace legal ideals, but in others, these structures are little more than symbolic gestures (Edelman 1992, 2016). In some cases, compliance professionals are enthusiastic proponents of legal ideals, becoming activists who confront organizational officials regarding rights violations. Where compliance professionals are granted authority and autonomy, and where these structures are designed to achieve specific goals, symbolic structures may be catalysts that engender the institutionalization of legal values within organizations (Edelman and Petterson 1999; Kalev, Dobbin, and Kelly 2006). In some such cases, organizational efforts at compliance may even exceed what was envisioned by proponents of the law (Gunningham, Kagan, and Thornton 2003). In other cases, symbolic structures serve as little more than window dressing and fail to advance the ideals of EEO law (Edelman 1992, 2016). Symbolic structures range from being both symbolic and substantive (or effective) to merely symbolic (or pure shams).

Irrespective of their effectiveness, symbolic structures such as policies banning discrimination and later sexual harassment, grievance procedures, affirmative action offices and officers, and affirmative action recruitment and training programs quickly diffused throughout organizational fields. Later, many of these structures would come to be known as diversity structures, including diversity training programs, offices of diversity (and later equity and inclusion) and the like. By demonstrating attention to law without committing employers to a particular course of action, symbolic structures proved a successful solution to the dilemma that employers faced given competing legal and business demands. Employers could create symbolic and substantive structures that would elevate legal principles over business interests, or they could create merely symbolic structures that privileged business interests over legal principles.

The creation of symbolic legal structures and formal governance structures is only the beginning of the process through which organizations define the meaning of compliance. Once in place, symbolic structures become the sites in which the requirements and meaning of law are confronted and negotiated in the context of everyday organizational events. Where legal ideals conflict with business goals, compliance professionals tend to interpret the meaning of legal requirements in ways that render law closer to business values and managerial prerogatives. Over time, the meaning of law tends to be understood in ways that incorporate managerial logic, values, and ways of understanding the world. As this occurs, law becomes *managerialized* within organizations, or infused with managerial values and interests, which in turn tends to lead to symbolic structures that are further from being both symbolic and substantive, and closer to being merely symbolic.

10.2.2 *The Managerialization of Law*

Managerialization can result from intentional efforts to circumvent legal requirements, but it is more often the unintentional result of addressing everyday problems in ways that subtly infuse law with managerial values and objectives. As compliance professionals use professional networks to fill in the details that law has left ambiguous, law within organizations acquires a managerial flavor that may differ in important ways from law within the public legal order. The forms of managerialization are likely to vary from one legal regime to another. However, there are at least four forms of managerialization that may lead symbolic structures to become less substantive, and in some cases, merely symbolic. These forms are: (1) internalizing dispute resolution (IDR); (2) contracting or managing away legal risk; (3) decoupling legal rules from organizational activities; and (4) rhetorically reframing of legal ideals. These four forms of managerialization, discussed briefly below, may coexist within particular organizations, and certainly coexist within organizational fields (Edelman 2016).

Internal Dispute Resolution (IDR): Since the 1960s, internal dispute resolution in the form of grievance or appeals procedures has become increasingly common in organizations. Internal complaint procedures tend to managerialize the law as complaint handlers subtly reframe law as consistent with good management, and complaints of rights violations as instances of poor management. Thus, even when corporations take complaints seriously, they often fail to recognize employees' legal rights or to take action that prevents further rights violations. Complaint handlers, for example, frequently treat allegations of sexual harassment as instances of poor management or treat complaints of gender discrimination as evidence of personality problems or interpersonal difficulties. Consequently, remedies to the problems that employees complain about tend to focus on repairing relationships or providing counseling rather than on eliminating discrimination or harassment from the workplace. The therapeutic orientation of IDR tends to deemphasize law and rights. Further, it gives employers far greater control over the resolution of disputes than is the case when those disputes are handled through the formal legal system (Edelman, Erlanger, and Lande 1993; Edelman 2016).

Contracting or Managing around Legal Risk: Another form of managerialization occurs as compliance professionals navigate around legal assumptions or standards, in a manner somewhat akin to taking advantage of a tax loophole. Organizations may revise their rules or employment contracts to navigate around legal risk through predispute mandatory arbitration clauses in their employment contracts or employment handbooks, which require employees to waive their right to sue for certain types of violations (Stone 1995; Roma 2011; Resnik 2016). Very few employees make use of arbitration provisions (Resnik 2016), and when they do, the results favor employers even more than when employees litigate (Colvin 2011). Organizations may also navigate around legal risk by insuring against the risk of legal liability (Mootz 1997; French 2012; Talesh 2015). Employment Practices Liability Insurance (EPLI) often comes with the requirement that employers adopt "best practices" to avoid discrimination (Talesh 2015), yet these best practices are often little more than symbolic gestures and fall short of guaranteeing a discrimination-free workplace (Edelman 2016). Employers may engage in risk avoidance and also alter their employment policies to reduce discrimination. But contracting or managing around legal risk makes it easier for employers to elevate business values above legal values, which in turn tends to produce organizational structures that are closer to merely symbolic than to symbolic and substantive (Edelman 2016).

Decoupling: Perhaps the most common form of managerialization is what Weick (1976) called "decoupling," or disconnecting organizational practices from formal organizational policies. Decoupling occurs where organizations have formal commitments to diversity or formal policies that ban discrimination or harassment yet fail to implement those commitments or policies into the everyday operations of the organization (Baron, Mittman, and Newman 1991; Edelman and Petterson 1999; Edelman, Uggen, and Erlanger 1999; Kalev, Dobbin, and Kelly 2006; Edelman 2016). Managers may overtly ignore the policies on the books, but decoupling may be subtler, as in the case of subjective standards for hiring or promotion that favor whites or males. Critical race theorists have pointed to other, even more subtle processes. For example, in their book *Acting White*, Devon Carbado and Mitu Gulati (2013) show how employers penalize members of minority groups who fail to assimilate to white behavioral norms or continue to associate predominantly with other minorities.

Rhetorically Reframing Legal Ideals: The subtlest form of managerialization is through the rhetorical reframing of legal ideals. Two parallel developments reframed legal ideals in the EEO context: the framing of EEO law as a requirement for good management, and the reframing of civil rights as diversity. Together these trends led employers and legal actors alike to envision symbolic structures not just as tools for achieving compliance, but rather as the achievement of compliance in and of themselves.

10.2.2.1 EEO Law Reframed As Consistent with Management "Best Practices"

During the first twenty years after the passage of the Civil Rights Act of 1964, the HR profession, management lawyers, and management consultants gradually began to believe that compliance with EEO law simply required employers to engage in good personnel practices, now commonly called "best practices." For example, an article titled "Fair Employment Practices: The Compliance Jungle," published in the journal *Personnel*, discussed the difficulty of complying with "the jungle of laws, executive orders, and regulations designed to provide equal employment opportunities," but then went on to argue that the law in essence only required employers to engage in good management practices:

> It could be argued that the laws simply require the employer to do what he should be doing anyway in the interest of management ... Policies which are clearly based on sound business reasons will generally, but not always, provide the employer with a supportable defense against charges that the policies are discriminatory (Thorp 1973, 646).

A few years later, another article in *Personnel* sought to attribute discrimination not to illegal bias but to ineffective personnel policies:

> Systemic discrimination does not result from racial, sexual or religious bias. Rather it is caused by ineffective personnel or human resource development systems that

do not sufficiently match objective capabilities of employees with the growth and production requirements of the organization (Giblin and Ornati 1975, 50).

Once compliance professionals framed law as a requirement for good personnel practices, the next step was to claim that these practices would insulate employers from legal liability. By the early 1980s, HR professionals argued explicitly that in sexual harassment cases, employers could avoid liability by having a policy banning sexual harassment and by responding promptly to any complaints placed through a formal grievance procedure. For example, an article in *Personnel* in 1981 claimed that:

> Liability may be avoided if two conditions have been met: (1) The employer has a policy discouraging sexual harassment, and the employee failed to use an existing grievance procedure and (2) the sexually harassing situations are rectified as soon as the employer becomes aware of the them (Linenberger and Keaveny 1981).

This claim was not legally correct at the time, but it did accurately forecast a legal development that would occur seventeen years later in the *Faragher* and *Ellerth* cases, which I discuss in the next section.

10.2.2.2 Civil Rights Reframed As Diversity

A second form of rhetorical reframing, which transformed the legal emphasis on race- and gender-based civil rights to a much broader requirement for policies that emphasized diversity, began in the mid-1980s. The HR profession embraced diversity as good for business but simultaneously suggested that employers should not limit diversity to those groups that were legally protected by the civil rights mandates of the 1960s and 1970s. By the 1990s, civil rights law was receiving less attention and diversity more attention. HR and legal professionals were constructing the presence of diversity programs as meeting the legal burden of nondiscrimination. Yet diversity rhetoric deemphasized the legal focus on race and gender equality and replaced it with a much broader notion that placed nonlegal dimensions of diversity on equal footing with those protected by law, including diversity based on lifestyle, dress style, geographic origin, communication style, problem-solving style, attitude, and prior experience (Edelman, Fuller, and Mara-Drita 2001; Edelman 2016).

As legal ideals are rhetorically reframed, it becomes increasingly possible for organizations to comply with law without reforming practices that perpetuate discrimination and inequality. Further, the symbolic structures themselves attain the status of legality, irrespective of the extent to which they curtail discriminatory actions. Social psychological studies conducted by Brenda Major and Cheryl Kaiser show that when subjects know that an organization has a diversity structure in place, they tend to overlook very clear evidence of inequality or discrimination (Kaiser and Major 2006; Dover, Major, and Kaiser 2014; Kaiser et al. 2013). Although

Kaiser and Major measure perceptions, their findings may be explained by a "managerialization of legal consciousness" (Edelman 2016). As legal consciousness, or the way in which people tend to think about EEO law, becomes managerialized, people increasingly understand the presence of symbolic structures not simply as tools to achieve legal compliance, but as the achievement of legal compliance itself.

All of these forms of managerialization tend to render organizational diversity structures less effective, that is, to move them closer to becoming merely symbolic and further from substantively achieving legal ideals. There is of course substantial variation across organizations. In some organizations, leaders and managers work hard to reduce discrimination and bias, and to provide real opportunity for men and women of color and white women as well as other disadvantaged groups. But importantly, a substantial body of research now shows that, in part due to managerialization, diversity structures are often ineffective and may undermine legal ideals (Edelman, Erlanger, and Lande 1993; Edelman and Petterson 1999; Edelman, Uggen, and Erlanger 1999; Edelman, Fuller, and Mara-Drita 2001; Kalev, Dobbin, and Kelly 2006; Edelman et al. 2011; Edelman 2016).

10.2.3 How Judges Are Influenced by Symbolic Structures

Judges are in theory selected because of their expertise in law but they are not immune to institutionalized ideas about symbolic structures. Just like employers, employees, compliance professionals, and lawyers, judges over time come to equate the symbolic structures that organizations create in response to civil rights law with the achievement of civil rights in organizations. (Edelman 2016). Symbolic structures provide a heuristic for judges, facilitating the intuitive assessment that all is in order, and that there is no discriminatory behavior. The findings by Kaiser, Major, and their colleagues suggest that the mere presence of symbolic structures causes people to overlook evidence of discrimination or inequality, including evidence that organizational practices deviate from antidiscrimination policies (Kaiser and Major 2006; Dover, Major, and Kaiser 2014; Kaiser et al. 2013). Similar studies have not yet been conducted on judges, and it may be that judges are more able than those without judicial experience to avoid the "illusions of fairness" that arose from the presence of diversity structures. However, research in social psychology suggests that judges are susceptible to the same heuristics as are lay decisionmakers (Guthrie 2007; Guthrie, Rachlinski, and Wistrich 2002, 2007). Further, judges are disproportionately white males (Stubbs 2016), and Kaiser and Major's work suggests that white males tend to be susceptible to these illusions (Kaiser et al. 2013).

Both management lawyers and plaintiffs' lawyers, moreover, contribute to the heuristic that symbolic structures constitute compliance by reinforcing assumptions about the fairness and rationality of symbolic structures. Management lawyers argue in court that their clients' symbolic structures constitute evidence of good faith, and of an absence of intent to discriminate, and when they cite judicial precedent that legitimates those structures. The more management lawyers rely on symbolic structures as evidence of compliance, the more judges are exposed to the idea that these structures advance civil rights values. Plaintiffs' lawyers, for their part, view organizations with symbolic structures in place as difficult targets of litigation precisely because they look fair, and often discourage plaintiffs from pursuing actions where those structures exist (Bisom Rapp 1999; Edelman 2016).

10.2.4 Judicial Deference to Symbolic Structures

I use the term "judicial deference" to refer to cases where judges fail to engage in adequate scrutiny of organizational structures, instead inferring nondiscrimination from the mere presence of those structures. Adequate scrutiny would mean that the judge looks beyond the mere existence of a structure and gives serious attention to any evidence that the structure operates in a discriminatory manner or coexists with discriminatory practices. Although it is the province of plaintiffs' lawyers to present the relevant evidence, judges should avoid inferring nondiscrimination from the mere presence of an antiharassment procedure, especially where there is evidence that employees are discouraged from exercising their right to complain.

Judges in employment cases frequently defer to organizations' symbolic structures without paying adequate attention to evidence suggesting that these structures are failing to protect employees' legal rights (Edelman et al. 2011; Edelman 2016). Consider, for example, *Grubb v. W.A. Foote Memorial Hospital, Inc.* (741 F.2d 1486, 6th Cir. 1984), a 1984 case in the Sixth Circuit Court of Appeals. Grubb, a black male laundry worker, aged sixty-one, sued for age and race discrimination after he was terminated. The company claimed that Grubb was dismissed as part of a reduction in force, but Grubb's lawyers pointed out that the company did not terminate a white female employee who had less seniority. Furthermore, there was substantial evidence of discriminatory intent, including reports that Grubb's supervisor had made repeated racist comments and suggested that it was time for Grubb to retire. Grubb tried to use the company grievance procedure but was told by a member of management that it would be of no use (741 F.2d at 1491). The circuit court ruled in favor of the employer without evaluating the adequacy of the grievance procedure, and explicitly rejecting the district court's finding that the reduction in force had been a pretext for race discrimination.

I examined judicial deference to organizational structures over time in a representative sample of 1,188 federal district and circuit court EEO opinions from 1965–2014 (Edelman 2016). Data were collected continuously from 1965–99 and

Judicial Deference in the Modern State

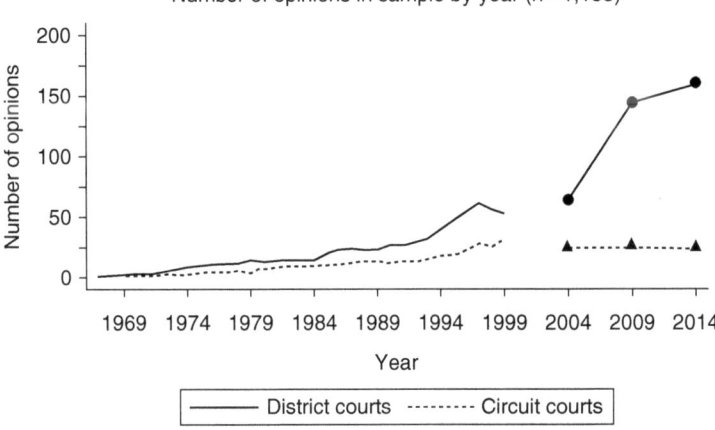

Note: The pre-2000 sample is based on a 2.0 percent sample of all opinions in Westlaw for the years 1965–1999. The post-2000 sample is based on a 2.0 percent sample of circuit court opinions and a 0.5 percent sample of district court opinions in Westlaw for the years 2004, 2009, and 2014. The post-2000 district court sample was multiplied by four to make it comparable to the remainder of the sample.

FIGURE 10.1: Number of opinions in sample by year ($n = 1,188$)

then at five-year intervals through 2014. Figure 10.1[2] shows the number of opinions in the sample by year for the district and circuit courts, respectively.

The study showed a dramatic rise in judicial deference without adequate scrutiny over time in both the district and circuit courts. As shown in Figure 10.2,[3] there was a gradual increase over time in the likelihood that judges would defer to symbolic structures, with a substantial increase after 2000. By 2014, judges deferred without adequate scrutiny in about 75 percent of district court cases, and in about 49 percent of circuit court cases.

Several factors help to explain the significant increase in judicial deference since 2000. First, since about 1990, there has been a substantial rise in the proportion of EEO cases that are terminated through grants of employers' motions for summary judgments or denials of appeals of summary judgment motions. Employers win roughly 80 percent of these cases. The legal standard for granting a motion for summary judgment is that the judge should draw all reasonable inferences in the light most favorable to the nonmoving party, which in civil cases is nearly always the employee. When judges use symbolic structures as a heuristic to infer a lack of discrimination, they are in essence drawing inferences in the light most favorable to

---

[2] Figure 10.1 was previously published in Lauren B. Edelman, *Working Law: Courts, Corporations, and Symbolic Civil Rights* (Chicago, 2016).
[3] Figure 10.2 is adapted from a figure published in Lauren B. Edelman, *Working Law: Courts, Corporations, and Symbolic Civil Rights* (Chicago, 2016).

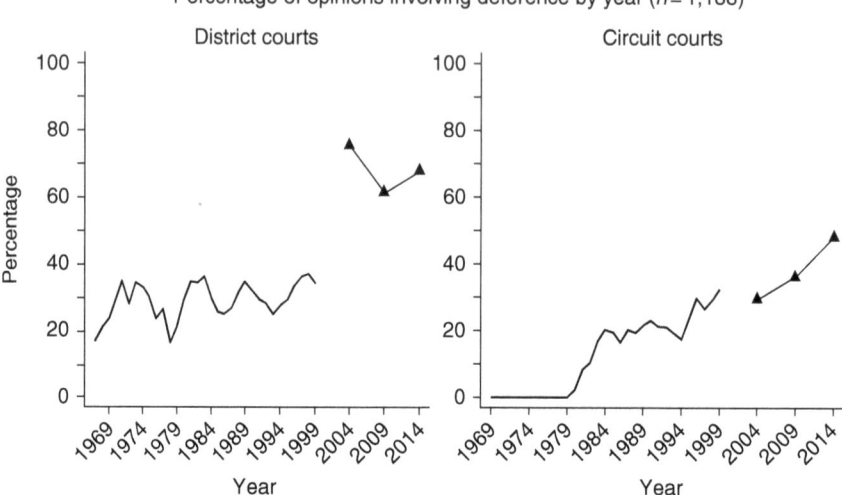

Note: Deference is shown as a five-year moving average based on the pre-2000 sample and as discrete points based on the post-2000 sample (which includes the years 2004, 2009, and 2014).

FIGURE 10.2: Percentage of opinions involving deference by year ($n = 1,188$)

the moving party, employers. Yet over the past twenty years, judges have deferred more in summary judgment cases than in fully adjudicated cases (Edelman 2016).

The second explanation for the significant increase in judicial deference since 2000 is the rise in the number of hostile work environment sexual harassment cases coupled with a pair of decisions issued by the US Supreme Court in 1998. In *Faragher v. City of Boca Raton* (524 U.S. 775, 1998) and *Burlington Industries, Inc. v. Ellerth* (524 U.S. 742, 1998), following a logic similar to that articulated seventeen years earlier in the 1981 *Personnel* article discussed above, the Court created an affirmative defense to allegations of hostile work environment harassment. Under the affirmative defense, an employer may avoid liability by proving that it exercised reasonable care to prevent and correct sexually harassing behavior and that the employee unreasonably failed to take advantage of any corrective opportunities provided by the employer (*Ellerth* 524 U.S. at 765; *Faragher* 524 U.S. at 807). The Court goes on to specify that an anti-harassment policy and a complaint procedure will generally suffice to meet the employer's burden of proof (*Ellerth* 524 U.S. at 744; *Faragher* 524 U.S. at 778).

Importantly, the Supreme Court *followed* trends in the lower courts toward deferring to employers' symbolic structures; as shown in Figure 2 above, deference to symbolic structures had been increasing steadily in the district and circuit courts long before the Supreme Court ruled in *Faragher* and *Ellerth* in 1998. The Society for Human Resource Management (SHRM), moreover, had filed an amicus brief in

Faragher, which strongly advocated that the Supreme Court adopt the affirmative defense. SHRM argued that employers, and not courts, were best suited to address sexual harassment. The EEOC, in amicus briefs submitted on behalf of the employees in both *Faragher* and *Ellerth*, also took the position that employers should be able to avoid liability by creating effective antiharassment policies and grievance procedures (Edelman 2016). The *Faragher* and *Ellerth* decisions, however, do appear to have influenced judicial deference to symbolic structures in the lower courts, as deference in hostile work environment sexual harassment cases increased substantially following the 1998 decisions, not just in sexual harassment cases but in all EEO cases (Edelman 2016).

Judicial deference to symbolic structures does not necessarily mean that an employer wins the case, since other factors are usually relevant in EEO cases. Nonetheless, increasing judicial deference in EEO cases does help to explain the dramatic rise in employer victories over time in EEO cases (Krieger, Best, and Edelman 2015; Edelman 2016). Since 2000, employers have won on average about 75 percent of district court cases and 81 percent of circuit court cases (Edelman 2016). Furthermore, although the courts have become more conservative over time (Martin and Quinn 2002), judicial deference to employers' symbolic structures cannot be explained by judicial politics. Liberal judges are actually somewhat more likely than conservative judges to defer to symbolic structures, perhaps because liberal judges are more impressed by the trappings of due process (Edelman et al. 2011; Edelman 2016). Further, the more symbolic structures that a judge defers to within a case, the more the outcomes look the same, irrespective of judges' political orientations (Krieger et al. 2015; Edelman 2016). Judicial deference, then, is in part responsible for employees' low likelihood of prevailing in EEO cases.

10.3 SYMBOLIC COMPLIANCE AND SOCIAL CHANGE IN THE PRISON CONTEXT

Feeley and Rubin's (1998) analysis of the civil rights era prison litigation in some of the most egregious state prison systems shows how judicial deference to organizational practices can produce meaningful change when coupled with careful monitoring to ensure that standards are met. My analysis of judicial deference in the EEO context, however, illustrates that judicial deference to organizational fields can instead serve to condone and institutionalize ineffective organizational structures. These different outcomes raise the question of whether judicial deference in the carceral field is generally more likely to bring about social change than is judicial deference in the EEO context. This does not appear to be the case, however, as research by other scholars of prison governance points to instances where legal authorities defer to ineffective forms of prison compliance.

Heather Schoenfeld (2010), for example, documents prison recalcitrance and symbolic compliance in the *Costello* v. *Wainwright* litigation in Florida (397

F. Supp. 20, M.D. Fla. 1975).[4] When the lower court ruled that prison populations be reduced to "normal capacity," the Florida Department of Corrections responded by: defining "capacity" as "maximum capacity" rather than "design capacity," moving prisoners to temporary facilities, reducing the space for each inmate, and normalizing the use of double bunking (Schoenfeld 2010). The special master characterized these efforts as a good faith effort to comply, and the state legislature modified prison capacity to allow for 50 percent over "design capacity," illustrating legislative deference to prison practices. In a quantitative analysis of overcrowding litigation from 1971 to 1996, Guetzkow and Schoon show that overcrowding litigation, rather than easing prison crowding, led to increased funding for prisons that did not have a statistically significant impact on overcrowding (Guetzkow and Schoon 2015). Prison conditions litigation often involves multiple issues, so it may be that the litigation led to improvements in other areas. Nonetheless, Guetzkow and Schoon's study illustrates judicial deference to a form of compliance that was in part merely symbolic.

Keramet Reiter (2012) illustrates another form of judicial deference to symbolic compliance in the context of litigation over the constitutionality of solitary confinement. She describes how prison architects designed supermax prisons to meet the most minimal standards set by previous litigation, and that they used the technical language of the earlier litigation to devise conditions that were more repressive than had previously been the case. For example, in response to earlier rulings that required adequate lighting in prison cells, some supermax prisons installed extremely bright fluorescent lighting that was left on twenty-four hours per day. Even as human rights activists and psychologists point out that this and other conditions of solitary confinement pose serious risks to prisoners' mental health, courts engage in the most superficial review of prison practices, deferring to compliance that is more symbolic than substantive (Reiter 2012).

The clearest evidence of judicial deference to symbolic compliance in carceral fields may be found in analyses of prison grievance systems. As prison conditions litigation gained traction in the 1960s, especially after the Supreme Court endorsed due process protections for prison inmates in *Wolff* v. *McDonnell* in 1974 (418 U.S. 539), corrections departments throughout the nation began to create grievance procedures for inmates both as gestures of due process and to avoid further litigation (Bordt and Musheno 1988; Swearingen 2008). Initially, Congress mandated grievance procedures for federal prisons but merely created incentives for their use in state prison (Belbot 2004; Brakel 1983). But the large number of inmate lawsuits led to the passage of the Prison Litigation Reform Act (PLRA) in 1996, which mandated that inmates exhaust all internal procedures before filing a federal lawsuit. Under

---

[4] The case was originally decided in 1975 (37 F. Supp. 20, M.D. Fla. 1975). It was decided on appeal by the Fifth Circuit Court of Appeals in 1976 (539 F.2d 547) and then by the US Supreme Court in 1977 (430 U.S. 325).

the PLRA, federal judges are all but mandated to defer to prison grievance procedures (Schlanger and Shay 2009; Feeley and Swearingen (2017).

If prison grievance procedures were fair and effective, this might be another example of the type of judicial deference that led to positive change, much like the deference that Feeley and Rubin (1998) document in the early prison conditions litigation in select state prison systems. But it appears that inmate grievance systems provide little substantive justice. In a rich and comprehensive analysis of inmate grievances in the California state prison system, Calavita and Jenness (2015) show that although inmates use these internal grievance procedures extensively, they only rarely result in meaningful challenges to the authority of corrections officials. The California legislature adopted a comprehensive grievance procedure for prison inmates in 1973, creating a model that was later followed by other states. Under this system, inmates may appeal any departmental decision or action, conditions, or policies by filing a form known as a "602" (Calavita and Jenness 2015). The California Department of Corrections and Rehabilitation (CDCR) includes several levels of review, overseen by prison officials, an inmate appeals coordinator, and the warden within each prison. There is a final level of appeal to the Inmate Appeals Branch (IAB) located in Sacramento.

Calavita and Jenness show that prison complaint handlers view virtually all inmate complaints as unwarranted and frivolous. Officers' accounts are privileged over the claims of inmates at every level of the grievance system, and IAB members in Sacramento openly state that they nearly always believe prison officials (Calavita and Jenness 2015, 118–19). In the year 2005–06, for example, inmates' appeals at the final level of review were denied in 94 percent of cases, granted in part in 4.7 percent of cases, and granted in full in only 0.02 percent of cases (Calavita and Jenness 2015, 44–5). As Malcolm Feeley and Van Swearingen (2017) point out, grievances appear to be handled in a way that constitutes little more than a façade of due process.

These examples suggest that the positive results of judicial deference to organizational standards reported in Feeley and Rubin (1998) are not found throughout the carceral field. Why might the judges in the prison reform cases examined by Feeley and Rubin have been more reform-minded than those in the later prison cases and than judges in EEO cases? I consider that question in the following Section 10.4 of the chapter.

10.4 JUDICIAL DEFERENCE AND SOCIAL CHANGE

The success of the civil rights era prison-conditions litigation that Feeley and Rubin (1998) describe may be due to several factors that were present in the litigation they studied but not present in the EEO litigation that I studied (Edelman 2016), nor in the more recent prison litigation described by other criminal justice scholars. I raise these differences as possibilities, but further research would be necessary to determine whether they in fact explain the differences I have noted in this essay.

First, during the time period that Feeley and Rubin (1998) focus on, there was no legislation mandating fair prison conditions. Such legislation was not passed until 1980, when Congress passed the Civil Rights of Institutionalized Persons Act (CRIPA), a law that the Reagan administration failed to enforce in any case (Feeley and Rubin 1998, 382). By contrast, judicial deference to organizations' symbolic structures in the EEO context developed in the context of the Civil Rights Act of 1964, which was extremely ambiguous with respect to employers' obligations. The ambiguity of the 1964 Act helped to create the conditions under which organizations created structures that symbolized attention to legal values while often failing to effectuate employees' civil rights (Edelman 2016).

Second, the judges that Feeley and Rubin describe appear to have been highly motivated to reform the egregious state prison systems. By contrast, judges in federal EEO cases tend to be highly skeptical of many civil rights plaintiffs as well as of the more progressive theories of discrimination (Gertner 2012; Edelman 2016).

Third, and relatedly, the litigation that Feeley and Rubin (1998) describe was prolonged over many years; lawyers were committed to the cause and willing to try repeatedly to reform the prison system, and judges were willing to hear the issues on a repeated basis. By contrast, the more recent period has seen changes in civil procedure doctrine, including changes to the standards for motions to dismiss and motions for summary judgment that make it easy for employers to move to terminate cases and motivate judges to rule in favor of employers (Edelman 2016).

Fourth, and perhaps most importantly, the judges that Feeley and Rubin (1998) studied put in place special masters to assist with the implementation of their orders and to report violations. The use of special masters, who worked directly within the prison systems and monitored their day-to-day activities, would have made it far more difficult for prisons to engage in symbolic compliance of the type that employers often create. There is no parallel to special masters in the context of EEO litigation.

Judicial deference to organizational practices and structures is becoming increasingly common in the modern state. As the Feeley and Rubin (1998) example shows, judicial deference to organizational practices can produce important substantive change that benefits the social have-nots. The positive impact of judicial deference to organizational practices likely depends, however, on lawyers committed to change, judges willing to take cases seriously and to view organizations' symbolic structures with a degree of skepticism, and perhaps most importantly the use of special masters who can penetrate organizational bureaucracy in a way that judges alone cannot. Where employers can easily create symbolic structures that symbolize attention to legal ideals without effectuating the goals underlying law, as is the case in EEO litigation, judicial deference to organizational practices is likely to result in rights that are merely symbolic and law that fails to produce meaningful social change.

10.5 JUDICIAL DEFERENCE TO ORGANIZATIONS IN THE MODERN STATE

A final consideration is why judges defer to organizations – either prisons or work organizations – in the modern state. There are no doubt several factors at stake. A key factor is that organizational structures become so institutionalized that judges accept those structures as normative standards against which to measure organizational compliance. It also appears, however, that there is a strong reticence among judges to second-guess the decisions of organizational administrators with respect to organizational governance.

In the employment context, an early instance of this logic appears in the 1978 Supreme Court case *Furnco Construction Corp. v. Waters* (438 U.S. 567). The case involved a supervisor who turned away three black bricklayers from a worksite even though they were fully qualified, because he only hired people who he knew or who were recommended to him by trusted members of his social networks. This hiring practice was the industry-standard, but reliance on social networks had resulted in a disproportionately white workforce. The Circuit Court had found the practice to be racially discriminatory and had offered the employer advice on a less discriminatory method of hiring that would rely on written applications and evaluations based on qualifications and experience rather than on social networks. The Supreme Court, however, chastised the Circuit Court for interfering with the employer's business judgment, stating: "Courts are generally less competent than employers to restructure business practices, and, unless mandated to do so by Congress, they should not attempt it" (438 U.S. at 578).

The idea that courts should refrain from reviewing employers' business judgments appears frequently in opinions involving judicial deference to employers' symbolic structures. Although this idea is expressed in a number of ways, a common phrase found in these cases captures the essence of judicial reluctance to look beyond the facial legitimacy of organizational policies: the notion that a court should not act as a "super-personnel department." This term is typically used in a sentence such as: "this court has repeatedly stated that it is not a super-personnel department that second-guesses employer policies that are facially legitimate." (*Widmar v. Sun Chemical Corp.*, 772 F.3d 457, 464 (7th Cir. 2014).

The term first appears in a 1983 case in the Tenth Circuit, *Verniero v. Airforce Academy School District No. 20* (705 F2d. 388). Since then, the term has diffused quickly across courts. Figure 10.3[5] shows the percentage of cases using the term "super-personnel department" in Title VII cases involving grievance procedures, antiharassment policies, or diversity policies from its first use through 2014.

The diffusion of that term over time provides an informal indicator of the extent to which it resonated with judges. As of 2014, the term had been used in 498 Circuit

---

[5] Figure 10.3 was previously published in Lauren B. Edelman, *Working Law: Courts, Corporations, and Symbolic Civil Rights* (Chicago, 2016).

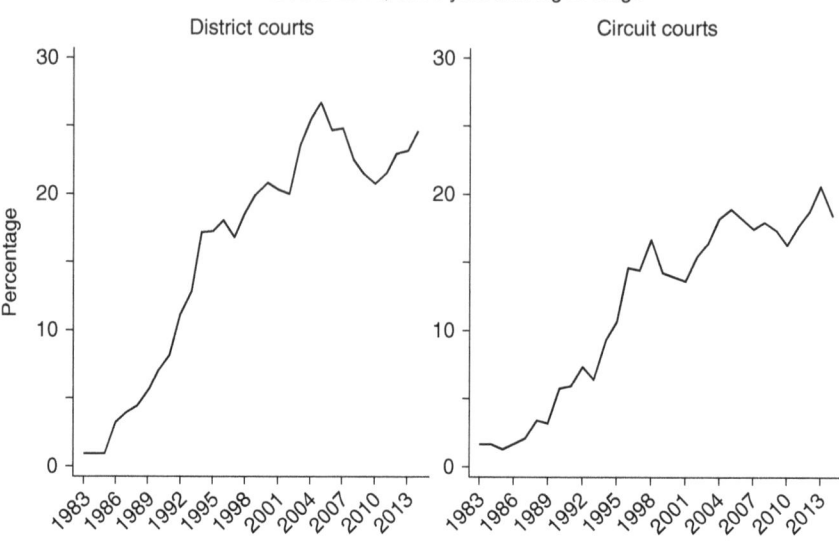

FIGURE 10.3: Percentage of opinions with the phrase *super-personnel department*, 1983 to 2014, three-year moving average

Court opinions and in 2,855 District Court opinions involving grievance procedures, antiharassment policies, or diversity policies. It is important to note, however, that the term appears only in a small fraction of EEO opinions that involve judicial deference, although the general reluctance of courts to interfere in employers' business judgments is apparent in most opinions involving judicial deference.

The logic apparent in judges' reticence to act as super-personnel departments in EEO cases is also apparent in prison reform cases, where courts reflect a strong deference to prisons' evaluations of their own objectives. In *Hudson v. Palmer* in 1984, for example, the Supreme Court held that "imprisonment carries with it the circumspection or loss of many rights as being necessary to accommodate the institutional needs and objectives of prison facilities, particularly internal security and safety" (468 U.S. 517, 517 [1984]). Similarly, in *Turner v. Safley* in 1987, the Supreme Court again reiterated that prison interests should trump prisoner rights: "[W]hen a prison regulation impinges on inmates' constitutional rights, the regulation is valid if it is reasonably related to legitimate penological interests" (482 U.S. 78, 89 [1987]).

The tendency toward judicial deference to organizational structures and standards, then, appears to be well-established in both the EEO and prison contexts. Where organizational structures are both symbolic and substantive – that is, when they appear just and advance the interests of justice – judicial deference to those structures advances the rights of prisoners, employees, or others subject to organizational power. Where organizational structures are merely symbolic, however, judicial deference to those structures will often fail to protect those most vulnerable to arbitrary organizational actions. Feeley and Rubin's (1998) analysis provides a powerful example of how judicial activism, together with an enforcement structure that reaches deep into organizations, can produce meaningful social reform and attention to civil rights. Judicial deference in the modern state, however, too often involves deference to organizational structures that appear legal but fail to protect legal rights.

REFERENCES

Baron, James N., Brian S. Mittman, and Andrew E. Newman. 1991. "Targets of Opportunity: Organizational and Environmental Determinants of Gender Integration within the California Civil Service, 1979–1985." *American Journal of Sociology* 96 (6): 1362–401.

Belbot, Barbara. 2004. "Report on the Prison Litigation Reform Act: What Have the Courts Decided So Far?" *Prison Journal* 84 (3): 290–316.

Bisom-Rapp, Susan. 1999. "Bulletproofing the Workplace: Symbol and Substance in Employment Discrimination Law Practice." *Florida State University Law Review* 26 (4): 959–1048.

Bordt, Rebecca L. and Michael C. Musheno. 1988. "Bureaucratic Co-Optation of Informal Dispute Processing: Social Control as an Effect of Inmate Grievance Policy." *Journal of Research in Crime and Delinquency* 25 (1): 7–26.

Brakel, Samuel Jan. 1983. "Ruling on Prisoners' Grievances." *American Bar Foundation Research Journal* 8 (2): 393–426.

Calavita, Kitty and Valerie Jenness. 2015. *Appealing to Justice: Prisoner Grievances, Rights, and Carceral Logic*. Oakland: University of California Press.

Carbado, Devon W. and Mitu Gulati. 2013. *Acting White? Rethinking Race in Post-Racial America*. New York: Oxford University Press.

Clayton, Cornell W. and Howard Gillman. 1999. *Supreme Court Decision-Making: New Institutionalist Approaches*. Chicago: University of Chicago Press.

Colvin, Alexander J. S. 2011. "An Empirical Study of Employment Arbitration: Case Outcomes and Processes." *Journal of Empirical Legal Studies* 8 (1): 1–23.

Dover, Tessa L., Brenda Major, and Cheryl R. Kaiser. 2014. "Diversity Initiatives, Status, and System-Justifying Beliefs: When and How Diversity Efforts De-Legitimize Discrimination Claims." *Group Processes & Intergroup Relations* 17 (4): 485–93.

Edelman, Lauren B. 1992. "Legal Ambiguity and Symbolic Structures: Organizational Mediation of Civil Rights Law." *American Journal of Sociology* 97 (6): 1531–76.

Edelman, Lauren B. 2016. *Working Law: Courts, Corporations, and Symbolic Civil Rights*. University of Chicago Press.

Edelman, Lauren B., Steven E. Abraham, and Howard S. Erlanger. 1992. "Professional Construction of Law: The Inflated Threat of Wrongful Discharge Doctrine." *Law & Society Review* 26 (1): 47–83.

Edelman, Lauren B., Howard S. Erlanger, and John Lande. 1993. "Internal Dispute Resolution: The Transformation of Civil Rights in the Workplace." *Law & Society Review* 27 (3): 497–534.

Edelman, Lauren B., Sally Riggs Fuller, and Iona Mara-Drita. 2001. "Diversity Rhetoric and the Managerialization of Law." *American Journal of Sociology* 106 (6): 1589–641.

Edelman, Lauren B., Linda H. Krieger, Scott R. Eliason, Catherine R. Albiston, and Virginia Mellema. 2011. "When Organizations Rule: Judicial Deference to Institutionalized Employment Structures." *American Journal of Sociology* 117 (3): 888–954.

Edelman, Lauren B. and Stephen Petterson. 1999. "Symbols and Substance in Organizational Response to Civil Rights Law." *Research in Social Stratification and Mobility* 17: 107–35.

Edelman, Lauren B., Christopher Uggen, and Howard S. Erlanger. 1999. "The endogeneity of legal regulation: Grievance procedures as rational myth 1." *American Journal of Sociology* 105 (2): 406–54.

Epstein, Lee, William M. Landes, and Richard A. Posner. 2013. *The Behavior of Federal Judges: A Theoretical and Empirical Study of Rational Choice*. Cambridge, MA: Harvard University Press.

Epstein, Lee and Jack Knight. *The Choices Justices Make*. Washington, DC: CQ Press, 1998.

Epstein, Lee and Jack Knight. 2000. "Toward a strategic revolution in judicial politics: A look back, a look ahead." *Political Research Quarterly* 53 (3): 625–61.

Feeley, Malcolm M. and Edward L. Rubin. 1998. *Judicial Policy Making and the Modern State: How the Courts Reformed America's Prisons*. New York: Cambridge University Press.

Feeley, Malcolm M. and Van Swearingen. 2004. "The Prison Conditions Cases and the Bureaucratization of American Corrections: Influences, Impacts and Implications." *Pace Law Review* 24 (2): 433–76.

Feeley, Malcolm M. and Van Swearingen. 2017. "Devolving Standards: California's Structural Failures in Response to Prisoner Litigation," in *Varieties of Legal Order: The Politics of Adversarial and Bureaucratic Legalism*, edited by John Barnes and Thomas Burke. New York: Routledge: 155–177.

French, Christopher C. 2012. "Debunking the Myth That Insurance Coverage Is Not Available or Allowed for Intentional Injuries or Damage." *Hastings Business Law Journal* 8 (1): 65–102.

Gertner, Nancy. 2012. "Losers' Rules." *Yale Law Journal Online* 122: 109–24.

Giblin, Edward J. and Oscar A. Ornati. 1975. "Beyond Compliance: EEO and the Dynamics of Organizational Change." *Personnel* 52 (5): 38–50.

Guetzkow, Joshua and Eric Schoon. 2015. "If you build it, they will fill it: The consequences of prison overcrowding litigation." *Law & Society Review* 49 (2): 401–32.

Gunningham, Neil, Robert A. Kagan, and Dorothy Thornton. 2003. *Shades of green: business, regulation, and environment*. Stanford: Stanford University Press.

Guthrie, Chris. 2007. "Misjudging." *Nevada Law Journal* 7: 420–56.

Guthrie, Chris, Jeffrey J. Rachlinski, and Andrew J. Wistrich. 2007. "Blinking on the Bench: How Judges Decide Cases." *Cornell Law Review* 93 (1): 1–44.

Guthrie, Chris, Jeffrey J. Rachlinski, and Andrew J. Wistrich. 2002."Judging by Heuristic–Cognitive Illusions in Judicial Decision Making." *Judicature* 86 (1): 44–50.

Kaiser, Cheryl R. and Brenda Major. "A Social Psychological Perspective on Perceiving and Reporting Discrimination." *Law & Social Inquiry* 31, no. 4 (2006): 801–30.

Kaiser, Cheryl R., Brenda Major, Ines Jurcevic, Tessa L. Dover, Laura M. Brady, and Jenessa R. Shapiro. 2013. "Presumed Fair: Ironic Effects of Organizational Diversity Structures." *Journal of Personality and Social Psychology* 104 (3): 504–19.

Kalev, Alexandra, Frank Dobbin, and Erin Kelly. 2006."Best Practices or Best Guesses? Assessing the Efficacy of Corporate Affirmative Action and Diversity Policies." *American Sociological Review* 71 (4): 589–617.
Krieger, Linda Hamilton, Rachel Kahn Best, and Lauren B. Edelman. 2015. "When 'Best Practices' Win, Employees Lose: Symbolic Compliance and Judicial Inference in Federal Equal Employment Opportunity Cases." *Law & Social Inquiry* 40 (4): 843–79.
Linenberger, Patricia and Timothy J. Keaveny. 1981. "Sexual Harassment: The Employer's Legal Obligations." *Personnel* 58 (6): 60–68.
Martin, Andrew D. and Kevin M. Quinn. 2002. "Dynamic Ideal Point Estimation Via Markov Chain Monte Carlo for the U.S. Supreme Court, 1953–1999." *Political Analysis* 10 (2): 134–53.
McGuire, Kevin T. "The Institutionalization of the U.S. Supreme Court." *Political Analysis* 12, no. 2 (2004): 128–42.
Mootz, Francis J., III. 1997. "Insurance Coverage of Employment Discrimination Claims." *University of Miami Law Review* 52 (1): 1–78.
Pritchett, C. Herman. 1948. *The Roosevelt Court: A Study in Judicial Politics and Values, 1937–1947*. New York: MacMillan.
Reiter, Keramet Ann. 2012. "The Most Restrictive Alternative: A Litigation History of Solitary Confinement in U.S. Prisons, 1960–2006." In *Studies in Law, Politics, and Society*, edited by Austin Sarat, 71–124. Bingley: Emerald Group.
Resnik, Judith. 2016."Lawyers' Ethics Beyond the Vanishing Trial: Unrepresented Claimants, De Facto Aggregations, Arbitration Mandates, and Privatized Processes." *Fordham Law Review* 85 (5): 1899.
Roma, Elizabeth. 2011. "Mandatory Arbitration Clauses in Employment Contracts and the Need for Meaningful Judicial Review." *Journal of Gender, Social Policy & the Law* 12 (3): 5.
Rubin, Ashley T. 2015. "A Neo-Institutional Account of Prison Diffusion." *Law & Society Review* 49 (2): 365–400.
Schoenfeld, Heather. 2010. "Mass Incarceration and the Paradox of Prison Conditions Litigation." *Law & Society Review* 44 (3-4): 731–68.
Schlanger, Margo and Giovanna Shay. 2009. "Preserving the Rule of Law in America's Jails and Prisons: The Case for Amending the Prison Litigation Reform Act." *Journal of Constitutional Law* 11 (1): 139–54.
Segal, Jeffrey A. and Albert D. Cover. 1989. "Ideological Values and the Votes of U.S. Supreme Court Justices." *American Political Science Review* 83 (2): 557–65.
Stone, Katherine Van Wezel. 1995. "Mandatory arbitration of individual employment rights: the yellow dog contract of the 1990s." *Denver University Law Review* 73: 1017–50.
Stubbs, Jonathan K. 2016. "Demographic History of Federal Judicial Appointments by Sex and Race: 1789–2016, A." *Berkeley La Raza Law Journal* 26: 92–128.
Sturm, Susan P. 1979. "Mastering Intervention in Prisons." *Yale Law Journal* 88 (5): 1062–91.
Swearingen, Van. 2008. "Imprisoning Rights: The Failure of Negotiated Governance in the Prison Inmate Grievance Process." *California Law Review* 96 (5): 1353–82.
Talesh, Shauhin A. 2015. "Legal Intermediaries: How Insurance Companies Construct the Meaning of Compliance with Antidiscrimination Laws." *Law & Policy* 37 (2): 209–39.
Thorp, Cary D., Jr. 1973. "Fair Employment Practices: The Compliance Jungle." *Personnel Journal* 52 (7): 642–49.
Weick, Karl E. 1976. "Educational Organizations as Loosely Coupled Systems." *Administrative Science Quarterly* 21 (1): 1–19.

Wahlbeck, Paul J., James F. Spriggs, and Forrest Maltzman. 1998. "Marshalling the Court: Bargaining and Accommodation on the United States Supreme Court." American Journal of Political Science 294–315.

CASES

Burlington Industries *v.* Ellerth, 524 U.S. 742 (1998).
Costello *v.* Wainwright, 397 F. Supp. 20, M.D. Fla. (1975).
Faragher *v.* City of Boca Raton, 524 U.S. 775 (1998).
Furnco Construction *v.* Waters, 438 U.S. 567 (1978).
Grubb *v.* W.A. Foote Memorial Hospital, Inc., 741 F.2d 1486 (6th Cir. 1984).
Hudson *v.* Palmer, 468 U.S. 517 (1984).
Turner *v.* Safley, 482 U.S. 78 (1987).
Verniero *v.* Airforce Academy School District No. 20, 705 F2d. 388, (10th Cir. 1983).
Widmar *v.* Sun Chemical Corp., 772 F.3d 457, 464 (7th Cir. 2014).
Wolff *v.* McDonnell, 418 U.S. 539 (1974).

11

The Law of the Workplace

Paul Frymer

Because of the fragmented and piecemeal development of federal labor policy in the United States, US courts have had many places of entry to participate in workplace regulation. This is, at least in part, ironic. The initial ambition of Progressive Era legislators and activists to develop a federal labor policy in the late nineteenth and early twentieth century was to counter the ongoing activism of the *Lochner* era judges who were striking down federal and state statutes in order to defend a more unbridled capitalist economy. Both the federal government and a majority of state governments responded by passing labor and workplace statutes designed to check courtroom intervention and substitute regulation, administration, and arbitration over litigation. During the 1930s, the efforts of legislators to overcome judicial activism restricting labor rights reached an apex. In 1932, Congress passed the Norris-La Guardia Act that declared federal support for the rights of workers to bargain collectively. A few years later, Congress passed the National Labor Relations Act (NLRA), authorizing the establishment of a regulatory agency designed to mediate conflicts between workers and employers by institutionalizing collective bargaining and allowing workers to organize unions of their own choosing. These statutory successes combined with Franklin Roosevelt's combative relationship with the courts marked the end of the *Lochner* era, the refutation of a constitutional right to economic liberty, and the establishment of a regulatory administrative state (e.g., Forbath 1989; Orren 1992).

From the perspective of the early twenty-first century, this state of workers' rights protected and authorized by government regulation and administration has largely been seen as a failure. Federal labor policy has struggled to maintain its statutory mission in the face of changes to the economy that include globalization and technological innovation, as well as partisan transformations that have given Republicans frequent governing majorities allowing them, in turn, to dominate the composition and scope of the National Labor Relations Board (NLRB) and squelch most union-led statutory reform. Certainly, the passage of the NLRA initiated a vibrant era for labor rights, and for decades roughly a third of the private workforce was unionized. Starting with the momentous, *Jones* v. *Laughlin Steel*

v. *NLRB* (301 U.S. 1, 1937), courts deferred to these statutes, recognizing congressional authority to regulate the economy under the commerce clause. The role of judges was to interpret labor statutes and largely defer to the administrative rulings of the Board. But as the New Deal era and Warren Court transcended into the Reagan Revolution and Roberts Court, judges increasingly weighed in on labor matters problematically. Early decisions such as *NLRB* v. *Mackay Radio and Telegraph Co.* (304 U.S. 333, 1938) weakened unions by denying opportunities for workers to strike in secondary markets. But recent decisions have been even more emphatic in delivering blows to unions and labor organizing. In *Hoffman Plastics Compounds* v. *NLRB* (535 U.S. 137, 2002), the Court sided with employers over the rights of unionized workers by disallowing the use of punitive provisions of the NLRA against companies that knowingly hired workers lacking worker permits or American citizenship. Most recently, in *Janus v. American Federation of State, County, and Municipal Employees* (585 U.S. __, 2018), a 5-4 conservative majority held that unions cannot rely on fees from employees who are not union members, although the union is legally required to represent them. Courts have hardly been the only problem that the New Deal labor state faced – globalization, violent attacks by employers on labor organizing, internal union problems with racism and sexism, and an outmoded statutory mandate that relied on private and local workers fighting for national and federal labor rights are just a few of the reasons for labor decline. But courts have contributed to this decline by failing to defend a more robust form of collective organizing, electoral opportunities for workers to choose unions without intimidation and violence, and the broader dynamics of labor institutionalism.

All areas of worker rights laws have been subjected to retrenchment from politicians and judges alike. But in contrast to judicial interpretations of the NLRA, other workplace statutes have received a more varied response, with frequent examples of judges interpreting the laws quite expansively. Most notably, the latter half of the twentieth century was a time when individual rights in the workplace were being greatly enhanced and expanded under judicial interpretations of statutes such as Title VII of the Civil Rights Act, the Americans with Disabilities Act, Title IX of the Education Amendments Act, the Pregnancy Discrimination Act, the Fair Labor Standards Act, and the Occupational Safety and Health Act. Moreover, judges have been interpreting common law doctrines within contracts and torts to establish employee rights that have dramatically altered the law of the workplace. The coexistence of different statutory and legal regimes – labor, employment discrimination, and employment – has resulted in a bifurcated and confusing law of the workplace that scholars are only slowly starting to engage as a whole. The traditional view of this complex and multifaceted law of the workplace has been to treat the statutory and legal areas completely separately. At most law schools, courses are taught in labor law and employment discrimination law, and they have almost nothing to do with each other; they are taught with their own textbooks and follow entirely different statutory and common law. In recent years, scholars have begun to examine this broader "law of the workplace" as a specific whole, attempting to make sense of these discrepancies across labor, employment, and employment discrimination law (Lichtenstein 2001; Sachs 2008; Schiller 2015). Some have focused on the discrepancy between employment and labor, noting how employment rights have thrived while labor rights have struggled; within this, some scholars note that employment discrimination law has directly and/or indirectly hurt union rights, by privileging individual rights over the collective bargaining model of the NLRA (Frymer 2008; Schiller 2015; Stein 1999). Other scholars have focused on the possibilities and opportunities that arise when the two realms are intersected. As scholars have increasingly argued, these rights in turn benefit unionizing and unionized workers as well (Crain and Kim 2013; Estlund 2006; Lee 2014; Sachs 2008). Finally, scholars have also looked outside of the labor-employment statutory world to incorporating political activism as a contributing if not primary mechanism for combatting union decline (e.g., Andrias 2016; Tomlins 1985). In this short essay, I continue this conversation and offer some ideas for why courts have provided opportunities in certain realms and not others – particularly in labor law – and what role courts and political actors can play to promote a future of enhanced labor rights.

11.1 LABOR LAW REDEFINES WORKPLACE RIGHTS

Workplace law and federal labor policy involve a wide array of statutory regulations, much of which was established during the early and middle decades of the twentieth century. But it is built on a beginning common law principle, with constitutional underpinnings, that most Americans are "at-will" in the workplace. At-will is a long-standing doctrine of American common law that gives both the employer and employee the right to terminate their professional relationship. The idea of at-will has deep historical roots, and its initial formation under English law stated that employers implied a one-year contract if they stated a yearly salary. It was arguably extended, at least implicitly, by the passage of the Thirteenth Amendment, which abolished slavery and promoted the idea of a free right to one's own labor, establishing for all people a voluntary right, subject to a range of contractual obligations, to terminate their employment (e.g., Estlund 1996; Feinman 1976).

By the mid-1870s, legal theorists were beginning to extract the idea out of pieces of common law: the at-will worker was "a person who, by contract or operation of law, is for a limited period subject to the authority or control of another person in a particular trade, business or occupation" (Wood 1886). What was critical was that either party could end the relationship, and at the beginning of the twentieth century the Supreme Court added teeth to this doctrine. In *Adair v. United States* (208 U.S. 161, 174–75, 1907), the Supreme Court found regulations infringing on an employee's right to at-will treatment to be "repugnant" to the Fifth and Fourteenth Amendments' right of due process and liberty of contract. Since both employees and employers had the same right to sell and buy labor, it followed that "the right of the employee to quit the service of the employer, for whatever reason, is the same as the right of the employer, for whatever reason, to dispense with the services of such employee." In *Bailey v. Alabama* (219 U.S. 219, 241, 1911), the Court overturned peonage laws, this time on grounds of the Thirteenth Amendment that prohibited workers be held to an employer by indentured contract. Involuntary servitude had a "larger meaning than slavery," and the Thirteenth Amendment prohibited a person working for another without choice. In reality, America was hardly a nation of "at-will" – throughout the country, workers of all races and sexes were bound to undesired work establishments that made the idea of individual freedom simply that. But for understanding the development of labor policy, this legal claim of "at-will" sets a critical baseline that all regulatory efforts need to confront. Worker protections, whether statutory or legal right, are portrayed as exceptions that need to be justified as such. And because the at-will doctrine remains, statutory provisions designed to protect workers are consistently hampered by the presumption that an employer need simply find a legitimate reason for termination (Estlund 1996).

Although in certain ways an ideal of workplace freedom, at-will also quickly became a doctrine used to stifle state and federal efforts to aid suffering workers in the increasingly inhospitable workplace of the industrial revolution. *Adair* is emblematic here. There, the Court struck down the Erdman Act, passed by Congress seeking to protect union members against discrimination by the employer on the grounds that neither side should have regulated advantages in workplace bargaining. Judges have long displayed skepticism towards many of the features of labor activism, from collective action to boycotts and job stoppages. As far back as *In re Debs* (158 U.S. 564 (1895)), when a unanimous Court held that a union strike could be enjoined and striking union members (including Eugene Debs, the president of the American Railway Union) jailed, the Supreme Court has taken a skeptical view of collective action that seemingly suppresses individual and minority rights. Both state and federal labor policy in the Progressive Era began working quickly to chip away at the at-will doctrine. Following the precedents set by earlier government organizations such as the Freedmen's Bureau, federal labor bureaus both examined and attempted to more vigorously protect worker rights. By the 1920s, numerous states had passed minimum wage laws, maximum daily hour laws, worker insurance and compensation programs, and established industrial welfare commissions (Douglas 1919; Forbath 1989; Skocpol 1992; Witt 2004). Until 1937, however, these efforts were frequently stymied by the Supreme Court, which relied on theories of individual liberties and economic laissez faire to strike down statutory efforts at regulation (Gillman 1993).

The National Labor Relations Act of 1935 changed all of this profoundly, for a period of time, but it did not entirely displace the at-will baseline. A centerpiece of the creation of the New Deal administrative state, the Act prohibits employers from denying or retaliating against employees who engage in their rights to organize on behalf of a labor union and participate in collective bargaining with the employer.

Heralded by some at the time as the "Magna Carta" of the labor movement, the Wagner Act significantly extended democracy to the workplace by authorizing workers to elect representatives of their own choosing. Once elected, the federal government through the National Labor Relations Board would oversee the process by which union representatives negotiate with their employers to obtain binding contracts governing wages, benefits, hiring and firing, and general workplace conditions. The Supreme Court famously approved of the constitutionality of the Act under the Commerce Clause in 1937 in *NLRB v. Jones and Laughlin Steel Corp.* (301 U.S. 1 (1937)), and for a brief period, labor found itself on the winning side of both Supreme Court and NLRB cases, leading to more than three decades of a strong national labor movement. Buoyed by these new laws, unions immediately won a number of dramatic victories in the automotive and steel industries. National membership in unions doubled in the first two years after the Act, and reached a third of the nation's nonagricultural workforce by 1945.

For a time, the labor movement survived and even thrived in the face of conservative efforts to reign in union rights, particularly the Taft-Hartley Act of 1947, which made secondary boycotts illegal, legitimized "right to work" laws that allow workers to opt out of union dues, and expanded unfair labor laws targeted at union organizing while giving employers more freedom to campaign against labor unions. But the New Deal labor regime remained emboldened and entrenched, with the institutionalization of federal administrative oversight over workplace organizing and collective bargaining. Other areas of workplace protection, most notably rights against discrimination on the basis of race and other discrete demographic categories, initially evolved through or compatibly with the NLRA's statutory mandate, with the NLRB and the Supreme Court working (albeit extremely slowly) to implement civil rights through either provisions within established unfair labor practices or a duty to fair representation (Frymer 2008).

Unions remained solidly about a third of the private workforce well into the 1970s, with the overall number of members in the private workforce even peaking in the early 1980s. The numbers of members in public unions, meanwhile, were soaring during this time in response to statutory amendments that provided them greater opportunities to thrive. But changes to the economy, particularly as more jobs became part-time and outsourced, and others moved across national borders, as well as Republican administrative power with the rise of Ronald Reagan and subsequent deregulation of many industries, led to severe declines in the labor ranks. Over two decades, the percentage of workers in nonpublic unions was cut in half, a number whose steady and significant decline has continued. This has taken place despite studies that show workers favor unionization (Freeman and Rogers 1999; Freeman 2007; Rosenfeld 2014), and federal data has consistently reported that nonunion workers make only about 80 percent of the weekly salaries that unionized workers do, and are far more likely not to receive health care benefits, retirement benefits, and an array of worker protections on the job (Dunn and Walker 2016).

Since then, union membership has plummeted to rates reaching those of the Gilded Era, when unions were still without federal statutory protection; today, roughly 10 percent of the nation's workforce is unionized, and only 6 percent of nongovernment workers, as the number of public employees who are unionized now matches that of the private sector.

Courts are not the sole, and quite arguably not the primary precipitator of this trend, and many focus the blame on changes to the global economy, partisan politics, racial divisions, and the limits of the statute itself, especially as it has aged over the decades with little statutory revision (Frymer 2008; Rosenfeld 2014; Warren 2010). But the Supreme Court has not been a bystander, either. The Court has continued to strike down critical statutes of the NLRA designed to protect and promote union organizing and collective bargaining, beginning early on with the use of dicta in a decision that privileged the employers' ability to hire strike breakers (*NLRB v. Mackay Radio and Telegraph Co.*, 304 U.S. 333 (1938)). Court rulings shrunk these ranks further, in part by narrowing the population within a workplace that was subject to union laws, weakening security agreements, and enabling the workplace repression of union organizing. As early as the 1980s, leading labor law scholars were referring to the law as "an elegant tombstone for a dying institution" (Weiler 1983). Most recently, the Supreme Court targeted public unions, a sector that has until recently remained a place of union strength and stability. In *Janus*, the Court held that a public employee could refuse to pay union fees, a decision expected to weaken union spending in national political campaigns. Consistently, the Court has ignored a central premise of the NLRA; that the law is designed to regulate the widely recognized collective action problems that union organizations face when attempting to coerce members into paying dues and participating actively in labor organizing, particularly in contrast to a singular powerful voice of the employer.

Perhaps the biggest problem is that the Supreme Court has made it difficult for the NLRB to enforce labor law against resistant employers. Employers are not required under the NLRA to bargain in good faith with a union until a majority of workers have established their support for the union in a certification election. Employers are given quite a bit of latitude under the law to make this difficult for the union, particularly being allowed to express and describe in no uncertain terms their opposition to the union. In *Lechmere, Inc. v. NLRB* (502 U.S. 527 (1992)), the Court held that union organizers do not have a right to organize on private property. Even with the law prohibiting specific types of activities by the employer, such as threat, intimidation, and unlawful firing, and the potential for the NLRB to impose a bargaining order in the face of employer intimidation, research has shown that unfair labor practices by employers in the context of union campaigns have risen markedly as they recognize the limits of the NLRB's ability to punish them within the Court's interpretation of the law (*NLRB v. Gissel Packing Co.*, 395 U.S. 575 (1969)). In *H.K. Porter Co. v. NLRB* (397 U.S. 99 (1970)), the Court stripped much of the enforcement power of the Board when employers refuse to bargain. The Supreme Court ruled that the NLRB does not have the power to impose a contract even in the event of employer activity designed explicitly to frustrate the bargaining process. The Dunlop Commission during the Clinton Administration found a marked increased in illegal conduct by employers (Commission of the Future of Worker-Management Relations 1994), as employers had become far more aggressive in intimidating, threatening, and coercing workers with a seeming willingness to accept the frequently trivial sanctions they faced as a result. Corporations are accused of violating these laws constantly, but little has been done to mandate a change in behavior (Bronfenbrenner 2009; Lichtenstein 2008).

Moreover, what was once thought to be the strength of labor law, a strong administrative agency seemingly impervious to major legislative and judicial reform where workers and employers were forced under government supervision to iron out their differences in a way that would be beneficial and fair to both sides, has in many ways become its weakness. As Cynthia Estlund (2002) has argued, labor law has in many ways simply "ossified," as there has been almost no statutory reform for decades, with the last moment of opportunity before Congress occurring (without the passage of legislation) in the 1970s. Unlike other laws of the workplace, the lack of a private right of action limits courts stepping in on behalf of individuals denied rights and opportunities within unionized workforces, something Estlund has argued has limited opportunities for energy, innovation, and revision that are identifiable in other areas of the law. Even during the earliest years of the Obama administration, when Democrats held majorities in Congress and the executive branch, labor reform was never a priority; the proposed Employee Free Choice Act, which would have given union organizing more security against employer threats, failed to get out of committee.

11.2 THE EXPANSION OF EMPLOYMENT AND EMPLOYMENT DISCRIMINATION LAW

But there are additional components to the declining effectiveness of labor rights; and as we move outside of the institutional sphere of the NLRA, we see both further challenges and opportunities in the broader environment of the law of the workplace. Again, continuing to hover over these possibilities is the at-will baseline, which has made labor protections seem extraneous and excessive, an unnecessary and restrictive addition to the Americans supposed "opportunity" and "freedom" to work or not work without intrusion from employer, union, and government alike. Exemplary of this are right to work laws that have proliferated with the passage of the Taft-Hartley Act. Right to work states started to develop, initially in the South, as a way of defending individual workers who wished to be employed at unionized workplaces without having to pay union fees. Taft-Hartley was not all that was responsible for this: in particular, labor's internal problems with racism and sanctioned discrimination led the Supreme Court to intervene prior to Taft-Hartley to protect individual worker rights, such as in *Steele v. Louisville and Nashville Railroad* (323 U.S. 192, 1944), which established a duty on the part of the union to represent all workers in the bargaining unit. Laws passed in the second half of the twentieth century further reinforced this baseline of individual rights, even if largely unintentionally, by protecting individual workers from discrimination, seemingly creating a whole new sphere of protections without the restrictions on freedoms and rights that increasingly characterized labor laws. These laws were not intended to be in opposition to labor law (indeed, the AFL-CIO was a prominent supporter of most of them), and they were all necessary to respond to the significant amount of discrimination that existed and continues to exist in the workplace. But the law of the American workplace only further exacerbated the division between the at-will doctrine and the labor union regulations of the NLRA. Rights in the workplace have evolved dramatically over the long twentieth century, and today involve many different components that are separated institutionally, the result of different federal statutes passed many decades apart.

FEPC laws in the 1940s began a multi-decade process of developing federal statutes denying employment discrimination on the basis of certain protected categories. Title VII of the Civil Rights Act of 1964 protects a different set of American workers on the basis of specific individual characteristics including race, sex, and national origin. These categories expanded in subsequent decades through legislation such as the Age Discrimination in Employment Act of 1967, which protects employees over the age of forty from discrimination in hiring and employment, and the American with Disabilities Act of 1990, which protects disabled people otherwise qualified to perform job standards with or without a reasonable accommodation. Still others, such as the Fair Labor Standards Act, the Clean Air Act, and the Occupational Safety and Health Act forbid employers from terminating employees who complain about workplace violations, as governed by these statutes. State and local laws often go even further, with some states establishing varying degrees of "just cause" standards for termination. Together, these statutes start to protect workers against discharge for a variety of reasons. Like with the NLRA, enforcers of these statutes struggle with the at-will baseline, as successful claims of discrimination must overcome the presumption that the employer has a legitimate reason to dismiss or injure the appellant employee. Unlike the NLRA, these statutes tend to place a great deal of responsibility on the individual plaintiff to protect their rights; they also substitute judicial decision-making for that of the participants in the workplace (Gould 2000).

Courts have also been active in refining the doctrine of at-will, relying on contract and tort law to establish certain workplace protections from arbitrary firings. A 1974 decision out of New Hampshire, *Monge v. Beebe Rubber Co.* (114 N.H. 130, (1974)), began a process among state courts in recognizing individual rights against employer discharge without cause. There, the state high court held that employment decisions to terminate should be grounded in good faith, and that doing so will enhance the state's goal of improving labor relations. Courts have frequently found implied contracts for workers who were initially hired under at-will provisions, drawing from employer-employee relationships and conversations, length of employment, and employee handbooks. Some state courts have found an implied right to "good faith and fair dealing," with the assumption that neither party will injure the other without cause. Judges have also employed features of tort law, such as intentional infliction of emotional distress, to enable workers additional remedies and weapons to fight against workplace inequality and poor treatment.

More dramatic have been the ways in which courts have expanded anti-discrimination law, developing an ambiguous and arguably weak statutory provision within the Civil Rights Act of 1964, and giving it both wide-ranging legal significance and real-world teeth. The passage of Title VII was built on bipartisan and ambivalent support, and it led to a provision riddled with qualifiers and an agency given authority to defend it seemingly mortally weakened by the absence of enforcement power (Frymer 2008; Skrentny 2002). But courts, including the Supreme Court, ignored many of the qualifiers, embracing affirmative action in employment even when the Act seemingly directly forbid it, running around provisions designed to shelter workplaces built on segregation and discrimination, altering seemingly precise and narrow definitions of what constituted an act of prejudice and discrimination, and expanding the categories of protected classes as defined under the Act (Lee 2014; Skrentny 2002). Employers, and particularly large corporations, have embraced versions of these laws, often arguing that the laws are *good* for their business, in ways and results that simply are unmatched and rarely seen within labor law (Delton 2009; Kalev et al. 2006; Lieberman 2002).

I do not mean to minimize the quite significant problems that potential plaintiffs face when attempting to utilize these private rights of action. It is hardly easy for individuals to protect themselves by placing the burden entirely in their hands to file a complaint, be prepared for the cost and duress of litigation, and defend their rights before an administrator or judge (Bumiller 1988; Edelman 2016). Evidence is clear that most people will not file claims because of the cost and the conflictive nature of litigation, the high hurdles they need to scale to get to the courtroom, as well as the fear of retaliation (Albiston et al. 2014; Haltom and McCann 2004). The legal system has established an apparatus that makes successful litigation difficult, increasingly encouraging, with judicial sanction, mandatory arbitration clauses, pre-trial settlement, and fewer remedies (e.g., Edelman 2016; Staszak 2015). Employers have established human relations offices designed to mute and mitigate potential employee protestations (Edelman 2016). And a more conservative Court, comprised of a majority of judges appointed by Republican presidents, have narrowed some of the more radical decisions that initially gave statutes such as Title VII and the ADA important authority in the earliest years of their existence. This does not deny a revolutionary reshaping of the workplace that has taken place – not all workplaces, and certainly not in the most ideal forms, but a transformation that has significantly changed the functioning and understanding of identity, diversity, and workplace rights. That said, neither does it mitigate the attack from conservative forces against workers in all terrains of policy and law.

11.3 WHAT IT MEANS

Scholars are correct to move to synthesize these different areas of workplace statutory protections. There is both an intellectual and practical reason; intellectually, workplace law has never been of one piece, and for too long we have treated it that way, championing an institutional mechanism more than a substantive policy (though, admittedly, one that has itself emphasized the institutional mechanism over a broader substantive agenda). Certainly, this is in part because of a normative vision that unions democratize the workforce, enabling employees to participate in the decision-making of their workplace. Unions provide many public goods and collective efficacy in a manner not comparable to individual rights regimes. They also are a critical force in democratic politics, funding workers rights movements and laws in both local and national campaigns. No proworker statute of the twentieth and twenty-first century has come without significant aid and support from labor unions. At the same time, reformers always seize on their best opportunities and when rights emerge in one realm, they are going to draw on them to their benefit. Labor laws are insufficient, but are vitally needed; employment laws seemingly have more bite to them and provide an opportunity to expand worker protections into sectors where employees are currently struggling.

Moreover, both laws have the potential to be strengthened by being connected with each other. In general, the administrators and adjudicators of labor law have resisted merging with civil rights law, something that is seemingly consistent with privileged pieces of the labor movement itself. While the AFL-CIO endorsed the Civil Rights Act and helped promote and fund civil rights organizations (some of which were importantly fused with local labor organizations), a significant number of unions struggled with discrimination within their own locals. Some unions, particularly in the building trades, maintained constitutional provisions that explicitly discriminated against people of color and women. The NLRB struggled for decades to incorporate civil rights within its regulatory mission, with frequent internal resistance and limited success (Frymer 2008). The Board continues to be ambiguous on matters such as Title VII. Although the NLRB established racial discrimination as an unfair labor practice, it has been reluctant to incorporate civil rights more directly. Its policy remains that discrimination is a Title VII issue, not an NLRA matter (see *Handy Andy* 228 NLRB 447 (1977); *Penn Plaza, LLC v. Pyett* 556 US 247 (2009)).

This has always been a point of contention within one of the largest democratic organizations in America. As long as union activists have pushed back against racial and gender diversity, other union activists have pushed ahead, working directly with progressive causes within and without the union movement. In recent decades, labor has made further efforts to incorporate what has become some of their largest growing sectors, people of color and women. Unions and union lawyers are assisting low-wage workers in nonunion settings, providing knowledge, resources, and mobilization (Fisk 2002); furthermore, the decline of these union actors cannot help but hurt broader efforts to mobilize on behalf of marginalized workers in all sectors (Fisk 2015; Lichtenstein 2001). And no movement to provide additional rights in the workplace, whether it involves the minimum wage, family leave, or workplace standards, can or does take place without union mobilization and resources. It is also increasingly the case that workplace laws are being brought together, and this might in turn create greater opportunities for mobilization as workers start to see further common cause. But to do so requires overcoming some longstanding legacies. One of those legacies is the isolated nature of labor law.

It remains notable how labor protections have failed so dramatically while employment and employment discrimination laws have thrived and expanded. What explains this discrepancy? In part, it is tied to the existence of different and historically separate social movements. The labor movement of the late nineteenth and early twentieth century drove the creation of the NLRA, while workplace activism such as strikes and worker protests drove many of the early successes under the NLRB in the 1930s. The civil rights movement of the mid-twentieth century similarly drove early success under Title VII, and waves of new movements, from women's rights to disability rights to LGBT rights, have continued to push the boundaries on workplace law. It is hardly accidental that a thriving and mobilized movement is directly correlated with new frontiers in the law.

Labor law has also struggled with ideological and partisan politics in a way in which civil rights law has not, or at least not to the same degree. Many of the critical Supreme Court decisions embracing the expansion of civil rights laws have been written or included important support from justices on the right side of the bench. Perhaps the Supreme Court's most radical decision on Title VII law, *Griggs* v. *Duke Power Co.* (401 U.S. 424 (1971)), which established the principle of disparate impact treatment to adjudicate whether discrimination was a factor in workplace hiring and firing, was a unanimous decision. One of the keys to garnering a majority of the Court in deciding *Price Waterhouse* v. *Hopkins* (490 U.S. 228 (1989)), one of the most famous expansions of workplace sex discrimination law to date, was a concurrence from Justice Sandra Day O'Connor. *Oncale* v. *Sundowner Offshore Services, Inc.* (523 U.S. 75 (1998)) expanded Title VII's protection against workplace discrimination and harassment on the basis of sex stereotypes with importantly crosscoalitional majorities; the holding, that discrimination by a member of the same sex is unconstitutional under Title VII, was the result of a unanimous decision written by Justice Antonin Scalia. The American Disability Act of 1990 was importantly bipartisan and signed by Republican President George H. W. Bush, as were the amendments to civil rights law in 1991. I do not want to make too much of the conservative support for employment rights; for every *Price Waterhouse*, there is a decision like *Wal-mart Stores* v. *Dukes* (564 U.S. 338, 2011), which, while ignoring employment rights, relies on weakening the rules of class action to deny women the right to sue for sex discrimination against the nation's largest employer (Staszak 2015).

Certainly, the NLRA has never received support from corporate America in the way that anti-discrimination measures have (Skrentny 1996, 2014). Indeed, corporate America has attempted to sabotage labor law from very early on, while coming to embrace civil rights laws in a much different way. There is a longer conversation to be had about why this is the case, but it is obviously critical to understanding the differing paths that these workplace protections have had.

Finally, there is no doubt a stronger, or at least easier link for lawyers and judges to make with individual rights under anti-discrimination laws and contract law than with a law that emphasizes administrative collective bargaining. Certain workplace protections have received greater support from judges, even strongly conservative judges, because they tap into certain ideas of individual rights in a manner that labor law, and its emphasis on collective mobilization and representation, do not. By contrast, conservatives opposed to labor law have seized on individual rights to counter workplace opportunities, with successful proposals to establish right to work states and enable "conscientious" employees to express their First Amendment rights to withhold dues from an organization they oppose. Many liberals also struggle to understand, let alone embrace the normative assumptions that underlie labor law, with its emphasis on maintaining collective action by restraining individual free riders and its privileging of administrative authority and binding procedures. This is clearly a matter of degree, and the move to retrench employment rights is certainly in gear, but the individual rights model remains politically powerful in a way that the levers of the administrative regulatory state do not.

11.4 CONCLUSION: MALCOLM FEELEY'S IMPACT ON OUR AND MY UNDERSTANDING OF LAW AND SOCIAL POLICY

As a law student at UC Berkeley, I took separate courses in labor and employment discrimination law, and learned about contractual and tort opportunities for workplace rights in a third and fourth class; I was taught about the topic of "race" and how it impacts the law in yet a fifth class. The labor law course dealt minimally and marginally with the subject of race and civil rights in the workplace; the employment discrimination course did not incorporate labor unions, and the erudite professor of the course admitted to having little knowledge about labor law and little experience encountering labor unions. In one of my last semesters of law school, I took Malcolm Feeley's seminar on law and social policy, where I wrote a paper that attempted to intersect these academic disciplines (Frymer 2003).

The paper was inspired by Malcolm's worldview that he communicated to us throughout the class: that we should stop thinking about traditional disciplinary and administrative boundaries, whether those that divide judging from policy making, doctrines from substance, and states and regions from nations. The law was a part of the broader governing process, and lawyers and judges worked within this context in ways that were both similar to and importantly different from other policy makers (Feeley and Rubin 1998). He told us time and again to look broadly at the universe of what constitutes the law, as well as what constitutes the goal of the policy. In the case of the workplace, he told me when I met with him to discuss my seminar paper, think of it as a whole and be cognizant of, but not bound by, doctrinal divisions nor divisions between federal courts judges and administrative officials on the NLRB. Malcolm Feeley has continued to challenge the orthodoxies of legal academia by forcing all of us not to rely on easy and legally and politically *constructed* ideals, from the false dichotomy between the judge and bureaucrat to the false demarcation of federal lines. In addition to the great enthusiasm, generosity, mentoring, and friendship that he showed me both then and since then, he fundamentally taught me how to think about law and policy by not over-privileging artificially constructed boundaries that do not match the broader goals of public policy and political power.

REFERENCES

Albiston, Catherine R. et al. 2014. "The Dispute Tree and the Legal Forest." *Annual Review of Law and Social Sciences* 10 (1): 105–31.

Andrias, Kate. 2016. "The New Labor Law." *Yale Law Journal* 126 (1): 2–100.

Bronfenbrenner, Kate. 2009. "No Holds Barred: The Intensification of Employer Opposition to Organizing." Briefing Paper #235, Economic Policy Institute.

Bumiller, Katherine. 1988. *The Civil Rights Society: The Social Construction of Victims.* Baltimore: Johns Hopkins University Press.

Commission of the Future of Worker-Management Relations. 1994. "Fact Finding Report." Washington, DC: Department of Labor and Department of Commerce.

Crain, Marion and Pauline T. Kim. 2013. "A Holistic Approach to Teaching Work Law." *St. Louis University Law Journal* 58 (1): 7–26.

Delton, Jennifer. 2009. *Racial Integration in Corporate America, 1940–1990.* New York: Cambridge University Press.

Douglas, Dorothy W. 1919. "American Minimum Wage Laws at Work." *American Economic Review* 9 (4): 701–38.

Dunn, Megan and James Walker. 2016. "Union Membership in the United States." U.S. Bureau of Labor Statistics. Washington, DC.

Edelman, Lauren B. 2016. *Working Law: Courts, Corporations, and Symbolic Civil Rights.* Chicago: University of Chicago Press.

Estlund, Cynthia. 2005. "Rebuilding the Law of the Workplace in an Era of Self-Regulation." *Columbia Law Review* 105 (2): 319–404.

Estlund, Cynthia. 2002. "The Ossification of American Labor Law." *Columbia Law Review* 102 (6): 1527–1612.

Estlund, Cynthia L. 1996. "The Changing Workplace: Wrongful Discharge Protections in an At-Will World." *Texas Law Review* 74: 1655–92.
Feeley, Malcolm M. and Edward L. Rubin. 1998. *Judicial Policy Making and the Modern State: How Courts Reformed America's Prisons.* New York: Cambridge University Press.
Feinman, Jay M. 1976. "The Development of the Employment at Will Rule." *American Journal of Legal History* 20 (2): 118–35.
Fisk, Catherine. 2002. "Union Lawyers and Employment Law." *Berkeley Journal of Employment and Labor Law* 23(1): 57–105.
Fisk, Catherine L. 2015. "Law and the Evolving Shape of Labor: Narratives of Expansion and Retrenchment." *Law, Culture, and the Humanities* 11 (1): 17–29.
Flynn, Andrea, Susan R. Holmberg, Dorian T. Warren, and Felicia J. Wong. 2017. *The Hidden Rules of Race: Barriers to an Inclusive Economy.* New York: Cambridge University Press.
Forbath, William. 1989. "The Shaping of the American Labor Movement." *Harvard Law Review* 102 (6): 1111–256.
Freeman, Richard B. and Joel Rogers. 1999. *What Workers Want.* New York: Russell Sage Foundation.
Freeman, Richard B. 2007. "Do Workers Still Want Unions? More than Ever." Briefing Paper #182, *Economic Policy Institute.*
Frymer, Paul. 2003. "Acting When Elected Officials Won't: Federal Courts and Civil Rights Enforcement in U.S. Labor Unions, 1935–1985." *American Political Science Review* 97 (3): 483–99.
Frymer, Paul. 2008. *Black and Blue: African Americans, the Labor Movement, and the Decline of the Democratic Party.* Princeton: Princeton University Press.
Getman, Julius G. 2016. *The Supreme Court on Unions: Why Labor Law is Failing American Workers.* Ithaca: Cornell University Press.
Gillman, Howard. 1993. *The Constitution Besieged: The Rise and Demise of Lochner Era Police Powers.* Durham: Duke University Press.
Gould, William B. 2000. "The Third Way: Labor Policy Beyond the New Deal." *University of Kansas Law Review* 48 (4): 751–64.
Haltom, William and Michael McCann. 2004. *Distorting the Law: Politics, Media, and the Litigation Crisis.* Chicago: University of Chicago Press.
Kalev, Alexandra, Frank Dobbin, and Erin Kelly. 2006. "Best Practices or Best Guesses? Assessing the Efficacy of Corporate Affirmative Action and Diversity Policies." *American Sociological Review* 71 (4): 589–617.
Lee, Sophia Z. 2014. *The Workplace Constitution from the New Deal to the New Right.* New York: Cambridge University Press.
Lee, Sophia Z. 2015. "A Signal or a Silo?: Title VII's Unexpected Hegemony," in *A Nation of Widening Opportunities: The Civil Rights Act at 50*, edited by Ellen Katz and Samuel Bagenstos. Ann Arbor: University of Michigan Press.
Lichtenstein, Nelson. 2001. *State of the Union.* Princeton: Princeton University Press.
Lichtenstein, Nelson. 2008. "How Wal-Mart Fights Unions." *Minnesota Law Review* 92 (5): 1462–501.
Lieberman, Robert C. 2002. "Ideas, Institutions, and Political Order: Explaining Political Change." *American Political Science Review* 96 (4): 697–712.
Orren, Karen. 1992. *Belated Feudalism: Labor, the Law, and Liberal Development in the United States.* New York: Cambridge University Press.
Rosenfeld, Jake. 2014. *What Unions No Longer Do.* Cambridge: Harvard University Press.
Sachs, Benjamin I. 2008. "Employment Law as Labor Law." *Cardozo Law Review* 29 (6): 2685.

Schiller, Reuel Edward. 2015. *Forging Rivals: Race, Class, Law, and the Collapse of Postwar Liberalism*. New York: Cambridge University Press.

Skocpol, Theda. 1992. *Protecting Soldiers and Mothers: The Political Origins of Social Policy in the United States*. New York: Cambridge University Press.

Skrentny, John David. 1996. *The Ironies of Affirmative Action: Politics, Culture, and Justice in America*. Chicago: University of Chicago Press.

Skrentny, John D. 2002. *The Minority Rights Revolution*. Cambridge: Harvard University Press.

Skrentny, John D. 2014. *After Civil Rights: Racial Realism in the New American Workplace*. Princeton: Princeton University Press.

Staszak, Sarah. 2015. *No Day in Court: Access to Justice and the Politics of Judicial Retrenchment*. New York: Oxford University Press.

Stein, Judith. 1999. *Running Steel, Running America: Race, Economic Policy and the Decline of Liberalism*. Chapel Hill: University of North Carolina Press.

Stone, Katherine V. W. 2004. *From Widgets to Digits: Employment Regulation for the Changing Workplace*. New York: Cambridge University Press.

Tomlins, Christopher. 1985. *The State and the Unions: Labor Relations, Law, and the Organized Labor Movement in America, 1880–1960*. New York: Cambridge University Press.

Warren, Dorian T. 2010. "The American Labor Movement in the Age of Obama: The Challenges and Opportunities of a Racialized Political Economy." *Perspectives on Politics* 8 (3): 847–60.

Weiler, Paul. 1983. "Promises to Keep: Securing Workers' Rights to Self-Organization Under the NLRA." *Harvard Law Review* 96 (8): 1769–827.

Witt, John Fabian. 2004. *The Accidental Republic: Crippled Workingmen, Destitute Widows, and the Remaking of American Law*. Cambridge: Harvard University Press.

Wood, H. G. 1886. *A Treatise on the Law of Master and Servant Covering the Relation, Duties, and Liabilities of Employers and Employees*. Albany: John D. Parsons, Jr.

12

Administrative "States" of Judicial Policy on Gender-Motivated Violence

Christine B. Harrington[1]

In what sense is the rise of the modern administrative state a catalyst for judicial policymaking? *Judicial Policy Making and the Modern State* (1998), Malcolm Feeley and Edward Rubin's treatise on judicial policymaking examines this dynamic in the context of prison reform litigation carried out by US federal courts in the mid to late twentieth century. Before 1965, federal judges had not reviewed the authority of prison wardens, who under the common law oversaw the implementation of internal prison practices.[2] This changed after a judge in the US District Court for the Eastern District of Arkansas declared conditions of overcrowding at Cummins Frame State Prison "cruel and unusual punishment" in violation of the Eighth Amendment of the US Constitution. Through investigative processes, the deployment of court orders, and much more, Feeley and Rubin trace how Judge Henley (a President Ford appointee) established jurisdiction for "constitutional courts to concern themselves with modes of punishment, thus creating general boundaries within which they could exercise their power" (Feeley and Rubin 1998, 13, 72). These actions not only shaped comprehensive court orders issued by federal judges in twenty-five states, they also generated new government programs, which in turn provided a rationale for judicial policymaking as a mode of judicial action.

The processes of judicial policymaking resemble how other branches make policy except for the fact that judges rather than elected officials are the agents (340). This is not to suggest that all judges and all elected officials have similar routines, political ideologies, or doctrines. Policymaking understood as a mode of *judicial action* takes seriously the practices of doctrinal creation.[3] Creating legal doctrine is a complicated process. Judges engage with preexisting practices and principles in the process of making a decision. In general, we recognize doctrinal creation,

---

[1] I would like to thank Bob Kagan for his generous comments on the initial presentation of these ideas. Matt Canfield's critical engagement and comments on the last draft were invaluable, and so very much appreciated. My thanks to Sharon Turret, research assistant and 2018 graduate of NYU Law School, for hunting down leads, visualizing congressional data, and working with "Gender in Law" students, who I also want to thank for inspiring this work. All errors are my own.
[2] For a discussion of the "hands-off doctrine," see Feeley and Rubin (2000, 31–34).
[3] For details on the concept of "mode of judicial action," see Feeley and Rubin (2000, 23).

interpretation, and so forth as juridical practices. In particular, Feeley and Rubin draw our attention to *"constraints, internal to the processes"* by which doctrine is created and judicial policymaking is carried out (242, added emphasis). In this sense, doctrine *performs as* a constraint on policymaking. However, not all elements of doctrinal productions, in their view, directly address the structure of the administrative state. Though three of four doctrinal aspects in their framework – analogies, metaphors, and labeling – constitute modes of policymaking, they argue these methods "predate the administrative state and characterize the development of the common law" (340). Analogies, metaphors, and labeling are "not necessarily specific to an institution, although they can be, and do not typically involve implementation by the judiciary itself, although this too can vary."

The fourth doctrinal element, institutional conceptualization, differs from the other three in that it "addresses the structure of the administrative state in a direct, context-specific manner" (Feeley and Rubin 1998). Feeley and Rubin also refer to "institutional conceptualization" as "the bureaucratic element" of doctrine. For example, in the Eighth Amendment prison condition cases, plaintiffs' lawyers successfully translated the "underlying problem confronting many inmates" to mean the "totality of their conditions-overcrowded, out-worn facilities; overextended staffs; brutality; dangerous conditions; lack of medical and food service; poor sanitation, heating, and ventilation-an endless list of problems" (Feeley and Rubin 1992, 126–27). The judges in these cases conceived of the institution "as the problem" and judicial oversight a potential remedy. As they responded to questions, complaints, and even disputes concerning the implementation and enforcement of their institutional conception, they exercised judicial management. They supervised compliance mechanisms (e.g., court orders, consent decrees) and brought in a range of new specialists, certified experts hired to investigate and verify whether the newly designated prison administrators complied with the law.[4]

The "bureaucratic element" often interacts with other institutional logics and coordinating procedures. For example, Feeley and Rubin maintain that the modern administrative state weakened well-established legal principles, such as federalism, separation of powers, and the rule of law:

> Just as the administrative state provides the model for judicial policymaking, it is the principal force behind the decreasing relevance of federalism, separation of powers and our traditional notion of the rule of law. (Feeley and Rubin 1992, 23)

The modern administrative state, however, is not treated as an abstract apparatus by Feeley and Rubin, nor by me. Courts ignore well-established legal principles for a number of reasons.[5] Consider a different historical context and another political

---

[4] For an analysis of the prison modernization project, see Feeley and Swearingen (2004, 455).
[5] For "pragmatic reasons courts tend to ignore federalism and separation of powers [when] these principles no longer describe the governmental system in which they exist and no longer carry any normative force." These "operational changes" are often "accompanied by epistemological ones" (Feeley and Rubin 1998, 343–44).

time, such as the rise of the contemporary judicial conservative legal movement during the late twentieth century and its ability to challenge the entrenched "liberal-legal network" (Teles 2008) by replacing well-established legal principles for national economic and social regulation with an updated version of the "freedom of contract doctrine" (Twiss 1962) known as the "takings doctrine" (Decker 2016).

This chapter examines the relationship between law and the modern administrative state,[6] turning our attention to a different set of legal and political struggles over the meaning and implementation of "bureaucratic elements" in policymaking. It focuses on the decade-long battle (1990–2000) between Congress and the federal courts over creating a civil right to be free from "gender-motivated violence," as defined by the 1994 Violence Against Women Act.[7] When the Violence Against Women Act (VAWA) passed both houses of Congress, supporters characterized it as a "consummate bipartisan effort," noting that Senator Orrin Hatch, R-Utah, was the lead cosponsor, along with "67 Senate cosponsors and 225 cosponsors in the House, from both sides of the aisle" (Goldfarb 1996, 396).[8] The effort may have been bipartisan from the advocates' perspective, but the votes were not. There was a significant partisan divide in both chambers. In the Senate, 96 percent of Democrats and only 16 percent of Republicans voted in favor of VAWA, while in the House of Representatives, 80 percent of Democrats and 20 percent of Republicans voted in favor of the bill.[9] Nonetheless, today VAWA is still widely recognized as a "capstone achievement of the late twentieth century anti-rape movement" to make "rape as well as domestic violence programs eligible for over $1.5 billion in federal funding to improve both law enforcement responses to assault and services for victims" (Freedman 2013, 286). These and other funding provisions survived four subsequent Reauthorization Acts (2000, 2005, 2012, and 2013); however, the heart of the Act – the federally protected civil right to be free from gender-motivated violence – was removed by the US Supreme Court in *U.S. v. Morrison* (2000).[10] In this 5–4 decision, the Court terminated the authority of

---

[6] The phrase "modern administrative state" broadly includes early twentieth-century Progressive reforms, the New Deal, and the Great Society. Also see Grisinger, 2012.

[7] The Act defines "gender-motivated violence" as "a crime of violence committed because of gender or on the basis of gender, and due, at least in part, to an animus based on the victim's gender;" and defines a "crime of violence" as "an act or series of acts that would constitute a felony against the person or that would constitute a felony against property if the conduct presents a serious risk of physical injury to another, and that would come within the meaning of State or Federal offenses described in section 16 of title 18, United States Code, whether or not those acts have actually resulted in criminal charges, prosecution, or conviction and whether or not those acts were committed in the special maritime, territorial, or prison jurisdiction of the United States." See 135 42 U.S.C. § 13981 (1994).

[8] This legislation passed as an amendment to the Omnibus Crime Control and Safe Streets Act of 1968. It is also in the legislative record as part of the Violent Crime Control and Law Enforcement Act of 1994, PuB. L. No. 103-322, 108 Stat. 1796. 42 U.S.C.A. § 13981(b)-(c) (1995).

[9] The vote for-against on VAWA in the Senate was 61–38, www.govtrack.us/congress/votes/103–1994/s295 and in the House 235–195, www.govtrack.us/congress/votes/103–1994/h416.

[10] See 529 U.S. 598 (2000). Caroline S. Schmidt's study of VAWA litigation during the 4.6 years *before* the civil rights provision was removed by the US Supreme Court, found that courts had decided sixty cases. Of these, fifty-two cases were filed in federal court, eight in state court. Only five of the sixty

federal courts to concern themselves with gender-motivated violence[11] by rejecting Congress' understanding of its authority to legislate under the Commerce Clause and the Fourteenth Amendment's enabling clause.

Scholars and activists characterize the Court's decision in *Morrison* as an instance of "backlash" against the rights revolution era of the 1960s–70s[12] and the legal gains made by the feminist anti-rape movement in particular in the 1980s–90s.[13] VAWA declared that violent crime, motivated by gender, was a form of unlawful discrimination. The scope of the Act "extended to date rape, marital rape, and spousal battering – acts that, on the surface, appear [to some as if] they have nothing to do with the market" (Goldfarb 2004, 523–24). Based on feminist critiques of the ways in which the familiar public-private dichotomy in American law maintains and reinforces gender subordination by protecting violence within status relationships, such as marriage, VAWA's civil rights remedy provided access to federal court for victims of gender-motivated violence.[14] The Court's decision in *Morrison* eclipsed these legislative goals while furthering the judicial revival of federalism as justification for overturning Congress' authority to create this civil right.[15]

This chapter offers an interpretative sociolegal analysis[16] of civil rights policy-making (VAWA) in a "political time"[17] when judicial conservatism re-emerges (late twentieth century) and effectively competes for control over the administrative state both from the bench[18] as well as *off the bench*. I argue that in this political time,

    cases went to the appellate level, including the *Morrison* litigation. She concludes that "VAWA did not produce many cases, which meant that VAWA did not bring relief to a significant number of individual victims of gender-motivated violence" (2015, 510). For additional commentary on federal cases involving the constitutionality of VAWA, see Weiss (1997) and Axelrad et al. (1999).
[11] Until the Rehnquist Court's decision in *Morrison*, the Court had previously invalidated only one other federal antidiscrimination law since Reconstruction. See MacKinnon (2000), 135.
[12] See Tushnet (2008) and Staszak (2010). For critiques of the backlash thesis, see Keck (2009) and Gash (2015).
[13] In particular see Freedman (2013) and Corrigan (2013).
[14] For data on the pervasiveness of violence against women in families and intimate relations, see Goldfarb (2004, 30–44 n.38, citations to 1990 Senate Report No. 101–545). Also see Olsen (1983) for analysis of the structure of consciousness in legal ideology concerning the treatment of women.
[15] See *U.S. v. Lopez*, 514 U.S. 549 (1994) decided just prior to *Morrison*, and the *Civil Rights* Cases, 109 U.S. 3 (1883), which were both cited as judicial precedent in *Morrison*.
[16] On interpretative sociolegal analysis, see Harrington and Yngvesson (1990).
[17] For a discussion of "political time" see Thelen (2000). My particular focus on VAWA addresses effects of pre-established and ongoing political, social, and legal arrangements (e.g., within family law, legislative-executive dynamics, legislative-judicial dynamics) as they related to "institutional conceptualizations" (Feeley and Rubin 1998) of judicial policy on gender-motivated violence.
[18] See Thomas Keck on the US Supreme Court (1937–2004), and in particular the re-emergence of judicial conservatism beginning with the Rehnquist Court. Based largely on doctrinal and decision-making analyses, Keck argues that this form of judicial conservatism was "born in reaction to the liberal judicial activism of the Warren Court" and was "not judicial restraint but its own version of judicial activism" (Keck 2004, 2). Also see Robert Post (2006, 3) on judicial conservatism during "the brief constitutionalization of prohibition" and the Taft Court's realization that "the administrative state was an unalterable reality."

judicial conservatives operationalized the norms of judicial administration for the purpose of expanding the judiciary's institutional role in shaping civil rights legislation. Judges and legislators are situated in regimes of inherited administrative norms that often condition internal processes and affect external interactions. Operating with these constraints and opportunities, judges and legislators provide administrative justifications for their policy preferences that may affect how policy problems/ disputes are framed and interpreted. In other words, legal as well as administrative judicial decisions are constituted when inheritance and agency intersect.[19] Rather than "weakening" the administrative state forged during the New Deal-Great Society era as much of the judicial backlash literature suggests, this chapter shows how judicial administration resources were deployed by the administrative arm of the judicial branch and developed into an enduring challenge to the entrenched comprehensive rational policymaking norms[20] structuring so much of civil rights policy after the 1960s.

There are two parts to this argument. Section 12.1 provides an interpretation of the institutional conceptualization of "gender-motivated violence" and the "private right of action remedy" for redress under VAWA. I draw on two main sources: (1) legislative histories produced by those who crafted the legislation and commented on the legal and political policy aspects of VAWA in law review articles and students notes published at that time; and (2) research about interbranch approaches to legislating civil rights enforcement policy. My purpose is not to determine the veracity of these works per se, but to interpret the core claims as a method or way of seeing administrative states in this policy field.[21] Section 12.2 explains how, when, why, and to what effect judicial opposition to this civil rights policy mobilized and deployed techniques of judicial administration off the bench. Building on a rich body of contemporary scholarly work on the conservative legal movement, federal court decisions, and jurisprudential frameworks,[22] this chapter examines how administrative judicial processes play a role in constituting modern administrative states.

---

[19] In general, see Teles (2008). In particular, Feeley and Rubin: "The point, rather, is that they [doctrines] do not become relevant and usable in a modern administrative state by virtue of that lineage. Each mechanism must be judged by its contemporary performance; if one is beginning with the governmental furniture delivered by tradition, each inherited item must be judged by its ability to fit the place we currently inhabit" (2000, 345). Also see Barnes's (2017, 28 n.2) discussion of law and American political development, specifically his reference to Orren and Skowronek's concept of "courts in time" (2004), and Frymer (2008).

[20] For historical-institutional analysis of pre- and post-1960s US administrative law policy paradigms, see Diver (1981).

[21] See Scott (1998) on legibility of the state; Tomlins (2012) on critical legal histories.

[22] For examples, see Teles (2008); Hollis-Brusky (2014) on the Federalist Society; Decker (2016) on the conservative turn to juridical activism. For discussion of conservative women's organizations against VAWA, see Schreiber (2008).

12.1 INSTITUTIONAL CONCEPTUALIZATION

Shortly after the Fourth Circuit Court of Appeals (*en banc*) held VAWA's civil rights provision unconstitutional,[23] the bill's chief sponsor, Senator Joseph R. Biden Jr., D-Del., defended VAWA once again; this time in the *Harvard Journal on Legislation* (2000).[24] Self-conscious of the fact that the US Supreme Court had just granted certiorari, Biden seized the "opportunity ... to explain the need for the remedy and its constitutional basis" (Biden 2000, 5). His account of VAWA's policy history begins with a detailed review of the Senate Judiciary Committee's four-year investigation (1990–94). It heard testimony from experts, including law enforcement officials, judges, social scientists, professors, and physicians, as well as victims. It heard testimony from state officials and read their task force reports, which "concluded themselves that their state justice systems were rife with gender bias in addressing domestic violence, rape, and sexual assault." All of this activity "generated a massive record" which Congress determined was strong evidence that "state legal systems institutionalized the historic prejudices against victims of rape or domestic violence by erecting 'barriers of law, of practice, and of prejudice not suffered by other victims of discrimination'" (Biden 2000). These findings of "widespread gender bias" in *state* legal systems were more than enough reason for Congress to act (on the rational basis standard), and Biden insists Congress did not act alone. Quoting a letter of support from forty-one state Attorney Generals to emphasize that "the problem of violence against women is a national one, requiring

---

[23] *Brzonkala v. Virginia Polytechnic Inst. & State University* (1999) 169 F.3d 820, USCA 4th Circuit, *en banc* (7–4). This decision reversed the Fourth Circuit's (2–1) opinion in *Brzonkala v. Virginia Polytechnic Inst. & State University* (1997) 132 F.3d 949, which "held that appellant [Christy Brzonkala] a female freshman college student properly stated a claim for gender discrimination under the Title IX of the Education Amendments of 1972, and Title III of the Violence Against Women Act of 1994 after appellee state university [Virginia Polytechnic Institute and State University] failed to seriously discipline two college football players [Antonio J. Morrison and James Crawford] who raped appellant." After two hearings, the university (VPI) found that Mr. Morrison had "sexually assaulted" Ms. Brzonkala. His two-semester suspension was "upheld on internal appeal. After the second *de novo* hearing – held, the school maintained, to cover a procedural technicality – the charges were, without notice or explanation to Ms. Brzonkala, changed from 'sexual assault' to 'using abusive language.' Then, without notice to Ms. Brzonkala, Mr. Morrison's punishment was set aside – a fact she learned in a newspaper – and he was welcomed back to the campus on a full athletic scholarship. Unable to continue with her education under these circumstances, suicidal and depressed as many raped women become, Ms. Brzonkala withdrew from school and sued the perpetrators under the Violence Against Women Act" (MacKinnon 2000, 140–41).

[24] Sally F. Goldfarb, staff attorney with the National Organization for Women (NOW) Legal Defense and Education Fund, who advised legislative staff during the drafting phase, attributes the passage of VAWA "largely to the stalwart support" of Senator Biden "and also to the support of Senator Orrin Hatch [R-Utah], who became the lead cosponsor of the bill after a series of compromises in the bill language ... Important help was also provided by Senator Barbara Boxer [D-Cal.] when she was in the House and later when she joined the Senate. And House passage of the Violence Against Women Act took place under the able leadership of Representatives Pat Schroeder [D-Colo.], Chuck Schumer [D-N.Y.], Louise Slaughter [D-N.Y.] and Connie Morella [R-Md.]" (Goldfarb 1996, 394).

federal attention, federal leadership, and federal funds," Biden says, "in fact, state officials *invited* Congress to pass the Violence Against Women Act" (Biden 2000).[25]

As a well-established senior legislator (thirty-six years in the US Senate) who held prominent leadership positions (chaired Senate Committees for twenty-two years) and had acquired policymaking experience with six presidents, Biden performed the role of an "institutionalized entrepreneur."[26] He took on the "hard work of channeling promising trends, compromising on actionable proposals, and building coalitions to gain wide acquiescence" (Grossman 2014, 189). Relying on conventional methods of comprehensive rational policymaking,[27] he worked closely with co-sponsors in the House and in the Senate to assemble what would eventually be "touted as an important measure to promote consistent crime control across states, improve funding and enforcement, and allow for court remedies for state inaction that constituted a form of discriminatory treatment" (Bumiller 2008, 140). As an example of rationalist policy goals, VAWA "aimed at comprehensiveness, covering everything from domestic violence hotlines, to evidentiary matters in sexual harassment cases, to rape kit exams" (Nourse 1996, 2).

Although policymaking is generally concerned with finding solutions to perceived social problems, the rationalist paradigm searches for "prophylactic" remedies.[28] This approach promises to yield predictable outcomes, with verified statistical techniques and long-range planning models. In the legislative hearings, the FBI's crime statistics were marshaled to represent the problem and illustrate "an epidemic of violence" disproportionately impacting women (Schumer, 1992, 1). If "crime prevention" was the solution to combatting this epidemic, then reformers thought it might become a unifying political rational for a civil rights protection against gender violence. The process of conceptualizing this statutory right closely resembles the process of doctrinal creation because the "coordinating ideas," as Feeley and Rubin might agree, are rights-based. Historical and institutional processes also shaped the political formation of this statutory right. However, before legislative allies were assembled or deals negotiated, staff attorneys on the Senate Judiciary Committee would grapple with existing legal categories and vocabularies.

12.1.1 *Addressing Law's Violence*

"Marital rape," "domestic violence," "date rape," and "acquaintance rape" were deeply problematic legal categories for Senate Judiciary Committee staff attorney Victoria

---

[25] In 1991, Attorneys General from forty-one states did urge for the passage of VAWA.
[26] See Grossman (2014) on policy networks, actors, and entrepreneurs.
[27] See Diver's discussion of the contrasts between New Deal "incrementalism" and "comprehensive rationalist" policy approaches (1981).
[28] Senator Biden described VAWA as "prophylactic legislation" and argued that, as such, it was "in keeping with Congress's prophylactic power to effectuate the purposes of the Fourteenth Amendment" (2000, 30, 42).

Nourse, whose job it was to make sense of these acts as civil rights violations. Such crimes of violence were by the very language of the law conceptualized as private relationship problems. "The crime did not exist without that relationship [martial, domestic, acquaintance], and yet, it was that relationship that had helped to make the crime something 'lesser,' some 'inferior' kind of crime, both in the eyes of the law and popular imagination" (Nourse 1996, 1). If this was "a story of the law working against its own language and rhetoric, a law struggling to try to change its own understanding of violence against women," as Nourse understood it (Nourse 1996), then decoupling the violent conduct (rape) from the relationship status (marital, domestic, date, acquaintance) was at the heart of conceptualizing this civil rights policy.[29]

The task of exposing violence in a body of law (criminal or civil), while simultaneously drawing upon legal norms to redress this "legal violence," is not uncommon in histories of legal reform movements. Law professor Reva Siegel's account of reforming marital chastisement laws during the Reconstruction Era by introducing "the language of privacy and love associated with companionate marriage in the industrial era," demonstrates how that law reform process "actually revitalize[d] a body of status law, *enhancing* its capacity to legitimate social inequalities that remain among status-differentiated groups" (1996, 2120). She specifically cautioned VAWA's drafters to "remain in critical dialogue with the evolving rules and rhetoric of any status regime it aspires to disestablish" (2207).[30] So too, we are forewarned by law professor Patricia Williams that the "attempt to split bias from violence has been this society's most enduring and fatal rationalization" (1987, 139; quoted in Hallock 1993, 577).

To begin with, the reformers framed their objectives – to address the status regime – as a whole, rather than particular doctrinal problems in need of fixing. The discourse of "affective privacy" was not only a "myth – an unfortunate legacy of the common-law 'rule of thumb'" as Senator Biden suggested (2000, 4), it was also a technique of reinscribing gender hierarchies.[31] More specifically, the regime's primary norm (affective privacy) operates through a web of legal institutions: policing, the exercise of prosecutorial discretion,[32] judging, and even pretrial criminal referral programs employed by the state.[33] The reformers' task seemed nothing short

---

[29] See Strebeigh (2009, chapters 21–22) for a detailed account of Nourse's research strategy.
[30] See Siegel's analysis of how federalism claims "perpetuate traditional discourse of marital status in new idiomatic form." She suggests federalism claims were likely to serve as a basis for the Court's legal reasoning in a future challenge to the constitutionality of VAWA's civil rights remedy (1996, 2207). Indeed, Siegel's insight did predict *U.S. v. Morrison* (2000).
[31] See Berry, Nelson, and Nielson's research (focusing on federal employment litigation) and analysis of what they call the "legal reinscription processes of race, sex, disability and age hierarchies" (2017, chapter 9 in particular).
[32] See Schneider (2000) on feminist lawmaking and battered women; Bumiller (2008) on how neoliberalism appropriated the feminist movement against violence; Corrigan (2013) on medical and legal practices of marginalizing victims of rape.
[33] In particular see Feeley (1979) on the punishing effects of certain lower criminal trial court administrative processes.

of pulling back and piercing the veil of relationship status; unmasking discriminatory (legal, social, and economic-based) norms and practices as justification for the proposed civil right.[34]

The motivation for conceiving this new civil right was twofold: (1) a recognition that the norm of affective privacy concealed the existence of gender-motivated violence; and (2) evidence that this body of status law was well-established in *state* institutions. The concept of a right to be free from gender-motivated violence embraced the "directionality"[35] of civil rights legislation. Also, familiar elements of legal reasoning, such as analogy, labeling, and metaphor, were as central in formulating policy arguments for this new civil right as they were in constituting the prison conditions doctrine a quarter of a century earlier. *Analogies* between federal laws against lynching and a civil right be to free from gender-motivated violence were made "to make plain (and to make true) that federal law tolerated no violence based on race" nor should it tolerate violence based on gender (Resnik 2010, 560).[36] Labeling "gender-motivated violence" as a form of discrimination "tracks the development of other forms of sex discrimination law, most notably sexual harassment" (Goldscheid 1999, 125–26),[37] which became a form of discrimination under Title VII of the Civil Rights Act as a result of the mid-1970s feminist movement's litigation strategy against sexual harassment (MacKinnon 1979; Baker 2008). Visual *metaphors*,[38] such as the "veil of relationship," exposed while questioning how "relationship" operates to reproduce gender subordination.

---

[34] This phrase is derived from Siegel's concept "to pierce the veil of privacy" (1996, 2173). She shows that during the Reconstruction Era, in both criminal and tort law, "formal and informal immunity rules" developed. For example, if a legally prohibited conduct, such as assault, occurs between subjects classified as being in a "relationship status," then "judges no longer insisted that a husband had the legal prerogative to beat his wife [as would be the holding under chastisements law]; instead, they often asserted that the legal system should not interfere in cases of wife beating, in order to protect the privacy of the marriage relationship and to promote domestic harmony. Judges most often invoked considerations of marital privacy when contemplating the prosecution of middle- and upper-class men for wife beating" (2120).

[35] For discussion of "directionality" in "coordinating ideas," see Feeley and Rubin (2000, 238–39).

[36] On the affirmative effect of civil rights, Resnick argues: "Creating a cause of action for people treated violently because of their gender that gave them access to the federal courts was one way to help women be physically safe when they used public transportation to participate in commercial activities as they went to schools and universities and when they worked in their homes" (2010, 560).

[37] In 1999, Julie Goldscheid was Senior Staff Attorney, National Organization for Women (NOW) Legal Defense and Education Fund. At the beginning of her article, in an "Editors' Note" she writes: "As this Article was going to press, the Fourth Circuit Court of Appeals, sitting *en banc*, issued a ruling declaring the Civil Rights Remedy unconstitutional. The decision contrasts starkly with each of the 11 other district courts to rule on this issue, each of which has upheld the law as constitutional. A petition for certiorari to the U.S. Supreme Court would be due in June" (1999, 123). Goldscheid would later represent plaintiff Christy Brzonkala before the Court in *U.S. v. Morrison* (2000). Her oral argument before the Court can be listened to at www.oyez.org/cases/1999/99-5.

[38] For example, Feeley and Rubin observe that "there is a visual quality to metaphor; it is like a picture where one sees the totality at a glance and then fills in the details on closer examination" (2000, 237).

Are gender-motived crimes "private matters" simply because there had been a "personal relationship" between the litigating parties?[39] And if so, what are the social, economic, and psychological harms/costs of continuing a policy that tolerates such violence?

Simultaneously representing the socioeconomic facts of gender-motivated violence and appealing to the legal authority of antidiscrimination law, reformers worked on translating their goals into rational policy arguments and credible legal claims.[40] New rhetoric, such as "break the silence of violence," emerged and amplified the symbolic value of challenging the preexisting status regime's normative role in preserving gender-motivated violence under the cover of relationship modifiers. Policy arguments for creating a *substantive* right to be free from gender-motivated violence (i.e., "break the silence of violence" to reduce violence against women) reflected the vision of law's ability to uncover injustices and perhaps even compensate the injured.[41]

Policy arguments for the *procedural* remedy (private right of action) shifted. Yet it is not clear whether this occurred because of the speaker's intended audience, or as the result of an actual policy change. The procedural remedy was a "means of compensating for the state's denial of equal protection," and/or a method of "preserv[ing] the states' voice in enforcing the civil right" (Biden 2000, 30, 26). In an effort to reconcile these conflicting perspectives, Biden cast VAWA as a bill with "different complementary strategies" and "carefully drafted to harmonize federal and state policies" (Biden 2000, 6, n.26). By averting explicit challenges to the status relationship regime's grip on state courts, this sort of procedural ambiguity[42] tends to preserve legislative-policy coalitions.[43]

---

[39] On the operation of metaphor and judging, Nourse suggests that "relationship operates as a metaphor or a screen by which we judge women's claims of autonomy, whether those claims actually arise in a relationship or not" (1996, 5 n.21).

[40] On the practice and political theory of legal translation, see Paris (2010).

[41] For example, as represented within liberal-legal ideology, the "myth of rights rests on a faith in the political efficacy and ethical sufficiency of law as a principle of government" (Scheingold 2004, Foreword to second edition by Malcolm Feeley; 16–17). While reformers (liberal and conservative) frequently make broad appeals to the myth of rights, the tools of legal reasoning have: (1) a "high level of indeterminacy" in legal translation processes because, as in the creation of doctrine, the "search for labels, metaphors, analogies, or institutional conceptualizations is necessarily an open-ended one" (Feeley and Rubin 1998, 239); and (2) a high level of individualism in rights-reform strategies, as in the VAWA policy debates, the "underlying premise of this seemingly universalistic appeal," Crenshaw argues, "functions to politicize the problem [of violence against women] only in the dominant community," "intended or not to exclude or ignore the needs of poor and colored women" (1991, 1259–60).

[42] For a discussion of "legal ambiguity" and "ambiguous principles" in employment compliance laws, see Lauren B. Edelman (1992) and Edelman, Smyth, and Rahim (2016).

[43] On "dislodging" entrenched governance structures and how the "challenges of countermobilization are more severe when the governance structure of a field is well defended," see Teles (2008, 15–17).

12.1.2 Judicial Enforcement of Civil Rights

The mechanism for enforcing VAWA's statutory right did address the judiciary's role in a direct, context-specific manner. Congress' bureaucratic element (Title III, Section 13981 of WAVA) extended federal court jurisdiction to enforce the civil right to be free from gender-motivated violence by providing plaintiffs access to federal court via a private right of action. If plaintiffs were successful, then under VAWA's provision they could recover "compensatory and punitive damages, injunctive and declaratory relief, attorney's fees, and 'such other relief as the court may deem appropriate'" (Goldfarb 2002, 65). Reform advocates viewed the Title III enforcement provision as "a logical extension" of federal civil rights laws designed to "fight discriminatory violence" (Siegel 1996, 2196; n.287, citation to S. REP. No. 138, 103d Cong, 1st Session, 51, 1993). Senator Biden said that Title III was "modeled after other traditional civil rights legislation providing a private right of action for victims of discrimination," such as 42 U.S.C. §§ 1981, 1983, 1985, 1994, and incorporated the Section 13981 standard (Biden 2000, 25). While political liberals and conservatives in Congress had agreed to use the private litigation enforcement model, going back even further than the early 1980s, the advocates' depiction of it as a "traditional model" obscures the historical and institutional processes shaping the politics of civil rights policy and judicial enforcement.[44]

During the era of the "Long Great Society"[45] both parties eschewed traditional administrative enforcement (agency adjudication), choosing instead to shape civil rights through private right of action suits (citizen suits). Political scientist Sean Farhang argues that this choice was "neither natural nor inevitable," but rather a "radical departure" from administrative state-building "motivated by legislative-executive conflicts over control of the administrative state" (2012, 659).[46] In 1964, Republicans, seeking to protect the rights of employers whom they believed were subject to "fishing expeditions by investigators, in their zeal to enforce title VII,"

---

[44] Nourse makes an important distinction between existing civil rights remedies that "appear to be the templates from which drafters copied the formal 'cause of action' under Title III and VAWA's cause of action." She writes,

> those remedies provide no analogue for the substantive right created by Title III "to be free" from gender-motivated violence. Section 1981 provides a cause of action to protect the rights of nonwhites "to make and enforce contracts, to sue, be parties, give evidence," and enjoy the equal "benefit" of all laws. Section 1983 provides a cause of action for violations of existing federal constitutional or statutory rights. Of the Reconstruction-era civil rights statutes, section 1985(3) comes closest to the substance of Title III because it addresses violent conduct. However, it differs in several important respects. For example, section 1985(3) is limited to those acts perpetrated by a conspiracy whose purpose is to deprive the plaintiff of "equal protection of the laws." VAWA's cause of action does not depend upon a showing that the defendant consciously intended to deprive another of "equal rights," but, instead, upon proof of violent acts "motivated" by gender. (1996, 8–9)

[45] On policy networks during this period, see Grossman (2014, chapter 4).

[46] On the political development of private enforcement regimes for civil rights, see Farhang (2010, chapters 4–6).

introduced the amendment to Title VII replacing agency adjudication with private litigation (Farhang 2012, 669).[47] In the 1980s, congressional Democrats opposed to what they believed to be the Equal Employment Opportunity Commission's (EEOC) bias under Presidents Reagan and Bush "in favor of employers and as *willfully* obstructing and sabotaging enforcement," were able to pass the Civil Rights Act of 1991 by "substantially increasing the economic incentives for private lawsuits to enforce Title VII" (Farhang 2012, 670). In those political times, congressional liberals and conservatives moved away from the New Deal consensus favoring agency enforcement, fearing that the negative impact of perceived executive influence on administrative decisions could harm their faction's substantive civil rights policy preferences. It is an open question as to whether or not the private enforcement model produced some measure of congressional autonomy vis-à-vis executive control of the bureaucracy. We do know that congressional Democrats and Republicans favored the private enforcement model over agency adjudication, though each "for very different reasons" (Farhang 2010, 162). Partisan factions thus agreed to not disagree about their ideological differences on civil rights in exchange for avoiding the risk of excessive executive influence over the bureaucratic element of enforcement.

In the early stage of VAWA's legislative development (1990–92), there are faint traces of Farhang's legislative-executive dynamic. On the same day that Senator Biden reintroduced VAWA as S.15[48] and Representative Barbara Boxer, D-Cal., reintroduced the House companion bill (January 14, 1991; 102nd Congress), Republican Senator Bob Dole, R-Kan., introduced a bill "intended to be a political alternative to the Biden-Boxer bill but one that *omitted* the controversial civil rights remedy" (Nourse 1996, 13, emphasis added).[49] During that month, the George H. W. Bush administration came out against the civil rights remedy in S.15, "urging Senators to conclude that the bill was unconstitutional" (Nourse 1996). Republicans in both branches (legislative and executive) were allied against the civil rights remedy in S.15. Nonetheless, the civil rights remedy Senate Republicans and Bush's Department of Justice initially opposed survived.[50] The next version of VAWA (S.11), reintroduced in the 103rd Congress during November of 1993, passed with bipartisan support, as clarified above, and then signed into law by President Clinton on September 13, 1994. Despite early Republican opposition, coming from Congress and the executive, Title III endured over three Congresses, spanning both

---

[47] On the question of why civil rights groups lobbied for the Civil Rights Fees Act of 1976, see Farhang's analysis of efforts by House Republicans in 1972 to eliminate class actions under Title VII (2010, 162).
[48] Previously S. 2754 (1990) 101st Congress.
[49] The name of the bill was "Women's Equal Opportunity Act," 137 Cong. Rec. S. 2189 (1991).
[50] The most extensive legislative history of VAWA to date is by Victoria Nourse. She notes that "VAWA took several different forms in both the House and the Senate: all told, there are at least fourteen versions of VAWA. Each of the three Senate bills and at least one of the three House bills were introduced in one form and then approved by committee after significant alterations. In addition, further changes were made during consideration on the floor of the Senate, and in conference committee" (1996, 6–7).

Republican and Democratic administrations. The judicial countermobilization against VAWA, however, proved to be more consequential.

12.2 JUDICIAL ADMINISTRATION IN ACTION

Organized judicial opposition[51] went public two weeks after S.15[52] was introduced (Nourse 1996, 16). On the surface, it may have appeared as if state judges were leading the offense. Their national organization, the National Conference of State Chief Justices (NCSCJ),[53] attacked VAWA on jurisdictional grounds, calling it "sweeping," and alleging that access to federal courts for gender-motivated violence intruded into areas of "domestic relations law" traditionally ceded to their courts. The NCSCJ also alleged that VAWA's civil rights remedy (Title III) would be used by parties as "a bargaining tool within the context of divorce negotiation,"[54] and "cause major dislocations in the processing of domestic relations cases." Within months, the Judicial Conference of the United States (herein Judicial Conference) endorsed NCSCJ's objections to S.15's "broad definition" of gender-motivated acts.[55] The federal judges (Judicial Conference) agreed with the state judges (NCSCJ) that VAWA would be a bargaining device in divorce negotiations, and as such it would "add a major complicating factor to an environment which is often acrimonious as it is" (Judicial Conference, Sept. 1991, 58). Independently of each other, both national judicial administrative organizations expressed general support for the legislation's substantive goal of reducing violence against women. The Judicial Conference announced it was prepared to work with Congress "to ensure the most efficient utilization of scarce judicial resources and to fashion an appropriate response to violence directed against women."

Meanwhile, in between sessions at the biannual meetings of the Judicial Conference (Judicial Conference 1991, 47), the Executive Committee, chaired by Chief Justice Rehnquist, announced the Chief Justice had appointed a special "Ad Hoc Committee on Gender-Based Violence" to advise the Conference on "whether it should take a position on the Violence Against Women Act that then-Senator Biden had introduced into Congress" (Resnik 2010, 560).[56] The Ad Hoc Committee

---

[51] However, not all judicial organizations opposed VAWA. "For example, as early as 1992, the National Association of Women Judges expressed its support for the remedy" (Nourse 1996, 6 n.24), and reaffirmed support in 1993 (Goldfard 2000, 67 n.47).
[52] On the Senate side, the first version was S.2754, 101st Congress, introduced by Senator Biden on June 19, 1990 and adopted by voice vote in October 1990. On the House side, Representative Pat Schroeder introduced H.R. 5468, 101st Congress.
[53] Founded in 1949; see Conference of Chief Justices Homepage – http://ccj.ncsc.org/.
[54] For further analysis of the Conference of State Chief Justices position on VAWA in 1991 see Nourse's comments on this testimony before the US Senate Committee Hearings (1996, 6 n. 24).
[55] By "broad definition," NCSCJ was referring to misdemeanors and other minor threats against persons and property.
[56] Law professor Judith Resnik was "one of six law professors who wrote an amicus brief filed on behalf of about 100 professors of constitutional law, the federal courts, and jurisprudence, in support of congressional authority to enact the Violence Against Women Act" (2000, 269). See her analysis of

was actually established a year earlier. In September 1990, the Conference Committee on Federal-State Jurisdiction reported, under the topic heading "federal question citizen suits," the "Conference postponed consideration of S.2754 [the first version of VAWA], a bill to create federal question jurisdiction for a victim of any rape, sexual assault, or abusive sexual contact motivated by gender-based animus to recover compensatory and punitive damages" (Judicial Conference 1990, 82). The following year, the Executive Committee reported, under the topic heading "Violence Against Women Act," that "three Conference committees *had reviewed* the legislation [S.15] and reported concern about its potential impact on the federal courts" (Judicial Conference 1991, 47, emphasis added). The three Conference committees, all of whose members were appointed by Chief Justice Rehnquist, included the Committee on Federal-State Jurisdiction, Ad Hoc Committee on Gender-Based Violence, and Executive Committee. Their recommendations to the Judicial Conference were developed at roughly the same time the National Conference of State Chief Justices (NCSCJ) announced its opposition to VAWA. Thus, when NCSCJ "vehemently" argued VAWA would "wreak major unforeseen changes in a large area of civil litigation which is not federal in nature" (McTaggart 1998, 1142), the Judicial Conference was prepared to launch its own "most lasting and vehement criticism" of VAWA's enforcement mechanism (Weiss 1997, 733).

12.2.1 Interbranch Ideological Competition over the Administrative State

The campaign they waged initially focused on the danger of involving the federal courts in "a whole host of domestic relations disputes" (Rehnquist 1992, 3). In public speeches, some of which were aired on local TV news,[57] and publications (newsletter of the Judicial Conference "The Third Branch") reported on by the Associate Press, the Chief Justice's vision of "domestic relations disputes" overwhelming the federal courts reached larger audiences. The message usually included some numbers, such as "over three million domestic relations cases were filed in state courts in 1989," and was followed by an interpretation: "If a party to one-tenth of those suits were to seek collateral recourse under S.15, those cases alone would exceed the total of all cases now pending in the district courts" (Judicial Conference 1991, 75). As the Chief Justice praised Congress for recognizing the predicament of the federal court's civil dockets and passing the Civil Justice Reform Act (1990), he criticized them for proposals he said would add to "those dockets causes of action now actionable in state courts, as S.15 would do, or as sections 202 and 121 3(G) of S.1241 (the Violent Crime Control Act of 1991) would do, the serious problem will become much worse" (Rehnquist 1992, 3). *Newsday* and *The Washington Post*, among other media outlets,

---

the Ad Hoc Committee on Gender-Based Violence, and documentation of Chief Justice Rehnquist's role in creating this Ad Hoc Committee (272 n.11).

[57] For examples, see Indiana local news coverage (Hallock 1993, 612 n.224) and the Chief Justice's convocation address at Wake Forest University (Easterling 1996, 950 n.120).

quoted the Chief Justice as saying that Congress' "initiative" to "let women sue those who victimize them" was "endangering" the federal courts and "degrading" justice: "Congress is endangering the quality and credibility of federal courts by trying to make federal cases of too many crimes and noncriminal disputes, Chief Justice William Rehnquist says. Unless checked, the result will be a degradation in the high quality of justice the nation has long expected of the federal courts, Rehnquist said in his 1991 year-end report on the federal judiciary" (Associated Press *Newsday* 1992, 15; *Washington Post* 1992, 29).

At the same time "the nation's highest-ranking judge" opposed allowing "domestic relations disputes" to become "federal cases," it was also reported that according to the Chief Justice "workloads for federal trial judges actually declined in 1991" (Associated Press *Newsday* 1992).

> Criminal case filings fell 4 percent, the first drop in over a decade, despite a 21 percent rise in fraud prosecutions stemming from the savings and loan crisis. Civil, or noncriminal, case filings in federal trial courts also declined in 1991, by 5 percent to 208,000. The number of new bankruptcy cases continued to increase, up more than 21 percent – to nearly 900,000. Personal bankruptcy cases rose 23 percent, far higher than the 7 percent rise in business bankruptcies. (*Washington Post* 1992)

When asked whether additional resources should be allocated, Rehnquist told *The New York Times* that increases in federal case files might justify "the provision of some additional judicial resources ... in the short run," but "adding more judges is not the solution" (Associated Press *Newsday* 1992). Why not? Why would additional resources *not* enhance the capacity of the federal courts to enforce a civil right to be free from gender-motivated violence?

Rehnquist replied to the media, telling them the "long-term implications of expanding the federal judiciary should give everyone pause" because "the writers of the Constitution intended the Federal judicial system to have only a limited role, reserved for issues where important national interests predominate" (Greenhouse 1992).[58] While judicial conservatives at this time often found authority for constitutional interpretation in "the Founders' intent," here, the Chief Justice finds justification for federal court administration in "original intent." It is not clear whether invoking "the Founder's intent" was meant to be understood as a constraint on federal judicial administrative institutions (which would otherwise support judicial enforcement of the civil right), or a foundational principle of judicial administration.

---

[58] In his 1991 annual address, Chief Justice Rehnquist reports that the Judicial Conference created a committee on long-range planning because of the need to "reexamine the role of the federal courts" (Resnik 2000, 271). Discussing mounting caseload pressures, he advocated against increasing the number of judges, stating that "modest curtailment of federal jurisdiction is important; equally important is self-restraint in adding new federal causes of action" (Rehnquist 1992, 3).

Either way, in this context, fidelity to "original intent" ignited an interbranch competition over the structure of the administrative state. That is, instead of deferring to Congress' bipartisan compromise on civil rights enforcement (favoring judicial over agency enforcement), the judicial countermobilization charged that Title III of VAWA (S.15) "significantly threatens the ability of the federal courts to administer this Act, and other Acts of Congress, promptly, fairly, and in accordance with their objectives" (Judicial Conference 1991, 57).

The first part of the charge – "the ability of the federal courts to administer this Act" – references a set of administrative claims: (1) VAWA's "sweeping" jurisdiction intrudes upon state domestic relations law; and (2) the creation of a private right of action (Title III) "clogs the federal courts' civil docket with domestic disputes." The second part – "and in accordance with their [Congress'] objectives" – claims that judicial administration is a legitimate restraint on the enforcement of legislative objectives. Both parts read together serve as a self-reinforcing administrative bias against judicial deference to Congress' objectives. Politically, the administrative rationale serves as a reassuring symbolic expression that there is "order in the courts" (judicial restraint on politics) and downplays (conceals) what original intent intends (i.e., domestic relations disputes are not important national interests), thus keeping the veil of relationship status in place, preserving the entrenched norm of affective privacy.[59]

This judicial challenge was unfolding while Congress was attempting to reverse nine Supreme Court decisions. On the bench, under the leadership of the newly appointed Chief Justice Rehnquist (1986), judicial conservatives came together to form a slim majority. In a series of employment discrimination cases, this new conservative majority decided to significantly narrow the reach of Title VII and reduce remedies available to employees alleging employer discrimination. Congress responded in 1990 by passing legislation that would have overturned these decisions, but it was vetoed by President Bush. After working out a compromise bill with the White House, a second bill was endorsed and signed by the president. The Civil Rights Restoration Act of 1991[60] affirmed Congress' interpretation of Title VII's "statutory intent" and overturned nine Supreme Court decisions. So, at the same time these "robed judges" on the Court faced defeat of their doctrinal attempt to cut back Title VII's private right of action enforcement regime, organized judicial opposition to VAWA was underway. The interbranch ideological struggle (judicial-congressional) over civil rights shifted ground from judicial review to judicial administration, a far less visible policymaking arena.

---

[59] On "the administrative system as symbol" see Murray Edelman (1974, chapter 3).
[60] Also known as the Civil Rights Act of 1991 (S. 1745), it passed the House 381–38 and the Senate 93–5. See Congressional Quarterly Almanac 102nd Congress, 1st Session (1991). For an excellent analysis of this legislation see Farhang (2010, chapter 6).

12.2.2 Bureaucratic Autonomy off the Bench

The rise of the modern administrative state has been a catalyst for bureaucratic judicial policymaking at least since the early twentieth century era of state rationalization,[61] when Congress created the Judicial Conference (1922). The legislative objective for this new institution was to facilitate communication and policymaking among the decentralized federal courts by providing for "a meeting at which the requirements of all the districts can be considered and compared" (Fish 1973, 34). Congress delegated authority "to prepare plans for assignment and transfer of federal judges to or from congested districts or circuits," which soon became known as "intercircuit assignment power" (Fish 1973, 33). The internal protocols and procedures of the Judicial Conference were largely left to be determined by its members, the chief justice and the senior circuit judges. Chief Justice William Howard Taft, whose political entrepreneurship[62] is credited for convincing Congress "judicial governance" would advance "administrative integration" in the federal courts, was a fan of the scientific management movement. His advocacy on behalf of "efficient judicial administration" led to an increase in the number of federal district court judges (Fish 1973), creating an opportunity to expose a new cohort of twenty-four federal judges to the idea of building "judicial governance" through administration.[63]

The Judicial Conference gained control over more areas of federal judicial administration after Congress passed the Administrative Office Act of 1939. This legislation transferred all fiscal, business, and data services from the Department of Justice (DOJ) to a new agency within the judicial branch – the Administrative Office of the US Courts (the Administrative Office). Political scientist Peter Graham Fish argues that while the DOJ's depression budget and the growing number of federal case filings were factors on the horizon, President Franklin Roosevelt's 1937 Court Bill ("the court-packing plan") is what motivated proposals from the Judicial Conference (chaired by Chief Justice Charles Even Hughes), endorsements and lobbying on the part of the American Bar Association's President Arthur T. Vanderbilt, and the passage of legislation (Fish 1973, chapters 3 and 4). Congress moved quickly to approve their reorganization plan, including a stipulation for the chief justice to appoint the director of the Administrative Office. Situating the new agency inside the judicial branch was more than

---

[61] See e.g., Kolko (1976) and Wiebe (1967). For a critique of the revisionist historians' perspective see Gilbert (2016).
[62] In addition to Fish (1973), see also Crowe (2012, 199–212) on Taft as a "political entrepreneur."
[63] However, research by political scientist Marie Provine found that "governance is a low-profile activity within the judiciary. Judges are reluctant to exercise authority over each other outside the realm of appeals; they value decentralization, local autonomy, and ample room for individual initiative in the organization of their work. Judicial independence means not just freedom from control by other branches of government, but freedom from control by other judges. The ideal of autonomous judges, with roots deep in American legal culture, powerfully influences contemporary debates about efficiency and accountability within the judiciary" (1988, 83).

a defensive response to FDR's court-packing plan; it provided new resources and institutional opportunities for the Third Branch to engage in bureaucratic state-building beyond the confines of adjudication. The new agency acquired the status of "secretariat for the Judicial Conference,"[64] with responsibilities the DOJ never had, including the administration of committees and programs for the federal courts, as well as liaison between the judicial branch, Congress, and individual judges. The invention of the Administrative Office "liberated the Judicial Conference from bureaucratic management" (Crowe 2015, 232), transformed the Judicial Conference into a "centralized-policymaking institution" (Fish 1973, 228), and further legitimized judicial policymaking through administration. The experts staffing the Administrative Office, advising and lobbying on behalf of the Judicial Conference, are the progeny of Progressive Era administrative state-building.[65] The project of "efficient judicial administration," and scientific management more generally, transposed the idea of "administration" into a specialized body of knowledge, skills, training, and certification (e.g., degree-granting programs in judicial administration).[66]

As interlocutor for the judicial branch, the Administrative Office facilitates and generates interbranch communications, particularly among congressional committees. While at the same time, the judicial branch's administrative capacity to coordinate legislative policy is enhanced by these professional networks and institutional ties. In addition, "under the auspices of providing advice regarding pending legislation and its impact on the federal judiciary," political scientist Dawn Chutkow shows how the appointments chief justices (from Rehnquist to Roberts) make to Judicial Conference committees "use the administrative structure and the incentives it creates to influence policy both internal and external to the judiciary" (2014, 304, 301). The scope of the chief justice's plenary appointment powers includes the allocation of administrative authority within the Judicial Conference and between the Administrative Office. The chief justice chooses who will be a member of which Judicial Conference committee, the committees' chairs, as well as the Director of the Administrative Office. These discretionary institutional powers enhance the chief justice's ability to direct and oversee multiple sites of judicial administration off the bench.

In 1986, leadership change on the Supreme Court transferred these plenary prerogatives to a new chief justice. In June of that year, President Ronald Reagan nominated Associate Justice Rehnquist to replace Chief Justice

---

[64] The Director of the Administrative Office also has the title of Secretary of the Judicial Conference.
[65] On professionalizing legal projects and political development see Harrington (1994).
[66] Yet, as historian Brian Balogh cogently puts it, "the revolt against Parsonian structure-functionalism in the social sciences challenged historians' lockstep conceptualization of bureaucratization, professionalization, technological advance, and evolution from entrepreneurial to corporate capitalism" (1991, 121).

Warren Burger. A few months after he was confirmed by the Senate in September, the new chief justice initiated a reorganization plan that commenced in December to study the "potential restructuring of the entire Judicial Conference" (Judicial Conference 1987, 57). The stated goals for this reorganization were "to operate more expeditiously" and develop "effective resources allocation." These goals are among the inherited norms of "efficient judicial administration," emblematic of the bureaucratic judicial regime developed in the early twentieth century. They were reinforced once again, this time in two of the four recommendations put forth by the commission appointed by Chief Justice Rehnquist:[67] (1) "improve communications among the Conference, its committees, the courts, the judges, supporting personnel, and the Administrative Office"; and (2) "ensure greater knowledge of, and allow greater participation in, the activities of the Conference and its committees by personnel throughout the judicial system" (Judicial Conference 1987).[68] The other recommendations, both of which were also approved, resulted in: (3) "strengthening the authority of the Executive Committee to deal with internal and external Conference business" by elevating its authority as a new "senior executive arm of the Conference" with a "newly-constituted Executive Committee";[69] and (4) consolidating delegation powers in the office of the chief justice, specifically for the purpose of "providing the Conference with an entity capable of implementing its policies between sessions" (of the Conference's annual meeting), such as "establish[ing] a legislative liaison group to monitor the legislative situation and maintain improved judicial/legislative relations" (Judicial Conference 1987, 58). As a consequence of this reorganization, the following year the chief justice created the Committee on Federal-State Jurisdiction. It would become something of a clearinghouse for "monitoring the legislative situation,"[70] coordinating with ad hoc committees. A network of ad hoc committees, authorized and appointed by the chief justice, would review, comment, and make recommendations to the executive committee on particular pieces of legislation.

The establishment of new plenary powers, along with the decision to consolidate them under the authority of the chief justice and executive committee he chaired, produced a more flexible policy network capable of interacting with multiple branches and governmental agencies, establishing cross-cutting ties, and developing

[67] On committee appointments as particularly important opportunities for political entrepreneurs in the judicial branch, see Chutkow (2014).
[68] See Provine (1988) on the Judicial Conference's concern with improving inter-court communications; see Barrow, Zuk, and Grytski (1996, 108) on the Administrative Office's circuit court governance work, in particular their findings that these efforts had "not proven much of a bulwark against ... the individualism of judges, even in the Ninth Circuit, where circuit institutions are strongest."
[69] Chaired by the chief justice, this is a six-member committee consisting of three circuit judges and three district judges. For data establishing a positive correlation between chief justices' appointments to Judicial Conference committees and partisanship (1986–2012), see Chutkow (2014).
[70] This committee's recommendations, including forming the committee itself, were approved by the Judicial Conference (Judicial Conference 1987; Federal Judicial Center 1987).

policy expertise. With this apparatus in place, opportunities for bureaucratic judicial policymaking expanded beyond responding to requests from Congress concerning judicial procedure and federal court caseload management. That is, with greater "operational latitude,"[71] the Judicial Conference achieved bureaucratic autonomy to compete in legislative policy arenas. Three years after the "restructuring of the entire Judicial Conference," the special Ad Hoc Committee on Gender-Based Violence was created (1990). VAWA was one of the Administrative Office's "high priority project" for the Judicial Conference. Its task was to focus on "securing revisions that would minimize the negative impact on the federal court system of proposed legislation creating a civil rights remedy in the federal courts for victims of gender-based violence" (Judicial Conference 1992, 7).[72]

12.2.3 *Judicial Bargaining in the Arena of Civil Rights*

If the first phase of the judicial countermobilization against VAWA was to challenge S.15, the next was the process of "securing revisions" through bipartisan negotiations with the Senate Judiciary Committee. In order to avoid some of what they feared would be "hostile floor amendments," the Senate Judiciary Committee's majority (Joe Biden) and minority (Orrin Hatch) leaders agreed to "negotiate a mutually acceptable bill" in May 1993 (Nourse 1996, 27). The Committee's agenda focused on addressing those challenges put forth by the judicial countermobilization. Indeed, their opposition to the definition of "gender-motivated violence" as well as to the enforcement mechanism structured the negotiations. First, the Senate Judiciary Committee approved procedural and jurisdictional amendments to the S.15 version of Title III: (1) giving state courts concurrent jurisdiction to enforce the statute; (2) prohibiting removal of any state court action asserting a claim under Section 13981 to a federal court; and (3) explicitly denying[73] any federal court to exercise "supplemental jurisdiction over any state law claims regarding divorce, alimony, the distribution of marital property, or child-custody decree" (Biden 2000, 7). In Biden's words, these changes were made to *"preserve the states' voice in enforcing the new right* to be free from gender-based violence" (Biden 2000, 26, emphasis added). They also, in his view, secured "a supplemental remedy for victims that minimally interferes with state prerogatives" (Biden 2000, 11). Second, the Committee approved the removal of all violent acts classified as misdemeanors from Title III coverage, and then also limited the cause of action to violent acts

[71] See Daniel Carpenter's conception of "bureaucratic autonomy" as a form of judicial-bureaucratic autonomy (Carpenter 2000, 124 n.7). I do not intend to claim, however, that this 1986–87 reorganization alone achieved a new form of judicial-bureaucratic autonomy *over* legislative policymaking.

[72] The Administrative Office predicted that VAWA's civil rights remedy would "significantly affect the federal courts and their administration by generating as many as 53,800 civil tort cases annually, with a projected 13,450 annual case filings expected in the federal courts" (Biden 2000, 26).

[73] Biden emphasized that it was "difficult to see how § 13981 arrogates jurisdiction to the federal courts over family law matters when the statute explicitly precludes such jurisdiction" (2000, 27 n.160).

that "rise to the level of a felony against the person or ... would constitute a felony against property if the conduct presents a serious risk of physical injury to another" (Nourse 1996, 28). For many in the civil rights and feminist movements, legislative reformers and staff attorneys in particular, these changes went against a core objective to "disestablish" the norm of affective privacy. As Victoria Nourse observed, this limit on the private right of action remedy excludes "many cases the act was intended to cover – cases in which state and local laws effectively 'downgraded' a crime (to a misdemeanor) because of the relationship of the parties" (Nourse 1996).

However much the Committee yielded to the opposition's position that VAWA threatened state court/federal court administration, the opposition remained unremittingly against the civil right provision until "a major concession to the judiciary" was accepted by the bill's sponsors (Goldfarb 2002, 68). According to law professor and political scientist Catherine MacKinnon, the Judicial Conference "conditioned its withdrawal of opposition to the bill" on inserting an "animus requirement" in the bill's definition of a "crime of violence motivated by gender" (MacKinnon 2000, 139).[74] Once the Committee accepted this condition, the Judicial Conference withdrew its objections based on jurisdiction but took no position on the civil right remedy. The final bill required plaintiffs to establish the violence inflicted on them was "due, at least in part, to an animus based on the victim's gender" (Public Law 1994, 103–332). The victim of a serious felony would therefore need to show the defendant had a specific intent or purpose to injure the victim, based on the victim's gender (Nourse 1996, 32).

What effect did "securing revisions" have on this civil rights legislation? In Biden's view, the requirement further clarified the meaning of the phrase "motivated by gender" by distinguishing the new civil right from state tort law and, importantly, responding to misrepresentations of VAWA as "supplanting state tort law" (2000, 27). He argued that "by enacting a civil rights statute that requires *invidious discriminatory motivation*, Congress also avoided creating a 'general federal tort law'" (Biden 2000, emphasis added). And, by his account, this means plaintiffs must present evidence that respondents' acts of violence were due, at least in part, to an "invidious discriminatory motivation" based on the victim's gender. Yet, four years earlier, Senate Judiciary staff attorney Victoria Nourse questioned whether the term "animus" necessarily required VAWA plaintiffs to establish an invidious discrimination motivation. She acknowledged that the term "animus" is "frequently associated with 42 U.S.C. sec. 1985(3)" and its use in civil rights case law "is synonymous with the word 'purpose'" (Nourse 1996, 33). However, Nourse cautioned against assuming

---

[74] MacKinnon, who was "involved in formulating the Violence Against Women Act and signed the Brief of Law Professors as Amici Curiae in Support of Petitioners, U.S. v. Morrison, 120 S. Ct. 1740 (2000) (Nos. 99–5, 99–29), also draws our attention to Justice Souter's dissent in Morrison, where he notes that the Judicial Conference withdrew its opposition "after the word animus was added" (2000, 135, 139 n.15).

that Section 1985(3) is precedent for Title III. She believed that the Supreme Court's narrow reading of the word "equal" in Section 1985(3), which required plaintiffs to show an "invidiously discriminating," "class-based animus or purpose," had wrongfully conflated two very different understandings of "the purpose" for bringing a cause of action in Section 1983(3) cases with "the purpose" for a cause of action in VAWA cases. Under 1985(3), "the purpose must be to deprive a person of 'equal' rights." While under VAWA, "the purpose must be 'based on the victim's gender'" (Nourse 1996). Further, her research on the legislative history of VAWA led her to conclude that "there is no textual language in VAWA, nor are there references in any of the many Committee reports, to the terms 'invidious' or 'class-based animus.'" And finally, even after the animus requirement was inserted (during the 1993 Biden-Hatch compromise), Nourse found that Senate Judiciary Committee reports continued to refer to Title VII case law as the "appropriate reference-point for assessing 'discrimination' under Title III" (Nourse 1996, 33 n.178).

While there may be good jurisprudential and/or political reasons for not conflating the Court's interpretation of "animus" in Section 1985(3) with Congress' intentions regarding the meaning of the term "animus" in VAWA's Title III, some advocates continued to refer to "animus" in Section 1985(3) as precedent for Title III.[75] For example, in the context of developing her argument about "congressional hearings on the Fourteenth Amendment and its enforcement acts provid[ing] a striking parallel to the hearings on the VAWA," law professor and political scientist Catherine MacKinnon shows that a "substantial amount of the Ku Klux Klan's violence, [was] the basis for the Third Enforcement Act that became Section 1985(3)" (2000, 155). MacKinnon, like Biden, views the Supreme Court's decision in *Griffin v. Breckenridge* (1971), as having established Section 1985(3) precedent on "animus" motivating those acts actionable under Section 13981 through VAWA (MacKinnon 2000). Her interpretation of VAWA's "mental element" (animus) speaks to the "practical effect" of the invidious discriminatory motivation standard. Its practical effect, MacKinnon says, "was to make it impossible for many victims to seek relief in court: not because the acts against them were not violent, not because their injury was not because of sex or gender, and not because adequate relief had already been provided. It was because evidence of the mental element, uniquely elusive and under defendants' control, would foreseeably be

---

[75] Julie Goldscheid (Senior Staff Attorney for NOW Legal Defense and Education Fund) argued that prior to VAWA Section 1985(3) and "other cases reveal that the same evidence establishes bias regardless of whether the standard for assessing animus is articulated as 'because of' a protected category, based on 'animus' or driven by 'invidiously discriminatory animus' ... the type of evidence used to show gender or other bias motivation does not vary, regardless of the particular statutory formulation. In addition, other federal civil rights cases also confirm that even under Section 1985(3), gender-based animus does not require proof of malice or hatred. As with other discrimination and bias crime cases, the essential inquiry is whether the crime was committed solely for random or non-discriminatory reasons. The use of the term 'animus' in the Civil Rights Remedy [in VAWA] does not alter that essential inquiry for gender- based bias crime cases" (1999, 151).

unavailable in many cases. Thus, were many women, through action taken by judges even before the law's enactment, excluded from access to relief for violence committed against them because they were women" (MacKinnon 2000, 139). The higher standard for proof of discrimination, in her view, had the practical effect of reinscribing gender inequality. Biden's interpretation speaks to practical effects, as well. He saw the practical effect of the animus requirement as "helping to clarify" the limits of the new civil right. He sought to reassure judicial opponents the practical effect of incorporating the animus requirement into the VAWA would reduce the size of the potential plaintiff pool and would "not preempt, invalidate, or duplicate" other bodies of law (state domestic relations and tort laws; federal tort laws) (2000, 11).

One difference between Biden's and MacKinnon's interpretation might be due to the timing of their interpretations relative to when the Court decided *U.S. v. Morrison*. According to Biden, who was writing on the eve of the Court granting cert to hear the case, the compromise of 1993 "was carefully crafted in the very best spirit of cooperative federalism" (Biden, 2000). MacKinnon's analysis, however, comes as a postmortem, written in the aftermath of *U.S. v. Morrison*. In contrast, she argues VAWA (with the animus requirement) was "constrained by the very laws it was passed to supersede. Foreshadowing rather than precluding its demise, when the VAWA built deference to federalism in, it cut violated women out" (2000, 139). What was not disputed, however, was that the "Committee limited the statute so that it did not reach even all violent crimes motivated by gender animus" (Biden 2000, 27; see also Nourse 1996 and Resnik 2010). Thus, the conservative judicial countermobilization was able to secure a legislative compromise off the bench, in favor of federalism, which had the effect of diminishing the scope of the right to be free from gender-motivated violence even before a five-member majority of the Court struck down this provision from the bench.

12.3 CONCLUSION

Within the legislative process, policymakers and feminist advocates found themselves interacting with at least four institutional logics, each reflecting institutional as well as political conceptualizations of civil rights policy in the late twentieth and early twenty-first century: (1) legal norms of relationship status (marital, domestic, date, acquaintance) operating in the state courts that diminished violent conduct (rape); (2) the lack of political will in the EEOC to enforce civil rights under Title VII; (3) the effect of congressional-executive interbranch dynamics on enforcement options, which favored creating a private cause for action (Title III); and (4) the conservative judicial movement's turn toward reviving federalism and reducing "administrative burdens" on the state. Rather than responding to federal judicial administrators' budgetary estimates, caseload management plans, and proposals to accommodate yet another private cause of action, the judicial opposition to VAWA's civil right raised the stakes, transforming the arena of interbranch coordination into an opportunity to compete with Congress over directionality of the administrative state – specifically, the power to administer civil rights legislation.

The political resources and possibilities that may enable, activate, or constrain federal judicial administrative mobilizations are nested in and shaped by intersecting historical processes[76] and institutional dynamics. For example, "administrative integration," the early twentieth-century state building project that created and financed the Judicial Conference (1922–present), established an administrative apparatus for judicial governance and policymaking. In other political times, struggles over directing the administrative state, such as Roosevelt's court-packing plan, transferred administrative tasks from the executive to the judicial branch, ironically assisting in building judicial capacity in the field of bureaucratic policymaking, as evidenced by coordination between the Judicial Conference and the Administrative Office. These historical and institutional processes constitute something that we might refer to in the plural – administrative "states." Finally, in exchange for adding a higher standard for proof of discrimination to the Violence Against Women Act, the judicial countermobilization achieved the "ability to administer legislation"[77] off the bench.

BIBLIOGRAPHY

Associated Press. 1992. "Rehnquist Carps at Congress." *Newsday*, January 1, 1992. ProQuest doc. ID: 278465596.

Axelrad, Danielle R., Derek W. Kelley, Judith Feinberg, Jennifer E. Sherven. 1999. "A Survey of Federal Cases Involving the Constitutionality of the Violence Against Women Act." *Public Interest Law Journal* 9: 133–59.

Balogh, Brian. 1991. "Reorganizing the Organizational Synthesis: Federal-Professional Relations in Modern America." *Studies in American Political Development* 5: 119–72.

Barnes, Jeb. 2007. "Bringing the Courts Back In: Interbranch Perspectives on the Role of Courts in American Politics and Policy Making." *Annual Review of Political Science* 10: 25–43.

Barrow, Deborah J., Gary Zuk, and Gerard S. Gryski. 1996. *The Federal Judiciary and Institutional Change*. Ann Arbor: University of Michigan Press.

Berry, Ellen, Robert L. Nelson, and Laura Beth Nielson. 2017. *Rights on Trial: How Workplace Discrimination Law Perpetuates Inequality*. Chicago: University of Chicago Press.

Biden, Senator Joseph R. 2000. "Essay: The Civil Rights Remedy of the Violence Against Women Act: A Defense." *Harvard Journal on Legislation* 37: 1–45.

Byrd, Richeé A. 2002. "Specific Provisions of the Violence Against Women Act." *Georgetown Journal of Gender and the Law* 3: 595–608.

Bumiller, Kristin. 2008. *In an Abusive State: How Neoliberalism Appropriated the Feminist Movement Against Sexual Violence*. Duke University Press.

---

[76] On the "nesting of systems" in particular see Orren (2004), and on the field of law and American political development more generally see Frymer (2008).

[77] For a discussion of "concerns" raised about the potential of the Judicial Conference to influence legislative outcomes, see Chutkow (2014, 304).

Carpenter, Daniel P. 2000. "State Building through Reputation Building: Coalitions of Esteem and Program Innovation in the National Postal System, 1883–1913." *Studies in American Political Development* 14 (2000): 121–55.

Chutkow, Dawn W. 2014. "The Chief Justice as Executive: Judicial Conference Committee Appointments." *Journal of Law and Courts* 2: 301–25.

Clayton, Cornell W. and Mitchell Pickerill. 2006. "The Politics of Criminal Justice: How the New Right Regime Shaped the Rehnquist Court's Criminal Justice Jurisprudence." *The Georgetown Law Journal* 95: 1385–425.

Congressional Quarterly Almanac 102nd Congress, 1st Session. 1991.

Corrigan, Rose. 2013. *Up Against a Wall: Rape Reform and the Failure of Success*. New York: New York University Press.

Crenshaw, Kimberlé. 1991. "Mapping the Margins: Intersectionality, Identity Politics, and Violence Against Women of Color." *Stanford Law Review* 43: 1241–99.

Crowe, Justin. 2012. *Building the Judiciary: Law, Courts, and the Politics of Institutional Development*. Princeton: Princeton University Press.

Decker, Jefferson. 2016. *The Other Rights Revolution: Conservative Lawyers and the Remaking of American Government*. New York: Oxford University Press.

Diver, Colin. 1981. "Policymaking Paradigms in Administrative Law." *Harvard Law Review* 95: 393–434.

Easterling, Michelle W. 1996. "For Better or Worse: The Federalization of Domestic Violence." *West Virginia Law Review* 98: 933–53.

Edelman, Murray. 1974. 6th edn. *The Symbolic Uses of Politics*. Urbana: University of Illinois Press.

Edelman, Lauren B. 1992. "Legal Ambiguity and Symbolic Structures: Organizational Mediation of Civil Rights Law." *American Journal of Sociology* 97: 1531–76.

Edelman, Lauren B., Aaron C. Smyth, and Asad Rahim. 2016. "Legal Discrimination: Empirical Sociolegal and Critical Race Perspectives on Antidiscrimination Law." *Annual Review of Law and Social Science* 12: 395–15.

Epp, Charles R. 2009. *Making Rights REAL: Activists, Bureaucrats, and the Creation of the Legalistic State*. Chicago: University Chicago Press.

Farhang, Sean. 2012. "Legislative-Executive Conflict and Private Statutory Litigation in the United States: Evidence from Labor, Civil Rights, and Environmental Law." *Law & Social Inquiry* 37: 657–85.

Farhang, Sean. 2010. *The Litigation State: Public Regulation and Private Lawsuits in the U.S.* Princeton: Princeton University Press.

Feeley, Malcolm M. 1979. *The Process is the Punishment: Handling Cases in a Lower Court*. New York: Russell Sage.

Feeley, Malcolm M. and Edward L. Rubin. 1998. *Judicial Policy Making and the Modern State: How the Courts Reformed American's Prisons*. New York: Cambridge University Press.

Feeley, Malcolm M. and Edward Rubin. 1992. "Prison Litigation and Bureaucratic Development." *Law & Social Inquiry* 17: 125–45.

Feeley, Malcolm M. and Van Swearingen. 2004. "The Prison Conditions Cases and the Bureaucratization of American Corrections: Influences, Impacts and Implications." *Pace Law Review* 24: 433–75.

Federal Judicial Center. 1987. *Education and Research Agency US Courts*. Accessed January 16, 2018. www.fjc.gov/history/home.nsf/page/admin_01_01_02.html

Fine, David M. 1998. "The Note: Violence Against Women Act of 1994: The Proper Role in Policing Violence Against Women Act of 1994." *Cornell Law Review* 84: 252–303.

Fish, Peter G. 1973. *The Politics of Federal Judicial Administration*. Princeton: Princeton University Press.
Freedman, Estelle B. 2013. *Redefining RAPE: Sexual Violence in the Era of Suffrage and Segregation*. Cambridge: Harvard University Press.
Frymer, Paul. 2008. "Law and American Political Development." *Law & Social Inquiry* 33: 779–803.
Gash, Alison L. 2015. *Below the Radar: How Silence Can Save Civil Rights*. New York: Oxford University Press.
Gilbert, Jess. 2016. *Planning Democracy: Agrarian Intellectuals and the Intended New Deal*. New Haven: Yale University Press.
Goldfarb, Sally F. 2004. "Public Rights for 'Private' Wrongs: Sexual Harassment and the Violence Against Women Act." In *Directions in Sexual Harassment Law*, edited by Catherine A. MacKinnon and Reva B. Siegel, 516–34. New Haven: Yale University Press.
  2002. "The Supreme Court, the Violence Against Women Act, and the Use and Abuse of Federalism." *Fordham Law Review* 71: 57–146.
  2010. "Viewing the Violence Against Women Act Through the Lenses of Feminist Legal Theory." *Women's Rights Law Reporter* 31: 198–205.
  1996. "The Violence Against Women Act of 1994: A Promise Waiting to Be Fulfilled." *Journal of Law and Policy* 4: 391–97.
Goldscheid, Julie. 2005. "Civil Rights Remedy of the 1994 Violence Against Women Act: Struck Down but Not Ruled Out, The." *Family Law Quarterly* 39: 157–80.
  1999. "Gender-Motivated Violence: Developing a Meaningful Paradigm for Civil Rights Enforcement." *Harvard Women's Law Journal* 22: 123–58.
  2000. "The Second Circuit Addresses Gender-Based Violence: A Review of Violence Against Women Act Cases." *Brooklyn Law Review* 66: 457–71.
  2000. "*United States v. Morrison* and the Civil Rights Remedy of the Violence Against Women Act: A Civil Rights Law Struck Down in the Name of Federalism." *Cornell Law Review* 86: 109–39.
Greenhouse, Linda. 1992. "Ease Load on Courts, Rehnquist Urges." *New York Times*, January 1, 1992. ProQuest doc. ID: 428369420.
Grisinger, Joanna L. 2012. *The Unwieldy American State: Administrative Politics Since the New Deal*. New York: Cambridge University Press.
Grossmann, Matt. 2014. *Artists of the Possible: Governing Networks and American Policy Changes Since 1945*. New York: Oxford University Press.
Hallock, W.H. 1993. "The Violence Against Women Act: Civil Rights for Sexual Assault Victims." *Indiana Law Journal* 68: 577–617.
Harrington, Christine B. 1994. "Outlining a Theory of Legal Practice." In *Lawyers in a Postmodern World: Translation and Transgression*, edited by Maureen Cain and Christine B. Harrington: 49–69. New York: New York University Press.
Harrington, Christine B. and Barbara Yngvesson. 1990. "Interpretive Sociolegal Research." *Law & Social Inquiry* 15: 135–48.
Hollis-Brusky, Amanda. 2014. *Ideas with Consequences: The Federalist Society and the Conservative Counterrevolution*. New York: Oxford University Press.
  2013. "It's the Network: The Federalist Society as a Supplier of Intellectual Capital for the Supreme Court." *Studies in Law, Politics and Society* 61: 137–78.
  2011. "Support Structures and Constitutional Change: Teles, Southworth, and the Conservative Legal Movement." *Law & Social Inquiry* 36: 516–36.
Judicial Conference of the US Courts "Resolution on Violence Against Women" and Letter of Judge Stanley Marcus, Chairman, Ad-Hoc Committee on Gender-Based Violence.

March 16, 1993. H.R. Hearing, reprinted in "Crimes of Violence Motivated by Gender: Hearing Before the Subcommittee on Civil and Constitutional Rights of the Committee on the Judiciary." Committee on the Judiciary, House of Representatives, 103rd Cong., 1st Sess. 51, 70–73.

Judicial Conference of the US Courts. *Report of the Proceedings of the Judicial Conference*, September 21, 1987. Washington, DC: Administrative Office of the US Courts. www.uscourts.gov/about-federal-courts/reports-proceedings-1980s

Report of the Proceedings of the Judicial Conference, September 12, 1990. Washington, DC: Administrative Office of the US Courts.

Report of the Proceedings of the Judicial Conference, September 23–24, 1991. Washington, DC: Administrative Office of the US Courts.

Report of the Proceedings of the Judicial Conference, March 16, 1992. Washington, DC: Administrative Office of the US Courts.

Report of the Proceedings of the Judicial Conference, March 16, 1993. Washington, DC: Administrative Office of the US Courts.

Keck, Thomas. 2009. "Beyond Backlash: Assessing the Impact of Judicial Decisions on LGBT Rights." *Law & Society Review* 43: 151–86.

2004. *The Most Activist Supreme Court in History: The Road to Modern Judicial Conservatism*. Chicago: University of Chicago Press.

Kolko, Gabriel. 1976. "The Foundations of the Political Economy 1875–1920." In *Main Currents in Modern American History*. New York: Harper & Row.

Kotkin, Minna J. 1995–1996. "The Violence Against Women Act Project: Teaching a New Generation of Public Interest Lawyers." *Journal of Law and Policy* 4: 435–61.

MacKinnon, Catharine A. 2000. "Disputing Male Sovereignty: On *United States v. Morrison*". *Harvard Law Review* 114: 135–77.

1979. *Sexual Harassment of Working Women*. New Haven: Yale University Press.

Maloney, Kerrie E. 1996. "Gender-Motivated Violence and the Commerce Clause: The Civil Rights Provision of the Violence Against Women Act After *Lopez*." *Columbia Law Review* 96: 1876–939.

McTaggart, Kelli C. 1998. "The Violence Against Women Act: Recognizing a Federal Civil Right to Be Free from Violence." *Georgetown Law Journal* 86: 1123–51.

Minow, Martha, Michael Ryan, and Austin Sarat, eds. 1995. *Narrative, Violence and the Law: The Essays of Robert Cover*. Ann Arbor: University of Michigan Press.

Conference of Chief Justices. 2009. *The History of the Conference of Chief Justices: 60th Anniversary*. Williamsburg, VA: National Center for State Courts.

Nourse, Victoria F. 1996. "Where Violence, Relationship, and Equality Meet: The Violence Against Women Act's Civil Rights Remedy." *Wisconsin Women's Law Journal* 11: 1–36.

Olsen, F. E. 1983. "The Family and the Market: A Study of Ideology and Legal Reform." *Harvard Law Review* 96: 1497–578.

Orren, Karen and Stephen Skowronek. 2004. *The Search for American Political Development*. New York: Cambridge University Press.

Paris, Michael. 2010. *Framing Equal Opportunity: Law and the Politics of School Finance Reform*. Stanford: Stanford University Press.

Post, Robert C. 2003. "The Supreme Court 2002 Term Forward: Fashioning the Legal Constitution: Culture, Courts, and Law." *Harvard Law Review* 117: 4–112.

Post, Robert C. 2006. "Federalism, Positive Law, and the Emergence of the American Administrative State: Prohibition in the Taft Court Era." *William and Mary Law Review* 48: 1–183.

Provine, Doris Marie. 1988. "Judicial Government." *Law and Contemporary Problems* 51: 83–109.
Rehnquist, William. 1992. "Chief Justice's 1991 Year-End Report on the Federal Judiciary." *The Third Branch: Newsletter of the Federal Courts* 24: 1–12.
Resnik, Judith. 2010. "Drafting, Lobbying, and Litigating VAWA: National, Local, and Transnational Interventions on Behalf of Women's Equality." *Georgetown Journal of Gender and Law* 11: 557–69.
   2000. "The Programmatic Judiciary: Lobby, Judging, and Invalidating the Violence Against Women Act." *Southern California Law Review* 74: 269–93.
Rubin, Edward L. and Malcolm M. Feeley. 1993. "Federalism: Some Notes on a National Neurosis." *UCLA Law Review* 41: 903–52.
Scheingold, Stuart A. 2004. *The Politics of Rights: Lawyers, Public Policy, and Political Change*. Ann Arbor: University of Michigan Press.
Schmidt, Caroline S. 2015. "What Killed the Violence Against Women Act's Civil Rights Remedy Before the Supreme Court Did." *Virginia Law Review* 101: 501–57.
Schneider, Elizabeth M. 2000. *Battered Women & Feminist Lawmaking*. New Haven: Yale University Press.
   1996. "Introduction: The Promise of the Violence Against Women Act of 1994." *Journal of Law and Policy* 4: 371–76.
Schreiber, Ronnee. 2008. *Righting Feminism: Conservative Women & American Politics*. New York: Oxford University Press.
Schumer, Representative Charles. "Opening Statement of U.S. House of Representatives, Subcommittee on Crime and Criminal Justice, Committee on the Judiciary." 102nd Congress, Second Session, Serial No. 42, February 6, 1992: 1–6.
Scott, James C. 1998. *Seeing Like a State: How Certain Schemes to Improve the Human Condition Have Failed*. New Haven: Yale University Press.
Siegel, Reva B. 1996. "'The Rule of Law': Wife Beating as Prerogative and Privacy." *Yale Law Journal* 105: 2117–208.
Staszak, Sarah. 2010. "Institutions, Rulemaking, and the Politics of Judicial Retrenchment." *Studies in American Political Development* 24: 168–89.
   2015. *No Day in Court: Access to Justice and the Politics of Judicial Retrenchment*. New York: Oxford University Press.
Strebeigh, Fred. 2009. *EQUAL: Women Reshape American Law*. W.W. Norton & Company.
Teles, Steven M. 2008. *The Rise of the Conservative Legal Movement: The Battle for Control of the Law*. Princeton: Princeton University Press.
Thelen, Kathleen. 2000. "Timing and Temporality in the Analysis of Institutional Evolution and Change." *Studies in American Political Development* 14: 101–08.
Tomlins, Christopher. 2012. "What is Left of the Law and Society Paradigm after Critique? Revisiting Gordon's 'Critical Legal Histories.'" *Law & Social Inquiry* 37: 155–66.
Tushnet, Mark. 2008. "The Rights Revolution in the Twentieth Century." In *The Cambridge History of Law in America*, vol. 3, edited by Michael Grossberg and Christopher Tomlins: 377–402. New York: Cambridge University Press.
Twiss, Benjamin R. 1962. *Lawyers and the Constitution: How Laissez Faire Came to the Supreme Court*. New York: Russell & Russell Inc.
Washington Post. 1992. "Expanding Federal Court Role Opposed; Rehnquist Says Congress Is Endangering Quality and Credibility." January 1, 1992. ProQuest doc. ID: 307488732.
Williams, Patricia. 1987. "Spirit-Murdering the Messenger: The Discourse of Finger Pointing as the Law's Response to Racism." *University of Miami Law Review* 42: 127–57.

Weiss, Carolyn Peri. 1997. "Title III of the Violence Against Women Act: Constitutionally Safe and Sound." *Washington University Law Quarterly* 75: 723–49.

Wiebe, Robert H. 1967. *The Search for Order, 1877–1920.* New York: Hill and Wang.

CASES

Brzonkala *v.* Virginia Polytechnic Inst. & State University (1997) 132 F.3d 949, USCA 4th Circuit, vote 2–1.

Brzonkala *v.* Virginia Polytechnic Inst. & State University (1999) 169 F.3d 820, USCA 4th Circuit, en banc vote 7–4.

Civil Rights Cases (1883) 109 US 3; vote 8–1.

Griffin *v.* Breckenridge (1971) 403 US 88; vote 9–0.

U.S. *v.* Lopez (1995) 514 US 549; vote 5–4.

U.S. *v.* Morrison (2000) 529 US 598; vote 5–4.

Amici Curiae Brief of Law Professors in Support of Petitioners, U.S. *v.* Morrison, 120 S. Ct. 1740 (2000) (Nos. 99–5, 99–29).

U.S. Reply Brief, U.S. *v.* Morrison (1999).

LEGISLATION

Violence Against Women Act (VAWA), 135 42 U.S.C. § 13981 (1994); (P.L. 103–322)
Violent Crime Control and Law Enforcement Act of 1994, PuB. L. No. 103–322, 108 Stat. 1796. 42 U.S.C.A. § 13981(b)-(c) (1995).

13

Can Courts Abolish Mass Incarceration?

Jonathan Simon

INTRODUCTION: THE SLOW ROAD TO DECARCERATION

The extraordinary growth in American prison populations from the late 1970s through the first decade of the twenty-first century has largely ended, and calls for reversing mass incarceration, as it has come to be known, abound from all sides. Yet as of this writing progress toward "decarceration" remains unsteady, and the likelihood of a systematic national decarceration effort led by the federal government has declined in the transition from the Obama to the Trump administration (Gottschalk 2015). Can courts enforcing federal constitutional and statutory rights play a role in moving the endgame along through conventional political institutions that appear blocked? The leading study of court-based prison reform in the United States, Malcolm Feeley and Edward Rubin's *Judicial Policy Making and the Modern State* (1998), examined the last great and successful effort by the judiciary to dismantle a discredited penal system, the plantation model that continued to operate in most southern states on a largely black prisoner population despite the legal defeat of segregation and the beginnings of voting rights enforcement in the South.

It is tempting to draw a direct connection between the plantation prisons and mass incarceration (or to see them as a form of survival through transformation in the process highlighted by Michelle Alexander (2010)), and there are similarities. Yet at minimum mass incarceration is a much broader phenomenon, extending to more states than plantation prisons ever did. While the plantation prison was an anomaly against a national consensus (thin as it proved to be) that demanded prisons apply some form of rehabilitative penology, mass incarceration today is or at least until very recently has been a consensus (which we can hope proves as thin).

Feeley and Rubin themselves observed the reasons that judicial reform had largely fallen silent as of their writing. One of their signal insights was that court-based reform relied heavily on trends inside the administrative state itself, especially the then national consensus behind rehabilitative penology and professionalization of correctional bureaucracies, modeled in the influential practices of organizations like the Federal Bureau of Prisons. These features were important to judges not simply for their internal institutional implications, but because they could provide a framework at once both enabling and limiting to guide prison officials' potentially limitless discretion, offering ways for courts to limit their authority and positive norms to fill that part of limiting their discretion the courts undertook. Yet precisely these features of American penality have long since eroded or changed in the process of creating mass incarceration. Rehabilitation, while enjoying something of a comeback under the slogan of "evidence-based corrections" is far from penological common ground across the states. Bureaucracy, by now well established in every penal system in the United States partially as a result of judicial policy making, has become an engine of mass incarceration and inhumanity (Simon 2014; Reiter 2016); a result that after the Holocaust should have surprised no one (Baumann 1992).

This chapter reviews the present situation facing courts and prisoners with Feeley and Rubin's pathbreaking phenomenology of judicial policy making in mind. The present conjuncture, seen from this perspective, points to a number of reasons for optimism that court-based reform of mass incarceration could be poised for progress. Three developments in particular and together can offer the limits and norms that judicial reform requires. The first is an ironic one indeed. The Prison Litigation Reform Act of 1996 (PLRA) was meant to largely kill off prison litigation, and it largely did. However, with its landmark ruling upholding a massive prison population reduction order for California, the Supreme Court in *Brown* v. *Plata* (2011) signaled strongly that the PLRA, while "strict in theory," is perhaps not "fatal in fact," and that courts can act within it to remedy longstanding constitutional violations. The Act now appears to be a source of positive limits by which courts can limit and legitimate their authority while addressing constitutional violations. Indeed, with its sweeping moral language about "human dignity" and the nature of prisons in "civilized" societies, Justice Kennedy's *Plata* opinion could be read as providing today's federal judges a legal reason to intervene in prison conditions and a pathway through the PLRA.

The second factor is the arrival (long anticipated by some of us) of a "new penology" that can replace (and even to some extent revitalize) the rehabilitative penology that played such a productive role in guiding court reform in the previous period (Feeley and Simon 1992).[1] Data-based risk assessment has begun to emerge as a potential hegemonic penal rationality in the American carceral state after decades of discussion. This new penology comes encumbered with many potential flaws tied to our constructions of crime data, but from the perspective of judicial policy making it also provides a positive discourse for courts to internalize into the Eighth

---

[1] Malcolm Feeley and I claimed that signs were abundant of a turn toward a risk-based penology dominated by actuarial methods and a scientific ethos. As we later acknowledged (Simon and Feeley 1995; 2003), our prediction was premature as far more populist forms of risk thinking dominated penology in the last decade of the twentieth century and much of the first one of the next. Only today, under pressure from cases like *Plata*, does risk seem to be gaining rapid ascendance.

Amendment analysis of violations and remedies. Blanket prison claims of security needs will become subject to their own data systems.

Finally, the need that courts have to match their moral sense of outrage with law-like rules that apply to the prison context without creating chaos or dictatorial judicial rule finds new resources in the present moment that were undeveloped the last time judicial policy making over prisons was in full swing. One extremely relevant source is the very substantial development of domestic disability rights law in the prison field. Another source, which has always been in the background but could gain more traction for contemporary courts seeking to address the problems of mass incarceration, is the considerable growth in the field of transnational and international human rights law for prisons.. Both bodies of law offer plenty of authoritative norms to courts seeking to establish just what should be provided by prisons that respect human dignity.

None of this will matter if individual trial judges turn away from the evidence and refuse the still unpopular task of investigating correctional systems. As Feeley and Rubin showed, the moral sentiments of judges are a starting point. Growing evidence suggests such judges exist all over the country (perhaps thanks to two terms of Obama appointments). The most recent example, *Braggs v. Dunn* (2017), follows closely the model laid down recently by the Supreme Court in *Plata* (2011). It will take more than courts to abolish mass incarceration. But state-by-state legal condemnation of the worst mass incarceration practices, calling out the indiscriminate incarceration of people of all risk levels under conditions that threaten the health and safety of many, coupled with strong population caps, can provide the dynamic needed in the most intransigent states to move toward the abolition of mass incarceration. Abolishing mass incarceration is not the same as abolishing the prison altogether, but as a partial abolition it can frame the conditions under which prisons are acceptable in civilized societies, if they are.

After revisiting Feeley and Rubin's phenomenology of judicial policy making in the previous prison reform era, I turn to each of the three developments and their implications for courts and prisoners today.

13.1 THE FIRST PRISON ABOLITION: ENDING THE PLANTATION PRISON

Recent studies suggest that in at least some states, the prison reform litigation movement that Feeley and Rubin celebrated actually helped to accelerate the trend toward mass incarceration in the succeeding decades (Lynch 2009; Schoenfeld 2010; Guetzkow and Schoon 2015). We will return to this troubling analysis, which is a potent reminder that litigation, like everything else, can produce unintended consequences. Yet we should not lose sight of the goal of litigation in this period nor read our own goals into the past. Then the mission was not to end mass incarceration (which had yet to take shape), but within an already shrinking prison population in the 1960s and 1970s to force an end to what many imagined to be most brutal expressions of the nineteenth-century penal imagination, i.e., forced labor and especially the "plantation" type agricultural labor prisons common throughout the South and clearly modelled on slavery (Feeley and Rubin 1998, 151).

The first thing we can take from Feeley and Rubin's account is that the abolition of this distinct form of penality was the primary intention of the judges who ultimately were the prime actors in placing prison systems under court order. Between 1969, when *Holt* v. *Sarver* placed the Arkansas prison system under exacting decrees, and the 1980s, these judges largely drove this form of penality from the United States. Because it played such a central role in their account of twentieth-century prison reform and how legitimate judicial policy making in fact happened in the US constitutional system, it is worth quoting at length from their more precise definition of practices they had in mind with what they called the "plantation model" (Feeley and Rubin 1998, 157–58).

> All these efforts were focused on the distinctive aspects of the plantation model, the aspects that distinguished southern prisons from prisons in other sections of the nation. This was the problem that the judiciary had defined as its basis for action. Over time, the judges declared that "driving" the prisoners to perform agricultural labor was unconstitutional, that plantation-style barracks, subsistence diets, and minimal medical care were unconstitutional, and that relying on the whip as the major method of discipline was unconstitutional. Less explicitly, but just as definitively, the entire concept of prisoners as a pool of labor, sentenced to sustain the institution that held them in bondage, was declared to be a violation of the Eighth Amendment.

It is this constellation of practices, rooted in slavery and making up a viable form of penality at work in many southern states in the last third of the twentieth century, which formed the definition of the "problem" to which a constitutional solution was needed and was fashioned. It is this "body of forbidden practices" according to Feeley and Rubin (1998, 157) "that created the Eighth Amendment." While the prison reform wave ultimately swept the nation, it was only these plantation-model systems where the institutions were put under systemic and radical transformational orders. In other states, it was by analogy to those "divergent and reprehensible" practices (Feeley and Rubin 1998, 157) that courts found Eighth Amendment violations, and then typically only particular practices, not whole systems (158).

Yet defining a moral problem with a possible legal solution was only the starting precondition for the judicial policy making involved in abolishing the plantation model. According to Feeley and Rubin's "phenomenological" account of judicial activism, courts in policy-making mode seek legitimacy in the constraining and enabling frameworks provided by law, or more precisely legal doctrine like structures of rules (Feeley and Rubin 1998, 210). Law in this sense is both an enabler and a constraint on judicial behavior (as it is perhaps for us all) (Feeley and Rubin 1998: 204–05).

In the case of some of the early prison cases around religious liberty or access to books, specific constitutional provisions, like the First Amendment, or the Due Process clause of the Fourteenth Amendment, provided direct access to well-established bodies of doctrine with relatively straightforward application to correctional settings. Not so those broader prison conditions challenges that relied on the sparse terminology of the Eighth Amendment with little historical and no direct textual application to correctional settings. "The broad language of the cruel and unusual punishment clause must be seen as a grant of jurisdiction" (Feeley and Rubin 1998, 210). In order to manage the anxiety of operating in this limitless grant, the courts needed what Feeley and Rubin call "coordinating ideas" (Feeley and Rubin 1998, 234) to form the primary material of doctrine-like rules. Seeking coordinating ideas to operationalize their moral intuition that the southern plantation prison was a moral outrage, federal courts found these ideas in the broad national consensus which they shared along with other members of their class in both major political tendencies "that prisons are supposed to be designed to rehabilitate the prisoner, and that prisons are supposed to be bureaucratically organized" (Feeley and Rubin 1998, 211).

As Feeley and Rubin further specify, successful "coordinating ideas" have to have a number of features to do the work of both enabling and constraining, including: being "fully realized," i.e., not awaiting specification or development; being "delimited," i.e., providing internal constraints on overreach; and "directional," i.e., providing an objective basis for how to replace discredited penal practices with viable alternatives. Rehabilitative penology, and independently the bureaucratization of prison management, fulfilled these functions perfectly when it came to abolishing the plantation prison. For rehabilitation, it was not the depth of its ideological support (which turned out to be thin and was already under attack), but because these institutionalizations provided a ready-to-hand system of operations that had proven to "work" in the sense of maintaining a morally acceptable order within prisons. In the terms of the rehabilitative model, the plantation prison and its close cousin, the forced industrial labor prison, were an anathema that degraded and made social integration more difficult (which of course was exactly its purpose). Moreover, rehabilitation was not a utopian idea, but existed as a set of accreditation standards of the American Correctional Association, and in the operational manuals of the Federal Bureau of Prisons, which was easily translated into a legal doctrine capable of enabling change without destabilizing prison authority. While critics were already claiming that "nothing works" because scientific evidence of lower recidivism tied to specific rehabilitative techniques was not available, courts were confident that rehabilitation worked in a different sense, "not rehabilitation at all but the creation of a prison that judges regarded as morally acceptable" (Feeley and Rubin 1998, 265). Bureaucracy was equally compelling as a coordinating idea.

By the last third of the twentieth century most of the large industrial states had already transformed their prison systems from individual warden-run prisons to correctional systems coordinated by a centralized bureaucracy subject to the administrative rules governing state action. This was true both internally, where prison workers were being upgraded to "correctional officers" expected to follow administrative procedures, and externally, where central administrators held wardens accountable. As with rehabilitation, the plantation prison was not only underdeveloped bureaucratically, it was organized around a whole different principle, that of charismatic authority reinforced with violence at the discretion of every power holder in the chain of authority and unbound by anything like rules (Feeley and Rubin 1998, 272). Against such an evil, demanding bureaucracy was a readily implementable strategy that seemed workable from a control perspective and which fit to a tee the formal model of doctrine-like rules.

Through demanding prisons that were rehabilitative in orientation and bureaucratic in organization, courts cut scissor-like through the heart of the plantation model, forcing southern states to adopt at least the rhetoric of "corrections" and more deeply embrace the mechanisms of bureaucracy. The plantation prison was dead by the 1990s, but in its place was growing an even larger prison system, although indeed one less reliant on violence and more bureaucratic in organization.

13.2 COURTS AND THE ABOLITION OF MASS INCARCERATION

Can we think about mass incarceration as a penal practice capable of being sufficiently discredited in the eyes of a new generation of federal judges to be seen by them as a moral problem? Even if so, what resources will allow the remarkable lawmaking role that rehabilitation and bureaucracy played in the past? In this section I argue that the *Brown v. Plata* decision in 2011 and similar recent decisions of a district court in Alabama point to reasons for optimism on both fronts.

At first blush it seems that mass incarceration is too big a phenomenon and too generalized to be characterized as "divergent and reprehensible" in the way southern plantation prisons came to be seen (Feeley and Rubin 1998, 157). It all depends, of course, on how we define mass incarceration. If we focus simply on the shift in the scale of imprisonment, as many now-classical accounts do (Zimring and Hawkins 1993; Garland 2001), or even the related phenomenon of racial hyper-concentration (Western 2006; Alexander 2010), mass incarceration is of course very general, crossing all regional lines and penological variations. But if we focus more on its qualitative dimensions, especially the toxic combination of chronic overcrowding, neglect of medical and mental health infrastructures, and the reliance on extreme forms of segregation to maintain discipline (Haney 2006; Fleury-Steiner and Longazel 2013; Simon 2014), we have a picture of mass incarceration penality that is at once fewer in the number of states included (at least in comparison to the all-states picture we get if we look only at the quantitative dimension of prison population growth), more compact in its distribution across the country, and more extreme and repellant in its manifestations; in short, to quote Feeley and Rubin, "divergent and reprehensible."

While states whose correctional systems meet these criteria are not few, neither are they the majority of states. Only five states in 2015 had overcrowding that crossed the *Plata* threshold line of 137 percent of design capacity (Alabama, Delaware, Hawaii, Illinois, and Nebraska; California, which had just dipped below that figure, was nearly 200 percent at the time the population cap was sought). One of these, Alabama, has just been found in violation of the Eighth Amendment in *Braggs* v. *Dunn* (2017) and seems likely to end up under a population cap in the remedy phase. As of 2015, another six states had prison overcrowding at over 120 percent of design, and thus stood in danger of tipping past the point where population cap litigation would be successful.

In *Brown* v. *Plata*, and more recently in *Braggs* v. *Dunn*, courts have used strong language to communicate outrage about the risk of untreated medical and mental health problems leading to suffering and premature death among prisoners:

> A prison that deprives prisoners of basic sustenance, including adequate medical care, is incompatible with the concept of human dignity and has no place in civilized society. (*Brown* v. *Plata* 2011, 1928)

This language suggests that courts are beginning to coalesce around a picture of a certain kind of mass incarceration as being morally unacceptable and illegitimate notwithstanding the strong appeals of federalism in this field (Simon 2014b), the kind of mass incarceration that puts a whole prisoner population at risk of degrading and even tortuous conditions if they have a health crisis. While this does not cover the broader phenomenon of mass incarceration, it does, I would argue, target the extreme policies that have driven the larger practice but are more constrained in some states than others. While there is no obvious cultural logic to the states that have embraced extreme mass incarceration in the way slavery formed the mold for plantation prisons, there is now a moral standard for action, one based on respect for human dignity. California's experience suggests that quite unlike the last period of judicial activism, intervention today based on conditions of extreme overcrowding may lead to a broader process of decarceration (Verma 2017).

The second question is what coordinating ideas replace rehabilitation and bureaucracy in providing a realized program for reform, implementable by courts in the language and style of legal doctrine. Recent overcrowding cases point in three directions that individually and in combination can enable more such interventions, and possibly can set in motion the wave of actions across the dozen or so states with hyper-overcrowding that would fulfill the promise of a judicial abolition of mass incarceration in its worst form.

13.2.1 The Prison Litigation Reform Act

The Prison Litigation Reform Act of 1996 was one of several federal laws in the mid-1990s designed to make court intervention in state prison systems more difficult and broad remedies less common. The Act contained measures aimed at curbing federal court filings by prisoners (usually through petitions mailed directly to courts with no lawyer involved) and measures aimed at limiting remedies. The most important limitation on filing was the requirement of administrative exhaustion, which forces prisoners to follow almost invariably futile administrative appeals to internal prison authorities, while the most trivial procedural failure in such appeals can result in a complete ban on federal courts hearing those cases. Other measures barred prisoners whose past filings have been deemed frivolous, and increased filing fees and decreased damages and potential attorneys' fees for civil rights lawyers taking on these cases. On the remedy side the PLRA set new limits on injunctive settlements previously limited to those established in litigation, subjected all remedies to a narrow relationship to the constitutional violation established, and imposed "least intrusive" intervention standards on all injunctive relief cases and a requirement that significant weight be given to potential impacts on public safety. Population caps and other orders resulting in compelling states to release prisoners were further restricted by a requirement that overcrowding be shown by the petitioners to be directly related to the constitutional violation, and that such orders are both necessary to its remedy and not too much of a risk to public safety.

Early observers, including Feeley and Rubin (1998, 382–84), wondered if the law might turn out to be symbolic. It turned out not to be, as Margo Schlanger's analysis shows (Schlanger 2006, 2015): the law brought about a major drop of sixty percent in the number of prisoner cases filed in the decade following the PLRA, a decline which has plateaued but not reversed according to 2012 data. Yet Feeley and Rubin (1998, 383) may have been more prescient in observing that the PLRA and other contemporaneous legislation might in fact provide congressional validation for the extraordinary body of judicial policy making that had already been accomplished by the time of the Act. "The statutes can be regarded as a validation of judicial policy making... Congress' ability to take action of this sort demonstrates that courts are not so imperial, or unstoppable, as their critics have claimed even when grounding their authority in the Constitution."

Indeed, in the aftermath of the Supreme Court's upholding of a massive and sweeping population reduction order in *Brown v. Plata*, we now see how the PLRA can provide legitimacy to judicial policy making that follows its dictates. Judicial fears that Eighth Amendment authority to order reforms might be boundless is directly addressed by the PLRA, such that courts now have a direct path to address morally outrageous prison practices so long as they can meet the PLRA requirements (Sullivan 2013). Administrative exhaustion and other limits on filings clearly have done huge harm to the ability of federal courts to monitor and enforce rights against unconstitutional prison conditions at a time when mass incarceration remains entrenched. Although a cooperative Congress is not likely in the near term, it should be a major priority of criminal justice reformers to see the PLRA repealed, or better yet, to retain its validation of previous court interventions, substantially amended. Yet it may be crucial that a revised PLRA or its successor creates a framework that both enables and restrains courts. Once a court becomes convinced a constitutional violation exists, they have Congress to thank for a safety zone around going too far in interfering with state penal autonomy. If remedies are narrowly shaped to address constitutional violations, if they take public safety into account, courts have a congressional template for finding their orders legitimate, limited, and law-like.

Perhaps most significantly, after *Brown* v. *Plata* overcrowding cases based on failure to remedy underlying constitutional violations seem to have a secure path through the PLRA, and it is not likely to be the only one (Johal 2014). Thus the Act validated not only past judicial activism but also future acts of judicial policy making.

13.2.2 The New Penology

Part of the drama in the story that Feeley and Rubin told in *Judicial Policy Making and the Modern State* (1998) was the quickly fading power of rehabilitative penology to provide consensus discourse about morally acceptable prisons and a ready-to-hand set of law-like standards for courts to use in implementing reform. Judges, like most other legal elites in that generation, had long come to accept rehabilitation not so much on empirical as normative grounds that it suited a civilized and democratic society (Rubin 2001). In terms of state policies, it was only in the most advanced industrial states of the North, Midwest, and far West that rehabilitative penology (along with other "progressive" ideas) took hold strongly. In other states, like Florida and Arizona, it was only under the pressure of the federal courts that rehabilitation replaced (briefly) an earlier history of punitive but cheap confinement (Lynch 2009; Schoenfeld 2010). Even as the reforms continued through the 1980s and 1990s, rehabilitation was being replaced in many states by an emphasis on deterrence and later incapacitation (Zimring and Hawkins 1995). The American Correctional Association and the Federal Bureau of Prisons, both sources for support for rehabilitation and resources for rising standards, have become more managerialist in their penal ideology.

These developments, more or less exogenous to the courts' own actions in the penal field, would likely have reduced court-based prison intervention to the enforcement of existing legal rules rather than more expansive policy making even if the PLRA had not choked off many cases (leading to underenforcement as well as lack of expansion).

There are signs today of a revival of rehabilitation across the United States. California, once a leader in abandoning rehabilitation, is now re-embracing the notion. It has done so most recently through Proposition 57, passed in California by voter initiative in November 2016; the law authorizes early prison release for prisoners convicted of nonviolent crimes for achieving key milestones in programs shown to be effective in reducing recidivism. Yet even if this cautious trend toward rehabilitation gains momentum, it is unlikely to regain its hegemonic role as a penal rationale. Even if it did, in its current neoliberal form, in which the responsibility is on prisoners to achieve their own success, rehabilitation is unlikely to be the productive source of rights it was in the 1960s and 1970s.

Yet if rehabilitation is unlikely to drive new policy formation by courts in the penal field, another development, the rise of data-based risk assessment tools, may (Feeley and Simon 1992). Risk tools based on statistical models of aggregate data have been growing in significance since the 1920s, when they were introduced into parole decision making in Illinois and other states. It was in the 1970s and 1980s, when more clinical forms of risk assessment came under sustained attack and cultural discrediting, that data-based risk assessment began to gain status as a method for rationalizing flawed individual decision making in parole and other correctional processes. During the rise of mass incarceration, the extreme commitment to incapacitation overrode considerations of individual risk or attempted to address it only crudely through criminal record-based scores (as in the Federal Sentencing Guidelines). It is only in the last decade, as mass incarceration has come under increasing strain, and the legitimacy of undifferentiated confinement has been called into question, have we seen data-based individual risk assessment coming to the fore as a solution to problems from the front end of the system (bail) to the back end (parole and diversion).

Risk assessment is not so much an alternative to rehabilitation as a goal for imprisonment or correctional supervision, as it is a new credible framework for operating prisons that are secure and moral. Moreover, prison systems, facing endless pressures to address overcrowding, have widely taken to risk assessment of their prisoners with improved and updated data-based models. Importantly, many of the recent court interventions around overcrowding have explicitly questioned the need for incarceration given the wide availability of low-risk prisoners who could be released (or not sent to prison in the first place). Indeed, with its command that federal courts give heavy weight to public safety, the Prison Litigation Reform Act puts risk front and center. It is here, of course, that courts until recently have felt a need to defer to prison managerial expertise. But if courts know that prisons have their own data-based and credible risk assessments available, and that these would identify individuals unlikely to pose a risk to the community if released, the road to population cap is greatly aided. Risk assessment also gives courts something they can use to produce limitations on their own discretion, such as exempting sentenced prisoners with high risk assessments from a cap.

13.2.3 Disability Rights and Human Rights

As they search for additional sources of rules and standards that can take on the shape of legal doctrine, courts will also be aided by two bodies of law that have largely come into existence after the end of the last great wave of judicial policy making: disability rights and human rights. The Americans with Disabilities Act of 1991 (ADA) was the most significant addition to US civil and employment rights in a generation, requiring that employers, landlords, and other commercial and educational establishments provide "reasonable accommodation" to people whose qualifications or suitability for the position, place, or opportunity could thereby be achieved. Only recently has this statute been brought into prison litigation, but it is now commonly used alongside the Eighth Amendment (as it is in *Braggs* v. *Dunn*). The aging of the prison population, a key feature of late mass incarceration, is likely to drive its use even higher. Importantly, the ADA can not only supplement the Eighth Amendment but it can also inform the substance of that Amendment. Respect for human dignity, which, according to the Supreme Court in *Plata* "animates the Eighth Amendment," requires more than just an end to torture, but under the "evolving standards of decency" seeks to protect access to a recognizably human form of life whose parameters expand with the insights of a "maturing society" (*Trop* v. *Dulles*, 101). The case law of the ADA in many fields can now enter the penal field as informing what dignity requires prisons to respect in order to comply with the Eighth Amendment.

Another highly productive field creating law-like rules and norms for the penal field is human rights law. The European Community adopted a comprehensive code of norms in 2006 specifically addressed at imprisonment. Enforcement of these norms is not a right, but they have influenced the European Court of Human Rights in interpreting Article III of the European Convention of Human Rights, which prohibits "torture" as well as "inhuman or degrading treatment or punishment" and which, like the Eighth Amendment, suffers from extreme vagueness (van Zyl Smit and Snacken 2009).

In 2015, the United Nations, in a unanimous vote of the General Assembly, updated the UN Standard Minimum Rules for the Treatment of Prisoners (SMRs) first adopted in 1955, before the initial wave of judicial policy making in the penal field. Then there was perceived to be little interest in such international standards given the leadership of the United States in the international penological ideals of rehabilitation. Today these much-enhanced standards, developed by international experts in an extraordinary process fostered by South Africa (a country ruled by former prisoners) and called the Nelson Mandela Rules, may indeed be a useful tool for reforming US prisons by creating targets for correctional standards independent of litigation. The norms the Rules express would eliminate mass incarceration as we have known it in the United States, including such standards as a requirement for single celling (Rule 12.1), nondegrading climate appropriate clothing (Rule 19.1), community standard of health care (Rule 32.1) and a prohibition on "prolonged" solitary confinement defined as more than fifteen days of continuous solitary (Rules 43, 44).

13.3 CONCLUSION

The voices of judges in the California and Alabama cases are indicative that a new wave of outrage is spreading within the federal judiciary around the toxic combination of overcrowding and poor mental and medical health care in prisons. After *Brown v. Plata* (2011) the PLRA is not a fundamental obstacle to judicial policy making in this space, and indeed seems to legitimize just that when necessary to protect constitutional rights. Risk assessment, while not a panacea, can provide courts with a defensible way to address public safety and limit their own discretion while at the same time opening up areas for potential challenges by those denied liberty. Disability rights under national law and international treaties offer standards and monitoring protocols along with growing bodies of positive law with ready application to the US if courts are willing to adopt them.

Of course, the key question begged by the title is of abolition. One of the most original and eye-opening aspects of Feeley and Rubin's *Judicial Policy Making and the Modern State* is their emphasis on the abolition of plantation-style prisons. Some may have hoped that large-scale prison conditions cases would force states to reduce prison populations further (they were still dropping in the 1960s and 1970s); this was a hope that did not endure, but for the judges who took up this task of judicial policy making it was not the prison in general (which they believed could be redeemed by rehabilitative penology) but this specific, discredited cluster of practices, including the whip, forced agricultural labor, inmate trustees, etc. at which they took aim. And they did abolish it. Their use of rehabilitation in the end could not deliver on sustained protection of human dignity in the age of mass incarceration, but it did abolish this one set of practices that had come to be seen consensually as "divergent and reprehensible" (Feeley and Rubin 1998, 157).

Today I believe there is a growing consensus that the combination of sustained overcrowding and poor mental and medical health care in prisons is morally obnoxious and cannot be justified penologically. States whose systems approximate or approach the conditions condemned in California and Alabama have every reason to expect that if they do not take the policy steps necessary to dismantle these conditions themselves, sooner or later a federal court will order them to do so.

Is this the end of mass incarceration? Not in the broader sense that includes historically high rates of incarceration, nor sadly in the concentration of incarceration on Latinx and Black people. Those can only be changed by policy making that no courts are likely to attempt, changes in sentencing laws and policing and prosecution practices. Yet there is reason to be optimistic that once a number of states have undergone substantial prisoner reductions without unacceptable rises in crime (the experience thus far in California and a number of other states; see Pew 2017), the logic of decarceration will have political momentum of its own. After all, the deeper changes necessary to reduce the scale of imprisonment and its racial concentration, a different approach to serious and violent crime (Urban Institute 2017), changes that courts are never likely to order, are ones that will be necessary if states are to avoid the heavy prison health care delivery investments necessary to stay out of trouble with the courts.

REFERENCES

Alexander, Michelle. 2010. *The New Jim Crow: Mass Incarceration in the Age of Colorblindness*. New York: New Press.
Bauman, Zygmunt. 1989. *Modernity and the Holocaust*. Cambridge, MA: Polity Press.
Feeley, Malcolm M. and Edward L. Rubin. 1998. *Judicial Policy Making and the Modern State: How the Courts Reformed America's Prisons*. Cambridge: Cambridge University Press.
Feeley, Malcolm M. and Jonathan Simon. 1992. "The New Penology: Notes on the Emerging Strategy of Corrections and Its Implications." *Criminology* 30 (4): 449–74.
Fleury-Steiner, Benjamin and Jamie G. Longazel. 2013. *The Pains of Mass Imprisonment*. London: Routledge.
Gottschalk, Marie. 2015. *Caught: The Prison State and the Lockdown of American Politics*. Princeton: Princeton University Press.
Guetzkow, Joshua and Eric Schoon. 2015. "If You Build It, They Will Fill It: The Consequences of Prison Overcrowding Litigation." *Law & Society Review* 49 (2): 401–32.
Haney, Craig. 2006. *Reforming Punishment: Psychological Limits to the Pains of Imprisonment*. Washington, DC: American Psychological Association.
Johal, Kiira J. 2014. "Note: Judges Behind Bars, the Intrusiveness Requirement's Restrictions on the Implementation of Relief under the Prison Litigation Reform Act." *Columbia Law Review* 114: 715–44.
Lynch, Mona. 2009. *Sunbelt Justice: Arizona and the Transformation of American Punishment*. Stanford: Stanford University Press.
Reiter, Keramet. 2016. *23/7: Pelican Bay and the Rise of Longterm Solitary Confinement*. New Haven: Yale University Press.
Rubin, Edward L. 2001. "The Inevitability of Rehabilitation." *Law & Inequality* 19: 343–77.
Schlanger, Margo. 2006. "Civil Rights Injunctions over Time: A Case Study of Jail and Prison Court Orders." *New York University Law Review* 81: 550–630.
Schlanger, Margo. 2015. "Trends in Prisoner Litigation as the PLRA Enters Adulthood." *University of California Irvine Law Review* 5: 154–78.
Schoenfeld, Heather. 2010. "Mass Incarceration and the Paradox of Prison Conditions Litigation." *Law & Society Review* 44 (3–4): 731–68.
Simon, Jonathan. 2014. *Mass Incarceration on Trial: A Remarkable Court Decision and the Future of American Prisons*. New York: New Press.
Simon, Jonathan. 2014b. "An Unenviable Task: How Federal Courts Legitimized Mass Incarceration," in *Legitimacy and Criminal Justice: An International Exploration*, edited by Justice Tankebe and Alison Liebling. Cambridge: Cambridge University Press. 227–46.
Sullivan, Kyle T. 2013. "To Free or Not to Free: Rethinking Release Orders under the Prison Litigation Reform Act after *Brown v. Plata*." *Boston College Journal of Law & Social Justice* 33 (2): 419–51.

van Zyl Smit, Dirk and Sonja Snacken. 2009. *Principles of European Prison Law and Policy: Penology and Human Rights*. Oxford: Oxford University Press.
Western, Bruce. 2006. *Punishment and Inequality in America*. New York: Russell Sage Foundation.
Zimring, Franklin E. and Gordon J. Hawkins. 1993. *The Scale of Imprisonment*. Chicago: University of Chicago Press.
Zimring, Franklin and Gordon Hawkins. 1995. *Incapacitation: Penal Confinement and the Restraint of Crime*. Oxford: Oxford University Press.

CASES

Braggs v. Dunn, United States District Court for the Middle District of Alabama, Civil Action No. 2:14cv601-MHT (WO), June 17, 2017

Brown v. Plata (2011) 563 U.S. 493, 131 S.Ct. 1910

Holt v. Sarver (1969) 300 F.Supp. 825 District Court for the District of Arkansas

Trop v. Dulles (1958) 356 U.S. 86

14

Policy-Making by Out-of-Court Settlements: Palestinian Informers at the Israeli High Court of Justice

Menachem Hofnung[1]

INTRODUCTION

In their seminal work on *Judicial Policy Making and the Modern State*, Feeley and Rubin (1998) demonstrate how trial courts have been very successful as policy-makers in reforming prison conditions. As a result, court rulings and their implementation have become instrumental in introducing significant changes into US correctional institutions.

Using Feeley and Rubin's theoretical framework as a starting point, I will try to go one step further and ask whether courts serve as effective policy-makers not only by writing authoritative binding decisions, but rather by avoiding detailed rulings. In such cases the court may install legal standards through negotiations with the litigating parties and pushing state agencies to accept either one of two outcomes: a) out-of-court settlement of the case; b) an agreement to make undesirable concessions in return for which the court will formally reject the petition, concluding that there is no point in further litigation as a valid legal claim of the petitioner was already met by the respondent.

The database for this research is comprised of more than 700 petitions by thousands of Arabs (mostly Palestinians) who are turning to the Israeli High Court of Justice (HCJ) and asking to be formally recognized as "informers" (a term commonly used in Israel to denote Palestinian collaborators with the Israeli secret services). In the absence of direct legislation, the court handles dozens of such petitions every year, and the numbers are steadily rising.

Since the Six Day War (1967), in which Israel seized control of the Gaza Strip and the Sinai Peninsula from Egypt, the West Bank from Jordan and the Golan Heights from Syria, thousands of Palestinians (along with their family members) have come to Israel from the West Bank and Gaza, many of them trying to gain recognition as "informers" or alternatively "threatened persons." The latter is a less desirable status

---

[1] I am grateful for suggestions and comments by Nir Barak, Alon Burstein, Ofir Hadad, Tamar Hofnung Yaniv Levy, Liora Norwich and the editors of this book.

that grants temporary asylum in Israel without the full range of benefits accorded to informers.

The largest group of people seeking asylum in Israel by claiming that they are entitled to the benefits accorded to informers are those defined in court files as "threatened." The term "threatened" denotes that even if there was some cooperation with Israeli authorities, it did not develop into full working relations, and therefore the person seeking refuge is not entitled to the benefits granted to informers who are formally relocated in Israel. Informers receive housing, work training, state assistance in schooling their children, health care, national insurance and more. Threatened persons may get only a temporary permit to reside in Israel on account of a threat to their life when accused by their fellow countrymen of collaboration with the Israeli security authorities (Hofnung 2017).

The dilemma the court faces is what to do with dozens of petitions by persons asking for rights based on claims that they are threatened by their own people due to suspicion of collaborating with Israel, when these claims are routinely challenged by the state? To make matters even more complicated, even if the petitioners' claims were fabricated from start to end, by the mere filing of a petition claiming that they are Israeli informers, those persons placed themselves in grave danger to their life unless asylum in Israel is granted. In other words, even if the case had no merit whatsoever at the outset, by the mere submission of a petition to the HCJ, the petitioner's life is placed under serious threat.

What should the court's policy in such a case be? How should it handle cases in which, regardless of the facts, by filling a petition, petitioners put their life in danger and a court order to deport such persons can result in their death? What are the political implications if the HCJ accepts the claim that scores of Palestinians and their family members have the right to settle in Israel on account of their prior recruitment and subsequent deception by Israeli officials?

14.1 STATUS OF INFORMERS AND THREATENED INDIVIDUALS

The entire process of recruiting, training, deploying and rescuing exposed informers is regarded as a state secret. Therefore, there is hardly any scholarly research on collaborators and informers. There have been several articles looking at infringements of human rights (Cohen and Dudai 2005; Cohen and Dudai 2007; Teplow 2010; Levenkorn 2012). In addition, one can find memoirs of intelligence operators describing their connections with agents. There are some reports in the media, but these focus on specific incidents and not on the entire phenomenon. In order to cope with the challenges imposed by lack of nonconfidential and reliable resources, the data for this study was mainly gathered from unrestricted open court files, since court files, and especially the final decisions in court rulings, are accessible in large unrestricted databases (some of which are commercial, though accessible after payment) with no limits in terms of censorship.

Recruitment of informers dates back to the early days of Zionist settlement in the land of Israel as part of the struggle against the British Mandate and the Palestinian National Movement (Gelber 1992; Lefen 1997; Cohen 2004; Nimrodi 2003). However, the scope and intensity of information gathering, and specifically the use of informers, grew dramatically after 1967 (Maimon 1993, 160–64; Ronen 1990; Peri 1999, 48–53). Relocation and integration of informers in Israel in large numbers took a sharp upward turn beginning in the 1980s, correlated with Israel's recognition that it cannot permanently stabilize its borders in the territories seized in the 1967 Six Day War.

The relocation and incorporation of large numbers of collaborators within Israeli society is highly associated with state contraction from 1982 onwards. Initially, following the takeover of Arab lands in 1967, recruitment of collaborators was deemed a necessary method in order to hold on to the conquered territories and to stabilize the borders around them. Withdrawing from these territories and contracting into more internationally accepted borders led to the process of relocation and rehabilitation of these collaborators. The relocation waves were largely a result of political decisions to withdraw from occupied territory (the Sinai Peninsula in 1982, consecutive withdrawals from parts of Lebanon's territory in 1983 and 1985, the Oslo Accords of 1993 that led to the withdrawal from areas of the West Bank, a second withdrawal from Lebanon in 2000 and the disengagement from Gaza in 2005). In between, the existence of the Palestinian Authority had been perpetuated as a semiautonomous institution in the West Bank along with the continuation of a massive Israeli presence in most of the territory. Given the ongoing tense relations between the Palestinian Authority and Israel, and the Palestinian security forces' use of counterintelligence and measures taken against collaborators, Israel recruited a large array of informers in order to secure a constant large flow of information.[2]

People in the occupied territories were recruited as informers and agents through a variety of temptations and pressures including financial payments, work permits, approval or denial of exit permits from the territories into Israel or abroad, authorization or prevention of medical treatment in Israel for family members, suspension of legal proceedings, release from detention or imprisonment, extortion and the like (Peri 1999, 49; Gillon 2000, 206; Hassan 2010). Controlling the territory from which

---

[2] In PH (Serious Crimes) District Court, Tel Aviv 1/98 *State of Israel* v. *Anonymous* (Ploni in Hebrew), two Palestinian informers who had been resettled in Israel were convicted on charges of providing the Palestinian Intelligence Service with secret information of their activities on behalf of the Israeli Shin Bet. In Criminal Case (District Court Haifa) 221/02, a former informer was convicted on charges of placing a bomb on a railway line and expressing readiness to help in smuggling a car full of explosives and a suicide bomber into Israel. In HCJ (High Court of Justice) 3372/05, the court rejected a petition by a former informer to regain his entitlement to benefits after his accorded rights were rescinded following a conviction on charges of spying against Israel. Several other court cases detail the activity of the Palestinian Security Services in executing or torturing people accused of being Israel collaborators: TA (Family Court, Haifa) 8898-05-11; Appeal 3555/05 (Military Court of Appeals, Judea and Samaria); Appeal 2176/07 (Military Court of Appeals, Judea and Samaria); BS 9107/09 (District Court Jerusalem).

informers are recruited enables the deployment of a wide variety of means, but also encourages wasteful and inattentive use of informers. The gap between the expectations of informers and the intentions of their operators gave way to situations in which people who may have brought some minor or insignificant information mistakenly assumed that Israel would protect them in troublesome times. When they were labelled or exposed as informers, they fled into Israel, only to discover to their dismay that the information that they had given and their exposal as informers did not grant them the type of protection they thought they deserved in return for risking their lives.[3] In cases like this, these people may have been denied the status of an informer, though they might have gained a less-desired status of a "threatened" person: a status that granted them temporary residency permits but no financial aid for the purposes of resettlement.

After the signing of the Oslo Accords in 1993, the fate of informers became a pressing policy problem. During the negotiations that led to the establishment of the Palestinian Authority, the fate of existing informers was assessed and it was concluded that the informers would be in mortal peril if they remained in their previous place of residence. Upon this assessment it was decided that the informers would be relocated in Israel, and in January 1994 the Israeli government adopted resolution b/118, which led to the establishment of the Security Aid Administration (hereafter SAA). The decision states:

> Towards the new deployment in the West Bank and the Gaza Strip, the Israeli government believes it is necessary to allow assist the agents and informers (hereafter informers), that worked with Israel's security forces to relocate along with their family members and to restart their lives within Israel.

The SAA was instantly assigned to prepare an immediate solution for hundreds of informers and their family members. In addition, the SAA assigned personnel to work directly with the state's welfare and education authorities in order to secure a prompt and efficient relocation process. To protect its informers, Israel encouraged the heads of about 1,400 households to relocate with their families into Israel (Peri 1999, 260).[4] Since 1994, the SAA has been the body entrusted with the relocation and integration of informers; it guides the process of resettlement and rehabilitation to its completion, a trajectory that takes between five and ten years.

A few years after the implementation of the Oslo Accords, the relations between Israel and the Palestinian Authority soured, especially following the election of Benjamin Netanyahu as Prime Minister in 1996. A crackdown on suspected collaborators caused many of them to flee to Israel and claim that they should be given all the benefits accorded to informers. When their claims were denied, they petitioned the HCJ. To cope with the stream of people coming to Israel and seeking the status of "informer," an administrative advisory tribunal called "the Threatened

---

[3] See for example HCJ 3295/02; HCJ 3283/03; HCJ 6939/11; HCJ 3729/13.
[4] Knesset 13th, meeting no. 279 (November 30, 1994).

Committee" was set up by Israel's Attorney General, without legislation or even applicable administrative regulations.[5] Soon enough, more petitions piled up at the HCJ and the Court was asked to solve individual cases without clear guidance (or a formal mandate) from the legislature.

The working guidelines of the Threatened Committee were not published, they were not known to lawyers, and became public only in February 2015, nearly sixteen years after the committee's establishment.[6] In the meantime, the HCJ has been faced with an increasing number of individual petitions, without applicable legislation or even guiding standards set in administrative regulations. With dozens of petitions piled onto the HCJ docket every year, the court was free, if not asked, to engage in policy-making.

14.2 COURTS AND POLICY-MAKING

Unlike elected executive officials who are expected to form and implement public policies, judges are commonly expected to determine facts and interpret authoritative legal texts (Feeley and Rubin 1998, 1). The power of judges to make policy decisions is highly contested by scholars, elected officials and even ordinary people. In spite of the fact that judicial policy-making has been heavily discussed in the literature for several decades, agreement about the scope and nature of this judicial function is far from being achieved (Cichowski 2007; Dotan 2014; Martinsen 2015; Rosenberg 2008; Silverstein 2009; Sweet 2000).

Much of the literature on judicial policy-making centers on either the court's involvement in rendering landmark cases nullifying major legislative acts or executive policies (and setting guiding principles for future actions), or selected policy areas in which courts become very active. The common way to evaluate what the court is doing is to analyze the content of the decisions that determine the outcome of legal disputes. Another way to look at a court's policy-making powers is to weigh the preventive nature of court action. Namely, when political actors choose to change course rather than take the risk of facing a legal battle in court (Dotan 2014, 44).

What we observe in the case of Palestinian informers is judicial policy-making of a different nature. Petitions from threatened persons are brought to the highest court of the land on almost a weekly basis, the court deliberates these cases and makes

---

[5] A Supreme Court Justice, Elyakim Rubinstein, who was the Attorney General from 1997–2004, gave in one decision an account of how the Threatened Committee was formed: "I was at the cradle of the Threatened Committee as an Attorney General when it was created. It was found that the existing arrangement that set up the Security Aid Administration, did not apply to those who provided very little assistance and we had to address their pleas." HCJ 3870/12 *Ploni* v. *Minister* of Interior.

[6] The publication made after an administrative petition based on the Freedom of Information Law, 1998, was submitted to the District Court in Tel Aviv. ATM 51147-05-14 *Gisha* v. *Coordinator of Government Activities in the Territories.*

decisions – in which the state formally never loses – and in spite of this statistical oddity, petitioners come to court in ever-increasing numbers.

The fact that petitioners claim partial wins in less than 1 percent of their petitions, yet they still keep submitting petitions, is a signal to the curious observer that something odd is happening in the courtroom, something that cannot be picked up by looking simply at the statistics of wins and losses. People don't simply go to court to engage in a lost cause. They may take a big risk, but they must perceive that they have at least some chance of beating the odds. Statistically speaking, this is not the case here. To analyze what is transpiring in the courtroom, we first have to explain the proceedings and powers of the HCJ before turning to the cases of threatened persons.

14.3 THE HIGH COURT OF JUSTICE

The Israeli Supreme Court has a dual function: it serves both as the highest appeals court in civil and criminal matters, as well as sitting as the High Court of Justice (HCJ). As the latter, it has *original and final* jurisdiction in petitions brought against the state and its organs in matters that fall outside the jurisdiction of other courts. It is within this latter capacity that litigation between public petitioners and policy-makers takes place. This is particularly the case with petitions concerning national security, where the respondents are almost always cabinet ministers, state agencies entrusted with security powers or the Israeli army.

The HCJ's jurisdiction is set out in section 15(c) of Basic Law: The Judiciary, according to which the High Court shall hear matters in which it deems it necessary to grant relief for the sake of justice. Unlike the "case or controversy" requirement of the US Constitution (Article III), the Israeli Supreme Court's power extends to any matter it finds necessary to decide in order to forward the administration of justice.

The HCJ has the power to intervene in almost any type of decision-making process and to issue orders to almost any state agency. Its decisions are closely followed and intensively covered by both the media and the public (Dotan and Hofnung 2005; Hofnung and Weinshall-Margel 2010; Davidov and Reichman 2010).

Additionally, when sitting as the HCJ, special procedural rules apply, resulting in an altogether more relaxed and simplified legal process. This simplified procedure – coupled with the finality of its decisions – has turned the HCJ into a relatively accessible and attractive institution for both individuals and public petitioners (Dotan 2014, 25).[7] This easy access and fairly low cost has seen the HCJ become a very attractive forum for persons claiming a mortal threat to their life because they are suspected of being Israeli informers.

---

[7] Each year the Supreme Court disposes of about 11,000 cases, many of them HCJ files (Dotan 2014, 25).

14.4 THREATENED PERSONS AT THE HCJ

Petitions by non-Israeli citizens claiming threat to life based on suspicion of collaborating with Israeli authorities can be heard by either the HCJ or a district court, with the latter sitting as an administrative court. The differences in parallel authority between the two instances are not of major importance for the purposes of this chapter, especially as close to 90 percent of all petitions submitted in the last twenty years were heard at the HCJ sitting as the court of first (and last) instance.[8]

The first petitions claiming threat to life in the Occupied Territories on the basis of collaborating with Israel came before the HCJ in 1996. In the first three years, the average number of petitions was three per year. In 1998, the HCJ started to evaluate the claims of threatened persons more closely and the Threatened Committee was formed. In 1999, the number of petitions rose to nine and remained at that level during the years 1999–2003. With the end of the second Intifada (uprising) in the West Bank and Gaza there were thirty-one petitions in 2004. An average of thirty-five petitions a year was seen in the period of 2004–09, and in 2010 we see another leap to fifty-two petitions. In 2010–14, the yearly average is forty-nine, with a peak of seventy-nine petitions in 2014.[9]

As one can see from Figure 14.1, the number of yearly petitions has constantly risen, reaching an all-time high in 2014. How do threatened persons fare in court? Not very well, if one looks only at the success rates of the petitions submitted to the HCJ and takes the numbers seriously. Out of 501 cases (between 1996 and 2014) there is not one single full victory for the petitioner in a binding precedent-setting decision of the court. There are four rulings in which the court has acknowledged that petitioners were right in part of their claims. Combining what the court finds to be full victories (none) and partial victories (four), the success rate remains at less than 1 percent of the 501 cases.

However, when we qualitatively assessed the decisions that are classified by the court as rejections or dismissals, we found that many of these can be classified as partial successes, including minor legal achievements that conclude with the state's approval to extend the residency permit of the petitioner, delay the petitioner's expulsion, or reconsider the petitioner's appeal in the Threatened Committee. Thus, the actual success rate (including partial success) jumps to about 38 percent of all cases that have been concluded with published results (144 partial successes out of 382 final verdicts). The common denominator to what we classify as partial

---

[8] The only year in which a significant number of petitions was heard at the District Court was 2013, in which there thirty-nine petitions (out of the fifty-six petitions handled by that judicial instance from 1996 to 2014). That number does not reflect criminal or civil proceedings involving threatened individuals.

[9] Almost all of the administrative petitions to district courts came in the years 2010–14. If we add together the petitions claiming threat to life in the two judicial instances (HCJ and district court) during the five-year period of 2010–14, we reach 303 petitions, or sixty-one per year.

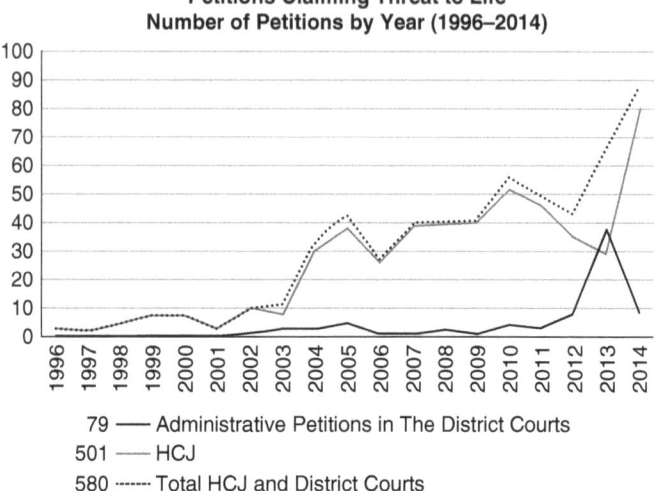

FIGURE 14.1: Petitions Claiming Threat to Life: Number of Petitions by Year (1996–2014)

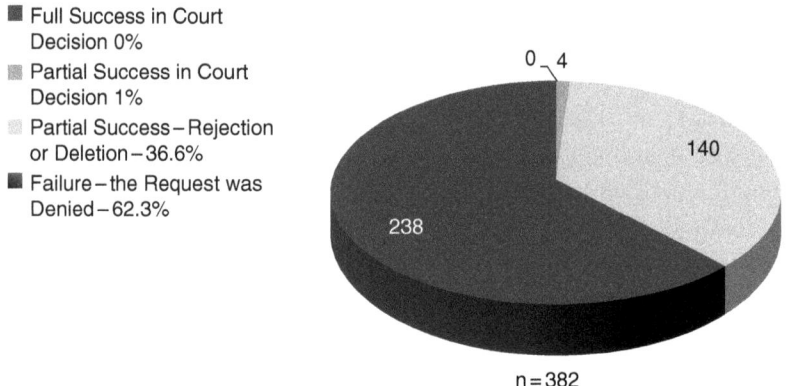

FIGURE 14.2: Success Rate of Threatened Persons Petitions to the High Court of Justice 1996–2015, Cases with Clear Final Decision.

success cases is that they provide the petitioner with a permanent or temporary legal residence status in Israel.

Being recognized as a threatened individual is far better than the other alternatives open to petitioners who have failed to obtain the status of informers. This small victory still prohibits the petitioner from obtaining the benefits that are given to informers, but obtaining legal residency in Israel is a highly desired accomplishment. Legal residency with a work permit is even more valuable. Thus, cancellation or dismissal of a petition is considered as a success from the perspective of the state's attorneys if the petitioner receives a temporary ninety-day permit to live in Israel with the status of a threatened individual. This is the case even though dismissal or rejection does not create a binding precedent, and it also implies that the petitioner will not be funded by the state like a recognized informer. The elusive fact is that a person who petitions the HCJ (even only once) by using the pretext of being an informer will remain in Israel formally or informally as a permanent resident. Regardless of the final outcome, petitioning the court is many times the victory in and of itself. The petitioner has a lawyer, a place to live, social ties and in many cases even a profitable job. Some people have petitioned the court four, five and even seven times, lost all cases, and still come back again and petition the court by utilizing the claim of changing circumstances (marrying an Israeli citizen, having a child with an Israeli spouse, etc.). The cost of relocation does not appear on the national security budget in cases where the petitioner is not recognized as an informer, though the social price becomes evident in different ways, including the stresses caused by integration into Israeli society of what is de facto a weak and detached population that lacks a permanent legal status.

14.5 POLICY-MAKING AT THE HCJ

In the cases of threatened persons the court found itself in a peculiar situation. On the one hand, it had to hear cases of desperate individuals, many of them having fled to Israel while leaving behind everything they had. By the mere act of petitioning the HCJ they had placed upon themselves the despised tag of Israeli collaborator. On the other hand, in all cases where petitions were filed, state lawyers appeared before the court and challenged the facts presented by the petitioner. The state's lawyers usually argued that either one or more of the following facts was present in the case: A) There is no threat to the life of the petitioner; B) The petitioner did not follow protocol by failing to present a case in front of the Threatened Committee before petitioning the HCJ; or C) Allowing the petitioner to stay in Israel poses a serious threat to public safety, in most cases due to the past criminal record of the person involved.

As the State of Israel created the Threatened Committee as a professional tribunal for hearing the pleas of threatened persons, the HCJ could have thrown out the majority of the cases on mere technicality by deciding that it would not hear the case before an initial decision was made by the appropriate administrative authority, i.e., the Threatened Committee. The HCJ did not take that route. Instead, the HCJ has heard almost every case, and in most cases has written a decision that brought the petition to a close. In the meantime it has been engaged in policy-making.

The Threatened Committee was created out of necessity; it has never been given a clear mandate, its procedure was secret and initially its decisions were given without explanation. In this situation the court had to hear and decide cases without having clear guidelines regarding its authority and the limits of the power of the Threatened Committee.

How has the HCJ operated as a policy-maker? By closely reading the HCJ's final decisions regarding threatened persons, we were able to define fifty-four cases (out of 382 files with a ruling closing the case) as having policy-making directives or making recommendations. By the term policy-making, we refer to decisions in which the HCJ sets procedures or standards of behavior that apply to all cases of threatened persons. There was no clear distinction between decisions rejecting the petition and decisions deleting the case (meaning that the case is removed from the docket) in which the petitioner can come back to the HCJ (with another petition based on similar facts). In fact, rejections, usually carrying out a full decision, were more likely to bring policy suggestions from the justices over decisions removing the case. In the latter instances it was sometimes difficult to trace the reasoning leading the court to delete the case.[10]

With the rising number of petitions from three in 1996 to the peak of seventy-nine in 2014, the justices developed an expertise and knowledge of the Threatened Committee's procedures. In the last couple of years it has been exceedingly difficult to trace a week on the docket of the HCJ in which the court has not deliberated petitions by threatened persons. Because the claim of threat to life is regarded seriously, the court rarely applies the "res judicata" principle. Hence the numerous examples of petitioners that petitioned the HCJ several times, and each time the court reviewed the case on the merits.[11]

In the first four years of hearing petitions by threatened persons, we could identify only two minor policy-making decisions, both of them made in January 1998 before the creation of the Threatened Committee. Then, in 2000 came the first case in which the HCJ set its own standards of treatment.

In May 2000, the court handed down its decision in HCJ 1562/98. Although the petition was ultimately rejected, the story and procedure that preceded the rejection make this case a significant one. The petition was filed by a young Palestinian from Gaza with a heavy criminal record who was recruited by the Israeli GSS (General Security Service, also known by its Hebrew acronym, Shin Bet) in 1993 as an informer. The connection between the new informer and GSS ended after a short time. The state's lawyers claimed that the contribution of the petitioner was

---

[10] Examples of phrases that appear in deleted petitions: "As agreed and requested, the petition is deleted," HC 7251/14 *Ploni v. Coordinator of Government Activities in the Territories*; or, "With the consent of the petitioner the petition is deleted." HC 3749/14 *Ploni v. Minister of Interior*.

[11] In HCJ 8643/10 the HCJ decided a case which was the seventh petition of the same person over a span of thirteen years. In HCJ 8619/12 the court heard the fourth petition of the same person in thirteen years; In HCJ 10604/06 the court heard the fourth petition of the same person in ten years.

miniscule, that there would be no threat to his life if he were deported to Gaza and that due to his past record of criminal convictions for fraud and theft he was not entitled to relocation or even a permanent permit to live in Israel. During the deliberations, the justices (in their words) discovered that the petitioner had a severe untreated eye injury that occurred during a brawl in an Israeli prison. At that point the justices took a proactive action.

At first the Court requested that the state lawyers allow for an administrative rehearing (a request that, practically speaking, cannot be refused by the lawyers representing the state). Then, a temporary writ requiring the state to explain its position was given. Another writ gave the petitioner temporary residence in Israel until the case was decided. The Court also ordered the respondent to explore the possibility of granting the petitioner a work permit. In addition, it told the Supreme Court's registrar to nominate a lawyer to represent the petitioner at the state's expense. A lawyer was nominated to both represent the petitioner at the HCJ and to file a civil suit for the damage that happened in Israeli prison. At that point, the Court sat again and heard that the state was willing to reconsider its position and allow the petitioner to remain in Israel for renewable forty-five-day periods as long as he could refrain from criminal activity. The court further asked the respondent (the state) to extend the renewable periods for ninety days at a time, and only when consent was given was the petition rejected. Thus, we see that the "losing" petitioner indeed achieved quite a lot, but from the respondent's position, the case did not set a binding precedent.

In the following years, and especially after Israel's withdrawal from Gaza (2005), the Hamas organization's win in the Palestinian elections (2006) and the subsequent takeover of Gaza[12] by Hamas (2007), the HCJ became much more active in making policy regarding threatened persons. In one case it supplied the petitioner with a list of the procedures and the relevant authorities he needed to contact for getting the treatment and benefits to which he was entitled.[13] In another it established the right of rehearing before the Threatened Committee if new information became available.[14] The HCJ also came up with a detailed outline of how to maintain due process of law and allow the petitioner access to all of the documents that can be provided without a risk to state security.[15] It also has suggested an outline of

---

[12] Since the Oslo Accords were signed, and especially after Mahmoud Abbas was elected in January 2005 as President of the Palestinian Authority, there has been official coordination between the security agencies of Israel and the PNA. After the Hamas takeover of Gaza (2007), Palestinian officials and members of the PLO fled to Israel due to the threat to their life. In addition, during the withdrawal from Gaza (2005), Israel evacuated several hundred residents of Dahaniya, a village in which families of Gazan informers lived under Israeli protection. See more on Dahanyia: HCJ 11121/08 *Abu Grarah v. Minister of Defence*; HCJ 2177/09 *Ashtiwi v. Minister of Defence*; HCJ 6549/12 *Ashtiwi and 110 others v. Prime Minister*; HCJ 533/13 *Armilat v. Minister of Interior*.
[13] HCJ 9394/10 *Ploni v. General Security Service*.
[14] HCJ 4414/11 *Ploni v. Prime Minister*.
[15] HC 1448/12 *Ploni v. the Threatened Committee*.

procedures to be applied at the Threatened Committee and restated those procedures when it found that they had not been closely followed.[16]

The HCJ was able to install legal standards into the workings of the Threatened Committee without infuriating the elected branches of government. In a country where national sentiments run high and vicious attacks on the judiciary are common political practices, this is by no means a small achievement. The court was able to do so by adopting a case-by-case treatment and avoiding sweeping landmark decisions in favor of the Palestinian petitioners.

14.6 CONCLUSION

How significant is the policy-making initiated by the HCJ? There is nothing better than the following story to provide a clue to answering this question. In 2014, a petition based on Israel's Freedom of Information Act was submitted at the district court in Tel Aviv.[17] To prevent a decision setting a binding precedent against the military, the state's attorneys agreed in November 2014 to present sixty different sets of internal regulations within six months, among them the procedures of the Threatened Committee.[18] That set of regulations was published in February 2015. Comparing the regulations put forth in 2015 with the hundreds of decisions by the HCJ in petitions against the Threatened Committee over almost twenty years, it is obvious that the state's attorneys' new set of regulations embraced the principles and guidelines suggested by the Court during that period. For almost any given regulation we can pinpoint to a corresponding decision of the HCJ.[19]

This small empirical study is in line with Feeley and Rubin's (1998) claim that courts engage in policy-making as an integral part of their judicial function. What this research adds to their ground-breaking work is a theoretical contribution backed by empirical evidence, which is that courts can engage in policy-making not only by reaching landmark binding decisions, but rather by purposely adopting a piecemeal approach of treating each case on an individual basis. By constantly using the implied threat of coming with a binding precedent in favor of the petitioner, the HCJ was able to coerce the state into settling scores of cases, and in doing so change and virtually set a written manual for treating threatened persons. Acting thusly while avoiding a fierce clash with the elected authorities was possible only because the HCJ refrained from writing decisions in favor of the petitioners, and thus

---

[16] HCJ 9482/11 *Ploni v. Minister of Interior*. HCJ 5476/14 *Ploni v. State of Israel*; HCJ 2409/15 *Ploni v. Prime Minister*.
[17] ATM 51147-05-14 *Gisha v. Coordinator of Government Activities in the Territories*.
[18] Procedures of Treating Thretened Individuals (2015), available at: www.cogat.idf.il/Sip_Storage/FILES/7/4677.pdf (last accessed June 30, 2016).
[19] Examples of HCJ rulings containing HCJ directives that were later put into the Procedures of Treating Threatened Individuals: HCJ 4535/96, HCJ 1199/97, HCJ 7370/11, HCJ 9482/11, HCJ 1562/98, HCJ 11216/04, HCJ 2205/05, HCJ 5449/08, HCJ 5763/09.

avoiding further erosion of public trust. How viable are the policy guidelines made by the judiciary? Only future research can tell.

REFERENCES

Cichowski, Rachel. 2007. *The European Court and Civil Society, Litigation, Mobilization and Governance*. Cambridge: Cambridge University Press.
Cohen, Hillel. 2009. *An Army of Shadows: Palestinian Collaborators in the Service of Zionism*. Oakland: University of California Press.
Cohen, Hillel and Ron Dudai. 2005. "Human Rights Dilemmas in Using Informers to Combat Terrorism: The Israeli-Palestinian Case." *Terrorism and Political Violence* 17 (1–2): 229–43.
Cohen, Hillel and Ron Dudai. 2007. "Triangle of Betrayal: Collaborators and Transitional Justice in the Israeli-Palestinian Conflict." *Journal of Human Rights* 6: 37–58.
Davidov, Guy and Amnon Reichman. 2010. "Prolonged Armed Conflict and Diminished Deference to the Military: Lessons from Israel." *Law & Social Inquiry* 35: 919–56.
Dotan, Yoav. 2014. *Lawyering for the Rule of Law: Government Lawyers and the Rise of Judicial Power in Israel*. Cambridge: Cambridge University Press.
Feeley, Malcolm and Edward Rubin. 1998. *Judicial Policy-making and the Modern State*. Cambridge: Cambridge University Press.
Gelber, Yoav. 1992. *Growing a Felur-de-Lis: The Intelligence Services of the Jewish Yishuv in Palestine 1918–1947*. Tel Aviv: Ministry of Defense.
Gillon, Cami. 2000. *Shin-Bet between the Schisms*. Tel Aviv: Yedioth Ahronoth Books and Chemed Books.
Hassan, Yousef Mosab. 2010. *Son of Hamas*. Carol Stream: Tyndale Momentum.
Hofnung, Menachem 2017. "The Price of Intelligence Collection: Relocation of Palestinian Informers in Israeli Towns." *Misphat Umimshal* (Haifa Law Review, in Hebrew) 18: 55–97.
Hofnung, Menachem and Keren Weinshall-Margel. 2010. "Judicial Setbacks, Material Gains: Terror Litigation at the Israeli High Court of Justice." *Journal of Legal Empirical Studies* 7: 664–92.
Lefen, Asa. 1997. *HaShai: The Roots of the Israeli Intelligence Community*. Tel Aviv: Ministry of Defense.
Levenkron, Naomi. 2012. "Who Knows the Man on the Wall." *Et Siyoua* 2.
Maimon, David. 1993. *The Vincible Terror*. Tel Aviv: Steimatzky.
Martinsen, Dorte Sindbjerg. 2015. "Judicial Influence on Policy Outputs? The Political Constraints of Legal Integration in the European Union." *Comparative Political Studies* 48: 1622–60.
Nimrodi, Jackob. 2003. *My Life's Journey*. Tel Aviv: Maariv.
Peri, Yaakov. 1999. *Strike First*. Tel Aviv: Keshet.
Ronen, David. 1990. *The Year of Shabak*. Tel Aviv: Ministry of Defense.
Rosenberg, Gerald. 2008. *The Hollow Hope: Can Courts Bring About Social Change?* Chicago: University of Chicago Press.
Silverstein, Gordon. 2009. *Laws Allure: How Law Shapes, Saves, and Kills American Politics*. Cambridge: Cambridge University Press.
Sweet, Alex Stone. 2000. *Governing with Judges: Constitutional Politics in Europe*. Oxford: Oxford University Press.
Teplow. Michael. 2009. "The Collaborators in Israel." *Legal Forum for Eretz Israel*.

PART IV

Political Liberalism and the Legal Complex

15

The International Legal Complex: Wang Yu and the Global Response to Repression of China's Rights' Lawyers

Terence C. Halliday[1]

INTRODUCTION

On June 15, 2015, China's official media launched an unprecedented public disinformation campaign against Wang Yu, a commercial lawyer who had emerged as a bold rights activist in the several years following her imprisonment by the Railway police for what she asserted was a false charge of beating someone on a station platform in Tianjin, a coastal city near Beijing. The coordinated nationwide attack, labeled by many of her supporters as a "smear campaign," included coverage in official newspapers, including *People's Daily*, online at People's Net, and on CCTV, China's multi-channel TV network. The articles alleged that this petite ex-prisoner had beaten someone to death, and then the official press "sarcastically" questioned whether she could be an authentic advocate to "represent justice and human rights" (B1610).[2]

Wang Yu's activist peers responded immediately with their own campaign to defend her reputation. Nevertheless, as a relative newcomer to the vanguard of rights activists, Wang Yu did not have strong connections outside China to strengthen her support. However, her name had arisen in connection with her defense in some newsworthy cases, not least that of the Five Feminists, which received extensive media coverage and heightened political awareness overseas.

All that changed on Wednesday, July 9, 2015, after Wang Yu dropped her lawyer husband, Bao Longjun, and sixteen-year-old son off at Beijing International Airport, where her son was headed to Australia for further study. She returned to her apartment. At 3:00 a.m. on Thursday, Wang Yu texted that her electricity and internet connections were turned off, and at 4:17 a.m. that someone was trying to

---

[1] This chapter draws on a research project on China's legal activists jointly led with Sida Liu, University of Toronto. The research reported here focuses on the twelve months from the July 9, 2015 crackdown to its first anniversary in 2016. I thank Sida Liu, the editors of this volume, and conference participants for their comments.

[2] In order to protect the anonymity of interviewees, quotations are assigned alpha-numeric codes.

pry open her front door. Then, all contact with her went dead. Neighbors later reported that some twenty to thirty police officers had gathered in the early hours for a so-called drug raid, and they left the area with someone in custody (China Human Rights Lawyers Concern Group 2015). In the following hours it became immediately apparent that Wang Yu's disappearance – since no one knew who took her or where she was being held – was the beginning of a preplanned attack on her Beijing Fengrui Law Firm, one of China's boldest centers of activity for such notable activist lawyers as Zhou Shifeng and Liu Xiaojuan, who had long represented the controversial artist Ai Weiwei. Zhou Shifeng, the managing partner, was detained from a hotel in which he was staying, while several other lawyers and administrators in the firm were also detained elsewhere in Beijing. Public security officers entered the firm itself and seized files and computers.

These disappearances and detentions were almost instantly conveyed to lawyer networks inside China, and within hours to networks in Hong Kong and across the world. Wang Yu's case, and the widening crackdown on activist lawyers across China that it heralded, provide a contemporaneous research site to extend Feeley's extensive work on the legal complex, courts, and political liberalism. This chapter begins with an overview of the concept of "legal complex," raises the question of whether it might be extended from domestic to international contexts, examines briefly mobilization in response to China's current crackdown on lawyers, and concludes by opening up the promise of this theory and research for the study of international legal complexes (Jothie 2010). While Wang Yu was eventually released into a harshly restrictive form of house arrest after many months of "enforced disappearance" (Wang Yu 2017), the events and dynamics that attracted international reactions in her first twelve months of detention continue to have a lingering impact, in significant part kept alive by an international legal complex and its allies in the media, civil society, and foreign offices of some states.

15.1 THE LEGAL COMPLEX AS A POLITICAL ACTOR

A nexus of struggle accompanies the formation and reformation of politics within many modern states. That nexus involves lawyers and a legal complex mobilizing collectively on behalf of a particular concept of political society (Bell 1994; Burrage 1989; De 2012; Karpik 1998; Rueschemeyer 1997; VonDoepp 2012).

Attention to this politics grows out of an intellectual biography in the sociology and later history of professions. In the Anglo-American scholarly sphere, the sociology of professions from the 1930s to 1970s adopted the view that other-interested and altruistic occupations called professions made functional contributions to the provision of professional services and the constitution of modern societies. A sharp backlash in US scholarship in the 1970s insisted that the so-called naïve assumption of professional altruism must be rejected in favor of a realism about professions, in which professional individual and collective action was oriented to upward mobility in social status and to control of markets in order to extract monopoly rents. Professions used their relative autonomy through self-regulation to restrict the supply of professionals and thus maintain economic privileges.

From the 1970s, both sociologists and historians of legal professions led a counterattack and insisted that lawyers' politics were directed not only to a functional social order, or the capture of a market for professional services, or for the ascendancy of a certain social stratum, but to specific ideals of a certain kind of political society. Whether in seventeenth-century England (Burrage 1997), eighteenth-century France (Bell 1997; Karpik 1988a), nineteenth-century Germany (Rueschemeyer 1997), twentieth-century India (De 2012; Mate 2012) and Singapore (Rajah 2012), or twenty-first-century China (Halliday and Liu 2007b), empirical research in enormously diverse times and places demonstrated that lawyers mobilized in various forms of collective action for a bundle of issues on which a quite heterogeneous body of legal professionals might find a homogeneity of interests.

That bundle of actions comprises three core elements (Halliday and Karpik 1997b; Halliday, Karpik, and Feeley 2007a; Halliday, Karpik, and Feeley 2012; Karpik 1997). First, lawyers fought for *basic legal freedoms* that restrained arbitrary state power. They demanded that rulers could not arbitrarily seize persons without cause, nor hold them indefinitely without legal process, nor torture, summarily execute, or "disappear" those persons that rulers did not like. They insisted upon rules, legal representation, trials where evidence could be presented and tested, and fair adjudication. Alongside these quite legal restrictions on unbridled state power, and indeed as a condition of counterbalancing the power of the state, lawyers were often in the vanguard of advocates for foundational political freedoms so that they themselves and other citizens could be able to speak freely, associate with whom they wished, and move about a country at will. And alongside these fundamental political freedoms lawyers very often were drawn into the defense not only of persons, but property as well, so that it could not be seized by individuals or the state without legal process and appropriate redress.

Second, lawyers, as actors in a private market of legal representation, insisted that they could act collectively through associations or networks outside the control of the state. They insisted other citizens should have similar capacities to join associations in an open *civil society* where social affiliations were not controlled or authorized or unduly monitored by the state. Their associations, sometimes clandestine (Ginsburg 2007; Graver 2015; Liu and Halliday 2016), usually public, would serve as anchors of a vocal civil society. And lawyers themselves, as advocates, might speak on behalf not only of individuals but express the views of publics as their spokespersons (Karpik 1988a; Karpik 1998).

Third, lawyers' politics sought not only a *moderation of the state* by social organizations outside the state, but in the very constitution of the state itself, most notably through various means of fracturing power within the state. Most commonly their goal was to achieve some autonomy for law and the courts so judges could act fairly, justly balancing the prosecutorial and coercive powers of the state against the vulnerabilities of the individual (Nonet and Selznick 1978). Judges themselves should be protected from all the various means of pressures exogenous to law that might influence their decision making.

This bundle of issues on which lawyers were most likely to mobilize despite whatever else divided them – basic legal freedoms, civil society, the moderate state – has been labeled "political liberalism" (Halliday and Karpik 1997a; Karpik 1988b; Karpik 1995; Karpik 1999). In retrospect, this might not have been the most felicitous term since "liberalism" came to connote far more than the eighteenth- and nineteenth-century activism displayed by lawyers. Nonetheless, it presented a counterpoint to mobilization of lawyers for economic liberalism. That is, research demonstrated that lawyers were as capable, if not as often, of engaging in collective action for a liberal political order as they were for a certain kind of economic order.

It became very apparent in studies in a revisionist history and sociology of professions from the 1980s that a politics of lawyers could not be separated from the politics of judges. Until the 1990s, in fact, scholarship on lawyers and judges in sociology and political science had been contained in hermetically sealed silos of rich interior conversations, while discussions between them were impoverished.

Malcolm Feeley, as an active leader in scholarship on courts, led a charge to break out of an otherwise robust body of scholarship on political jurisprudence (Feeley 2012; Halliday 2013) in order to engage the burgeoning cross-national studies on professions. This in no small part was stimulated by the research of young scholars at Berkeley (Couso 2007; Ghias 2012; Massoud 2011; Mate 2012; Moustafa 2007a; Moustafa 2007b; Munir 2012), who demonstrated in Chile, Pakistan, Sudan, India and beyond that the politics of lawyers and judges were frequently intertwined. Indeed, part of the explanatory challenge for transitions to a liberal political society was to understand the political dynamics between lawyers and judges.

In fact, however, repeated studies of lawyers and judges across the world showed that this potential dyad or structural relationship was itself too limiting. When lawyers or judges mobilize they often do so inside a wider matrix of legal occupations. The properties of that matrix led to the naming of a new political actor – the legal complex (Karpik and Halliday 2011a; Halliday, Karpik, Feeley 2007a). Feeley's leadership in studies of the British post-colony and in Nordic societies seeks to elaborate the properties and dynamics of that complex.

We may summarize its five essential features here (Karpik and Halliday 2011a). A legal complex:

(1) *comprises all legally trained occupations in a given society whose work involves legal practice.* It can include occupations such as advocates or barristers, solicitors, judges and magistrates, civil servants acting in legal capacities, military

lawyers and judges, lawyers acting as lawyers inside corporations, and legal academics.

(2) *refers to legally trained occupations in action.* That is, it refers not to all persons in a society with a law degree or legal training, but to those practising law at any given moment. It refers not only to heroic leaders, but it attends particularly to collective action, such as lawyers and judges mobilizing through networks, associations, marches, and various symbolic gestures.

(3) *focuses on action with respect to specific issues.* A legal complex that forms around particular issues may not form around other issues. The broadest-based legal complex is likely to be found on the narrow legalistic grounds of political liberalism. Other legal complexes may rise or fall on one (e.g., freedom of speech) or another freedom (e.g., protection against torture). In that sense it is possible to distinguish between *the* legal complex, where very occasionally an entire legal complex will mobilize, and *a* legal complex, where some segments of the legal complex take action while others do not.

(4) *has structural configurations.* On any issue, the structural ties of potential segments of the legal complex can be mapped, both in terms of proximity among the segments or the type of association they forge. We can expect to see alliances and lines of conflict within and among segments of a legal complex.

(5) *has temporal dynamics.* Legal complexes rise and fall. In some periods they will be passive, in others active. Part of the theoretical challenge for studies of the legal complex is to isolate those proximate and distal conditions under which a legal complex will act at one historical moment but not another.

"In sum, the legal complex denotes legal occupations that mobilize on a given issue at a given historical moment, usually through collective action that is enabled through discernible structures of ties" (Karpik and Halliday 2011, 221). The contingencies of mobilization extend in two directions – one with respect to combinations and orientations of action within the legal complex, the other with respect to relationships outside the legal complex, most notably in civil society.

Studies in many comparative and historical sites show quite different combinations among segments of the legal complex. For instance, lawyers alone mobilized *for* basic legal freedoms in Japan (Feeley and Miyazawa 2007) and China (Halliday and Liu 2007a), but were complicit or acted *against* basic legal freedoms in Sudan in the 1980s–2000s (Massoud 2012). Lawyers led antiliberal "revolutions" in contemporary Hungry and Russia (Scheppele 2019, chapter 18 this volume). Lawyers acted together with judges *for* basic legal freedoms in Sudan in the 1950s–60s (Massoud 2012), Taiwan in 1970–90 (Ginsburg 2007), and Namibia (VonDoepp 2012), but for the most part allied *against* political liberalism in fascist Italy and Germany (Guarnieri 2007; Ledford 1997). A wider legal complex joined forces to press *for* basic legal freedoms in Hong Kong (Jones 2007) and Venezuela (Perdomo 2007), but they were *inactive* or *opposed* to an opening of a liberal political society in Pakistan in the 1970s to 1990s (Aziz 2012) and in Chile between 1973 and 1990 (Couso 2007).

The legal complex has limited capacity to resist attacks on basic legal freedoms or to effect shifts to a more liberal political society unless it has allies. Those allies are found in civil society – e.g., labor and women's organizations, religions, media – and the market, and they rely on information technologies from print to the internet to social media (Gould 2012; Halliday 2010; Liu and Halliday 2016; Munir 2012).

In all of these cases the ideals of a legal complex for basic legal freedoms are nested within norms of constitutionalism, United Nations conventions, and jurisprudential traditions, among others. In other words, domestic legal complexes are invariably nested within international and historical currents of thought and lineages of law. The case of Wang Yu, and international reactions to China's unprecedented attack on lawyers, exemplify the dimensions of this embeddedness.

15.2 CHINA'S REPRESSIVE TURN AGAINST LAWYERS

On July 9, 2015, one hundred and one activist lawyers from across China, including some of Beijing's most notable activists, such as Li Heping, Jiang Tianyong, Li Fangping, and Tang Jitian, took the daring step of issuing a public call for Wang Yu's release, which they circulated on social media as widely as possible given the control of censors inside China (China Human Rights Lawyers Concern Group 2015). Radio Free Asia, an invaluable source for those Chinese who can penetrate the Great Firewall, broadcast on July 10 that Wang Yu was missing and "believed detained" (Radio Free Asia, "Beijing Rights Lawyer 'Missing,' Believed Detained," July 10, 2015).

By Friday, July 10, international scholars, lawyers' and human rights groups close to the activists, and activists residing outside China, including exiled crusader Teng Biao, began to mobilize rapidly to inform media, states, and intergovernmental bodies of a crackdown that quickly covered all of China. The lawyers daring to sign the petition to release Wang Yu seemed to be targeted at the outset.

Within twenty-four hours of the initial detentions, the political section of the US Embassy in Beijing was in direct contact with notable activists, some before they were detained and interrogated, and others after they had been released, to discover why China's government had taken drastic steps against lawyers not seen for decades. On July 10, the Hong Kong-based China Human Rights Lawyers Concern Group, a highly vocal and prestigious NGO with close ties to China's activist lawyers, put out a statement via its internet listserve calling for help and detailing in microscopic detail the timeline of the initial attack on Wang Yu, her family, and her Fengrui law firm colleagues.

International networks came alive. An article in Hong Kong's *South China Morning Post* on the disappearances (South China Morning Post 2015) was distributed on July 10 to an international network of over 1,500 specialists on

China's politics who communicate on the ChinaPol listserve, a message board that includes diplomats and many of the most influential journalists covering China for prominent overseas media. Amnesty International released a statement on July 11 cataloguing in detail the detainees by name, location, and occupation, criticizing China's top leadership, and demanding "unconditional release of all those detained solely for their work defending human rights" (Amnesty International 2015). On July 12, the US Department of State issued a statement condemning the detention of human rights defenders and strongly urging China "to release all those who have recently been detained for seeking to protect the rights of Chinese citizens" (Kirby 2015). The European Union issued a statement three days later which pressed China to "release all those detained for seeking to protect ... the rights of all citizens as recognised by the Chinese Constitution" and enshrined in the Universal Declaration of Human Rights (European Union External Action 2015).

Rapid exchanges crisscrossed the world among lawyers, INGOs, and UN advocacy groups. A nexus of lawyers' groups, human rights NGOs and INGOs, and international media exchanged information, discussed tactics, confirmed facts, as activist human rights groups and organizations of the legal complex sought mutual support, and caucused about forms of leverage on China's government, amid parallel releases of stories by the media. The UN Human Rights Council Special Rapporteur issued a statement that "Lawyers need to be protected not harassed – UN experts urge China to halt detentions" (UNHCR 2015). The INGO International Service for Human Rights reinforced that view in its July 11 statement that "China must immediately cease its coordinated targeting of human rights defenders." It connected the new incursions on the rights of lawyers to China's rejection of the expression of concern by the UN High Commissioner for Human Rights over China's new National Security Law, which "leaves the door wide open to further restrictions on the rights and freedom of Chinese citizens" (International Service for Human Rights 2015). Lawyers' defense organizations issued human rights appeals for information and demands for release and forbearance in the ongoing "raids, abductions, detentions, disappearances, summons and searches" (Chinese Human Rights Defenders 2015).

As Amnesty International's comprehensive and regular updates reinforced the extraordinary scope of the security move against lawyers and activists, divergences in the international legal complex, and even between lawyers' groups within a national profession, revealed fissures in forms of response to China.

By Monday, July 13, national and international bar associations in Asia, Australia, North America, and Europe had caucused with members and together about appropriate responses. The varieties of responses were instructive. The top leadership of the American Bar Association (ABA) had been alerted about the crackdown by its human rights leaders, and academic networks and discussions began on July 11 among the ABA, the International Bar Association, the Council of Bars and Law

Societies of Europe (CCBE), and the Francophone Union des Internationale des Avocats (UIA).

Many European lawyers' organizations issued independent statements. These were brought together by the Dutch group, Lawyers for Lawyers, as twenty-four organizational signatories to a July 21 letter addressed to President Xi Jinpeng and the Minister of Public Security. The letter, widely circulated on the internet and posted on its website, strongly condemned "the recent unprecedented and seemingly well-coordinated detention of a large number of human rights lawyers in China" (Lawyers for Lawyers 2015). It criticized China's security apparatus against the standards of global norms on the role of lawyers, human rights, fundamental freedoms, and human rights defenders.

The following day, July 22, the world's peak association of lawyers' organizations, the International Bar Association, issued an open letter through its Human Rights Institute (IBAHRI),

> to His Excellency Mr Xi Jinping, President of the People's Republic of China, to express its deep concern at the unprecedented number of lawyers, human rights activists and support staff who have faced arrest, questioning and detention in China since 9 July 2015. The IBAHRI understands that, at the time of writing, 132 lawyers who work to protect human rights and fundamental freedoms have been summoned, arrested, questioned and/or detained by Government authorities across 24 provinces of China. The IBAHRI is gravely concerned by reports that some individuals have been detained incommunicado; without access to legal counsel; unable to notify family members; and/or detained under residential surveillance and not in an officially recognised place of detention. (International Bar Association 2015)

If they were not already aware of the situation in China, this letter gave notice to its membership of 55,000 individual lawyers and more than 190 bar associations and law societies spanning all continents of the gravity of the crackdown, and set a tone for reactions by lawyers.

The United States, however, provides a snapshot of the longstanding paradox of lawyers' ability to mobilize collectively across the diversity of their ideological and economic interests, reproducing a pattern earlier documented by Powell (Powell 1988) and Halliday (Halliday 1987). The New York City Bar conceives of itself as a:

> 145 year-old organization of more than 24,000 members in New York City, throughout the U.S., and in over fifty countries across the globe, including China. Our membership includes judges, prosecutors, government officials, and defense lawyers, as well as corporate attorneys representing nearly every major law firm and corporation in the U.S. (Raskin 2015)

Following the lead of its Committee on International Human Rights, the President of the City Bar wrote a letter which expressed "grave concern" about the "intimidation, arrest, detention, and in many cases enforced disappearance" of lawyers, activists, support staff, and families. Informed by close ties between the City Bar's own members and China's activists, together with a detailed spreadsheet updated regularly by Amnesty International's Hong Kong office, President Raskin could write explicitly about 228 people targeted and twenty-two that remained missing or in custody. She named those individuals. She aligned the City Bar with "the protected scope of lawyers' legitimate work" as practised by the Fengrui Law Firm. She extensively contrasted China's actions with international UN standards and China's own Criminal Procedure Law and, indeed, Xi Jinping's Four Comprehensives, which included a commitment to "govern the country according to the law." She ended with a call for immediate release of detainees and for detentions to adhere to international standards, including access to legal counsel and detention in "official detention facilities."

This strong, detailed, and forthright letter contrasts noticeably with the American Bar Association, whose internal politics immediately registered sharp divides. For more than seventeen years the ABA Rule of Law Initiative (ROLI) had an office in Beijing, and it had cooperated with the government in many projects to advance rule of law. ROLI and most ABA leaders preferred no statement at all from the ABA in case it impaired a future ABA presence in Beijing or might harm ABA employees in its Beijing office, especially Chinese citizens. By contrast, the ABA Human Rights Center and segments of the International Law Section, among other ABA members, preferred a strong statement which registered grave concern at the detentions and urged China to respect the rights of lawyers inscribed in China's own laws and constitution, as well as in UN standards. Both sides brought specialist academics and lawyers to buttress their cases. In the weeks following the crackdown the ABA President did issue a statement, but it placed emphasis on future cooperation with China's authorities and scarcely mentioned the historically unprecedented treatment of lawyers in the crackdown (American Bar Association 2015).

As the rolling magnitude of the crackdown continued, the international response began to shift into a different register. One organization called upon the International Olympic Committee to reject China's bid for the 2022 Winter Olympics (Initiatives for China 2015a). Several rights and lawyers' groups within the Untied States targeted the US–China Rights Dialogue, scheduled for August 13–14 in Washington, DC, as a focal point for protest. An NGO Rights Defense Network called for the Dialogue "to have muscle to improve [the] rapidly deteriorating rights situation." It demanded that the United States exert "significant pressure" and tangible "results on the ground" to demonstrate the value of a continuing dialogue with China. A coalition of "overseas Chinese organizations in the greater Washington DC region" staged a small public demonstration in front of the Chinese Embassy on August 13, where it read "A Letter of Protest against China's Arrest of Rights Lawyers" (Initiatives for China 2015b).

More remarkable was a public statement directed to the Dialogue by twenty-five lawyers and eleven human rights defenders, most of whom were still inside China, and several of whom, such as Chang Boyang, Tang Jitian, and Jiang Tianyong, had themselves suffered physical and other injuries under previous crackdowns. The statement explicitly requested that:

"1. The Chinese government should release all lawyers and activists who have been arbitrarily detained and forcibly disappeared ...
2. The US government should pay close attention to the latest legislative trend and urge Chinese authorities to abolish or substantially amend the clauses and articles of law and regulations that breach the Constitution of the People's Republic of China or the international standards of human rights ..."

In addition, persons expressing views to or about the Dialogue should have their safety assured and results of the Dialogue should be publicly reported.[3]

In the event, the "on-the-record briefing" conducted on August 24 by US Assistant Secretary of State Tom Malinkowski registered explicitly the "growing sense of alarm in the US about human rights developments in China," and went so far as to catalog reports about denial of access to legal counsel, forced public confessions, and named individual lawyers including Wang Yu, Zhou Shifeng, Li Heping, and Liu Xiaoyuan. The Secretary further stated that these issues "will be a very prominent issue at the summit" between Presidents Obama and Xi Jinping.[4]

While media stories continued to roll out across the world, the register shifted again as the United States prepared to host a state visit of President Xi Jinping coupled with Xi's appearances at the United Nations. The prospective meetings sharpened the focus of activists in the United States and beyond.

Already the State Department had been active on several fronts – through direct contacts with activist lawyers by Beijing Embassy officials, internal discussions at the highest levels in the State Department (Halliday, private communications, 2015), through public statements by its Assistant Secretary, and in the Human Rights Dialogue with China, which occurred in August. The tone of the State Department's messages hardened when Ambassador Saperstein, Ambassador at Large for International Religious Freedom at the State Department, learned that on his fact-finding mission to China in late August 2015 that a leading Christian rights lawyer, Zhang Kai, had been arrested the night before he was scheduled to meet with the Ambassador (Buckley 2015; China Change 2015). With the full authority of the State Department, Saperstein issued a strong public statement "condemning" China's detention of lawyers.[5]

As Xi's state visit approached, numerous groups urged the Obama administration variously to cancel the visit, to invite China's exiled human rights lawyers to the White House, to leave empty seats signifying "disappeared lawyers" at the State

---

[3] Chinese Lawyers' Statement on 2015 China–US Dialogue on Human Rights.
[4] www.state.gov/r/pa/prs/ps/2015/08/24/246092.htm
[5] See different statements by Saperstein and the Press Office.

dinner, and for Obama to take a strong position vis-à-vis the detained rights lawyers in his face-to-face meetings with Xi.

In the meantime, Ambassador Samantha Power launched a US State Department publicity initiative at the UN entitled "#FreeThe20 campaign," in anticipation of the forthcoming UN Conference on Women presided over by China (US Department of State 2015). The first woman featured in the public launch was Wang Yu.

Xi's visit to the United States was met with public protests outside China's Embassy, a protest breakfast by rights protesters, NGOs, and lawyers' groups, and private meetings by Secretary Kerry with Chinese activists (China Aid 2015). Human Rights Watch China Director, Sophie Richardson, attended the State dinner, where she took the opportunity to represent the plight of human rights lawyers and activists to President Obama, President Xi, and those senior China officials who would speak to her, albeit very briefly in this regimented diplomatic milieu. Activism then shifted to other forthcoming events that sharpened international attention, such as President Xi's visit to Britain in November 2015, and a scheduled meeting in late 2015 by the American Bar Association President with Chinese officials in Beijing.

Mobilization by lawyers and rights groups outside China spiked sharply in January 2016 as the six-month deadline approached for China to either release or charge its disappeared lawyers held under the "residential surveillance" provisions of Article 73 of the Criminal Procedure Law. In the event, those charged faced long-term prison sentences for offences of inciting subversion of the state or actual subversion of the state, charges far in excess of previous crackdowns (Phillips 2016).

Again, strong public statements were issued by lawyers' rights groups in Hong Kong and the Unites States, the International Bar Association's Human Rights Institute, European national, specialist, and coalitions of bar associations, and the New York City Bar. Legal notables from across the world, UN human rights bodies, and many governments, including the United States, joined the chorus of criticism and demands on China's government to adhere to universal legal standards. Many stories centered on Wang Yu and Li Heping, whose bold rights advocacy inside China resonated with eclectic international publics, including feminists, Christians, minorities, labor rights activists, and environmentalists, among others.

Since the international pressure on China may have shamed its leaders in the perceptions of international public opinion, it did bring several of the charged lawyers to trial, although some trials were held in secret and all were stage-managed for wider public consumption. In fact, the government doubled down on its repression by keeping detainees isolated from family and diplomats, and adopted the cynical practice of dismissing lawyers chosen by the detainees and replacing them with lawyers acceptable to the security apparatus.

A stronger wave of international criticism therefore responded to China's abuse of fundamental legal rights as the crackdown approached its one-year anniversary in early July 2016. After a long internal set of negotiations within the American Bar Association, its leadership announced on the anniversary of Wang Yu's abduction that she had been awarded the first ABA International Human Rights award, an announcement that sufficiently stung China's leaders that the *Global Times*, widely read by Chinese Communist Party cadres and officials, editorialized against the ABA and all other ways that the "West wilfully provokes over rights lawyers."[6] The ABA was joined in its outspokenness by bar associations in the United States, Europe, and elsewhere, and by prestigious bodies of jurists such as the International Commission of Jurists. The International Bar Association's Human Rights Institute released a strong public statement over the signatures of its joint chairs, Baroness Kennedy (United Kingdom) and Hans Corell, former UN Under-Secretary-General for Legal Affairs.

15.3 AN ACTIVIST INTERNATIONAL LEGAL COMPLEX

The international response to the July 9, 2015 crackdown shifted and turned, adjusted and adapted in the long year of struggle inside and outside of China up to the one-year anniversary of the crackdown in July 2016. In these varieties of mobilization, patterns of activism can be observed that embraced lawyers, an international legal complex, and international civil society. An overview of this activism begins to lay bare the contours of national struggles for political liberalism now translated into international and global milieux.

15.3.1 *Who Mobilized?*

The dynamics and structure of responses outside China can be observed in the inter connectedness and cross-reliance of many types of lawyers' organizations and networks.

The most immediate responses came from NGOs focused on law and lawyers in China. Within twenty-four hours, Hong Kong's China Human Rights Lawyers Concern Group (hereafter HK Concern Group) began posting detailed tracking, by the minute, of the disappearance of Wang Yu, the detention of her Fengrui law firm colleagues, and the rapid expansion of the campaign in the following days. The HK Concern Group has maintained accurate up-to-the-minute reporting on all detentions and steady and reliable commentary on developments.

As the magnitude of the nationwide crackdown became evident, the mix of signatory organizations to the Lawyers for Lawyers letter indicates the growing texture of the international legal complex and its ability to mobilize rapidly. There are national bar associations (DeutscherAnwaltVerein, Norwegian Bar Association, The Law Society of England Wales, Syndicat des Avocats de France), provincial or

---

[6] *Global Times*, Editorial, July 11, 2016, p.14.

city generalist bar associations (The Law Society of Upper Canada, Ordres des Avocats des Geneve, Amsterdamse Orde van Advocaten), specialty national and international criminal defense associations (European Criminal Bar Association), human rights sections of national and international bar associations (Bar Council of Ireland Human Rights Committee, Solicitors' Internnational Human Rights Group, Bar Human Rights Committee of England and Wales), and other international organizations for human rights or political segment of the lawyer population including The Observatory for the Protection of Human Rights Defenders, European Democratic Lawyers/Advocats Europeens Democrates, and the International Association of People's Lawyers. It is noteworthy that this coalition was forged within twelve days of Wang Yu's detention. Its activism and immediacy rested heavily on instant and regular online reporting and monitoring by human rights INGOs and international lawyers' groups, and the permeability of China's information firewall in both directions.

On July 22, 2015 the world's most inclusive peak association of 190 bar associations and 55,000 individual members, the International Bar Association, released publicly its own letter to President Xi (see Section 15.2). While focused almost entirely on the rights of lawyers, both to be protected in their representation of others, and to be able to defend others, the letter juxtaposed the reported actions of China's authorities with a wide-ranging set of universal norms and China's own constitution and laws (see Table 1). In addition, the prestigious International Commission of Jurists (ICJ), based in Geneva, was a signatory to the Lawyers for Lawyers letter. The ICJ explicitly constitutes itself as a body representing distinguished private lawyers, judges, government officials, and international civil servants acting in juristic capacities.

On July 28, 2015 the local bar association with arguably the most global reach, certainly to the worlds of commerce, trade, and finance, and possibly of human rights, the New York City Bar, released a strong and detailed three-page letter of its own to President Xi (see Section 15.3.2). A year later, the American Bar Association released a much strengthened statement when it announced the awarding of the International Human Rights Prize to Wang Yu (American Bar Association 2016).

Several academics in Hong Kong, the United States, and the United Kingdom who specialize in rights and activist lawyers in China functioned as conduits of information between China's activists and lawyers' associations, and indeed anchored in many respects both the facts and interpretations of unfolding events. An early but unsuccessful effort was made to forge an academic alliance, if their law schools would not, to release a public statement.

Partly in an effort to exert a different form of leverage on China's leaders, a small group of academics and international NGO China specialists drafted a letter to President Xi Jinpeng to which they sought eminent jurists around the world as signatories. Published simultaneously in *The Guardian* (2016), with accompanying articles in the *New York Times* (Buckley 2016), *Die Zeit*, and *Le Monde*, the public letter drew current and former notable judges, legal academics, government law ministers, and renowned practitioners into a momentary, cross-national appeal that was disseminated widely, particularly through electronic news outlets.

Analytically, it can be seen that this international response loosely mirrored the elements of a domestic legal complex. Within and across these varieties of mobilization could be found practising solicitors and barristers, judges and legal academics. They unified around a particular issue. And consistent with studies of legal complexes within a state, this international legal complex displayed a temporal dynamism, yet to be fully analyzed, which showed ebbs and flows of mobilization, unfolding internal struggles within leading associations, and shifting tactics as events unfolded on the ground.

Yet, as the international response unfolded it was also clear that internal divides within practising legal professions kept large numbers of practitioners on the sidelines, or they quietly dissented from associational and network activism. That is, the international legal complex that did mobilize was a fraction of the full population of legal occupations that might have activated on the lawyer crackdown in China. Three months after the crackdown began on July 9, 2015, no judges' association nor organization of legal academics or of prosecutors had taken a public position. Their involvement, if at all, came within bar associations that count large numbers of legal academics and judges among their members and, for a few, as signatories to public letters of appeal to China's leaders.

Hence the "international" in the international legal complex manifested itself in multiplex ways – domestic associations with international orientations; international professional associations constituted to transcend state borders; alliances of state and supra-state associations; networks and single-issue expressions of solidarity by notables; and the indications of an international professional "public" brought together through listserves (e.g., ChinaLaw, ChinaPol) and social media among others.

15.3.2 *The Rhetoric of Mobilization*

It is instructive to parse the rhetorical and substantive components of the letters released by the International Bar Association Human Rights Institute, Lawyers for Lawyers, and the New York City Bar. The statements, letters, and appeals to China's leaders invoked three principal sets of norms: international standards, China's constitution, and China's statutory law.

International standards: All the letters appeal to UN norms to which China can be held accountable (Table 1).

As befits organizations of lawyers, a strong emphasis in these representations is placed on rights of access to lawyers, the recognition that a lawyer's role in a system of justice must not be conflated with the acts or views of a lawyer's client(s), that lawyers themselves should be free of fears or harms against them for carrying out their professional mandate, and that "lawyers, like other citizens, are entitled to freedom of expression, belief, association and assembly" (Raskin 2015). The appeals widen to

TABLE 1 *China's Breaches of UN Norms*

UN standards	Specific provisions within standards	In public letter from:
Universal Declaration of Human Rights (UDHR)		New York City Bar Lawyers for Lawyers
	Art 9 – prohibition against arbitrary detention	New York City Bar International Bar Association
	Art 14 – persons should be notified of the charges against them at the time of arrest	International Bar Association
UN Basic Principles on the Role of Lawyers	Principles 1, 5, 7 – persons should have prompt access to lawyers when detained or arrested	Lawyers for Lawyers International Bar Association
	Article 16 – "Governments shall ensure that lawyers (a) are able to perform all of their professional functions without intimidation, hindrance, harassment or improper interference ... and (c) shall not suffer, or be threated with, prosecution or administrative, economic or other sanctions for any action taken in accordance with recognized professional duties, standards and ethics."	International Bar Association New York City Bar
	Article 17 – rights of lawyers to be "safeguarded" in the carrying out of their professional functions	International Bar Association
	Article 18 – "lawyers shall not be identified with their clients ...."	International Bar Association New York City Bar New York City Bar
	Article 23 – "lawyers, like other citizens, are entitled to freedom of expression, belief, association and assembly."	International Bar Association
The Internatl Covenant on Civil and Political Rights (ICCPR)	Article 9 – prohibition against arbitrary detention	Lawyers for Lawyers New York City Bar

TABLE 1 (continued)

UN standards	Specific provisions within standards	In public letter from:
UN Declaration on Human Rights Defenders		Lawyers for Lawyers
UN Body of Principles for the protection of all persons under any form of detention or imprisonment	Principle 19 on informing family members of whereabouts Art 37 – prohibition against arbitrary detention	Lawyers for Lawyers International Bar Association New York City Bar

universal norms on rights of detainees (against arbitrary detention, notification of charges, access to lawyers) and beyond those to rights accorded the families of detainers (e.g., rights of notification). China is in breach of all these standards for the twenty-three currently "disappeared" persons and virtually all those still in custody.

China's constitution: The letters maintain that China's security apparatus is in breach of China's own legal standards as they are institutionalized in the country's constitution and laws. Article 35 of China's constitution, states the New York City Bar and IBA, guarantees "rights to free speech, assembly, association, and demonstration." Article 37 prohibits "unlawful detention or deprivation of restriction of citizens' freedom of the person." Moreover, states the IBA, China's constitution aligns in these articles with UN norms in the ICCPR and UDHR, and thus China is in breach simultaneously of its own governing laws and the universal standards to which it supposedly assents.

China's statutes: The New York City Bar protests that the security measures do not conform to Article 37 of China's Lawyers Law, which protects lawyers in carrying out their professional duties. And both the IBA and City Bar observe that the crackdown breaks China's Criminal Procedure Law provisions that state criminal suspects have right to appointment of a defender (Article 33) at the date where the person is first interrogated, and that family members should be informed of the rights of detained persons within twenty-four hours (Article 83).

Not least, the crackdown belies President Xi's own statements in the Four Comprehensives that he is committed to "govern the country according to law" and to advance the rule of law (New York City Bar). And, not to put too fine a point on it, the International Bar Association discreetly reminds China's leaders that "as an applicant" to membership in the UN Human Rights Council, its current actions may impair its election to that body.

15.3.3 *For Basic Legal Freedoms and Political Liberalism*

A substantive analysis of the content of public appeals and the normative ideals they embody reveals that the international legal complex centered on the bundle of values observed in studies of the legal complex and political liberalism. While the norms in each of these letters appeal to "the rule of law" as a conventional idiom of international legal and political discourse, in fact the self-description of the IBA more properly points to ideals more expansive than procedural rule of law.[7] The IBA seeks "to promote and protect human rights and the independence of the legal profession under a just rule of law." This admixture of different albeit complementary ideals can be better captured by the concept of political liberalism, as a bundle of commitments and behaviors observed by bar associations and the legal complex in many contexts.

Like classic formulations of rule of law, the discourse against China's leaders is built on a fundamental fear of rulers that appears to be a historical and comparative constant – the fear that persons will be "arbitrarily deprived of their liberty" (Lawyers for Lawyers) and thereafter indefinitely detained, held incommunicado, tortured, or executed without any protections in law or restraint of the ruler.

The China letters of protest demand basic legal freedoms from "intimidation, arrest, detention, and in many cases enforced disappearance" (Raskin 2015; International Bar Association 2015); from being "detained, arrested, held incommunicado, summoned, or otherwise having their freedom temporarily restricted" (Lawyers for Lawyers 2015; International Bar Association 2015); from being "missing" "held in their homes" and "under residential surveillance" (Raskin 2015); from "harassment" and "questioning" (Raskin 2015); from being held "not in an officially recognized place of detention" (Raskin 2015). In other words, cast negatively, the international legal complex demands that harms to civil liberties be forestalled by adherence, cast positively, to internationally inscribed norms that protect legal freedoms through "due process guarantees" (Raskin 2015; International Bar Assocation 2015), respect of *habeas corpus*, and other foundational civil rights.

As a condition of such protections, the international bodies place particular emphasis on lawyers' capacities to effect the protection of a subject's core rights. That has two sides: one is to give lawyers immediate access to clients; the other is that lawyers themselves in their everyday practices and lives be free from varieties of coercion and threat listed accurately by the Lawyers for Lawyers coalition and documented extensively in empirical research (Liu and Halliday 2016; Pils 2015).

---

[7] There is, of course, a massive literature on rule of law, its meanings, opposites or alternatives, and we do not treat that here. The concept of political liberalism, as it relates to the politics of the legal complex, contains most elements of a procedural or due process rule of law, but goes beyond it as an empirically derived bundle of activities for which lawyers will broadly mobilize in diverse times and places.

The subtext of the appeals to China's leaders, however, reveals that a premise for protection of basic legal freedoms inheres in foundational political freedoms that permit and encourage a robust civil society as a counterweight to the power of the state and the ever-present temptations to arbitrary rule. It is not simply that lawyers as individual counsel for clients are at risk. The letters and the crackdown make clear that it is lawyers acting collectively, as a professional or civil society group, that multiplies the fears of a repressive regime.

Moreover, it is notable that appeals to international norms point to a double characterization of lawyers. On the one hand, the lawyers and their relationships with each other, including rights to speak, associate, and assemble together, should permit them, we might interpolate, to establish some autonomy as a collectivity. That is, they should be permitted to act in microcosm as a civil society group.[8] This expectation is explicitly stated in the New York City Bar's reference to Article 23 of the UN Basic Principles on the Role of Lawyers. On the other hand, by implication, they should also be able to lead, combine, and advise other parts of civil society. It is instructive, then, that the letter by the Lawyers for Lawyers coalition is also copied to the UN Special Rapporteur on the promotion and protection of the right to freedom of opinion and expression, and that letter explicitly asserts that China's actions violate the UN Declaration on the Rights and Responsibility of Individuals, Groups and Organs of Society to Promote and Protect Universally Recognized Human Rights and Fundamental Protections.

Finally, it can be inferred that all the appeals for due process and adherence to universal norms are premised on a moderate state, that is, a state where it is possible to get a "fair trial," as the IBA demands. Significantly, these three letters scarcely mention trials, courts, or judges. It is true that the Lawyers for Lawyers coalition copied its letter to the UN Special Rapporteur on the Independence of Lawyers and Judges, and the IBA characterizes itself as an organization committed to the "just rule of law," which by implication requires an institution that has degrees of freedom to exercise legal restraint on arbitrary executive power. Yet perhaps there is also a realism in these letters that a one-party state cannot tolerate a moderation of its power in this way since it would challenge the very coercive foundations of that power.

15.4 INTERNATIONAL CIVIL SOCIETY AND THE PUBLIC SPHERE

To be effective, mobilization by legal complexes, indeed the integrity of the legal complex itself, requires constructive relations with civil society and public support.[9]

---

[8] This view is reinforced by the appeal on October 8, 2015 by many Chinese lawyers that they *not* be compelled to join the All China Lawyers Association, which they view as a coercive arm of the very state that fails to protect them.

[9] In practice, this proposition needs qualification because there are instances where a purely *legal* mobilization has an authority and effectiveness that might be eroded by certain types of civil society or public support. In general, however, being able to appeal to publics or build civil society coalitions has repeatedly been shown to be consequential (Gould 2006; Ghias 2012; Karpik 1999).

At least four types of support or leadership by international civil society are evident in the politics of the Wang Yu and lawyer crackdown.

First, rights organizations focused specifically on China have taken the lead; Human Rights in China, based in New York, and China Human Rights Defenders, based in Washington, DC. Initiatives for China: Citizen Power for China has been very active in its own right (e.g., through its listserve and online updates) and in alliance with others.[10]

Second, several international human rights organizations gave the China crackdown high priority. Amnesty International's Hong Kong Office, as we have seen, monitored developments daily and regularly updated its spreadsheet of information on every one of the more than 300 individuals caught up in this wave of repression. The tracking gave names, gender, professional status, date of detention, allegations against detainees (if known), type of detention (e.g., residential surveillance at designated location, criminal detention, unknown), criminal charge (if known), and whereabouts (almost all unknown). Human Rights Watch has issued public statements deploring the crackdown and has taken behind-the-scenes actions to strengthen the resolve of bar associations thought to be timid or quiescent in their response. And to reflect the broader civil society ramifications of the crackdown, Freedom House and Reporters without Borders have issued statements in alliances and coalitions with the legal complex and other civil society groups.

Third, insofar as the China crackdown threw a shadow over China's minorities and religious groups, these joined the protests. ChinaAid, an advocacy organization for rule of law and religious freedom, based in the US and with strong ties to China's Christian rights lawyers and US evangelicals, was active at events (e.g., the protest breakfast held in Washington during Xi's visit) and in publicizing information from its rich information channels inside China. Wang Yu and many of the other lawyers arrested and detained have championed China's minorities, and so the International Campaign for Tibet and the Uyghur Human Rights Project co-wrote the letter of appeal to President Obama.

Finally, and perhaps most importantly, the crackdown attracted extensive international media coverage. In English this included not only prestigious old print media (e.g., *South China Morning Post, New York Times, Washington Post, Guardian, Melbourne Age*), religious media (e.g., *Christian Post*), and broadcast media (e.g., Radio Free Asia, BBC World Service, Voice of America), but also new media, including the *Buzzfeed* story on Wang Yu and wide-ranging instantaneous coverage on Twitter. To a lesser degree coverage has been visible in French, German, and Spanish media.

---

[10] For instance, a public letter to President Obama from Initiatives for China was co-signed by Amnesty International, Freedom House, Human Rights Watch, Human Rights in China, ChinaAid, among others.

15.5 GOING FORWARD

This chapter has proposed that the logic of inquiry that Feeley and his collaborators have applied extensively to the politics of legal complexes within nation-states can and must be extended to an emergent concept of international legal complexes. However, the very preliminary findings and analysis offered here require far more extensive empirical investigations and theoretical elaboration. Feeley's singular contributions to the politics of judges over many years lead naturally to the question of the ways in which judges, either in their own voices or through other means of expressing their views on and off the bench, are able to join international mobilization on issues beyond their jurisdictions. Presumbly the complexity of configurations within an international legal complex will also magnify beyond those already observed in studies of nation-states.

In a world where politics for and against globalization have intensified, Feeley once again has pointed scholarship to new horizons where the prospects and limits of mobilization for basic legal freedoms can be focused on the legal profession and beyond. These vistas will also require attention to judges where Feeley's writings have been so influential and, as Feeley himself has shown, the embeddedness of judges in a more complex structure of legal occupations which we may observe in an international legal complex.

15.6 POSTSCRIPT

By her own admission, after long refusing to provide a televised false confession of her errors, and in the wake of receiving the American Bar Association International Human Rights Award on July 8, 2016, Wang Yu ultimately was coerced to confess on television to the complicity of her son with "anti-China forces" (Wang Yu 2018) as a condition of getting out of detention and her son getting to Australia. In August 2016, she and her husband were "released on bail" and exiled to Ulanhot in eastern Inner Mongolia, where they remained under 24/7 surveillance and frequent de facto house arrest. Her son was permitted to travel to Australia for further studies in January 2018. Wang Yu and her husband, Bao Longjun, now reside in Beijing, where their activities and movements remain closely monitored. They are prevented from practising law.

REFERENCES

American Bar Association. 2015. "ABA President William C. Hubbard statement on Lawyers in China." Accessed August 3, 2015. www.americanbar.org/news/abanews/aba-news-archives/2015/08/aba_president_willia.html.
  2016. "Chinese Lawyer Wang Yu to Receive Inaugural ABA International Human Rights Award." Accessed July 8, 2016. www.americanbar.org/news/abanews/aba-news-archives/2016/07/chinese_lawyer_wango.html.

Amnesty International. 2015. "China: Dozens of human rights lawyers targeted in nationwide crackdown." Accessed July 11, 2015. www.amnesty.org/en/lastest/news/2015/07/china-lawyers-targeted/

Aziz, Sadaf. 2012. "Liberal Protagonists? The Lawyers' Movement in Pakistan." In *Fates of Political Liberalism in the British Post-Colony: The Politics of the Legal Complex*, edited by Terence C. Halliday, Lucien Karpik, and Malcolm M. Feeley, 305–49. New York: Cambridge University Press.

Bell, David A. 1994. *Lawyers and Citizens: The Making of a Political Elite in Old Regime France*. Oxford: Oxford University Press.

———. 1997. "Barristers, Politics, and the Failure of Civil Society in Old Regime France." In *Lawyers and the Rise of Western Political Liberalism: Europe and North America from the Eighteenth to Twentieth Centuries*, edited by Terence C. Halliday and Lucien Karpik, 65–100. Oxford: Oxford University Press.

Buckley, Chris. 2015. "Lawyer Who Represented Churches in China Is Missing." *New York Times*, August 27, 2015. www.nytimes.com/2015/08/28/world/asia/lawyer-who-represented- churches-in-china-is-missing.html.

———. 2016. "Charges Against Chinese Rights Lawyers Draw Foreign Criticism." *New York Times*, January 18, 2016. www.nytimes.com/2016/01/19/world/asia/china- lawyers-arrest- reaction. html?rref=collection%2Ftimestopic%2FChina&action=click&contentCollection=world&region=stream&module=stream_unit&version=search&contentPl acement=8&pgtype=collection.

Burrage, Michael. 1989. "Revolution as a Starting Point for the Comparative Analysis of the French, American, and English Legal Professions." In *Lawyers in Society*, edited by Richard Abel and Philip Lewis. Berkeley: University of California Press.

———. 1997. "Mrs Thatcher Against the 'Little Republics': Ideology, Precedents, and Reactions." In *Lawyers and the Rise of Western Political Liberalism*, edited by Terence C. Halliday and Lucien Karpik, 125–66. Oxford: Oxford University Press.

Caster, Michael. 2017. *The People's Republic of the Disappeared: Stories from inside China's System for Enforced Disappearances*. United States: Safeguard Defenders.

China Aid. 2015. "Radio Free Asia: American Secretary of State Kerry meets relatives of China's Dissenting Prisoners." Accessed September 24, 2015. www.chinaaid.org/2015/10/rfa-american-secretary-of-state-kerry.html.

China Change. 2015. "The Work of Lawyer Zhang Kai: 'I Have God as My Backer.'" Accessed August 31, 2015. https://chinachange.org/2015/08/31/the-work-of- lawyer-zhang-kai-i-have-god-as-my-backer/.

China Human Rights Lawyers Concern Group. 2015. "101 China Lawyers' Statement Concerning Lawyer Wang Yu Disappearance." Accessed July 10, 2015. www.chrlawyers.hk/en/content/china-lawyers-statement-concerning-lawyer-wang-yu%E2%80%99-disappearance.

Chinese Human Rights Defenders. 2015. "China: Halt Police Operations Targeting Human Rights Lawyers as 'National Security' Threat." Accessed July 13, 2015. www.nchrd.org/2015/07/china-halt-police-operations-targeting-human-rights-lawyers-as-national-security-threat/.

Couso, Javier A. 2007. "The Role of Chile's Legal Complex in the Configuration of a Moderate State." In *The Legal Complex and Struggles for Political Liberalism*, edited by Terence C. Halliday, Lucien Karpik, and Malcolm M. Feeley, 315–44. Oxford: Hart Publishing.

De, Rohit. 2012. "Emasculating the Executive: The Federal Court and Civil Liberties in Late Colonial India: 1942–1944." In *Fates of Political Liberalism in the British Post-Colony:*

The Politics of the Legal Complex, edited by Terence C. Halliday, Lucien Karpik, and Malcolm M. Feeley, 59–90. New York: Cambridge University Press.

European Union External Action. 2015. "Statement by the Spokesperson on Recent Developments in the Human Rights Situation in China." July 15, 2015.

Feeley, Malcolm M. 2012. "Judge and Company: Courts, Constitutionalism and the Legal Complex." In *Fates of Political Liberalism in the British Post-Colony: The Politics of the Legal Complex*, edited by Terence C. Halliday, Lucien Karpik, and Malcolm M. Feeley, 493–522. New York: Cambridge University Press.

Feeley, Malcolm M. and Setsuo Miyazawa. 2007. "The State, Civil Society, and the Legal Complex in Modern Japan: Continuity and Change." In *The Legal Complex and Struggles for Political Liberalism*, edited by Terence C. Halliday, Lucien Karpik, and Malcolm M. Feeley, 151–92. Oxford: Hart Publishing.

Ghias, Shoaib A. 2012. "Miscarriage of Chief Justice: Lawyers, Media, and the Struggle for Judicial Independence in Pakistan." In *Fates of Political Liberalism in the British Post-Colony: The Politics of the Legal Complex*, edited by Terence C. Halliday, Lucien Karpik, and Malcolm M. Feeley, 340–77. New York: Cambridge University Press.

Ginsburg, Tom. 2007. "Law and the Liberal Transformation of the Northeast Asian Legal Complex in Korea and Taiwan." In *Fighting for Political Freedom: Comparative Studies of the Legal Complex and Political Change*, edited by Terence C. Halliday, Lucien Karpik, and Malcolm M. Feeley, 43–64. Oxford: Hart Publishing.

Gould, Jeremy. 2012. "Postcolonial Liberalism and the Legal Complex in Zambia: Elegy or Triumph?" In *Fates of Political Liberalism in the British Post-Colony: The Politics of the Legal Complex*, edited by Terence C. Halliday, Lucien Karpik, and Malcolm M. Feeley, 412–54. New York: Cambridge University Press.

Graver, Hans Petter. 2015. "The Legal Complex: Denmark and Norway under German Occupation 1940–1945." Presented at the workshop, The Legal Complex and Political Liberalism in the Nordic Countries: A Case of Exceptionalism? University of California, Berkeley, Boalt School of Law, October 3, 2015.

Guardian. 2016. "China Must End Its Intimidation and Detention of Human Rights Lawyers." Letters, January 17, 2016. www.theguardian.com/world/2016/jan/18/china-must-end-its-intimidation- and-detention-of-human-rights-lawyers.

Guarnieri, Carlo 2007. "Lawyers and Statist Liberalisms in Italy." In *The Legal Complex and Struggles for Political Liberalism*, edited by Terence C. Halliday, Lucien Karpik, and Malcolm M. Feeley, 439–62. Oxford: Hart Publishing.

Halliday, Terence and Sida Liu. 2007a. "Birth of a Liberal Moment? Looking through a One-Way Mirror at Lawyers' Defense of Criminal Defendants in China." In *The Legal Complex and Struggles for Political Liberalism*, edited by Terence C. Halliday, Lucien Karpik, and Malcolm M. Feeley, 65–108. Oxford: Hart Publishing.

Halliday, Terence C. 1987. *Beyond Monopoly: Lawyers, State Crises, and Professional Empowerment*. Chicago: University of Chicago Press.

2010. "The Fight for Basic Legal Freedoms: Mobilization by the Legal Complex." in *Global Perspectives on the Rule of Law*, edited by James J. Heckman, Robert L. Nelson, and Lee Cabatingan, 210–40. London: Routledge-Cavendish.

2013. "Why the Legal Complex is Integral to Theories of Consequential Courts." In *Consequential Courts: Judicial Roles in Global Perspective*, edited by Diana Kapiszewski, Gordon Silverstein, and Robert A. Kagan, 337–48. New York: Cambridge University Press.

Halliday, Terence C. and Lucien Karpik. 1997a. *Lawyers and the Rise of Western Political Liberalism: Europe and North American from the Eighteenth to Twentieth Centuries.* Oxford: Clarendon Press.

    1997b. "Politics Matter: A Comparative Theory of Lawyers in the Making of Political Liberalism." In *Lawyers and the Rise of Western Political Liberalism: Europe and North American from the Eighteenth to Twentieth Centuries*, edited by Terence C. Halliday and Lucien Karpik, 15–64. Oxford: Clarendon Press.

Halliday, Terence C., Lucien Karpik, and Malcolm M. Feeley. 2007a. *Fighting for Political Freedom: Comparative Studies of the Legal Complex for Political Change.* Oxford: Hart Publishing.

    2007b. "The Legal Complex and Struggles for Political Liberalism." In *Fighting for Political Freedom: Comparative Studies of the Legal Complex for Political Change*, edited by Terence C. Halliday, Lucien Karpik, and Malcolm M. Feeley, 1–42. Oxford: Hart Publishing.

    2012. *Fates of Political Liberalism in the British Post-Colony: The Politics of the Legal Complex.* New York: Cambridge University Press.

Halliday, Terence C. and Sida Liu. 2007b. "Birth of a Liberal Moment? Looking through a One-Way Mirror at Lawyers' Defense of Criminal Defendants in China." In *Fighting for Political Freedom: Comparative Studies of the Legal Complex and Political Change*, edited by Terence C. Halliday, Lucien Karpik, and Malcolm M. Feeley, 65–108. Oxford: Hart Publishing.

Initiatives for China. 2015a. "Joint Open Letter to International Olympic Committee regarding Beijing's bid for the Winter Olympics 2022." Accessed July 23, 2015. www.initiativesforchina.org/?p=1990.

    2015b. "Protest Against Arrest of Human Rights Lawyers in China." Accessed August 11, 2015. www.initiativesforchina.org/?p=2002.

International Bar Association. 2015. "Open letter to His Excellency Mr Xi Jinping, President of the People's Republic of China, from the IBAHRI." Accessed July 22, 2015. www.ibanet.org/Article/NewDetail.aspx?ArticleUid=fbd9f17b-5a7e-4111-bec3-fb5ad75066df.

International Service for Human Rights. 2015. "China: Release Wang Yu and other detained and disappeared human rights defenders." Accessed November 11, 2015. www.ishr.ch/news/china-release-wang-yu-and-other-detained-and-disappeared-human-rights-defenders.

Jones, Carol. 2007. "'Dissolving the People': Capitalism, Law and Democracy in Hong Kong." In *Fighting for Political Freedom: Comparative Studies of the Legal Complex and Political Liberalism*, edited by Terence C. Halliday, Lucien Karpik, and Malcolm M. Feeley, 109–50. Oxford: Hart Publishing.

Karpik, Lucien. 1988a. "Lawyers and Politics in France, 1814–1950: the State, the Market, and the Public." *Law and Social Inquiry* 13 (4): 707–36.

    1995. *Les Avocats: Entre l'Etat, le public et le marche.* Paris: Editions Gallimard.

    1997. "Builders of Liberal Society: French Lawyers and Politics." In *Lawyers and the Rise of Western Political Liberalism: Europe and North America from the Eighteenth to Twentieth Centuries*, edited by Terence C. Halliday and Lucien Karpik, 101–23. Oxford: Oxford University Press.

    1999. *French Lawyers: A Study in Collective Action, 1274–1994.* Oxford: Oxford University Press.

Karpik, Lucien and Terence C. Halliday. 2011a. "The Legal Complex." *Annual Review of Law and Social Science* 7: 217–36.

Kirby, John. 2015. Press Statement. US Department of State. July 12, 2015.
Lawyers for Lawyers. 2015. "China: Open Letter to President for Massive Wave of Arrests." Accessed July 22, 2015. www.advocatenvooradvocaten.nl/10870/china-open-letter-to-president-for- massive-wave-of-arrests/.
Ledford, Kenneth F. 1997. "Lawyers and the Limits of Liberalism: the German Bar in the Weimar Republic." In *Lawyers and the Rise of Western Political Liberalism: Europe and North America from the Eighteenth to Twentieth Centuries*, edited by Terence C. Halliday and Lucien Karpik, 229–64. Oxford: Oxford University Press.
Liu, Sida and Terence C. Halliday. 2016. *The Politics of Defense: Lawyers and Criminal Justice in China*. New York: Cambridge University Press.
Massoud, Mark. 2012. "Lawyers and the Disintegration of the Legal Complex in Sudan." In *Fortunes and Misfortunes of Political Liberalism: The Legal Complex in the Post-Colony*, edited by Terence C. Halliday, Lucien Karpik, and Malcolm M. Feeley, 192–218. New York: Cambridge University Press.
Mate, Manoj. 2012. "'Priests in the Temple of Justice': The Indian Legal Complex and the Basic Structure Doctrine." In *Fates of Political Liberalism in the British Post-Colony: The Politics of the Legal Complex*, edited by Terence C. Halliday, Lucien Karpik, and Malcolm M. Feeley, 112–48. New York: Cambridge University Press.
Moustafa, Tamir. 2007a. "Mobilising the Law in an Authoritarian State: The Legal Complex in Contemporary Egypt." In *The Legal Complex and Struggles for Political Liberalism*, edited by Terence C. Halliday, Lucien Karpik, and Malcolm M. Feeley, 193–281. Oxford: Hart Publishing.
  2007b. *The Struggle for Constitutional Power: Law, Politics, and Economic Development in Egypt*. New York: Cambridge University Press.
Munir, Daud. 2012. "From Judicial Autonomy to Regime Transformation: The Role of the Lawyers' Movement in Pakistan." In *Fates of Political Liberalism in the British Post-Colony: The Politics of the Legal Complex*, edited by Terence C. Halliday, Lucien Karpik, and Malcolm M. Feeley, 378–411. New York: Cambridge University Press.
Nonet, Philippe and Philip Selznick. 1978. *Law and Society in Transition: Towards Responsive Law*. New York: Harper Books.
Perdomo, Rogelio Perez 2007. "Lawyers and Political Liberalism in Venezuela." In *The Legal Complex and Struggles for Political Liberalism*, edited by Terence C. Halliday, Lucien Karpik, and Malcolm M. Feeley, 345–60. Oxford: Hart Publishing.
Phillips, Tom. 2016. "China's Pursuit of Rights Lawyers Signals Aggressive Push Against 'Subversion.'" *Guardian*, January 14, 2016. www.theguardian.com/world/2016/jan/14/chinas-pursuit-of-human-rights-lawyers-signals-aggressive-push-against-subversion.
Pils, Eva. 2015. *China's Human Rights Lawyers: Advocacy and Resistance*. London and New York: Routledge.
Powell, Michael J. 1988. *From Patrician to Professional Elite: the Transformation of the New York City Bar Association*. New York: Russell Sage.
Rajah, Jothie. 2010. "Can the Foreign Lawyer Speak? Singapore Encounters Foreign Bar Associations." Paper presented at the *Law and Society Association Annual Meeting*, May 23, 2010, Chicago, IL.
  2012. "Lawyers, Politics and Publics: State Management of Lawyers and Legitimacy in Singapore." In *The Fates of Political Liberalism in the British Post-Colony: The Politics of the Legal Complex*, edited by Terence C. Halliday, Lucien Karpik, and Malcolm M. Feeley, 149–92. New York: Cambridge University Press.

Raskin, Deborah. 2015. Letter on behalf of NYC Bar Association to Xi Jinping. July 28, 2015. www.hrichina.org/sites/default/files/nyc_bar_association-letter_to_h.e._xi_jinping_re_chinese_lawyers_7.28.15.pdf.

Rueschemeyer, Dietrich. 1997. "State, Capitalism, and the Organization of Legal Counsel: Examining an Extreme Case – the Prussian Bar, 1700–1914." In *Lawyers and the Rise of Western Political Liberalism: Europe and North America from the Eighteenth to Twentieth Centuries*, edited by Terence C. Halliday and Lucien Karpik, 207–28. Oxford: Oxford University Press.

South China Morning Post. 2015. "Chinese rights lawyers and staff of law firm missing as police search office." July 10, 2015. www.scmp.com/news/china/society/article/1835741/chinese-rights-lawyers-and-staff-law-firm-mission-police-search.

United Nations Human Rights: Office of the High Commisioner. 2015. "'Lawyers need to be protected not harassed' – UN experts urge China to halt detentions." Accessed July 16, 2015. www.ohchr.org/EN/NewsEvents/Pages/DisplayNews.aspx?NewsID=16241&LangID=E.

US Department of State. 2015. "U.S. Ambassador to the United Nations Samantha Power to Launch #FreeThe20 Women Political Prisoners and Prisoners of Concern Campaign." Accessed August 31, 2015. https://2009-2017.state.gov/r/pa/prs/ps/2015/08/246491.htm.

VonDoepp, Peter. 2012. "Legal Complexes and the Fight for Political Liberalism in New African Democracies: Comparative Insights from Malawi, Zambia and Namibia." In *Fates of Political Liberalism in the British Post-Colony: The Politics of the Legal Complex*, edited by Terence C. Halliday, Lucien Karpik, and Malcolm M. Feeley, 455–90. New York: Cambridge University Press.

Wang Yu. 2017. "My Endless Nightmare." In *The Peoples Republic of the Disappeared: Stories from inside China's System for Enforced Disappearances*, edited by Michael Caster, 65–84. United States: Safeguard Defenders.

2018. "709 Crackdown Three Years On: Mother and Lawyer Reveals Brutality Against Her Teenage Son for the First Time." Accessed October 24, 2018. https://chinachange.org/2018/07/01/709-crackdown-three-years-on-mother-and-lawyer-reveals-brutality-against-her-teenage-son-for-the-first-time/.

16

The Legal Profession's Promise of Justice: Choices and Challenges in Legal and Sociolegal Work

Mark Fathi Massoud[1]

INTRODUCTION

This chapter provides a socio-legal perspective on justice in the legal profession and in legal scholarship by bringing together the values of idealism and humanism with ambition, materialism, and science. For lawyers and judges, the practice of justice may be guided by contradictory pulls toward public-spirited idealism (for instance, helping an indigent client or promoting social transformation) and self-serving materialism (for instance, increasing personal earnings or improving reputation). For legal scholars, studies of law emanate from sometimes conflicting impulses to build social theory and the rule of law, adopt social scientific research designs, and achieve personal goals that improve one's renown. Exposing these tensions in pursuing justice and in writing about justice reveals the promises and perils of legal practice and legal scholarship. Just as lawyers and judges face their own conflicting commitments between materialism and idealism, scholars who study them must decide whether and how to insert empirical materials and normative values into their research. In the long term, understanding how scholars use empirical materials and promote normative values involves questioning conventional wisdom, paying attention to context, and thinking comparatively.

Malcolm M. Feeley's oeuvre, which inspired this chapter and book volume, exemplifies how lawyers and judges work to secure justice and how legal scholars can combine empirical methods with humanistic values to study the legal profession. Feeley's solo and collaborative scholarship, spanning more than forty years, has been central to literature on the practices of judges and lawyers in diverse political contexts, from lower courts in the United States to apex courts in East Asia and former British colonies (Feeley 1979, 1983; Becker and Feeley 1973; Feeley and Rubin 1998, Feeley and Miyazawa 2002; Halliday, Karpik, and Feeley 2007, 2012).

---

[1] The author thanks Marjory Ruiz for valuable research assistance and Richard Abel, Philip Lewis, Adam Millard-Ball, Gordon Silverstein, Martin Shapiro, and the editors and anonymous reviewers for helpful feedback. This chapter would also not be possible without the generosity of respondents in Sudan, South Sudan, Somalia, and Somaliland, where the author has studied the legal profession's promise of justice.

Feeley's scholarship is also known for its robust contribution to social theory and social equity, including through his self-reflective dedication to racial justice (Feeley 2010; see also Lempert 2010; Gómez 2010; Seron 2016). Feeley's commitments to social theory and social equity are models for students of law and politics, and form part of his career engagement with social and legal theorists. These theorists include, most notably, Philip Selznick (who spent much of his career urging social scientists to consider the values of morality, humanity, and personhood) and Martin Krygier (who has devoted much of his professional life to building a social theory of the rule of law). Together, the examples of Feeley, Selznick, and Krygier encourage legal scholars to understand the influences on lawyers and judges, and to reflect upon the scholarly urges to provide empirical data that shape policy solutions or to put forward a humanistic commitment to values, social theory, and the rule of law.

This chapter proceeds in three parts. In Section 16.1, I explain how a culture of materialism and idealism exists in the legal profession and shapes how lawyers and judges commit to and practice social justice. Next, I explain in Section 16.2 how scholars face their own tensions related to promoting justice, as they draw on a combination of data-driven social science practices, policy goals, and humanistic or theoretical aspirations. Finally, I conclude with implications of these tensions in the legal and scholarly pursuits of justice, including for socio-legal scholars thinking comparatively about the legal profession and, more generally, about law's power in society. In addition to interpreting Feeley's writing on law and courts, I also draw from scholarship in legal and social theory, my own research in Sudan and Somalia, and a ninety-minute personal interview I conducted with Malcolm Feeley.

16.1 THE LEGAL PROFESSION'S MATERIALISM AND IDEALISM

The culture of the legal profession – lawyers practicing law and judges hearing cases – exists along a spectrum between two contradictory goals. On the one hand, lawyers and judges commit in their personal and work lives to professionalism and securing the rule of law and the rights of their clients or the underserved. On the other hand, as a profession they also protect themselves by restricting entry – tempering the profession's idealism with its materialism. Thus, the legal profession seems at once self-serving and other-regarding. This section analyzes these tensions between materialism and idealism in the legal profession.

16.1.1 *The Legal Profession's Materialism*

Sociologists have long debated problems associated with allocating work to professions, from architects and accountants to real estate agents, physicians, and firefighters (Barber 1963; MacDonald 1995; Albert and Weeden 2011). On the one hand, professions promote a "community interest" as an alternative to self-interest (Barber

1963, 672). They also act as "stabilizing elements in society" and "centers of resistance to crude forces which threaten . . . peaceful evolution" (Carr-Saunders and Wilson 1933, 497). But professions also enable selected persons to gain a monopoly over problem solving and routinized tasks in a specialized area. Ultimately, this monopoly helps members of a profession to maximize material gain, including economic wealth, political power, or social prestige.

The legal profession is no exception to the critiques mounted on professions. In the United States, for instance, the legal profession controls "the production of producers" through high-cost entry requirements, including professional examinations (Abel 1985). These barriers disproportionately impact ethnic minorities, women, and those with lower incomes, who may be unable to afford the time or money associated with entry into the profession. To that end, an industry has emerged in the United States and overseas for aspiring legal professionals: coaching for law school admissions tests, hornbooks and outlines for law school course examinations, and preparation programs for bar exams. Once in the profession, experienced lawyers control access to resources and will opt to fight or settle disputes when it suits their clients' goals (He and Su 2013). Likening lawyers to a self-determined priestly class, legal historian Robert W. Gordon (1996, 1013) writes that American lawyers since the nineteenth century have portrayed themselves as sacred "statesmen" with "a direct line to God's mind through their knowledge of the principles of legal science."

Private lawyers in the United States – including corporate defense counsel billing hourly rates and personal injury lawyers taking contingency fees – typically choose clients and cases most likely to cover attorneys' fees, ensure practice growth, and improve reputation. Lawyers in China have also been known to screen potential clients to avoid representing persons with labor claims, due to lawyers' own economic insecurity (Michelson 2006). In the United States and overseas, even pro bono practices and legal aid programs – assisting clients unable to afford lawyers – seem to take place within a system that promotes materialism. Law school clinics and "privileged lawyers" must decide between worthy and unworthy calls for assistance while "relying on private philanthropy" (Abel 2010, 2443–44; see also Cummings 2004, cited in Abel 2010, n. 8).

Originally published in 1976, Gerald Stern's book *The Buffalo Creek Disaster* is a remarkable example of how pro bono practices may help lawyers and their firms garner prestige or achieve other material goals (Stern 2008). Among the most widely assigned texts to first-year law students – and taught for years in Malcolm Feeley's undergraduate courses at the University of California, Berkeley – the book is a personal account of Stern's representation of hundreds of clients in a class-action environmental disaster suit against a coal mining company and its parent corporation, Pittston. Stern describes how his law firm, which worked more than 40,000 hours on the case from 1972 to 1974, received nearly $3 million in contingency fees from a $13.5 million settlement agreement between plaintiffs' lawyers and the Pittston corporation. Although Stern was unable to obtain Pittston's acceptance of responsibility for the disaster, he concludes that private law firms nevertheless "do well by doing good" (Stern 2008, 302). In the end, the law firm prevails in this book about the legal profession's spirit of justice. But as a class-action lawyer, Stern laments how he gradually lost touch with his clients and their stories of suffering while he became absorbed in discovery, other pretrial actions, settlement hearings, and the choices of venue, remedies, and defenses (Stern 2008). Indeed, litigation can often be consumed by this kind of "legalism," defined as rule-following, formalism, and the pursuit of technical legal details and procedures (Shklar 1964).

Lawyers seeking to do good overseas may also end up doing better for themselves and other elites, and potentially harming the welfare of the poor. In the 1960s and 1970s, American and European aid groups, lawyers, and legal scholars rushed to add legal development to foreign economic development programs, particularly through legal reform projects aimed at Latin America, Africa, and elsewhere in the global South. This wave of what became known as "law and development," however, began to collapse by the mid-1970s, when Western scholars began to question openly whether the export of a "liberal legalism" paradigm benefitted repressive leaders in countries with weak rule-of-law infrastructures (Trubek and Galanter 1974; see also Dezalay and Garth 2002). While those involved in these projects did not persist once they felt their activities were bringing about more harm than good, they also did not endure the harms that the poor suffered. Instead, their experiences helped to build their professional careers.

A half-century after these law and development programs reached their heyday, lawyers involved in international human rights projects in war-torn contexts continue to face similar critiques that well-meaning programs designed to build legal institutions may instead thwart democracy and the rule of law (for a review, see Massoud 2016a; see also Branch 2011, 2007; Kennedy 2002; Mutua 2008). These lawyers may also be creating competitive markets for civil society groups to use the discourse of human rights strategically in order to receive funds from foreign aid agencies, whether or not the members of these new civil society groups actually believe that human rights discourse is a moral or legal call to action (Bob 2002; Englund 2004, 2006; Massoud 2016c). During my own fieldwork in Sudan just after the country's civil war (Massoud 2013), I recall meeting a European lawyer working for a United Nations agency; he told me frankly that he hoped the United Nations would renew his employment contract for another year not because of his work to build the rule of law in Sudan, but because his high expatriate salary would facilitate a home purchase upon his return to Europe.

More recently, lawyers I met in Somaliland, the autonomous northern region of Somalia, discussed the growing legal aid industry in post-conflict settings. Law students and graduates regularly receive educational scholarships, training, and job offers from United Nations agencies and UN-funded legal aid offices that encourage new lawyers to represent indigent clients in courts. These international and nongovernmental organizations provide stable employment and, in the long term, they build a new kind of legal profession in war-torn societies (Massoud 2015).

Lawyers have also sought to dominate international business transactions and dispute resolution. Private international lawyers have become principal actors in the global marketplace, helping to formalize business deals across national borders and to resolve disputes behind closed doors, using international arbitration tribunals (Dezalay and Garth 1996). These transactions and dispute processes not only serve the legal profession's bottom line. They also function at the behest of resource-rich authoritarian regimes that use the guarantee of private international arbitration schemes to attract foreign investment and maintain control over domestic courts (Massoud 2014).

Critical turns in the research on the legal profession continue to reveal how legal professionals' materialism shapes their political or pecuniary ambitions, across contexts and epochs. Notable examples come from the work of Richard Abel, Philip Lewis, Yves Dezalay, and Bryant Garth, who show how lawyers and judges use the profession's prestige to catapult themselves to political or financial power (Abel and Lewis 1988a, 1988b, 1989, 1996; Dezalay and Garth 1996, 2002, 2010). In England, for instance, lawyers since the eighteenth century have sought market dominance by controlling the number of barristers and solicitors, in part by focusing on technical competence and tutelage. In so doing, lawyers have limited both "competition from fellow professionals" and dispute resolution services offered by nonprofessionals (Abel 1986, 5, 18).

In colonial Egypt, lawyers in the late nineteenth century perpetuated ideas of the universality of the rule of law and Egyptian nationalism while they simultaneously supported "landowners ... the king's power, and British influence" (Ziadeh 1968, 407). Similarly, in contemporary Russia and Hungary, politicians trained in the law use legal language and "governance checklists" – for instance, touting their trained judiciaries, enforced laws, and rights to appeal – to create legal "loopholes" that repress opposition groups while facilitating the material gains of political inner circles (Scheppele 2015, 2013).

In East and South Asia, legal elites co-opted by colonial and postcolonial state building projects wielded enormous political power to create a legal industry that serves empire (Dezalay and Garth 2010; see also Silverstein 2008). Similarly, following Sudan's 1956 independence from British and Egyptian colonial rule, judges and lawyers working in the Sudan High Court sought to build the rule of law on the foundation of English common law (Massoud 2018, 2013). But later, for more than a generation after the 1970s, some of these same democratic-minded legal elites – still carrying banners of nationalism or the rule of law – used legal discourse and their respected knowledge and positions to justify authoritarian governments' systematic dismantling of the rule of law. In some cases, they openly took advantage of opportunities to join military coups and achieve political goals and ambitions, such as attempting to annex Sudan to Egypt (Massoud 2012).

In sum, materialism exists in various forms within the legal profession, and even lawyers engaged in pro bono and legal aid programs may end up serving their own or their profession's monopolistic interests. For centuries, across the spaces that humans have occupied from East Asia to Africa and Eastern Europe to North and South America, lawyers and judges at best have served themselves or their profession, and at worst they have been the human weapons of dictators.

16.1.2 The Legal Profession's Idealism

An alternative account can be given of the work of lawyers and judges. It is an account of the role that those with legal training play in securing political and democratic freedoms, sometimes in hostile settings and at great personal risk. Reading this account of legal idealism alongside its counterpart of materialism, described above, reveals how the legal profession's pursuit of materialism is tempered by a sense of moral duty to pursue justice and defend human rights and freedoms (Simon 2000).

In this account of the legal profession's promise of justice, courts become central institutions in the fight for political liberalism as lawyers and judges navigate between complex institutional ideals and incentives (Feeley 1973, 2012; Halliday, Karpik, and Feeley 2007). Lower courts are particularly important sites in the fight for political freedoms. Whereas the complexity of a court bureaucracy may leave a novice bewildered, under the right conditions this bureaucracy may also help this novice to achieve justice (Ewick and Silbey 1998; Feeley 1973).

Legal idealism matters insofar as institutions and structures allow it to flourish. That is, while judges are often tasked with delivering judgments on politically salient matters, courts rarely can act alone, particularly because their power is limited vis-à-vis other branches of government (Bickel 1962; see also Dworkin 1986; Rosenberg 2008). In addition, judges who join the fight for political liberalism – in democratic and authoritarian states alike – require responsive government institutions and an active bar or civil society to bring causes and cases forward (Feeley 2012; see also Ghias 2011; Massoud 2011; Moustafa 2007).

Given these substantial constraints that judges and lawyers face in the practice of justice, scholars have sought to account for legal idealism. Malcolm Feeley's scholarship provides an example of how scholars have responded to decades of research in comparative sociology and comparative law that documents how legal professions coalesce into groups of elites. In his empirical studies of criminal trials, Feeley watched prosecutors, defense lawyers, and judges toil for justice, despite the obstacles they faced and regardless of whether they succeeded (Feeley 1979). Even prosecutors, he found, felt a sense of role morality, or moral duty to their profession and the people it serves. These empirical findings seemed to contradict those of other scholars who were busy exposing lawyers' "grubby materialism" (personal interview with Malcolm M. Feeley, June 2015). Feeley's accounts reveal how the legal profession's idealism may be taken seriously in scholarship on courts. Like repetitive religious practices that generate conviction, the routinized practices of prosecutors, defense lawyers, and lower court judges are the daily tools of ethical persons, and they come to represent a new faith in the adversarial system of justice (Feeley 1987).

It is this desire to account for idealism that attracted Feeley to collaborate on two books with Terence Halliday and Lucien Karpik. According to Feeley, he joined Halliday and Karpik after reviewing their earlier book (Halliday and Karpik 1998) and telling them that they needed to add judges and judicial politics to their study of lawyers, at which point Halliday and Karpik invited Feeley to join them as a coeditor of the next two volumes (personal interview with Malcolm M. Feeley, June 2015). In their 2007 and 2012 books, the three authors then examined this practice of legal idealism across national contexts. Their organizing rubric is a "legal complex" of "legally-trained occupations, centered on lawyers and judges" (Halliday, Karpik, and Feeley 2007, 3). Their books reveal how – across cases in Africa and Asia, from Egypt, Malawi, and Sudan to Pakistan, India, and Singapore – lawyers are present, and, with judges, they have labored to produce social justice and political change through their legal work and status. That is, rather than seeking to gain political power, to increase salary, or to earn other material benefits, these professionals have engaged in "political lawyering" to build national independence, defend human rights, and promote basic human dignities.

16.1.3 *From the Legal Profession to the Legal Complex*

The cases contributing to contemporary studies of the legal complex are united by their common investigation into the work that lawyers and judges do, both inside and outside of courtrooms. Together they ask a range of important questions about the practices of legal professionals. For instance, in what ways do the repetitive practices of law – taking cases before courts, asking judges to resolve disputes, administering justice through the work of executive branch agencies – shape politics and society? To what extent do lawyers and judges use politically important cases to fight against colonial domination and hoist the flags of national independence and political liberalism? And to what extent do higher courts in British postcolonies use English common law to promote the rule of law? This comparative examination of the legal complex concludes that lawyers and judges across countries and time periods have engaged in a common set of practices: lobbying and working – often at great personal risk – to ensure that their societies promote judicial independence, a moderate state, and a robust interpretation of the rule of law that citizens can rely on for security.

The book at the heart of this investigation into the legal complex is Halliday, Karpik, and Feeley's 2012 volume, *Fates of Political Liberalism in the British Post-Colony*. Using cases from diverse countries across Africa and in South and Southeast

Asia, the authors show how different types of political regimes shape the extent to which lawyers help themselves, help their societies, or both. Developing theory inductively, Halliday, Karpik, and Feeley categorize three regime types that influence the extent to which the legal complex can achieve the goal of political liberalism. First are *liberal-legalist regimes* in which legal elites in a newly independent country emphasize the importance of the rule of law, diversity, or fundamental rights. Second are *absolutist regimes* in which, unlike liberal-legalist regimes, legal elites promote law to coerce or repress citizens or minority groups. In absolutist regimes, political liberalism becomes a grave threat to political authority. Third are *volatile regimes* in which legal elites move along a spectrum between promoting and destroying the rule of law, depending on their relative power or threats from minority groups, war, or economic crisis. Sometimes liberal-legalist, absolutist, and volatile regimes appear in the same places across different time periods, just as in some volatile cases the same legal elites might adopt a liberal-legalist approach or an absolutist approach when different political opportunities emerge (Massoud 2012).

Additional examples of a spirit of justice within the legal profession extend the work of Halliday, Karpik, and Feeley. In China, for instance, lawyers who initially resisted involvement in politically salient cases or prodemocracy movements often are pushed into the fight unwittingly after being arrested by the regime. State media also influence how the public views the legal profession, by either lionizing or demonizing lawyers (Jacobs and Buckley 2015). Research on Tunisian lawyers reveals how they became the overseers of the new government in the extraordinary moments following the government's collapse during the Arab Spring (Gobe and Salaymeh 2016). Indeed, two of four organizations awarded the 2015 Nobel Peace Prize for bringing stability to Tunisia in the aftermath of its 2011 revolution – the Tunisian Human Rights League and the Tunisian Order of Lawyers – were law-related groups. Those with legal training who take government jobs in zones of extreme conflict, then, may quickly be maneuvering themselves from persons who resist the law to persons who write the law.

Feeley and his colleagues and contemporaries have urged scholars to think about justice with caution. That is, justice is not so much a "thing" as much as it is a contingent and layered process. Achieving the promise of justice (or democracy or political liberalism) depends on the court venue, the kind of legal system, the particular political philosophy animating that legal system, and the political conditions and regime type (Feeley 1987). Thus, any theory of justice must reflect the political, historical, and social context of the system in which legal professionals operate, and their relative ability to adopt an idealistic approach to their work.

To summarize so far, the two accounts in this section of the chapter underscore the complexity of the pursuit of justice, as lawyers and judges are pulled toward materialistic and idealistic goals. These legal professionals, in the long term, may be serving the two masters of materialism and idealism (Bell 1995). Acknowledging the divergent goals of lawyers and judges is a first step toward studying how they choose between materialism and idealism, and whether and how they combine or circumscribe these goals.

16.2 TAKING VALUES SERIOUSLY IN LEGAL SCHOLARSHIP

An analogous story may be told of tensions within legal scholarship. One could first draw a contrast between legal scholars' commitments to social justice and the protectionism of the legal academy – an academic guild of highly paid professors whose students control who can publish in law reviews that charge costly submission fees and use a unique citation system (Tamanaha 2012). A more useful contrast, however, may be found by seeing empirical study as another version of materiality. That is, scholars may be torn between presenting their normative values and opinions, conducting empirical research, or both.

This section outlines how law has made itself into both a positive and a normative discipline, as legal scholars draw themselves into social science, social theory, and social change. On the one hand, scholars commit to empirical data, methods, and rigor. On the other hand, they often also commit to values, such as the promotion of the rule of law and human rights. Discussing these sometimes conflicting commitments – in relation to the conflicting commitments that lawyers and judges face – helps to illuminate how lawyers, judges, and the scholars who study them each approach their professions, and the tensions and contradictions they face in their work.

16.2.1 *Producing Social Science through Empirical Claims*

Legal and socio-legal scholars have long been attracted to producing empirically grounded claims and using data to study the functions of law in politics and society. Similarly, "new institutionalist" approaches in political science have been based on a quest to promote empirical and scientific rigor in the study of law and courts (Gillman 2004; Smith 1988). Studies of the ways that rights discourse or litigation impact citizens' decisions and legal work have drawn on various methods, including fieldwork, surveys, ethnography, and participant-observation research (Bumiller 1987; McCann 1994; Nielsen 2000; Chua 2014a; Massoud 2016b). Drawing in part from quantitative approaches in law and economics and in behavioral economics, the expanding field of empirical legal studies has led to the creation of major university centers on the topic – at Berkeley, Cornell, and University College London, among other places – and to a number of national and international conferences devoted to empirical legal studies. An increasing number of scholarly studies of law in the United States and overseas use archival, qualitative, or quantitative evidence to understand discourses of law and the political functions of courts. (For some recent examples, see Obasogie 2014 and Gómez 2010 on race in the United States; Cichowski 2007 and Kawar 2015 on Europe; Couso 2003, Brinks 2007, and Kapiszewski 2012 on Latin America; Ellett 2013, Klug 2000, and Massoud 2013 on Africa; Moustafa 2007 on Egypt and Moustafa 2013a and Moustafa 2013b on Malaysia; Sharafi 2014 on South Asia; Stern 2013 and Erie 2016 on China; and Chua 2014a and Cheesman 2015 on Southeast Asia. For empirical legal scholarship that investigates international courts and arbitration tribunals, see Huneeus 2013, Hafner-Burton 2013, Massoud 2014, Merry 2006, Shaffer 2012, and Stacy 2009.)

Malcolm Feeley's work has taken a central role in the chorus of scholars who promote a deep, contextual, and empirical understanding of the work of lawyers and judges. Scholars too focused on the goals of the legal profession, Feeley has argued, risk losing touch with the organizational procedures and bureaucratic processes that create incentives to comply or sanctions for noncompliance (Feeley 1973). Thus, studies of the goals of legal professionals are incomplete without an empirical understanding of the structures within which lawyers and judges operate, and the compliance incentives created by those structures. These incentives may be revealed through site-intensive study of bureaucracies at work.

Feeley's award-winning book *The Process is the Punishment* is the result of an in-depth investigation of how lower courts in New Haven, Connecticut, administer criminal sanctions (Feeley 1979). To collect materials, Feeley adopted a mixed-method approach involving surveys, ethnography, and participant observation. In the book, Feeley discusses how the result of his quantitative analysis of a survey of 1,600 criminal cases was only the beginning of other methodological approaches (Feeley 1979, 153). Ethnographic and participant-observation methods allowed Feeley to understand the complex nature of sanctioning in the American criminal justice system, including other personnel and processes at work, like external actors (e.g., police officers) and negotiation (Feeley 1979, 197). The combination of empirical methods also allowed Feeley to come to his widely cited conclusion that courts function as a result of the interplay of many diverse actors, as judges often prioritize procedures and substantive justice over formal justice (Feeley 1979).

Committing to empirical rigor may involve conducting in-depth case studies, but it also may entail thinking and writing about those cases comparatively. Feeley has long seen the value of comparative work; one of his first books was a comparative study of state courts in the United States (Becker and Feeley 1973). I asked Feeley about his turn decades later to study the legal profession outside the United States and, referencing a statement by his Berkeley colleague, Martin Shapiro, Feeley replied, "We have to keep up with our students" who study non-US jurisdictions (personal interview with Malcolm M. Feeley, June 2015). The two books that Feeley coedited on the legal complex have a total of twenty-five case study chapters on the role of lawyers and judges in twenty-two countries on five continents (Halliday, Karpik, and Feeley 2007, 2012). Feeley and his coauthors are not alone in subscribing to the notion that doing justice in contemporary scholarship may also involve generating or testing theories using comparative empirical scholarship. Another recent example is scholarship on the "new legal realism," which promotes empirical methods for studying law and society at close range and in a self-reflective manner (Klug and Merry 2016; Mertz, Macaulay, and Mitchell 2016).

In sum, there are numerous examples of socio-legal scholars using empirical methods to help make sense of the social and political world in which lawyers, judges, and citizens operate. The works presented here represent a portion of the range of methods that scholars are using to study law empirically. Research in socio-legal studies is also revealing the circumstances under which judges and lawyers move between idealism and materialism (Cummings 2011) as academics continue to call for a broad commitment to engaged scholarship that draws on empirical data related to courts and public policy (Seron 2016). As the field grows, scholars are beginning to reflect on questions of methodology, for instance in fieldwork with courts and judges in new democracies (Ellett 2015; Ellett and Massoud 2016) or in conflict zones and authoritarian states (Massoud 2016b). Large-scale programming efforts are creating web-based repositories of qualitative data in law and social science (Qualitative Data Repository 2018; for a critique, see Isaac 2015).

16.2.2 Producing Social Theory through Normative Claims

Just as many legal researchers are pulled toward collecting empirical data and producing social science, many also are pulled toward producing social theory and making jurisprudential and normative claims. Legal philosophers have long been interested in the morality of law or the relationship between law, justice, and morals, including H. L. A. Hart (1961), Lon Fuller (1964), and Ronald Dworkin (1986), among others. The commitment to legal philosophy has also extended beyond the boundaries of jurisprudence to build social theory and social policy. Abram Chayes (1976) entered the debate by investigating the role of courts in the rise of impact litigation geared toward social policy and the public interest, rather than toward the resolution of past disputes between private individuals or enterprises.

Some legal historians have equally been committed to jurisprudence and social theory. In his groundbreaking book *Persons and Masks of the Law*, John Noonan (2002 [1975]) writes about how America's great judges and legal thinkers have used the formalism of jurisprudence to "mask" the humanity behind litigants or citizens. When applied to persons, for instance, the legal concept of property provided a licit justification for the institution of slavery. In other words, law creates an artificial language in which abstract rules, rather than persons, are the units of analysis. While these rules can be helpful for consistency, fairness, and efficiency in adjudication, they also may remove human dignity from the legal process (Noonan 2002).

The socio-legal scholar perhaps best known for a deep commitment to social theory and the study of values is Philip Selznick (for a detailed examination of Selznick's work and legacy, see Krygier 2012a). Selznick's work draws in no small part from Lon Fuller's jurisprudence on law's inner morality (see Selznick 1992; Krygier 2014a). It also draws from the mid-twentieth century pragmatist philosopher John Dewey, who, as Selznick writes in the preface to his final book, A *Humanist Science*, "regarded the separation of fact and value as a 'pernicious dualism'" (Selznick 2008, xviii). Selznick emphasizes that "the wants and needs of human beings cannot be attributed to a generic human nature; they are determined by specific settings. A link is thereby forged between the scientific demand of close observation and the values realized in social life" (Selznick 2008). Thus, empirical rigor is important, but it must not come at the cost of losing the importance of values, ideals, and moral and social theory. Those who study crimes, for instance, often have a humanist impulse that gives attention to "how ideals arise from recurrent human needs and strivings" (Van Seters 2012).

Similarly, lawyers' and judges' needs, strivings, and values are shaped by the context within which they operate as legal professionals and, perhaps just as importantly, by those contexts in which they do not operate as legal professionals but as friends, parents, adult children, siblings, loved ones, colleagues, or even commuters and consumers of news and social media. And, similarly, scholars have values, strivings, and needs to see justice (however defined) achieved in the world and, perhaps more importantly, to have feelings or even actions of justice emanate from their writing.

Philip Selznick's body of scholarship, which invites scholars to take social theory more seriously, and to link facts with values, is not alone. Martin Krygier has also been at the forefront of a wave of writing that is committed to normative values like the rule of law, or attributes of limited government that ensure judicial independence, human rights, and that no person – government official, police officer, or otherwise – is above laws designed to protect citizen and society alike. Krygier's commitment is not only to the practice of the rule of law but also to a social theory of the rule of law. Grounding social theory with an understanding of rule-of-law programs worldwide, Krygier has sought to understand the puzzling gap between the rule of law in theory and practice (Krygier 2016; Krygier 2011; Krygier 2009). In so doing, Krygier has taken a stand on Selznick's call for understanding the place of values and ideals in the world (Krygier 2012a; Krygier 2012b).

Selznick and Krygier emphasize that what is needed is not just scholarship in which social theory and legal doctrine contribute to one another, but in which social context and legal ideals and practices come together to produce social theory, not dissimilar from Malcolm Feeley's approach (Krygier 2014b, 327, citing Cotterrell 2006). In Feeley's work, even plea bargaining – a process that scholars have criticized for decades – is the result of a combination of factors that, each on their own, ought to be highly desirable (Feeley 1982). The prosecutors Feeley met in New Haven "really believed" in what they were doing as a form of justice for society, which is what attracted him to study courts and the legal profession (personal interview with Malcolm M. Feeley, June 2015).

16.2.3 *A Grounded Social Theory of Justice*

Adopting a grounded social theory of justice is one way to unite divergent strands of legal scholarship by combining facts and values with empirical and normative claims. Joining together the findings of Feeley, Selznick, and Krygier reveals how a commitment to grounded social theory means thinking comparatively and paying attention to context. It also showcases the importance of questioning conventional wisdom and, for some scholars, adopting a posture that is contrarian, by rebuffing widely accepted assumptions (personal interview with Malcolm M. Feeley, June 2015). Values – whether an academic study takes certain values into account or argues for particular values – can give direction to social science. But they, too, "are subject to criticism and revision in light of social science findings" (Selznick 2008, xvii). Thus, the commitment to social theory is as tempered by social science as data may be tempered by social theory.

Feeley's promotion of grounded social theory may not be immediately obvious to readers of his work on lower courts, or even to readers of his work on the legal profession. But it is clearest in Feeley's response to Rick Lempert's 2009 presidential address to the Law and Society Association. Feeley's essay, "The Personal and the Professional: Assessing the Ambivalent Commitment to Racial Justice in the United States," is perhaps his strongest public call for legal scholars not to abandon social theory. In it, he encourages scholars to adopt not only a policy-oriented approach but also a more explicitly normative approach. Building on decades of personal experiences and a strong sense of value and self-reflection, Feeley writes movingly of his experience as a young boy in segregated schools in Texas and being drawn to the study of law and society for a "combination of scholarly and social justice reasons" (Feeley 2010, 504). He uses first-person narrative and life experience to urge his professional colleagues to give more attention to racial inequality, not just for the sake of policy change but also for the sake of social theory and a better understanding of values and ideals (Feeley 2010; Lempert 2010). Critical race theorists have similarly drawn on a combination of personal experience and theoretical grounding to improve scholarship on racial and gender justice (see, for instance, Williams 1991).

Socio-legal scholars like Feeley, Selznick, and Krygier are not alone. A range of scholars are also holding values up to empirical scrutiny, and vice versa, by chronicling injustices and revising social (and socio-legal) theory using their observations. These include early indictments of socio-legal scholarship that promoted the field as a "policy science" in order to secure external funding, rather than encouraging self-reflexive critiques of law's claims to authority (Dezalay et al. 1989; Sarat and Silbey 1988). Socio-legal scholars continue to move in new directions that link empiricism with social theory, most notably through groundbreaking research on the history and social psychology of prisons, punishment, and juries (Haney 2005, 2006; Lynch and Haney 2015; Reiter 2016); on critical race theory (Williams 1991; Obasogie 2014); and on queer politics in authoritarian states (Chua 2014a, 2014b, 2012). These are a few examples of socio-legal scholarship that, as with Malcolm Feeley's work, have sought to channel social justice concerns and empirical rigor into works simultaneously of scholarship and of conscience. Sustaining this kind of engaged scholarship that is equally unafraid to question empirical data and social theory will help future socio-legal scholars answer the field's dominant questions better and, more importantly, to ask more refined questions, just as Selznick urged his contemporaries to do (Rosen 2012).

CONCLUSION

In this chapter, I have sought to respond to Malcolm Feeley's call for scholarship that pursues justice by contributing to both social theory and social policy. To do so, I have provided examples of the tensions within the legal profession's and legal scholars' pursuits of justice. As scholars work to uncover the ambitions, fears, and values of lawyers and judges, they also put on display their own values, privileges, and challenges. Situating scholarship self-reflectively and in its social, political, and historical context facilitates deeper explanations of the contradictions in how legal professionals act and in how researchers study those actors. That is, justice and equity are values that travel, and they travel into and out of lawyers' and judges' minds just as they travel into and out of scholars' minds. A more robust commitment to understanding the diverse cultures within which scholars work may illuminate more clearly the diverse cultures within which lawyers and judges work.

Illusions exist in legal work, that lawyers are either self-serving private practitioners or that they are selfless pursuers of justice (but not both), and that selfless lawyering somehow paves the way to an ideal state of liberal democracy. Just as a spectrum exists in regime types between democracy and dictatorship, the legal profession's commitments are much more complex and layered, involving a spectrum of attractions from materialism to idealism. Perhaps, then, it is through these overlapping and conflicting commitments that the path to justice is revealed – a path that is winding, shadowed, and fraught.

The threads woven together here are not simply about legal professionals who are, in the words of Philip Selznick, the agents of what ought to be accessible bureaucracies. These threads also form an understanding of how scholars chronicle the work of lawyers and judges who use law's power to create change. The oeuvre of Malcolm Feeley encourages us to ask how, and at which point, we insert ourselves into our chronicles of those who pursue justice. Perhaps we do so in as messy a fashion as those who pursue their own conceptions of justice, equally lured by materials and values. It involves linking social science methods with humanistic inquiry and a deep concern for humanity and historical context. The question remains for scholars to continue to unravel how we, and those whom we study, migrate between layered formations of materials and values. This work may be simultaneously confining and liberating.

These reflections resurrect a question first posed by Richard Abel and Philip Lewis (1996, 285) when they concluded their major study of the legal profession:

"How do lawyers shape polities?" Their reply, after more than a decade of work, was unexpectedly blank: "We really do not know the answer to this question." A few sentences later, however, they added the following: "Legal training may imbue graduates with fidelity to legality" (Abel and Lewis 1996). This response, had it come two decades earlier, could easily have triggered Feeley's impulse to study lawyers and judges as persons torn apart by conflicting impulses. It is these conflicting impulses that drive the profession to balance the pursuit of material gain with a fidelity to legality. For scholars, studying justice and being part of the pursuit of justice involves balancing their own impulses to produce materials that let data speak and that let conviction speak.

While this chapter analyzed some of the dissonances, parallels, and overlaps in the legal profession and scholarship on it, it leaves open the question of how political, social, and economic circumstances shape the ways that cultures of materialism and idealism emerge in legal work, and how and why legal professionals reverse course from working to realize the rule of law to working to realize contradictory political goals. Answering these deeper questions may also help scholars to understand the ways that we, too, are guided by conflicting commitments and multiple ends – methodological, normative, and personal – in our common pursuit of justice.

Writing successfully about justice may involve moving readers – as would a novel, film, or other work of art – to rethink easily held beliefs about the agents of power. Socio-legal scholars may ultimately succeed at the Herculean task of challenging apathy and evoking response, as Malcolm Feeley has encouraged us to do, when our writing about justice embraces both close observation and social theory, and when our scholarship moves easily between these goals.

REFERENCES

Abel, Richard. 1985. "Comparative Sociology of Legal Professions: An Exploratory Essay." 10 *Law & Social Inquiry* 1: 5–79.
Abel, Richard. 1986. "The Decline of Professionalism?" 49 *The Modern Law Review* 1: 1–41.
Abel, Richard. 2010. "The Paradoxes of Pro Bono." 78 *Fordham Law Review*: 2443–50.
Abel, Richard L. and Philip S. C. Lewis, eds. 1988a. *Lawyers in Society: The Common Law World (Volume 1)*. New York: Beard Books.
Abel, Richard L. and Philip S. C. Lewis, eds. 1988b. *Lawyers in Society: The Civil Law World (Volume 2)*. New York: Beard Books.
Abel, Richard L. and Philip S. C. Lewis, eds. 1989. *Lawyers in Society: Comparative Theories (Volume 3)*. New York: Beard Books.
Abel, Richard L. and Philip S. C. Lewis, eds. 1996. *Lawyers in Society: An Overview*. Berkeley and Los Angeles: University of California Press.
Abel, Richard and Philip S. C. Lewis. 1996. "Putting Law Back into the Sociology of Lawyers." In *Lawyers in Society: An Overview*, edited by Richard L. Abel and Philip S. C. Lewis. Berkeley and Los Angeles: University of California Press.
Albert, Kyle and Kim Weeden. 2011. "Occupations and Professions." *Oxford Bibliographies*. DOI: 10.1093/obo/9780199756384–0038.

Barber, Bernard. 1963. "Some Problems in the Sociology of the Professions." 92 *Daedalus* 4: 669–88.
Becker, Theodore L. and Malcolm M. Feeley, eds. 1973. *The Impact of Supreme Court Decisions*. Oxford: Oxford University Press.
Bob, Clifford. 2002. "Political Process Theory and Transnational Movements: Dialectics of Protest among Nigeria's Ogoni Minority." 49 *Social Problems* 3: 395–415.
Bell, Derrick A. 1995. "Serving Two Masters: Integration Ideals and Client Interests in School Desegregation Litigation." In *Critical Race Theory: The Key Writings that Formed the Movement*, edited by C. West., K. Crenshaw, N. Gotanda, G. Peller, and K. Thomas. New York: New Press.
Bickel, Alexander M. 1962. *The Least Dangerous Branch: The Supreme Court at the Bar of Politics*. New York: Bobbs-Merrill.
Branch, Adam. 2007. "Uganda's Civil War and the Politics of ICC Intervention." 21 *Ethics & International Affairs* 2: 179–98.
Branch, Adam. 2011. *Displacing Human Rights: War and Intervention in Northern Uganda*. Oxford: Oxford University Press.
Brinks, Daniel M. 2008. *The Judicial Response to Police Killings in Latin America: Inequality and the Rule of Law*. Cambridge: Cambridge University Press.
Bumiller, Kristin. 1987. "Victims in the Shadow of the Law: A Critique of the Model of Legal Protection." 12 *Signs* 421–39.
Carr-Saunders, A. M. and P. A. Wilson. 1933. *The Professions*. Oxford: Clarendon Press.
Cichowski, Rachel A. 2007. *The European Court and Civil Society: Litigation, Mobilization, and Governance*. Cambridge: Cambridge University Press.
Chayes, Abram. 1976. "The Role of the Judge in Public Law Litigation." 89 *Harvard Law Review* 7: 1281–316.
Cheesman, Nick. 2015. *Opposing the Rule of Law: How Myanmar's Courts Make Law and Order*. Cambridge: Cambridge University Press.
Chua, Lynette J. 2012. "Pragmatic Resistance, Law, and Social Movements in Authoritarian States: The Case of Gay Collective Action in Singapore." 46 *Law & Society Review* 4: 713–48.
Chua, Lynette J. 2014a. *Mobilizing Gay Singapore: Rights and Resistance in an Authoritarian State*. Philadelphia: Temple University Press.
Chua, Lynette J. 2014b. "Rights Mobilization and the Campaign to Decriminalize Homosexuality in Singapore." 1 *Asian Journal of Law and Society* 1: 205–28.
Cotterrell, Roger. 2006. "The Concept of Legal Culture." In *Law, Culture and Society: Legal Ideas in the Mirror of Social Theory*. Aldershot: Ashgate. 81–96.
Couso, Javier. 2003. "The Politics of Judicial Review in Chile in the Era of Democratic Transition, 1990–2002." 10 *Democratization* 4: 70–91.
Cummings, Scott L. 2004. *The Politics of Pro Bono*. 52 UCLA Law Review 1: 18–25.
Cummings, Scott L., ed. 2011. *The Paradox of Professionalism: Lawyers and the Possibility of Justice*. Cambridge: Cambridge University Press.
Dezalay, Yves and Bryant G. Garth. 1996. *Dealing in Virtue: International Commercial Arbitration and the Construction of a Transnational Legal Order*. Chicago: University of Chicago Press.
Dezalay, Yves and Bryant G. Garth. 2002. *The Internationalization of Palace Wars: Lawyers, Economists, and the Contest to Transform Latin American States*. Chicago: University of Chicago Press.
Dezalay, Yves and Bryant G. Garth. 2010. *Asian Legal Revivals: Lawyers in the Shadow of Empire*. Chicago: University of Chicago Press.

Dezalay Yves, Austin Sarat, and Susan Silbey. 1989. "D'une Démarche Contestataire à un Savoir Méritocratique: Éléments pour une Historie Sociale de la Sociologie Juridique Américaine." *Actes de la Recherche en Sciences Sociales* 78: 79–93.
Dworkin, Ronald. 1986. *Law's Empire*. Cambridge, MA: Harvard University Press.
Ellett, Rachel. 2013. *Pathways to Judicial Power in Transitional States: Perspectives from African Courts*. New York: Routledge.
Ellett, Rachel. 2015. "Interviewing African Judges: Reflections on Fieldwork and Data Collection in Comparative Judicial Politics." Paper presented at the annual meeting of the American Political Science Association (on file with author).
Ellett, Rachel and Mark Fathi Massoud. 2016. "Not All Law is Public: Reflections on Data Transparency for Law and Courts Research in Africa." 12 *American Political Science Association African Politics Conference Group (APCG) Newsletter* 2: 8–10.
Englund, Harri. 2004. "Towards a Critique of Rights Talk in New Democracies: The Case of Legal Aid in Malawi." *Discourse & Society* 15 (5): 527–51.
Englund, Harri. 2006. *Prisoners of Freedom: Human Rights and the African Poor*. Berkeley: University of California Press.
Erie, Matthew. 2016. *China and Islam: The Prophet, the Party, and Law*. Cambridge: Cambridge University Press.
Ewick, Patricia and Susan S. Silbey. 1998. *The Common Place of Law: Stories from Everyday Life*. Chicago: University of Chicago Press.
Gordon, Robert W. 1996. "The Path of the Lawyer." 110 *Harvard Law Review*: 1013–18.
He, Xin and Yang Su. 2013. "Do the 'Haves' Come Out Ahead in Shanghai Courts?" 10 *Journal of Empirical Legal Studies* 1: 120–45.
Feeley, Malcolm M. 1973. "Two Models of the Criminal Justice System: An Organizational Perspective." 7 *Law & Society Review*: 407–25.
Feeley, Malcolm M. 1979. *The Process is the Punishment: Handling Cases in a Lower Court*. New York: Russell Sage Foundation.
Feeley, Malcolm M. 1982. "Plea Bargaining and the Structure of the Criminal Process." 7 *Justice System Journal* 3: 338–54.
Feeley, Malcolm M. 1983. *Court Reform on Trial: Why Simple Solutions Fail*. New York: Basic Books.
Feeley, Malcolm M. 1987. "The Adversary System." In *Encyclopedia of the American Judicial System: Studies of the Principal Institutions and Processes of Law (Volume II)*, edited by Robert J. Janosik. New York: Charles Scribner's Sons.
Feeley, Malcolm M. 2010. "The Personal and the Professional: Assessing the Ambivalent Commitment to Racial Justice in the United States." 44 *Law & Society Review* 3/4: 503–14.
Feeley, Malcolm M. 2012. "Judge and Company: Courts, Constitutionalism, and the Legal Complex." In *Fates of Political Liberalism in the British Post-Colony: The Politics of the Legal Complex*, edited by Terence C. Halliday, Lucien Karpik, and Malcolm M. Feeley. Cambridge: Cambridge University Press.
Feeley, Malcolm M. and Edward Rubin. 1998. *Judicial Policy Making and the Modern State: How the Courts Reformed America's Prisons*. Cambridge: Cambridge University Press.
Feeley, Malcolm M. and Setsuo Miyazawa, eds. 2002. *The Japanese Adversary System in Context: Controversies and Comparisons*. London: Palgrave Macmillan.
Fuller, Lon L. 1964. *The Morality of Law*. New Haven: Yale University Press.
Ghias, Shoaib. 2011. "Miscarriage of Chief Justice: Judicial Power and the Legal Complex in Pakistan under Musharraf." 35 *Law & Social Inquiry* 4: 985–1022.

Gillman, Howard. 2004. "Martin Shapiro and the Movement from 'Old' to 'New' Institutionalist Studies in Public Law Scholarship." *Annual Review of Political Science* 7: 363–82.
Gobe, Eric and Lena Salaymeh. 2016. "Tunisia's 'Revolutionary' Lawyers: From Professional Autonomy to Political Mobilization." 41 *Law & Social Inquiry* 2: 311–45.
Gómez, Laura. 2010. "Looking for Race in All the Wrong Places." 46 *Law & Society Review* 2: 221–45.
Hafner-Burton, Emilie M. 2013. *Making Human Rights a Reality*. Princeton: Princeton University Press.
Halliday, Terence C. and Lucien Karpik, eds. 1998. *Lawyers and the Rise of Western Political Liberalism: Europe and North America from the Eighteenth to Twentieth Centuries*. Oxford: Oxford University Press.
Halliday, Terence C., Lucien Karpik, and Malcolm M. Feeley, eds. 2007. *Fighting for Political Freedom: Comparative Studies of the Legal Complex and Political Liberalism*. Oxford: Hart Publishing.
Halliday, Terence C., Lucien Karpik, and Malcolm M. Feeley. 2007. "The Legal Complex and Struggles for Political Liberalism." In *Fighting for Political Freedom: Comparative Studies of the Legal Complex and Political Liberalism*, edited by Terence C. Halliday, Lucien Karpik, and Malcolm M. Feeley. Oxford: Hart Publishing. 1–42.
Halliday, Terence C., Lucien Karpik, and Malcolm M. Feeley, eds. 2012. *Fates of Political Liberalism in the British Post-Colony: The Politics of the Legal Complex*. Cambridge: Cambridge University Press.
Halliday, Terence C. and Lucien Karpik. 2012. "Political Liberalism in the British Post-Colony: A Theme with Three Variations." In *Fates of Political Liberalism in the British Post-Colony: The Politics of the Legal Complex*, edited by Terence C. Halliday, Lucien Karpik, and Malcolm M. Feeley. Cambridge: Cambridge University Press.
Haney, Craig. 2005. *Reforming Punishment: Psychological Limits to the Pains of Imprisonment*. Washington, DC: American Psychological Association (APA) Books.
Haney, Craig. 2006. *Death by Design: Capital Punishment as a Social Psychological System*. Oxford: Oxford University Press.
Hart, H. L. A. 1961. *The Concept of Law*. Oxford: Clarendon.
Huneeus, Alexandra. 2013. "International Criminal Law by Other Means: The Quasi-Criminal Jurisdiction of Human Rights Courts." 107 *American Journal of International Law* 1: 1–44.
Isaac, Jeffrey C. 2015. "For a More *Public* Political Science." 13 *Perspectives on Politics* 2: 269–83.
Jacobs, Andrew and Chris Buckley. 2015. "China Targeting Rights Lawyers in a Crackdown." *New York Times*, July 22, 2015. http://nyti.ms/1LDjrXE.
Kapiszewski, Diana. 2012. *High Courts and Economic Governance in Argentina and Brazil*. Cambridge: Cambridge University Press.
Kawar, Leila. 2015. *Contesting Immigration Policy in Court: Legal Activism and its Radiating Effects in the United States and France*. Cambridge: Cambridge University Press.
Kennedy, David. 2002. "The International Human Rights Movement: Part of the Problem?" *Harvard Human Rights Journal* 15: 99–125.
Krygier, Martin. 2009. "The Rule of Law and the 'Three Integrations.'" 1 *Hague Journal on the Rule of Law* 1: 21–27.
Krygier, Martin. 2011. "Four Puzzles about the Rule of Law: Why, What, Where? And Who Cares?" 50 *Nomos*: 64–104.
Krygier, Martin. 2012a. *Philip Selznick: Ideals in the World*. Stanford: Stanford University Press.

Krygier, Martin. 2012b. "Missing All That Matters." 10 *Issues in Legal Scholarship* 1: 5–17.
Krygier, Martin. 2014a. "Reply to Patrick Emerton, 'Naturalising Natural Law? Reflections on Martin Krygier's *Philip Selznick: Ideals in the World* and Kristen Rundle, *Forms Liberate: Reclaiming the Jurisprudence of Lon L. Fuller.*'" 39 *Australian Journal of Legal Philosophy*, 176–88.
Krygier 2014b. "The Rule of Law after the Short Twentieth Century: Launching a Global Career." In *Law, Society and Community: Socio-Legal Essays in Honour of Roger Cotterrell*, edited by Richard Nobles and David Schiff. Aldershot: Ashgate. 327–46.
Krygier, Martin. 2016. "The Rule of Law Between England and Sudan: Hay, Thompson, and Massoud." 41 *Law & Social Inquiry* 2: 480–88.
Klug, Heinz. 2000. *Constituting Democracy: Law, Globalism, and South Africa's Reconstruction*. Cambridge: Cambridge University Press.
Klug, Heinz and Sally Merry. 2016. *The New Legal Realism: Studying Law Globally (Volume II)*. Cambridge: Cambridge University Press.
Lempert, Richard. 2010. "A Personal Odyssey Toward a Theme: Race and Equality in the United States, 1948–2009." 44 *Law & Society Review* 3/4: 431–62.
Lynch, Mona and Craig Haney. 2015. "Emotion, Authority, and Death: (Raced) Negotiations in Mock Capital Jury Deliberations." 40 *Law & Social Inquiry* 2: 377–405.
Macdonald, Keith M. 1995. *The Sociology of the Professions*. Thousand Oaks: Sage.
Massoud, Mark Fathi. 2011. "Do Victims of War Need International Law? Human Rights Education Programs in Authoritarian Sudan." 45 *Law & Society Review* 1: 1–32.
Massoud, Mark Fathi. 2012. "Lawyers and the Disintegration of the Legal Complex in Sudan." In *Fates of Political Liberalism in the British Post-Colony: The Politics of the Legal Complex*, edited by Terence C. Halliday, Lucien Karpik, and Malcolm M. Feeley. Cambridge: Cambridge University Press.
Massoud, Mark Fathi. 2013. *Law's Fragile State: Colonial, Authoritarian, and Humanitarian Legacies in Sudan*. Cambridge: Cambridge University Press.
Massoud, Mark Fathi. 2014. "International Arbitration and Judicial Politics in Authoritarian States." 39 *Law & Social Inquiry* 1: 1–30.
Massoud, Mark Fathi. 2015. "Work Rules: How International NGOs Build Law in War-Torn Societies." 49 *Law & Society Review* 2: 333–64.
Massoud, Mark Fathi. 2016a. "Ideals and Practices in the Rule of Law: An Essay on Legal Politics." *Law & Social Inquiry* 41 (2): 489–501.
Massoud, Mark Fathi. 2016b. "Field Research on Law in Conflict Zones and Authoritarian States." *Annual Review of Law & Social Science* 12: 85–106.
Massoud, Mark Fathi. 2016c. "The Politics of Islamic Law and Human Rights: Sudan's Rival Legal Systems." In *The New Legal Realism: Studying Law Globally*, edited by Heinz Klug and Sally Engle Merry. Cambridge: Cambridge University Press.
Massoud, Mark Fathi. 2018. "How an Islamic State Rejected Islamic Law." *American Journal of Comparative Law* 66 (3): 579–602.
McCann, Michael. 1994. *Rights at Work: Pay Equity Reform and the Politics of Legal Mobilization*. Chicago: University of Chicago Press.
Merry, Sally Engle. 2006. *Human Rights and Gender Violence: Translating International Law into Local Justice*. Chicago: University of Chicago Press.
Mertz, Elizabeth, Stewart Macaulay, and Thomas W. Mitchell. 2016. *The New Legal Realism: Translating Law-and-Society for Today's Legal Practice*. Cambridge: Cambridge University Press.
Michelson, Ethan. 2006. "The Practice of Law as an Obstacle to Justice: Chinese Lawyers at Work." 40 *Law & Society Review* 1: 1–38.

Moustafa, Tamir. 2007. *The Struggle for Constitutional Power: Law, Politics, and Economic Development in Egypt*. Cambridge: Cambridge University Press.

Moustafa, Tamir. 2013a. "Liberal Rights versus Islamic Law? The Construction of a Binary in Malaysian Politics." 47 *Law & Society Review* 771–802.

Moustafa, Tamir. 2013b. "Judging in God's Name: State Power, Secularism, and the Politics of Islamic Law in Malaysia." 2 *Oxford Journal of Law and Religion* 1: 1–16.

Mutua, Makau. 2008. *Human Rights: A Political and Cultural Critique*. Philadelphia: University of Pennsylvania Press.

Nielsen, Laura Beth. 2000. "Situating Legal Consciousness: Experiences and Attitudes of Ordinary Citizens about Law and Street Harassment." 34 *Law & Society Review* 4: 1055–90.

Noonan, John. 2002. *Persons and Masks of the Law: Cardozo, Holmes, Jefferson, and Wythe as Makers of the Masks*. Berkeley and Los Angeles: University of California Press.

Obasogie, Osagie K. 2014. *Blinded by Sight: Seeing Race through the Eyes of the Blind*. Stanford: Stanford University Press.

Qualitative Data Repository. 2018. Available at: https://qdr.syr.edu/about.

Reiter, Keramet. 2016. *23/7: Pelican Bay Prison and the Rise of Long-Term Solitary Confinement*. New Haven: Yale University Press.

Rosen, Robert Eli. 2012. "All Fact is Beautiful Theory: The Romantic Philip Selznick." 10 *Issues in Legal Scholarship* 1: 63–70.

Rosenberg, Gerald N. 2008. *The Hollow Hope: Can Courts Bring About Social Change?* (2nd edn.) Chicago: University of Chicago Press.

Sarat, Austin and Susan Silbey. 1988. "The Pull of the Policy Audience." 10 *Law & Policy* 2/3: 97–166.

Scheppele, Kim Lane. 2013. "The Rule of Law and the Frankenstate: Why Governance Checklists Do Not Work." 26 *Governance: An International Journal of Policy, Administration, and Institutions* 4: 559–62.

Scheppele, Kim Lane. 2015. "Common Template, Diverse Agendas: The Futility (and Danger) of Legislating for the World." Paper presented at the Annual Meeting of the Law and Society Association (on file with author).

Seron, Carroll. 2016. "The Two Faces of Law and Inequality: From Critique to the Promise of Situated, Pragmatic Policy." 50 *Law & Society Review* 1: 9–33.

Selznick, Philip. 1992. *The Moral Commonwealth: Social Theory and the Promise of Community*. Berkeley and Los Angeles: University of California Press.

Selznick, Philip. 2008. *A Humanist Science: Values and Ideals in Social Inquiry*. Stanford: Stanford University Press.

Shaffer, Gregory, ed. 2012. *Transnational Legal Ordering and State Change*. Cambridge: Cambridge University Press.

Sharafi, Mitra. 2014. *Law and Identity in Colonial South Asia: Parsi Legal Culture, 1772–1947*. Cambridge: Cambridge University Press.

Shklar, Judith. 1964. *Legalism: Law, Morals, and Political Trials*. Cambridge, MA: Harvard University Press.

Silverstein, Gordon. 2008. "Singapore: The Exception That Proves Rules Matter." In *Rule by Law: The Politics of Courts in Authoritarian Regimes*, edited by Tom Ginsburg and Tamir Moustafa. Cambridge: Cambridge University Press.

Simon, William H. 2000. *The Practice of Justice: A Theory of Lawyers' Ethics*. Cambridge, MA: Harvard University Press.

Smith, Rogers M. 1988. "Political Jurisprudence, the 'New Institutionalism,' and the Future of Public Law." 82 *American Political Science Review* 1: 89–108.

Stacy, Helen. 2009. *Human Rights for the 21st Century: Sovereignty, Civil Society, Culture.* Stanford: Stanford University Press.

Stern, Gerald. 2008 [1976]. *The Buffalo Creek Disaster: How the Survivors of One of the Worst Disasters in Coal-Mining History Brought Suit against the Coal Company and Won.* New York: Vintage.

Stern, Rachel. 2013. *Environmental Litigation in China: A Study in Political Ambivalence.* Cambridge: Cambridge University Press.

Tamanaha, Brian Z. 2012. *Failing Law Schools.* Chicago: University of Chicago Press.

Trubek, David M. and Marc Galanter. 1974. "Scholars in Self-Estrangement: Some Reflections on the Crisis in Law and Development Studies in the United States." 1974 *Wisconsin Law Review* 4: 1062–102.

Van Seters, Paul. 2012. "Selznick and Dworkin: The Importance of Values in Moral and Social Theory." 10 *Issues in Legal Scholarship* 1: 43–53.

Williams, Patricia. 1991. *The Alchemy of Race and Rights: Diary of a Law Professor.* Cambridge, MA: Harvard University Press.

Ziadeh, Farhat J. 1968–1969. "Abstract of the Role of Lawyers in Egypt." 3 *Law & Society Review*: 407–08.

17

The Varieties of Judicial Independence and the Judiciary's Role in Political Reform

Edward L. Rubin

One of the most significant contributions that scholarship can offer is to call attention to something that everyone sees but no one has yet noticed. Malcolm Feeley's work with Terrence Halliday, Lucien Karpik and Setsuo Miyazawa on the liberal legal complex falls into this favored category (Halliday, Karpik and Feeley 2007; Feeley and Miyazawa 2007). Judges and lawyers are among the most visible members of our society, they are known to play important roles, and their interactions are sufficiently familiar to serve as the subject matter of movies, television shows and popular fiction. But it is only recently, as a result of Feeley's work with his colleagues, that the relationship between judges and lawyers has been recognized as a functional component of political liberalism. As his surveys of nations on five continents reveal, the quality of the relationship between judges and lawyers can powerfully contribute to the process of securing basic human rights and imposing constraints on governmental power – the hallmarks of political liberalism, in Feeley's view. Thus, this relationship, which lies at the center of the legal complex, is a major factor that determines whether liberal regimes flourish or founder.

Among the crucial factors that determine the nature of the legal complex and its role in political liberalism is judicial independence. This is, of course, a well-recognized feature of political liberalism, something that we celebrate as a motherhood and apple pie component of a just society. But in bringing the judge-lawyer interaction into focus, Malcolm Feeley's work invests this issue with renewed significance. This chapter builds upon the insights of his work by revisiting the familiar subject of judicial independence. The existing literature amply assesses the reasons why it is important and what mechanisms can establish and protect it (Burbank and Friedman 2002; Russell and O'Brien 2001; Shugerman 2012; Tarr 2012; Tate and Vallinder 1997). But less attention has been devoted to its basic character and the different forms it can assume. If one wants to understand the way the legal complex operates in a variety of different political contexts, however, the character and varieties of judicial independence become a matter of primary importance.

The starting point of the analysis is the observation that independence is not an inherent quality but a relationship. It does not make much sense to ask whether something is independent as an abstract matter. An infant is the very image of dependence, but if it is an American infant, it is independent of the President of France. Thus, the useful question will be whether something is independent of another thing that it might be expected to depend upon. In the case of judges, they – and more precisely their decisions – might depend upon other actors in the political and legal system. In the political system, the obvious possibilities are the other institutions identified as branches, that is, the executive and the legislature. In the legal system, the most obvious possibility is practicing lawyers. To limit the inquiry to these obvious possibilities represents a simplification of both systems, of course, but as the following discussion will demonstrate, at the very least, it is complicated enough to justify an inquiry.

The first part of the inquiry, Section 17.1, will focus on the judiciary's independence from lawyers, from the legislature and from the constitution. Judicial independence from the executive will not be discussed separately, but only in connection with these other relationships. The reason lies in its familiarity; independence from the executive, it will turn out, is what we ordinarily mean by judicial independence. It can thus serve as a baseline for evaluation of the other, less familiar relationships. Section 17.2 of the inquiry will then use the categories in Section 17.1 to assess the way that judicial independence functions as a component of the legal complex, and the role it plays in advancing political liberalism.

17.1 THE VARIETIES OF JUDICIAL INDEPENDENCE

17.1.1 *Independence from the Litigants*

It might appear, on first impression, that judges' independence from the litigants who come before them is so basic and essential that it does not merit much discussion. To be influenced by the litigants themselves, as opposed to the substance of their factual presentations and legal arguments, would seem to be nothing other than corruption (Ackerman 1999; Thompson 1987; Underkuffler 2013). Even courts that lack independence of any other kind often feature this apparently obvious and primal form of it. As recent scholarship reveals, judges in authoritarian regimes such as fascist Germany and Italy, and in the authoritarian regimes of Brazil, China, Singapore and Spain, have eschewed bribery and decided nonpolitical cases even-handedly, in large part because unbiased adjudication is advantageous for private enterprise, which these regimes supported (Bosworth 2007, 308–12; Ginsburg and Moustafa 2008; De Grand 2004, 47–56; Guarnieri 2007, 441–42; Paxton 2004, 145–48).[1] George Orwell's Burmese judge

---

[1] Needless to say, the fascist regimes did not hesitate to mount totally one-sided and savagely vindictive trials in political cases. Interestingly, however, these political cases were often handled by newly organized courts that were kept separate from the previously established ones that continued to handle ordinary civil and criminal cases (Deutscher 1960, 369–85; McCauley 1993, 100–08; Ortner 2018; Shirer 1960, 1069–73).

took bribes from both sides and then decided on the merits, (Orwell 1934, 6–7), but few modern regimes would feel comfortable relying on this way of achieving orderly adjudication.

It is necessary, however, to be more precise about what it means to say that a judge is independent of the litigants. Does it mean that she is free of the litigants' direct influence and control, or does it also mean that she had no knowledge of the litigants beyond the information that is presented and assessed in open court? When two private individuals are before a modern court in a politically liberal society, we usually expect the judge to recuse herself if she has outside information about one of the litigants.[2] This is not an invariable rule, however. To begin with, there are some industries, the US entertainment industry being one example, where arbitrations are carried out by private attorneys who typically have had business dealings with one or both of the litigants. Industry members prefer the potential bias that might result to the greater uncertainty of submitting their case to a court of general jurisdiction, where the judge may be more neutral but is unfamiliar with industry practices.[3] Second, the rule against outside knowledge of the litigant is difficult to apply if one of the litigants is a celebrity, and impossible if it is a large corporation, a labor union, an important public interest organization or the government. For a contemporary American judge to be unaware of the character and motivation of the United Automobile Workers, the Sierra Club or Exxon Corporation would indicate stupidity, not neutrality. A modification of the rule, therefore, is that, in cases where knowledge of the litigant cannot be avoided, the judge may not regard her knowledge as relevant to her decision.[4]

According to the legal realists, contemporary judges are simply unable to sustain the assertion that they treat knowledge of the litigants as legally irrelevant. When then Judge Alex Kozinski described an independent judiciary as one "where the person who appoints you doesn't own you," (PBS Newshour 2005), he was overlooking the possibility that the judge's decision making might be equally influenced by his own attitudes toward the litigant, a possibility he amply demonstrated in his intemperate decision against Sea Shepherd (*Institute of Cetacean Research* v. *Sea*

---

[2] See Judicial Conference of the United States (2014):

> (1) A judge shall disqualify himself or herself in a proceeding in which the judge's impartiality might reasonably be questioned, including but not limited to instances in which:
> (a) the judge has a personal bias or prejudice concerning a party, or personal knowledge of disputed evidentiary facts concerning the proceeding.

[3] Based on author's personal knowledge from practicing entertainment law in New York City, and from redacted copies of Directors' Guild and Writers' Guild arbitrations on file with the author.

[4] It is worth noting that independence of this sort is a fairly recent development; formerly, the judge's knowledge of the litigant, and specifically the litigant's character, was often regarded as the most important consideration. Weber's *kadi*, for example, was certainly familiar with the litigants (Weber 1978, 976–78). English juries were originally a form of royal inquest (of the sort that produced the Domesday Book) and were assembled to report whether they knew of any crimes that had occurred in their neighborhood (Pollock and Maitland 1952, vol. 1, 138–54). For centuries, English petit juries continued to base their decisions, at least in part, on their knowledge of the accused person's character.

Shepherd Conservation Society 2012).[5] Moreover, as Yoav Dotan demonstrates in his study of the Israeli judicial system, when the government is a litigant, its character is often treated by courts as legally relevant (Dotan 2014; see also Devins 1994; Lee 1988; Salokar 1992). Observers might attribute this to the fact that the judges are themselves government employees, or that they are conventional people who share the government's views, or that they are being intimidated. The explicit rationale, however, is that government lawyers, unlike private lawyers, review the merits of the case in advance and will only bring actions that they regard as valid. There is much to be said in favor of this approach, most notably that it moderates governmental force by filtering out weak cases before the private person has been subjected to the expense and reputational damage that results from public accusation. But it also raises a question about whether the judge in this situation can be truly described as independent of the government.

Another contemporary situation where the government's identity as a litigant is treated as legally relevant appears in administrative procedure, where the agency acts as both prosecutor and adjudicator. The resulting potential for unfairness was one of the major motivations behind the enactment of the US Administrative Procedure Act, which included provisions (subsequently strengthened) to separate these functions (US Code, Title 5 § 557(d)(1)). At present, many agency adjudications are decided by an Administrative Law Judge (ALJ), whose neutrality is assured by safeguards that rival those of any other judicial officer in the United States (US Code, Title 5: §§ 1305, 5372). But ALJs must be granted jurisdiction by specific statutory provision; in other cases, the decision is made by a hearing officer or administrative judge (AJ), who is simply an agency employee, like the person who initiates the case. Moreover, preliminary agency action, such as cease and desist orders, continue to be determined by the same officials who initiate them. These orders are subject to judicial review, but their impact is often sufficient for them to be considered as adjudicatory decisions in their own right. While such procedures should be monitored to avoid unfairness, the need to impose preliminary, informal sanctions in administrative enforcement is an insistent one. If the agency could not impose costs on regulated parties until it obtained a judicial judgment, the opportunities for delay and obstruction would render the regulation itself ineffective.

In all the above situations, including those involving the government, the question involves the influence of the litigants on the judicial decision maker. These situations thus remain on one side of a crucial boundary, a boundary that is crossed if the government influences the decision maker in its capacity as an executive, rather than

---

[5] Judge Kozinski described Japanese whalers, who are widely regarded as having violated international law, as having been "hounded on the high seas for years by a group calling itself Sea Shepherd Conservation Society and its eccentric founder, Paul Watson"). He has openly proclaimed his politically conservative views, as well as having posted images of naked women painted to look like cows on a personal website. More recently, Judge Kozinski resigned after allegations emerged that he had sexually harassed his female law clerks.

a litigant. For present purposes, the executive capacity can be regarded as the authority to punish rather than persuade. At the extreme, it would involve a fine or imprisonment, which dictatorial regimes often inflict on noncompliant judges, but it also might also involve civil sanctions such as dismissal, salary reduction or demotion. Any such sanction clearly undermines judicial independence; in fact, insulation from such sanctions is the way that judicial independence is typically defined.

This is obvious, but it implies two collateral principles that are not as extensively recognized. First, the executive may be able to threaten judicial independence with less obvious sanctions. The authority to make resource allocation decisions regarding the construction, maintenance and usage of public buildings is regarded by virtually everyone as falling within the authority of the executive. Egregious uses of this authority, such as transferring judges to a decrepit facility in a remote location, might well elicit public criticism, which would act as a control on the executive's ability to threaten judicial independence in this manner. But more subtle actions, such as failing to proceed with construction of a new facility, might escape such notice. The research that Malcolm Feeley carried out in the study of the US prison reform cases that I authored with him revealed that the Santa Clara County Board of Supervisors, faced with a series of decisions declaring that its operation of its jails violated the Eighth Amendment, "delayed on long-standing plans to build a new county courthouse for the entire judiciary" (Feeley and Rubin 1998, 124).

A second collateral principle is that the authority to dismiss or sanction judges, and thus the potential threat to judicial independence, might be exercised by someone other than the executive. In American state government, this authority often resides with the populace, which elects judges and can remove them, either in the next election or by separate recall votes (Carrington 1998; DuBois 1980). Such provisions were generally the products of the late nineteenth-century Populist movement, which saw appointed judges as members of a narrow ruling elite, or of subsequent efforts that drew upon Populism's continuing appeal. The instinct is a creditable one, but the mechanism for achieving it is seriously flawed. Voters cannot educate themselves about the credentials of any but the most important public offices, and state judges rarely achieve this level of political salience. The result is that judicial elections are either pro forma or can be bought with campaign funds. The problem was exacerbated by the Supreme Court's ill-considered decision in *Republican Party* v. *White* (2002), which held that provisions forbidding candidates for judicial office from announcing their views on disputed legal or political issues violated the First Amendment. This electoral control over the judiciary, like executive control, represents a clear threat to judicial independence.

17.1.2 *Hyper-Independence – Independence from the Legislature*

While independence from the executive can be considered the essential feature of judicial independence generally, independence from the legislature might be regarded as judicial misbehavior. In a democratic polity, after all, the legislature makes the law, and surely judges should follow the law in deciding individual cases. If one wants to get jurisprudential about the matter, then one can say that the legislature either is the sovereign or represents the sovereign people, and is thus the necessary source of legal rules. In the US Constitution, both the Bill of Attainder Clause in the original document (Art. 1, Sec. 9. Cl. 3) and the Due Process Clause of the Fifth and Fourteenth Amendments, can be understood – with a few exceptions involving substantive due process – as providing that the political process produces general rules that impose punishments or disadvantages. The role of the courts is to follow prescribed procedures and determine when an individual is subject to those rules (Rubin 2017, 408–10; Rubin 2013, 585–90).

In the Anglo-American legal system, however, there is an obvious and important exception to this understanding – the common law. Common law courts make legal rules. They do not do so all at once, of course, the way a legislature does, but incrementally (Eisenberg 1991; Shapiro 1981, 65–131). Nonetheless, they make legal rules, and for the last century, at least, observers have recognized the justification that they are merely applying the in-dwelling principles of Anglo-Saxon law to be a legal fiction. In thus making rules, the courts are acting independently of the legislature. Just as ordinary judicial independence means that the courts decide cases without instruction from the executive, which otherwise is granted the authority to implement legal rules of general application, common law means that the courts make rules of general application without instruction from the legislature, which otherwise is granted the authority to enact such rules. Common law might therefore be described as judicial hyperindependence.[6]

To be sure, there is a significant difference between the judiciary's independence from the executive and its independence from the legislature. In the American constitutional system, and to some extent in the British system as well (Shapiro 1981, 71–74), independence from the legislature is revocable but independence from the executive is not. That is, we recognize the authority of the legislature to displace the judiciary's common law rule making by enacting statute, and this was true even before the advent of the administrative state, when such authority was only occasionally exercised. In contrast, it is never considered acceptable for the executive to displace judicial independence by imposing punishments or disadvantages on specific individuals. The executive cannot do so, and the legislature cannot authorize the executive to do so. That is exactly what the Bill of Attainder Clause and the procedural aspect of the Due Process Clause of the US Constitution, and equivalent provisions in the constitutions of other nations, are understood to mean.

In order to explore the significance of judicial hyperindependence in more depth, it is useful to consider its origin in the English-speaking world. The standard account

---

[6] Agencies that are insulated from executive supervision are called independent agencies, and are sometime described as depoliticized. I have previously described agencies that are insulated from legislative supervision as well as executive supervision (a relatively rare device) as hyperdepoliticized (Rubin 2012).

of its origins was based on myth – the myth that judges were applying in-dwelling principles that emerged from ancient custom. To the premodern mind, this gave common law a noble pedigree, second only to divine inspiration, because custom was regarded as the product of divinely granted rationality (Aquinas 1948, 1022–25, I-II, Q.97). This myth was invoked by Sir Edward Coke as an instrument of opposition to the Stuarts, since it made the common law more venerable than the English monarchy, and it still serves as a conceptual basis for America's hopelessly outdated legal education system (Pocock 1987, 30–55).

Modern historical research, however, reveals that the common law was in fact the result of statutory enactments by King Henry II during the latter part of the twelfth century (Mortimer 1994, 53–63; Pollock and Maitland 1968, 136–73; Warren 1977, 317–61). Prior to these enactments, England, like other parts of Christian Europe, possessed a complex patchwork of feudal jurisdictions, with each baron, earl and sometimes lowly subvassal maintaining a separate court to resolve disputes within his fiefdom (Bloch 1961, 359–74; Ganshof 1996, 158–67; Gies and Gies 1990, 172–94; Mortimer 1994, 51–54). Henry did not abolish these courts,[7] but he established royal courts to displace them in important cases, which generally meant cases involving land ownership. His main motivation for doing so was that he had come to power as a result of the civil war between Stephen and Maude, who had issued conflicting land grants in an effort to secure support, and he wanted to resolve those disputes with a single set of uniform, or common rules.[8] He also wanted to collect the court fees, which were a substantial source of income, rather than having them go to the truculent barons who presided over the various feudal courts. Given these motivations, Henry did not care what rules were implemented by the courts, so long as the rules were uniform and he received the fees. Thus, he delegated the task of developing the rules to the judges themselves, which is why we use the misnomer "common" to refer to incremental, judge-made legal rules.

Once the Enlightenment had begun the work of demolishing the Western world's mythology, common law became vulnerable to systematic displacement by the newly developing administrative state. Its partial, albeit increasingly attenuated, survival can be attributed to the reasons that derive from its historical reality, rather than the myth. Unlike France, which ushered in a modern, administrative state by revolution, and Austria, which did so through the efforts of an enlightened but intemperate despot, Britain's modern state evolved in a gentle and gradual way (Rubin 2005, 29–36). Its domestic concerns were the need for professional administrators, the abolition of slavery in the colonies, the impact of enclosure in the countryside and industrialization in the cities, the slovenly harshness of its criminal justice system and the desperate

---

[7] In fact, one of the provisions that Henry's son, King John, agreed to in Magna Carta (Ch. 34) was that the baronial courts would be protected against the writ of *praecipe* (Holt 1992, 173–79, 277).

[8] Thus, his statutes, or assizes, authorized the writs of *novel disseisin* and *mort d'ancestor*, to bring disputes about land between two contestants, or between one contestant and the heirs of another, into the royal courts (Pollock and Maitland, 1952, 145–54).

plight of the poor throughout the realm (Churchill 1957, 237–51; Tevelyan 1948, vol. III, at 64–156). These issues were not seen as involving common law rules regarding contracts, torts or property, and only tangentially regarded as requiring changes in the common law definitions of crime. Thus, nineteenth-century British reformers were content to leave the common law in place.

In the newly formed United States, the view was largely the same. Modern historians have declared the American Revolution to be "radical" or "ideological," but such terms apply only in the political realm (Bailyn 1992; Wood 1991). The zeal of the Revolution's leaders did not extend to the details of personal relations or business arrangements. In these areas, they were content to leave the status quo intact (Friedman 2005, 65–104). In other words, the nineteenth-century Americans, like the nineteenth-century British, simply did not care about the areas governed by common law. It did not matter to them whether a defect in a manufactured product was regarded as foreseeable negligence, whether contractual terms of adhesion were enforceable, or whether one property owner could sue another for nuisance because of the smell produced by the second owner's pigs. In preserving common law in the interest of tradition and convenience, they were securing judicial hyperindependence – the insulation of the courts from the legislature as well as the executive.

By the end of the nineteenth century, however, the situation had changed. One of the major causes of this change was the introduction of Uneeda Biscuits by the newly organized National Biscuit Corporation in 1898. Nabisco had decided that it needed to find a way to market crackers so they would not spoil when stored in the proverbial cracker barrel at a general store. It came upon the idea of packaging the product at its factory in waxed paper and selling the packages directly to the public. All at once, it needed to give the product a distinctive name, design its package, and advertise it to the public. Working in reverse, Nabisco hired an advertising agency which named the product Uneeda Biscuits on the basis of the slogan it invented ("Do you know Uneeda Biscuit"), and designed a package featuring a little boy in a raincoat to emphasize the product's resistance to moisture (Fox 1997, 13–39; Sivulka 1998, 4–100). This seemingly modest event, and a few similar ones from the same period, signaled the advent of modern marketing. No longer was the buyer engaged in a personal transaction with the producer, as she was in the traditional village where she went to the baker to buy crackers or the carpenter to buy her furniture. Instead, an increasing range of products were now produced entirely at factories remote from the consumer, advertised in the mass media, and sold in large retail stores. These products rapidly became essential, in part because an increasingly urbanized population depended on them for basic necessities, in part because they provided conveniences and created desires that became the very substance of people's daily lives (Leach 1993).

A second, equally momentous change could be observed in the Nabisco plant that produced Uneeda Biscuits. Here, as elsewhere in industrial America, there was no longer a personal relationship between the employer and the employee. No longer was the employee a relative of the employer, or a future fellow member of his guild, or a parishioner in his church. Every vestige of personal connection or even paternalism was gone from the employment relationship as hundreds or thousands of workers trooped into giant factories each morning and carried out prescribed and regimented tasks under the supervision of professional managers.

When those workers went home in the evening, moreover, they most likely returned to rental property, not a cottage on their employer's land but one unit in a block of tenements owned by a corporation headquartered in a different – and much nicer – part of town. If the worker owned a home, it might well be downwind from the Nabisco plant, where industrial processes had curdled the formerly sweet smell of baked goods into nauseating fumes.

With these changes, the personal relationships that had existed in the past between buyer and seller, employer and employee, landlord and tenant, and adjoining property owners disappeared, and ordinary people found themselves confronting massive, impersonal corporations that lacked feelings in general, to say nothing of feelings for their consumers, employees, tenants and neighbors. Through the democratic process, people turned to the government for protection, redress and equalization. The result was that the law of contract, tort and property, previously seen as even handed and uncontroversial, became a matter of public concern. People demanded legislation, and the enactments that resulted defined an entire segment of American history as the Progressive Era (Chambers 1992; Goldman 1952; Hofstadter 1955; McGerr 2003; Sanders 1999; Wiebe 1967). In other words, the American public – the voting public – was no longer willing to tolerate the hyperindependence of the judiciary that defined the common law. Now they cared, as Henry II had not, about the specific rules governing personal relations, and they demanded that the government displace existing rules and establish new ones.

The federal courts, and specifically the Supreme Court, were distressed by this shift in public attitudes. Their response was a series of decisions, extending through the first third of the twentieth century, striking down various Progressive enactments as unconstitutional (*Adair v. U.S.*, 1908; *Coppage v. Kansas*, 1915; *Jay Burns Baking Co. v. Bryan*, 1924; *Lochner v. New York*, 1905; *New State Ice Co. v. Liebmann*, 1932; *Weaver v. Palmer Bros.*, 1926). Assessments and reevaluations of the Supreme Court's decisions during this period – often described as the Lochner Era after a leading case – have become something of a cottage industry among legal academics (Berstein 2011; Gillman 1993; Kens 1998; Mayer 2011; Morag-Levine 2003, 63–85). One possible explanation that is relevant to the present discussion is that the Court was trying to safeguard common law against displacement by Progressive legislation. Perhaps the justices believed the medieval argument that laws that evolved gradually over time, reflecting the accreted views of many persons, were more rational than those written and enacted all at once. Perhaps they felt that the judiciary's independence from the legislature was an essential feature of this third branch of our government, and could only be overcome with a strong showing of necessity.

In any event, this body of doctrine was definitively rejected in 1937–38 (*West Coast Hotel v. Parrish*, 1937; *United States v. Carolene Prods. Co.*, 1938; Cushman, 1998) and seems unlikely to be revived (Chemerinsky 2006, 625). The result is that judicial independence from the legislature has been recognized as a revocable grant of authority. Unlike independence from the executive, this hyperindependence is not required by any normative principle. It continues in our system because it is familiar and because there remain important areas, such as contracts between businesses, or torts between individuals, where the applicable rules are not of major policy concern. In jurisprudential terms, the legislature either constitutes or represents the sovereign and can exercise all authority within its constitutional limits. Common law, or the independence of the judiciary from the legislature, should be viewed, as Kelsen (2007) points out, as a delegation of authority from the legislature to the courts. Like any other delegation by the sovereign, it can be revoked, and history indicates that it will in fact be revoked whenever its subject matter becomes a source of public attention or concern.

17.1.3 Hyperindependence and Independence from Constitutional Provisions

The distinction between judicial independence and judicial hyperindependence provides a way to conceptualize the role of the courts in a constitutional regime, that is, a regime where a founding or organizational document is recognized as legally authoritative. Such regimes are now the standard form of modern democratic governments, and they are of particular importance in Feeley's account of the way the legal complex can advance and secure political liberalism. Typically, courts are empowered to enforce the terms of the founding document, and this gives them the authority, unique since the time of the Hebrew prophets, to countermand the decisions of the institutions that are in actual, hierarchical control of the governmental apparatus, including its deployment of physical force.[9]

From the perspective of judicial independence, a constitution typically has two effects. First, it almost always secures the judiciary's independence from the executive as a matter of basic fairness to individuals, a principle we describe as procedural due process. This is, as just discussed, the essential component of judicial independence. Second, a constitution typically establishes some measure of judicial hyperindependence, that is, independence from the legislature, defined as the nation's supreme rulemaking institution. The national judiciary of a modern state plays an extremely important role by interpreting the statutes that are enacted by the legislature. In doing so, however, it has no independence. Its role is to interpret statutes in accordance with the legislature's intent (Katzmann 2016). The legislature can always reverse its decisions by revising the

---

[9] In other words, judicial review provides the first functional way since the time of the Hebrew prophets (e.g., Nathan's condemnation of David for sending Uriah the Hittite to the front [2 Samuel 12:1–13]) to institutionalize the widely recognized norm that a duly enacted provision that violates a society's prevailing norms should not be obeyed (Rubin 2008).

legislation, something that the US Congress has done on a regular basis. Quite often, the revision is designed to render the judiciary's decision unsupportable, and thus achieve what the legislature regards as its original purpose in enacting the statute. As long as this capability is only used prospectively, a limit established by the Ex Post Facto Clause of the original US Constitution, no one regards it as a source of unfairness. It simply means that the legislature does not approve of the interpretation that the courts have given to its statute, and therefore decides, by the same procedure as it used to enact that statute, that it will now enact a differently worded one to secure the interpretation that it wants.

But most modern constitutions also provide for judicial review, either explicitly, or, in the case of the US Constitution, where the device originated, by judicial interpretation (*Marbury v. Madison*, 1803). In this case, the judiciary is partially independent of the legislature because it can reach decisions that the legislature cannot overrule. Such independence, unlike the judicial independence granted by the common law, is not revocable. Once the nation's highest court has decided that a statute violates the constitution, the legislature cannot overrule the decision. Of course, it can, and often does, revise the statute to pass judicial scrutiny, but it must do so by complying with the interpretation that the court has imposed, not by precluding that interpretation.

In order for the judiciary to act in this manner, it must also be independent of the executive; that is, judicial independence is a necessary but not sufficient condition for judicial hyperindependence. If the executive could control the decisions of the courts, then the legislature, which controls the executive (always in theory and at least sometimes in practice) can enlist the executive to compel the decision that it wants. It is therefore quite common for courts possessing the power of judicial review to use that power to protect their constitutionally established independence from the executive; this was in fact, the rationale for the US Supreme Court's decision in *Marbury v. Madison* (1803) that established the mechanism in the first place.

Although the judiciary is partially independent of the legislature in regimes that authorize judicial review, it is not independent of the Constitution itself. That is, the authority granted to the judiciary is not the authority to make its own decisions, but the authority to enforce the provisions that appear in the constitutional text. What makes this dependence different from subordination to the executive or the legislature is that a constitution, by definition, is written by an authority that is no longer in existence. Typically, that authority is a specially convened convention, or a specially convened convention and a specially organized vote by some or all of the regime's future citizens.[10] This grants the judiciary a sort of independence from

---

[10] John Elster gets this wrong in his well-known discussion of self-commitment, when he analogizes a constitution to the myth of Ulysses and the Sirens (Elster 2000, 88–174). Ulysses bound himself to the mast of his ship so that he would be unable to succumb to the enticements of the Sirens. A constitution is drafted by a convention which does not bind itself, but rather binds its subordinates (the government and citizens) and then passes out of existence. Thus, it more closely resembles a testamentary document (Rubin, 637–58).

the constitution that can be regarded as midway between its independence from the executive and its independence from the legislature in a common law regime. It is not as complete as independence from the executive, because constitutional courts are supposed to follow the instructions embodied in the constitution itself, whereas, as discussed above, the executive may not issue instructions to a truly independent judiciary. On the other hand, it is more complete than the independence of common law courts from the legislature because it cannot be revoked. This is not because it cannot be revoked in theory, but because there is no one around to exercise the revocation. Some constitutions, including the American, establish a procedure for calling a new constitutional convention, which does have the power to revoke judicial interpretations of the document, but it is a difficult and often impossible process to use, and that makes an enormous difference.

The significance of the hyperindependence from the legislature that a constitution with judicial review provides will depend on the ambiguity of the constitution's provisions. Suppose there is a provision in the constitution whose meaning everyone in the society regards as clear, such as a limit on the number of times the president can be reelected. There is simply no role for the judiciary in these circumstances because a judicial interpretation would add nothing to the understanding of other members of the government and the society. Of course, the president might choose to ignore this accepted meaning, and even give an extra-constitutional excuse for doing so such as emergency, but in this case she would ignore any decision by the judiciary as well. In contrast, where the constitution's provisions are ambiguous, the judiciary's hyperindependence, that is, its independence from the legislature, provides it with the opportunity to declare legal rules, just as it does under a common law regime. In fact, observers have noted that the way the US Supreme Court reaches its decisions bears a close resemblance to the decision process of common law courts.

Conventional discourse in the United States and elsewhere either denies the existence of linguistic ambiguity in the constitutional text or treats it as an unfortunate defect that clear thinking and judicial humility should minimize. By this point, the US Senate confirmation ritual, where nominees pledge to enforce the Constitution "as written," and not according to their own interpretation, has become so wearisome that even the declarations of its absurdity have become clichés. But full appreciation of textual ambiguity's central role in the mechanism of judicial review remains elusive, and here a focus on the varieties of judicial independence can be of assistance.

The US Supreme Court has produced an authoritative and convincing discussion of textual ambiguity in what is perhaps the leading case in modern administrative law, *Chevron, U.S.A. v. NRDC* (1984). The case concerned interpretation of a statute, rather than a constitutional provision. The Court was reviewing a regulation by the agency charged with implementation of the statute, and the question was whether the agency, in drafting its regulation, had interpreted the statute correctly. According to prevailing doctrine, the Supreme Court, in considering the case on appeal, should have interpreted the statutory language itself, since appellate courts traditionally decide questions of law de novo. Instead, the Court held that it would defer to the agency's interpretation. Its rationale was that Congress, in choosing an administrative agency to implement the statute, had intended the agency to resolve statutory ambiguities. In other words, linguistic ambiguity should not be regarded as a drafting error, but rather as explicit grant of rulemaking authority to the institution charged with interpretation of the language in question.

The *Chevron* opinion states that its conclusion applies whether the linguistic ambiguity was consciously intended, was inadvertent, or simply resulted from the failure of the drafters to agree upon more precise linguistic formulations (*Chevron, U.S.A. v. NRDC* 1984, 865). It reaches these conclusions in connection with statutory drafting, but the rationale applies just as well, and perhaps even better to the drafting of a constitution. The constitution's drafters will consciously choose open-ended or ambiguous language in many cases because the document's authority is supposed to extend into a vaguely imaginable or truly unimaginable future. We know for a fact that this concept, having been generated by the Enlightenment, was fully available to the framers of the US Constitution (Bury 1982; Gay 1969, 98–125; Pagden 2013, 341–71; Williams 2004, 92–97, 277–87), and thus to any subsequent constitution drafter. But even if there is no conscious intent, it is a fair conclusion that the drafters were granting rulemaking authority to the interpreter because they knew perfectly well that they could not imagine or provide for every future contingency. To put the matter simply, one does not know what one does not know, and everyone knows that. Drafting even an ordinary statute necessarily involves the recognition that unanticipated situations will arise, and the authority to make new law for those situations is thus implicit in the general grant of interpretive responsibility. Finally, there will be situations where all the drafters know what they want to say but are unable to agree with one another, and conclude passage of the overall instrument to be more important than any individual point. The proliferation of homey metaphors to describe this situation, such as punting or kicking the can down the street, attests to its familiarity. Again, everyone understands that compromises leaving agreed-upon language ambiguous grant rulemaking authority to the interpreter.

Such authority can be understood as partial hyperindependence from a constitution as drafted. It is partial because legal and social norms place limits on the range of possible interpretation, and a court that exceeded such limits might not be obeyed. It is hyperindependence because it involves the authority to make rules, and not merely to adjudicate particular cases. In theory, a constitution need not grant this additional level of independence. It might consist of a limited number of highly detailed provisions; in fact, some American state constitutions have this character, and run to several hundred pages in length. But the US Constitution, and most other modern constitutions, contains a great deal of broadly worded language. Thus, in addition to defining the judiciary as independent of the executive, and granting it the hyperindependence to make rules independent of the legislature, a constitution grants the judiciary the further hyperindependence of making rules independent of the constitution itself.

17.2 THE JUDICIARY'S ROLE IN POLITICAL REFORM

The foregoing discussion of judicial independence can shed some additional light on Malcolm Feeley's insights about the role of what he calls the legal complex in advancing political liberalism. Each form of independence affects the legal complex in a different way. As Feeley and his colleagues reveal in their studies, the actual results vary from one nation and one culture to another, and a full account can only be provided through a microanalysis of the way in which a wide variety of factors interact in each particular situation (Rubin 1996). Nonetheless, it is possible to offer some general observations about the process Feeley has identified. Doing so helps illuminate additional aspects of this process. Conversely, it demonstrates the way in which Feeley's insights clarify the often discussed but insufficiently analyzed subject of judicial independence.

17.2.1 *Independence from the Litigants and the Executive*

Judicial independence from the litigants does not appear to bear any direct connection to political liberalism, or to the general influence of the legal complex on the surrounding society. For the most part, it means that the adjudicatory process is not corrupt, that the litigants can only affect the outcome of their case through the substantive arguments that are recognized as relevant by prevailing legal rules. It is certainly possible for politically liberal regimes to have corrupt judiciaries, just as it is possible for dictatorial regimes to have honest ones. On the other hand, corruption generally favors members of the society's elite, and thus the status quo, in part because they have the resources to bribe judges, in part because judges, who are themselves members of the elite, will be favorably inclined to them where favoritism is acceptable. As such, it is likely to serve as an impediment to reform. It can also serve as a target of reform, however, because corruption is difficult for a regime to justify, even a regime that rejects liberalism in the name of defense, internal order or efficiency. The People's Republic of China, for example, has advanced the justification that its current government represents an "Asian" alternative to democracy and political liberalism. But the notorious corruption of the nation's judiciary has tended to undermine this argument, even among those who find it otherwise convincing.

The essential form of judicial independence, which is independence from the executive, has a more organic relationship to political liberalism. To begin with, this form of independence is a necessary condition for such a regime; no polity can be said to have achieved conditions of political liberalism if those in control of the government can decide to impose criminal punishments on citizens or disrupt their business relationships for political purposes. The reverse is not true, of course; many regimes that are not politically liberal find the regularity and reliability of judicial independence from the executive to be useful. This was the situation in England between the time the common law was initiated by Henry II in the late twelfth century and the time that parliamentary democracy became ascendant in the late eighteenth century. The value of a fair, independent judiciary was almost immediately apparent; what the famous Chapter 39 of the Magna Carta (1215) means when it says that no one will be punished "except by . . . the law of the land" is that the barons who signed the document would be judged by the same rules that governed their inferiors, that is, common law, rather than being subject to feudal duties as direct vassals of the grasping and mercurial King John (Holt 1992, 126–35).

Although judicial independence is not inevitably linked to political liberalism, it does provide opportunities for the legal complex to move society in that direction. Most obviously, it removes one instrument of oppression from the ruling forces, that is, the political trial, just as Chapter 39 of the Magna Carta removed feudal exactions from King John's greedy hands. The analogy is more accurate than it might first appear. It is obvious that in a feudal society such as twelfth- and thirteenth-century England, the ability to rely on feudal custom to exercise control and intimidation over unruly members of the warrior elite was an effective weapon, in large part because it was perceived as legitimate or legal. In postfeudal societies such as the Early Modern and High Modern West, trials can serve a similar function. The Court of Star Chamber, originally a court of equity and a means of imposing justice upon powerful nobles who might overawe an ordinary judge, became an instrument of oppression for the Stuart monarchs (Ackroyd 2015, 140–69). The show trials of the both the Soviet and Nazi regimes are of course notorious (Deutcher 1960, 369–85; Fitzpatrick 1999, 194–217; McCauley 1993, 100–08; Ortner 2018; Shirer 1960, 1069–73). That the Stuarts, facing powerful opposing forces in society, limited in their own authority by long-standing tradition and dealing with a deeply entrenched legal culture, would rely on trials to suppress their enemies is to be expected. But it is somewhat surprising to see totalitarian dictators, in complete control of the awesome apparatus of a modern state, and fully prepared to murder millions of their citizens, nonetheless relying upon trials to convict perceived enemies that they could have murdered with impunity. Apparently, in Western culture, the legitimating force of trials is sufficiently strong that even the absolutely powerful see it as a powerful weapon.

Judicial independence from the executive removes this weapon from the ruler's hands. It will remain possible for the ruler of a nonliberal regime to enact a statute that criminalizes dissent and then obtain convictions under that statue from an independent judiciary. Statutes of this sort were standard for the European monarchies of the Early Modern Era (Beam 2007, 189–209; Kamen 1983, 170–05). Even regimes where political liberalism is well established may enact such legislation when their courage falters, as the United States did during and after both World Wars (Stone 2004). But there is always the risk that an independent judiciary will acquit the accused, either because the ruler hesitated to draft the law in sufficiently oppressive terms or because the ruler drafted it in such oppressive terms that judges purposefully misinterpret it. Such acquittals not only set an opposition leader free, but serve as a public humiliation for the ruler. Thus, an independent judiciary enables the legal complex to serve as an arena for resistance and reform.

There is, moreover, a more diffuse but possibly more significant way in which judicial independence might contribute to political reform. Independence from the executive creates a social space, an arena, where governmental action can be challenged and criticized in a relatively safe way. Lawyers can use that space to establish their own independence, that is, a sense of a professional identity that involves formulating and following norms that are not established by the government but are generated by their own practices before the court. This has at least two possible effects that might favor political reform. First, it establishes a pattern for civil society; other institutions can then use the judicially protected independence of lawyers as a model for establishing their own independent norms and modes of action (Cohen and Arato 1994). Second, an independent judiciary and bar provides protection for individuals and institutions acting in other areas or by other modes, since the state cannot impose legal punishments on such people at will, but must face opposition from their legal representatives and prove its case to an independent judiciary.

17.2.2 Hyperindependence from the Legislature

It might at first appear that judicial independence from the legislature, that is, the ability of the judiciary to make rules as well as adjudicating cases, would provide an even more favorable arena for the legal complex to advance the cause of political liberalism than standard judicial independence. Generalizations of this sort are difficult, however, because all the examples of common law regimes in Western history consist of England and its possessions, and are thereby embedded in a single historical experience. It would appear, however, that the English common law courts and their progeny, whose defining feature was their independence from the legislature, played a fairly minor role in the advance of political liberalism, despite a certain amount of mythology to the contrary. To be sure, they used their rulemaking power to protect their own independence from the executive, which is no small thing. But it is difficult to ascribe the dramatic advances toward political liberalism in either Britain or America as the work of common law courts.

One reason for this relates to the origin of common law and the revocable nature of the independence it grants to the judiciary. Henry II was willing to permit royal judges to develop rules regarding possession of landed property because his main concern was that disputes between the previously contesting parties be resolved. Precisely how these disputes were resolved was not of primary concern to him so long as civil order was established and maintained. The common law judiciary's continued independence from the legislature – its authority to make legal rules – depends on the legislature's continued perception that the substance of the law created by the courts does not have major policy implications. That is at least one meaning of the familiar maxim that it is more important for the case to be resolved than for the case to be resolved correctly. The need for consideration in creating an enforceable contract, the role of contributory negligence in determining tort liability and the extent of the encumbrances that a testamentary document can impose on landed property are important common law rules, but they are not likely to be of great concern to political leaders who are dealing with foreign affairs, domestic conflict and the health of the economy.

This indifference to the issues that were left to the judiciary to resolve by common law extends even to the definition of criminal offenses. While the general level of crime in society is often a matter of public policy concern, the particular ways in which offenses are defined at their margin are not. In the contemporary United States, where crime policy has proved so useful as an instrument for mobilizing partisan politics and coding otherwise offensive racial attitudes, attention has been directed almost entirely to the length of sentences, not to the definition of crime. Similarly, totalitarian regimes that dominated and politicized so many aspects of society were generally content to treat ordinary crimes in the same way that their predecessors did. Even the harshest dictator has little interest in changing the law of theft so that loyal, tax-paying subjects are arrested under an idiosyncratic definition of theft. Thus, in the criminal as well as civil area, the common law rules that developed in the English-speaking world were generally of little concern to political leaders or the general public. What was of concern was the existence of the common law itself, which was seen, perhaps as a matter of mythology, as something that distinguished Anglo-American society from the more oppressive regimes of continental Europe. These two factors operated in tandem to preserve the judiciary's hyperindependence, while simultaneously rendering it of limited value in efforts to advance political liberalism.

The relatively low political profile of common law rules may seem surprising in light of the general view that the common law is animated by deep and abiding principles embodying the very essence of Anglo-American legal culture. This is once again a matter of mythology, a way that the judiciary justified its rulemaking authority without emphasizing the fact that this authority was granted by the legislative function and could be revoked at the will of whatever institution exercised that function. In fact, common law seems to develop and extend its rules incrementally, by analogy, and without a general plan, like ants building a bridge across an open space by attaching their bodies to each other. To the extent that common law is truly generated by underlying principles, rather than by day-to-day predicaments, however, the principles involved tend to be conventional standards of behavior. They provide that people should know the normal consequences of their actions, that they should avoid harming other persons or their property, and that they should take reasonable precautions against the possibility that others will harm them. Principles such as these, even assuming they are embedded in the legal culture, may instantiate an irenic and efficient social order, but they are unlikely to be the basis for political reform.[11]

There are exceptions to this general pattern, but some of them support the basic observation. In 1709, the British Parliament enacted the Statute of Anne, which provided copyright protection for published work (Parliament of Great Britain 1710; Deazley 2004; Rose 1993). Common law judges might have developed legal rules regarding such work over time, as they had developed rules regarding other forms of property. But published books had been controlled by a royal monopoly, precisely because English monarchs, particularly during the Reformation (Edwards 2004; Eisenstein 1980, 303–451; MacCulloch 2004, 70–83), recognized that this particular form of property, unlike cows or clocks, could exercise powerful effects on public opinion. The Statute of Anne was thus enacted to address an issue that had already been identified as a matter of political concern, and thus outside the ambit of common law and the competence of common law judges.

In contrast, American consumer legislation, such as the Truth in Lending Act (US Code, Title 15 §§ 1600–13, 1631–41, 1671–77) and the Magnuson Moss Warranty Act (US Code, Title 15, § 2301–2312) imposed statutory rules on subjects previously governed by the common law, in effect revoking the grant of hyperindependence to the judiciary in the areas it covered. These statutes were enacted because modern mass marketing had undermined the factual premises on which common law rules were based, and because a social movement, focusing on consumer rights, had turned issues involving financial transactions between large companies and ordinary people into a major social policy issue. Significantly, the rationale for both statutes was that common law had failed to develop fair rules of contract and tort in the modern marketing context. In other words, the common law, for all its vaunted fairness and flexibility, was generally regarded as a failure, not only clinging to an outmoded concept of neutrality, but allowing powerful institutions to use that false neutrality as an engine of oppression.

This is not to say that common law courts played no role in advancing political liberalism in English-speaking nations due to their status as hyperindependent, as opposed to simply independent institutions. There were certain judicial doctrines, most notably involving criminal procedure but also concerning freedom of conscience and freedom of speech, that made some progress in premodern common law

---

[11] Thus, one of the reasons why it is educational malpractice to teach only common law to first-semester or first-year law students, aside from the fact that it is no longer our dominant source of legal rules, is that such a curriculum can be delivered without ever referring to the democratic nature of American government (Rubin 2007).

courts. Whether this occurred because of the legal complex or in spite of it has been a matter of some controversy. Leonard Levy argued that the common law courts generally developed and elaborated the common law crimes of blasphemy and seditious libel; his view is that the demand for freedom of speech and conscience was primarily generated by civil society, and that common law doctrine served to impede, rather than advance this demand (Curtis 2000; Eldridge 1995; Levy 1960). This view has come under attack from other observers, however, who regard the correlation between common law regimes and political liberalism as an indication that there is a causal relationship between the two (Klug, Starmer and Weir 1996).

A famous American case that could be regarded as a common law contribution to political liberalism was the trial of John Peter Zenger during the colonial period (Butler 2000, 112–15; Kluger 2016).[12] Charged with seditious libel, Zenger was acquitted through what can be best described as jury nullification. Thus, the case did not provide a doctrinal precedent, but it may well have been more important as an indication that American juries would not display the solicitude for public officials that made the common law crime a useful instrument of political control. In this sense, it could be said to have advanced the cause of political liberalism. But it did so through the independence of the courts, whose outcomes could not be dictated by government officials, rather than through hyperindependence, which would have denied those officials the ability to try Zenger in the first place.

17.2.3 *Hyperindependence and the Constitution*

Judicial hyperindependence beyond common law is provided by judicial review under a constitution. As stated above, this independence only confers rulemaking authority, akin to common law, if the constitution contains ambiguous terms. But if this mode of judicial independence is to serve as a means of advancing political liberalism, there needs to be a certain level of specificity about those terms, that is, they need to indicate that issues contributing to political liberalism are within the ambit of judicial concern. Virtually all modern constitutions display this dual feature: they guarantee many of the basic features of political liberalism, but do so in general or ambiguous terms. The result is that constitutional courts are in fact guided by embedded principles that provide them with a foundation on which new legal doctrines can be built. These are different from the animating principles of common law, which, as just described, are often mythological constructions or, if real, are cabined within politically insignificant areas. Rather, they create the possibility of instantiating basic elements of a politically liberal regime: constrained government authority and individual rights.

Here as well, however, there has been controversy over whether this possibility has been, or even can be realized. According to Gerald Rosenberg, it is a "hollow hope,"

---

[12] Zenger himself wrote an account of the trial (Zenger 2010).

an expectation that the judiciary is in fact unable to fulfill (Rosenberg 2008). Rosenberg's account of the US Supreme Court's meager achievements in advancing political liberalism have recently been joined by Geoffrey Stone's meticulous analysis of free speech protection during wartime (Stone 2004) and by Erwin Chemerinsky's reassessment of the Court's performance during the entirety of its existence. Feeley and Miyazawa reach a similar conclusion regarding the Japanese Supreme Court's performance in that nation's post-World War II democratic era (Feeley and Miyazawa, 2007). The generality of their conclusions points to basic structural impediments in a constitutional court's ability to initiate or implement genuine political or social change. These might include the almost inevitable membership of judges in the ruling elite, the difficulty of carrying out a coordinated program by means of individual decisions, the judiciary's lack of administrative resources, its inability to mobilize other forces in society, and the judges' awareness of these limitations, combined with a debilitating timidity about risking the legitimacy of their position and their institution.

It is here that Malcolm Feeley's concept of the legal complex offers one of its most valuable insights. In assessing the mechanisms by which the cause of political liberalism is, and can be advanced, it is more useful to treat the legal complex rather than the judiciary as the unit of analysis. That is, the question should not be what constitutional courts can do on their own, because courts simply cannot act on their own. Their cases are initiated by attorneys for the moving party, their information is provided by attorneys for both parties and their decisions are implemented by attorneys for the parties or by executive officials. The impact of the legal complex, therefore, cannot be measured solely by results in decided cases, but rather is determined by the interaction of judges, private lawyers, government lawyers and even legal academics.

As stated above, ordinary judicial independence creates an arena of action that has the effect of establishing an independent legal profession and of protecting individuals that the government attempts to punish. The hyperindependence produced by ambiguous and rights-oriented constitutional provisions politicizes that arena. First, it allows for arguments that are directed at state policies, and not merely state practices, to be advanced. In an ordinary case before an independent judge, the attorney for the accused can argue that his client's speech did not fall into the category of seditious libel, but he cannot challenge the common law or statute that defines this crime. Such challenges become possible under a constitution. As a result, political or issue-oriented groups of lawyers can develop; there can be a civil rights bar, a gay rights bar, an environmental bar, a prisoners' rights bar and so forth.

Although these groups must experience a certain modicum of success if they are to continue functioning, their influence does not depend on winning most of their cases or securing a major precedent in their favor. There was an active civil rights bar before *Brown* v. *Board of Education* (1954), and despite the somber shadow of *Plessy* v. *Ferguson* (1896) (see Brown-Nagin 2012, 17–131; Mack 2014; Tushnet 1996). There was an active gay rights bar before *Lawrence* v. *Texas* (2003) (see Cain 2000; Stein 2012). These groups of lawyers, having organized around potential constitutional protections, then provide ordinary law protection for their clients in individual cases, combatting government efforts to accuse them of crimes and private efforts to take advantage of their unpopularity. They establish a normative discourse that partially validates the group within civil society, even if it fails to achieve the legal protection it desires. In other words, the mere presence of an organized bar, generated and sustained by the possibility of constitutional validation, can produce important advances in political liberalism even if full validation from the courts is not forthcoming.

The second effect produced by action within the arena created by ambiguous, rights-oriented constitutional provisions is to ally the legal complex with broader social movements (Della Porta and Diani 1999; Gamson 1990; Melucci 1989; Oberschall 1996; Tarrow 1994; Touraine 1981). The sorts of principles that animate constitutional provisions are likely to connect with nonlegal reform efforts within civil society to a much greater extent than any in-dwelling principles of common law. People are more likely to take to the streets in favor of the right to vote than in favor of the nonenforceability of contracts without consideration, and women's rights will attract more support than the reasonable man. Ultimately, social movements with broad support are likely to affect legal doctrine. It may look as if the causal arrow is moving in only one direction, but in fact the arena of legal hyperindependence may have played an important role in mobilizing the social movement in the first place. Conversely, even if the social movement does not produce a change in legal doctrine, the effort to effect such a change, and even the failure to achieve it, may serve as a means of mobilizing change by other means. Despite the urging of many political and legal theorists, for example, the US Supreme Court has never recognized an affirmative right to subsistence, education or health care, but the idea that these should be recognized may well have facilitated the enactment of statutory provisions to the same effect.

CONCLUSION

Judicial independence is a widely discussed subject, and both its contours and its rationale have become familiar. We know that it involves the insulation of the courts from control by the executive, and that its purpose is to ensure fair treatment of individual litigants. But Malcolm Feeley offers us a new way of thinking about both the structure and meaning of this subject, as he has about so many others. Judicial independence, he informs us, is not simply the creation of a single barrier to influence, but rather a component of the legal complex, a dynamic, polymorphic interaction among judges, lawyers, legislators and executive officials. Its purpose is not simply to provide fairness for litigants, but also to secure basic human rights and impose constraints on governmental power, thereby advancing the political liberalism of the regime as a whole.

In providing these insights, he reveals new relationships and issues regarding the role of the judiciary. These include the independence of the judiciary from private lawyers, its independence from the legislation through common law and constitutional law, its ability to serve as an arena for mobilizing the forces that support political liberalism and its authority to make rules on its own that advance a liberal agenda.

REFERENCES

Ackerman, Susan Rose. 1999. *Corruption in Government: Causes, Consequences, and Reform*. New York: Cambridge University Press.
Ackroyd, Peter. 2015. *Rebellion: The History of England from James I to the Glorious Revolution*. New York: St. Martin's Press.
Aquinas, Thomas. 1948. *Summa Theologica*. Translated by Fathers of the English Dominican Province. Notre Dame: Ave Maria Press.
Bailyn, Bernard. 1992. *The Ideological Origins of the American Revolution*. Rev. edn. Cambridge, MA: Harvard University Press.
Beam, Sara. 2007. *Laughing Matters: Farce and the Making of Absolutism in France*. Ithaca: Cornell University Press.
Bernstein, David E. 2011. *Rehabilitating Lochner: Defending Individual Rights Against Progressive Reform*. Chicago: University of Chicago Press.
Bloch, Marc. 1961. *Feudal Society*. Translated by L. A. Manyon. Chicago: University of Chicago Press.
Bosworth, R. J. B. 2007. *Mussolini's Italy: Life under the Fascist Dictatorship, 1915–1945*. New York: Penguin.
Brown-Nagin, Tomiko. 2012. *Courage to Dissent: Atlanta and the Long History of the Civil Rights Movement*. New York: Oxford University Press.
Burbank, Stephen B. and Barry Friedman, eds. 2002. *Judicial Independence at the Crossroads: An Interdisciplinary Approach*. Thousand Oaks: Sage.
Bury, J. B. 1932. *The Idea of Progress: An Inquiry into its Growth and Origins*. New York: Dover Publications.
Butler, Jon. 2000. *Becoming America: The Revolution Before 1776*. Cambridge, MA: Harvard University Press. 112–15.
Cain, Patricia A. 2000. *Rainbow Rights: The Role of Lawyers and Courts in the Lesbian and Gay Civil Rights Movement*. New York: Routledge.
Carrington, Paul. 1998. "Judicial Independence and Democratic Accountability in the Highest State Courts." 61 *Law & Contemporary Problems* 61: 79.
Chambers II, John Whiteclay. 1992. *The Tyranny of Change: America in the Progressive Era, 1890–1920*. New Brunswick: Rutgers University Press.
Chemerinsky, Erwin. 2015. *The Case Against the Supreme Court*. New York: Penguin.
  2006. *Constitutional Law: Principles and Policies*. 3rd edn. New York: Wolters Kluwer.
Churchill, Winston S. 1957. *A History of the English-Speaking Peoples*. New York: Dodd, Mead & Co.
Cohen, Jean L. and Andrew Arato. 1994. *Civil Society and Political Theory*. Cambridge: MIT Press.
Curtis, Michael Kent. 2000. *Free Speech, "The People's Darling Privilege": Struggles for Freedom of Expression in American History*. Durham: Duke University Press.

Cushman, Barry. 1998. *Rethinking the New Deal: The Structure of a Constitutional Revolution.* New York: Oxford University Press.
De Grand, Alexander J. 2004. *Fascist Italy and Nazi Germany: The 'Fascist' Style of Rule.* 2nd edn. New York: Routledge.
Deazley, Ronan. 2004. *On the Origin of the Right to Copy: Charting the Movement of Copyright Law in Eighteenth Century Britain, 1695–1775.* Portland: Hart Publishing.
Della Porta, Donatella and Mario Diani. 1999. *Social Movements: An Introduction.* Oxford: Blackwell.
Deutscher, Isaac. 1960. *Stalin: A Political Biography.* New York: Vintage.
Devins, Neal. 1994. "Unitariness and Independence Solicitor General Control over Independent Agency Litigation." *California Law Review*, 82: 255.
Dubois, Philip L. 1980. *From Ballot to Bench: Judicial Elections and the Quest for Accountability.* Austin: University of Texas Press.
Dotan, Yoav. 2014. *Lawyering for the Rule of Law: Government Lawyers and the Rise of Judicial Power in Israel.* Cambridge: Cambridge University Press.
Edwards, Mark U. 2004. *Printing, Propaganda and Martin Luther.* Minneapolis: Augsburg Fortress Press.
Diarmaid, MacCulloch. 2003. *The Reformation: A History.* 70–87.
Eisenberg, Melvin A. 1991. *The Nature of the Common Law.* Cambridge, MA: Harvard University Press.
Eisenstein, Elizabeth L. 1980. *The Printing Press as an Agent of Change.* Cambridge: Cambridge University Press.
Eldridge, Larry. 1995. *A Distant Heritage: The Growth of Freedom of Speech in Early America.* New York: New York University Press.
Elster, Jon. 2000. *Ulysses Unbound: Studies in Rationality, Precommitment and Constraints.* Cambridge: Cambridge University Press
Feeley, Malcolm and Setsuo Miyazawa. 2007. "The State, Civil Society and the Legal Complex in Modern Japan: Continuity and Change." In *Fighting for Political Freedom: Comparative Studies of the Legal Complex and Political Liberalism*, edited by Terrence C. Halliday, Lucien Karpik and Malcolm Feeley, 151. London: Bloomsbury.
Feeley, Malcolm and Edward L. Rubin. 1998. *Judicial Policy Making and the Modern State: How the Courts Reformed America's Prisons.* Cambridge, UK: Cambridge University Press.
Fitzpatrick, Sheila. 1993. *Everyday Stalinism: Ordinary Life in Extraordinary Times: Soviet Russia in the 1930s.* Oxford: Oxford University Press.
Fox, Stephen. 1997. *The Mirror Makers: A History of American Advertising and its Creators.* Urbana: University of Illinois Press.
Friedman, Lawrence. 2005. *A History of American Law.* 3rd edn. New York: Touchstone.
Gamson, William A. 1990. *The Strategy of Social Protest.* 2nd edn. Belmont: Wadsworth Publishing.
Ganshof, F. L. 1996. *Feudalism.* Translated by Philip Grierson. Toronto: University of Toronto Press.
Gay, Peter. 1969. *The Enlightenment: The Science of Freedom.* New York: W.W. Norton & Co.
Gies, Frances and Joseph Gies. 1990. *Life in a Medieval Village.* New York: Harper & Row.
Ginsburg, Tom and Tamir Moustafa. 2008. *Rule by Law: The Politics of Courts in Authoritarian Regimes.* New York: Cambridge University Press.
Goldman, Eric. 1952. *Rendezvous with Destiny: A History of Modern American Reform.* New York: Alfred A. Knopf.
Gillman, Howard. 1993. *The Constitution Besieged: The Rise and Demise of Lochner.* Durham: Duke University Press.

Guarnieri, Carlo. 2007. "Lawyers and Statist Liberalism in Italy." In *Fighting for Political Freedom: Comparative Studies of the Legal Complex and Political Liberalism*, edited by Terrence C. Halliday, Lucien Karpik and Malcolm Feeley, 439. London: Bloomsbury.

Halliday, Terrence C., Lucien Karpik and Malcolm Feeley. 2007. "The Legal Complex and Struggles for Political Liberalism." In *Fighting for Political Freedom: Comparative Studies of the Legal Complex and Political Liberalism*, edited by Terrence C. Halliday, Lucien Karpik and Malcolm Feeley, 1. London: Bloomsbury.

Hofstadter, Richard. 1955. *The Age of Reform: From Bryan to FDR*. New York: Vintage.

Holt, J. C. 1992. *Magna Carta*. Cambridge: Cambridge University Press.

Kamen, Henry. 1983. *Spain, 1469–1714: A Society of Conflict*. New Haven: Yale University Press.

Katzmann, Robert. 2016. *Judging Statutes*. New York: Oxford University Press.

Kens, Paul. 1998. *Lochner v. New York: Economic Regulation on Trial*. Lawrence: University of Kansas Press.

Kelsen, Hans. 2007. *General Theory of Law and State*. Translated by Anders Wedberg. Clark: Lawbook Exchange.

Klug, Francesca, Keir Starmer and Stuart Weir. 1996. *The Three Pillars of Liberty: Political Rights and Freedoms in the United Kingdom*. New York: Routledge.

Kluger, Richard. 2016. *Indelible Ink: The Trials of John Peter Zenger and the Birth of America's Free Press*. New York: W.W. Norton.

Leach, William. 1993. *Land of Desire: Merchants, Power, and the Rise of a New American Culture*. New York: Vintage.

Lee, Rex E. 1988. "Lawyering in the Supreme Court: The Role of the Solicitor General." *Loyola Los Angeles Law Review*, 21: 1059.

Levy, Leonard W. 1960. *Legacy of Suppression: Freedom of Speech and Press in Early American History*. New York: Harper Torchbook.

Mack, Kenneth. 2014. *Representing the Race: The Creation of the Civil Rights Lawyer*. Cambridge, MA: Harvard University Press.

Mayer David. 2011. *Liberty of Contract: Rediscovering a Lost Constitutional Right*. Washington, DC: Cato Institute.

MacCulloch, Diamaid. 2003. *The Reformation: A History*. New York: Penguin.

McCauley, Martin. 2014. *The Soviet Union, 1917–1991*. London: Longman.

McGerr, McGerr. 2003. *A Fierce Discontent: The Rise and Fall of the Progressive Movement in America*. New York: Free Press.

Melucci, Alberto. 1989. *Nomads of the Present: Social Movements and Individual Needs in Contemporary Society*. Translated by John Keane and Paul Mier. Philadelphia: Temple University Press.

Morag-Levine, Noga. 2003. *Catching the Wind: Regulating Air Pollution in the Common Law State*. Princeton: Princeton University Press.

Mortimer, Richard. 1994. *Angevin England, 1154–1258*. Oxford: Blackwell.

Oberschall, Anthony. 1996. *Social Movements: Ideologies, Interests and Identities*. New York: Routledge.

Ortner, Helmut. 2018. *Hitler's Executioner: Roland Freisler, President of the Nazi People's Court*. Barnsley: Frontline Books.

Orwell, George. 1934. *Burmese Days*. New York: Harcourt, Brace.

Pagden, Anthony. 2013. *The Enlightenment and Why It Still Matters*. New York: Random House.

Paxton, Robert O. 2004. *The Anatomy of Fascism*. New York: Vintage.

PBS Newshour. 2005. "Debate Brews over Splitting Ninth Circuit Court." www.pbs.org/newshour/bb/law-jan-june05-controversial_1–17.

Pocock, J. G. A. 1987. *The Ancient Constitution and the Feudal Law*. Cambridge: Cambridge University Press.

Pollock, Frederick and Frederic Maitland. 1952. *The History of English Law Before the Time of Edward I*. Edited by S. F. C. Milsom. Cambridge: Cambridge University Press.

Rose, Mark. 1993. *Authors and Owners: The Invention of Copyright*. Cambridge, MA: Harvard University Press.

Rosenberg, Gerald. 2008. *The Hollow Hope: Can Courts Bring About Social Change*. 2nd edn. Chicago: University of Chicago Press.

Rubin, Edward L. 2017. *Lochner and Property, in Nicholas Parrillo, Administrative Law from the Inside Out: Essays on Themes in the Work of Jerry L. Mashaw*. New York: Cambridge University Press.

  2013. "The Illusion of Property and a Right and Its Reality as an Imperfect Alternative." *Wisconsin Law Review*, 2013: 573.

  2012. "Hyperdepoliticization." *Wake Forest Law Review* 47: 631.

  2008, "Judicial Review and the Right to Resist." *Georgetown Law Review* 97: 61.

  2005. *Beyond Camelot: Rethinking Politics and Law for the Modern State*. Princeton: Princeton University Press.

  2007. "What's Wrong with Langdell's Method, and What to Do About It." *Vanderbilt Law Review*, 60: 609.

  1996. "The New Legal Process, the Synthesis of Discourse, and the Microanalysis of Institutions." *Harvard Law Review*, 109: 1393.

Russell, Peter H. and David M. O'Brien, eds. 2001. *Judicial Independence in the Age of Democracy: Critical Perspectives from around the World*. Charlottesville: University of Virginia Press.

Salokar, Rebecca M. *The Solicitor General: The Politics of Law*. Philadelphia: Temple University Press.

Sanders, Elizabeth. 1999. *Roots of Reform: Farmers, Workers, and the American State 1877–1917*. Chicago: University of Chicago Press.

Shapiro, Martin. 1981. *Courts: A Comparative and Political Analysis*. Chicago: University of Chicago Press.

Shirer, William L. 1960. *The Rise and Fall of the Third Reich: A History of Nazi Germany*. New York: Simon & Schuster.

Shugerman, Jed Handelsman. 2012. *The People's Courts: Pursuing Judicial Independence in America*. Cambridge, MA: Harvard University Press.

Sivulka, Juliann. 1998. *Soap, Sex, and Cigarettes: A Cultural History of American Advertising*. Belmont: Wadsworth.

Stein, Marc. 2012. *Rethinking the Gay and Lesbian Movement*. New York: Routledge.

Stone, Geoffrey R. 2004. *Perilous Times: Free Speech in Wartime: From the Sedition Act of 1798 to the War on Terrorism*. New York: W.W. Norton.

Tarrow, Sidney. 1994. *Power in Movement: Social Movements, Collective Action and Politics*. Cambridge: Cambridge University Press.

Tarr, G. Alan. 2012. *Without Fear or Favor: Judicial Independence and Judicial Accountability in the States*. Stanford: Stanford University Press.

Tate, C. Neil and Torbjorn Vallinder, eds. 1997. *The Global Expansion of Judicial Power*. New York: New York University Press.

Thompson, Dennis F. 1987. *Political Ethics and Public Office*. Cambridge, MA: Harvard University Press.

Touraine, Alain. 1981. *The Voice and the Eye: An Analysis of Social Movements*. Translated by Alan Duff. Cambridge: Cambridge University Press.
Trevelyan, G. M. 1948. *History of England*. 3rd edn. Garden City: Doubleday & Co.
Tushnet, Mark. 1996. *Making Civil Rights Law: Thurgood Marshall and the Supreme Court, 1931–1961*. New York: Oxford University Press.
Underkuffler, Laura S. 2013. *Captured by Evil: The Idea of Corruption in Law*. New Haven: Yale University Press.
Warren, W. L. 1977. *Henry II*. Berkeley: University of California Press.
Weber, Max. 1978. *Economy and Society*. 8th edn. Edited by Guenther Roth and Claus Wittich. Berkeley: University of California Press.
Wiebe, Robert H. 1967. *The Search for Order, 1877–1920*. New York: Hill and Wang.
Williams, David. 2004. *Condorcet and Modernity*. Cambridge: Cambridge University Press.
Wood, Gordon S. 1991. *The Radicalism of the American Revolution*. New York: Vintage.
Zenger, John Peter. 2010. *A Brief Narrative on the Case and Tryal of John Peter Zenger*. Edited by Paul Finkelman. New York: St. Martin's Press.

CASES

Adair v. U.S., 1908. 208 U.S. 161.
Brown v. Board of Education, 1954. 347 U.S. 483.
Chevron v. NRDC, 1984. 467 U.S. 837.
Coppage v. Kansas, 1915. 236 U.S. 1.
Institute of Cetacean Research v. Sea Shepherd Conservation Society, 2012. No. 12–35266 (Ninth Cir., Oct. 9).
Jay Burns Baking Co. v. Bryan, 1924. 264 U.S. 504.
Lawrence v. Texas, 2003. 539 U.S. 558.
Lochner v. New York, 1905. 198 U.S. 45.
Marbury v. Madison, 1803. 5 U.S. 137.
New State Ice Co. v. Liebmann, 1932. 285 U.S. 262.
Plessy v. Ferguson, 1896. 163 U.S. 537.
Republican Party v. White, 2002. 536 U.S. 765.
United States. v. Carolene Products Co., 1938. 304 U.S. 144.
Weaver v. Palmer Bros., 1926. 270 U.S. 402.
West Coast Hotel v. Parrish, 1937. 300 U.S. 379.

STATUTES

Judicial Conference of the United States, 2014. Code of Conduct for United States Judges (2014), Canon 3(C).
Parliament of Great Britain, 1710, Statute of Ann or Copyright Act.
US Code, Title 5. Administrative Procedure Act, P.L. 79–404, 60 Stat. 237 (1946), amended by P.L. 94–409, 90 Stat. 1247 (1976).
US Code, Title 15. Truth in Lending Act, P.L. 90–321, 82 Stat, 146 (1968).
US Code, Title 15. Magnuson Moss Warranty Act, P.L. 93–637, 88 Stat. 2192 (1975).

18

The Legal Complex and Lawyers-in-Chief

Kim Lane Scheppele

18.1 LAW, LEGALISM AND ANTILIBERALISM

In their thought-provoking work on the "legal complex," Terry Halliday, Lucien Karpik and Malcolm Feeley posit that those who have been trained as lawyers are likely to act on behalf of political liberalism to advocate for the realization of basic civil liberties and access to justice (Halliday and Karpik 1998; Halliday, Karpik and Feeley 2007, 2012). By broadening studies of the legal profession to the study of legally educated elites more generally and examining the way that these elites act in a variety of politically challenging contexts, Halliday, Karpik and Feeley (HKF) have imagined a new relationship between law and politics. In their hands, law is more than persons or institutions; law generally embeds a set of liberal ideas that guide the development of politics. Legally trained people are the carriers of these ideas and, while their ability to articulate liberal values and their success in making those values real are contingent on social circumstances, the many case studies in the HKF volumes show that people trained in law are often in the vanguard of political liberalism.

In this chapter, I will take on the HKF agenda but will explore the dark side of the force, so to speak. While lawyers have a well-deserved reputation for defending political liberalism, they also have a reputation for being "legalistic." Legalistic lawyers pay scrupulous attention to law, advocating a sort of law-following that denies law's liberal spirit. Legalism identifies technically correct uses of law that are either indifferent or hostile to political liberalism in the sense described by HKF. For example, the valorization of the legal loophole over legal principle is often associated with "legalistic" conduct. So while HKF have shown how very often legally trained people turn out to defend liberalism in politics, I want to explore how often legally trained people can turn out to be legalists in politics in order to undermine liberal values. This effort should not be taken to undermine the HKF project, but instead to open the question of variation: when, and under what circumstances, do legally trained people press for political liberalism, and when do they use their legal talents to stall or block liberal reform – or, worse yet, use law for illiberal purposes?

Just as HKF started with suggestive case studies and built out more general theories from there, I will do the same. In this chapter, I will examine Hungary and Russia, both countries that are presently led by lawyers-in-chief. Viktor Orbán, prime minister of Hungary, and Vladimir Putin, president of Russia, were deeply trained as lawyers and their governing styles reflect their legal education in important ways. Each has introduced antiliberal reforms in his respective country in a highly legalistic manner. Each has developed a regime that could be characterized as "legalism from the top." Each – with an impeccable use of legal tools – has engaged in monopolization of constitutional power within a constitutional system. Both Putin and Orbán have used similar tactics in dealing with their opponents in ways that were effective at least in part because those who opposed them were not so legally clever.

Building from these case studies, I will argue that a certain type of lawyer in a key executive position – possessed of a lawyer's skills with a drive to monopolize power – can use the law to tie his or her opponents in knots. Law, in the hands of the illiberal lawyer, can be used as a force against liberalism just as easily as it can be used for liberalism. Law, after all, is a neutral tool that gains its content in the hands of its users. This assertion should not be surprising to those who have seen that rule of law reform is no barrier to illiberalism (Massoud 2013). First, however, we should explore the plausible connections between law, legalism and antiliberalism to explain why law is not hard-wired for liberal purposes.

Law is famously difficult to understand for those without legal training, even though one justification for the value placed on the rule of law is that it enables those governed by law to know where they stand. The rule of law is, at a minimum, supposed to be associated with legal certainty, predictability, public rules and consistent enforcement. And those who equate the achievement of the rule of law with emancipatory projects often argue that the reduction of arbitrariness alone produces liberal effects. E. P. Thompson studied the Black Act in England, which was perhaps the purest example of a law explicitly written to preserve noble privilege against the starving peasantry. But as he famously found, even the most illiberal law in the end constrains the powerful and creates openings for the disadvantaged to claim victories and the realization of rights. His conclusion, that law is an "unqualified human good," grew from his findings that clear, predictable and regularly enforced rules eventually gave those at the bottom of the social scale a chance to defend themselves against arbitrary uses of power (Thompson 1975, 263).

But even if law has the potential to rein in arbitrary power, it may not always feel that way to those who are to be governed by law. From Franz Kafka's famous account in *The Trial* of the person doomed to wander around the legal system without knowing the charges or the evidence against him, to the peasant in Anton Chekhov's *The Malefactor* who unscrews a nut from the ties of railroad tracks to use as a fishing weight and then finds himself called before a judge as a criminal defendant because his actions could have caused a hypothetical train accident that never occurred, the ordinary person befuddled by law is a frequent character in fiction across diverse cultures. Law may have the power in the abstract to constrain arbitrariness, but perhaps only if one can know and work within the rules of the system. Law, to the uninitiated, may appear only to baffle and confuse. Law's very technical complexity allows it to be used as a deep resource for the stealth accumulation of power.

The portrayals of the legalistic and obstructionist lawyer conflict with the image one gets of legally trained liberals in the HKF volumes. Their "legal complex" singles out those with legal training as a potentially powerful group to mobilize for liberal values. The HFK corpus shows that liberalism often has a particular power among those who have been educated in law – but not always. Sometimes, of course, legally trained people fail to mobilize. They can be threatened, put off by legal causes that fall outside their narrow window of concern or ineffective when they attempt to enter politics (Halliday, Karpik and Feeley 2007). Failing at a noble cause or even remaining silent in the face of threat would not generate the sort of vicious portrayals we see, however. These negative images of lawyers suggest that they seem to be especially capable of succeeding at ignoble causes. Their occasional absence on the front lines of social causes may be due less to an inability to mobilize and more to the opportunities they see to use the law for illiberal purposes. As Karpik and Halliday noted in their review of the legal complex literature, "ample evidence exists to show how the legal complex has supported regimes that violate the very basis of political liberalism" (Karpik and Halliday 2011, 224), though they do not have a theory about when such illiberal failures occur.

Perhaps we can get a handle on whether and when law tends toward liberalism by noting that a distinction is often drawn between "rule of law," used to describe the sort of legal certainty that is used to enhance liberal values, and "rule by law," where the predictability, clarity and power of the law is used for illiberal ends (Tamanaha 2004; Ginsburg and Moustafa 2008). In short, the uplifting power of law when used in defense of liberal values is matched by a less sunny side of law when it is used instrumentally in order to achieve the monopolization of power, the repression of dissent and the elimination of spaces for evidence and reason. The HKF line of work shows, however, that even in authoritarian governments, courts are not always all bad (Moustafa 2008), which is why political liberalism can succeed even in these challenging and illiberal spaces. It is probably this observation, well grounded in case studies, that provides the strongest case for the inherently liberal character of law.

The potential for lawyers to use their talents for repressive projects is not robustly explored in the HKF line of work. But sometimes authoritarian leaders trained in law do exactly what one would guess with law's powerful potential. Such leaders can turn the neutral potential of legal ideas into illiberal law, sometimes even pulling judges and other legal officials along with them. In Pinochet's Chile, for example, judges went over to the dark side of the force with alarming alacrity (Hilbink 2007). Contemporary Chinese criminal trials are conducted under the shadow of political influence, as lawyers and judges work within a system of illiberal law (Lan 2010). Even the Nuremberg Trials, now considered a model of uplifting legality, were micromanaged at the time on the Soviet side by Andrei Vyshinsky, Stalin's infamous justice minister, who had learned how effective show trials could be for public education (Hirsch 2008). In fact, much of the empirical attention to "rule by law" has examined how judiciaries, prosecutors and those who have legal training have been captured for illiberal purposes precisely through the operation of law.

Since HKF emphasize that legally educated people are often important vectors for political liberalism across a wide variety of special jobs (as judges, academics, private lawyers and prosecutors, for example), we can expand this range to consider other important state officials with legal training, particularly state leaders and especially effective executives. I use the term "effective executive" to designate the executive who carries the primary responsibility for the deployment of executive power under the constitution of the country. Thus, in the United Kingdom, the effective executive is the prime minister rather than the Queen; in Germany, it is the chancellor rather than the president; in France, the effective executive is a shared responsibility between the president (for foreign policy) and prime minister (for domestic policy) where they are of different parties, but the president is the effective executive if the president and prime minister are from the same party, and so on.

While some effective executives with legal training have been liberals, others have not. How can we understand lawyer-leaders against the backdrop of the HKF corpus?

As it turns out, effective executives very often start their careers as lawyers across a wide range of countries, both liberal and illiberal. Many of Canada's prime ministers – and almost all recent ones – have had a degree in law except the current Prime Minister Justin Trudeau, his predecessor Stephen Harper, and that other Albertan Joe Clark. Among recent US presidents, both Barack Obama and Bill Clinton were educated as lawyers. Among recent UK prime ministers, Tony Blair and Margaret Thatcher were lawyers too. Nestor and Cristina Kirchner met as law students before assuming the presidency of Argentina in sequence. Having lawyer/executives is not unique to constitutional-democratic countries. Vladimir Lenin was, famously, a lawyer (Burbank 1995). Singapore's founding Prime Minister Lee Kuan Yew (Mydans 2015) and Ferdinand Marcos of the Philippines were educated as lawyers as well. Perhaps their legal educations influenced the way they governed, too?

While I have never seen an official count, effective executives trained in law seem to be relatively common. Given the many and varied connections between law and politics, one might expect lawyers to govern differently than nonlawyers when they take up effective executive roles. If one believes the central HKF thesis, one would expect these "lawyers in chief" to govern liberally. But, as the list above suggests, this is obviously not uniformly true. Perhaps we should start with a more general hypothesis: that effective executives trained as lawyers will govern *as lawyers* – for good or for ill.

How would an executive govern "as a lawyer"? I hypothesize that a lawyer-executive would take law seriously as an instrument for exercising, consolidating and wielding power. Law, in short, is "the way the state talks to itself," so governing in a rule of law state is done through legal means. Law underwrites state routines and establishes a status quo against which one has to argue hard to win. Winning the law for one's side can defeat a lawyer-executive's political opponents, particularly if that individual is clever enough to design legal reforms that look reasonable (to sideline the critics) but that work in ways that consolidate power in the executive's hands (to use law to gain an edge).

When a lawyer-leader takes office, frenzied lawmaking – where the very speed of the lawmaking effort may put nonlawyers at a disadvantage because they cannot see as quickly or clearly what is going on – may then be accompanied by a period of aggressive legal reinterpretation. Lawyers know that law is always capable of being read in multiple ways. In fact, legal argument often works to the advantage of the disadvantaged when they have liberal legal counsel who can reinterpret the law in their direction, as the HKF line of work makes clear. But if an illiberal lawyer-executive gains the upper hand in the determination of authoritative legal interpretation, or heads off regime-undermining interpretation with strategic appointments or structural reforms that render these regime-undermining interpretations risky for those who might make them, then the lawyer-executive can win the battle over interpretation as well. In short, an illiberal lawyer-in-chief can use legal skills to gain a particular advantage in governing. While lawyering from an executive perch may be in principle a neutral skill – lawyer-leaders can govern liberally or illiberally – I would like to suggest that lawyering skills in an effective executive may be particularly consequential where that lawyer-executive wants to undermine liberal governance. This is true for precisely the reasons that the HKF project suggests: law can be an especially effective vector for political liberalism, so undermining it by law may be the most effective way to bring it down. If a lawyer-executive realizes this and can cut off that influence before it can be realized, liberalism may be hard-pressed to become ascendant any other way. Illiberals always have coercion to fall back on, but liberals are stuck with law.

So with this account of why lawyer-executives may be particularly adept at consolidating power in an illiberal way, let us turn to our case studies: Hungary and Russia.

18.2 LAWYER-EXECUTIVES AND THE CONSOLIDATION OF POWER: THE CASES OF HUNGARY AND RUSSIA

Hungary emerged from direct Soviet influence in 1989 and the Soviet Union itself collapsed two years later, making the Russian Federation – once the largest component piece of the much larger Soviet state – an independent country. The postcommunist transformation of what had been antiliberal states into liberal states was widely regarded as inevitable and a very good thing, more easily achieved in some parts of the former Soviet world than in others. States that had been once located in "Eastern Europe" began insisting that they were now in "East-*Central* Europe" in recognition of their aspirations to belong to the West generally and the European Union specifically. Former Soviet states – those that had been component parts of the Soviet Union – were not as exuberant in their liberal aspirations and were much more ambivalent about whether they "belonged" in the "West," but most took at least some steps in a liberal direction in the 1990s, and virtually all engaged in extensive legal reform.

The naïve language of "transition" assumed at the time that countries that had been in the Soviet orbit would have no other choice but to move toward market-driven constitutionally aspirational democracies on the western European model, signaling the "end of history." By and large, the "end of communism" was thought to signal the end of antiliberal dictatorships. We can now see that what happened was far more complicated and ambivalent across the whole region than that naïve first approximation suggested.

Hungary's "transition" was in many ways a major liberal model for the other states in the region. With the first reformed constitution adopted in the post-Soviet world as part of the roundtable process in 1989, Hungary appeared to be first out of the blocks and fast on its way toward becoming what the political scientists would later call a "consolidated democracy" (Linz and Stepan 1996). In a consolidated democracy, constitutional democratic institutions are the "only game in town," and liberalism is ascendant in a way that becomes hard to challenge. Consolidated democracies are, almost by definition, places where political liberalism has won.

In those early days after 1989, Hungary appeared to follow the HKF model, precisely because lawyers were very prominent in the transition. The first multiparty elections in 1990 brought six parties into the parliament. Five were headed by lawyers, including several from academia. Moving Hungary quickly toward consolidated political liberalism was on the agenda of all of the political parties. The transition was guided prominently by Hungary's powerful Constitutional Court, whose party-neutral judges nonetheless shared a common liberal political vision with the dominant political parties. Hungary was clearly a case of the legal complex in action – in which legally educated leaders were dominant in all of the key offices, guiding Hungary toward political liberalism (Scheppele 2006).

As a result, Hungary quickly settled into a stable multiparty democratic system with a liberal constitution robustly enforced by a Constitutional Court and rotations of party dominance at each election (until the 2006 election, when a sitting government was reelected for the first time). Hungary was in the first wave of postcommunist countries to join both NATO and the European Union with flying colors, with no doubts about its permanent move into the family of constitutional, democratic, liberal and rule of law states. Most observers, myself included, were convinced that Hungary had completed a model transition and had consolidated its democratic and constitutional gains – until the 2010 elections brought lawyer Viktor Orbán into the prime minister's office in a landslide. Orbán almost immediately began rolling back political liberalism, even overtly admitting in 2014 that he was building an "illiberal state" (Orbán 2014). And, as we will see, he used law as his primary tool.

Russia had a much less promising start in its political and legal transition. After 1991, when the Soviet Union collapsed into its federal pieces, a fractious parliament and a strong Constitutional Court in Russia proved to be rather too much of a challenge to emergent leader Boris Yeltsin, who was definitely not a lawyer and who, in fact, had little patience for or understanding of law. In 1993, after the parliament rejected Yeltsin's efforts to rewrite the constitution and after the Constitutional Court ruled repeatedly against his improvised extensions of executive power, Yeltsin called out the tanks to bomb the parliament, shutter the Constitutional Court and push through a new constitution with minimal consultation. After that illiberal flourish, he governed by decree, won a tainted second election and ruled with arbitrariness as his major hallmark. Perhaps that was because he was also an unsteady drunk. Though many thought he would find ways to stay in power forever, he abruptly gave up power in a surprise move by naming Vladimir Putin acting president on New Year's Eve 2000. While Putin then had to stand for election as president of Russia, no one doubted the outcome. Putin then set about to rein in the chaos of the Yeltsin years, starting with a flurry of new laws as befitted his background as a lawyer. Putin's "managed democracy" is routinely considered to have been more managed than democratic, and it surely was more legal than Yeltsin's chaotic democracy. According to Petrov (2005), a managed democracy features: (a) a strong presidency and weak institutions; (b) state control of the media; (c) control over elections allowing elites to legitimize their decisions; and (d) visible short-term effectiveness and long-term inefficiency. The result is an "unstable stability" based on the president's personality. He is actually a hostage of the system. Managed democracy has kept Putin in power for well into his second decade in office.

Russia's transition to a consolidated democracy was therefore much rockier than Hungary's, and the reason often given for the failure of Russia to achieve the status of consolidated democracy was that Russia had had more than seventy years of communism. The states of East-Central Europe had had only about half of that time under Soviet domination, so that the precommunist regimes were still within the living memory of the older population. That said, as Perry Anderson has so convincingly explained, the myth of difference between East-Central Europe and the rest of the Soviet-inflected world was the product of overt lobbying on the part of those who had become close to the dissident groups of East-Central Europe. Once the USSR collapsed, this alleged advanced status of Poland, former Czechoslovakia and Hungary became a self-fulfilling prophecy as foreign investment, special rule of law programs and other assistance (including, for Poland, debt relief) helped these countries "earn" their places at the front of the queue to join Europe (Anderson 1999).

Given what we know about the legal complex, however, we might have guessed that Hungary and Russia were different at the start of their political transitions because of the role of lawyers in the process. With the prominence of lawyers in the Hungarian democratic transition, political liberalism was assured while the general absence of lawyers in the Russian political transition after 1991 made political liberalism less likely. There is certainly an HKF story to tell about these two transitions that would make perfect sense.

With the rise to power of Orbán and Putin relatively far into the transitions, however, both Hungary and Russia came to be governed by very different sorts of lawyers than the sort that typically advance political liberalism. Instead, Hungary and Russia came to be led by lawyers with a will to personal power and a determination to stay in office as long as they could. And this is where the counter-HKF argument begins. Illiberal lawyers can deploy legal tools to wrong-foot the legal opposition.

Before the 2010 election, Orbán had made no secret of his plan to govern for a protracted period, but he was elected in a landslide over an incumbent government that presided over an economic crisis amidst overwhelming evidence of its own corruption. Orbán won the two-thirds majority of parliamentary seats needed to amend the constitution without the assistance of any other party, and that in a free and fair election, but many voted for him without realizing that Orbán would follow an illiberal path. Hungary's consolidated democratic institutions seemed certain to foil any illiberal ambitions he might have had, and he never mentioned that constitutional reform was part of his political program. As we will see, however, Orbán's rapid assault against the legal grounds of consolidated democratic institutions caused them to fail almost immediately. With a distinctively legalistic adjustment to the electoral laws, Orbán has succeeded in winning at least two more terms in office, with no likely successful opposition in sight.

Putin, having come into politics from the ranks of the Soviet KGB's foreign service, was immediately greeted with suspicion as someone who would surely try to stay in office as long as he could and kick the pins out from under the fragile democracy that Yeltsin had built. Putin's first election was chalked up to a general lack of choice combined with the already limited scope of Russian democratic discourse and institutions. Putin's subsequent elections – or at least their margins of victory – were attributed to fraud. Russia became the self-fulfilling prophecy of its critics: a state with a failed consolidation of democracy that once again refused to become properly liberal.

Analysts might have understood better what happened next in both Russia and Hungary once Putin and Orbán came to power if they had focused on the fact that the leaders of each state were clearly clever lawyers. In fact, both did surprisingly similar things to consolidate their own power, using the law as their key weapon against critics at home and abroad. Regardless of the prior state of their constitutional governments – with Hungary looking quite advanced and Russia seeming quite primitive in the development of constitutional democracy – both Orbán and Putin were able to undermine the new democratic institutions through law to substitute something far less liberal.

18.2.1 Constitutional Revolution in Hungary: 2010 and Beyond

After its election in 2010, the Orbán government created a constitutional frenzy. Orbán's Fidesz party won two-thirds of the seats in Parliament in a system where a single vote that garnered an absolute two-thirds majority was enough to change the constitution. Twelve times in its first year in office, it amended the constitution it inherited. Those amendments removed most of the institutional checks that could have stopped what the government did next – which was to install a new constitution. The new Fidesz constitution was drafted in secret, presented to the Parliament with only one month for debate, passed by the votes of only the Fidesz parliamentary bloc, and signed by a president that Fidesz had named. Neither the opposition parties nor civil society organizations nor the general public had any influence in the constitutional process, not least because they had so little time to react and because their ranks of lawyers were far less impressive than those on the Fidesz side. There was no popular ratification. The Fidesz constitution went into effect on January 1, 2012.

While the government claimed it had been given a mandate to make major changes, the general Hungarian public thought otherwise. During the election campaign in 2010, Fidesz never said it would change the whole constitutional system. Once the Fidesz governing program became clear after the party came to power, the popularity of Fidesz plummeted, even more so after the government undertook to replace the constitution. Public support for the government dropped to 17 percent when Fidesz introduced its new constitutional draft in March 2011 and the constitution came into effect in January 2012. But Fidesz's loss of support did not help any other party. Instead, public opinion polls showed that Fidesz' drop in support was accompanied by a rise of those who favored no party at all. This may be because the left opposition simply walked out of the Parliament and did not even both to vote against the new constitution, while the far-right opposition actually liked and supported some of the nationalist elements of the new constitution. Thus, there was nowhere for a voter who wanted to strongly oppose the governing party to go, because none of the other parties staked out a coherent alternative to the Fidesz plan.

Even though the government pushed through a one-party constitution on its own in the face of plummeting public support, this didn't stop the constitutional juggernaut. The government amended its own new constitution four times in the first fifteen months and once more two years later. Each time, the government did so with the votes of *only* its own political bloc, rejecting all proposals from the political opposition and from civil society groups. The current Hungarian constitution remains a one-party constitution.

In spring 2013, the Fidesz government passed a fifteen-page amendment to the new forty-five-page constitution. The Fourth Amendment nullified more than twenty years of rights-protecting case law of the Hungarian Constitutional Court that had been developed before the new constitution went into effect. This left a giant gap where firm legal protection of basic rights once stood. The government's legalistic rationale was that the old decisions went with the old constitution and could no longer be used as good law. But the Fourth Amendment also specifically overturned nearly all of the decisions that the Constitutional Court had made under the new constitution striking down controversial new laws the Fidesz government had championed, so it appeared rather that the government wanted to cut off all sources of potential opposition to its new constitution. The Fourth Amendment removed the Constitutional Court's power to evaluate on substantive grounds any new constitutional amendments, a move which then permitted the governing party to escape review by inserting any controversial new proposal directly into the constitution. The Fourth Amendment removed all traces that the Constitutional Court had once stood for a liberal constitutional order. It entrenched political control of the judiciary and gave the government new tools to prevent the opposition from gaining traction. Under cover of constitutional reform, the Fidesz government gave itself absolute power. With the new constitution the governing party could do virtually anything it wanted, even if civil society, the general public and all other political parties were opposed.

To avoid public discussion of the constitutional revolution, the government introduced many of the new laws, including the constitution itself, most of the constitutional amendments and nearly all of the supermajority laws required by the constitution through the established parliamentary procedure of a "private member's bill." This procedure bypasses the stage of public consultation and ministry review required of all government bills. That, combined with the fact that the Parliament instituted a new rule through which a two-thirds vote could cut off parliamentary debate on any topic, meant that most of these new laws received very little public discussion. It was not uncommon in those first few years of the Fidesz government for a constitutional amendment to go from first proposal to part of the working constitution in just a few weeks, and major laws could be proposed in the morning and could go into effect that same night.

Taken over the four years of Fidesz's first constitutional revolutionary term, the constitutional changes were complicated, detailed and spread out across a new constitution, a half-dozen major constitutional amendments and dozens of "cardinal" (supermajority) laws. In the end, thousands of pages of lawmaking produced a wholly new legal system passed in a giant legislative blur, sometimes in the middle of the night. I strongly suspect that most Hungarians did not understand the details of this new constitutional system, but they could see that it was all "legal." Even Hungarian lawyers were not able to keep up with the total revolution in the law, nor could they find much of a legal toehold to use to object to it, even though it undermined democratic liberalism in Hungary.

How did the new constitutional structure undermine democratic liberalism? To see this, one needs to know that, in the communist period, Hungary had a unicameral parliamentary system of government. This was not surprising, because an illiberal government had no need of checked power. In 1989, however, major constitutional changes in Hungary added a number of checks to this basic framework to turn it into a liberal and democratic government, but underneath the 1989 reforms, the major communist-era structure remained intact. In 1989, a Constitutional Court was created as the primary watchdog on the majoritarian dangers of this unicameral parliamentary system. In the new constitutional design, the Hungarian Constitutional Court conducted the primary oversight in a system that had little formal separation of legislative and executive power; it was the crucial check on power. In a transition where many of the key players were lawyers, putting all of their constitutional eggs in the basket of a powerful court was just the sort of thing that the key actors in a legal complex would do.

Given such weighty responsibility in the 1989 constitutional design, the Constitutional Court was made highly accessible to the new democratic public in Hungary. Literally anyone could ask the Constitutional Court to review a law for constitutionality using a so-called *actio popularis* petition. As a result, virtually every law was challenged in one way or another, so the Constitutional Court acted as if it were an upper legislative chamber. From the time it opened in January 1990, the active Constitutional Court kept each new government under constitutional constraint regardless of the government's political leanings. Opinion polls showed that the Constitutional Court was consistently the most highly respected political institution in Hungary.

The procedure for electing judges to the Constitutional Court before 2010 prevented the Court from being captured by any one political fraction. Because each judicial nominee to the Constitutional Court had to first be approved by a majority of parliamentary parties before then being elected to the Court by a two-thirds vote of the Parliament, the Court always had a balance of different political views represented on the bench.

The Constitutional Court was the primary, but not the only, substantial change made to the constitutional system in 1989 that provided more checks on Hungary's communist-era unicameral parliamentary government. Revamped parliamentary procedure required extensive consultation with both civil society and opposition parties before government bills could be put to a vote. Important issues of constitutional concern required a two-thirds vote of the Parliament. Private members' bills were made possible and also made easier to pass, giving power to those out of government but in the Parliament. The streamlined procedure for private members' bills was there for a reason: it encouraged even independent parliamentarians to participate fully in the lawmaking process to give political opposition more voice.

Four new ombudsmen were added after 1989 to the system of rights protection. Other independent institutions – the central bank, state audit office, prosecutor general's office, national election commission and media board – provided both expertise and additional checkpoints on the untrammeled use of majoritarian power. For example, both the national election commission and the media board were structured to ensure representation from across the political spectrum so they could not be easily dominated by the governing coalition. An independent judiciary ensured that the laws were fairly applied. The judiciary's political independence was assured by making it self-governing . There were so many different checks instituted after 1989 on the power of the prime minister and parliamentary majority that the post-1989 constitutional system worked reliably to ensure that the operation of majoritarian political power did not ride roughshod over democratic guarantees and constitutional limitations.

In contrast with this robust system of complementary powers, the new "Fidesz constitution" removed virtually all of the checks on the power of a unicameral parliamentary system provided by institutions that had been inserted in 1989. Under the Fidesz constitution, the Constitutional Court's power and independence were attacked first; not surprisingly, as the Court provided the most powerful limitation on what a government could do. The system for electing constitutional judges was changed so that a single two-thirds vote of the Parliament became sufficient to put a judge on the Court, abolishing the multiparty agreement that was once necessary for nomination. The Fidesz constitution also expanded the number of judges on the Court from eleven to fifteen, giving the governing party four more judges to name immediately, allowing it to pack the Court. As it happened, the Fidesz government also benefited from the fact that a large number of judges' regular terms ended shortly after the 2010 election. The combined effect of these factors allowed the Fidesz government to select nine of the fifteen judges on the Court in its first three years in office, and the Constitutional Court has rarely challenged the governing party's laws since that time.

Even if the Court is in Fidesz-friendly hands, however, a powerful Court might still be dangerous to a government that shuns checks on its freedom of action. This may explain why the jurisdiction of the Court was cut for good measure. The constitution was changed so that the Court no longer has the power to review laws based on *actio popularis* petitions, which are petitions that anyone can file. Now, the only individuals who can challenge laws must show first that they have been concretely injured by the application of a potentially unconstitutional law, and then that they have exhausted their remedies in the ordinary courts. This is the German system of "constitutional complaints," and it would have been a major boon to the general constitutionalism of the system if the powers of abstract review had not been largely removed at the same time, to the point where abstract review can virtually never be used. Now, if the Constitutional Court only hears cases that have concrete victims, it is hard for the Court to rule on matters pertaining to separation of powers and the structure of democratic institutions. For example, individuals rarely have "standing" to challenge a law that creates a new system for judicial appointments or a law that gives a government agency the power to issue decrees without parliamentary oversight, both laws that have been passed since Fidesz came to power.

In addition to limiting access to the Court, the Fidesz constitution restricted the jurisdiction of the Court in other ways as well. The Court is now barred from reviewing any law that deals with taxes or budgets when those laws are passed at a time when the national debt is more than 50 percent of GDP, a situation likely to exist for the foreseeable future. As a result, if a tax law infringes an individual's constitutionally guaranteed property rights or if such a tax is applied selectively to particular minority groups, there is nothing that the Constitutional Court can do. This opens up a space for the government to violate many personal rights without any constitutional oversight. Not surprisingly, many of the government's most rights-infringing measures have come in the guise of budget adjustments. Nationalizing private pensions, confiscating the assets of a series of rural savings and loans, forcing banks to take foreign-currency mortgage payments based on an artificially set exchange rate, retroactively taxing severance bonuses of public sector workers and targeting particular sectors of the economy for punitive taxes are matters that cannot be challenged before the Constitutional Court any longer – and all were eagerly carried out by the Fidesz government under cover of constitutional darkness. The Fourth Amendment, which eliminated the Court's prior jurisprudence, has also barred the Court from reviewing constitutional amendments for substantive conflicts with constitutional principles. As a result, if the constitution promises freedom of religion, but a constitutional amendment requires a two-thirds parliamentary vote before a church is officially recognized (a provision that was added to the constitution with the Fourth Amendment), the Court can do nothing about this. Or if the constitution says anyone may freely express her opinion, but an amendment says that no one may defame the Hungarian nation (a provision that was also added to the constitution with the Fourth Amendment), there is nothing the Court can do. As long as a sitting government can command a two-thirds majority, the government can directly amend the constitution any time it thinks the Constitutional Court might strike down some policy that the government wants to enact, regardless of how much these new amendments violate principles that have been guaranteed elsewhere in the constitution.

The Orbán constitutional revolution continued by bringing the ombudsman, the central bank, the media council and the election council all under party control – by law. With all of these changes, the popularity of the Fidesz party sank dramatically. This drop in the polls was accompanied by a new legal framework to regulate the

2014 election, which the governing party might well have imagined it would lose. Under the new rules, the fragmented "left" opposition was dramatically disadvantaged by eliminating the second-round run-off for individual constituencies. That, together with gerrymandered districts, meant that Fidesz was practically guaranteed a return to power as the single largest – even if not the majority – party. Added to this were rules that gave votes to ethnic Hungarians in neighboring states, particularly those who were sure to vote for the governing party, along with rules that made it hard for expats driven from the country by Fidesz policies to vote outside the country. There were many more rules that, in their detail, favored the governing party, to say nothing of the fact that the election commission – dominated by governing party members – kept making decisions that favored the government throughout the 2014 campaign and in the vote count. The end result was that Fidesz was returned to power with (just barely) two-thirds of the seats in the parliament despite having only won 43 percent of the domestic vote (Scheppele, 2014a, 2014b). The election monitors from the Office of Democratic Institutions and Human Rights of the OSCE declared that the election was nominally free but not fair. The governing party, as they noted, had a distinct advantage because it had effectively merged party and state (OSCE 2014). But it was all done legally.

Thinking about these changes from within the legal complex framework, one can see how incredibly *legalistic* they were. Each change that undermined the democratic liberalism of the system was accomplished with exquisite legality, passed as law according to the rules laid down. This was a revolution of a consolidated democracy that only a lawyer could love.

But the revolution was not, as HKF would predict, a democratic and liberal one. Rather the opposite. Fidesz's extraordinary attention to legal detail, however, reveals much the same sensibility that HKF admire. Viktor Orbán and his inner circle of lawyers designed a system that had not a single illegal or exceptional moment. I might add that the government went to great lengths to avoid violating European Union law, which might have called in a higher objecting power. But EU law only covers certain topics, so the Fidesz lawyers drew a big circle around those and only operated in the spaces that EU law left to national jurisdiction. The Fidesz revolution constituted a genius project of illiberal lawyers, in which their legal training played a huge role.

Lawyers, being lawyers, see the opportunities that law makes available and they avail themselves of these opportunities. What forces liberal power to collapse – and in this case, power had been on the side of democratic liberalism – is the strategic deployment of illiberal law.

18.2.2 *Legal Revolution in Russia: 2000 and Beyond*

Since 1991, when the Soviet Union broke apart, leaving an independent Russia as the largest of the separate pieces to emerge from that former federation, Russia has had a turbulent constitutional trajectory. Among other things, there were almost no lawyers in sight in political offices during the first decade of Russia's democratic evolution. The Constitutional Court, which attempted to intervene to make the transition more "legal," was beaten up and left for dead in a major constitutional conflict in 1993. Legal chaos was the order of the day until lawyer-in-chief Vladimir Putin came to power in 2000.

During the Soviet period, Russia had had its own subnational constitution. At first after 1991, this same constitution served as the legal basis of the new national Russian Federation. Of course, the Soviet-era constitution had to be amended to remove one-party control, add competitive elections, put the Parliament and the presidency on a more democratic footing, establish real federalism, create a Constitutional Court and add real rights. There were, therefore, more than 300 amendments in two years, which created a sort of legal chaos. In many ways, a chaotic constitution was no better than the Soviet one. With such constant constitutional change, the continually reformed institutions could only lurch on in constitutional ambiguity as the law swirled around them in an endless state of movement.

Under this patchwork constitution inherited from the Soviet era, Russian President Boris Yeltsin's position was precarious because the paper constitution set up a parliamentary system with a formally weak presidency, and the lower house of the Parliament refused to approve his initiatives at every turn. The lower house, still called the Supreme Soviet at that point, was able to oppose Yeltsin so effectively because it had a clear majority bloc consisting of the only strong and country-wide party at that time – the Russian Communist Party. Yeltsin had attempted repeatedly to destroy the Communist Party, but the Constitutional Court got in the way by first preventing him from disbanding the Communist Party, and then from seizing its property. The Communist Party returned the compliment by attempting to block nearly everything Yeltsin tried by way of reform. Yeltsin's response to having to govern with a Parliament that did not share his sense of the country's future was to govern not by statute, which would have required that he find a way to compromise with the Parliament, but instead to govern by *ukaz*, or executive decree (Ahdieh 1997, 56). In this way, the autocratic history of Russia was echoed in its usual legal form. (The ukaz was the traditional legal instrument of the tsars.) Having new laws on the books made relatively little difference in any event. As Robert Ahdieh notes: "Though many laws were adopted, the most essential ones were ignored" (Ahdieh 1997, 50).

In this legal chaos, when it was often not clear what the constitution was, it became clear that Russia needed constitutional reform – and probably a new constitution. At least, Russia needed a constitution that organized the state more comprehensively and workably than the incoherent bricolage of the ever-shifting ex-Soviet constitutional pieces. Yeltsin and his advisors had tried to bring a new constitution into effect from the time they took office, but this effort, too, was constantly blocked by the Parliament, which had its own ideas about the shape that the new constitution should take.

Finally, in the summer of 1993, Yeltsin unilaterally called a constitutional conference – something like a constituent assembly – to draft a new basic law (Ahdieh 1997, 56). The representatives were not elected; instead, they were all invited by Yeltsin. The draft produced by the constitutional conference seemed to promise a way around the presidential-parliamentary deadlock over constitutional reform by reconstituting the Parliament and requiring a new election for president. But not surprisingly, the office of the president strongly dominated in Yeltsin's version of the constitution.

Yeltsin's constitutional draft did not, in any event, settle the constitutional crisis. Instead, the battle of wills between Yeltsin and Parliament intensified as they headed into the fall of 1993. The Supreme Soviet took on Yeltsin by passing a new series of constitutional amendments to the former Soviet constitution, amendments that would have reduced the office of the president to a mere figurehead (Ahdieh 1997, 65). In short, Parliament countered Yeltsin's presidentialist draft constitution with a constitution of its own in which (not surprisingly) the Parliament was the leading power. To get around Parliament yet again, Yeltsin proposed taking his constitution to a series of regional ratifications, instead of using the then-valid constitutional amendment procedure of first submitting the constitution to the Parliament for a vote, and then to a national popular referendum. But the Parliament blocked Yeltsin's turn to the regions for approval, too, claiming that this novel procedure was not authorized under the existing constitution. As both sides dug in further and further, Yeltsin's patience snapped.

In a televised public speech on September 21, 1993, Yeltsin announced that the state was experiencing a profound constitutional crisis. He issued Decree No. 1400, called (without the slightest trace of irony) "On the Step-by-Step Constitutional Reform of the Russian Federation," which, first and foremost, suspended the existing constitution. He disbanded Parliament and halted the operation of the Constitutional Court. But some of the parliamentarians defied his order and refused to disband. A faction of the Constitutional Court – with some of the judges refusing to participate – met despite the ban to hastily vote that Yeltsin's Decree No. 1400 was unconstitutional.

Yeltsin's declaration of emergency and seizure of power were met with substantial resistance. The resistance was carried out in the name of the now-suspended constitution, with the rebel parliamentarians holed up in their offices claiming authority under the existing constitution while the rump Constitutional Court, declaring that the suspension of the constitution was itself unconstitutional, clung publicly to the old constitution as the justification for its decision.

When Yeltsin learned that the parliamentarians who were refusing to leave the White House (the parliamentary office building) were heavily armed, Yeltsin cut off all utilities to the building. A crowd supporting the rump parliamentarians surrounded the White House to defend it, took over the city's television broadcasting tower and occupied the Moscow mayor's office. In response, Yeltsin called out the tanks and ordered a huge artillery attack against the White House and those barricaded inside. After over 100 members of the opposition were killed, they surrendered. A curfew was imposed in Moscow and more than 6,000 people were arrested by the army. Censorship was pressed against those media still critical of Yeltsin. In Russia's regions, local leaders who opposed Yeltsin were fired, and all local parliaments were dissolved by presidential decree.

Still proclaiming constitutional reform but continuing to rule by decree, Yeltsin once again convened a constitutional conference in October 1993, and this new, smaller and even more loyal assembly changed the summer draft of the constitution. The biggest alteration was the stunning increase in presidential power, which became even more sharply superior to Parliament. "In its final form," Ahdieh explained, "the constitution was thus premised not on the separation of powers, but on presidential supremacy" (Ahdieh 1997, 72–73).

So sure was Yeltsin that this draft would be adopted as Russia's new constitution that he put it to a referendum and held elections for the newly constituted Parliament on the same ballot. The constitutional draft squeaked through, but many have long suspected that the fifty percent turnout required to make the constitutional referendum valid was not actually reached except in the official results reported after the fact. In any event, there had been virtually no public debate over the constitution, and it would appear likely that no more than a tiny fraction of Russia's population knew what was in it at the time it passed.

The 1993 Constitution created a presidentialist state which, even by the standards of presidentialist states, granted the president extraordinary powers. For example, in addition to being the head of state, the president is also the "guarantor of the Constitution" and the constitutional officer who "ensures concerted functioning and interaction of all bodies of state power" (Russian Constitution, Art. 80(2)). The holder of that office "defines the basic domestic and foreign policy guidelines of the state" (Russian Constitution, Art. 80(3)). There is virtually no part of the Russian government, regional or national, over which the Russian president does not have substantial influence or veto power in the 1993 Constitution.

As you can see from this description, Russia's rocky transition from communism revealed that law did not matter much, except as an object of political struggle. Apart from the Constitutional Court judges, who tried to mediate between the president and the Parliament, there were few lawyers in sight. Though it is always hard to prove a counterfactual, Russia's bumpy start after 1991 may have been because the legal complex actors largely stayed out of politics. Yeltsin, impatient with law, rammed through a new constitution giving himself nearly unlimited powers, and then simply governed by decree for much of the decade, leaving Russia's legal infrastructure in shambles. On New Year's Eve of the new millennium, when the Russian news media were all on holiday for several weeks, Yeltsin took to the airwaves and announced he was stepping down, with his prime minister, Vladimir Putin, immediately assuming the powers of the presidency. As Archie Brown noted at the time, this was not only a constitutionally unanticipated way to leave power, but it was not even disguised by Yeltsin's health woes. Instead, it was a naked attempt by Yeltsin to secure the election of his favored successor, a plan that worked (Brown 2001, 35).

While foreign commentary focused on Putin's background in the KGB as a guide to his future governing style and made much of the fact that his inner circle consisted of his KGB friends, commentators would have made much better sense of Putin's presidency had they focused on his background as a lawyer and on the common backgrounds of his circle of associates who shared his legal training. Putin had been a top law graduate, drafted into the KGB, as top lawyers were in his graduating class, and he was then posted abroad into the most prestigious assignments. This was also true of many of those whom Putin recruited to the ranks of his new government. In this new set of political actors, the legal training ran deep. Putin thinks like a lawyer, and many of his actions in his many years in power are explainable only if one sees them against the background of his legal training and his mobilization of legal tools.

Putin's first election campaign made his priorities clear. They also made clear his lawyerly tendencies. If elected, he promised, he would bring about "the dictatorship of the law!" (Sharlet 2001, 195). The phrase was meant to reassure voters that the chaos of rule by decree had ended, and that in its place would come substantial legal reform that would increase the strength and predictability of the Russian state. In pronouncing the dictatorship of the law, Putin used the Russian word *zakony* not *pravo* – which is to say he invoked the word for law in the sense of statutes rather than the word for law in the sense of justice or rights. Increased legal predictability would be the hallmark of his term in office, and this would come through formally enacted law.

At the first opportunity after his election, Putin proposed far-reaching legal reforms. In the space of just a few years, his administration drafted – and the Parliament duly passed – huge framework statutes that would provide the backbone of a new system of Russian law. Putin clearly wanted to govern as a lawyer (Scheppele 2005).

One month into office as president, Putin put forward an ambitious program to regularize Yeltsin's chaotic system of decrees and to substitute properly passed laws instead. He introduced comprehensive new framework statutes regulating land law, labor law and both civil and criminal procedure. One year later, he initiated a new tax code. These laws replaced the much-amended communist-era statutes that were an unholy mess after a decade of a nonlawyer running the government. According to Putin at the time, "we are suffocating from the absence of fundamental legislation adequate to the changing situation," adding that "it is impermissible that the country should be living according to laws written under a different system of government." Putin's onslaught of legislation renovated major swaths of Russian substantive law, giving judges more concrete guidance. To help with the enforcement of these laws, Putin also increased by nearly one-third funding to the ordinary judiciary to strengthen them as they began to enforce all of this new law.

The biggest threat to Putin's ability to bring legal order to constitutional chaos was the countervailing power of regional governors. Throughout Yeltsin's presidency, he had played the regions against the center and won, which was how he had managed to stay in office so long. But by the end, the regions were playing the president and weakening his powers. Putin took on the task of radically altering – by law – the key bases of support for the Russian governors (Sharlet 2001). In many ways, these reforms restored the original conception of the 1993 constitution, which had always been intended to standardize relations between the center and the regions. With an executive decree, Putin created supergovernors, a set of positions between the center and the regional governors designed to keep an eye on the governors and limit their freewheeling ways. Putin then restructured the Federation Council, the Parliament's upper house in which each region had two representatives, so that regional governors could no longer sit in that body.

While Putin had to buck the resistance of the Federation Council in the implementation of these news laws, he easily had enough votes in the Duma to override the Council's first veto of the plan to reign in the regional governors. But in reducing the governors' legal powers, Putin did not cross any obvious constitutional lines. Yeltsin's constitution said nothing about how the representatives to the Federation Council should be appointed, and Putin just filled in the blanks with his new legislation. To mollify the miffed governors, Putin revived and institutionalized the old State Council that gave governors an advisory role in the national government, even as he took away their lawmaking powers. Annoyed, the governors nonetheless traded real power for the appearance of power.

The Constitutional Court had battled the centrifugal tendencies of the regional governors under Yeltsin; this made the Constitutional Court Putin's best friend on this issue. Putin then pushed a law through the Parliament that removed the retirement age for sitting constitutional judges. This, Putin's critics said, ensured that the judges who had supported the centralization of state power – in particular Constitutional Court President Marat Baglai – could stay on until the constitutional challenges to Putin's legal amputation of the powers of the regional governors could work their way through the system.

Putin then expanded the ordinary court system, creating a system of administrative courts, bolstering the system of justices of the peace, and increasing the total number of judges, while also increasing the budget for the courts by a massive amount. It seemed that he really did want to empower judges, once he had constrained them with many new laws to apply.

Putin's tsunami of legislation constituted the first time since the Russian Federation gained its independence in 1991 that a president had taken concrete steps to govern the Russian Federation by law. As lawyer-in-chief, Putin's style of governance was dramatically different from that of nonlawyer Yeltsin.

But Putin's ambitions to consolidate power did not end there. History handed him an opportunity to pass another wave of legislation fundamentally changing the organization of state power in Russia – and it did so around the horrible terrorist attack on the school in Beslan in 2004 that resulted in the deaths of 330 people, 150 of whom were schoolchildren.

Putin reacted to Beslan by springing into legal action. First and foremost, he announced that he would strengthen what Russians call the "vertical of power," the direct command structure of the government. And how would he do this? By getting rid of the remains of the messy federalism that had developed during the Yeltsin period, when the regions went their own way and governors dominated the scene. (Even with all of these efforts to contain them, Putin was still fighting the governors.) According to Putin (2004):

> The most important factor in strengthening the state, I consider, is a single system of executive power in the country, a single system stemming from the spirit and the letter of Article 77 of the Constitution of the Russian Federation ... The bodies of executive authority in the [center] and in the constituent parts of the Russian Federation will be formed by a single system of authority. And correspondingly, they must work as a single integrated organism with a clear structure of subordination.

To accomplish this task, he proposed replacing the regional elections for local governors with a system in which the president (not surprisingly) would appoint the governors. As a check, the respective local *dumy* (regional parliaments) would have to confirm the appointments, but the initiative and the nomination would come from Putin.

Putin's Beslan proposal was raced into law. The bill that quickly passed the Parliament and was signed by President Putin, however, added a new detail not in Putin's original speech: if a local duma rejected the president's candidate for governor twice, then the president could dissolve the regional parliament, call new elections, and start again. While Article 77 Section 2 of the Russian Constitution permits the executives of the regions and the national government to coordinate their efforts, it says nothing about the national president having any control over a regional legislature. The constitutionality of Putin's program for appointing regional governors was therefore certainly not clear, and would seem to be directly contradicted by Article 77 Section 1, which preserved the independence of regional governments. But despite questions about its constitutionality, the plan became law.

Putin's Beslan speech also proposed making a modification to the way that the lower house of the national Parliament (the *Duma*) itself was elected in order to more effectively respond to terrorism. At the time, half of the seats in the *Duma* were determined on the basis of proportional representation from party lists, and the other half of the seats were elected through first-past-the-post single-member districts. In the fall 2003 parliamentary election, parties supporting President Putin swept the election and would have had an overwhelming majority in the *Duma* (instead of merely a substantial majority) if the single-member constituency elections had not put into the *Duma* a number of independents, liberals and others whose parties did not get enough votes to get them over the five-percent threshold to win a party fraction. Putin proposed doing away with the single-member districts, creating a Parliament where all of the seats were filled directly from party lists. Given that Putin's party was the only truly country-wide party in the country, this further consolidated his power.

But was this proposal unconstitutional? Given the way that the 1993 Constitution was written, there was little direct text to contradict it because the Constitution itself left the election law for the federal Parliament to adopt through ordinary legislation. If an ordinary statute could be passed changing the basis for elections, it was hard to see how this would violate the Constitution, which envisages precisely this way of establishing the electoral system. The only element fixed in the constitution was the number of representatives, 450, and their four-year terms, not the method of their selection. So Putin did not propose a change in the constitutionally clear aspects of the Duma's structure; he only changed the parts that were not constitutionally specified. It was therefore hard to see how constitutional objections could succeed. Legalism, all around.

Interestingly enough, however, the *Duma* initially stalled at passing these changes, perhaps because some of their own number saw their political fates as implicated in the change. But eventually, with Putin's party dominating the Parliament, they voted for his plan.

The Beslan tragedy produced a huge wave of lawmaking designed to cope with terrorism. More than 200 draft laws were proposed to fight terrorism, with most of the proposals eventually consolidated into about forty more complex statutes. The ones I have mentioned here are the most sweeping in their implications for the organization of the basic constitutional system of Russia, but these laws with constitutional implications avoided direct confrontation with clear constitutional language and took advantage of weaknesses in the original constitution, whose language had not been crafted with lawyerly precision in the first place.

Putin, in lawyerly fashion, aimed his crucial power-consolidating reforms at precisely the places in the constitution where the specification of detailed institutional arrangements was weak. He took aim instead at the places where the institutions were not spelled out specifically in the constitutional text. As a result, it was not clear that there was any particular constitutional prohibition against changing the statutes that specified how the institutions were to be structured. Where the constitution was vague, new proposals could be floated without directly running up against constitutional plain language.

Nonetheless, it would be hard to say that these proposals, sweeping as they were, did not affect the basic constitutional structure. But when Russia's constitution was written under a strong executive (but nonlawyerly) hand in 1993, enough was left out or left vague for major constitutional changes to look "constitutional enough" to pass later. Yeltsin's basic lawlessness in 1993 left open the door for Putin the lawyer to turn the constitution in a deeply illiberal direction in a perfectly legalistic way.

18.3 CONCLUSION: ILLIBERAL LAWYERS-IN-CHIEF

As we have seen with this discussion of Viktor Orbán and Vladimir Putin, lawyers-in-chief, illiberal effective executives can govern impeccably *as lawyers*. Both Orbán and Putin had been star pupils of the constitutional systems they inherited, systems that had been set up earlier in their countries' transitions from communism. Each constitutional system had its own characteristic weaknesses – the disproportionate election law combined with the easy constitutional amendment rules in the Hungarian case, and the fill-in-the-blanks quality of the institutions in the Yeltsin constitution in the Russian case. Each lawyer-in-chief knew precisely how to guide legal and legalistic reform through these constitutional structures to fundamentally change the balance of power so that no one else could challenge them in the constitutional order. In fact, both lawyers-in-chief consolidated power so effectively that now it will take a very clever constitutional trick – or a very messy revolution – to get rid of either of them.

How does this bear on the political liberalism thesis of HKF? Halliday, Karpik and Feeley are right that lawyers approach politics in a distinctive and law-guided way. Where their theory may need a friendly amendment is on the question of when governing as a lawyer means governing as a liberal.

We have demonstrated here that sometimes lawyers are illiberal. And illiberal lawyers can promote illiberal legal change. More constitutions than we might guess have Achilles' heel problems that would enable perfectly legal methods to undermine a previously liberal constitutional order. Max Weber, a key founder of modern social science but also a lawyer, already saw this well. He noted that, on the economic side of the law, it would be possible to change an economy from a free-market system to communism through the free, contractual acquisition of all private property by the state – all without fundamentally changing the formal qualities of the legal order. The examples of Viktor Orbán and Vladimir Putin show that the same is true on the political side. Winning a big election with a large enough parliamentary majority to make major changes can result in the free, legislative abolition of whatever liberal principles a constitution has to offer. If the illiberal lawyers-in-chief are clever enough, they can disable existing checks that would prevent a future constitutional revolution through law before they concentrate all power in their hands through formally correct legislation. This paper has shown that illiberal legal revolutions can be accomplished more easily under the umbrella of a liberal constitution than one might guess.

Halliday, Karpik and Feeley were onto something when they noted that lawyers entered politics *as lawyers*. What we can now see, however, is an ever-greater variety of ways in which not all lawyers tilt liberal. What remains to be determined is when lawyers will act as liberals and when they will succumb to the inevitable temptations of illiberal power.

REFERENCES

Abdullaev, Nabi. 2004. "Putin Tells Judiciary to Clean Up Its Act." *Moscow Times*, December 1, 2004.

Ahdieh, Robert B. 1997. *Russia's Constitutional Revolution*. University Park: Penn State University Press.

Anderson, Perry. 1999. "A Ripple of the Polonaise: Review of Timothy Garten Ash, A History of the Present." *London Review of Books*, November 23, 1999. www.lrb.co.uk/v21/n23/perry-anderson/a-ripple-of-the-polonaise.

Brown, Archie. 2001. "From Democracy to 'Guided Democracy.'" *Journal of Democracy* 12 (4): 35.

Burbank, Jane. 1995. "Lenin and the Law in Revolutionary Russia." *Slavic Review* 54: 23–44.

Finn, Peter. 2004. "Putin Close to Winning New Power over Judiciary." *The Washington Post*, October 2, 2004, A15.

Ginsburg, Tom and Tamir Moustafa. 2008. *Rule by Law: The Politics of Courts in Authoritarian Regimes*. Cambridge: Cambridge University Press.

Halliday, Terence and Lucien Karpik. 1998. *Lawyers and the Rise of Western Political Liberalism: Legal Professions and the Constitution of Modern Politics*. Oxford: Oxford University Press.

Halliday, Terence, Lucien Karpik and Malcolm Feeley. 2007. *Fighting for Political Freedom: Comparative Studies of the Legal Complex for Political Change*. Oxford: Hart Publishing.

Halliday, Terence, Lucien Karpik and Malcolm Feeley. 2012. *Fates of Political Liberalism in the British Post-Colony: The Politics of the Legal Complex*. Cambridge: Cambridge University Press.

Hilbink, Lisa. 2007. *Judges beyond Politics in Democracy and Dictatorship: Lessons from Chile*. Cambridge: Cambridge University Press.

Hirsch, Francine. 2008. "The Soviets at Nuremberg: International Law, Propaganda, and the Making of the Postwar Order." *American Historical Review* 113: 701.

Karpik, Lucien and Terry Halliday. 2011. "The Legal Complex." *Annual Review of Law and Social Science* 7: 217–36.

Lan, Rongjie. 2010. "A False Promise of Fair Trials: A Case Study of China's Malleable Criminal Procedure Law." *UCLA Pacific Basin Law Review* 27: 153.

Linz, Juan and Alfred Stepan. 1996. "Toward Consolidated Democracies." *Journal of Democracy* 7:14–33.

Massoud, Mark. 2013. *Law's Fragile State: Colonial, Authoritarian, and Humanitarian Legacies in Sudan*. Cambridge: Cambridge University Press.

Moustafa, Tamir. 2008. "Rule by Law." Paper prepared for the Yale Workshop on the Rule of Law, March 2008, available at www.yale.edu/macmillan/ruleoflaw/papers/yalepaper3.pdf.

Mydans, Seth. "Lee Kuan Yew, Founding Father and First Premier of Singapore Dies at 91." *New York Times*, March 23, 2015. www.nytimes.com/2015/03/23/world/asia/lee-kuan-yew-founding-father-and- first- premier-of-singapore-dies-at-91.html?_r=0.

Orbán, Viktor. 2014. Speech at Baile-Tusnad, translation available at http://budapestbeacon.com/public-policy/full-text-of-viktor-orbans-speech-at-baile-tusnad-tusnadfurdo-of-26-july-2014/10592.

OSCE/ODIHR Election Observer Mission. 2014. "Preliminary Analysis and Conclusions for the Parliamentary Election of 6 April 2014." Available at www.osce.org/odihr/elections/117205?download=true.

Petrov, Nikolay. 2005. "The Essence of Putin's Managed Democracy." Carnegie Endowment for International Peace, October 8, 2015. Available at https://carnegieendowment.org/2005/10/18/essence-of-putin-s-managed-democracy-event-819.

Putin, Vladimir. 2004. "Sympathy for the Victims Is Not Enough" (RTR television broadcast, September 13, 2004), available as "Russia's Rulers and Public Must Unite Against Terrorism." Putin, BBC Worldwide Monitoring, September 13, 2004. Available at LEXIS, Nexis Library, Bbcmir File.

Scheppele, Kim Lane. 2014a. "Hungary, an Election in Question." *The Conscience of a Liberal* (blog), *New York Times*. February 28, 2014. https://krugman.blogs.nytimes.com/2014/02/28/hungary-an-election-in-question-part-1/.

Scheppele, Kim Lane. 2014b. "Legal but not Fair: Viktor Orbán's New Supermajority," *The Conscience of a Liberal* (blog), *New York Times*. April 13, 2014. http://krugman.blogs.nytimes.com/2014/04/13/legal-but-not-fair-hungary/.

Scheppele, Kim Lane. 2005. "'We Forgot About the Ditches:' Russian Constitutional Impatience and the Challenge of Terrorism." 53 *Drake Law Review* 963–1027.

Scheppele, Kim Lane. 2006. "Guardian of the Constitution: Constitutional Court Presidents and the Struggle for the Rule of Law in Post-Soviet Europe." *University of Pennsylvania Law Review* 154: 1757–851.

Sharlet, Robert. 2001. "Putin and the Politics of Law in Russia." *Post-Soviet Affairs* 17: 195.

Tamanaha, Brian. 2004. *On the Rule of Law: History, Politics, Theory*. Cambridge: Cambridge University Press.

Thompson, E. P. 1975. *Whigs and Hunters: The Origins of the Black Act*. London: Breviary Stuff Publications.

Index

administrative state, judicial policymaking and. *see* judicial policymaking
adversarial bias. *see* bias
alternative dispute resolution processes, problems with, 82
assault. *see* gender-motivated violence

baby farms and infanticide in Victorian England, 176, 187
behavioral science perspectives
  on adversarial bias in criminal process, 20, 25
  on miscarriages of justice, 27
best practices, law reframed as, 199
bias
  adversarial bias in criminal process, 19, 23
  behavioral science perspective on, 20, 25
  measures to reduce, 31
  MF's concept of adversarialism, 20
  MF's contribution to scholarship on, 19
  miscarriages of justice, 27
  phenomenon of adversarial bias, 20
  reconciliation of perspectives on, 20, 29
bureaucratic autonomy of judges, 246
bureaucratic element in judicial policymaking, 231

children. *see also* infanticide in Victorian England
  criminological effect of early childhood trauma, 58
  effects of exposure to courts
    brutalization by court environment, 63
    court process as intergenerational punishment, 55
    effects of parents' court experiences, 55, 57
    home environment negatively compared to court, 65
    lessons from research on, 56, 68
    loss of respect for parents, 62
    manipulative uses of children by defense lawyers, 64
    measures to reduce, 56, 68
    normalization of wrongdoing, 60
    offender perspectives, 66
    prosecutorial perspectives, 60
    research methodology and data, 59
    traumatic effects, 58
  effects of parents' imprisonment, 56
China
  courts' role in e-cigarettes regulation, 116
  e-cigarettes regulation, 98, 99, 101, 106, 107, 113
  repression of rights lawyers
    arrest and disappearance of Wang Yu, 289
    disinformation campaign against Wang Yu, 289
    response by international civil society and public opinion, 306
    response by international legal community, 290, 294, 300, 302
  tobacco regulation, 111, 116
civil procedure
  alternative dispute resolution processes, problems with, 82
  class action process, problems with, 80
  costs of invoking rights outweigh rights themselves, 91
  discovery rules, problems with, 76
  due process, gap between ideal and reality, 73, 90
  Federal Rules of Civil Procedure (1938), 73, 90
  MF's contribution to scholarship on problems of, 72
  pleading process, problems with, 74
  reduction of due process protections, 73, 90
  summary judgment process, problems with, 78
civil rights. *see* rights
class action process, problems with, 80

comparative law
  criminal court reform, 140
  MF's contribution to scholarship on, 98, 116
  prisons, 165
complex policy choices. *see* policy
compliance
  as defined by compliance professionals, 196
  symbolic compliance, social change and, 205
constitutional provisions, judicial independence from, 344, 353
constitutional reform as tool for repression, 369, 374
costs
  of criminal pre-trial processes, 55
  of invoking civil due process rights, 91
counsel. *see* lawyers
court reform. *see also* prisons
  criminal courts. *see* criminal courts
  Japan. *see* Japan
  MF's contribution to scholarship on, 122, 135
  US, 122
Court Reform on Trial: Why Simple Solutions Fail? (book). *see* Feeley, Malcolm
courts. *see also* civil procedure; criminal courts
  and complex policy choices, 116
  and e-cigarettes regulation, 114
criminal courts
  adversarial bias, 19, 23
  behavioral science perspective, 19
  children's exposure to. *see* children
  costs of pre-trial processes, 55
  institutional power in American society, 55
  organizational theory perspective, 19, 23
  reform
    comparative law perspective, 140
    criteria for success, 144
    Italy, 141, 143, 146, 147
    Japan. *see* Japan
    MF's contribution to scholarship on, 139, 152
    and politics of criminal justice, 147
    reasons for failure, 141, 152
criminal justice, politics of, 147
criminological effect of early childhood trauma, 58
culture of legal profession. *see* lawyers

decision making. *see* judicial reasoning
defense lawyers. *see* lawyers
deference. *see* judicial deference
Dewey, John
  concept of law, 36
  influence on MF, 43
disability rights and mass incarceration, 269
discovery rules, problems with, 76
diversity, rights reframed as, 200
due process. *see* civil procedure; legal process

e-cigarettes, regulation of
  China, 98, 99, 101, 106, 107, 113, 116
  classification of e-cigarettes, different approaches to, 99
  convergence and divergence in regulatory policy, 99
  courts' role, 114
  definition of e-cigarettes, 102
  emergence of e-cigarettes, 97
  EU, 98
  financial regulation compared, 100
  globalization and, 97, 100
  health perspectives on, 101, 105
  health risks of e-cigarettes, 104
  Japan, 98, 99, 101, 106, 107, 111, 116
  MF's concept of comparative law applied to, 98, 116
  national variations, 97
  popularity of e-cigarettes, 103
  reasons for regulatory divergence, 101
  tobacco regulation and, 107
  UK, 97
  US, 98, 99, 101, 105, 107, 109, 114
education and training reform. *see* Japan
employment. *see* equal employment opportunity (EEO) litigation; workers rights regulation
England. *see* infanticide in Victorian England; United Kingdom
equal employment opportunity (EEO) litigation
  civil rights reframed as diversity, 200
  compliance as defined by compliance professionals, 196
  EEO law equated with management best practices, 199
  judicial deference in, 195
  managerialization
    and legal risk, 198
    decoupling of organizational practice and policy, 198
    internal dispute resolution (IDR), 198
    of law, 197
    rhetorical reframing of legal ideals, 199
European Union (EU), e-cigarettes regulation, 98
executive branch, judicial independence from, 348

families, intergenerational punishment of. *see* children
Fates of Political Liberalism in the British Post-Colony (book). *see* Feeley
Federal Rules of Civil Procedure (1938), 73, 90
Feeley, Malcolm (Referred to elsewhere in the index as MF)

concept of law, 36, 48
contributions to scholarship
    adversarial bias, 19
    comparative law, 98, 116
    complex policy choices, 99, 116
    costs of pre-trial processes, 55
    court reform, 122, 135
    criminal court reform, 139, 152
    due process, 72
    grounded social theory of justice, 325
    idealism of lawyers, 319, 321
    international legal community, 292
    judges as policy makers, 193
    judicial independence, 335, 355
    judicial policymaking in prison reform
        litigation, 230
    law and society scholarship, 36
    lawyers in politics, 361, 382
    legal complex concept, 320
    politics of criminal justice, 147
    prison reform, 259, 270
    socio-legal perspective on legal profession,
        314, 315
    workers rights regulation, 226
*Court Reform on Trial: Why Simple Solutions
    Fail?* (book), 122, 135, 139, 147
and Dewey, John, 43
empirical basis of his research, 314, 323
*Fates of Political Liberalism in the British Post-
    Colony* (book), 320
Judicial Policy Making and the Modern State
    (book), 259, 270
normative basis of his research, 325
Process is the Punishment, The (book)
    arguments and themes, 37
    concept of law, 48
    empirical basis of research, 323
financial regulation, globalization and, 100
freedoms. *see* rights

gender stereotypes in murder cases, 187
gender-motivated violence
    civil rights and judicial bargaining, 249
    institutional conceptualization of, 235, 252
    judicial enforcement of civil rights, 240
    judicial policymaking and administrative state
        in relation, 232
    legal language of violence, 236
    right to freedom from
        creation of, 232, 236
        ideological conflict over administrative
            state, 243
        judicial administration in opposition to, 242
        removal of, 232

gender-motivated violence
globalization
    and convergence in legal policy, 100
    and e-cigarettes regulation, 97, 100
    and financial regulation, 100

heads of state. *see* lawyers as heads of state
health perspectives on e-cigarettes regulation, 101
human rights and and mass incarceration, 269
Hungary. *see* Orbán, Viktor

ideals. *see* rhetorical reframing of legal ideals
IDR. *see* internal dispute resolution
illiberal state in Hungary, 367
illiberalism. *see* lawyers as heads of state
incarceration. *see* prisons
independent judiciary. *see* judicial independence
inequality. *see* economic inequality
infanticide in Victorian England
    attitudes to, 182, 186
    baby farms, 176, 187
    cases
        examples, 172, 173, 174, 185
        number of, 173, 174, 183
        outcomes, 180
    creation of special offense of, 184
    leniency, 182, 185, 186
    in literature, 174, 177
    modern times compared, 184
    neonaticide
        definition and distinction of, 172
        incidence of, 172
    prosecution difficulties, 178
    reasons for, 173, 184
    seduced and abandoned women, 174, 186
    share of all infant deaths, 183
    unwritten law as to, 187
    as women's crime, 173
informer status applications by Palestinians. *see*
    Israel
institutional conceptualization
    of gender-motivated violence, 235, 252
    in judicial policymaking, 231
intelligence informers. *see* Israel
intergenerational punishment of families. *see*
    children
internal dispute resolution (IDR) as
    managerialization of law, 198
international legal community
    activism, 300
    defense of basic legal freedoms, 305
    interconnectedness, 300
    legal complex concept, 290, 308
    liberal political values, 305

international legal community (cont.)
  MF's contribution to scholarship on, 292, 308
  process of mobilization, 300
  public support for, 306
  response to China's repression of rights lawyers, 290, 294, 302
  rhetoric of mobilization, 302
Israel
  High Court of Justice (HCJ)
    effectiveness of policy changes, 284
    hearing of, 279
    hearing of informer status applications, 279
    policymaking by, 277, 281
    role of, 278
  informer status applications by Palestinians
    effectiveness of policy changes, 284
    HCJ policymaking, 277, 281
    HCJ's dilemma over policy, 274
    number of, 273
    recruitment of informers, 275
    status of informers and threatened persons, 274
    by threatened persons, 274
  threatened persons
    hearing of informer status applications, 279
    status as, 274
Italy, criminal court reform, 141, 143, 146, 147

Japan
  court reform
    expectations from, 122, 136
    MF's insights applied to, 135
    scope of, 122
  courts' role in e-cigarettes regulation, 116
  criminal court reform
    background to, 123
    changes, 127
    continuity, 129
    lay judges, 122, 123
    reasons for, 125
  e-cigarettes regulation, 98, 99, 101, 106, 111, 116
  legal education reform
    aim of, 122
    change and continuity in tension, 134
    professional law schools, 131
    reasons for, 131
  tobacco regulation, 110
judges
  bureaucratic autonomy outside court, 246
  civil rights and judicial bargaining, 249
  enforcement of civil rights, 240
  independence. see judicial independence
  lay judges reform in Japan, 122, 123
  policymaking. see judicial policymaking
  and political reform, 335
judicial deference
  equal employment opportunity (EEO) litigation, 195
  influences on judicial reasoning, 193
  and managerialization of law, 197
  MF's insights applied to, 194
  organizational theory perspectives, 194
  to organizations, 209
  prison conditions litigation, 194, 205
  social change
    and judicial deference, 207
    and symbolic compliance, 205
  symbolic structures
    deference to, 202
    influence of, 201
judicial independence
  bureaucratic autonomy of judges, 246
  and common law, 340
  historical development of
    UK, 340, 349, 352
    US, 342, 352
  independence
    from constitutional provisions, 344, 353
    from executive, 348
    from legislature, 339, 350
    from litigants, 336, 348
    as relationship, 335
  liberalism and, 335
  MF's contribution to scholarship on, 335, 355
  and political reform, 348
Judicial Policy Making and the Modern State (book). see Feeley, Malcolm
judicial policymaking
  bureaucratic autonomy outside court, 246
  by out-of-court settlements, 273
  civil rights and judicial bargaining, 249
  controversy about, 277
  example of, 242
  ideological conflict over administrative state, 243
  institutional conceptualization, 231
  judges as policy makers, 193
  as judicial action, 230
  MF's contribution to scholarship on, 230, 259, 270
  and modern administrative state, 230
  modes of, 231
judicial policymaking
judicial reasoning, influences on, 193
jurisprudence. see also law and society scholarship; philosophy of law

justice
  grounded social theory of justice, 325
  miscarriages of justice, 27
  politics and criminal justice reform, 147
  promise of justice, 319, 321
  socio-legal perspective on justice in the legal profession, 314

labor law. *see* equal employment opportunity (EEO) litigation; workers rights regulation
law
  managerialization of. *see* managerialization of law
  reframing of legal ideals. *see* rhetorical reframing of legal ideals
  theories of
    Dewey, John, 43
    MF's concept, 36
law and society scholarship. *see also* jurisprudence; philosophy of law; socio-legal work
  MF's contribution to, 36, 226
law schools reform in Japan. *see* Japan
lawyers. *see also* international legal community; lawyers as heads of state
  collective activism, 291
  defense of basic legal freedoms, 291
  humanistic values, 314
  idealism, 319, 321, 327
  legal complex concept, 290, 308, 320
  legal scholarship approach to professional values, 322
  manipulative uses of children by defense lawyers, 64
  materialism, 315
  moderation of state power as aim of, 291
  prosecutorial perspectives on children in court, 60
  social science approach to
    empirical basis of, 322
    grounded social theory of justice, 325
    justice in the legal profession, 314
    legal complex concept, 320
    legal scholarship's role in, 327
    normative basis of, 324
    shaping of legal culture, question of, 328
    tensions within legal culture, 315, 327
lawyers as heads of state
  anti-liberalism, 362, 382
  case studies, 362
  effective heads of executive with legal training, 364
  liberal or illiberal, 365
  position of, 364

failure of liberalism in legal complex, 363
Hungary. *see* Orbán, Viktor
law and arbitrary power, 362
law making as tool of repression, 365
and legal complex, 363
legal interpretation as tool for repression, 365
legal training as tool for repression, 362, 363
legalism, 361
liberal political inclination, 361
MF's contribution to scholarship on, 361, 382
rule by law, 363
and rule of law, 362, 363
Russia. *see* Putin, Vladimir
lay judges reform in Japan, 122, 123
legal complex concept, 290, 308, 320, 363
legal culture. *see* lawyers
legal education
  lawyers and politics. *see* lawyers as heads of state
  reform in Japan. *see* Japan
legal freedoms, lawyers' defense of, 291, 305
legal ideals. *see* rhetorical reframing of legal ideals
legal language of violence, 236
legal policymaking. *see* judicial policy
legal process. *see also* civil procedure; courts; criminal courts; judges; lawyers
  adversarial bias. *see* bias
  costs of pre-trial processes, 55
  intergenerational punishment of families. *see* children
  MF's contribution to scholarship on problems of, 72
legal profession. *see* lawyers
legal risk, managerialization of, 198
legalism and anti-liberal government, 361
legislature, judicial independence from, 339, 350
liberalism
  international legal community, 305
  and judicial independence, 335
  lawyers and politics. *see* lawyers as heads of state
  and legal complex concept, 320
literature and infanticide in Victorian England, 174, 177
litigants, judicial independence from, 336, 348
lower criminal courts. *see* criminal courts

managed democracy in Russia, 367
managerialism in prisons, 159
managerialization of law
  decoupling of organizational practice and policy, 198
  internal dispute resolution (IDR), 198
  legal risk, 198

managerialization of law (cont.)
  process of, 197
  rhetorical reframing of legal ideals, 199
mass incarceration. see prisons
miscarriages of justice, adversarial bias and, 27
murder
  gender stereotypes, 187
  infanticide and neonaticide. see infanticide in Victorian England
  unwritten law as to, 187

neonaticide. see infanticide in Victorian England

Orbán, Viktor
  anti-liberalism, 362
  constitutional reform as tool for repression, 369
  democracy and liberalism in post-communist Hungary, 365
  election as prime minister, 367
  illiberal state as aim, 367
  legal education and governing style in relation, 362
  legal training as tool for repression, 368, 382
  legalism, 362
organizational theory perspectives
  adversarial bias, 19, 23
  consequences of punishment's organizational context, 158
  decoupling of organizational practice and policy, 198
  judicial deference, 194, 209
  prisons. see prisons
out-of-court settlements, judicial policymaking by, 273

Palestinian informers in Israel. see Israel
parental experiences of court and prison, effects on children. see children
penology. see prisons
philosophy of law. see also jurisprudence; law and society scholarship
plantation prisons, abolition of, 259, 261, 270
pleading in civil proceedings, problems with, 74
policy
  complex policy choices
    courts' role in, 116
    MF's contribution to scholarship on, 99, 116
  globalization and convergence in regulatory policy, 100
  judges as policy makers. see judicial policymaking
  social policy and workers rights regulation, 226

political leadership. see lawyers as heads of state
political reform, judges' role in, 335
political repression of rights lawyers. see China
politics of criminal justice, 147
prisons
  and colonial-era executions, 155
  comparative law perspective, 165
  decarceration movement, 259
  disability rights and human rights, 269
  effects of parents' imprisonment on children, 56, 57
  failure
    criminal court reform failure compared, 152
    persistence of prisons in spite of, 152, 166
    responses to, 165
  judges as policy makers, 193
  judicial deference in prison conditions litigation, 194, 205
  judicial policymaking in prison reform litigation, 230
  mass incarceration
    consensus on, 259
    courts and abolition of, 264
    developments towards reform, 260
    disability rights and human rights, 269
    judges' support for reform, 261, 270
    Prison Litigation Reform Act 1996, 266
    prospects for ending, 270
    rehabilitative penology, 267
    MF's contribution to scholarship on, 259, 270
    MF's insights applied to, 153, 193, 230
  modern prisons, 156
  as organizations
    administrative and official discretion, problem of, 161
    ambiguity and conflict in goals and rules, 162
    beginning of penal organization, 157
    consequences of organizational context, 158
    growth of informal structures, 163
    historical development, 155
    managerialism, 159
    organizational framework as cause of failure, 153, 164
    organizational theory perspectives, 154
  persistence and repeated failure of, 152, 166
  plantation prisons, abolition of, 259, 261, 270
  Prison Litigation Reform Act 1996, 266
  rehabilitative penology, 267
  symbolic compliance and social change in relation, 205
Process is the Punishment, The (book). see Feeley, Malcolm
process of law. see legal process

Index

promise of justice, 319, 321
prosecutors. *see* lawyers
psychological perspectives
   criminological effect of early childhood trauma, 58
   effects of childrens' exposure to courts. *see* children
punishment
   consequences of organizational context, 158
   intergenerational punishment of families. *see* children
   prisons. *see* prisons
Putin, Vladimir
   anti-liberalism, 362
   communist legacy and democratic failure in Russia, 367
   constitutional reform as tool for repression, 374
   democracy and liberalism in post-communist Russia, 365, 367
   election as president, 367
   legal education and governing style in relation, 362
   legal training as tool for repression, 368, 382
   legalism, 362
   managed democracy, 367

rape. *see* gender-motivated violence
reason. *see* judicial reasoning
reform. *see* courts, reform of; criminal courts, reform
rehabilitative penology, 267
repression. *see* political repression
rhetorical reframing of legal ideals
   civil rights reframed as diversity, 200
   EEO law equated with management best practices, 199
   managerialization and, 199
rights
   civil rights and judicial bargaining, 249
   costs of invoking rights outweigh rights themselves, 91
   disability rights and mass incarceration, 269
   freedom from gender-motivated violence. *see* gender-motivated violence
   human rights and and mass incarceration, 269
   and judicial bargaining, 249
   judicial enforcement of civil rights, 240
   lawyers' defense of basic legal freedoms, 291, 305
   reframing of civil rights as diversity, 200
   repression of rights lawyers. *see* China

workers rights. *see* workers rights regulation
risk, managerialization of legal
   risk, 198
rule by law, and rule of law, 363
rule of law
   nature of, 362
   and rule by law, 363
Russia. *see* Putin, Vladimir

separation of powers. *see* judicial independence
smoking. *see* e-cigarettes
social change
   and judicial deference, 207
   and symbolic compliance, 205
social policy. *see* policy
socio-legal perspective on justice in the legal profession, 314
summary judgment process, problems with, 78

theories of law. *see* law, theories of
threatened persons applications by Palestinians. *see* Israel
tobacco. *see* e-cigarettes
trauma in early childhood, criminological effect of, 58
trials, costs of pre-trial processes, 55

United Kingdom (UK). *see also* infanticide in Victorian England
   development of legal complex in former colonies, 320
   e-cigarettes regulation, 97, 106
   illiberal laws and rule of law, 362
   judicial independence, historical development of, 340, 349, 352
United States (US)
   children's exposure to criminal courts. *see* children
   court reform, 122
   courts' role in e-cigarettes regulation, 114
   criminal court reform. *see* criminal courts
   e-cigarettes regulation, 98, 99, 101, 105, 107, 109, 114
   judicial independence, historical development of, 342, 352
   jury trials, 131
   legal community's response to China's repression of rights lawyers, 296
   as organizations. *see* prisons
   tobacco regulation, 107

United States (US) (cont.)
  unwritten law, 187
unwritten law, 187

vaping. *see* e-cigarettes
Victorian England. *see* infanticide in Victorian England
violence against women. *see* gender-motivated violence

Wang Yu
  arrest and disappearance, 289
  Chinese government disinformation campaign against, 289
  support from international legal community, 290
women
  infanticide by. *see* infanticide in Victorian England
  violence against. *see* gender-motivated violence
workers rights regulation
  consequences of reform, 224
  courts' role, 215
  development of different statutory and legal regimes, 216
  expansion of employment and employment discrimination law, 221
  failure of, 215
  labor law redefinition of workplace rights, 217
  law and social policy in relation, 226
  MF's insights applied to, 226
wrongful convictions. *see* miscarriages of justice

Books in the Series

Diseases of the Will: Alcohol and the Dilemmas of Freedom
Mariana Valverde

The Politics of Truth and Reconciliation in South Africa: Legitimizing the Post-Apartheid State
Richard A. Wilson

Modernism and the Grounds of Law
Peter Fitzpatrick

Unemployment and Government: Genealogies of the Social
William Walters

Autonomy and Ethnicity: Negotiating Competing Claims in Multi-Ethnic States
Yash Ghai

Constituting Democracy: Law, Globalism and South Africa's Political Reconstruction
Heinz Klug

The Ritual of Rights in Japan: Law, Society, and Health Policy
Eric A. Feldman

Governing Morals: A Social History of Moral Regulation
Alan Hunt

The Colonies of Law: Colonialism, Zionism and Law in Early Mandate Palestine
Ronen Shamir

Law and Nature
David Delaney

Social Citizenship and Workfare in the United States and Western Europe: The Paradox of Inclusion
Joel F. Handler

Law, Anthropology, and the Constitution of the Social: Making Persons and Things
Edited by Alain Pottage and Martha Mundy

Judicial Review and Bureaucratic Impact: International and Interdisciplinary Perspectives
Edited by Marc Hertogh and Simon Halliday

Immigrants at the Margins: Law, Race, and Exclusion in Southern Europe
Kitty Calavita

Lawyers and Regulation: The Politics of the Administrative Process
Patrick Schmidt

Law and Globalization from Below: Toward a Cosmopolitan Legality
Edited by Boaventura de Sousa Santos and Cesar A. Rodriguez-Garavito

Public Accountability: Designs, Dilemmas and Experiences
Edited by Michael W. Dowdle

Law, Violence and Sovereignty among West Bank Palestinians
Tobias Kelly

Legal Reform and Administrative Detention Powers in China
Sarah Biddulph

The Practice of Human Rights: Tracking Law between the Global and the Local
Edited by Mark Goodale and Sally Engle Merry

Judges beyond Politics in Democracy and Dictatorship: Lessons from Chile
Lisa Hilbink

Paths to International Justice: Social and Legal Perspectives
Edited by Marie-Bénédicte Dembour and Tobias Kelly

Law and Society in Vietnam: The Transition from Socialism in Comparative Perspective
Mark Sidel

Constitutionalizing Economic Globalization: Investment Rules and Democracy's Promise
David Schneiderman

The New World Trade Organization Knowledge Agreements: 2nd Edition
Christopher Arup

Justice and Reconciliation in Post-Apartheid South Africa
Edited by François du Bois and Antje du Bois-Pedain

Militarization and Violence against Women in Conflict Zones in the Middle East: A Palestinian Case-Study
Nadera Shalhoub-Kevorkian

Child Pornography and Sexual Grooming: Legal and Societal Responses
Suzanne Ost

Darfur and the Crime of Genocide
John Hagan and Wenona Rymond-Richmond

Fictions of Justice: The International Criminal Court and the Challenge of Legal Pluralism in Sub-Saharan Africa
Kamari Maxine Clarke

Conducting Law and Society Research: Reflections on Methods and Practices
Simon Halliday and Patrick Schmidt

Planted Flags: Trees, Land, and Law in Israel/Palestine
Irus Braverman

Culture under Cross-Examination: International Justice and the Special Court for Sierra Leone
Tim Kelsall

Cultures of Legality: Judicialization and Political Activism in Latin America
Javier Couso, Alexandra Huneeus, and Rachel Sieder

Courting Democracy in Bosnia and Herzegovina: The Hague Tribunal's Impact in a Postwar State
Lara J. Nettelfield

The Gacaca Courts, Post-Genocide Justice and Reconciliation in Rwanda: Justice without Lawyers
Phil Clark

Law, Society, and History: Themes in the Legal Sociology and Legal History of Lawrence M. Friedman
Edited by Robert W. Gordon and Morton J. Horwitz

After Abu Ghraib: Exploring Human Rights in America and the Middle East
Shadi Mokhtari

Adjudication in Religious Family Laws: Cultural Accommodation, Legal Pluralism, and Gender Equality in India
Gopika Solanki

Water on Tap: Rights and Regulation in the Transnational Governance of Urban Water Services
Bronwen Morgan

Elements of Moral Cognition: Rawls' Linguistic Analogy and the Cognitive Science of Moral and Legal Judgment
John Mikhail

Mitigation and Aggravation at Sentencing
Edited by Julian V. Roberts

Institutional Inequality and the Mobilization of the Family and Medical Leave Act: Rights on Leave
Catherine R. Albiston

Authoritarian Rule of Law: Legislation, Discourse and Legitimacy in Singapore
Jothie Rajah

Law and Development and the Global Discourses of Legal Transfers
Edited by John Gillespie and Pip Nicholson

Law against the State: Ethnographic Forays into Law's Transformations
Edited by Julia Eckert, Brian Donahoe, Christian Strümpell and Zerrin Özlem Biner

Transnational Legal Ordering and State Change
Edited by Gregory C. Shaffer

Legal Mobilization under Authoritarianism: The Case of Post-Colonial Hong Kong
Waikeung Tam

Complementarity in the Line of Fire: The Catalysing Effect of the International Criminal Court in Uganda and Sudan
Sarah M. H. Nouwen

Political and Legal Transformations of an Indonesian Polity: The Nagari from Colonisation to Decentralisation
Franz von Benda-Beckmann and Keebet von Benda-Beckmann

Pakistan's Experience with Formal Law: An Alien Justice
Osama Siddique

Human Rights under State-Enforced Religious Family Laws in Israel, Egypt, and India
Yüksel Sezgin

Why Prison?
Edited by David Scott

Law's Fragile State: Colonial, Authoritarian, and Humanitarian Legacies in Sudan
Mark Fathi Massoud

Rights for Others: The Slow Home-Coming of Human Rights in the Netherlands
Barbara Oomen

European States and Their Muslim Citizens: The Impact of Institutions on Perceptions and Boundaries
Edited by John R. Bowen, Christophe Bertossi, Jan Willem Duyvendak, and Mona Lena Krook

Environmental Litigation in China: A Study in Political Ambivalence
Rachel E. Stern

Indigeneity and Legal Pluralism in India: Claims, Histories, Meanings
Pooja Parmar

Paper Tiger: Law, Bureaucracy and the Developmental State in Himalayan India
Nayanika Mathur

Religion, Law and Society
Russell Sandberg

The Experiences of Face Veil Wearers in Europe and the Law
Edited by Eva Brems

The Contentious History of the International Bill of Human Rights
Christopher N. J. Roberts

Transnational Legal Orders
Edited by Terence C. Halliday and Gregory Shaffer

Lost in China? Law, Culture and Society in Post-1997 Hong Kong
Carol A. G. Jones

Security Theology, Surveillance and the Politics of Fear
Nadera Shalhoub-Kevorkian

Opposing the Rule of Law: How Myanmar's Courts Make Law and Order
Nick Cheesman

The Ironies of Colonial Governance: Law, Custom and Justice in Colonial India
James Jaffe

The Clinic and the Court: Law, Medicine and Anthropology
Edited by Ian Harper, Tobias Kelly, and Akshay Khanna

A World of Indicators: The Making of Government Knowledge through Quantification
Edited by Richard Rottenburg, Sally Engle Merry, Sung-Joon Park, and Johanna Mugler

Contesting Immigration Policy in Court: Legal Activism and Its Radiating Effects in the United States and France
Leila Kawar

The Quiet Power of Indicators: Measuring Governance, Corruption, and Rule of Law
Edited by Sally Engle Merry, Kevin Davis, and Benedict Kingsbury

Investing in Authoritarian Rule: Punishment and Patronage in Rwanda's Gacaca Courts for Genocide Crimes
Anuradha Chakravarty

Contractual Knowledge: One Hundred Years of Legal Experimentation in Global Markets
Edited by Grégoire Mallard and Jérôme Sgard

Iraq and the Crimes of Aggressive War: The Legal Cynicism of Criminal Militarism
John Hagan, Joshua Kaiser, and Anna Hanson

Culture in the Domains of Law
Edited by René Provost

China and Islam: The Prophet, the Party, and Law
Matthew S. Erie

Diversity in Practice: Race, Gender, and Class in Legal and Professional Careers
Edited by Spencer Headworth and Robert Nelson

A Sociology of Constitutions: Constitutions and State Legitimacy in Historical-Sociological Perspective
Chris Thornhill

A Sociology of Transnational Constitutions: Social Foundations of the Post-National Legal Structure
Chris Thornhill

Shifting Legal Visions: Judicial Change and Human Rights Trials in Latin America
Ezequiel A. González Ocantos

The Demographic Transformations of Citizenship
Heli Askola

Criminal Defense in China: The Politics of Lawyers at Work
Sida Liu and Terence C. Halliday

Contesting Economic and Social Rights in Ireland: Constitution, State and Society, 1848–2016
Thomas Murray

Buried in the Heart: Women, Complex Victimhood and the War in Northern Uganda
Erin Baines

Palaces of Hope: The Anthropology of Global Organizations
Edited by Ronald Niezen and Maria Sapignoli

The Politics of Bureaucratic Corruption in Post-Transitional Eastern Europe
Marina Zaloznaya

Revisiting the Law and Governance of Trafficking, Forced Labor and Modern Slavery
Edited by Prabha Kotiswaran

Incitement on Trial: Prosecuting International Speech Crimes
Richard Ashby Wilson

Criminalizing Children: Welfare and the State in Australia
David McCallum

Global Lawmakers: International Organizations in the Crafting of World Markets
Susan Block-Lieb and Terence C. Halliday

Duties to Care: Dementia, Relationality and Law
Rosie Harding

Insiders, Outsiders, Injuries, and Law: Revisiting "The Oven Bird's Song"
Edited by Mary Nell Trautner

Hunting Justice: Displacement, Law, and Activism in the Kalahari
Maria Sapignoli

Injury and Injustice: The Cultural Politics of Harm and Redress
Edited by Anne Bloom, David M. Engel, and Michael McCann

Ruling Before the Law: The Politics of Legal Regimes in China and Indonesia
William Hurst

The Powers of Law: A Comparative Analysis of Sociopolitical Legal Studies
Mauricio García-Villegas

A Sociology of Justice in Russia
Edited by Marina Kurkchiyan and Agnieszka Kubal

Constituting Religion: Islam, Liberal Rights, and the Malaysian State
Tamir Moustafa

The Invention of the Passport: Surveillance, Citizenship and the State, Second Edition
John C. Torpey

Law's Trials: The Performance of Legal Institutions in the US "War on Terror"
Richard L. Abel

Law's Wars: The Fate of the Rule of Law in the US "War on Terror"
Richard L. Abel

Transforming Gender Citizenship: The Irresistible Rise of Gender Quotas in Europe
Edited by Eléonore Lépinard and Ruth Rubio-Marín

Muslim Women's Quest for Justice: Gender, Law and Activism in India
Mengia Hong Tschalaer

Children as 'Risk': Sexual Exploitation and Abuse by Children and Young People
Anne-Marie McAlinden

The Legal Process and the Promise of Justice: Studies Inspired by the Work of Malcolm Feeley
Jonathan Simon, Rosann Greenspan, Hadar Aviram

Sovereign Exchanges: Gifts, Trusts, Reparations, and Other Fetishes of International Solidarity
Grégoire Mallard

Measuring Justice: Quantitative Accountability and the National Prosecuting Authority in South Africa
Johanna Mugler

Negotiating the Power of NGOs: Women's Legal Rights in South Africa
Reem Wael

Indigenous Water Rights in Law and Regulation: Lessons from Comparative Experience
Elizabeth Jane Macpherson

The Edge of Law: Legal Geographies of a War Crimes Court
Alex Jeffrey

Everyday Justice: Law, Ethnography and Injustice
Sandra Brunnegger

Lightning Source UK Ltd.
Milton Keynes UK
UKHW020840150522
402927UK00019B/405